Trademark Acknowledgem

Wrox has endeavored to provide trademark information about all the companies and products mentioned in this book by the appropriate use of capitals. However, Wrox cannot guarantee the accuracy of this information.

Credits

Authors
Charles Arehart
Nirmal Chidambaram
Shashirikan Guruprasad
Alex Homer
Ric Howell
Stephan Kasippillai
Rob Machin
Tom Myers
Alexander Nakhimovksy
Luca Passani
Chris Pedley
Richard Taylor
Marco Toschi

Additional Material
Simon Robinson
Karli Watson

Technical Architect
Victoria Hudgson

Technical Editors
Amanda Kay
Chanoch Wiggers

Index
Michael Brinkman

Project Administrators
Marsha Collins
Avril Corbin

Cover
Shelley Frasier

Production Coordinator
Mark Burdett

Illustrations
William Fallon

Technical Reviewers
Terry Allen
Graham Brown
Jeremy Michael Crosbie
Armand Datema
Simon Ellis
Alastair France
Tone Grimstad
Costantinos Hadjisotiriou
Mark Harrison
Jeremy Hill
Alex Homer
Kamran Kordi
Karen Little
Hank Murphy
Stephan Osmont
Luca Passani
Chris Pedley
Iztok Polanic
John Raikou
Simon Robinson
Marco Rondelli
Gianluca Rosa
Erik Saastad
Jordon Saardchit
Beau Smith
Oliver Southgate
Harald Stegavik
Richard Taylor
Jan Teerlinck
Joao Vieira
Karli Watson
Mark Wilcox

Category Manager
Jan Kolasinski

Proof Readers
Mira McMullen
Diana Skeldon

G000070376

About the Authors

Charles Arehart

Charlie Arehart is a veteran information systems developer, educator, and industry analyst with nearly 20 years experience. His company, SysteManage, is a web application development firm now focusing on wireless applications. Charlie is an Allaire Certified Instructor, who's taught hundreds of students, and he's a regular speaker to User Groups throughout the country. He's a seasoned developer who delights in helping others become more effective in their practice. He's also a prolific writer, contributing a monthly "Journeyman" column in the ColdFusion Developer's Journal and serving as tips editor for CF Advisor. He was also tech editor and contributor to the recently published ColdFusion for Dummies, from IDG, and is contributing to an upcoming IDG book on DreamWeaver UltraDev.

Charlie would like to thank the publishers for giving him the opportunity to contribute, as well Ben Forta-(noted ColdFusion maven) for writing an article in the ColdFusion Developer's Journal that started Charlie's interest in WML. He'd also like to acknowledge his former employer, Fig Leaf Software, and all the great folks there who permitted him to join for a time in their highly regarded contributions to the CF community. Finally, thanks to Kim for her patience through the process and for helping me see that it's through God's grace that this work is done. Thanks be to Him.

Nirmal Chidambaram

Nirmal Chidambaram currently works for Geologik Software, but first started programming when he had just left school. With a growing fascination for computers, he continued studies related to any computer topic, even though his engineering discipline was in Mechanical branch. He still fondly remembers the day when he first eyes on Windows 1.0 and the thrill of running his first 16-bit program for windows – a *Hello World!* program. Nirmal's expertise ranges from topics such as Distributed Object Computing to Graphics programming using OpenGL. Now, his main area of interest is in developing Multi-Modal interfaces. He is also currently developing GeoXML, a XML vocabulary for representation of geological data.

My sincere thanks to Mr. Thomas Roehrich and Mr. Gulzar Nazim for their support, encouragement and for their critical comments on my chapter. My special thanks to my parents also. And, last but not the least, my thanks to Victoria for giving me this chance and for her valuable suggestions. I can be reached at nirmal@reflexmicrobyte.com

Shashikiran Guruprasad

Shashikiran Guruprasad is currently working with Silicon Automation Systems (SAS, http://www.sasi.com/) in Bangalore, India and has been involved in the development of Nortel Networks' GSM/GPRS products for more than two years now. WAP has caught his fancy for the past year after he realized that there are (or soon will be) more mobile phone users than users of the Internet. His current interests include Distributed Systems, Wireless Networks and Mobile Computing. He likes reading technology news and seems to have a ready opinion on anything remotely related to technology!

I would like to extend my special thanks to my manager Sanjay Tamwekar, who gave me the thumbs up sign as soon as I informed him of my writing venture and Santosh Xavier, the head of SAS WAP Gateway team who showed so much more enthusiasm in giving me ideas and encouragement, than I had expected. I would like to thank Deepak Veliath, a long time friend and co-author of Professional PHP, who put me on to this. I would like to appreciate my family who shared my highs and lows during the writing and my editor Victoria Hudgson for having a lot of fortitude to oversee such a large scale effort from so many writers.

Alex Homer

Alex came to writing computer books through an unusual route, including tractor driver, warehouse manager, garden products buyer, glue sales specialist, and double-glazing salesman. With this wide-ranging commercial and practical background, and a love of anything that could be taken to pieces, computers were a natural progression. Now, when not writing books for Wrox, he spends his spare time sticking together bits of code for his wife's software company (Stonebroom Software – http://www.stonebroom.com) or just looking out of the window at the delightfully idyllic and rural surroundings of the Peak District in Derbyshire, England.

Ric Howell

Ric Howell is Chief Technology Officer for Concise Ltd, a London-based business and software consultancy serving Financial, Insurance and Banking markets. He provides consultancy for clients on enterprise IT Architecture and the utilization of technology in meeting corporate strategy. With over 15 years experience in the IT industry, he can remember the days when mainframes were the only computers and structured-development was hot technology. He has survived down-sizing, up-sizing, right-sizing, the invention of LANs, the rise of client-server development models, the object-oriented development revolution, the 'demise' of Transaction Monitors, the invention of distributed computing, the rise of the Internet, thin-client computing, the rebirth of server-centric computing, the component-based development revolution, and the re-invention of OTMs and application servers. He is haunted by a strange sense of deja vu. Since the mid-nineties, Ric has been working with Internet technologies, Java and component based distributed systems development. He was a founder and CTO of a start-up software company producing an EJB based CRM solution, where he was responsible for the design of the product. Currently, Ric is involved in helping Concise's clients develop their WAP and Mobile initiatives, and was instrumental in initiating Concise's Mobile Solutions practice. A particular area of concern for many of Concise's clients is security, so this is an area that he does considerable investigation into, but experience has taught him that where security is concerned, no one is an expert.

Stephan Kasippillai

Stephan is a senior management consultant and has been following developments in the world of mobile computing and wireless technology for several years. His role as Principal Consultant with the Concise Group involves the conception, development and deployment of leading edge wireless solutions for the Investment Banking and Asset Management industries. Having conceived and driven the formation of a wireless solutions practice within the Concise Group, he is currently engaged in a number of projects with major investment banks to help them understand and benefit from the application of mobile data technology. This involves developing and implementing global wireless strategies that can adapt to the rapid changes in technology whilst delivering clearly defined business objectives.

Rob Machin

Rob Machin graduated from Durham University in 1994 with a First in Mathematics and Philosophy. Since then he has discarded Fermat and Sartre, and become a specialist in mobile commerce, n-tier systems architecture and new technologies, developing object-oriented software using both Smalltalk and Java. He is currently working as a Technical Consultant with the Concise Group Ltd, advising on the construction of WAP applications and mobile commerce solutions for the financial markets and investment banking sector of the City of London. Rob can be contacted at RobMachin@bcs.org.uk.

Dedicated to Clara, with thanks to Mo and Nell for their love and support.

Tom Myers

Tom has a BA (cum laude), St. John's College, Santa Fe, New Mexico ("Great Books" program), 1975 and a PhD in computer science from the University of Pennsylvania, 1980. He taught computer science at the University of Delaware and Colgate before becoming a full-time consultant and software developer. He is the author of "Equations, Models, and Programs: A Mathematical Introduction to Computer Science" Prentice-Hall Software Series, 1988, several articles on theoretical computer science, and two joint titles with Alexander Nakhimovsky: *Javascript Objects*, Wrox, 1998, and *Professional Java XML Programming with Servlets and JSP*, Wrox, 1999.

Alexander Nakhimovsky

Alexander Nakhimovsky received an MA in mathematics from Leningrad University in 1972 and a PhD in general linguistics from Cornell in 1978, with a graduate minor in computer science. He taught general and Slavic linguistics at Cornell and SUNY Oswego before joining Colgate's computer science department in 1985. He published a book and a number of articles on theoretical and computational linguistics, several Russian language textbooks, a dictionary of Nabokov's Lolita, and, jointly with Tom Myers, *Javascript Objects*, Wrox, 1998, and *Professional Java XML Programming with Servlets and JSP*, Wrox, 1999.

Luca Passani

Luca is an Italian IT-professional who lives in Oslo, Norway. He has extensive experience with client-side and server-side scripting in web technologies. Over the past year he has been working extensively with WAP. Luca received recognition in the WAP community after two articles on WAP were published on ASPToday.com. He has also published other articles in many prestigious international IT magazines. His company, Cell Network, is one of the major Internet consultancy companies in Europe (http://www.cellnetwork.com).

I would like to thank the following people: Bente, Erling, Monica and Christel, who run my company, have faith in me and are totally cool; Dino Esposito and the people at Wrox for introducing me to the wonderful world of technical writing; all of the nice people on the WML programming mailing list; all the people at Phone.com who provided me with valuable assistance and information: Heidi who succeeded in understanding why I needed to sit in front of a PC after 10 hours spent in front of a PC and my beloved daughter Sandra who did not switch off my PC in the most crucial moments.

Chris Pedley

Chris joined a software company based in Oxfordshire last year undertaking a year's industrial placement as part of his degree in Computer Science from the University of York. His first task at the company was to look at the new technology of WAP, which proved to be very relevant to many business areas of the company. Since then, he has worked on WAP solutions for a variety of different purposes ranging from banking information to healthcare solutions. His aim after graduation next year is to continue working in the sector of the IT industry where IT and telecommunications meet.

Richard Taylor

Richard Taylor is the co-founder of Poqit.com, a WAP development consultancy and content conversion specialist. Prior to this, Richard has coded and project-managed his way through every computing fad since 1982, and has worked in the object-oriented field for the past 8 years. In his spare time, Richard likes to dream of Laverda motorbikes with perfect electrics. A cold sweat usually ensues. He can be reached at rct@poqit.com.

To Julia, Alys and Jamie

Marco Toschi

Marco is an Italian engineer who has been working for two and a half years in Oslo as a consultant for Consafe Infotech, an international consultancy company based in Sweden. Originally from Milano, Italy, Marco took my Master of Science degree in telecommunication engineering before moving to Norway. He loves music of whichever genre and also playing his three guitars. In his spare time, he enjoys skating and cycling around in the woods. During the last two years, he has been developing Internet and mobile solutions for Scandinavian telecom operators and companies using the latest technologies available, such as Java, WAP and GPRS. Recently, he has written an article on WML and WMLScript for an Italian technical paper.

I'd like to thank Luca, for suggesting my involvement with this project. I would also want to thank everyone at the Consafe Infotech office in Oslo, for welcoming me so nicely in Norway and Cesare, of course, who took me here. I finally thank my mom and dad, who made me this good…

Table of Contents

Table of Contents

Table of Contents

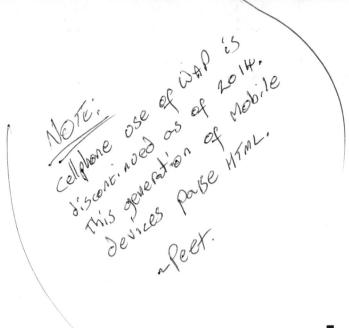

NOTE:
cellphone use of WAP is
discontinued as of 2014.
This generation of mobile
devices parse HTML.
~Peet.

Introduction

Over recent years, the trend toward smaller and faster devices, coupled with the need for information access on the move, has paved the way for a new technology that brings together the two worlds of the Web and the mobile phone. The Wireless Application Protocol (WAP) is an industry-wide standard, defining a communications protocol and application environment that allows us to access Internet content and services from mobile phones. Designed from the ground up for low-power, small-screen devices with limited input capabilities and low bandwidth, WAP has enabled the development of a new breed of Internet-ready phones at mass-market prices.

As a developer, you need to keep up-to-date with changing technology, and WAP is no exception. This book will not only introduce WAP, the underlying protocols and the markup language WML, but will show you how WAP fits in with the Web as we know it, and how you can leverage existing web technologies to create advanced WAP applications. Practical examples will illustrate what it is possible to do using today's technologies, but we also include a discussion of what we can expect to see happening in this area over the next couple of years.

Who is this Book For?

The book is for anyone who wants to find out about WAP, what it is, how it works, and how they can apply this new technology in their own work. Web developers with some experience in HTML, scripting, and some server-side technology will get the most of out of the book, learning how to apply their existing skills in the WAP environment. However, it will also be useful for project managers, application architects or other professionals who want to gain an understanding of WAP technologies and the benefits they can provide to today's businesses.

What's Covered in this Book

This book is divided into five main sections:

❏ The first section (Chapters 1 - 3) starts with an overview of WAP, its place in the wireless world, and a discussion of how the underlying protocols work. It also covers the basic architecture of WAP, all the tools that you'll need to get started with WAP, and in depth coverage of WAP gateways.

❏ Over Chapters 4 - 7, we move on to a thorough introduction to WML and WMLScript, with many practical examples. Differences between the implementations of WML in different devices are discussed, and illustrated in the examples. This section concludes with a look at some usability issues and design guidelines specific to wireless devices.

❏ Next, we look at how we can leverage existing server-side web technologies in WAP development. Chapters 8 - 11 include coverage of ASP, XML, XSLT, JSP, Servlets and ColdFusion. Practical case studies are included, illustrating how to make the most of your existing knowledge in the development WAP applications. Even if you're not familiar with the technologies covered in this section, short introductions at the beginning of each chapter should provide enough background information for you to be able to understand the applications.

❏ The fourth section (Chapters 12 - 15) focuses on more advanced techniques that should help you on your way toward developing m-commerce applications. Starting with the conversion of existing sites to WAP, we move on to see how we can incorporate e-mail and directory services into WAP applications, with examples illustrating this in both Java and ASP. The section concludes with a discussion of the security issues associated with wireless applications.

❏ The final section of book looks to the future and some of the technologies not yet implemented in the first generation of WAP devices, such as push features and WTA (Wireless Telephony Applications). Coverage of a related technology, VoiceXML, is also included in this section. We conclude with a brief look at the long-term future of wireless applications.

The appendices include complete references for WML tags (including details of browser support), WMLScript syntax, WMLScript Standard Libraries and WTAI functions.

What You Need to Use this Book

As you can see from the discussion above, the subjects covered in this book include a diverse set of technologies. To some extent, the tools you'll need depend on which technologies you are most interested in and what platform you are running on. For full details of where these resources are available from, we suggest you check out Appendix H.

Listed below is a summary of the main tools you'll need to try out the code examples:

❏ WAP development kit / WAP emulator: Many emulators are available – for details you should consult Chapter 2. The two that are mainly used throughout the book are those that come with the Nokia and Phone.com toolkits.

❑ Platform: The code has been developed and tested on Windows NT 4 / Windows 2000, but much of the code (the Java examples) should also run on UNIX platforms.

❑ Web server: We've used either IIS (version 4.0 or 5.0 will do) or Apache throughout most of the book. However, two chapters use Gefion Lite Web Server. Note that you'll need to be running IIS or have an ASP plugin for your web server in order to run the ASP examples.

❑ Java: To test the Java examples, you'll need to have JDK 1.3 installed. You'll also need the JSWDK 1.0 (Java Server Web Development Kit) for servlet and JSP support. For running servlets and JSP, we've used Tomcat 3.1 together with Apache (see Appendix F for details).

❑ XML: For chapters 9, 10 and 12, you'll need an XML parser and an XSLT processor. We've used a variety in this book, namely, MSXML that comes as part of IE5, Sun's JAXP 1.0, Apache's Xerces, James Clarke's XT, and Xalan (which comes with Cocoon, see below). Note that the version of MSXML that is shipped with IE5 (and used in Chapter 9) contains an XSLT processor that only works with an older version of XSLT. A new version of the processor is available for download from the Microsoft site.

❑ To run the ColdFusion code, you'll need ColdFusion Studio and Server (evaluation versions are available).

❑ Chapter 12 (*Converting Existing Sites*) uses Apache's Cocoon, an XML-based web publishing framework.

❑ For Chapter 13, in addition to the above Java tools, you'll need JAF (Java Activation Framework) and JavaMail 1.1.3, available from Sun, as well as access to an SMTP server and a POP3 server. However, to run the final example you'll just need IIS 5.0.

❑ For Chapter 14, you need access to an LDAP server – we used Netscape's Directory Server. You'll also need Sun's JNDI and / or Microsoft's ADSI.

❑ To try out any VoiceXML examples, you'll need a voice browser (available from IBM Alphaworks), and also IBM's ViaVoice if audio browsing is required.

All source code from the book is available for download from: http://www.wrox.com.

Conventions

To help you get the most from the text and keep track of what's happening, we've used a number of conventions throughout the book.

For instance:

> **These boxes hold important, not-to-be forgotten information that is directly relevant to the surrounding text.**

While this background style is used for asides to the current discussion.

As for styles within the text:

When we introduce them, we **highlight** important words.

We show keyboard strokes like this: *Ctrl-A.*

We show filenames and code within the text like so: `doGet()`

Text on user interfaces is shown as: Menu.

We present code in three different ways. Definitions of methods and properties are shown as follows:

```
protected void doGet(HttpServletRequest req, HttpServletResponse resp)
                throws ServletException, IOException
```

While example code is shown like this:

```
In our code examples, the code foreground style shows new, important,
    pertinent code
while code background shows code that's less important in the present context,
    or has been seen before.
```

Part One

WAP and the Wireless World

In 1997, Phone.com got together with Ericsson, Motorola and Nokia to form the WAP Forum, with the aim of creating a standardized solution to the problem of how to provide Internet access from mobile phones. In 1999, we saw this becoming a reality, as the first WAP phones hit the streets. This book is not just about WAP, but also about how you, as a developer, can take advantage of this new technology. Part One of the book will give you the necessary background information on the technology and tools, which will allow you to get started in WAP development. We won't be moving on to look at any practical WAP development until Chapter 4.

We'll begin in Chapter 1 with a general overview of WAP, including a discussion on why and how WAP came about, details on the architecture of WAP applications and on the WAP protocol stack.

Chapter 2 gives some practical help and advice, covering the variety of different tools currently available for WAP development, and going into detail on the installation, set up and use of the toolkits from four major vendors: Nokia, Phone.com, Ericsson, and Motorola. It's quick and easy to get going with WAP – and you should have your first "Hello World" program running in no time.

As will become clear in this part of the book, the WAP gateway plays a key part in translating between the familiar Internet protocols, such as TCP/IP and HTTP, and the WAP protocols, such as WSP and WTP. Chapter 3 focuses entirely on gateways, examining what they are and why they're needed – specifically, who needs to run their own gateway – and finishes off by comparing some of the gateways available and examining the installation process for two of these: the Nokia WAP Server and the Kannel Open Source Gateway.

1

Overview of WAP

In 1997 the term WAP hit the headlines all over the world and everyone started looking at it as the new 'money making machine' in the telecommunications area. The arrival of WAP coincided with a period of great interest in the wireless world, both in consumer and industry markets.

WAP – the **Wireless Application Protocol** – is a communications protocol and application environment for the deployment of information resources, advanced telephony services, and Internet access from mobile devices. In this chapter, we will be examining what this statement really means. We will take a broad overview of WAP – what it is, the factors that brought about its creation, and why it is suitable for giving us the power of the Internet via mobile phones and PDAs. We will see the advantages that it has, and the limitations that will be imposed upon us as developers. We will also compare it with more traditional web development to find out what the similarities and differences are. More importantly, we will look at how WAP is structured, the types of systems that are involved and what functions they implement.

All the ideas and concepts introduced in this chapter are analyzed in more depth in later chapters of the book. In the latter part of the book, we will analyze the interaction between WAP and existing technologies, such as dynamic content generation tools and directory services. We will look at specific case studies and help you set up your own WAP solutions.

WAP and the Wireless World

In recent years, wireless telecommunications have become a common subject of technical papers. The new trend in technology is to provide users with the ability to have all they could possibly need in a pocket sized device.

Smaller and smaller PDAs (Personal Data Assistants), laptop computers and mobile phones are hitting the market, incorporating brand new features designed to let the users work and access documents in whatever situation they are in. The Internet is considered with particular interest, given the fact that it is widespread and easy to access from almost anywhere in the world.

One of the latest innovations in the field – and the one that has shaken the telecommunications world to its roots – is WAP. It introduces a new way of looking at the wireless phenomenon – letting the applications 'follow' their customers and provide them with innovative services.

Mobility

Mobility is the new buzzword in the business world and over time, expectations have risen about exactly what this means. In the late eighties and early nineties, *mobility* was associated with the ever-reachable salesman and his mobile phone. This concept expanded (mainly across Europe and Asia) with the advent of Global System for Mobile communications (GSM) in 1991. It is also possible to connect your laptop to a phone, whether by cable, IR port or, in the near future, the much-anticipated **Bluetooth**.

> *Bluetooth is a new technology that is designed to provide a common way to connect mobile devices, such as PDAs, laptops and mobile phones. It was developed by a consortium including Ericsson, Nokia, Intel, IBM, Toshiba, Motorola, and Palm (3Com), and its final goal is to take the place of cables and IR, providing faster connection speeds. For more information you can refer to the site* www.bluetooth.com.

Here is a definition for mobility that might work in today's business world:

> **Mobility is the ability to access information and services any time, anyhow, anywhere.**

This information might be an e-mail that your boss sent you, asking for a report, the latest sales figures for this month, or the phone number of a client you need to talk to.

The services include banking applications, online shopping and checking stock quotes. What we are talking about is extending enterprise applications to incorporate the mobile client, i.e. extending the office to include any location the in which worker might be – at home, at a conference, traveling, and so on.

The increase in expectations of the mobile public over recent years has been driven by the rapid development of wireless technology. From mobile phones to PDAs and handheld computers, the devices being developed have become smaller, more powerful, and – as consumer demand increases – cheaper. This in turn drives the market forward. New technologies spread much faster than they did in the past, giving everyone the chance to experience new services. There is no longer a neat division between different categories of people. Technology available to businessmen is now equally available to teenagers. Although the markets for different categories of people are very different, they can all benefit from new and attractive services.

Changing the Way We Look at the Net

With the advance of the Internet, e-commerce has now grown to enormous proportions; online banking, trading and shopping have proven to be such a success that the goal of business has become the provision of services that are available from *anywhere*.

On top of this, the number of mobile phones in the world is increasing every day at an astonishing speed, with analysts forecasting that there will be more than a billion mobile phones in use within the next five years (Gartner Group) and that over half of Internet access will be through non-PCs (Meta Group). The mobile phone has become a part of daily life for many people, and together with a watch, is the only electronic device that many people carry around everywhere with them, all day long.

The graph below is from a report, *WAP Market Strategies*, from Ovum (http://www.ovum.com). It compares the forecasted growth of mobile phones, Internet enabled mobile phones, and Internet enabled mobile phones that are actually used to access the Internet:

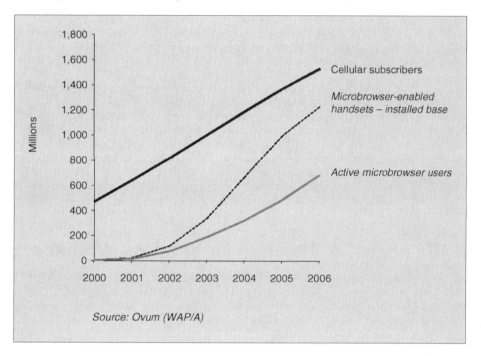

Wherever we are and whatever the topic, we have come to take for granted the availability of information, through the computer. However, a major bottleneck has been predicted for this data Utopia at the beginning of this millennium. That bottleneck is the computer itself. Constant improvements have kept the price of a PC reasonably high – high enough to keep the purchase of a computer at the bottom of many people's list of priorities. Furthermore, there are still many people that do not feel the need for, or do not feel like playing around with, devices that they see as too technical. Some others may be working behind a computer all day long, and therefore refuse to sit behind one during their spare time too.

It's time that the Internet moved on from the PC. This doesn't mean the end of the PC; radio didn't kill the newspaper, TV didn't kill the radio, and the VCR didn't kill cinema – there's always room for more than one media. It simply means that there is more than one way of accessing information from the Internet, and the method you choose depends on who you are, where you are and what you want.

We now have Internet capable televisions and games consoles, and within a few years, we should see the introduction of Internet enabled Hi-Fi systems. And, with the advent of cheap, reliable mobile phones capable of accessing the Net, there seems to be a major opportunity for a powerful and real mobile data service.

However, the Internet – as it is now – is not well suited to the mobile phone. It is typically too complex and takes up too much bandwidth; and a web page would generally not fit onto the screen of your average mobile phone. While the third generation of wireless technology (known as 3G) should go some way to easing the bandwidth issue, there are still other problems that need to be considered, before the Internet and mobile devices can be brought together. For example, there is typically no keyboard on a mobile phone, so it is much harder for a user to enter information on their phone compared to a PC. Also, the screen is very small, and so cannot display much text at any one time and will struggle with complex graphics. It goes without saying that your average phone is nothing like as powerful as a PC!

So, if we are going to allow Internet access from a mobile phone, we first need to take into account these limitations of the client device. The Internet protocols (TCP/IP and HTTP) are far from being suitable for use with mobile phone communications. They introduce far too many overheads, requiring many messages between clients and server just to set up a connection. These overheads call for a high processing power on the client device.

Furthermore, there is a second limitation connected to the internal structure of wireless networks. This is the sustained waiting time, called **latency**. Basically, the information coming from the Internet and going to the mobile phones has to go through various elements in the mobile network, each one introducing a little delay. Also, the air interface used to transmit data to mobile telephones has a bandwidth that is very limited, nowadays reaching 9600 bit per second in a GSM network, compared to a minimum of around 28 or 56 kbps on a wired network. Thus the Internet protocols, which send many large messages, naturally result in a large latency.

These reasons motivate the need for a new set of protocols more appropriate to communication with wireless devices.

The WAP Forum – A Standard for Wireless Web Access

Back in 1995, in the US, Unwired Planet introduced **HDML** – the **Handheld Device Mark up Language** – which is a cut-down version of HTML, designed to run on wireless devices. And, in Japan, the operator NTT DoCoMo introduced a service called **i-mode** in early 1999. This has become a very popular technology, with almost 7 million users accessing Internet services from mobile phones, which has been driven largely by the youth market.

These two technologies present us with an interesting question: which is the winning technology? Is it the one providing the best technical solution to a given problem, or is it the one that is most widely adopted? This was probably the question that was asked at Unwired Planet (now Phone.com) during 1996 and early 1997. Recall that Unwired Planet was the first company involved in the development of a new technology devised to port Internet services to wireless users. They could have kept on focusing just on the development of HDML, letting it grow in the US as NTT DoCoMo have done with I-mode in Japan. However, they chose instead to get the major mobile phone manufacturers involved in their project, reckoning that the more devices there were that supported the technology in the world market, the more they could sell their wireless Internet solutions around the world. Involving other companies, each one with a large customer base in different parts of the world, has helped to promote the newborn technology.

Thus, the **WAP Forum** was created by Phone.com, Ericsson, Nokia and Motorola. Everyone got 'infected' by the WAP virus, with network operators and device manufacturers struggling to offer the new technology to their customers, just to stay competitive. The Phone.com WAP gateway – UP.Link – is the most mounted in operator networks. Also, the Phone.com software application – UP.Browser, which allows the mobile phones that it is installed in to receive WAP data – is present in a large fraction of the WAP compliant mobile phones around the world.

With the advent of the WAP Forum, Phone.com shared its knowledge, and the partnership soon evolved into the now all-encompassing **WAP specifications** that include complementary application, session, transaction, security, and transport protocol layers. A new markup language called **the Wireless Markup Language (WML)** has also been created. These protocols minimize the problems outlined above associated with the use of Internet protocols for wireless data transfer. They do this by eliminating unnecessary data transfers, and using binary code to reduce the amount of data that has to be sent. Also, wireless sessions are designed to be easily suspended and resumed, without the connection overheads associated with the Internet protocols. Thus the protocols are well suited to the low bandwidth associated with wireless communications.

The WAP forum has now grown to a membership of over 230, made up of carriers, handset manufacturers, software developers and other companies. Their mandate includes ensuring product interoperability and maintaining growth of the wireless market. With 90% of the handset market now being represented at the WAP Forum, along with many software companies and network operators, WAP will be the primary way of accessing the Internet.

The standardization of methods to access the Internet from mobile phones has brought many benefits to many different people. For the end users, a breadth of choice of devices, networks and applications has arisen in a competitive market, since the specifications are not biased towards any one company. The network operators have been able to extend their customer base due to the new services on offer, which are independent of the network used. For the service providers there are new functionalities, such as **push** technology and **WTA (Wireless Telephony Applications)**, which are discussed later, that could increase their revenue making potential. And for the device manufacturers, there is the opportunity to devise new innovative products in a wide open market, without a huge increase in expense since WAP tries to keep the necessary processing power to a minimum.

At the time of writing, the WAP Forum is working on version 1.3 of the WAP specifications, and version 1.2 is being implemented in the wireless networks. However, at present, mobile phones still only support version 1.1 of the WAP specifications. This book will focus on the aspects of the 1.1 specification that are implemented today, but we will take a quick look at some of the forthcoming features that will be important in the future.

The Business Perspective

As the new standard protocol for providing content to wireless devices, WAP has been accepted on the telecommunications market with enthusiasm from all sides, as the growth in the stock market of some of the companies involved with WAP can confirm. The high penetration rates for mobile phones across Europe, Japan and other parts of Asia – and increasingly in the US – mean that mobile commerce has become so significant it has even given birth to new jargon terms, such as **m-commerce** and **m-business**. Many businesses were caught out by the speed of change on the Internet and the rapid rise of e-commerce, and so have jumped quickly to supply WAP services in an effort not to be left behind. There are already plans in place for **mobile advertising** – advertising content aimed at mobile devices – to finance the investments made. This is somewhat hampered by the difficulties in profiling customers.

A new service, made available with WAP, is the **Location Information Service**. This can supply the position of a network subscriber to the WAP applications that use it. It is made possible by the many antennas network operators have distributed around the country to communicate with the mobile phones. The network operator always knows which antenna is receiving the signal from a given mobile phone, and of course the operator also knows where each antenna is located.

Location services provide a way of delivering location dependent information and advertising to subscribers. For example, it will allow us to find out where the nearest bank or the nearest travel agency is. These services, even though included in the WAP 1.1 specifications, are not yet implemented in the operator networks. When available they will provide many benefits.

Together with the push technology that is part of the WAP 1.2 specifications, this feature will give the developers the ability to design marketing applications that provide advertising information to subscribers when, for example they are close to a shop or a bank or a cinema. Push technology, which is discussed in more detail later on in this chapter, can be used to send information to subscribers without them sending any request for content.

We are now ready to analyze where the money comes from in the WAP world; some of the possibilities are shown in the diagram below:

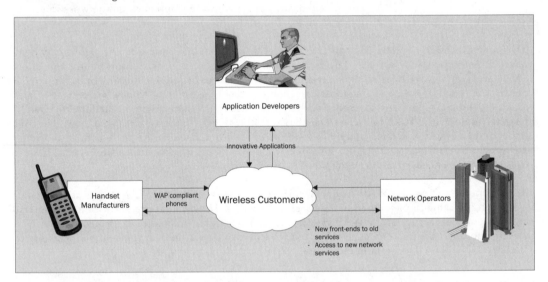

The additional data traffic in the network is the first real source of revenue, at least in the beginning when m-commerce and advertising are yet to become mainstream. The network operators are evidently the parties gaining the most advantage from this, since the more new users that the content providers attract to their WAP applications, the more the traffic will grow in the network. The other direct sources of income for network operators are the subscriptions from WAP-interested customers.

One interesting feature offered by network operators, but also sometimes by content providers, is a **WAP portal**. A WAP portal is similar to a web portal: it is a page containing many links to interesting applications, grouped by category. Since the network operator's portal will, in most cases, be the first page that a subscriber sees on their device when connecting, it is clear that the applications listed there will have an enormous advantage over those that are not.

Network operators will charge content providers and advertisers for the display of their links on the operator's portal. It is also probable that the operators will try to form partnerships with content providers who supply new and interesting services. In this way, they will monopolize their content, thus differentiating themselves from other operators, satisfying their own subscribers and attracting subscribers from other operators.

Application developers play an important role in the newborn WAP industry. In addition to providing **Value Added Services**, there is a strong demand for services that are available on the Web to be ported to WAP. One of the major advantages to WAP is that its markup language, WML, is based on **XML**. This effectively means that it should be easier to provide content in a device independent way. In practice, this is not always so, but this is a topic we'll come to time and again throughout the book. It is discussed in detail in Chapter 9.

Last but not least, content providers are the ones closing the WAP circle. As we have seen, they will be forced to pay to be listed on the operator's portal. They will also probably pay more than one operator, so that the service that they provide can reach a wider audience. If their service is attractive enough, they may try to share the revenues that the operators make, due to the traffic that their WAP application generates on the wireless network. Incomes will also be generated for the content providers if they decide to tax the subscriber to access their content or if they include advertisements on their pages.

What is WAP Able to Do?

As with all new technologies, the expectations of WAP were very high when it was first introduced. Before the first WAP phones were available, everyone was expecting to surf the Internet from their phones just like from a normal browser, with pixel-perfect content, images and sound. The reality of course is quite different...

WAP is intended to provide a common application environment for mobile devices and its protocols *are* based on the Internet protocols. However, this does *not* mean that WAP was devised with the intent of porting the entire content of the Internet to mobile devices.

The average HTML page is now very elaborate, filled with multimedia content, frames, colors, and dynamic effects. Such pages would lose all their appeal if translated into WAP pages and presented on a display of, for example, 5 lines of 20 characters, like the one shown in the screenshot here:

Even though there are now some products available for translating HTML pages into WAP ones (and we'll discuss these in Chapter 12), the results are less than convincing. Today, WAP applications are almost all primarily developed for WAP users, bearing in mind the limitations of mobile phones. This will probably continue to be the trend for the future.

Typical applications available over WAP today include trading applications, home banking applications, shopping applications and e-mail interfaces. Many sites offer news, radio and TV listings, and some of them will help you find a restaurant or a list of cinemas for the city you're traveling to. These are a few examples of URLs to current WAP sites:

Italian Giroscopio hotel booking:	`http://www.giroscopio.com/wap`
UK Entertainment Centre:	`http://www.ents24.com/index.wml`
WAP portal:	`http://wap.waportal.com`
WebCab.de:	`http://webcab.de/i.wml`
ElectricNews.Net - tech news via WAP:	`http://adlib.ie/enn/waphome.wml`

With limited or non-existent graphics, no multi-media, no complex user interaction, and no colors, what is left for us in WAP applications?

If you are willing to take a chance on building a successful WAP application, you will have to start thinking about the peculiarities of a mobile device and how people could take advantage of them. People are always on the move, so Location Information Services will have a major impact on the market. Push technology will probably supply a way to try to predict what people feel like doing and to suggest where and when they can do it, without them requesting anything from your site.

WAP Application Architecture

So far we have looked at what WAP is, and the reasons why it has been introduced. We will now embark on a more in depth description of its technical details.

The WAP protocols were designed with the web protocols in mind. The goal of WAP was to use the underlying web structure, but to render communication between content providers and mobile devices more efficient and less time consuming than if the web protocols themselves were used. In this section, we will start introducing the elements involved in mobile communications, and their role in the whole picture.

Let's start by comparing the different ways you can access information from the Internet using a WAP device. In the diagram below the main differences between (a) WAP used to access the Internet, (b) WAP used to access an intranet, and (c) the Internet architectures are shown.

Since the WAP architecture has been designed to closely follow that of the Web, the client-server paradigm used by the Internet has been inherited by WAP. The main difference, however, is the presence of the WAP gateway for translating between HTTP and WAP.

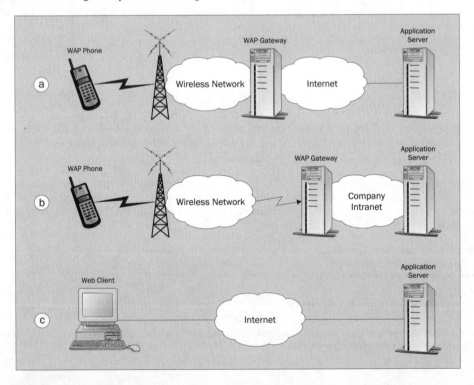

So far in this chapter, we may have introduced some terms that are new to you, as well as some that may already be familiar. Before continuing, we will take a closer look at these technical terms, which will be used in the rest of this chapter and, indeed, in the rest of the book.

- ❏ **WAP Device**: This term indicates the physical device that you use to access WAP applications and content. It doesn't necessarily have to be a mobile phone – it might be a PDA or a handheld computer. More generally, it's every WAP compliant device.

- ❏ **WAP Client**: In a network environment, a client is typically the logical entity that is operated by the user and communicates with the 'server entity'. In the WAP world, the client is the entity that receives content from the Internet via a WAP Gateway. This is usually (but not necessarily) the WAP browser. Commonly, 'WAP client' and 'WAP browser' are often used interchangeably.

- ❏ **WAP Browser**: This is software running on the WAP device that interprets the WAP content arriving from the Internet and decides how to display it on the screen of the WAP device. WAP browsers are available for all WAP devices, and are frequently referred to as **Microbrowsers**. There are also emulators available for some browsers, which run on PCs.

- ❏ **User Agent**: An agent is normally the software that deals with protocols, and WAP is no exception to this. The WAP client contains two different agents: the WAE User Agent and the WTA User Agent (each of which will be covered later in the chapter).

- ❏ **WAP Gateway**: This is the element that sits (logically) between the WAP device and the origin server. It acts as an 'interpreter' between the two, enabling them to communicate. It usually resides within the operator network, but you can also install your own gateway, as we will see later. Unless otherwise stated, when a gateway is discussed, we mean a gateway residing in the operator network, since this is the more common situation that one encounters.

- ❏ **Network Operator**: This is the company or organization that provides carrier services to its subscribers. As an example, the company you are paying your telephone bills to is your network operator. A network operator enables you to make calls to other phones from your telephone and, in addition, provides you with different services, such as voice mail, call diversion etc.

- ❏ **Bearer Services**: These are the different ways that a mobile phone can communicate with the wireless network. To send and receive data from an application server, mobile phones have to establish some sort of connection with the WAP gateway. A bearer service is the method they use to do this. In GSM networks, for example, we either use **SMS** (Short Message Service) or **CSD** (Circuit Switched Data). With the former bearer, the gateway has to divide the information that is to be sent to the phone into a lot of little messages (just like when you send a text message to a friend using your mobile). With CSD, we communicate with the gateway using a data connection, which is not dissimilar to the way the modem in your computer communicates with the Internet Service Provider that you have an account with.

- ❏ **Content/Origin/Application Server**: These three names are used throughout the book interchangeably. They denote the element that hosts the Internet content that is sent to clients when they make a request for it. A web server is an origin server, providing HTML content (but also WAP content if properly configured).

As you can see from the diagrams on the previous page, the WAP architecture resembles closely that of the Internet.

To access an application stored on the server, the client initiates a connection with the WAP gateway, and sends a request for content. The gateway converts the requests coming from the WAP client into the format used over the Internet (HTTP), and then forwards them to the origin server. On the way back, the content is sent from the server to the gateway, which then translates it to WAP format, and then sends it to the mobile device. The gateway allows the Internet to talk to the wireless network.

The concept of connection is left deliberately vague, since the goal of WAP is to provide a protocol that is able to adapt to any type of mobile network. The connection is established between the WAP phone and the gateway by means of the bearer used. Whether we are accessing WAP services by sending data packets or SMS messages, we see the same functionality. It may, however, affect the speed of the connection and therefore affect the cost of the connection, but this is less important to the developer.

As is the case with the Internet, content servers host the content or applications, but in the case of WAP these are sent to the clients as **WML** and **WMLScript** files, rather than HTML etc. WML (Wireless Markup Language) and WMLScript are the languages used to design and write WAP content. WML has some similarities to HTML and XML, and WMLScript doesn't differ much from JavaScript. They are described later in this chapter, and in more detail in Chapters 4, 5 and 6.

The WML and WMLScript files are sent, on request, to the WAP client via a WAP gateway, which translates the content into a form that is optimized for the narrow bandwidth radio interface. The clients contain a microbrowser that displays the received information to the user.

We'll now look at a few of the elements of the WAP architecture in a bit more detail.

WAP Client

The WAP specifications leave a great deal of autonomy to the device manufacturers. There is no WAP specification indicating what the WAP device should look like or how it should present and display the content it receives from the Internet. These kinds of decisions, together with those relating to the user interface and the internal organization of phone functionality such as the phonebook, are left to the vendor.

The only requirement for a device to be WAP compliant is that it must implement a **WAE User agent**, a **WTA User Agent** and the **WAP Stack**.

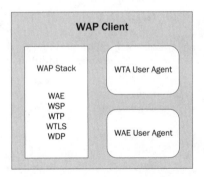

❑ The **WAE User Agent** (Wireless Application Environment User Agent) is the microbrowser that renders the content for display. It receives the compiled WML, WMLScript, and any images from the WAP gateway, and executes or displays them on the screen. Even if the implementation details are left to the vendor, the browser must implement all the functionality provided by WML and WMLScript. It must also manage the interaction with the user, such as text input, and error or warning messages.

❑ The **WTA User Agent** (Wireless Telephony Applications User Agent) receives compiled WTA files from the WTA server and executes them. The WTA User Agent includes access to the interface to the phone, and network functionality such as number dialing, call answering, phonebook organization, message management and location indication services, which we discussed earlier.

❑ The **WAP Stack** implementation allows the phone to connect to the WAP gateway using the WAP protocols. We'll be looking at all the WAP protocols in detail later in this chapter.

WAP Proxy, WAP Gateway Or WAP Server?

When you read articles, surf the Internet or attend conferences, you will certainly hear about WAP *gateways*, *servers* and *proxies*. These three terms are often used interchangeably and wrongly so. On the contrary, in the world of networks these three elements are quite different logically and they have different functionalities as well:

- ❑ **Content/Origin/Application Server**: This is the element in the network where the information or web/WAP applications reside. (Web servers belong to this category.)

- ❑ **Proxy**: This is an intermediary element, acting both as a client and as a server in the network. It is located between clients and origin servers; the clients send requests to it and it retrieves and caches the information needed by contacting the origin servers.

- ❑ **Gateway**: This is an intermediary element usually used to connect two different types of network. It receives requests directly from the clients as if it actually were the origin server that the clients want to retrieve the information from. The clients are usually unaware that they are speaking to the gateway.

These three terms are illustrated in the diagram below where (a) an origin server has a direct connection to the Internet, (b) access to the Internet is through a proxy server, and (c) a gateway server lies between two different types of networks.

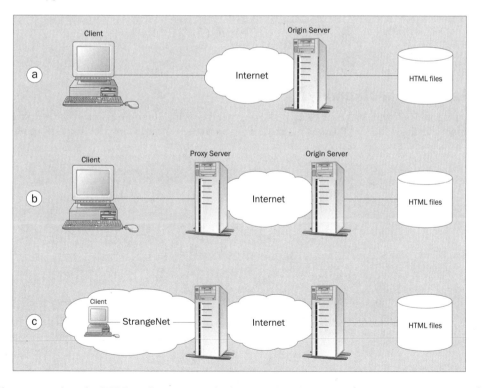

The element used in the WAP architecture, which we earlier defined as (and is commonly called) a WAP gateway, is actually a **proxy**. It is used to connect the wireless domain with the Internet one. However, it contains *protocol gateway* functionality plus *encoder/decoder* functionality.

The products at present on the market create the confusion of terms. What you are typically offered today when you search for such a WAP element is a mixture of all of the servers described above. It logically belongs to the proxy category but, as we have seen, has gateway functionality and in addition is equipped with server functionality. In other words it can run server-side scripts, Java servlets and do all the things that a standard web server can do.

The rule to survive this confusion is generally to consider a WAP gateway and a WAP proxy as the same thing; we will try to consistently use the term 'gateway' throughout this book. Also, it's a good idea to avoid the term 'WAP server'. WAP servers are usually a WAP gateway with server functionality added. It is probably better to refer to such an element as a "combined application server and gateway".

In the diagram below we illustrate the use of a WAP proxy/gateway. We will move on to consider exactly what the gateway does in the next section.

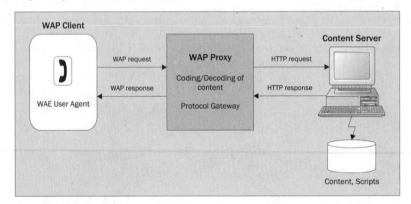

WAP Gateway Functionality

In the diagram below, a WAP gateway is shown, together with other elements in the wireless network. This highlights how the WAP Gateway has to collaborate and interface with all the other elements in order to provide a proper service:

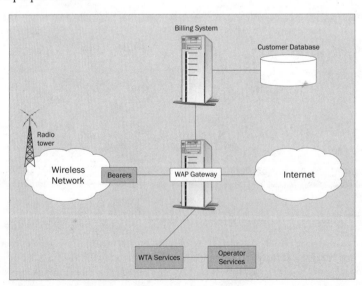

Whenever you start a WAP session on your mobile phone, the following steps are executed. (The details of the WAP protocols are dealt with in a later section.)

❏ A connection is created via WSP (Wireless Session Protocol) between the mobile device and the WAP gateway, which we assume is present in the operator network.

❏ As you enter the address of a WAP site (by typing it or selecting a bookmark, for example), the gateway is sent a request from the device's microbrowser using WSP. WSP is the WAP protocol in charge of starting and ending the connections from the mobile devices to the WAP gateway. We will discuss it in more detail in a later section.

❏ The gateway translates the WSP request into an HTTP request and sends it to the appropriate origin server.

❏ The origin server sends back the requested information to the gateway via HTTP.

❏ The gateway translates and compresses the information and sends it back to the microbrowser in the mobile device.

The gateway part of the WAP proxy takes care of translating all the requests that are sent and received by the client using WSP to the protocol that the origin server is using (HTTP for example). This is illustrated in the diagram below. The content provider sends its content using HTTP to the gateway. It then forwards all the content received to the WAP devices, using the WAP protocols.

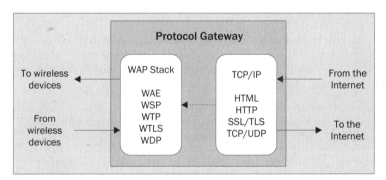

Functionally speaking, the gateway operates to some extent in a similar way to the current Internet web browsers. When you try to access an FTP or Gopher site using your web browser, you are completely shielded from the protocols and requests that your browser uses to contact the site. As far as you are concerned, both FTP and Gopher sites use the same protocol to communicate with the browser as a normal web site, since the information that is displayed on your screen is in the same format as when you access an HTML page.

The coder/decoder (CODEC) functionality within the gateway is used to convert the WML and WMLScript content going to and coming from the client into a form that is optimized for low-bandwidth networks. This is illustrated in the diagram on the following page.

Translation of encrypted data takes place in the memory of the gateway. No unencrypted data is ever stored on a secondary storage medium since this would create crucial security problems. This idea is discussed in more detail in Chapter 3 (on gateways) and Chapter 15 (on WAP security).

Content belonging to a non-secure session is cached on the storage media of the gateway, reducing the processing time and the resources required when someone else requests the same content.

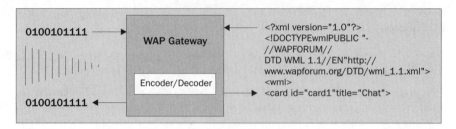

Another service that the CODEC functionality can provide is the translation of HTML or text to WML. However, this use of the gateway should be considered very carefully, since many limitations apply. HTML and WML are both based on tags and they can look very similar to each other – we can be fooled into thinking that translating HTML into WML is the easiest way of accessing Internet content from a wireless device. However, HTML has now grown into a fully-fledged language, allowing dynamic content and multimedia to be displayed. Many Internet sites around use frames, and take advantage of all the features of HTML and the use of multimedia such as sound, video and graphics. The result of the translation of such an HTML page into a WML one will therefore be quite poor. (Methods of translating existing content, with all the advantages and disadvantages this brings, and the situations in which translation is suitable are discussed in detail in Chapter 12.)

The HTML to WML translator, when present among the gateway features, is there mainly for giving us compatibility and to reassure us that if we really need something important that is stored in HTML format then we have a way to retrieve it.

The WAP gateway needs, of course, to have more functionality than just that listed above. Since it is usually the operator network element that is contacted by customers to access a service, it also has to include charging functionality. It can be connected to a billing system and a customer database for this purpose.

It also implements an interface for each of the bearers present in the wireless network of the operator. For example, if we install a gateway in a GSM network, it must implement an SMS (Short Message Service) and a CSD (Circuit Switched Data) interface.

The WAP gateway is also connected to the WTA server, present in the operator network, that provides the interface for accessing some of the network services the operator wants to provide.

Who Needs a Gateway?

So should you install your own gateway? There aren't too many reasons to do this, since the wireless network operator always provides the gateway. Furthermore, WAP gateways are designed for installation and use in an operator network and their use in another environment generates some difficulties, for example the adjustment of the gateway for the different bearers and handsets.

If you are involved in the design of an application that involves a high level of security, such as Intranet directory services, or involving the exchange of critical private data, you may be concerned with the security risks of a wireless connection. You will not want to be left with an insecure information exchange all the way between your hosted content and the mobile devices.

Instead, many companies wish to install their own gateway, ensuring that their content can be sent securely to the mobile phones authorized to access it, avoiding completely the Internet side of WAP. These issues will be discussed further in Chapter 3, but also see Chapter 15 for other security issues.

The installation of a fully-fledged WAP gateway will take time, effort, and usually cost a lot of money, so before undertaking this action, make sure there are no alternatives. When installing your own gateway, you will also have to choose whether to restrict the number of customers that can access your service, or to install an interface for each and every type of bearer available on the wireless network market.

Another problem with setting up your own gateway is that customers wishing to use it will need to change the way their phone is configured completely, and then change it back, if they are to use the original gateway provided with their phone. This will mean changing the IP address of the gateway, phone number and possibly the user name and password. One or two phones provide multiple settings. However, this is the exception rather than the rule.

If you work for an operator or if you have to implement an Intranet solution (and this last possibility is one of the only situations where you will really need your own gateway), then you can consider buying one of the software packages listed below. You will find more details on gateways in Chapter 3, but here is a brief summary of the current products available:

- **Ericsson Jambala**: product aimed at the TDMA network
- **Ericsson WAP gateway/proxy**: gateway package that will fit the GSM network
- **Nokia WAP Server**: gateway package that will fit the GSM network
- **Motorola Exchange (MIX)**: scalable gateway package that will adapt to different types of networks
- **Phone.com UP.Link**: gateway package that fits diverse types of network, including CDMA, CDPD, GSM, iDEN, PDC, PHS and TDMA

WAP Application Server

While on the Internet a web server is the content provider – a computer hosting the information we wish to share with the rest of the world. When considering WAP content/application servers you will see that the features that a server provides can vary greatly, depending on who you are speaking to. Out of the confusion come two definitions, which are given below:

- The WAP application/origin/content server has the exactly the same function as a web server and offers the same features to clients. The distinction between them is only a logical one, since the two can coexist on the same physical device, and some servers can provide both functions using the same piece of software. The only difference lies, of course, in the content that they store and send back to the clients. While the web server supports files such as HTML, JavaScript, multimedia, and all types of images, the WAP application server stores WML, WMLScript and **WBMP** (Wireless Bitmap) image files.

- A WAP server is usually just a WAP application server with gateway functionality added. It will provide all the services a normal origin server provides, but it will also act as a WAP gateway.

The WAP application server may, of course, also host all the technologies used to provide dynamic content. As you will see later in the book, you can use XML in conjunction with **XSLT, ASP,** and Java servlets, to name just a few, to dynamically generate WML content in the same way that you use them to generate HTML content on a web server. Chapters 8 to 11 will be focusing on this subject.

nable a web server to host WAP applications, you merely need to add the **MIME** types for
the configuration settings of the server. (We will see how we can do this in the next
IME (Multipurpose Internet Mail Extensions) is a method used to convert and transmit files
ernet. When transmitting the files, the server attaches a header to the file defining the type
ained in the files. The receiving client then knows what the file type is and can deal with it
y. Most WAP browsers accept only WAP MIME types, and sending a file with the wrong
leader will generate an error.

WAP Internal Structure

Before we look at the details of how the WAP protocols are structured, let us first briefly examine the definitions of a **protocol** and a **layer**.

Protocols

As anyone who has done any international traveling knows, it is quite important when you travel to adapt your clothing and behavior to the place you are in. It is also important to speak a common language that allows others to understand what you are saying. The same problem arises with telecommunication networks; there are many different devices, and networks, and to allow them to communicate with each other, you must provide them with a common language. **Protocols** are the answer to this problem. There are a lot of different kinds, from very simple ones, to very elaborate ones, but they all have the same property in common: they allow computers to communicate with each other.

> **A protocol defines the type and the structure of messages that two devices have to use when they are communicating with each other.**

This is what the Internet is all about: a set of common protocols (including HTTP) to let everyone speak with anyone else on the Net.

Layers

Since the protocols are functionally and logically divided into different groups of functionality, they are also physically framed into layers, each one providing a specific service to the next layer. One layer may provide methods to send bits down a physical cable; another may supply methods to establish a connection. The **protocol stack** is the set of all the layers that compose the set of protocols.

WAP Protocol Stack

In the next few pages, we will look at how the WAP protocol is structured and how the different WAP layers map into Internet protocol layers.

If your aim is to design WAP applications, you don't need to know very much about the WAP stack. The only two sections that have some relevance for developers are the ones dealing with WML and WMLScript. However, we provide details of all the WAP protocols here for completeness and for those of you who are curious about them.

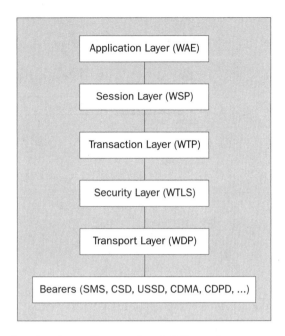

The WAP stack, illustrated in the above diagram, has 5 different layers:

- **Application Layer**: WAE (Wireless Application Environment) provides an application environment intended for the development and execution of portable applications and services.

- **Session Layer**: WSP (Wireless Session Protocol) supplies methods for the organized exchange of content between client/server applications.

- **Transaction Layer**: WTP (Wireless Transaction Protocol) provides different methods for performing transactions, to a varying degree of reliability.

- **Security Layer**: WTLS (Wireless Transport Layer Security) is an optional layer that provides, when present, authentication, privacy and secure connections between applications.

- **Transport Layer**: WDP (Wireless Datagram Protocol) is the bottom layer of the WAP stack, which shelters the upper layers from the bearer services offered by the operator.

The WAP stack was derived from, and inherited most of the characteristics of, the ISO OSI reference model [ISO7498]. The main difference between the two is the number of layers: WAP has just five layers, while the OSI model has seven of them.

For those of you not familiar with the OSI model, it is maybe useful to compare the WAP layers to the web protocol stack used in the web model. There are of course strong similarities between the two; the main differences being the compactness and lightness of the WAP protocols. As we saw earlier, the Internet protocols introduce high overheads and are not effective when used in the low bandwidth and high latency network such as the one used with mobile phones.

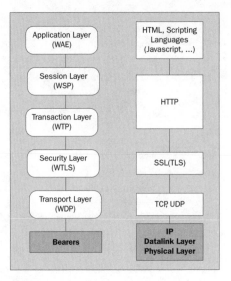

Both of the application layers, WAE and that of the web stack, provide a markup language and a scripting language for the development of applications. Bear in mind however, that this diagram is illustrative, and that it is not intended to imply a direct one-to-one correspondance between the protocols.

We'll now consider each of the WAP stack layers in turn.

Wireless Application Environment (WAE)

The application layer of WAP provides an environment that includes all the elements related to the development and execution of applications. The Wireless Application Environment (WAE) allows the developer to use specific formats and services, created and optimized for presenting content and interacting with limited capability devices. WAE consists of two different user agents located on the client side, the WAE user agent – including the microbrowser and the text message editor – and the WTA user agent. (WTA is discussed later on in this chapter, and also in more detail in Chapter 18.)

The WAE specifications say nothing about the implementation of the user agents. All the browsers, message editors, and phonebooks contained in WAP devices can vary greatly while still complying with the specifications. WAE formally specifies just the formats, such as images and text formats, that the user agents have to be compliant with. This is an important characteristic of WAP in general, as we will soon see when looking at WML.

Beginning with WAP 1.2, there will also be another scenario: it will be possible to push content towards a WAP client without any request made by the client. This will be covered later in this chapter, and also in more detail in Chapter 16.

The main building blocks of the WAE are the following:

❑ A lightweight markup language: WML

❑ A lightweight scripting language: WMLScript

❑ An interface to local services and advanced telephony services: WTA (not yet implemented)

We will look at WML and WMLScript in the next two sections, but these topics are covered in more detail in Chapters 4, 5 and 6.

Wireless Markup Language – WML

In the early days of the Internet, HTML was created with the intention of specifying the content to be displayed, leaving decisions as to *how* to display the content to the browsers. However, nowadays what is encapsulated in an HTML page is much more than the content. Layers, pictures, and special effects leave very little to the creativity of the browser.

With WML, WAP takes a step backwards in time to the old system. As application designers, we do not know to whom we are talking to, how big the screen of the client is, or how many keys the keyboard has. We simply know that a screen is available, and we assume that it is tiny. That's all. Keeping this in mind, we have to forget the beautiful images provided by our favorite web sites, the astonishing dynamic effects, the sounds and all the other fancy things that can be found when you browse the web.

WML has been designed to display mainly text-based pages. It is tag-based, shares elements of HTML4 and HDML2, and is defined as an XML document type. Each WML document is a single **deck**, which is made up of one or more **cards**. When the user accesses a WAP site, it sends back a deck; the user is shown the first card, reads the content, possibly can enter some information, and then moves to another card, the choice of which is dependent on the user's actions. The way in which the card is displayed is left to the browser; for example, different browsers will prompt the user for input in different ways. The browser decides how to best present the content depending on the device capabilities.

Although WML has limited capabilities when compared to HTML, it has nevertheless a wide range of features:

- ❑ **Support for text**: When including text in a card, the programmer can use emphasis elements (such as **bold**, *Italics*, <u>underlined</u>, etc...), line breaks and tables. You should remember, however, that the features each browser implements may vary, and some do not support tables.

- ❑ **Support for images**: A new format has been created for displaying images, called **WBMP** (Wireless Bitmap). Images compliant with this new standard are currently black and white. However, some browsers do not support images.

- ❑ **User input**: Cards can contain input elements. The browser decodes input tags and then decides the best way to prompt the user for the input requested. WML specifies tags for allowing the user to submit text entries, choose among a list of options, and start a navigation or history management task (such as going to the previous card or jumping to a specified link).

- ❑ **Variables:** Variables can be included in the WML code, to keep track of hidden information and to manipulate user input.

- ❑ **Navigation and history stack**: Common navigation and history functionalities are included.

- ❑ **International support**: The WML character set is UNICODE, which uses 16 bits to represent each character.

- ❑ **Optimization for narrow-band:** WML has been designed to adapt to the high-latency and narrow-band characteristics of wireless networks. The specifications say that connections with the origin server should be avoided unless absolutely necessary. This is accomplished by means of various technologies: variables that last longer than a single deck, cards grouped in decks, and client-side user input validation via WMLScript.

The following is an example of what WML code looks like (it is a simple 'Hello World' type example). For now we will not assume your understanding of it, as we will be studying WML in detail in Chapters 4 and 5.

```
<?xml version="1.0"?>
<!DOCTYPE wml PUBLIC "-//WAPFORUM//DTD WML 1.1//EN"
"http://www.wapforum.org/DTD/wml_1.1.xml">

<wml>
    <card id="card1" title="Hello World">
        <p>
            Hello WAP World!
        </p>
    </card>
</wml>
```

WMLScript

WMLScript is a lightweight procedural scripting language, which is based on ECMAScript, the standardized version of JavaScript. It adds intelligence to the client, providing a set of libraries for mathematical operations, string manipulation, etc., collaborates with WML, and helps prevent unnecessary connections with the server. In particular WMLScript supplies the programmer with:

❑ The capability of checking and validating the input submitted by the user before it is sent to the server, thus preventing the transmission of invalid data to the server.

❑ Access to the device facilities, such as the phonebook, calendar and list of messages (WTA).

❑ Methods of interacting with the user without the help of the content server, such as methods for displaying error and warning messages.

WMLScript files are separate to the WML decks from which they are called, unlike HTML where script can be embedded. Even if WML cards contain a link to WMLScript files, these are not sent to the client with the WML files, as happens with HTML. Currently, WMLScript files are sent to the WAP client only when the client tries explicitly to access functionality (typically a function) contained in one of them.

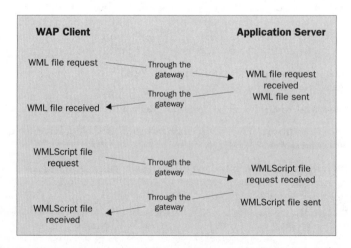

Wireless Session Layer – WSP

The Wireless Session Protocol enables services to exchange data between applications in an organized way. It includes two different protocols:

❑   **Connection oriented session services** – operates over the Wireless Transaction Protocol (WTP)

❑   **Connectionless session services** – operates directly over the Wireless Transport layer (WDP)

Session services are those functionalities that help to set up a connection between a client and a server. A service is delivered through the use of the primitives it provides. **Primitives** are defined messages that a client sends to the server to request a service facility. In WSP, for example, one of the primitives is S-Connect, with which we can request the creation of a connection with the server.

The **connection-oriented** session service provides facilities used to manage a session and to transmit reliable data between a client and a server. The session created can then be suspended and resumed later if the transmission of data becomes impossible. Also, once the push technology takes off, unsolicited data can be pushed from the server to the client in a confirmed or unconfirmed way. In **confirmed push** the server is notified upon reception of the data by the client, in **unconfirmed push** the server is not notified of the reception of the pushed data. Most of the facilities provided by the connection-oriented session service are confirmed, meaning that the client can send Request primitives and receive Confirm primitives and the server can send Response primitives and receive Indication primitives.

The **connectionless** session service provides only non-confirmed services; in particular only unreliable method invocation (asking the server to execute an operation and return a result) and unconfirmed push are available. In this case clients can only use the Request primitive and servers are only able to use the Indication primitive.

To start a new session, the client invokes a WSP primitive that provides some parameters, such as the server address, the client address and client headers. These can be linked to HTTP client headers and can, for example, be used by the server to retrieve the type of user agent within the WAP client (which might be both the version and type of the browser). This is useful when we want to format the output differently, depending on the client's device type. For example, one phone may have a 20 character wide display; another may have a 16 character wide display.

In some respects WSP is basically a binary form of HTTP. As previously mentioned, the binary transmission of data between a server and a client is an essential adaptation made for the narrow-bandwidth mobile network. WSP supplies all the methods defined by HTTP/1.1 and allows capability negotiation to gain a full compatibility with HTTP/1.1.

Wireless Transaction Layer – WTP

The Wireless Transaction Protocol provides services to accomplish reliable and non-reliable transactions and operates over the WDP layer or over the optional security layer, WTLS. WTP, as all the other layers in WAP, is optimized to adapt to the small bandwidth of the radio interface, trying to reduce the total amount of replayed transactions between the client and server.

In particular, three different classes of transaction services are supplied to the upper layers:

❑   Unreliable requests

❑   Reliable requests

❑   Reliable requests with one result message

Unreliable Request

The initiator (in this case a content server) sends a request to the responder (the user agent) who does not reply with an acknowledgment. The transaction has no state and terminates once the invoked message is sent:

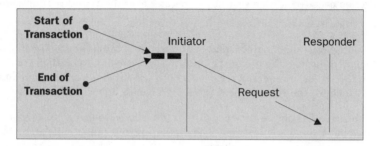

Reliable Request

The initiator sends a request to the responder who acknowledges it. The responder stores the transaction state information for some time, so that it can re-transmit the acknowledgement message if the server requests it again. The transaction ends at the initiator when the initiator receives the acknowledgement message:

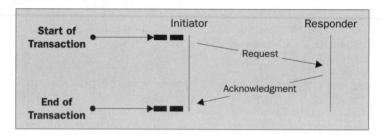

Reliable Request with One Result Message

The initiator sends a request to the responder who implicitly acknowledges it with a result message. The initiator then acknowledges the result message, maintaining the transaction state information for some time after the acknowledgment has been sent, in case it fails to arrive. The transaction ends at the responder when it receives the acknowledgement message.

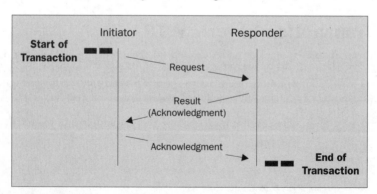

Wireless Transport Layer Security – WTLS

WTLS is the solution to the security issue, provided by WAP Forum. WTLS is an optional layer and is based on TLS (Transport Layer Security) v1.0, which in turn is based on SSL (Secure Sockets Layer) v3.0, which are Internet protocols. WTLS operates over the transport layer (WDP).

During the past few years, security over the Internet has become a big issue. E-commerce, e-banking and e-trade experienced a big evolution once SSL was standardized. By providing guaranteed privacy, confidentiality and authenticity over the TCP protocol, SSL enabled commercial solutions to expand their services.

For the companies that had to share financial or confidential data over the Net, the fact that everyone could read this data just by sneaking in during a transmission was an enormous limitation. SSL delivered methods to encrypt the data content and to make it accessible only to entrusted users. Furthermore, it gave the users the ability to check whether the content they were requesting was really coming from the origin server it was supposed to.

It should be obvious that WAP also had to adapt to this situation, by offering ways to protect, when needed, the data requested from or sent to the user. In WTLS we find the same fundamental characteristics we observed in all the previous layers in the WAP stack: it is an adaptation of an Internet protocol both to the high-latency, narrow-bandwidth air interface and to the limited memory and processing power of the WAP device. WTLS attempts to lighten the overheads associated with establishing a secure connection between two applications. It provides the same grade of security that is supplied by SSL 3.0, while reducing the transaction times. It provides services that ensure **privacy, server authentication, client authentication** and **data integrity**.

- ❏ **Privacy** guarantees that the data sent between the server and the client is not accessible to anyone else. No one can read the unencrypted message, although they can see the encrypted message.

- ❏ **Server authentication** ensures that the server really is who it claims to be, and that it is not an imposter.

- ❏ **Client authentication** provides a way for the origin server to limit the access to the content it provides. Just those subscribers that are recognized as trusted ones, can gain access to the site.

- ❏ **Data integrity** takes care that no one can alter the content of a message being transmitted between server and client without one of them noticing.

In the diagram that follows, we show how the WAP gateway handles secure sessions. A standard SSL session is opened between the web server and the WAP gateway and a WTLS session is initialized between the gateway and the mobile device. The encrypted content is sent through this connection from the server to the gateway, which translates it and sends it to the mobile phone.

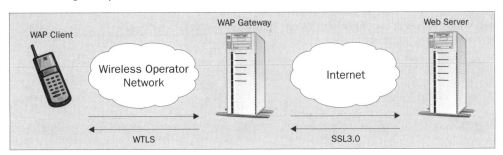

WTLS empowers the SSL protocol by adding effective features such as datagram support, optimized handshake and dynamic key refreshing.

Today, WAP gateways are available which provide public/private key encryption with a key length up to 1024 bits. To use a secure connection the origin server has to be installed as if we were setting up a secure connection over the Internet; the gateway will take care of matching the SSL connection to a WTLS one.

The translation between SSL and WTLS takes place in the memory of the WAP gateway. It is important that unencrypted information is not stored anywhere in the gateway, since this defeats all the security measures used to protect the stored data from being seen by unauthorized people.

Even though WAP gateways are provided with many features to supply the maximum level of security, there is still a lot of concern surrounding the WAP security solution. Banks and all the companies that really have to protect their data, still prefer to host and install their own gateway, giving them the ability to send encrypted data right to the mobile phones, with no need for translation. Time will show whether WTLS will be gradually adopted as the standard or if it will just be ignored.

WTLS is an optional layer in the WAP stack. This means that *security in WAP is only available on demand and is not a built in feature of the WAP architecture*. Hence, the information traveling to and from the WAP gateway is normally not encrypted, unless we use SSL connections to communicate between the origin servers and the gateway.

Security is discussed in detail in Chapter 15.

Wireless Datagram Protocol – WDP

WDP is the bottom layer of the WAP stack and is one of the elements that makes WAP, the extremely portable protocol that it is, operable on extremely different mobile networks. WDP shields the upper layers from the bearer services provided by the network, so allowing the applications a transparent transmission of data over the different bearers. Bearer services are the nitty gritty of communication between the mobile phone and the Base Stations (the antennas). They include SMS, CSD, USSD, DECT, and CDMA.

The physical layer prepares the data to be sent from the mobile device over the air interface, and sends the data using the bearer service implemented in the network that the device is operating in.

Getting a WAP Site on the Air

Now that we have discussed how the WAP protocols work, how a WAP gateway works, and which services an origin server provides, we will try to combine all these elements together. What does happen when you switch on your shiny new WAP phone and access a WAP site?

One main assumption made here is that the WAP phone is configured to connect to a WAP gateway and that it works properly. We will also assume, for simplification purposes, that the bearer used is not SMS (Short Message Service) or some similar bearer, but that a data connection is initiated between the mobile phone and the gateway (a typical bearer in GSM networks could be CSD for example). If SMS is used, the details contained in this section are still valid, with the exception that the expression 'place a call' should be replaced with 'make a connection'.

Wireless Networks

When we want to cover an area with a wireless network, we divide the geographic region into sections called **cells**. This is the reason why wireless networks are often called **cellular networks**. Every cell contains an antenna, also called a **Base Station**, which communicates with the mobile phones.

Base Stations are grouped and controlled by a **Base Station Controller** that is attached to a **Mobile Switching Center**. The Base Station Controller has access to the fixed network as well as the entire wireless network; in this way, subscribers are able to communicate both with normal telephones (in fixed networks) and with mobile telephones (in the same or a different wireless network).

While a mobile phone is switched on, it is communicating with a Base Station. Every time someone calls your mobile phone and you are under the coverage of a given Base Station, the Base Station attempts to contact the phone and, if the operation succeeds, your phone informs you of an incoming call (by buzzing, flashing, or whatever other method). If you are moving during a conversation, driving on the highway for example, every time you exit the area covered by a Base Station, a *Hand Over* procedure is initiated to pass the connection to the Base Station that covers the area you are moving into.

In the wireless networks where WAP is implemented, a WAP gateway is installed and connected to the wireless network **LAN** (Local Area Network). A new phone number is defined and assigned to an **Access Server**. When the subscriber initiates a browsing session, a call is placed to that number.

The only purpose of the Access Server is to authenticate the subscriber willing to get in contact with the gateway. It is connected to a database storing the valid subscribers, numbers. Once the subscriber has been validated, they will be connected to the internal LAN, and allowed to communicate directly with the WAP gateway.

Browsing WAP Sites

The first connection to the gateway is illustrated in the figure shown on the next page. The browser contained in the phone will automatically send the subscriber's details to the gateway together with a user name and password. The gateway checks them against a database as would a dialup connection to the Internet in a traditional PC session.

A WAP browser also has an associated 'home page' deck, determined by the service provider, which is loaded into the microbrowser after the user has been authenticated. This deck is a WAP portal, which was introduced earlier in the chapter. It lists available links and services from that gateway.

This process is illustrated below:

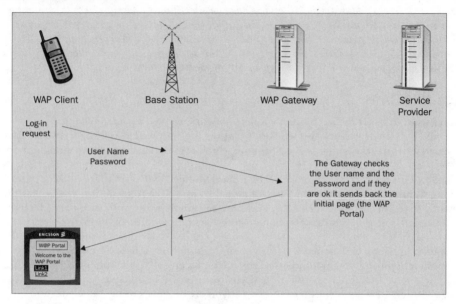

The login procedure that takes place at the gateway will cause the first, sometimes long, wait. However, during the login procedure the gateway doesn't access an external application server, since the WAP portal is stored on the gateway itself or on an application server located in the internal operator network. Once we are logged in, we can start the WAP browsing.

The latency associated with browsing via a mobile device is strongly dependent on the type of bearer used. The more advanced the bearer is, the faster the connection with the WAP gateway, and consequently the less time required to transfer data to and from the gateway. Let's take the GSM Network (the predominant implementation in Europe) as an example. GSM gives the user the choice from a diverse selection of bearers, for example SMS (Short Message System), CSD (Circuit-Switched Data) or the new (at the time of writing – still being tested) GPRS (General Packet Radio Switching).

When we run WAP over an SMS bearer, the WAP Gateway has to divide the content addressed to the WAP device into packets, each one containing at most 160 bytes. The device then has to reassemble the messages it receives to decipher the content. This procedure is very time consuming and accounts for the fact that SMS is the slowest bearer amongst the possible choices.

With CSD, a data connection is established between the WAP device and the WAP Gateway. The speed of the connection is 9600 bps, providing a faster medium for data exchange compared to SMS.

GPRS is a new technology for data transfer within the GSM wireless network. It has been designed to be an upgrade of the GSM network, supplying more bandwidth to wireless communication. It is still under development in many countries and, while many network operators are advertising its launch in autumn 2000, the lack of terminals and possible technical problems due to its early release may postpone its introduction in the commercial market to early 2001. The main slogan related to GPRS and the one that everyone will be hearing is "always connected, always online". It is a précis of the main capabilities of GPRS (if we forget about the bandwidth for a while).

With GPRS there will be a minimal connection setup procedure which will occur when you switch on your GPRS phone. After that, you'll be always online, ready to start receiving and sending data in less than one second. A second peculiar characteristic of GPRS is that the subscriber will be charged by the volume of data they send and receive and not, as it is now with the GSM data connection, by the length of time they are connected. When it enters the commercial market, GPRS will provide speeds of up to 171.2 kbit per second, with an average of 30 or 40 kbps, which will surely be a step forward for WAP and m-commerce in general.

When dealing with voice or data communication in a wireless network we have to take into consideration some more factors that can limit the bandwidth and therefore increase the already high latency. The main problem connected with a wireless network is that between the Base Station and the mobile phones there are obstacles which disturb the transmission. Such obstacles include buildings, tunnels, cars and people, which absorb waves and have a negative impact on the Signal to Noise Ratio (SNR). SNR is a way of measuring the amount of noise that is introduced to the signal before it is received. SNR decreases dramatically with distance.

A low SNR in a voice call will just result in strong disturbances and background noise while we are talking. However, in the case of data connections it is more critical. In WAP connections, low SNR will result in lost data, which will mean the retransmission of data that has been corrupted on its way to the mobile device from the gateway. The retransmission will, of course, increase the latency.

How Do I Get Started?

The most obvious way to get started with WAP is, of course, to buy a WAP-enabled device, such as a WAP phone or a WAP-enabled Personal Digital Assistant (PDA), and begin to look at the applications available. There are many applications on the market already, and by the time you read this book there will surely be an even larger choice.

An alternative is to use an emulator – a 'pretend' mobile device that can be used on your desktop computer. We will cover the more widely used emulators in Chapter 2.

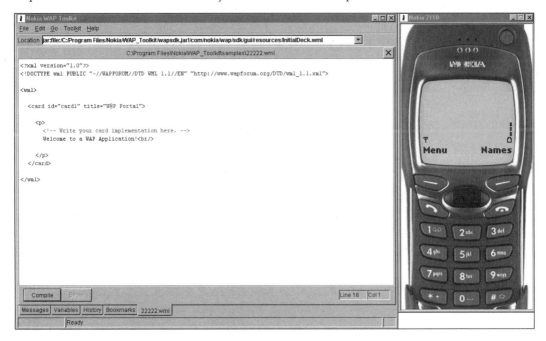

Emulators are available from the four founding members of the WAP Forum, as well as from various third party vendors. The majority of these do not promise an exact rendition of your application; they should be used as a guide and only approximate the final result. Some even depend on the WAP specifications, rather than basing themselves on any one phone. We will cover interoperability issues throughout the book, but the current implementations of WAP among the main players are by no means consistent, making the development of applications difficult. The emulators will, however, be more than adequate to test the logic of your applications. However, you'll find it useful to play around with a real WAP phone for a while, in order to gain a better understanding of the issues relating to data input and other limitations of a real device.

You can also use a WAP plug-in, which allows your standard Internet browser to display WAP content. We have included a list of resources in Appendix H. The majority of these are also useful resource centers for news, new applications and generally for keeping up with market information.

WAP Portal

A good place to start looking for applications is typically a WAP portal. We have already come across this concept a few times in this chapter. A portal provides lists of links, making it easier to navigate to different sites. Popular portals on the Internet include Yahoo.com and AltaVista. They provide links, grouped in categories, and allow you to search for useful resources and save keying in URLs. If you want some news sites or e-commerce sites for example, you simply have to look for the relevant category and follow the most appealing link.

WAP Portals supply you with two useful advantages:

❑   You do not have to browse and search for the sites that provide you with a certain service: you find sites already grouped by the service they provide. This, in the case of WAP, saves you a lot of time, since WAP browsing can be rather time consuming, since we have no proper keyboard or mouse available and the speed of the connection is pretty low.

❑   You don't have to remember or to write down the name of the site you want to visit, since you are automatically redirected by clicking on one of the links listed on the portal.

The address of the WAP portal owned by your network operator is normally specified in the settings of the WAP enabled device, so, just like on a web browser, you will be pointed there whenever you start a WAP session. This can be taken a step further to personal WAP portals. These are powered by a general portal which is customized to the user's preferences, and implements a favorites folder, screening out subjects that the user is not interested in.

WAP versus the Web

One of the main issues with the WAP technology is the wide spread confusion about its potential. When the first WAP phones were hitting the market, it was credited with magical powers, some of which were far beyond the scope of WAP itself.

Now things are clearer: WAP phones are available, people are beginning to use them and there is a better understanding of the opportunities and limitations presented by WAP. It may be said that one of the reasons for this is the similarity between WAP and the web, which results from the fact that WAP is based on the current Internet technologies. This has allowed the use of already proven methods, which have enabled the quick deployment of WAP, and also levered the experience and resources available on the Internet. It must be said, however, that there are major differences between the two. This section will examine some of these differences, and introduce some of the fundamental principles behind programming WAP applications, which we'll be examining in more detail throughout this book.

The first major difference between the web and WAP will be the services offered. While there will be common services such as mail access and reading the latest news, there are many web services that it will not be possible to port to mobile devices. Instead there will be opportunities for many new types of services such as those based on Location Information, which we saw earlier.

Another major difference between WAP and the Internet at the moment lies in the manner of browsing. When *surfing* on the Internet you are, most of the time, not concerned with the length of time you are connected, since nowadays the cost for an Internet call is quite cheap. On the other hand, a WAP user, for whom the connection costs are higher, will be more concerned with the issue of cost. Inputting data on a phone is relatively difficult, and so also increases the connection time. Therefore, WAP users will want fast access to services guaranteed to be useful to them.

Portals such as Yahoo and Excite, are present in both the Web and WAP scenarios, but in the case of WAP they have an even greater importance. Why go somewhere else to search for a particular service if the service you are searching for is already listed there, just a *click* away? There will of course be situations where the WAP user will wish to enter an exact URL; in this case the user is likely to save it permanently as a bookmark for easy subsequent retrieval.

The predicted growth in mobile phone use and their predominance in modern culture brings with it further issues about WAP usability. The typical WAP user will not necessarily be a computer or web user, so applications should not depend on the computer literacy of the user. WAP applications must therefore be as simple and as user-friendly as possible.

The user interface influences the usability of any given web or WAP service, though this is of higher importance in the case of WAP. With such small screens, information needs to be displayed in a neat and clear way in order to stimulate people into using the service.

On top of all this, you must also remember that WAP user tolerance to errors will be almost non-existent. While the web users are somewhat used to "ERROR 404. Server too busy" messages and are willing to put up with them, the average WAP user will probably be much less tolerant and will stop trying to access a service if errors pop up regularly. Furthermore if error messages have not been properly programmed, the user will be unable to browse back or to perform whatever action they want, other than typing in a new address. Developers should bear in mind that they should always give the user a chance to go a step backwards or to try again if something in their application has gone wrong. The usability problem is one of the biggest issues in today's wireless world and will be discussed at length in Chapter 7.

WAP 1.2 - WTA and Push Features

The WTA and push technologies, which have been mentioned occasionally within this chapter, are two features that increase the value of WAP. Unfortunately both the technologies are for the moment not yet available. WTA was defined in WAP 1.1, but it is not yet supported by many of the mobile devices and networks. The push feature has been defined in WAP 1.2 and should be implemented in the WAP phones and operator networks of the second generation.

Wireless Telephony Application Interface – WTAI

WAP has been created to give us the chance to interact with the Internet and Internet-like services from our mobile phones. Is it then natural to think the other way round? Can we give the Internet a way to use the mobile phone functionality? The answer to this question is supplied by the WTA framework. For now, we'll just look at a brief introduction to WTA, as it is discussed in detail in Chapter 17.

WTA is used to access the services that are present either locally on the client device or in the mobile network. An example of local services on the client might be retrieving or deleting names in the phonebook. Network services include voice mail interaction or cell location information. All of the WAP-compliant devices should support the WTA local services, so, theoretically, the WTA functions should work on every WAP-compliant phone. Currently, this does not apply, since WTA is not yet fully implemented on the first generation of WAP phones. However, it should be available on the second generation.

Both local and network services are executed by an entity contained in the mobile devices called **WTA User Agent**. This is responsible for the retrieval and execution of WTA functions. All the WTA functions, both local and network, are contained in libraries stored on the **WTA Server**, a server located in the operator network. An interface called **WTAI** (Wireless Telephony Application Interface) ensures the interaction of the WTA user agent with the device functionalities and the network services.

All these concepts are illustrated in the diagram below. When we want to access a WTA service, the WTA user agent sends a request to the WAP gateway which contains the name of the library with the function we want to use. The gateway requests the function code from the WTA server and then sends it back to the WTA user agent. The agent will now execute the code with the help of the WTAI, which is the interface in the phone to the device dependent functionalities (the phonebook for example) or the network functionalities (like placing a call).

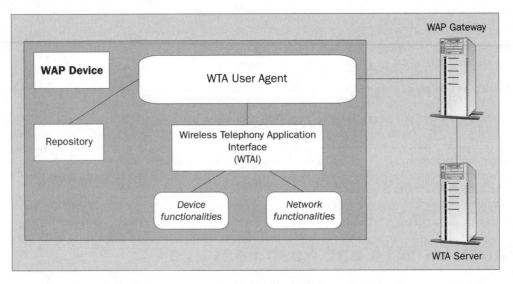

Since the retrieval of the proper file from the WTA server is quite time consuming, a repository in the mobile client can be used to store the most commonly used WTA functions. The size of the repository has not been defined yet by the WAP Forum and can therefore vary depending on the particular WAP device.

The WTA defines a set of functions that resemble WMLScript functions; they are accessible from WMLScript code and sometimes, depending on the service, from WML code as well. If for example we want to place a call from inside WMLScript, we can call a function like this:

```
WTAVoiceCall.setup("+39089456789", 1);
```

Here, `WTAVoiceCall` is the library where the function `setup()` is contained. The string and the number inside the parentheses are simply the parameters we are sending to the function.

If we want to place a call from inside WML instead, we would use something like this:

```
wtai://wp/mc;+39089456789,1
```

The diagram below illustrates the use of WTA. Notice how the WAP client must request the file from the gateway, which in turn, requests it from the WTA server:

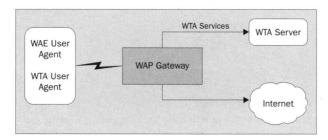

Unfortunately, WTA functions are not yet supported in the majority of the WAP mobile phones on the market now. Some phones give access to some of their internal functionality, but to fully experience the power of the WTA functions we will have to wait for the next generation of devices.

Push Technology

In November 1999 the WAP Forum released the specifications for WAP 1.2. The most important addition to this version is the launch of push technology to deliver content to WAP terminals, without the server receiving any request for it. Push will be discussed in detail in Chapter 16, so we'll just look at a brief overview here.

The potential of push technology has opened the door to an abundance of new services, and everyone in the WAP market is looking forward to being able to use it. WAP version 1.2 has introduced some problems as well, however. For example, some of the WAP mobile phones on the market today will not allow an upgrade from version 1.1, so services will need to make sure that they can cope with the first generation of WAP phones, as well as providing more powerful applications for the second.

With the advent of push technology, the WAP architecture has grown to include a new element, the **Push Proxy Gateway** (PPG), which receives the push requests from the origin servers and forwards them to the WAP terminals. The PPG and the WAP gateway can coexist on the same network element.

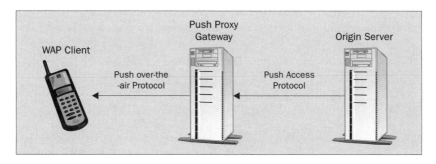

In the new architecture there are also two new protocols involved:

- ❑ **Push Access Protocol** (PAP)
- ❑ **Push over-the-air** (OTA) **Protocol**.

PAP is used by the origin server to communicate with the Push Proxy Gateway. It uses HTTP/1.1 and the HTTP POST method to transmit the information to the proxy. In the specification for the Push Access Protocol, it states that PAP has been designed so that it can be tunneled through other and future protocols although HTTP is the first to be supported. **Tunneling** is the capability to send protocol messages untouched over whatever other protocol is being used. With this in mind, it is clear from the above statement that the PAP protocol has been conceived to grant future scalability and compatibility with different Internet protocols such as SMTP or FTP.

Using the PAP protocol, the origin server can perform various different operations:

- ❑ Send content to a mobile phone (through the Push Proxy Gateway).
- ❑ Read the status of a previous push operation. This allows the origin server to request, via a message following the push one, information about whether the pushed content has arrived or not.
- ❑ Be notified when the content reaches the terminal. This feature is similar to the previous one; the difference being that here the origin server sends a push request to the Push Proxy Gateway asking to be sent a notification when the actual push content is delivered.
- ❑ Cancel a previous push operation.
- ❑ Request from the Push Proxy Gateway information about the type and capabilities of a specific device.

The Push over-the-air Protocol is based on WSP and is used by the Push Proxy Gateway to send the pushed content to the mobile device.

The Push Proxy Gateway itself has logically almost the same functions as the WAP gateway:

- ❑ Acts as a protocol gateway, converting from Push Access Protocol to Push OTA Protocol.
- ❑ Resolves the addresses and locates the devices to which the content is being pushed.
- ❑ Determines what kind of capabilities a given device in the network has and sends a report to the origin server if requested. This feature is useful for the adaptation of the content for a particular type of device.
- ❑ Identifies and authenticates the origin server from where the push requests arrive.
- ❑ Encodes the content it receives in the proper format for over the air transmission.

Summary

We are facing a new and exciting era. Telecommunications are spreading and the *mobility concept,* once just related to the possibility of *speaking* to someone independently of their location, has changed to assume a wider and deeper meaning. People that ask for mobility demand access to personal data, wherever they are in the world and at any time. The same people also demand ease of use. The simpler and more user-friendly a technology is, the more chance it has of becoming a winning technology. All these factors went into the design of a way to access the Internet and Internet-like services from a mobile device.

The Wireless Application Protocol (WAP) aims to become the standard for operators, device manufacturers, and application developers to bridge the gap between the Internet and the wireless network domain. The real power of WAP technology is that it provides everyone with opportunities: device manufacturers, application developers and network operators will increase their revenues by adopting WAP, while the final users will obtain a whole new set of services that will increase their mobility.

WAP is an open specification, meaning that every member of the WAP forum can contribute to its design. The WAP architecture is derived from that of the Internet, with clients and servers communicating via a new element – the WAP gateway. It has a key role in the WAP architecture, acting as a translator between WAP devices and web servers, since the two of them are placed in different networks and therefore use different protocols.

We have seen how the different layers composing the WAP stack are related to each other, and how they relate to the TCP/IP stack used in the Internet world. We have also clarified the concepts of the WAP gateway, the WAP proxy and, to some extent, the WAP server.

At the end of the chapter we began talking about the development of WAP applications. In the next chapter we will discuss the different platforms available and the different development toolkits we can use to design and test WAP software.

2

Setting up WAP

In the last chapter, we introduced the WAP technology and briefly described the architecture of the WAP environment. While understanding the WAP environment is an important step to begin developing WAP applications, we also need to understand the practical side of things – how to set up and use the relevant tools. Like XML and HTML, WML files are text files, which means that you can use your favorite text editor to develop your WAP pages if you prefer. However, although this is a relatively new technology, several products are already available which will allow us to develop and test our applications. At the time of writing, many of them are still in beta versions and some contain bugs, but they can nevertheless be very useful.

This chapter will point you in the direction of some of the currently available software, and take a look at some of the development products in more detail.

Available Software Products

There are currently a wide variety of different software products available that facilitate the development and hosting of a WAP application. However, the market is changing very quickly and more products are being developed all the time. Some are not distributable for legal reasons, but most are freely available on the Internet, downloadable from developer sites.

WAP Browsers

The WAP browser runs in the WAP device and displays the content that it receives. It also provides the front-end through which the user can navigate the WAP application. The browser may be built into the phone or mobile device, or into the SIM card the device contains. WAP browsers are also available which will run on PC's directly or through a web browser by means of a plug-in. Often a PC WAP browser is included in the downloadable SDK (Software Development Kit) available from various companies and it can be an important tool in testing the software, particularly if it emulates a real device. In some ways it can be easier than using a real device, since it makes it easier to test your application throughout its development. However, it is important to remember that the majority of emulators do not guarantee that they emulate the real handset exactly. They are just an indication of how the content is handled. For guaranteed testing of an application, you will need to finalize testing on the targeted device(s). In this way you can be sure that your application will work using the exact setup of your user.

Currently it is quite hard – if not impossible – to provide any one WML page which displays well in all browsers. While this may improve with further development, the current implementations will have to be catered for. There are several ways to deal with this problem, but broadly they can be divided into static and dynamic solutions. A static way to cater for differing browsers is to provide separate files for each. This will only work while your application is aimed at a limited number of devices, but with the rapidly growing market for WAP-enabled devices, this solution does not scale and will quickly become unmanageable. We anticipate that like HTML content, and especially with the experience and resources that are now available, the majority of WML content will be provided dynamically. By generating the appropriate content on the server, we can manage a variety of different devices. We will see plenty of examples of this later in the book.

In order to dynamically generate an application for a specific device, we parse the header of the request made by the device to find the name of the browser being used. There are then several sources on the Internet that allow us to submit the name of a browser to find out its capabilities.

As mentioned, the browsers contained within real devices have very different capabilities. For example the Nokia 7110 device was the first to mass market and its browser is very limited. It implements the minimum specified in order to be considered a WAP device, and in some areas even falls below what is required for a WAP device. However, phones making use of the Phone.com browser (which we will see a little later) have more capabilities than specified. Unfortunately, rather than merely implementing all of the WAP specifications, Phone.com have opted for implementing their own extensions that do not form part of the WAP 1.0 specifications. These extensions are causing incompatibility problems for developers, and throughout this book, these problems together with other issues will be highlighted.

Shown below is a summary of some of the WAP browsers currently available:

Browser	Description	Available from
WinWAP	Freely available browser that runs on Windows PCs	`http://www.slobtrot.com/`
Nokia	Several browsers are available with the Nokia toolkit, which is covered in more detail later in this chapter.	`http://forum.nokia.com/`

Browser	Description	Available from
UP.Browser	Available with the Phone.com toolkit, which is also covered later in the chapter.	`http://updev.phone.com/`
Ericsson	There are different browsers available with the Ericsson Development toolkit including the R320, which we cover later in the chapter. Ericsson (with Symbian) also has a simulator for the R380 browser (though the R380 devices are not yet available). This is different from other mobile phones in that it uses a touch screen, so the simulator works particularly well as a PC browser since you can simply use the mouse to click on links instead of using buttons to move around. Ericsson also has a browser for the MC218, which is a handheld computer rather than a mobile phone.	`http://www.ericsson.com/`
Motorola	Motorola have an offering similar to the other companies with their toolkit. It is covered in more detail later in the chapter.	`http://www.motorola.com/`
Gelon.net.	At this site, a WAP browser is run on-line within the web browser on your PC. Although this isn't yet a perfect browser it is worth investigating.	`http://www.gelon.net/`
Palm	A browser called WAPman is available for Palm OS handheld devices such as the Palm Pilot. These devices come under the category of PDAs (Personal Digital Assistants) rather than mobile phones.	`http://palmsoftware.tucows.com/`

WAP Gateways

The concept of a WAP gateway was introduced in the last chapter. It is basically a piece of software that acts as a translator between the Internet and the mobile device, allowing the two to communicate. Usually you will not need your own gateway, but just to make use of one owned by a network operator. However, the functionality of gateways is covered in more detail in the next chapter, including a section on how to set up your own gateway should you need to.

We won't be coming back to the subject of gateways in this chapter, as the entire next chapter is devoted to it.

WAP Application Servers

Of course, the most important part of a WAP application is where and how it is going to be hosted. This is very easy to do on a standard web server. As we will see, after the gateway, browser requests travel in the Internet domain, and the output is XML compliant. As such, a standard web server is able to provide that output. All that you will need to do is add the following MIME types to those that the web server knows about:

Content	MIME	Extension
WML	`text/vnd.wap.wml`	wml
Compiled WML	`application/vnd.wap.wmlc`	wmlc
WMLScript	`text/vnd.wap.wmlscript`	wmls
Compiled WMLScript	`application/vnd.wap.wmlscriptc`	wmlsc
Wireless bitmap (WBMP)	`image/vnd.wap.wbmp`	wbmp

MIME (Multipurpose Internet Mail Extensions) is a specification for the format of data that can be sent over the Internet.

When the server sends data in response to a request it receives, it sends a MIME type with it. This MIME type can also be explicitly set by the application. Normally, the file extension of the requested file is associated with a MIME type and so the server automatically issues the correct MIME type. Then, when a browser receives information from the server, it checks its MIME type to see what to do with it. If, for example, it sees that the data has a MIME type of `"image/vnd.wap.wbmp"` then it knows to display it as a picture. The MIME types accepted by the browser, can also be discovered dynamically by the server, using information included in the request for data. An application can explicitly set the MIME type by determining the supported MIME types of the device.

Now, as with static HTML content, static WML content has very limited scope for providing services. For more complex applications, dynamic generation of pages is a must. This essentially means deploying an application that will dynamically generate pages from a database, which keeps maintenance to a minimum. These applications are typically hosted on application servers. To include WAP support, once again, all you need to do is to configure them to use the above MIME types.

You may need to get your system administrator to configure the MIME types on the web or application server for you. The process for both IIS and Apache is outlined briefly below.

Configuring MIME Types with IIS

IIS 5.0 is provided as standard with Windows 2000 and IIS 4.0 is an optional service with Windows NT 4.0.

In order to configure the MIME types for IIS, we need to use the Internet Information Services snap-in for the MMC (Microsoft Management Console). You can open this from the Start menu under Administrative Tools in the Programs menu, or simply from the Control Panel:

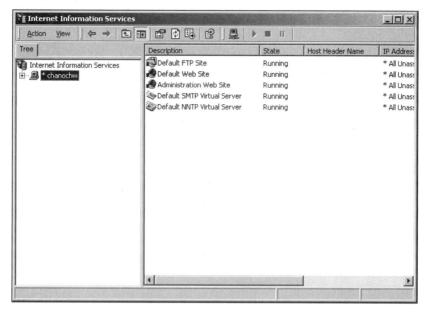

The next step is to open the Internet Information Services folder on the left-hand side. The name of the machine will appear as a sub-tree to that folder, as you can see in the diagram above. Right-clicking on the machine name brings up a menu from which the Properties option should be selected. A properties window should appear, from which you should select Edit under Computer MIME Map to bring up a window with a list of the recognized MIME types. Use this window to add each of the MIME types given in the table above. Remember to save the settings back to the console when you have finished. The MIME types have then been successfully configured.

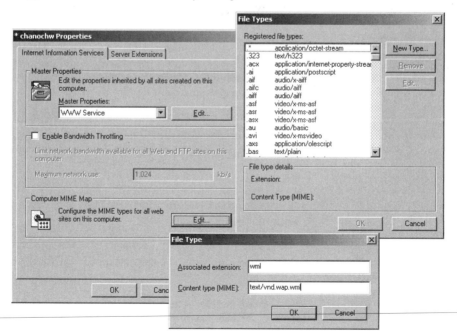

Configuring MIME Types with Apache

Apache is an application server in the public domain which was originally written for UNIX, but which is now available from other platforms. A discussion of how to install Apache is given in Appendix E.

One way to add the correct MIME types to the Apache server is to create a file called .htaccess within each directory that you have used to store WML files. This file should look something like this:

```
addtype text/vnd.wap.wml wml
addtype application/vnd.wap.wmlc wmlc
addtype text/vnd.wap.wmlscript wmls
addtype application/vnd.wap.wmlscriptc wmlsc
addtype image/vnd.wap.wbmp wbmp
```

When the server uses files from this directory or any of its subdirectories, it will send them to the requestor according to the rules in this file.

Note that in order to read these .htaccess files, the server must be configured to recognize them – they are sometimes ignored for reasons of security.

WAP Resources

As yet, WAP is a relatively new technology, but it is certainly causing considerable excitement in both the telecommunications and IT industries. As it is continuously developing, we can't hope to give an exhaustive list of resources here. However, most are available on the Internet, so keep an eye out for relevant sites.

Ericsson, Nokia and Phone.com all have good developer areas, but there are other independent resources for developers. The WAP Forum is the official site for specifications and the latest news on WAP, and they can be found at http://www.wapforum.com.

AnywhereYouGo.com claims to be "100% wireless application development and deployment" and has already been running successfully for some time under its previous name of Waptastic. Its WAP section is very comprehensive, including plenty of information for developers, as well as links to the latest news items. It can be found at http://www.anywhereyougo.com.

Another very popular site for WAP resources is Gelon.net. This site has already been mentioned in this chapter for its WAP browser. It also has discussion forums, a developer section and a most comprehensive set of links available to other resources on the Web. The web site is located at http://www.gelon.net.

Yourwap.com is another popular site, which is more customer focused. They include a combined WAP and web browser, which has so far performed most reliably. They can be found at http://www.yourwap.com.

You might also like to try http://www.hicon.nl which hosts a library of free downloadable WBMP (Wireless Bitmap) files.

A good site for getting in touch with like-minded developers and discussing WAP-related issues is The WAP Group, which can be found at http://www.thewapgroup.com.

The Development Toolkits

While it is easy enough to develop your site with a text editor, the use of a development toolkit will cut down on development time significantly. We will now discuss a few of these development toolkits, often referred to as SDKs (Software Development Kits) or ADKs (Application Development Kits). The majority of these include an emulator to quickly simulate the outcome of your code.

It is important to have access to emulators or simulators for all the types of device that a user may have. These devices vary in screen size and control panels. This is why development kits are created that have the potential for emulating different configurations – we'll see this in practice shortly. When testing your applications, it would of course be very expensive to buy every possible different WAP-enabled PDA and mobile phone, and this expense is spared if you can use free emulators for these configurations However, as we mentioned before, these emulators are not really sufficient for the final testing of your WAP applications. It is important that this is carried out on real WAP devices.

In this section we will look at the offerings from Nokia, Phone.com, Ericsson and Motorola. Each of these offerings contains emulators to test, and aid in the debugging of, your WAP applications.

Nokia

The Nokia WAP Toolkit can be downloaded from the Nokia forum. The download is free, but registration is required before access to this site is allowed. The Nokia forum is located at http://forum.nokia.com.

At the time of writing, the latest version of the Nokia Toolkit product is 1.3 beta. Earlier versions of the toolkit were particularly unstable, but the latest release doesn't seem to have any major problems. Although the Nokia 7110 part of this product is still very buggy, it never dies with the severity of previous versions of the toolkit. The non-Nokia 7110 elements of this toolkit are now very stable.

The requirements for running the Nokia WAP toolkit 1.3 beta are:

- ❑ 266MHz Pentium or better
- ❑ 64MB RAM / 128MB recommended
- ❑ Windows NT 4.0 SP3 or Windows 98
- ❑ 16 bit color
- ❑ 1024x768 resolution
- ❑ 20MB of hard disk space
- ❑ Java Runtime Environment (JRE) 1.2.2 (international version)

Installing the Nokia WAP toolkit involves simply running the downloaded executable and following the on screen instructions. However, one thing to note is that some developers have had problems with the toolkit in the past if it is installed in a path that has spaces in its name.

> *Installation of the toolkit on an operating system other than Windows 98 and NT is a tricky area. Officially the toolkit only works on these operating systems, and the installation utility will definitely only work under Windows. Since the actual toolkit is a Java program, it is just about possible to get the toolkit to run under Linux by installing it under Windows and then copying the JAR files across to a Linux installation.*

Launching the installed program should bring up the following two windows:

Here they are shown open with the default example file. If at first they don't appear, don't panic – the program can take quite some time to start up.

The window on the left is the toolkit window and is where the bulk of the work is done. From here it is possible to create and edit WML and to monitor the state of the application that is currently in use. The window on the right, is called the device window, and is the WAP browser. In here it is possible to test WAP applications. If the machine where the toolkit is running has Internet access, it is also possible to view any WAP site on the Internet.

When developing applications using this toolkit, it is best to turn off Fast Encoding. The fast encoding option generally speeds things up, but it also prevents the toolkit from giving meaningful error messages. When it is disabled the error message will include the line and column number where the error occurred. This is very helpful for debugging purposes, otherwise errors can be difficult to locate. To turn off fast encoding, simply select the Preferences option from the Toolkit drop down menu. On the Encoding tab, make sure that the Use Fast Encoding option is unchecked:

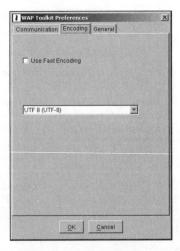

To create your very first WAP example, choose New from the File dropdown menu and select WML Deck. A template WML deck will appear in the toolkit window. It is actually a "Hello World" example that can be compiled and shown on the browser:

The "Hello world" program is loaded into an editor. Notice that the editor is color coded to mark different sections of the code. To display this WML in the browser, click on the Show button. You will be asked to save the file, and once you've done that it will be displayed in the emulator as illustrated in the screenshot above.

Notice how the toolkit window on the left is organized using a series of tabs along the bottom. Their respective roles are mostly intuitive. The following table summarizes what these tabs represent:

Tab	Use
Messages	This tab records all the error messages that the toolkit has reported.
Variables	This tab gives the details of all the WML variables that presently have a value. (WML variables are covered in Chapter 5.)
History	This is a list of locations where the emulator has been, and means that the emulator knows where to go when you click on the back button.
Bookmarks	A bookmark for a WML site that is frequently visited can be added here so that you don't have to keep typing in the full URL to go to that site.
WML Deck	This displays the WML for the deck presently being handled by the emulator.

Table continued on following page

51

Tab	Use
Session	This gives the details of all the items that have been used in the current session. This is not the same thing as the history, since it lists each individual item complete with their MIME type and size.
Editor tabs	Editor tabs are for editor windows where WML can be created or modified.

Any additional tabs will be files that are currently open, which could include scripts, decks and bitmaps. (Note that the kit includes a WBMP (wireless bitmap) editor.)

If you have skipped ahead and already know a bit of WML, you might like to try typing some in here now and trying it out. If you don't yet know any WML just try changing the "Hello World!!!" text.

If you try changing the text and then click on Show, you'll find the result unchanged in the right hand device window. This is because the toolkit only recompiles the WML source code if there is not an already compiled file available. So, in order to show the changes we must first compile the new WML – by hitting the Compile button – after which the browser will show the changes.

Most developers don't actually edit their WML inside the toolkit; they generally use another editor and then simply load it into the toolkit for testing and debugging. This is because the Nokia toolkit is quite a slow application and the editor doesn't boast the useful features of other editors. Developers tend to use their favorite editor – some may even prefer the Windows Notepad over the toolkit editor! To try this, create a text file in a text editor with the following content:

```
<?xml version="1.0"?>
<!DOCTYPE wml PUBLIC "-//WAPFORUM//DTD WML 1.1//EN"
"http://www.wapforum.org/DTD/wml_1.1.xml">

<wml>
    <card id="main" title="First Example">
        <p>
            Hello again!
        </p>
    </card>
</wml>
```

This can be loaded into an editor within the toolkit by selecting the Open option from the File dropdown menu and locating the file. It can then be displayed using the same system as before – just click on the Compile button and then on Show.

If you are confident that your deck will work as it is without any need for debugging, you can simply type in its URL in the Location textbox at the top of the left hand toolkit window. The location of the WML is given as a URL, and on the local machine this path is prefixed by file:/. So, to access a file called helloworld.wml in a directory called WAP on the C: drive, enter the following into the Location textbox:

    file:/C:/WAP/helloworld.wml

You may prefer to store your files on a web server and access them from there. If, for example, you put this same file in the root directory of the web server running on your machine, you would just type the following into the Location textbox and hit return:

```
http://yourmachinename/helloword.wml
```

You can type the URL of any WAP site on the Internet in here and it will be displayed in the browser. For example, try typing the following in to go to the WAP site of the WAP forum:

```
http://www1.wapforum.org/wml/home.wml
```

> **Remember, if you are behind a firewall, you will need to setup the browser to use a proxy, if you want to get at sites on the other side of the firewall. The proxy settings can be changed by selecting the Preferences option from the Toolkit dropdown menu. The proxy settings are on the Communication tab.**

The Browser

So how do you navigate around WAP sites using this browser? The important parts of the browser are labeled below:

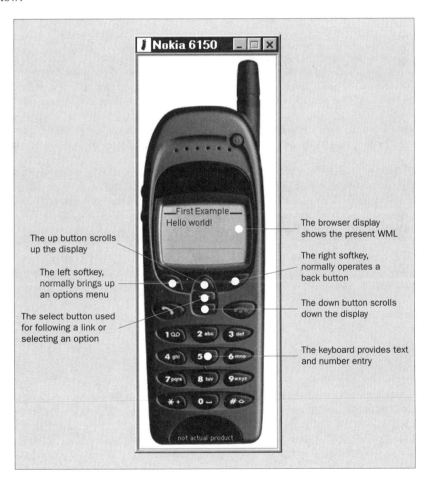

The up button scrolls up the display

The left softkey, normally brings up an options menu

The select button used for following a link or selecting an option

The browser display shows the present WML

The right softkey, normally operates a back button

The down button scrolls down the display

The keyboard provides text and number entry

It should be noted that this is not an emulator for a WAP browser contained within a Nokia 6150 mobile phone. The Nokia 6150 is a real device, but it doesn't contain any WAP browser. If you want to change the type of device that the toolkit uses, then simply select Preferences from the Toolkit menu, and go to the General tab. The WAP Device section of this window allows one of three different devices to be selected:

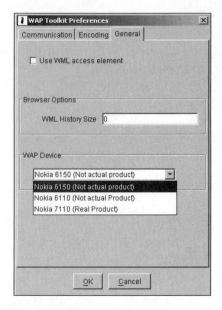

The first of these is the Nokia 6150, which we've already seen. The second is the Nokia 6110. Once again, although this phone does exist, it does not really have a WAP browser. The emulator is just a WAP browser that uses the same control layout of the Nokia 6110. The only real difference between the layout of the Nokia 6150 and 6110 devices is that the 6110 device does not have a select button. Instead, the left softkey fills the role of both bringing up an options menu *and* being the select button in this configuration. It does this by simply acting as the select key for a few seconds, and if the user then doesn't select anything, it changes to become the button that brings up an options menu.

It may seem strange to have WAP browsers in the toolkit that are based on phones that don't have WAP browsers, but remember that mobile network providers are beginning to develop WAP browsers to place in their SIM cards. The result of this is that devices, such as the 6110, that do not have controls intended for use with a WAP browser, could need to use techniques such as those shown above to enable them to be used as a WAP device.

Note that for both the 6150 and 6110 emulators, we have a choice as to whether to use HTTP or a WAP gateway for the delivery of content. This choice can be made in the Communications tab of the Preferences window, which is found on the Toolkit dropdown menu.

The third option on the WAP Devices menu is an emulator of a real device, one with a real WAP browser, namely the Nokia 7110. As this option does exist as a real phone, let's take a more detailed look at it now.

Nokia 7110 Emulator

When selecting the Nokia 7110 for the first time you will be prompted to enter the details for a WAP gateway. Since the 7110 device emulates a real phone, it requires a WAP gateway to work and you cannot use this part of the emulator without one. The name you give the gateway is not important – it can be anything you like. The important part is the WAP Gateway input box, which must contain the IP address of a valid WAP gateway. If you do not own one yourself, you will need to obtain access to a gateway run by someone else.

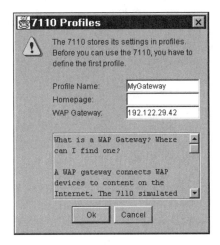

Many people have found the Nokia 7110 emulator to be quite unstable. If you find the phone does freeze up while you are using it, just click on the red button in the top right corner to reset the phone:

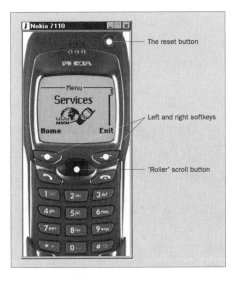

Returning to the main window of the emulator, note that the Nokia 7110 emulator doesn't have as many tabs as the other phone configurations in the Nokia toolkit. In particular, the WML Deck and Session tabs are not used with this configuration.

Phone.com

While Nokia have gained some early market domination in Europe due to the timely release of the 7110, when you look more internationally, it is generally Phone.com (formerly Unwired Planet) who are supplying most of the browsers to phone manufacturers. What this means for now is that many phones produced by third party manufacturers will be using the Phone.com browser. However, in the very near future, expect competitor browsers to be available in mobile phones as part of the SIM card provided by the network provider. Also remember it's not just mobile phones that will have WAP browsers.

Like Nokia, Phone.com also offers a development kit for free download from its website, named the UP.SDK. It is presently only available for the Windows and Solaris platforms. The most important program included with it is the UP.Simulator, which consists of a browser and an information window. Unlike the Nokia toolkit, there is no WML editor supplied with this toolkit.

Downloading and Installing the UP.Simulator

The UP.Simulator can be downloaded from `http://www.phone.com`, although you need to register with their developer program first. Once downloaded, the installation is straightforward and during the installation process, the UP.SDK menu item is installed on your startup menu. The UP.SDK comes with a comprehensive set of documentation, which includes:

- ❑ WML reference

- ❑ WMLScript reference

- ❑ WMLScript Developer's Guide

- ❑ Tools and APIs reference for developing WML services, like faxing and notifications (Push messages)

Besides the documentation, the SDK also includes numerous examples to help you get up to speed in developing WAP applications. Examples using ASP, Visual Basic, Visual C++, WML and WMLScript are available.

Shown below are the information and browser windows. The browser window naturally contains the WAP browser that you use to test your applications. The information window gives details of what is going on at that time. For example, in the information window below it can be seen that the WAP site at `http://phone.com` has just been fetched.

Note that there are no options or controls of any kind on the information window. All the options are provided from the menus on the browser window, everything that takes place being recorded in the information window. In order to view a WAP site, you just type the URL (local or otherwise) into the input box marked Go.

This input box and other important features of the browser window are labeled in the diagram below:

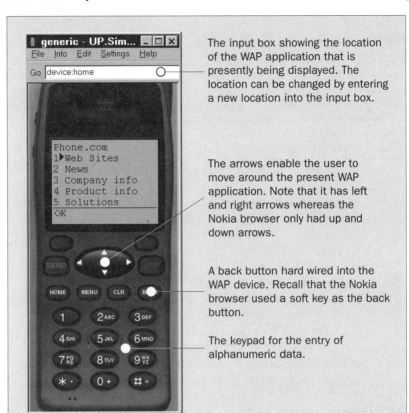

The input box showing the location of the WAP application that is presently being displayed. The location can be changed by entering a new location into the input box.

The arrows enable the user to move around the present WAP application. Note that it has left and right arrows whereas the Nokia browser only had up and down arrows.

A back button hard wired into the WAP device. Recall that the Nokia browser used a soft key as the back button.

The keypad for the entry of alphanumeric data.

Configuration Files

The Phone.com browser, known as the UP.Browser, is used in many different mobile phones. In order to provide emulation for each of them, the UP.Simulator can load **phone configuration files**. A phone configuration file changes the size of the screen and keypad layout of the UP.Simulator to mimic a particular device. To load a phone configuration simply select the Open Configuration option from the File menu and the simulator should change to look like the specified device.

The latest release of the UP.Simulator is version 4.0. This release includes four additional emulation devices, which are very helpful for testing your WAP application on the different target devices that your application may eventually be deployed on.

The four additional devices are from the following phone manufacturers:

- ❑ Alcatel
- ❑ Motorola
- ❑ Samsung
- ❑ Mitsubishi

For a complete list of phones utilizing the Phone.com browser, point your web browser to `http://updev.phone.com/dev/ts/`.

The Info Menu

The Info menu in the browser window, has a list of options that specify the different types of output sent to the information window. Much of the information that can be found on the various tabs in the Nokia toolkit, can also be examined in the UP.Simulator by selecting an option from this menu and examining the output in the information window. The following table summarizes the information that is available under each of these options:

Menu Option	Information Given
Alerts	This details any error messages that have been given by the UP.Simulator.
Source	This gives the source code for the WAP application that is currently being handled by the UP.Simulator.
Cache	This lists the location and other details of all the items that the simulator currently has cached.
History	A list of WAP sites that have been visited. It is this list that is used to calculate where to go when the back button is pressed.
Memory	The memory contents of the device – don't worry you should never have to use this information!
Vars	Details of all the WML variables that currently have a value assigned to them. This topic is covered in Chapter 5.
Cookies	Displays the details of any cookies. These are small pieces of data that represent the current state of an individual user within an application.

The Settings Menu

There is one very important option on the Settings menu: the UP.Link Settings option. Selecting this option produces the following configuration window:

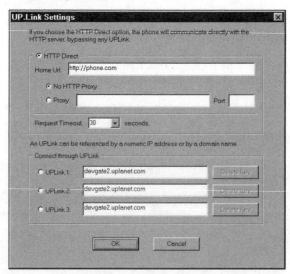

This window defines whether or not a WAP gateway should be used. With the UP.Simulator you have two options, namely HTTP Direct or using a gateway.

In the example shown above, the HTTP Direct option has been selected, so no WAP gateway is being used. This is useful if you do not want to use a gateway.

You may wish to test your WAP applications using a WAP gateway if, for example, you're testing compatibility issues with certain gateways. The UP.Link is a WAP gateway produced by Phone.com. Although the SDK is designed to be used with a UP.Link gateway, it should also work with any other WAP gateway although there are some exceptions, for example, at present it does not work with the WAP gateway written by Nokia.

Up to three WAP gateways can be configured in the above menu, the details of which should be added to the bottom section of the window. Only one is used in any one session and can be selected as required, this can test compatibility in applications that depend on the gateway and not the browser, the notable one being support for cookies.

> **Remember if you are going through a firewall you may need to use a proxy, which can also be set up from this window. Unfortunately, for practical reasons you can't use both an HTTP proxy and a WAP gateway.**

Testing your Applications

To test your WAP application locally, you can use any web server (which has had its MIME types set up as we saw earlier) and type the URL directly into the location input box. However, if you wish to test local files there is no mechanism for browsing to them: you must type in the full path using the file:// format.

If your WML deck is formed correctly without error, you should see your application in the browser window, for example like this:

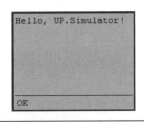

After the deck is loaded in the UP.Simulator, take a look at the information window:

The information window lists very clearly what is happening behind the scenes. We can see that the UP.Simulator is issuing a request for the `hello.wml` file from the web server and that the deck size is 227 bytes, before the compilation to WAP binary format. After compilation, the WAP binary is 128 bytes. This information is especially useful when you are concerned about the size of your application and it allows you to ensure that your deck size does not exceed the limit of each real WAP device.

Suppose that you now make a request for the same document again. This time round, you can see from the information window that the request has been answered by sending a file from the cache:

```
cache hit: <HTTP://LOCALHOST/hello.wml>
```

To see the WML source, hit *F5*:

```
*********************** Current WML *************************************
<?xml version="1.0"?>
<!DOCTYPE wml PUBLIC "-//WAPFORUM//DTD WML 1.1//EN" "http://www.wapforum.org/DTD
/wml_1.1.xml">
<wml>

<card id="main" title="UP.Simulator">
    <p>
        Hello, UP.Simulator!
    </p>
</card>
</wml>
*************************************************************************
```

To see how you can debug your WAP application using the UP.Simulator, you can modify the above WML document to insert a deliberate error. For example, if we changed the closing `</p>` tag to `<p>`, and tried loading the new WML document into the UP.Simulator, we would see the following screen:

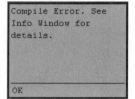

```
Compile Error. See
Info Window for
details.



OK
```

Upon examining the information window, we would see the WML source that has failed the compilation process:

```
======================= WML Errors =====================
WML translation failed.
(8) : error: Invalid element 'p' in content of 'p'. Expected PCDATA | em |
strong | b | i | u | big | small | br | img | anchor | a | table | input |
select | fieldset | do
(9) : error: Close tag 'card' does not match start tag 'p'
(10) : error: Close tag 'wml' does not match start tag 'p'
(10) : error: Expected the end tag 'card' instead of end of file

======================= End Errors =====================

*********************** Current WML *************************************
<?xml version="1.0"?>
<!DOCTYPE wml PUBLIC "-//WAPFORUM//DTD WML 1.1//EN" "http://www.wapforum.org/DTD
/wml_1.1.xml">
<wml>
```

```
<card id="main" title="UP.Simulator">
   <p>
      Hello, UP.Simulator!
   <p>
</card>
</wml>
****************************************************************************

Translation failed for content-type: text/vnd.wap.wml
```

As you can see, the information window has very clearly pointed to the error in the WML code. (If you're not familiar with the syntax rules of WML, note that these are covered in detail in Chapter 4.)

Extended WML Support

In addition to, the WML elements defined in the WML specification, the UP.Simulator also supports its own extensions to WML. However, you must be aware that these extensions do not work on other WAP browsers. It is best to avoid using these extensions unless you can be sure that all your users are equipped with the UP.Browsers. For more details, see Appendix A.

Ericsson

Ericsson offers a development kit called WapIDE. As with the other toolkits, this program is designed to be run under Windows, and may be downloaded from the Ericsson developer web site at `http://www.ericsson.com/developerszone`. The installation of WapIDE is in two parts: the WapIDE 3PP and the WapIDE SDK. The WapIDE SDK is the actual development kit and the WapIDE 3PP contains supporting files. Installation of these two items has the side effect of also installing the Xitami web server on your machine. You don't need this to be running in order to use the Ericsson WapIDE and you probably will want to remove it from your startup sequence. You don't need a web server to use the Ericsson toolkit, and if you are already running a web server, installing a second can cause difficulties.

If the installation has been successful, the WapIDE will be available from the Start menu. The actual WapIDE SDK can be run by selecting the WapIDE application from the WapIDE folder in the Start menu, after which the following window should appear:

As you can see, the Ericsson WapIDE consists of three main application areas: a WAP browser, an application designer and a set of server tools. We'll be looking at each of these in turn.

WAP Browser

The Ericsson WapIDE browser has similar features to the browsers in the other toolkits introduced earlier. The main features of the browser are labeled in the diagram below:

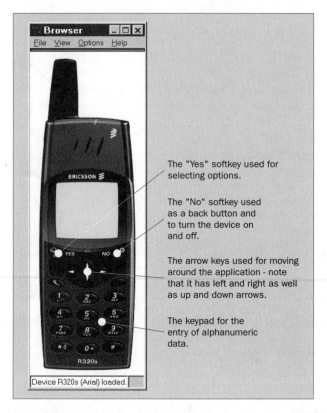

By default, the browser looks like the Ericsson R320 device. However, it is possible to change the configuration by loading a new device, using the Load Device option on the File menu of the browser.

Before anything can be done with the browser, the device first has to be turned on. This can be done by holding down the No button on the phone. After this, loading a WML application into the browser is straightforward – you just need to select the Load URL option from the File menu and type in the location of the file in URL form. If the file is located on the local machine it can be opened from this same window by selecting the Browse button and locating the file. Hence you do not necessarily need a web server to test your applications with this toolkit.

Like some of the other browsers that we have seen so far, it is not necessary to use a WAP gateway in order to view WAP applications using the WapIDE browser. However, if you do wish to use a WAP gateway with the browser then it is possible to do so. You may wish to do this if you are testing whether they will be any compatibility problems with certain WAP gateways. This can be configured from the Proxy Setup window that is opened by selecting Proxy Options from the Options menu:

The Ericsson WapIDE refers to a WAP gateway as a 'WAP Proxy', so to use a WAP gateway select this tab. Enter the address of the gateway in the window brought up by clicking on the Details button.

The useful monitoring facilities in the Ericsson toolkit are found under the View menu. There are two important options on this menu: Log window and WML Variables. WML Variables opens a window giving the names and values of any WML variables that have had a value assigned to them. (We'll be looking at the topic of WML variables later on in Chapter 5.) The Log window option opens a window from where many things can be monitored:

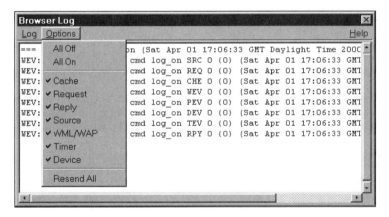

This window is similar to the information window with the Phone.com UP.SDK. The main difference here is that you can choose which information you would like to be written out. This is achieved via the Options menu by ticking the options required. You can see an example of this in the screenshot above.

Application Designer

When starting the Application Designer, an existing project has to be selected or a new one created. Try creating a new project called TestProject and set it up to use the R320 browser. To select the Ericsson R320 you will need to click on the Browse button and select the file r320s.dev.

The window should look like this:

Clicking on **Create New Project** opens the main window, within which two windows exist. The one on the left is the same browser as before, on the right is an editor window.

Type the following code into the editor window:

```
<?xml version="1.0"?>
<!DOCTYPE wml PUBLIC "-//WAPFORUM//DTD WML 1.1//EN"
"http://www.wapforum.org/DTD/wml_1.1.xml">

<wml>
    <card id="main" title="First Example">
    <p>
       Hello world!
    </p>
    </card>
</wml>
```

Save this file and then click on the **Toggle Project Test Mode** button. This is labeled in the diagram below. If all has gone well the words "Hello World" appear on the browser.

When you are in testing mode, the source can't be edited. In order to change it you will need to toggle the **Project Test Mode** back to developing.

Server Toolset

The tools under this option are not really needed when you first start out, but as you begin to develop more advanced WAP applications you may find some of the tools here useful. The server toolset is really just a collection of various utilities, of which the most useful are the WML and WMLScript compilers. When writing a WAP application it can sometimes be difficult to detect problems, particularly if the WAP browser is returning a message such as "Connection failed". Compiling the WML or WMLScript can often give more meaningful errors messages. In addition, the Ericsson toolkit includes a WML 1.1 syntax checker that is particularly useful when you are learning WML.

In order to start one of the server tools, select server toolset from the main SDK menu, which opens the following window:

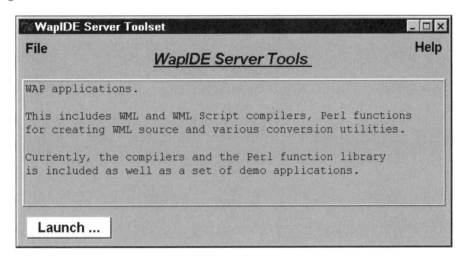

As an example, we'll try the WML Syntax checker here. To begin with create a file called `test.wml`, with the following content. There is an error in this example, don't correct it for now:

```
<?xml version="1.0"?>
<!DOCTYPE wml PUBLIC "-//WAPFORUM//DTD WML 1.1//EN"
"http://www.wapforum.org/DTD/wml_1.1.xml">

<wml>
    <card id="main" title="Using compiler">
    <p>
        <b>
            Hello world!
        <b>
    </p>
    </card>
</wml>
```

Select the WML 1.1 Syntax Analyzer option from the sub-menu that appears when you click the Launch button. You are prompted to load a file, so locate `test.wml` and load it.

Then click on the big VERIFY button. You should get the following error message:

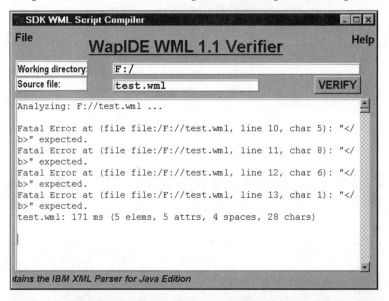

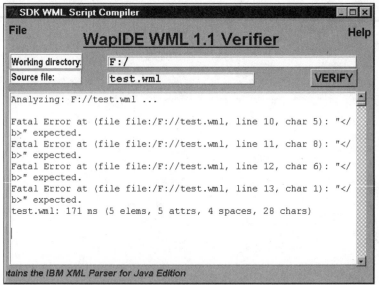

You may well have already spotted the error, but here is where it occurs:

```
    <b>
        Hello world!
    <b>
```

The second <b> should have been a </b>. The syntax checker says that there is an error in line 10 (and consequently every line following it) which is missing a closing </b> WML tag.

Motorola

The **Motorola Applications Development Kit** (MADK) is similar to those discussed so far in this chapter. It provides an editor and a WAP browser but has one extra feature that the other toolkits do not. The MADK can be used for editing and testing **VoxML**, which allows the development of applications that make use of voice interaction. VoxML is the precursor to VoiceXML, the adopted standard for voice based communication over the Web. This isn't incorporated into WAP, but it is certainly something to look forward to in the future. With the restrictive interfaces available on phones, VoiceXML could well provide an answer to the lack of intuitiveness of the WAP browser experience. VoxML, together with VoiceXML, is looked at in more detail in Chapter 19.

The MADK is another toolkit designed for Windows, but due to its voice recognition, which makes use of Microsoft Agents, installation can take some time. These agents are the characters that appear on the screen and communicate with you during the voice recognition process. They read out the responses to your commands and appear to be listening when you speak to them. The latest release at the time of writing requires an advanced, proprietary Microsoft Virtual Machine for Java (MSJVM).

> *A word of warning: this MSJVM is NOT uninstallable, may cause problems to your other Java machines, files and applications and, in addition, the ADK doesn't seem to recognize later builds of the JVM (than the one required by the ADK) so is quite difficult to install and run properly.*

When the application is run it consists of two windows, the Integrated Development Environment (IDE) window and the User Interface Simulator (UIS) window. Essentially the IDE is the editor environment and the UIS is its accompanying browser.

UIS

As with the Phone.com and Ericsson toolkits, the Motorola ADK can also read configuration files to setup the phone interface. This option is found under the Open Configuration option on the File menu. However, unlike the current offerings from Phone.com and Ericsson, the Motorola ADK actually includes quite a few sample configuration files. For example:

Even though the configurations are significantly different in the above examples, the method used to view a site in the UIS is the same – the location of the WAP application is just entered into the textbox labeled Go.

As is the case with the browsers in the other development kits, in the MADK it is possible to view WML with or without using a WAP gateway. By default, the software is setup not to access data through a WAP gateway. In order to change the configuration, bring up the Mobile Settings window that is found by selecting the Mobile Link Settings option on the Settings menu:

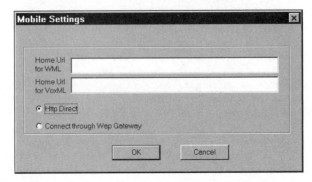

In order to select a WAP gateway simply check the Connect through Wap Gateway option and click OK.

IDE

We have seen a simple "Hello world" application in each of the other toolkits we've looked at so far. The method of doing this in the MADK is very similar to that of the Nokia toolkit or the Application Designer in the Ericsson toolkit. Select New from the File menu. In the opened window, select wml as the File Type, and give the File name, say HelloWorld:

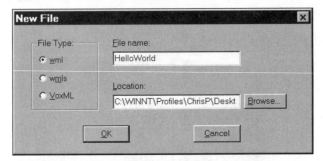

An editor window will then be produced. Type in the now familiar "Hello world" application:

```
<?xml version="1.0"?>

<!DOCTYPE wml PUBLIC "-//WAPFORUM//DTD WML 1.1//EN"
"http://www.wapforum.org/DTD/wml_1.1.xml">

<wml>

    <card id="main" title="Using MADK">
    <p>
```

```
        Hello world!
    </p>
    </card>
  </wml>
```

To test this, just select the **Start Simulate** option from the **Tools** menu. The UIS will then display "Hello World" as is shown in the two screenshots of the UIS given earlier.

You can just use the Motorola ADK to work on individual WML files, but the ADK also allows you to view and organize complete projects. By keeping all your WML files together in a project, the MADK can begin to help in the quite complex task of organizing large WAP development. To create a project, simply select **New Project** from the **Project** menu, and give your project a name:

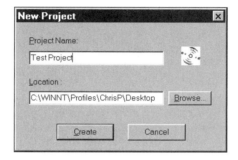

Once a project has been created, a Project Explorer window appears on the left of the IDE. WML files can be added to this window by selecting the relevant option on the context menu.

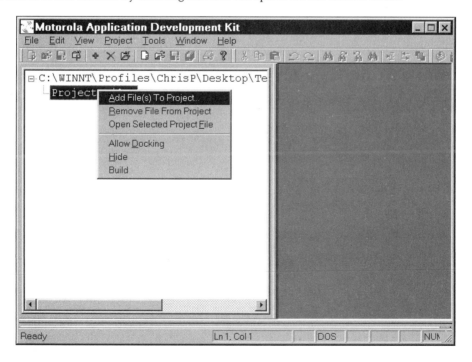

Unfortunately, the Motorola ADK also suffers in its current version from some quite unfortunate bugs. Its instability can prove to be a nuisance at times but if you can get to grips with the MADK it does have one very nice feature, its responsiveness. The MADK is fast, and perhaps this makes its failings more acceptable.

Which One to Choose?

The table below describes the functionality of the four main development toolkits that we have seen.

Toolkit	Performance	Emulator	Reliability	Editor	Notes
Ericsson	Relatively fast.	Difficult to say at time of writing due to availability of real products, but initial results suggest that it is a poor emulator of the real device.	Quite unstable.	Yes.	Offers a simple WML syntax checker without the hassle of starting up a WAP browser.
Nokia	Very sluggish, particularly the 7110 emulator.	7110 emulator is excellent, simulating the real device very well. 6110 and 6150 give possible alternatives.	Very stable except for the 7110 emulator which is exceptionally bug-ridden.	Yes.	Nokia 7110 has stolen an early lead in the market in Europe – making it important to test applications with the 7110 emulator.
Phone.com	Relatively fast.	If you can get hold of the configuration files for the phone that are being developed, this will offer a good emulator. Unfortunately these are not all readily available at present.	Very good but a few annoying problems.	None.	The UP.Browser is used in many phones, making it important that applications work with the browser.
Motorola	Very good.	Unknown, but the browser does not look much like a Phone.com browser. Since the Phone.com browser is being used in Motorola phones, this suggests it isn't a very good emulator.	Quite poor from installation onwards.	Yes.	Also includes VoxML development facilities.

There is no simple answer to the question of which one of these emulators to choose. The answer would depend very much on which device you expect most users to have when accessing your application? This is a fast moving market, as the new handsets become available the situation could quickly change.

As it stands at the time of writing, Europe is dominated by the Nokia 7110, where in some countries demand is outstripping supply, but in North America it looks more as if devices containing the UP.Browser will be the most popular. However, as devices using the Ericsson or Phone.com browsers are now on sale in Europe, the Nokia 7110 could be overtaken as the most popular WAP device.

The best solution is to test on all of them. How a WAP application looks in one phone can vary greatly to how it looks on another. For example, if you develop your application specifically for a device using the UP.Browser you may be very disappointed when you see it on the Nokia 7110. The main point to be aware of at all times is that you should "never trust a phone emulator". To re-iterate an earlier point, for guaranteed performance you must test with the real thing. This is where the cost of WAP development comes in – the toolkits mentioned in this chapter are all free, but of course WAP devices are not. A typical WAP phone costs between $100 to $200 in USA, £100 to £200 in the UK, so by the time you have built up your test bed of WAP devices you may well have made a large investment. This is not such a big problem for a huge organization or a startup company with plenty of venture capital, but not something the average amateur can afford to do to test their WAP applications.

Also remember that these are just the four most commonly used toolkits at present. Rumors are always flying around of new Visual WAP type environments that will soon be available. There is certainly a market for an all in one toolkit that offers all of the features of the present development toolkits complete with emulators for all the devices on the market.

Other Tools

So far we have looked at the main development kits available, and briefly examined the merits of each. In the final part of this chapter, we'll have a quick look at some of the other products that are available for WAP development.

Microsoft Mobile Explorer Emulator

Microsoft Mobile Explorer has already been incorporated into phones from both Benefon (Q) and Sony in their CMD-Z5. It includes support for both HTML and WML, graphics and cookies. It also claims some WTA functionality.

Here is a snapshot of the emulator for this browser and it's 'Configurator' or Properties manager:

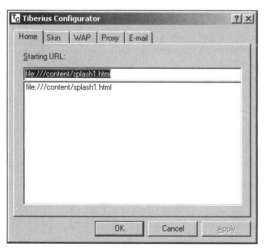 

The various decks produced throughout the book have been tested using this emulator, which seemed very stable although it is still in beta stage. Main issues relating to it are memory usage and its non-support for various WAP features and particular WMLScript. One thing to note is that, in an attempt to emulate phones more closely, the Microsoft Mobile Explorer cannot read un-compiled `.wml` code. It can only accept it in it's compiled form `.wmlc`.

This emulator is now available for download from the Benefon web site at `http://www.benefon.com`.

DotWAP

DotWAP provides a simple environment that creates WAP applications, hiding the intricacies of the code underneath. It doesn't, however, appear to include a working simulator and since most large scale WAP applications are likely to be making use of server-side technologies such as ASP and Cold Fusion, it isn't much use for big projects. If you wish to quickly create a very small WAP application it could be suitable though.

The screenshot below shows DotWAP in use:

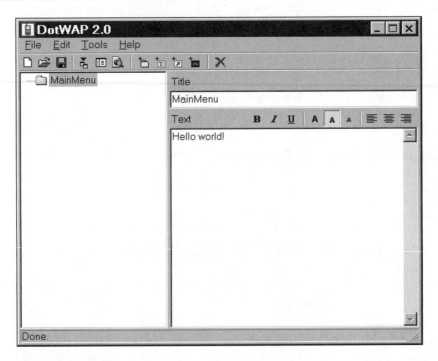

DotWAP can be downloaded from: `http://www.inetis.com/english/solutions_dotwap.htm`.

WAPtor

WAPtor is a better tool for the creation of small-scale WAP applications. It doesn't hide as much of the actual code away as DotWAP, making it a better tool for learning, and it does include a simulator.

The screenshot below shows WAPtor in use, with the markup language used to create the application on the left, and the simulator displaying it on the right:

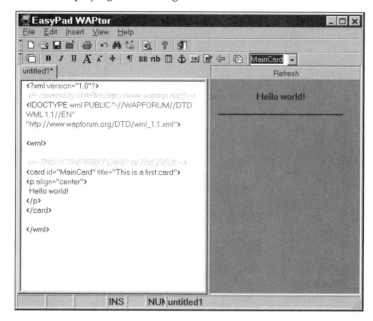

WAPtor can be downloaded from `http://www.waptop.net/waptor/`.

CardONE

Installation of this program can be a little daunting, unless you speak German. In fact, even once it's installed, there is the occasional dialog box that isn't in English, so you may need a German dictionary to hand if you wish to use this program. As you can see from the picture below, it is a very simple program that also hides the code from you. It does have strong abilities for organizing projects, but you are unlikely to be using a tool such as this on a large project.

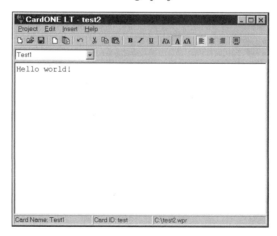

CardONE can be downloaded from `http://www.peso.de/wap_en/index.htm`.

Summary

There is a large amount of software available for use in developing and deploying WAP applications. On the server-side, all that most people will need to concern themselves with is adding MIME types to an existing web server solution. Later in the book it will be seen how current web technologies such as Cold Fusion or Active Server Pages can be used to develop WAP applications.

There are numerous browsers and numerous clients running these browsers. The large number of browsers is causing problems with development since every device is displaying WAP applications in a slightly different way. As far as development environments for WAP are concerned, there are a large number available and they have varying ranges of features.

We have covered the specifics of setting up and getting started with WAP in this chapter. In the next chapter we take a closer look at WAP gateways. After this, we will begin to learn the application development languages and skills that are used in the creation of WAP applications, including WML and WMLScript, as well as all the familiar server-side technologies.

3

WAP Gateways

This chapter will provide a detailed insight into all aspects of WAP Gateways. While in-depth knowledge of how a gateway works is not needed in order for you to develop WAP applications, it is useful for developers to have an overall understanding of the purpose and functionality of a gateway. With this in mind, it is recommended that you read the first parts of this chapter, while later sections may be skipped depending on your position within the WAP world.

The aim of the chapter is to answer the following questions, and perhaps arrive at answers to a few more, which aren't listed here, along the way:

- ❑   What is a WAP Gateway and why do we need one?
- ❑   What are the different functionalities of a WAP Gateway and how do they fit together?
- ❑   How does a WAP model compare with that of the World Wide Web?
- ❑   What are the possible locations of a WAP Gateway, and do I need one?
- ❑   How can you select the best WAP Gateway to suit your needs from amongst the ones available?
- ❑   How do you install the most commonly available Gateways?

What is a WAP Gateway?

A WAP gateway forms a bridge between two distinct worlds, the Internet (or another IP packet network) and the wireless phone/data network, which are fundamentally different in their underlying technologies.

Work is currently being done into the convergence of various technologies that will make life simpler for people who access information. Eventually we may see a day when a single predominant technology will be used for all types of network, supporting voice, data and video services. However, until then we need solution specific technologies, like WAP, to enable information flow towards users who are using different access mechanisms.

A WAP gateway is basically software that is placed between a network that supports WAP and an IP packet network such as the Internet. It acts as an intermediary that converts between the protocols of the packet network and the protocols on the WAP network (WSP, WTP, WTLS and WDP, which were discussed in Chapter 1). When cellular packet networks, such as GPRS, that can use TCP/IP directly are prevalent, it may still make more sense to use the WAP protocols as it's nature is to reduce the data transfer sizes required. In addition WAP, for the moment, presumes the use of WML, which is geared towards small screens and low processing power. If on the other hand you use a GPRS mobile connected to a laptop, we can access HTTP and TCP/IP directly to access information on the Internet. Among other things, the gateway converts WSP requests from wireless devices into HTTP requests, and vice versa for the HTTP responses.

A WAP gateway can be implemented as a single host or a cluster of servers for load balancing. However, regardless of the implementation, it can still be considered as a single box from a mobile user's perspective.

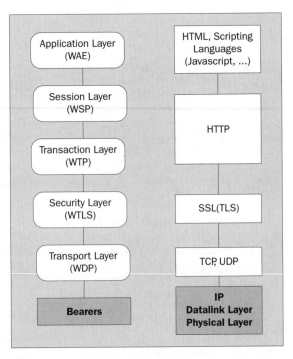

The Internet is based on the TCP/IP protocol stack, which is suited to wired networks and quite unsuitable for most types of wireless networks. This is because:

❑ TCP is a heavyweight transport layer protocol that has high overheads (or control data as a percentage of the total data transferred), especially during connection establishment. This is due to the **three-way-handshake** mechanism. It also transmits large amounts of data to handle the possibility of packets arriving in a different order to which they were sent. This could happen if the packets take different routes in an IP network.

Here is a simple illustration of the three-way-handshake mechanism in TCP:

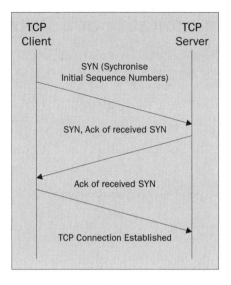

A connection is only considered as established when all three messages have been exchanged, a large overhead in wireless networks.

The round-trip delays (or **latency**) incurred are very high in wireless networks, which would mean that timer values used for retransmission of data in wired networks would cause unnecessary network congestion. When packets transmitted are not acknowledged by the remote entity within a fixed period, known as a retransmission timer value, the TCP layer at the sending end resends these packets. The median roundtrip time (that gives an idea of how long it would take for packets sent to be acknowledged) could be a reasonable value of 0.4 seconds in the case of an IP bearer in wireless networks (this is much less in wired networks). On the other hand, in the case of the Short Message Service (SMS) bearer, it could shoot up to 10 seconds. In the worst-case scenario, the value could very well be much larger than this, which is unacceptable for practical reasons when using browsing applications. Due to such large round-trip delays, the TCP layer that works fine on a wired network will cause a lot of retransmission of data because it believes that the data is lost. This causes severe network congestion in wireless networks. Although there has been enough academic as well as industry research in finding a wireless TCP/IP solution with moderate success, it will take some time before they are available for large-scale use.

By keeping the WAP communication protocol stack separate from that of the Internet, it is possible to implement WAP for a wide range of wireless bearer networks (Internet protocols are not suitable for all types of such networks). This ensures bearer independence for all layers of the stack except WDP. Because WDP has to interface with the idiosyncrasies of various bearer networks, WDP provides a consistent interface to the upper protocol layers, so it must have a bearer specific implementation. If a vendor develops the WAP protocol stack, WDP is the only layer that must be rewritten to support different bearer networks. The WTP layer implements a simple request-response transaction-oriented protocol instead of the three-way-handshake connection-establishment mechanism. WTP has been inspired by T/TCP or TCP for Transactions. T/TCP omits the three-way-handshake mechanism for starting a transaction and this is known as TCP accelerated open (TAO). Refer to *TCP/IP Illustrated, volume 3* by W. Richard Stevens, ISBN 9814053090 for an in depth discussion and analysis of TCP for transactions.

Functionality of a WAP gateway

We will now consider the functions that a WAP gateway performs in detail. Some of these functions are optional. This means that some gateway products may not provide certain functions because they are not mandatory. (Optional functions will be explicitly mentioned. Otherwise, they can be assumed mandatory). Below is a summary of the functions that a gateway carries out:

❏   Implementation of WAP protocol stack layers

❏   Access Control

❏   Protocol conversion: WSP ⇔ HTTP

❏   Domain Name resolution

❏   HTML to WML conversion

❏   Encoding of WML content

❏   WMLScript compilation

❏   Security

❏   Provide caching for frequently accessed content

Implementation of WAP Protocol Stack Layers

This is the most obvious function of a WAP Gateway and it contributes to most of the functionality of a gateway. Depending on whether the type of service is connection-oriented or connectionless, secure or not secure, the following stack layers need to be implemented:

❏   Non-secure Connection-oriented: WSP ↔ WTP ↔ WDP

❏   Secure Connection-oriented: WSP ↔ WTP ↔ WTLS ↔ WDP

❏   Non-secure Connectionless: WSP ↔ WDP

❏   Secure Connectionless :   WSP ↔ WTLS ↔ WDP

Access Control

This involves restricting specific content (like subscription services, or company intranet WAP services). Recognition of the device could be based on IP address or **MSISDN number** (its phone number). This depends on the bearer being used. For example, a WAP gateway using SMS as the bearer will use phone numbers because this information is the only one available to identify the device. In the case of an IP bearer, the gateway does *NOT* have access to the phone number of the device if there is one. In addition, not all devices have IP addresses. It depends on the bearer being used. If a bearer such as SMS is used, there is no need for the device to have an IP address associated with it. Even devices that use an IP bearer will typically not have IP addresses associated with it on a permanent basis. For example, if an IP bearer is used over circuit switched data through an ISP, the remote access server may have dynamically assigned an IP address while you were connected. However, in the case of wireless packet networks like GPRS, an IP address (or X.25 addresses if GPRS is used for X.25 services) will always be associated with the device as long as the device is switched on and a subscription for the service exists, even when the device is not transmitting or receiving packets.

A more fine-grained access control can be achieved by using user authentication. This could use the HTTP basic or proxy authentication mechanism. It would not only control which devices were allowed to retrieve content through the gateway, but also control what content is made available to each device.

Protocol conversion: WSP ⇔ HTTP

As described in Chapter 1, WSP supports complete HTTP/1.1 functionality. This includes extensible request-reply methods (like GET, POST, etc.), request, response and entity headers (like `"Accept: application/vnd.wap.wml"`, a request header that specifies the particular MIME types that a client can handle) and content negotiation. Content negotiation is the process of selecting the best representation suited for a client for a given response when there are multiple representations for the same content available from the server.

A **request header** is meta-information that is sent along with a HTTP request (like GET or POST requests). Similarly, a **response header** is meta-information in a HTTP response that is sent by the server as a response to a previous HTTP request. As part of the HTTP response, the server might also send an entity body (an HTML file for example) depending on the type of request. The meta-information sent to give more meaning to the entity body that was sent is known as an **entity header**.

However, WSP headers are in a compact binary **tokenized** form, as defined in the WSP specification. A **token** is a group of characters that has a specific meaning when used together as a string. For example, in the Accept header that you see below, `"Accept:"`, `"text/plain"`, `"text/vnd.wap.wml"` etc. are all string tokens. A binary token for these would be an octet representation.

For example, the HTTP/1.1 protocol request header below uses 122 octets (or bytes in other words):

```
Accept: text/plain, text/vnd.wap.wml, text/vnd.wap.wmlscript,
application/vnd.wap.wmlc, application/vnd.wap.wmlscriptc
```

The above request header indicates to the server that the client can accept content in any of the above MIME formats, plain text, WML in both compact and text form, WMLscript as text and in its compact form.

Using WSP, the same header is represented with just 5 octets:

```
0x80 0x83 0x88 0x89 0x94 0x95
```

For MIME types not defined in the WAP specifications, encoding is not done and the textual headers are sent as is.

Domain Name Resolution

Resolution of domain names, used in URLs, to IP addresses is done by Domain Name Server (DNS) services. (This is optional if the gateway uses an HTTP proxy to retrieve the content.) For example, let's say there is a WAP Gateway set up at your workplace that you normally use for accessing intranet WAP services. At the same time, your company network setup requires the use of an HTTP proxy server to access the Internet. Now if you wanted to retain the same gateway settings on your device to access WAP content both on your corporate intranet as well the public Internet, the only way to do this would be to configure the WAP Gateway to connect to the Internet through the HTTP proxy. The HTTP proxy has the responsibility of resolving Internet domain names instead of the WAP Gateway in this case.

HTML to WML Conversion

Note that this is an optional feature. This conversion can never be perfect, and it can never be guaranteed that after conversion an HTML page will be rendered properly on a wireless device. These issues will be discussed further in Chapter 7, which covers usability issues, and Chapter 12, which looks at methods of converting existing content to WAP. Despite any claims from vendors on the quality of conversion, it is recommended that content providers actually provide WML content separately if they are targeting wireless device users. One solution that origin servers could adopt is to have two formats for the same content (WML as well as HTML) and look at the "User-Agent" and/or "Accept:" HTTP request headers to decide which one to send in the response. If the specified URL references a server-side script, the format of the dynamically generated output is decided based on these two request headers.

Another suggested mechanism is to provide content in XML and convert this to HTML or WML, using XSLT for the transformation, as will be described in Chapter 9. However, you need to be aware that this transformation is in the origin servers and not in the WAP Gateway.

Encoding of WML Content

WML content – coming from the Internet or another provider – is encoded into a compact binary form at the gateway before it is sent to the wireless device. This process is known as tokenization. During this process, the gateway also performs checks to verify that the WML content has no errors and is **well-formed**. (Because WML is an XML language, it has to comply with the well formedness of XML, the rules set out to define correctly formed XML. This will be explained further over the next two chapters.) In the case where this verification fails, the gateway sends an error indication to the user agent on the wireless device. With this mechanism, the user agents on the device can assume all WML they receive is well-formed and avoid complex error handling implementations that might have otherwise made the user agent consume a lot more resources on the device.

WMLScript Compilation

The compilation of WMLScript on the gateway involves syntax and semantic checks, and the generation of bytecode according to the WMLScript Instruction Set (this is an assembly level instruction set defined in the WMLScript specifications, for a non-existent virtual machine), which has been optimized to generate code of minimal size. Although this procedure involves generating a binary stream of bytes, it is not entirely analogous to WML encoding. The differences are summarized in the table below:

WML Encoding	WMLScript Compilation
The structure and content of the WML documents are encoded into standard binary values that have been precisely defined in the specifications. The WML element tags, attributes, variable references and other common strings, like `http://` for example, are directly transformed into corresponding octet representation.	WMLScript is compiled in a manner similar to compilation of programs in other programming languages and therefore all the phases of a compiler, like syntax and semantic checks and code generation, are present here.
Encoded WML can be directly used to render the content on the device because a one-to-one mapping exists between tags, attributes etc.	The generated code is similar to Java bytecode. It consists of assembly program instructions for a non-existent architecture. The client needs the use of an interpreter (similar to a Java Virtual Machine) to interpret the instructions and execute on the client device. The interpreter maintains some state information, like Instruction Pointer, variables, operand stack and a function call stack, during the execution of the bytecode

The error detection during compilation need not keep track of the types of error that occur. Only the fact that there is an error is reported to the wireless device that made the request. The user of the device is not usually interested in understanding the error; they only want to know when one has occurred.

Security

This involves providing WTLS, between the gateway and the device, and SSL, between the gateway and the HTTP origin server. Refer to Chapter 15 for a discussion on this topic.

According to WAP specifications, it is optional for implementations to provide security features of WAP. It may be necessary to use a gateway product that implements security features, depending on the kind of content provided (like banking or m-commerce). Although it is necessary to use WTLS between the gateway and the device for secure WAP applications, the use of SSL between the gateway and the origin server may not be necessary even for secure applications. This depends on the position of deployment of the gateway that is being used for the secure application. The section, "*Positioning of a WAP Gateway in the Network*" later in this chapter will provide you with some insights about this.

Provide Caching for Frequently Accessed Content

This functionality is very similar to that of proxy servers, which are found in various organizations, that cache Internet content regularly accessed by members of the organization.

The Web Model Vs the WAP Model

In this section, we will compare the Web and WAP models. This should help to clarify the functionality of gateways described previously in more detail.

We start by considering the web model, and what happens when a user makes a request for some content:

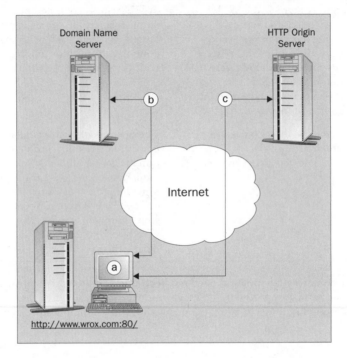

a. The user enters the URL of a website in the browser, selects a bookmark or clicks on a hyperlink of a previously loaded URL (`http://www.wrox.com:80` for example).

b. The browser parses the URL and typically uses its resolver library to resolve the domain name part of the URL into an IP address. The resolver library transparently sends DNS queries to a pre-configured Domain Name Server, which returns the required IP address. The Domain Name Server in turn might have to send queries to other servers on the Internet to resolve the address, but this is not relevant to the subject of the text.

c. The browser then makes a TCP connection to the IP address of the origin server, either at the port given in the URL if it is specified, or port 80 if it is not (443 for secure HTTP URLs that start with `https://`). The browser then sends a request for content, along with request headers, to the origin server. The server sends the response headers and entity headers if any, along with the requested content, back to the browser on this TCP connection.

The transaction need not happen exactly as specified above. It is quite common to have an intermediary or proxy server through which content is retrieved by the browser. This is frequently the mechanism used by corporate users to access the Internet for increased security and to reduce traffic by caching frequently accessed content in the proxy. The primary difference in this mechanism is that the client browser makes an HTTP request to the proxy rather than directly to the origin server. The proxy acts on behalf of the client in one of two ways. If the requested content exists in its own cache and hasn't expired, it is sent straight back to the client. If not, then the proxy makes an HTTP request to the origin server to retrieve the content, which it can then send back to the client. It is possible to extend this to a model where there are two or more proxies between the client and the origin server. However, in practice, there are hardly any situations where we might require more than one proxy.

The proxy mechanism in the Web brings us now to the model adopted by WAP to deliver content to wireless devices, since the gateway has some proxy functionality.

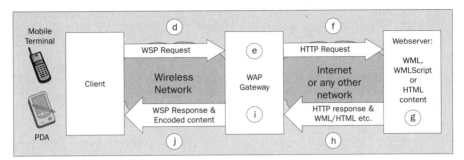

d. As soon as the mobile user chooses a URL, either by typing it in, following a hyperlink in a WML deck or selecting a pre-assigned bookmark, a WSP request is sent to a WAP gateway, the address of which is pre-configured (possibly by the user) in the mobile. The request method (GET or POST for example) together with any request headers is in encoded format. Here's an example (unencoded) request:

```
GET http://wap.wapportal.com HTTP/1.1

... ( other request headers )
```

This will be sent by the client in the encoded format as:

```
0x40 0x18 'h' 't' 't' 'p' ':' '/' '/' 'w' 'a' 'p' '.' 'w' 'a' 'p' 'p' 'o' 'r' 't'
'a' 'l' '.' 'c' 'o' 'm' ... ( other request headers in binary form)
```

In the above byte stream, 0x40 is the assigned number given in WSP specifications for the GET method. The second byte gives the length of the URL that follows. The rest of the byte stream consists of the binary value for the character in the UTF-8 character set (Universal Multiple-Octet Coded Transformation Format defined in the ISO standard, ISO10646). Note that the above binary stream does not include any of the lower protocol layer headers (like that of WTP or WDP).

e. The WAP Gateway transforms the encoded WSP request into an HTTP request. The request is then parsed. The gateway decides, using this request and request headers like Cache-control etc, whether the content identified by the URL is already present in its cache or whether an HTTP request needs to be sent to the origin server to retrieve the content. The domain name part of the URL is resolved into an IP address using similar methods to the web model. Refer to HTTP 1.1 RFC (Request for Comments) available at http://www.ietf.org/rfc/rfc2616.txt for a detailed description of the Cache-control header.

f. An HTTP or an HTTPS (secure HTTP) request is then sent to the origin server with the textual request headers and entity headers if any.

g. Depending on the URL, the origin server returns static content, for example WML, HTML or graphics files, or executes CGI/ASP /JSP scripts or another server-side technology that dynamically generates WML or HTML content. (See Chapters 8 through 11 for more detail on dynamically generating WAP content using server-side technologies.)

h. An HTTP or HTTPS response is sent back to the WAP Gateway with the requested content, along with response headers and entity headers if any.

i. The WAP gateway performs HTTP to WSP header conversion, WML encoding, WMLScript compilation if required, and HTML to WML conversion, followed by WML encoding if required. Some gateways may also perform conversions from graphics formats used on the Internet (GIF, PNG etc.) to WBMP.

j. The WSP response with the encoded content is sent to the mobile terminal along with WSP response headers and entity headers if any.

The following table gives a summary of the differences between the two models:

Web Model	WAP Model
TCP & IP are the transport and network layer protocols providing end-to-end communication.	A lightweight protocol stack WDP – WTP – WSP suited for wireless networks is used between the device and the WAP gateway. TCP/IP is used between the gateway and the origin server.
HTTP is the application layer protocol used.	WSP is the application layer protocol used, which can be considered as a binary form of HTTP. It has additional functionality in that it provides the concept of a session as opposed to the stateless model of HTTP. Of course, WSP also supports a connectionless mode that does not implement sessions.
The protocol headers and the content markup language tags are in a textual format. Typically, these are human readable.	The protocol headers (in most cases) and the content markup language tags are encoded into a compact binary form between the gateway and the device.
An HTTP proxy can be used as an intermediary.	A WAP gateway, which is somewhat comparable to an HTTP proxy, is always used.
Client-side scripting (such as JavaScript or VBScript) embedded in the content travels in the source code before being interpreted by the browser.	Client-side scripting (WMLScript is the only supported language) is in a separate file on the origin server. When there is a request for a script resource, it is delivered to the WAP gateway where it is compiled and bytecode is generated, before it is transported to the user agent in the WAP device. The user agent therefore needs to have a bytecode interpreter and a virtual machine environment similar, for example, to Java.
Browsers support a large number of image formats and other multimedia formats either directly or indirectly through plugins.	Mobile user agents currently support a much smaller number of multimedia formats because of the limited capabilities of the devices themselves and because of the available bandwidth. In fact, a black & white bitmap format known as WBMP is the only image format that is currently supported. But the WAP protocol stack does not in anyway restrict the type of the content it can transport over the network and is generic enough to allow any type of content, like streaming audio & video, to be delivered using WAP whenever it makes sense to do so.

Positioning of a WAP Gateway in the Network

Having read this far, it must be quite clear to you that a WAP gateway sits somewhere between the wireless device and the HTTP origin server. However, we will now evaluate in more detail the possible locations in which a WAP gateway can be situated, and the advantages and disadvantages of each choice. As a content provider, a network operator or a service provider, you would make the final choice.

Here is a summary of the useful locations of a WAP gateway:

❑ A WAP Gateway provided by the network operator

❑ A WAP Gateway provided by the content provider

❑ A WAP Gateway provided by the Internet Service Provider (ISP)

A WAP Gateway Provided by the Network Operator

We assume here that the bearer is IP over dialup circuit switched data (CSD). In the figure given below, it is clear that in this case the WAP gateway is part of the infrastructure that belongs to the cellular network operator. The WAP Gateway houses a pool of modems that take up phone ports on the Mobile Switch. The phone users would have to configure their phones with the access phone number(s) to dial into the Remote Access Server (RAS) setup.

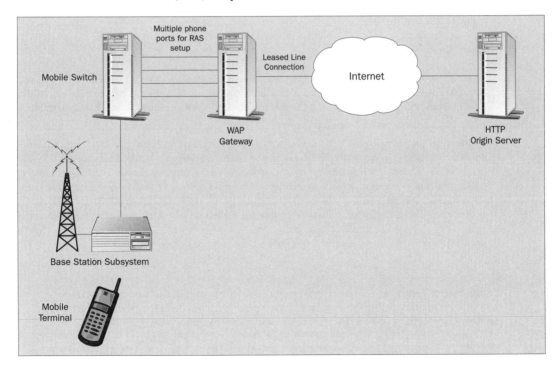

The network operator's infrastructure is comprised of:

❑ **Base Station Subsystem**: This is comprised of **Base Transceiver Stations** (BTS, or antennas) and the **Base Station Controller**, which is the master controller for all the BTSs.

❑ **Network Subsystem**: This is comprised of the **Mobile Switching Center**, which is a fixed telephone switch that has the added complexity of managing mobility.

❑ **Remote Access Server(s)**: Necessary for operator-provided WAP services using Circuit Switched Data.

❑ **Leased-line(s) to the Internet**: Necessary for operator-provided WAP services.

❑ **WAP Gateway**: Necessary for operator-provided WAP services.

Even in the case of packet networks such as GPRS, the network operator can put up a WAP Gateway just before the operator's infrastructure terminates on the Internet.

One of the advantages of the above setup is:

❑ The mobile device only needs a single gateway setting to access any Internet content. The user simply fires up the microbrowser in the mobile device to access information without having to fiddle with the configuration, since it is likely that the device came preconfigured when the mobile was bought in a packaged subscription. The network operator could also use an Over-the-Air (OTA) Configuration, using SMS to do this job. OTA provisioning strings are quite specific to each mobile vendor, though many WAP gateway vendors do support this feature.

Disadvantages for this scenario are:

❑ The network operator might introduce additional advertising content which will piggyback on the content from the Internet when it is sent to the wireless device. The content provider on the Internet will probably not like the idea of their content being obscured in this way.

❑ Even if secure HTTP (HTTPS) and SSL are used between the WAP gateway and the application server as well as WTLS between the user agent and the gateway, the requested content will be in an unencrypted form in the main memory and disk cache of the WAP gateway. Almost every operating environment provides mechanisms to read the memory of an executing process as long as administrative privileges are present. Because gateways cache content after it is received at the WSP layer, data will not be encrypted when stored on the disk cache. This could cause security problems, which will be a cause for concern in some cases such as banking applications. However, as long as a non-disclosure agreement for the data exists between the content provider and the network operator, this will not be an issue.

> **In the case of secure web applications, regardless of the number of intermediaries or proxy servers used, information is in an encrypted form between the browser and the secure website when secure HTTP is used (that is, end-to-end security is possible). WAP applications are dissimilar in this sense from those of the Web. This is because encryption is provided between the device and the gateway where it is decrypted. Data may be encrypted again (using SSL) between the gateway and the origin server.**

❑ The network operator may choose to block access to all but a few 'approved' WAP sites. Some subscribers might protest, move to a competitor or even use Internet access provided by an ISP to access a public WAP gateway. However, most subscribers either will be unaware of how to bypass the WAP gateway in the preconfigured settings on their mobile device, or not interested in fiddling with the provided settings. Many of them may not even bother to try to access services/hyperlinks other than the ones provided by an 'approved' WAP portal. Eventually, however, competition and awareness on the part of the subscribers should level the playing field.

A WAP Gateway Provided by the Content Provider

In the figure below, a gateway is shown which is part of the infrastructure of a content provider:

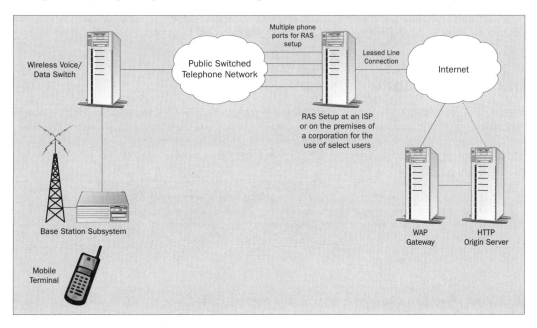

A content provider might decide to have its own WAP Gateway at its **web farm** (the location where a cluster of origin servers are located). They would then advertise the configuration information needed to use their gateway.

One advantage of this solution is:

❑ In the case of secure applications, like banking, access to the content on the origin servers through a WAP gateway other than the content providers own could be disabled for the sake of security. If mobile users try to access the secure content through another WAP gateway, they could be presented with a message asking them to configure their devices to use the content provider's gateway. In this manner, all data can be transferred between the device and the gateway using WTLS and the unencrypted data is present only on the private network of the content provider.

The disadvantages include:

❑ If every content provider chooses to adopt this solution, it will be impossible for the mobile user to have all the necessary gateway configurations set up on their device. For instance, Nokia 7110 supports up to a maximum of 10 gateway configurations. The user will also need to switch configurations every time they need to access a different WAP site.

A WAP Gateway Provided by the Internet Service Provider (ISP)

An ISP could also host a WAP Gateway. The architecture is very similar to the previous case except for the position of the WAP Gateway. The gateway will now be closer to the RAS server and will be one of the nodes on the ISP's network. Although this solution is technically possible, it would hardly make any sense commercially. Unless the ISP also has content to provide, it would be worthless to invest in a gateway.

Striking a Balance

Network operators should consider providing a WAP gateway as a value added service to subscribers, keeping it open so that users are allowed to connect to any site they choose. Otherwise, someone else will do this and take away your subscriber base. Exceptions to this are high level security applications such as banking, electronic buying/selling or credit card transactions.

> **If access control is not enforced – that is, in the case where *any* WAP gateways are allowed to retrieve a piece of content – it is possible that someone could setup a public WAP gateway, and then capture all the (unencrypted) information on the WAP gateway.**

Application Hosting

It is possible to have an origin server on the same host where a WAP gateway is run. This process is called **application hosting** and in Nokia's terminology, the gateway/application server is known as a **WAP Server** as discussed in Chapter 1.

In my opinion, the host which has the WAP gateway installed must avoid hosting content as much as possible. Storing content in say, a database backend on the same host, can be a drain on the system resources and would make it harder to implement clustered scalable solutions to be used when there are a large number of simultaneous users. If the host contains only the WAP gateway functionality, it could then service more users simultaneously than an application-hosting gateway.

If security is the only reason for the use of application hosting, it is suggested that a separate WAP gateway be provided within the same network as the origin server. The gateway host is distinct from the origin servers that store the content. This will ensure security, as discussed above, while still allowing the gateway to take a larger user load.

Combined content and gateway servers (on a single host) are more likely to be used by corporations to provide wireless information services for their employees, than network providers. In such a situation, it is quite evident that scalability is not an issue because the number of simultaneous users would be very small and a single server would be quite sufficient to handle the entire load. Besides, a single server with RAS setup on the same host is a lot easier to administer and manage when compared to a clustered solution, and is the best 'off the shelf' solution. For more information on corporate WAP services, refer to an excellent white paper by Nokia on deployment scenarios for corporate WAP services available at `http://www.forum.nokia.com/download/whitepaper_deploy_scenarios.pdf`

Who needs their own gateway?

Here's a summary of who needs their own gateway:

- ❑ Cellular/Wireless Network Operators.
- ❑ Corporations wishing to provide mobile information services on the company Intranet.
- ❑ Content providers who offer services like banking, e-commerce and online payment systems, may need to have their own gateway for security reasons. This can be avoided by signing contracts with network operators who will then protect the privacy of the content providers' critical data by enforcing restriction in physical access to the gateway host to very few people.

Selecting a WAP Gateway

The discussion in the previous section should have helped you to decide whether you really need your own gateway or not. In this section, we will consider the options for someone who does need a WAP gateway, and list some parameters/features that you should check and compare with each vendor.

What are your options?

There are quite a few vendors of WAP gateways, with prices for solutions ranging from completely free up to nearly half a million US dollars! The choice of solution would therefore depend on the scale of your operations.

There are only two freeware/open software solutions. Kannel, available free of charge under the open software licensing, and personal WAP Gateway (KNO Software), a freeware product.

Here is a list of vendors together with their current WAP Gateway product offerings:

- ❑ Audicode, Audicode WAP Server (`http://www.audicode.com/eng/index.html`)
- ❑ CMG, WAP Service Broker (`http://www.cmg.com/`)
- ❑ Dr. Materna Gmbh (`http://www.materna.com/`)
  - ❑ Anny Way – Carrier WAP Gateway
  - ❑ Anny Way - Corporate WAP Gateway

- Ericsson (http://www.ericsson.se/WAP/)

    - WAP Gateway/Proxy for GSM networks
    - Jambala WAP Gateway for TDMA networks

- Infinite Technologies (http://www.waplite.com/)

- Integra Micro Systems (http://www.integramicro.com/ or http://www.VSellinIndia.com/jataayu/index.html)

    - Jataayu Personal WAP Server
    - Jataayu Enterprise WAP Server
    - Jataayu Carrier WAP Server

- Kannel, Open-Source WAP Gateway (http://www.kannel.org/)

- KNO Software, Free Personal WAP Gateway (http://www.kno.fi/)

- Mobileways (http://www.mobileways.de/)

- Motorola (http://www.motorola.com/MIMS/ISG/wap)

- Nokia (http://www.forum.nokia.com/wap/tools.html)

    - Nokia Artus Messaging Platform
    - Nokia WAP Server

- Omnys Wireless Technology (http://www.omnys.it/eng/home.html)

- Phone.com, UP.Link Server Suite (http://www.phone.com/products/uplink.html)

- Silicon Automation Systems, SAS WAP Gateway (http://www.sasi.com/)

- Kipling Information Technology, Trinity WAP Gateway (http://www.kipling.se/wap.html)

- Virtuacom or Edge consultants (http://www.virtuacom.com/)

    - VirtuaCom WAPgate
    - VirtuaCom WAPgate lite

As a buyer of the product, it should be possible for you to request an evaluation copy of all the solutions listed in the previous section, so that you can choose the solution best suited to your needs. Points to consider are the bearers supported, approximate price and licensing terms, WAP standard compliance, availability, supported platforms, scalability, provisions for billing, remote administration, proprietary additions, present customers and any unique selling points amongst others.

Installing and Configuring WAP Gateways

WAP Gateways are available for many server platforms, including flavors of UNIX, or UNIX-like platforms, and Microsoft Win32 based platforms. We will discuss here the installation of two products:

- Kannel, the open-source WAP Gateway on a GNU/Linux box

- Nokia WAP Server on a Windows NT box

Building, Installing and Configuring Kannel

Kannel is an open-source WAP gateway developed by the Finnish company, WapIT Ltd., and is available for a free download from `http://www.kannel.org/`. The download is currently available only in source form, so you will need to compile the sources. It is not being released under the GNU Public Release licensing, but under a BSD-style open-source licensing.

The open-source gateway distribution consists of a WAP gateway and a separate SMS gateway. The SMS gateway could be used as a web interface to send short messages to GSM mobiles. Because we are not concerned with this here, we will not be going into the details of using the SMS gateway.

> *Even though there is bearer support for SMS and this bearer support is used by the SMS gateway, WAP over SMS is currently unsupported by Kannel.*

We will use RedHat 6.1 with Linux 2.2.12-20 configuration to build & install the Kannel WAP Gateway. The distribution should be fairly easy to build on any UNIX-like platform that has at least some of the GNU tools.

The requirements are:

- ❏ A C compiler. A GNU C compiler is preferred.
- ❏ GNU make. All GNU tools can be downloaded from `http://www.gnu.org`
- ❏ POSIX pthreads library. (Check for `libpthread.a` or `libpthread.so` in `/usr/lib`.)
- ❏ A socket library. (Depending on the flavor of UNIX that you have, it could either be a separate library `libsocket.a` or it could be part of the standard C library.)
- ❏ Gnome-XML library from `http://xmlsoft.org/xml.html`. This might also require `zlib`, depending on how it is configured.
- ❏ GNU Bison 1.28 if you are planning to modify the WMLScript compiler.

Kannel FAQ that addresses some of the common questions is available at `http://www.kannel.org/faq.shtml`

We first need to uncompress the distribution and extract the files:

```
$ gzip -cd gateway-0.8.tar.gz | tar xvf -
$ cd gateway-0.8
```

We then have to run the configure script before we can build the binaries. You might want to pass some additional options so that the binary installation is done in your home directory rather than the default `/usr/local` directory for which you might need root or administrative access:

```
$ ./configure --prefix=<install_directory>
$ make
$ make install
```

Here are the most important executables that will be created:

- ❏ `bearerbox-0.8` (Bearer interfacing for UDP/IP and WDP implementation of the SMS bearer.)

- ❏ `seewbmp-0.8` (A simple tool to print WBMP monochrome bitmaps as ascii graphics on a character terminal.)

- ❏ `smsbox-0.8` (SMS Gateway.)

- ❏ `wapbox-0.8` (Rest of the WAP Gateway.)

With this, we have finished the installation, but we still need to configure the different boxes.

bearerbox

We can find a sample `kannel.conf` file in the `gw/` subdirectory under the directory where we extracted the gateway package. This directory contains all the sample files required for configuration of the gateway. For the moment, to get the gateway up and running, we can accept the defaults provided in the file for all but a section called `CSD Router` and `heartbeat-freq`. Further dissection of the configuration files is required for fine-tuning. Enough documentation has been provided in the bearerbox configuration file making it easy to change and experiment with new settings. Therefore, we simply copy the sample configuration files available in the directory where you extracted the package.

```
$ cd <install_directory>/bin
$ cp <directory_where_package_was_extracted>/gateway-0.8/gw/*conf ..
```

Edit `kannel.conf` using your favorite editor. Under the `CSD Router` section (which is very easy to locate), add the following:

```
wap-udp = wap
interface-name = <IP address of the host where the bearerbox is running>
wap-service = "wsp/wtp"
```

The above `wap-service` part indicates that a non-secure connection-oriented mode is being used by the WAP gateway.

> **Kannel currently supports non-secure connection-oriented mode only. Circuit Switched Data with UDP/IP bearer is the only one supported.**

Each box (wapbox as well as smsbox) sends a message at regular intervals to the `bearerbox` that essentially says, "I'm alive and well". If the `bearerbox` does not receive such messages, it will assume that the other box in question has crashed, but not enough to make the TCP connection break gracefully. It then closes the connection and removes the box from its list of contents. When the other box is well again, it will re-open the connection. The regular interval that we mentioned, is known as `heartbeat-freq`.

The default value has been given a negative value so that the `bearerbox` doesn't start without you editing the configuration file first. Therefore, change the following lines:

```
#heartbeat-freq = 30
# this is here to prevent people from using this without editing
hearbeat-freq = -600
```

to

```
heartbeat-freq = 30
# this is here to prevent people from using this without editing
#hearbeat-freq = -600
```

Notice the moving of the # sign to comment out the default value. Run the `bearerbox` like this in a character terminal. (Or one that emulates a character terminal that provides a command-line interface under X Windows. One such program is called xterm. If you do not have X Windows installed, it doesn't matter. Run the program directly from the shell, say bash, on the console.)

This should give you an output like that shown below and start the `bearerbox`:

Unlike most other open-source or free software, this one doesn't have a huge number of command-line options. However, the downside is that it is not possible to find all the options using a `./bearerbox-0.8 -help|-h` command. The user guide lists one or two options, but in my opinion, this is quite incomplete.

```
bearerbox-0.8 [ <OPTIONS> ] [<conf_file_name>] [<internal_sms_box_conf_file> ]

The available <OPTIONS> are :
(-v|--verbosity) <level>     set stderr output level. 0 = DEBUG, 4 = PANIC
(-F|--logfile) <logfile>     set logfile name
(-V|--fileverbosity) <level> set logfile output level. Defaults to DEBUG

| has the usual meaning, only one option should be specified.

--verbosity, --logfile, --fileverbosity are aliased arguments. But they don't
actually follow the linux long option format that could be parsed in a C program
using the getopt_long(3) function
```

wapbox

In another xterm, we can now start the wapbox executable to produce a functional WAP gateway, which we can then begin to use. We have to change the configuration file wapbox.wapconf for a single parameter. This is to change the heartbeat-freq value. The procedure is very similar to the one mentioned in the previous bearerbox section.

```
  File   Edit   Settings   Help
$ ./wapbox-0.8
2000-06-18 20:33:35 [1024] INFO: Debug_lvl = -1, log_file = <none>, log_lvl = 0
2000-06-18 20:33:35 [1024] INFO: Config dump begins:
2000-06-18 20:33:35 [1024] INFO: filename = <kannel.wapconf>
2000-06-18 20:33:35 [1024] INFO: group:
2000-06-18 20:33:35 [1024] INFO:     <bearerbox-host> = <localhost>
2000-06-18 20:33:35 [1024] INFO:     <bearerbox-port> = <13002>
2000-06-18 20:33:35 [1024] INFO:     <heartbeat-freq> = <30>
2000-06-18 20:33:35 [1024] INFO:     <log-level> = <0>
2000-06-18 20:33:35 [1024] INFO: Config dump ends.
2000-06-18 20:33:35 [1024] INFO: --------------------------------------------------
2000-06-18 20:33:35 [1024] INFO: WAP box version 0.8 starting up.
```

The command-line options for the wapbox are almost the same as those of the bearerbox:

```
wapbox-0.8 [ <OPTIONS> ] [<conf_file_name>]
The available <OPTIONS> are:
(-v|--verbosity) <level>       set stderr output level. 0 = DEBUG, 4 = PANIC
(-F|--logfile) <logfile>       set logfile name
(-V|--fileverbosity) <level>   set logfile output level. Defaults to DEBUG
```

Kannel is designed in such a way that the bearer adapter functionality of the bearerbox is separated from the rest of the WAP gateway functionality. With this mechanism, it is possible to add any number of wapboxes on different hosts to distribute the load. The bearer adapter executable (or bearerbox) can be run on a dedicated host, which then interfaces with the mobile devices. Because this functionality is quite lightweight, a single bearerbox can support a much larger number of wapboxes.

Configuring Nokia 7110 to connect to Kannel

The following settings must be set:

❑ Home page: <URL of the home page you prefer to access>

❑ Connection type: continuous

Because Kannel supports only connection-oriented mode, the above setting must be used.

- ❑ Connection security: `off`

  Kannel has not implemented WTLS yet and so this should be off.

- ❑ Bearer: `data`

  Kannel does not support SMS bearer for WAP services, and this should be data.

- ❑ Dial-up number: `<phone number you dial for Circuit Switched Data>`

  If you are using the dialup access provided by an ISP, specify the dialup phone number of the ISP's RAS server. If you want to setup your own RAS Server on a GNU/Linux box that also runs the gateway, refer to `"doc/dialup.txt"` in the directory where you extracted the package. It gives basic information required to complete the setup.

- ❑ IP address: `<IP address of the host running bearer box>`

  The host where you run the `bearerbox` needs to be reachable from the RAS server where you connect.

- ❑ Authentication type: `normal`

- ❑ Data call type: `<analog or ISDN, depending on what your operator supports>`

  If your network operator supports the V.110 protocol between the mobile switching center and the RAS phone line, you can use `ISDN`, which gives you the advantage of quicker dialup connection times. If you are unsure, use `analog`.

- ❑ Data call speed: `9600`

  Your network may not support higher speeds. Use a higher value if you are sure that the networks support them.

- ❑ User name: `<PPP username for logging in to the RAS>`

- ❑ Password: `<PPP password for logging in to the RAS>`

Installing and Configuring a Nokia WAP Server on the Windows platform

The Nokia WAP Server is available only on Windows NT and cannot be installed on other Win32 platforms (Windows 95 or 98). The product is available on HP-UX and Solaris platforms as well, but we will stick with the NT 4.0 installation in this section, primarily because an evaluation copy of the product is only available for NT 4.0. This section will briefly explain the basics of getting Nokia WAP Server installed and the bare minimum of configuration options. For a detailed document on installation and administration of this product, you should refer to the "Getting Started Guide" and "Administration Guide" documents available at `http://www.forum.nokia.com`. Click on the links **WAP developers Nokia WAP Developer Forum** to reach the login screen, if you have registered already. If you have not registered yourself, click on the links **WAP developers Registration Form** to do so.

Once you have logged in, you can get the required documents from the links **Nokia WAP Server Documents**. Accessing/Downloading the documents require you to go through Nokia's licensing terms acceptance page. However, if you are impatient to go through all this, an alternative exists right now that does not require you to be logged in to the developer forum. (If too many people download the documents in this manner, there is a possibility that Nokia might change the links to avoid people bypassing the developer forum):

1. Nokia WAP Server Administration Guide:
`http://www.forum.nokia.com/download/techdoc_admin-guide.pdf`

2. Getting Started Guide: `http://www.forum.nokia.com/download/techdoc_get-started.pdf`

3. Guide for Setting up a Connection from Nokia 7110 to Nokia WAP Server via Win NT 4.0 RAS and a Modem:
`http://www.forum.nokia.com/download/sg_nokiawapserver_and_winnt4ras.pdf`

4. Nokia WAP Server Product Description:
`http://www.forum.nokia.com/download/techdoc_server1_0descrip-011299.pdf`

5. Nokia WAP Server API 1.0 programmers guide:
`http://www.forum.nokia.com/download/techdoc_prog-guide.pdf`

The Nokia WAP Server 1.0 and trial license keys can be downloaded from
`http://www.nokia.com/corporate/wap/trial_download.html`

In order to install the WAP Server on an x86 box, you need *at least* the following:

- Microsoft Windows NT 4.0 with Service Pack 4 or 5.0.

- 128 MB of RAM (256 MB recommended). For testing some of your content, even 64 MB would do.

- 100 MB of free hard disk space.

- Java Runtime Environment (JRE) 1.2.2.

- 16-bit colour depth setting on the Windows NT box.

- Administrative access to the Windows NT box.

If you want some performance improvement in the execution of Java applications and servlets, you should install the Java Hotspot Performance Engine 1.0.1 available for download from `http://java.sun.com/`. *You will need to register yourself with Java Developer Connection for this download.*

Installation

The installation process is quite simple and involves just clicking a few buttons. Use WinZip or any other zip file extractor to extract the distribution into a temporary folder. Run the program `setup.exe` to start an installation program similar to that of most other Windows software. After the installation program has displayed the license agreement for you to accept, it will move on to other dialog boxes that ask you for information, before copying all the files onto your installation folder.

Two types of setup are possible:

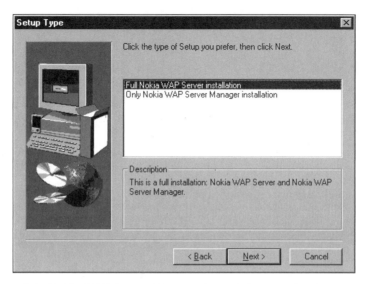

The second option, **Only Nokia WAP Server Manager installation**, installs the server manager, which could then be used to administer a previously installed Nokia WAP Server (on the same host or a different one). This option doesn't require the license strings either. However, we will choose the first option where we have a full installation of Nokia WAP Server.

The temporary license keys (valid for 30 days after the date of the first launch of the server) need to be obtained from Nokia download site after registration with Nokia WAP Developer Forum. Until then, you won't be able to complete the installation. The license keys are emailed to you and are of the form 2C9NM1-164MPJ-DKM2NS. Enter the first part of the license string, 2C9NM1-164MPJ in the **String 1** editbox and the second part of it, DKM2NS in the **String 2** editbox:

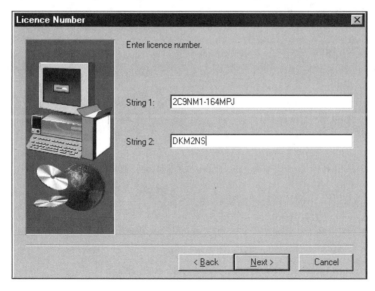

After clicking Next in several other self-explanatory dialog boxes, including one in which you can choose the installation directory, the installation will be complete.

Starting Nokia WAP Server

You can start the WAP Server either manually, or using the NT service.

However, if you are using the UDP bearer, first note that before starting the server, you will have to ensure that the WAP standard UDP/IP ports 9200-9203 are free on the host where Nokia WAP Server is being installed, and are not being used by any other program. Also, check whether TCP port 1099 is free as this is used for the server administration by Nokia WAP Server Manager. You will have to open the same set of ports on the firewall if your server is installed on a host that is inside a firewall and you want users outside the firewall to be able to connect. You can use a freely downloadable tool called *strobe* available from ftp://ftp.cert.dfn.de/pub/tools/net/strobe/strobe-1.03.tgz (You can get a list of port scanner software for different systems at http://www.softpanorama.org/Security/port_scanners.shtml to check what ports are being used by the system. Alternatively, you could use the netstat -a command, on Windows NT, HP-UX or Solaris, and look for all entries with protocol state LISTEN or LISTENING.

Manually Starting the Server

From the Start menu choose Programs|Nokia WAP Server|Nokia WAP Server. The following console window pops up and displays some trace messages during startup:

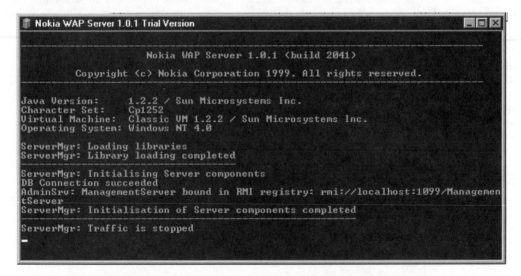

Starting Nokia WAP Server Using the Windows NT Service Mechanism

A Windows NT Service allows a program to be configured to start as soon as the system boot up is complete without anyone having to log in to the system. For someone having knowledge of UNIX based systems, this is analogous to Unix Daemon programs that start executing automatically during the boot up of the system. Ultimately when you have finished configuring the WAP Server and you ready to serve device users, you should set the server to be started in this manner so that the server is up and running even when no one is logged on. You can do this from the Start menu using Programs|Nokia WAP Server|Nokia WAP Server Service Installation. The following console window appears and if you type "*yes*" and press *Enter*, the NT Service is installed and the WAP Server will automatically be restarted if the system is rebooted.

Once the service has been installed, you can control how the service starts up from the Services dialog box in the Control Panel. For the moment, stop the service in the following dialog box by clicking the Stop button in case it has already been started. Start the WAP Service using the manual startup described in the previous section, so that you can view the startup screen and the logs ofwhen devices connect to the WAP Server and retrieve content. The console window that displays logs is not visible when the WAP Server is started as a Windows NT Service.

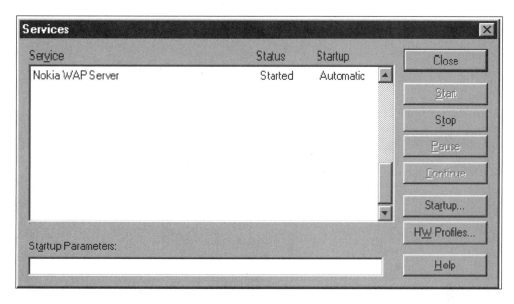

Administering and Configuring a Nokia WAP Server

Start the Nokia WAP Server Manager from the Start menu. If you are doing this for the first time, you will have to run the manager on the same host as the server. This is because, by default, remote administration is not enabled.

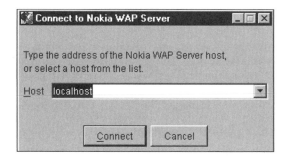

On clicking the Connect button, you will normally get a login dialog-box, as shown below. However, if it fails check whether a *localhost* entry is present in the file `%SystemDrive%\WINNT\system32\drivers\etc\HOSTS` and if not, add the following entry:

```
127.0.0.1   localhost
```

The default administrative userid is admin and the password is empty:

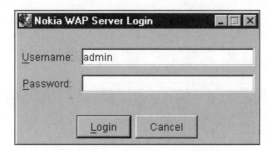

After a successful login, you get the Nokia WAP Server Manager window. The server status indicates that the server has not been started and so we will do this right away.

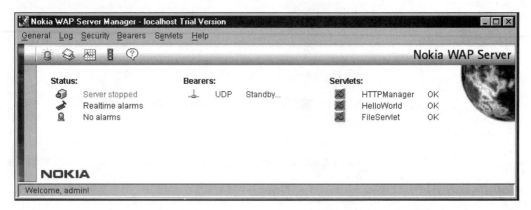

If you double-click on the Server stopped line, a dialog-box will pop up asking you: Do you want to start the traffic? Clicking Yes should start the service, change the status to Server running and change the Bearer status to: UDP running - OK.

Configuring the Server to Connect to the Internet

The Nokia WAP Server uses Java servlets for everything other than the basic gateway functionality. In fact, the responsibility of connecting to an HTTP origin server to retrieve content is handled by an `HTTPManager` servlet. You can configure this by selecting Servlets|HTTPManager from the menu so that the wireless devices that have been configured to use this server can retrieve WAP content from the Internet using HTTP. If you do not configure this servlet, devices can only retrieve content that either resides locally on the same host where the WAP Server is running or is generated dynamically by another Java servlet that may have been installed.

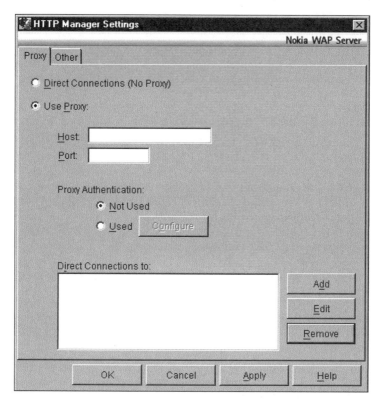

If you already have an Internet connection that does not require the use of proxy servers, you can choose Direct Connections (No Proxy). On the other hand, if you are setting up the WAP Server on a host on your corporate network that has a firewall, which allows only an HTTP proxy server to connect to hosts on the Internet, you will need to choose Use Proxy. You will also need to specify the host and the port where the proxy server is running. Additionally if your proxy server allows retrieving content from the Internet only after authenticating yourself using say, a userid and a password, you will need to change Proxy Authentication to Used and configure it. To have direct connections and not use the proxy server for content on the **corporate intranet**, you just need to specify the domain name and/or IP subnetwork in the Direct Connections to: edit box.

For example, if Wrox were to provide this facility, they would add wrox.com to the Direct Connections to edit box, so that any URL that has a *wrox.com* in it would cause the proxy server **not** to be used. Similarly, if for example they used the IP subnetwork 10.0.0.16 for their internal network, adding this to the edit box would ensure similar results.

It is possible to install a WAP gateway on a host with a dialup Internet connection. However, unless you are doing this for the most trivial of reasons (like checking the content that you authored in an emulator that requires the use of a gateway) and not for mobile subscribers, you wouldn't use this mechanism. With a dialup Internet connection, the IP address of the host connecting to the Internet Service Provider (ISP) is dynamically generated. This means that you cannot advertise the IP address of your WAP gateway for subscribers to configure their phones. In any case, the bandwidth is not sufficient for more than a few subscribers at the same time.

If you are providing access to corporate content and applications on an intranet for employees using mobile phones, you need a **Remote Access Server** setup for employees to connect to your intranet. This is discussed in the next section. As an extra facility for the employees, you can provide access to WAP content on the Internet using your corporate Internet connection, which is quite possibly a high-bandwidth leased-line connection. Since most corporate networks have a proxy server to access Internet content, you will have to fill in the details of the proxy server in the HTTPManager settings.

Configuring the Server to Connect to the Wireless Devices

We now have to configure the server so that wireless devices can connect to the WAP Server using one of the following network access mechanisms:

1. A dial-up network connection using Circuit Switched Data (similar to dialup Internet access from PCs where a dial-up modem is used and TCP/IP protocols operate over Point-to-Point Protocol, PPP).

2. Short Message Service (SMS) network connection.

3. Cellular/Wireless packet networks, like **Cellular Digital Packet Data (CDPD)** or **GPRS** networks.

In the case of **1.** and **3.**, UDP/IP will carry WAP data, whereas in **2.**, SMS will do the job.

❑ **UDP/IP Bearer**

There is nothing much to be done to configure the Nokia WAP Server for this bearer, since it is added by default. The only other thing that you might have to do is to setup a Remote Access Server (RAS) and the corresponding modem pool if you are using Circuit Switched Data. However, if you only have a WAP Server and assume that your subscribers will use their dialup Internet connections from a private ISP to connect to the Internet, then you don't have to worry about RAS setup. To get some information on how to setup RAS on Windows NT, Nokia has provided excellent documentation together with screenshots for which the URL has already been provided at the beginning of the current installation and configuration section. It is *NOT* necessary for the WAP Server and the RAS setup to be on the same host.

❑ **SMS Bearer**

Even though SMS is widely supported by most GSM operators and mobile devices alike, providing WAP access through a WAP gateway can turn out to be a non-generic solution.

> **Each Short Message Service Center (SMSC) vendor supports a different set of protocols for submitting and receiving short messages through their SMSCs. The Internet, dial-up ISDN/modem lines or leased lines are used as media for submitting and receiving messages from the WAP gateway. Some of these protocols require the sender/receiver of short messages to be authenticated by the SMSC. Typically, SMSC operators charge subscription and/or monthly fees for this facility.**

There are at least a few protocols to interface with the SMSCs from Nokia, CMG, Logica Aldiscon and other vendors. Some of these protocols, and the parameters to be configured on Nokia WAP Server to access different SMSCs, are listed here. However, it is not important to know about these protocols in detail as long as you know enough to configure the SMSC interface. The list of these protocols is by no means an exhaustive one, but these are currently the only ones supported by Nokia WAP Server and therefore they have been discussed here. To configure the SMS CIMD or UCP bearer in Nokia WAP Server, add the required bearer using the Bearers menu from the main window of Nokia WAP Server Manager. To configure the particular bearer you have added, double-click the adapter name in the Nokia WAP Server Manager main window. Select the required adapter and click on the Configure button in the Bearer Adapter Management dialog box. The properties described below are available in the Properties tab of the Configuration dialog box.

❑ **Computer Interface for Messaging Distribution (CIMD)**

This is the protocol used between Nokia's Artus SMSCs and a WAP Gateway supporting the SMS bearer. Such an SMSC is accessed using TCP/IP over the Internet. Therefore we need to specify values for the following Nokia WAP Server properties.

WDP_SMS_DRIVER_HOST	:	SMSC IP address
WDP_SMS_DRIVER_USER_ID	:	userid in SMSC
WDP_SMS_DRIVER_PASSWORD	:	password in SMSC
WDP_SMS_DRIVER_PORT	:	TCP port in SMSC

❑ **Universal Computer Protocol (UCP) / External Machine Interface (EMI)**

This is the protocol used between CMG's SMSCs and a WAP Gateway supporting the SMS bearer. An SMSC of this kind is accessed using dialup anolog or ISDN modems. The host where the WAP gateway/server is installed needs to have these modems connected to it. These are the properties of the Nokia WAP Server that need to be given values.

WDP_SMS_DRIVER_CFG_SMSC_HOST	:	SMSC IP address
WDP_SMS_DRIVER_CFG_SMSC_NUMBER	:	Phone number to dial
WDP_SMS_DRIVER_CFG_SMSC_PORT	:	TCP port in SMSC

Summary

In this chapter, we discussed the role of WAP gateways in providing content to a mobile user. Listing all the functions that a gateway carries out, we have highlighted the importance of a WAP gateway in enabling WAP-based information services. We went on to compare the WAP model with the web model, clarifying the functionality of the gateway and evaluated different locations in the network where a WAP gateway can be located, and evaluated the advantages as well as the disadvantages that each solution provides to the end user. We then listed some of the current WAP gateway product offerings. How to install, configure and get them working quickly was discussed for Kannel, the open-source WAP gateway, and Nokia WAP Server trial version.

Part Two

The Wireless Markup Language

So, now you have an understanding of WAP in general, and have got some tools installed to help you get started, it's time to find out how to make content available over WAP, and, to do that, we need to get to grips with its markup language, that is, WML. WML was designed from the start as a markup language to describe display of content on small screen devices. This is the subject of the next two chapters.

Chapter 4 starts with a brief examination of the language from which WML is defined, XML, and goes on to look at the basic card/deck structure of WML, and how this compares to HTML pages. The main focus of the chapter is the set of WML tags used for format and layout of content, such as text, links, tables, and images. Chapter 5 moves on to look at how we can use WML to provide a more interactive experience for the user by adding options menus and allowing them to input text.

WMLScript is the only client-side scripting language available for use on WAP-enabled devices. It is based on ECMAScript, so if you have some JavaScript experience, you should find the syntax very familiar. If not, you'll find full coverage of WMLScript syntax in Chapter 6, followed by coverage of the WMLScript Standard Libraries, and an example illustrating the use of WMLScript to implement client-side validation.

If you have had the chance to play around with a WAP-enabled phone, you'll be familiar by now with the limitations of such devices. The lack of a proper keyboard for entering text is tricky, as is trying to read large amounts of text on the small screen. These issues, along with many others associated with usability, are discussed in depth in the final chapter of this section.

4

Basic WML

Over the next two chapters, we'll be focusing on the markup language of WAP – the Wireless Markup Language, or WML. Here we will be introducing the basics, such as formatting text, adding links for implementing user navigation, and using tables and images to add a professional touch to applications. In the next chapter, we'll move on to see how we can allow the user to interact more with the application, by making selections, entering text, and so on.

While we will attempt to include all relevant aspects of WML here, this is not intended to be an exhaustive reference – the information presented here describes the most important and often used features, and will help you to get started in a practical context. For a complete listing of all the WML elements, please refer to Appendix A.

But before we even start with WML, let us first take some time to look at the roots of WML and examine the language from which it is derived – XML.

eXtensible Markup Language

Knowing XML is not vital to writing Wireless Markup Language applications, but having a little background XML knowledge can help to make learning WML a faster process. If you are familiar with XML then you may wish to skip to the next section. Otherwise you will find that this section gives you a good grounding in this technology and the implications of XML.

What is XML?

XML is a technology for creating structured documents that can be exchanged between systems. In XML, unlike HTML, the way that data is to be displayed is not described; rather, it is the structure and organization of the data that is defined. As a result of differences in protocols from system to system and the way that data storage and data transmission are implemented, data transfer between different platforms or applications has always been problematic. For example, the electronic transfer of documents between two different businesses can become troublesome and frequently this means the use of simple text files. Different approaches to security, operating systems and data storage techniques make data integrity issues complex and expensive to resolve.

XML was the product of the World Wide Web Consortium's effort to create a language for describing documents in a system independent way. It is a subset of SGML (Standard Generalized Markup Language) – a general purpose document storage mechanism, which was defined to enable storage of very large numbers of documents. In addition to document content, XML contains metadata – data that describes the content. In XML this was designed to be both operator-readable and machine-readable. This makes it a powerful technology that is available for both human and automatic agents, consumption.

Simple example

XML is a markup language that includes rules regarding how tags can be used, but the tags themselves may be defined for specific applications. For example, examine the following piece of XML that describes the recipe for a cornflake breakfast:

```xml
<?xml version="1.0"?>
<!-XML Recipe Example -->
<recipe name="cornflakes">
   <ingredients>
       <ingredient>
           <name>
               Cornflakes
           </name>
           <quantity>
               150g
           </quantity>
       </ingredient>
       <ingredient>
           <name>
               Milk
           <name/>
           <quantity>
               1/4 pint
           </quantity>
       </ingredient>
   </ingredients>
   <method>
       Place cornflakes in a bowl.
       Pour milk onto cornflakes.
   </method>
</recipe>
```

Let's start by defining a few of the concepts used. A **tag** is a part of the document delimited by angled brackets (< >). An **element** is a named section of the document that begins with a tag in the form *<tag>* and ends with a tag in the form *</tag>*. Where a tag does not delimit content, it takes the form *<tag/>*. You'll find that throughout the book we refer to both elements and tags.

In the above example, there are several elements. There is an `ingredient` element, a `recipe` element, a `method` element and so on. The `<recipe>` tag also contains an **attribute**. An attribute is an assignment placed within a tag to give additional meaning to that element. In this example the only attribute is the `name` attribute, but there can be as many as we like within a tag.

The first line of the code should be familiar since it is a comment. Anything between the `<!--` and `-->` is ignored by processors and doesn't form part of the data that is being structurally represented by the XML.

XML Parser

An XML parser is a component used to process XML documents. A document must meet certain criteria in order to be successfully parsed, and if it meets these, it is said to be **well-formed**. As well as the syntax illustrated above, in order to be well formed a document must have its elements nested correctly. A closing tag must always be used to close the closest opening tag pair. Therefore the following is invalid:

```
<tag1>
    <tag2>
</tag1>
    </tag2>
```

XML is also case sensitive, so all tags must consistently use the same case; `<hello>`, `<Hello>` and `<HELLO>` are distinct entities in XML. In addition, it must only have one root element, and element content must not include any reserved characters (for example, the & character and <, less than).

Other requirements are not relevant to us at this point or are very involved. If you are interested in detailed coverage of XML, you should consult one of the many good books available on the subject, for example, *Professional XML*, from Wrox Press.

How do we know what the tags mean?

Of course the tags need to be given meaning, and the rules of well-formed XML documents alone are not enough to make sure that data is presented in a meaningful way. For example, what is to stop a developer from producing the following document since it is well formed?

```
<ingredient>
    <name>
        Cornflakes
    </name>
    <quantity>
        150g
        <method>
            Place cornflakes in a bowl.
            Pour milk onto cornflakes.
        </method>
    </quantity>
</ingredient>
```

It should be obvious that the method element should not be allowed inside the quantity element. This is where **Document Type Definitions** (**DTD**) come in. An XML document can be associated with a DTD that gives further indication of its structure; the DTD describes the tags that may be inside a document conforming to the DTD, what tags may be nested within each tag and other information. The XML parser can then use the information given by the DTD to check that the document has the correct structure. If the XML document has the correct structure in relation to its associated DTD then it is said to be **valid**. (A detailed description of DTDs is beyond the scope of this book.

WML is an XML language that is defined by a DTD and therefore follows all the rules that have been mentioned above as well as the rules given in its DTD. Should you wish to examine this DTD it can be found at http://www.wapforum.org/DTD/wml_1.1.xml.

WML Structure

On the Web, a page is loaded into a browser. Several pages may be displayed with the use of frames and this fact is often used to separate navigation and text. A WAP device, on the other hand, loads not a page but a **deck** of **cards**. The WAP device displays only one card at a time, and the card contains both content and navigational controls. Although a WAP device can only display one card at a time, it can hold many different cards; an associated group of cards is known as a deck. This system of organizing the markup language into decks of cards, rather than pages as in HTML, is due to the latency associated with wireless devices. Delays in connection to the server become unacceptably high in the environment in which WAP devices operate. By returning several cards at once, trips to the server are reduced and additional content can be stored locally on the device whilst the user navigates around it.

The way that WAP browsers treat WML can be quite different from the way that web browsers treat HTML. Traditionally, web browsers are tolerant of badly formed HTML and will compensate for errors where they can, but this is not the same for WAP devices. According to the specifications drawn up by the WAP forum and with the assistance of the World Wide Web Consortium, an error in the document should result in an error in the browser; a WAP browser should not display erroneous WML.

A Basic WML Card

As with all new technologies, the best place to start is at the very beginning. Here we will start with our very own *Hello World* program. How we view this WML is somewhat device dependent, but the Chapter, "Setting Up WAP ", explained in detail how to view WML in some of the more common browsers and toolkits.

```
<?xml version="1.0"?>
<!-- ch4_ex01.wml -->
<!DOCTYPE wml PUBLIC "-//WAPFORUM//DTD WML 1.1//EN"
"http://www.wapforum.org/DTD/wml_1.1.xml">

<wml>
    <card id="main" title="First Example">
        <p>
            Hello world!
        </p>
    </card>
</wml>
```

All the code shown in this chapter has been tested in the Nokia 6110 emulator, the UP.Simulator, yourwap.com browser, WinWAP, Microsoft Mobile Explorer emulator and Ericsson's browser.

Bear in mind that although the Nokia 6110 does not actually simulate a real phone, it is a good choice to use in a development environment, because it does implement the current WAP standards extensively and supports the majority of the features.

Here is what the code above looks like on the Nokia 6110:

Let's take a moment now to look at this example, piece by piece, to see how it was put together and what each section does.

The Header

Every WML deck starts with the same XML header:

```
<?xml version="1.0"?>
<!DOCTYPE wml PUBLIC "-//WAPFORUM//DTD WML 1.1//EN"
"http://www.wapforum.org/DTD/wml_1.1.xml">
```

The first line of this simply states that what follows is an XML document and the version number used. The next line selects the document type and gives the URL of the Document Type Definition. This DTD gives the full XML definition of WML. The DTD referenced is that defined in WAP 1.1, but this header may change in future versions of WML. If you don't understand this header don't worry; as long as every WML document begins with a header *exactly* as it is shown above, a gateway or browser will not reject the document. Since this information is repeated in every file, you may discover that many toolkits will generate this for you automatically.

The Body

The WML code of a deck is enclosed in the `<wml></wml>` tag pair. This is the body of the document, and the cards are defined within it using the `<card></card>` tag pair.

This tag pair is our first encounter with attributes in WML. The `id` attribute gives a unique ID for this card within the deck, while the `title` attribute often describes the card and may be displayed by the browser:

```
<card id="main" title="First Example">
```

A card may have other attributes (see Appendix A), but we have only defined `id` and `title`. The `id` attribute gives the card an identifier that can be used to refer to it in other parts of the WML. When navigation is covered later, we'll see how this identifier is used to select the next card to be displayed on the device. It can also be used to refer to a particular section of a deck from an external deck. The `title` attribute gives the name of the card to be presented to the user. Not all WML browsers display the `title` attribute, so the design of a card should not rely upon a title, but it can be useful in guiding the user nonetheless.

113

An example of when we should *not* use the `title` attribute would be a card that asks a question in the title, and then presents a list of possible answers. A user using a phone with a UP.Browser, which does not display the title, for example, would be immediately lost!

Also used in our first simple example is the `<p></p>` tag pair. As in HTML, this tag simply marks a paragraph of text – but we'll look at this in more detail in the next section.

For now, we are examining the basic structure of a WML deck, and there is one more tag pair that can be very useful; the `<head></head>` pair and in particular the `<meta/>` tag that can be used within it. The following example WML uses these tags to declare to the device the character set that should be used to display the deck:

```
<?xml version="1.0"?>
<!DOCTYPE wml PUBLIC "-//WAPFORUM//DTD WML 1.1//EN"
"http://www.wapforum.org/DTD/wml_1.1.xml">

<!-- ch4_ex2.wml -->
<wml>
    <head>
        <meta content="charset" name="character-set=ISO-10646-UCS-2"/>
    </head>

    <card id="main" title="First Example">
        <p>
            Hello world!
        </p>
    </card>
</wml>
```

Note that there is a difference between this header and the WML document header given at the top of the document. This second header belongs to the WML deck and not the WML document itself.

The `<meta>` tag allows generic metadata about the deck to be defined. Metadata can literally be anything; it can be data of any sort. In this example it is used to define the character set that should be used to display the document's content. If the browser doesn't understand the data supplied with the `content` type, it simply ignores it.

One application of metadata is caching. WAP devices, in attempt to increase efficiency, may store previously downloaded data in a section of memory called a **cache**. When the user attempts to view a card, the browser will display information previously saved in the cache. However, you should use this with caution, because if the card displays time sensitive data that has changed on the server, the user will be seeing out-of-date information. In browsers with caches it is sometimes possible to set the maximum cache life of the card using some meta information or to direct the device not to cache the content at all.

If the WML is used on a device with a browser that has no cache, it doesn't matter, as the metadata will just be ignored. That is the wonder of metadata; it can be about anything and is therefore the only way that browsers can receive information which isn't part of the strict WML definition found in the WAP specifications. Of course, if you are not targeting one particular device with your WML code, you will need to consider carefully any application that depends on metadata for proper performance, since devices are notorious for varying widely in implementations.

Text Formatting

In this section, we're going to see the tags defined for formatting text. In particular, we'll be taking a look at how to handle paragraphs, line wrapping, and how to add different styles to plain text. How all these features are displayed is very device dependent and you may find that some WAP browsers ignore many, if not most, of these text formatting features.

It is also worth noting that many ignore whitespace in the same way as web browsers. This means that you should structure files in a way that makes them easy to read without being concerned at the resultant file size. It should be noted, however, that any whitespace before the `<?xml version="1.0" ?>` line constitutes an error and browsers and gateways alike should crash if this is the case. This is especially relevant with dynamic generation of WML code as described later in the book. In the case where the declaration may be preceded by other code (specific to the dynamic generation technology), there should not be any whitespace contained that will be passed to the browser/gateway.

Within the code, any whitespace characters read in are replaced by spaces and will cause lines to wrap. In other words, both text and markup can be arranged to maximize ease of reading for consequent updates of your code. So, our "Hello World" example shown earlier and the following alternative to it, which has had all its non-essential whitespace removed, are identical (within 1 byte or so) in size:

```
<?xml version="1.0"?><!-- ch4_ex01.wml --><!DOCTYPE wml PUBLIC "//WAPFORUM//DTD
WML 1.1//EN" "http://www.wapforum.org/DTD/wml_1.1.xml"><wml><card id="main"
title="First Example"><p>Hello world!</p></card></wml>
```

For readability purposes, you probably agree the first is better.

Paragraphs and the `<p>` Tag

In the first example given above, the phrase "Hello world!" was enclosed in `<p></p>` tags. These tags mark a section of text as a paragraph element.

> **In WML, all text to be displayed on the main part of the screen must be inside a paragraph element.**

Of course, you can have more than one paragraph inside a card, but remember not to try and fit too much text onto one card. The typically small displays on the majority of WAP devices makes large quantities of data cumbersome for a user to absorb. In addition, large quantities of data will have an affect on the fetch speed and may decrease user satisfaction.

The card shown below is illegal and would generate an error in the browser because the WML is not conforming to the definition given in the DTD:

```
<!-- ch4_ex03.wml -->
<card id="main" title="First Example">
   Hello world!
</card>
```

The missing `<p></p>` tags will generate an error in this case.

The following example illustrates how to make use of more than one paragraph in a card:

```
<?xml version="1.0"?>
<!DOCTYPE wml PUBLIC "-//WAPFORUM//DTD WML 1.1//EN"
"http://www.wapforum.org/DTD/wml_1.1.xml">

<!-- ch4_ex04.wml -->
<wml>
   <card id="main" title="Wrox press">
   <p>
      Professional WAP by Wrox Press gives a broad overview of WAP and
      associated technologies.
   </p>
   <p>
      To learn more, join us at the Wrox Wireless Developer conference in San
      Francisco, U.S.A, 6th October!
   </p>
   </card>
</wml>
```

We have defined two <p></p> tag pairs here. The browser will separate the text into two separate blocks. If you scroll down the card, you'll see how the two paragraphs have been separated; in the Nokia browser this causes the indentation shown in this screenshot:

Remember that the WML needs to be well-formed, so it is crucial to always add a closing </p> tag at the end of a paragraph. Unlike HTML browsers (which are very forgiving and do not demand that all tags are closed), WML browsers will not display content that is not well-formed. Finally, remember also that since WML is case-sensitive, using <P></P> will also generate an error.

Line Wrapping and Breaking Lines

In addition to breaking up the text, it may also be desirable to control the layout of a paragraph in more detail. For example, if displaying a timetable of events, it would make the information clearer if the time was aligned to the left and the details aligned centrally. You may wish to display a paragraph aligned to one side of the display or maybe even in just one line, but remember the small screen size severely limits this. The <p> tag has attributes for this purpose, mode and align. The align attribute can be assigned left, right or center and the mode attribute wrap or nowrap. They perform exactly as their names suggest, and in particular, the align attribute is the same as in HTML. The following example and commentary should clarify their use:

```
<?xml version="1.0"?>
<!DOCTYPE wml PUBLIC "-//WAPFORUM//DTD WML 1.1//EN"
"http://www.wapforum.org/DTD/wml_1.1.xml">

<!-- ch4_ex05.wml -->
<wml>
   <card id="main" title="Wrox press">
   <p align="center">
      Professional WAP by Wrox Press gives a broad overview of WAP and
      associated technologies.
   </p>
```

```
    <p mode="nowrap">
        To learn more, join us at the Wrox Wireless Developer conference in San
        Francisco, U.S.A, 6th October!
    </p>
    </card>
</wml>
```

The `align` attribute aligns the text centrally:

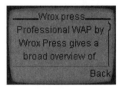

The `mode` attribute is used to specify whether the browser should automatically wrap lines when it gets to the end of the screen. In the second paragraph, the mode has been set to `nowrap` to turn off wrapping. The result is that the entire paragraph appears as one line, which in the Nokia 6110 browser has the unfortunate consequence that you can't read it since there is no horizontal scrolling:

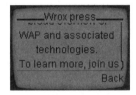

However, in the UP.Simulator this line scrolls across the screen so that it can be read:

If wrapping is turned off, the text can be broken by inserting line breaks using the `<br/>` tag. A `<br/>` tag forcibly inserts a line break into the text. This simply means that a new line is started for all content immediately following a `<br/>` tag:

```
<?xml version="1.0"?>
<!DOCTYPE wml PUBLIC "-//WAPFORUM//DTD WML 1.1//EN"
"http://www.wapforum.org/DTD/wml_1.1.xml">

<!-- ch4_ex06.wml -->
<wml>
    <card id="main" title="Wrox press">
        <p align="center">
            Professional WAP by Wrox Press<br/>
            gives a broad overview of WAP and<br/>
            associated technologies.
        </p>
        <p mode="nowrap">
            To learn more, join us at the <br/>
            Wrox Wireless Developer conference <br/>
```

```
            in San Francisco, U.S.A, 6th October!<br/>
        </p>
    </card>
</wml>
```

This example shows `<br/>` tags being used to break lines in the second paragraph. Notice however, that in the first paragraph a `<br/>` is also used. A `<br/>` can be used to force a line break at any point in some text, no matter what wrapping mode has been set for the paragraph. So, if you don't want to worry about line breaks, set the mode to `wrap`; remember the `<br/>` will still work as specified.

Styles

With all this text on such a small screen, picking out the important information can be quite difficult. What is needed is a way to mark certain parts of the text as noteworthy. Applying a style such as 'bold text' to a section of text would achieve this and WML provides several tags for this purpose. The way the browser chooses to implement this varies, so it should be considered only as an indication of the way text should be treated – it is merely a hint to the browser. Some browsers will ignore the styles altogether. The styles defined by the WML specification are:

Style	Tag	Description
Bold	`<b></b>`	Makes something **stand** out more.
Italic	`<i></i>`	Use *slanted* text.
Underline	`<u></u>`	Draw <u>a line under</u> the text.
Emphasis	`<em></em>`	Emphasise the text in some way, the choice is left to the device in this case.
Strong	`<strong></strong>`	Similar to emphasis, device may apply a style to indicate the text is significant.
Big	`<big></big>`	Increases the size of the text.
Small	`<small></small>`	Reduces the size of the text.

The following example makes use of four of these styles:

```
<?xml version="1.0"?>
<!DOCTYPE wml PUBLIC "-//WAPFORUM//DTD WML 1.1//EN"
"http://www.wapforum.org/DTD/wml_1.1.xml">

<!-- ch5_ex07.wml -->
<wml>
    <card id="main" title="Wrox press">
    <p align="left" mode="wrap">
        <i>Professional</i><br/>
        <u>WAP</u> by <b>Wrox Press</b><br/>
        <big>Wireless Developer conference</big> <br/>
        <small>Copyright (c) Wrox Press 2000</small>
    </p>
    </card>
</wml>
```

The example Wrox Press WAP site presented in the last section, has now been extended to make use of styles. The `<i></i>` tag pair has been used around 'Wrox' to apply an italic font to it. The details of the wireless conference have been highlighted by using the `<big></big>` tag pair to increase the size of the font. A copyright notice doesn't need to stand out on a page, so it has been reduced in size using the `<small></small>` tag pair. The result is shown in the Nokia 6110 toolkit emulator and the UP.Simulator:

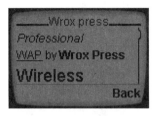 

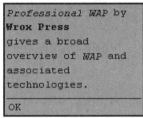 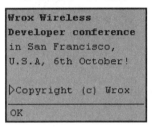

Currently, not all WAP devices on the market have browsers that support styles; as you can see in the UP.Simulator, neither small nor underline are supported. This doesn't mean that styles should be avoided. If a browser identifies a valid WML tag, such as a style tag, that it doesn't support it won't produce an error and it will still display the text. You should not be surprised if, when testing your WAP applications on a real device, the styles don't appear to have any effect. The Nokia 7110 is one example of a device that has minimal support for styles. The `<b></b>`, `<u></u>`, `<i></i>`, `<big></big>`, `<small></small>`, `<em></em>` and `<strong></strong>` style tag pairs are all unsupported.

Special Characters

There are some characters that have a special meaning in WML. We have already seen that all tags are encased in < and > characters. If one of these characters needs to be displayed on the screen of a WAP device, it is possible to enter the character using its ASCII number, in the form `&#number`. In addition, there are shortcut forms, so for example > can be represented as `&#62;` and `&gt;` . Another character that has a special meaning in WML is the ampersand (&) character; if we wish to output it to the screen we can use `&#38;`.This is the same encoding as is used in HTML. The following example shows this in use, to display the less than, and greater than, characters that have ASCII codes 60 and 62:

```
<?xml version="1.0"?>
<!DOCTYPE wml PUBLIC "-//WAPFORUM//DTD WML 1.1//EN"
"http://www.wapforum.org/DTD/wml_1.1.xml">

<!-- ch4_ex08.wml -->
<wml>
    <card id="main" title="Maths facts">
    <p>
        1 &#60; 2 = True <br/>
        1 &#62; 2 = False <br/>
    </p>
    </card>
</wml>
```

This displays as:

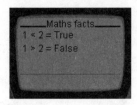

The following table shows some commonly used characters, and the names by which we refer to them within WML code:

Character	WML name
Quote	quot
Apostrophe	apos
Ampersand	amp
Less than	lt
Greater than	gt
Soft hyphen	shy
Non-breaking space	nbsp

The following code gives an example of named special characters being used in WML:

```
<?xml version="1.0"?>
<!DOCTYPE wml PUBLIC "-//WAPFORUM//DTD WML 1.1//EN"
"http://www.wapforum.org/DTD/wml_1.1.xml">

<!-- ch4_ex09.wml -->
<wml>
    <card id="main" title="Maths facts">
    <p>
        1 &lt; 2 = &quot;True&quot; <br/>
        1 &gt; 2 = &quot;False&quot; <br/>
    </p>
    </card>
</wml>
```

Notice how the ASCII numbers have been replaced with lt and gt. Also, it is simple to surround the true and false statements with quotes. This displays as:

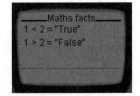

If we look again at the table above, we see the last entry is non-breaking space. As the name suggests, a non-breaking space character is one that cannot be replaced with a line break. Earlier in the chapter, we saw how a paragraph could be set to automatically wrap lines when they reached the edge of the display. As you might imagine, this is achieved by replacing a space between words with a line break. If there is one particular point where you don't wish a line break to be inserted, a non-breaking space character can be used; and when a WML browser encounters an nbsp, it cannot start a new line. It may decide to cause a line break at an earlier stage in the line, or it may decide to force the line over the edge of the screen. You should be aware that this does cause problems for some browsers, though. For example, the following WML:

```
<?xml version="1.0"?>
<!DOCTYPE wml PUBLIC "-//WAPFORUM//DTD WML 1.1//EN"
"http://www.wapforum.org/DTD/wml_1.1.xml">

<!-- ch4_ex10.wml -->
<wml>
    <card id="main" title="Wrox press">
    <p align="left" mode="wrap">
        To learn more, join us at the <br/>
        Wrox Wireless Developer conference in
        <big>San Francisco</big> U.S.A&nbps;6th October!
    </p>
    <p align="center" mode="nowrap">
        <small>Copyright (c) Wrox Press 2000</small>
    </p>
    </card>
</wml>
```

The above example doesn't behave quite as expected on many WAP devices. It is a mandatory requirement of the WAP specification that all browsers should be capable of displaying lines, in an unbroken manner, that are too wide for the display. It states that horizontal scrolling or some other mechanism should be used in order to achieve this. Unfortunately some device manufacturers have ignored this, and this fact must be taken into account. In the example code above, the line "San Francisco 6th October" should all appear on one line, but don't be surprised if it is split over several lines, or it disappears off the screen and there is no way to read it. For example, the above WML when displayed on a Nokia 7110 is displayed with no white space, it has just ignored the   character altogether:

If this device were used to browse your WML, you wouldn't be able to use non-breaking spaces. Therefore, unless you are sure of what type of device your user will be browsing your content with, you should exercise caution when using non-breaking spaces.

Navigation

Implementing good navigation around a WAP application is important since very little can be displayed on the small screen the device has. In addition, choices can often be confusing and increase the frustration a user feels. This section examines how to write WML to allow a user to move around.

Anchor Links

An anchor link is a part of the display that, when the user selects it, takes the user to a new location within the current application or another application altogether. The concept of an anchor link is used all over the Web to provide links from one resource (page content) to another. In order to specify the resource location, WAP has adopted the familiar **Uniform Resource Locator** (**URL**). A URL takes the form:

```
protocol://domain/filepath/filename#offset?variable1=value&variable2=value
```

The protocol being used is normally HTTP. Although the browser is communicating with the gateway via WAP protocols, the resources are being fetched by the gateway from the origin server using HTTP. The domain is the location of the machine that is being accessed, an alias or familiar name for it's IP address. This normally takes the form `www.company.com` or, often in the case of WAP, `wap.company.com` or `mmm.company.com`, although it can actually be anything. Strictly speaking the domain is just the `company.com` part. Alternatively, the IP address of the machine can be used. The `filepath` is the location of the file on the machine. So if you are looking for a file called `index.wml` inside a directory called `wapfiles` then the URL has the form:

```
http://wap.company.com/wapfiles/index.wml
```

Remember that although a single file contains one deck, a deck can contain many cards. The offset specifies which card to display. The offset is specified using the `id` attribute of a card, as was discussed earlier. So to visit a card with `id="main"` we would use:

```
http://wap.company.com/wapfiles/index.wml#main
```

If a card isn't specified, then the first card in the deck (in sequential order in the deck code) will be displayed.

Entering any URL into a device when you don't have a proper keyboard is difficult. The longer the URL, the more difficult it is. In addition, special characters on a mobile device may require many key presses to get at. For example, the / character can be entered by pressing the 1 key 15 times on the Nokia browser. Some mobile phones have predictive text input to reduce the number of key presses required to enter text. However, this works by recognizing words and won't be of much help when entering URLs. This difficulty means that most users will simply access WML cards by following links, and will rarely actually enter a URL directly into the device. If they do, they will be likely to bookmark it so as not to have to enter the URL again. If a service is being launched where the user will need to enter a URL, even if this will only be on one occasion, the URL should be kept as short as possible. The initial deck could be given a short name like `a.wml` instead of `index.wml` and if the web server being used supports default documents, this could be used to prevent the user having to type in the name of a file at all. For the same reason, you should avoid nesting the first deck deep in many sub-directories as this also creates a long URL.

Attaching a variable to the end of a URL is a good way to send data back to the server where your WML decks reside. It is however, very unusual to manually add variables to the end of a URL. The use of this is examined in a moment.

In order to move around in WML, a section of text or an image can be marked as being an **anchor**. An anchor is a method specifying navigation between cards. This is exactly the same process as in HTML. The anchor specifies the location of the card that is being linked, as well as the text or image that is serving as an anchor. The browser then displays the text in a different way to normal text, to show that it is a link. Again, the WAP specification does not specify how this difference should be indicated and this will vary between browsers. In the Nokia 7110 a link is indicated by underlining the anchor text, whereas in the UP.Browser, a link is surrounded by square brackets. When a user selects a link, the browser navigates to the specified link if it is in the same deck, or alternatively submits a subsequent request to the gateway for the specified resource. An example is presented to show this in use:

```
<?xml version="1.0"?>
<!DOCTYPE wml PUBLIC "-//WAPFORUM//DTD WML 1.1//EN"
"http://www.wapforum.org/DTD/wml_1.1.xml">
```

```
<!-- ch4_ex11.wml -->
<wml>
    <card id="main" title="Wrox press">
        <p align="center">
            Professional WAP by Wrox Press<br/>
            gives a broad overview of WAP and<br/>
            associated technologies.
        </p>
        <p mode="nowrap">
            To learn more, join us at the <br/>
            Wrox
            <anchor>
                <go href="ch4_ex13.wml"/>
                    Wireless Developer conference
            </anchor><br/>
            in San Francisco, U.S.A, 6th October!<br/>
        </p>
    </card>
</wml>
```

Notice how the various devices show that the text Wireless Developer conference is a link:

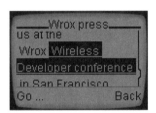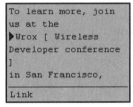

"Wireless Developer conference" has now been enclosed within a <anchor></anchor> tag pair and bound to an action. This effectively means that the browser associates a particular action with a selection of this text and we will look at some alternatives to simple hyperlinks. The action is specified in the <go> tag, which is also inside the anchor. This tag signifies that when the text inside the anchor is selected, the WML card pointed to by the href attribute of the <go> tag is displayed, replacing the currently displayed card. This may well be in a different deck, in which case the filename also needs to be given, as on this occasion.

In this example, we have assumed that the linked resource is local to the current deck, that is, it resides in the same directory as the WML file, with the card containing the link to it. Otherwise we would specify its absolute address including the domain name and full virtual or actual pathname.

```
<go href="http://domainname/pathname/ch4_ex13.wml"/>
```

In addition, we can reference any one particular card within a deck by specifying it as shown previously by a hash (#) followed by the card's ID.

Specifying the full absolute URL can also be used to access a deck that is located in a different domain on the Internet. The following code demonstrates this in use:

```
<?xml version="1.0"?>
<!DOCTYPE wml PUBLIC "-//WAPFORUM//DTD WML 1.1//EN"
"http://www.wapforum.org/DTD/wml_1.1.xml">

<!-- ch4_ex12.wml -->
<wml>
   <card id="main" title="Manufacturers">
   <p>
      The following are WAP pages of mobile phone manufacturers.
      <br/>
      <anchor>
         Ericsson
         <go href="http://mobileinternet.ericsson.se/emi/default.asp"/>
      </anchor>
      <br/>
      <a href="http://wap.nokia.de/">
         Nokia
      </a>
      <br/>
   </p>
   </card>
</wml>
```

In this example, we have introduced a new tag in this piece of code; the `<a></a>` tag pair. It is very common when producing WAP applications to mark a section of text to link to another card. As it is so common, the `<a></a>` is provided as a shortcut for doing this. The tag simplifies content linking; rather than including a `<go>` element, we simply provide a value for the `href` attribute and enclose the text that will serve as a link.

So, the following WML:

```
<a href="http://wap.nokia.de/">
   Nokia
</a>
```

is identical to the much longer:

```
<anchor>
   <go href="http://wap.nokia.de/"/>
   Nokia
</anchor>
```

In the next chapter we will see the benefits of using the longer version, since the `<go>` tag has another useful attribute.

Going Backwards

Returning to our previous example, if the users wish to return to the previous card, we will need to implement a back function. WML has a tag defined to allow the user to return to the previous card, namely `<prev/>`. Whenever the user follows a link in a WAP browser, the browser keeps a list of the cards that have been visited. When the `<prev/>` tag (or task, as it is sometimes called) is used, the browser will look up the last card that has been visited, and return to it. In the next example, the second deck ch4_ex13.wml could include some text to return to the previous card:

```
<?xml version="1.0"?>
<!DOCTYPE wml PUBLIC "-//WAPFORUM//DTD WML 1.1//EN"
"http://www.wapforum.org/DTD/wml_1.1.xml">


<!-- ch4_ex13.wml -->
<wml>
   <card id="main" title="Conference Details">
   <p align="center">
      <b>Wireless Developer conference</b><br/>
      in San Francisco<br/>
      U.S.A<br/>
      <i>6th October</i><br/>
      <anchor>
         <prev/>
         Go back
      </anchor>
   </p>
   </card>
</wml>
```

When this WML is displayed on a WAP device, the back option is displayed as a normal anchor link:

This enables the user to return to their original card. However, remember that some mobile phones (including the Nokia 7110 and Ericsson R320) have a soft button underneath and to the right of the screen, which is normally the back button. The following code attaches the `<prev/>` task to this button:

```
<?xml version="1.0"?>
<!DOCTYPE wml PUBLIC "-//WAPFORUM//DTD WML 1.1//EN"
"http://www.wapforum.org/DTD/wml_1.1.xml">


<!-- ch4_ex14.wml -->
<wml>
   <card id="main" title="Conference Details">

   <do type="prev">
      <prev/>
   </do>

   <p align="center">
      <b>Wireless Developer conference</b><br/>
      in San Francisco<br/>
      U.S.A<br/>
      <i>6th October</i><br/>
   </p>
   </card>
</wml>
```

This code now produces a **Back** button on the mobile device. In the Nokia emulator, this is the right soft key. Notice how the **Back** button is on the right of the screen display:

The `<do></do>` tag pair used in the above code will be covered in more detail in the next chapter, when we examine how to build up an options menu. The `type` attribute of the `<do>` tag is the button or other such mechanism that is having a task assigned to it. However, the `type` attribute cannot be relied upon as the browser is under no obligation to pay any attention to this. There is no way of knowing how the value of the `type` attribute will be interpreted on any given device. We cannot make the assumption that something assigned to the `prev` type will automatically be assigned to the back button.

It is possible to label the back button by making use of the `label` attribute of the `<do>` tag. We may wish to change the above so that the right soft key is called **Previous**, so that it looks like:

The only change in the above code is the addition of the `label` attribute in the use of the `<do>` tag, see ch4_ex17.wml:

```
<do type="prev" label="Previous">
    <prev/>
</do>
```

On some devices, the use of this `label` attribute is essential. If the device doesn't recognize the `prev` type, it may just label the option as **prev** instead of **Back** or **Return**, which is a lot less obvious for our users to follow. However, there are some situations where the use of the `label` attribute is better avoided. For example, if the device is allowed to choose a label for its back key, then when the phone is switched into different languages, it will automatically use the correct word for the current language.

One of the WML tags that may seem a little peculiar at first is the `<noop/>` tag. It does nothing at all, and yet it is still a useful tag. So, when are we going to want to use a tag that does nothing at all? Well, some browsers automatically allow the user to return to the previous card, whether the WML has catered for this or not. For example, the UP.SDK does this using its hard-wired back button. If you want to prevent the user from being able to step back to the previous card, then we can assign the `<noop/>` task to the back button. At first we may be concerned about the fact that WML provides a facility to do this, but consider an m-commerce solution where the user has just accepted a purchase. We don't want the user thinking they have cancelled the order because they have stepped back through the purchase. The following example demonstrates `<noop/>` in use:

```
<?xml version="1.0"?>
<!DOCTYPE wml PUBLIC "-//WAPFORUM//DTD WML 1.1//EN"
"http://www.wapforum.org/DTD/wml_1.1.xml">
```

```
<!-- ch4_ex18.wml -->
<wml>
   <card id="main" title="Conference Details">

   <do type="prev">
      <noop/>
   </do>

   <p align="center">
      <b>Wireless Developer conference</b><br/>
      in San Francisco<br/>
      U.S.A<br/>
      <i>6th October</i><br/>
   </p>
   </card>
</wml>
```

This code makes the assumption that the back button has been assigned to a button with type prev. Being able to stop a user going back may seem odd, but as we saw above, there are occasions when we might wish to do this. In the next chapter we will see many other tasks that can be stopped using the <noop/> tag, but it's more likely that we'll wish to change the meaning of the back button, instead of simply preventing it. Suppose an advert is inserted between two cards – it would be good if, when the user clicked to go back from the second card, they went straight back to the first card instead of through the advert. The following example illustrates this:

```
<?xml version="1.0"?>
<!DOCTYPE wml PUBLIC "-//WAPFORUM//DTD WML 1.1//EN"
"http://www.wapforum.org/DTD/wml_1.1.xml">

<!-- ch4_ex20.wml -->
<wml>

   <card id="main" title="Wrox press">
   <p align="left" mode="wrap">
      <i>Wrox</i> provides <b>professional programmers</b> with titles
      that provide a path through their development careers.
   </p>
   <p align="left" mode="wrap">
      Our last conference was a success and the next will be a
      <anchor>
         <go href="#advert"/>
         a Wireless Developer conference
      </anchor>.
      </p>
      <p align="center" mode="nowrap">
         <small>Copyright (c) Wrox Press 2000</small>
      </p>
   </card>

   <card id="advert" title="Advert">
      <p align="center">
         <big>Professional Active Server Pages 3.0</big>
         <br/>
         <i>Available now</i>
         <br/>
         <small><a href="#details">
         Get conference details
         </a></small>
      </p>
      </card>
```

```
<card id="details" title="Conference Details">
    <do type="prev">
        <go href="#main"/>
    </do>

    <p align="center">
        <b>Wireless Developer Conference</b><br/>
        San Francisco <br/>
        U.S.A <br/>
        <i>6th October</i><br/>
    </p>
</card>

</wml>
```

Running through a sample user session, the behavior of this code can be examined. The now familiar first card presents the user with a link to the conference details, which they find by scrolling down:

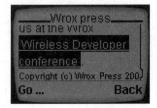

After following this link, an advert is displayed on the screen. In the next chapter, timers will be introduced which will allow us to show a card for a short interval. For now though, the code requires the user to scroll down and follow a link onto the information they have requested:

The conference details then appears and a back option is available on the right soft key.

When the user selects the back option they are returned to the original Wrox press home page and not the advert:

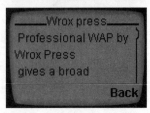

In this example all the cards have been brought into one deck. Notice how in the third card the contents of the <do></do> tag pair have been altered to go back to the main card and not the advert as might be expected by normally pressing the back button. The WML extract is:

```
<do type="prev">
   <go href="#main"/>
</do>
```

If you have tried this out, don't worry if it hasn't performed as expected. As has already been noted, the handling of the type attribute in the <do> tag is very device dependent. For example in the Nokia 7110, this WML adds a "Back" item to its list of options instead of changing the function of the right soft key.

Advanced Display Features

In this section we will examine some of the more advanced display features provided by the WML specification. As has been commented on above, the current browser implementations seem to be having a hard enough time supporting even the most basic of the features of WML, so don't be surprised if the features introduced in this section don't work on your browsers at all.

Tables

Any serious WAP application or service is likely to have a database behind it. Often, we want to extract information from the database and display it to the user in a useful and intuitive way. The information retrieved from databases is frequently suited to being displayed in a tabular manner. WML tables are based upon and work much like HTML tables.

At the time of writing it makes sense to consider tables an advanced display feature. This is because, again, support for tables varies greatly from one browser to another and many do not support them at all. As with all WML, if a browser does not support tables, it will not produce an error or neglect to display the data. Instead, it may simply ignore the table format and display the table data in a single column (like the browser in the Nokia 7110). Other devices have other quirks when displaying tables, such as that displayed by UP.Simulator. The UP.Simulator displays tables as expected, unless some of the data in the table is also an anchor, in which case it doesn't display this data in a tabular form.

Here is an example of the use of tables. Of course in this WML example the table data is hardwired in, but in real world applications this is unlikely to be the case.

```
<?xml version="1.0"?>
<!DOCTYPE wml PUBLIC "-//WAPFORUM//DTD WML 1.1//EN"
"http://www.wapforum.org/DTD/wml_1.1.xml">

<!-- ch4_ex21.wml -->
<wml>
  <card id="main" title="Recent books">
  <p align="left">
    <table columns="2">
      <tr><td>Professional Linux Deployment</td><td>Blackburn et al</td></tr>
      <tr><td>Professional Symbian Programming</td><td>Allin et al</td></tr>
      <tr><td>Professional ASP Web Techniques</td><td>Homer</td></tr>
      <tr><td>Beginning E-Commerce with VB, ASP, SQL Server 7.0 and
      MTS</td><td>Reynolds</td></tr>
      <tr><td>Beginning Site Server</td><td>Huckaby et al</td></tr>
    </table>
  </p>
  </card>
</wml>
```

129

This displays as:

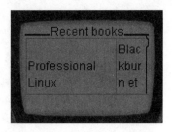

Three new tag pairs have been introduced here, `<table></table>`, `<td></td>` and `<tr></tr>`. Note that there is no equivalent to HTML's `<TH>` tag. The whole table has to be contained within the table tags. Each row is contained within a `<tr></tr>` tag pair and each item within a row is contained within a `<td></td>` tag pair. It is important to remember the ordering here: data items go inside a row, which go inside tables. The number of columns in a table is specified as an attribute inside the `<table>` tag:

```
<table columns="2">
```

Sometimes it is helpful to emphasize some of the data in a table, and it is possible to alter the style of the table using all the style tags introduced earlier. In addition to this, it is also possible to alter the alignment of a table.

```
<?xml version="1.0"?>
<!DOCTYPE wml PUBLIC "-//WAPFORUM//DTD WML 1.1//EN"
"http://www.wapforum.org/DTD/wml_1.1.xml">

<!-- ch4_ex22.wml -->
<wml>
    <card id="main" title="Recent books">
    <p>
        <table columns="2" align="LR">
            <tr>
                <td>Professional Linux Deployment</td>
                <td><small>Blackburn et al</small></td>
            </tr>
            <tr>
                <td>Professional Symbian Programming</td>
                <td><small>Allin et al</small></td>
            </tr>
            <tr>
                <td>Professional ASP Web Techniques</td>
                <td><small>Homer</small></td>
            </tr>
            <tr>
                <td>Beginning E-Commerce with VB, ASP, SQL Server 7.0 and MTS</td>
                <td><small>Reynolds</small></td>
            </tr>
            <tr>
                <td>Beginning Site Server</td>
                <td><small>Huckaby et al</small></td>
            </tr>
        </table>
    </p>
    </card>
</wml>
```

In this example, a couple of things have been changed. Notice that in some of the table cells a style has been applied; in this case the `small` style has been used to reduce the size of the author names. Also the `align` attribute of the `<table>` tag has been used here. This attribute doesn't perform the same as the `align` tag that we have already seen with the `<p>` tag. The attribute is assigned a letter for each column in the table, and the letter determines how that column is to be aligned. L denotes left alignment, R for right alignment and C for center alignment.

So if you had a three column table and you wanted the first column to be left aligned and the next two columns to be centered, assign `"LCC"` to the `align` attribute. The above example used a "LR" alignment and this displays as:

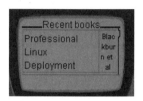

As you can see, tables do not work very well on devices with such small screens. The limited width of the screen means that fitting one column on can be a nuisance, let alone several. In this case it appears that it is the browsers that *do* implement tables that may cause 'unsightly' rendering of the content and it may be, that for now, it is best to avoid using them.

Images

The Web is full of many graphically intensive pages, but in WAP applications this simply isn't possible. Graphics can be used sparingly to display logos or perhaps adverts, but using them as part of the interface, possibly as arrows to navigate the content, should be avoided due to the current inconsistent support from WAP devices. The WAP standards define a brand new image format, the **Wireless Bitmap**, which is more commonly referred to by its acronym **WBMP**. This is a very simple picture format with no compression, which only supports black and white images. The bandwidth limitations imposed on WAP devices, may suggest compression would be an attractive solution. However, you should remember that small wireless devices typically have low processing power. The code needed to decompress graphic images on such devices would run slowly.

When developers first began producing WAP applications, tools for the creation and editing of WBMPs were not yet available. WBMPs were produced by creating two color BMPs, and then editing their headers. The WBMP format is supplied in Appendix E should you wish to experiment with this method. Thankfully, there are now a few WBMP tools available.

Images are inserted into a card by the use of the `<img/>` tag. Let's look at an example first, before we examine the tag in more detail:

```
<?xml version="1.0"?>
<!DOCTYPE wml PUBLIC "-//WAPFORUM//DTD WML 1.1//EN"
"http://www.wapforum.org/DTD/wml_1.1.xml">

<!-- ch4_ex23.wml -->
<wml>
    <card id="main" title="Welcome">
    <p align="center">
        <img src="wroxlogo.wbmp" alt="Wrox : Programmer to programmer"/><br/>
        <a href="wrox6.wml">Enter site</a>
    </p>
    </card>
</wml>
```

This simple deck displays the Wrox logo and allows the user to enter the rest of the site via a hyperlink. Even this simple logo makes the WAP application look much more professional.

The `<img/>` tag has been used to insert the image into the card. This card has two notable attributes, `src` and `alt`. The `src` attribute gives the location of the image and follows exactly the same rules as for the `href` attribute of the `<a>` and `<go>` tags we saw earlier. Yet again, the handling of this part of WML varies from device to device. If the device is not capable of displaying the image pointed to by the `src` attribute, it may instead display the text assigned using the `alt` attribute. In addition to lack of support for images, there are a variety of reasons why it may not be able to display the image. The path stated in the `src` attribute may be incorrect or the image may not be in the correct WBMP format.

For these reasons, it is always good practice to assign meaningful text to the `alt` attribute. Of course once again simply because the WAP specification says that a browser should do something, it doesn't mean it will, and the present offerings from Phone.com and Ericsson don't appear to do this. In this case, this applies both to the display of images and the display of the `alt` text, neither of which display in some browsers.

Who was it that said 'a picture is worth a thousand words'? With such small screens, small images instead of text can be very useful, allowing us to get more information across to the user in the small space available. Images can be particularly useful when used as links. For example, an application could be navigated using small icons instead of lots of text.

Let's look at our example again. The card we've just seen can be modified to do away with the Enter site text by making the image itself a link.

```
<!-- ch4_ex24.wml -->
<wml>
    <card id="main" title="Welcome">
    <p align="center">
        <a href="wrox7.wml">
            <img src="wrox.wbmp" alt="Wrox : Programmer to programmer"/>
        </a>
    </p>
    </card>
</wml>
```

Of course, by now it should be obvious that every way in which WML is treated varies from device to device. For example, the Nokia 7110 will display images, unless they are links, in which case it displays the text assigned to the `alt` attribute.

These images show the above WML in the Nokia 6110 emulator (on the left) and then in a Nokia 7110 emulator (on the right):

When working with images, it is important to remember the small memory capabilities of WAP devices. Some WAP gateways will perform conversion of images to WBMPs, if they are not in that format already. In this case it must still be established in advance whether the amount of memory images required will cause problems.

Finally, when working with images, simply converting an old image to WBMP will rarely be effective. When pictures are converted to black and white they can lose much of their original detail and remember that the pictures need to be scaled down. Using the Nokia 7110, images should really be no bigger than around 96x44 since the device crops any part of an image that will not fit on the display at once. In addition, this browser will not allow images and text on the same line and this will need consideration when designing an application. We do not recommend using automatic image conversion since the results could end up unacceptable.

Summary

We've covered the basics of WML in this chapter, and seen how we must follow the rules of XML when coding our WML. We've examined how WML needs to be organized into decks and cards, and looked at a basic WAP site, that illustrated the use of text, tables, links and images.

We have seen that current standards mean inconsistent browser behavior, however, this language is fairly robust and errors should not occur due to unsupported functionality. This does leave us, as developers, with this question: should we use functionality that may fail depending on the browser viewing our application, when the current industry trends point towards variety of clients? We will discuss these issues in Chapter 7.

Several tags have been introduced which are summarized in Appendix A.

There is still a lot more WML to be covered. The <do></do> tag is yet to be discussed in detail, and WML has other tricks the developer can use to eke that extra functionality from our applications. With the tags we know at the moment, the amount of interaction with the user is minimal; all they can do is follow links. In the next chapter we will see how to make use of some much more advanced WML features.

5

Interacting with the User

In the previous chapter, we focused mainly on the displaying of content using WML. However, WML can be used for more than simply displaying pre-formatted documents – we can use it to a much greater extent by enabling the user to interact with the WAP device. We can draw a parallel with the Internet; in the early days of the Web, the content was very static, yet today the Web is full of dynamic applications that interact with the user. This chapter covers WML's option menu, select lists and input fields. In order to make use of these features more effectively, events and variables of WML are covered.

Given the limitations in memory and processing of current devices, the real power of the wireless Internet lies not just with the WAP device, but with the server. This chapter covers the techniques for sending information back to the server for further processing or storage, which opens up endless opportunities for WAP applications.

Making a Selection

With the breadth of options available on the Web, it will not be too long before an application will require the user to make a decision as to what they want to do next. WML provides us with several ways to allow a user to make a selection on a WAP device. We will look at the options menu, and select lists, two mechanisms provided to create a list of options.

The Options Menu

Many WAP browsers attach an option menu to each card. The user typically brings up this menu on a mobile phone by using the left softkey. On other devices these options may simply appear as a list on the top of the display. The way in which this is handled varies from one device to another, and we'll see more on this later in the book. This option menu is built up through use of the `<do></do>` tag pair. When the user makes a selection from the option menu, an action is carried out which is specified by whatever is inside this element – usually a link. The name of the option is given as the `label` attribute of the `<do>` tag and this is typically the text the user will see on the screen. The `<do>` tag also has a `type` attribute that must be assigned a value. This `type` is the button, menu or other user selection item where this option is to go. This is very device specific, but using the `accept` type typically adds an item to the option menu. The following example is a card that has a simple options menu:

```
<?xml version="1.0"?>
<!DOCTYPE wml PUBLIC "-//WAPFORUM//DTD WML 1.1//EN"
"http://www.wapforum.org/DTD/wml_1.1.xml">


<!-- ch5_ex01.wmp -->
<wml>
    <card id="main" title="Wcommerce">
        <do type="accept" label="Who are we?">
           <go href="#who"/>
        </do>
        <do type="accept" label="Products">
           <go href="#products"/>
        </do>
        <do type ="accept" label="Services">
           <go href="#services"/>
        </do>
    <p>
        Welcome to the Wcommerce wireless shopping site
    </p>
    </card>
</wml>
```

Now of course we have not implemented the destination cards in this example, so if you attempt to click through you will get a `'card not found'` error. However, it illustrates an options menu. You will find that if you try this WML code on a variety of WAP browsers, the way it is rendered varies from one device to another. While some browsers will add these to the options menu (accessed using the left soft key), some, like the UP.Browser, add the first choice to that menu and create an additional menu using the right soft key for the remaining options.

The option menu is a very useful part of WML. As a general rule, if the WAP device you are targeting has good support for an options menu, you should try to move links out of the body of the card and onto this menu. The user of the device is likely to be familiar with making selections using this method and valuable space on the screen will be saved. Of course there is nothing stopping you from using a combination of options menu links with links on the card. It may be better to separate essential services from others by placing them on the card itself, providing the rest as an options menu.

Let's see what this looks like on the Nokia 7110 emulator and the UP.Simulator respectively – the deck would be displayed as follows:

 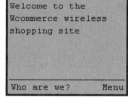

Clicking on the Options button (or on the Menu button in the case of the UP.Simulator) produces:

 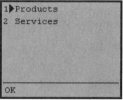

The Microsoft Mobile Explorer renders the options at the top of the card. On loading the deck these options are shown:

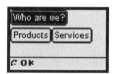

If you then scroll down, you will find the welcome screen:

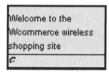

Templates

Now if we extend the above example to include the 'who', 'products' and 'services' cards, we may well wish to have the options menu on every card. This allows the user to go to any of the main cards simply by selecting it from the options menu, a little like having a frame down the left hand side of a web site with links to all the main pages. Adding the options menu to every card has the undesirable effect of increasing the size of the deck rapidly:

```
<?xml version="1.0"?>
<!DOCTYPE wml PUBLIC "-//WAPFORUM//DTD WML 1.1//EN"
"http://www.wapforum.org/DTD/wml_1.1.xml">

<!-- ch5_ex02.wml -->
<wml>
   <card id="main" title="Wcommerce">
      <do type="accept" label="Who are we?">
         <go href="#who"/>
      </do>
      <do type="accept" label="Products">
         <go href="#products"/>
      </do>
      <do type ="accept" label="Services">
```

```
        <go href="#services"/>
    </do>
<p>
    Welcome to the Wcommerce wireless shopping site
</p>
</card>

<card id="who" title="Who are we?">
    <do type="accept" label="Who are we?">
        <go href="#who"/>
    </do>
    <do type="accept" label="Products">
        <go href="#products"/>
    </do>
    <do type ="accept" label="Services">
        <go href="#services"/>
    </do>
<p>
    Wcommerce is a new internet retailer ready for the wireless world.
</p>
</card>

<card id="products" title="Products">
    <do type="accept" label="Who are we?">
        <go href="#who"/>
    </do>
    <do type="accept" label="Products">
        <go href="#products"/>
    </do>
    <do type ="accept" label="Services">
        <go href="#services"/>
    </do>
<p>
    We supply a range of wireless products.
</p>
</card>

<card id="services" title="Services">
    <do type="accept" label="Who are we?">
        <go href="#who"/>
    </do>
    <do type="accept" label="Products">
        <go href="#products"/>
    </do>
    <do type ="accept" label="Services">
        <go href="#services"/>
    </do>
<p>
        We can help you to book film tickets, restaurants or
        hotel rooms, online in the wireless world.
</p>
</card>
</wml>
```

What is needed is some way to apply the options menu across the entire deck without repeating it. A more sensible way of handling this would be to have a mechanism that allows us to define our option menu once, yet have it available from each card. The way that we can achieve this is by using a **template**. A template is given at the start of deck, directly following the <wml> tag, and is specified using the <template></template> tag pair. Everything that is between the <template></template> tags is automatically inserted into every card within the deck.

This simplifies our code enormously:

```
<?xml version="1.0"?>
<!DOCTYPE wml PUBLIC "-//WAPFORUM//DTD WML 1.1//EN"
"http://www.wapforum.org/DTD/wml_1.1.xml">
<!-- ch5_ex03.wml -->
<wml>
    <template>
        <do type="accept" label="Who are we?">
            <go href="#who"/>
        </do>
        <do type="accept" label="Products">
            <go href="#products"/>
        </do>
        <do type ="accept" label="Services">
            <go href="#services"/>
        </do>
    </template>

    <card id="main" title="Wcommerce">
    <p>
        Welcome to the Wcommerce wireless shopping site
    </p>
    </card>

    <card id="who" title="Who are we?">
    <p>
        Wcommerce is a new internet retailer ready for the wireless world.
    </p>
    </card>

    <card id="products" title="Products">
    <p>
        We supply a range of wireless products.
    </p>
    </card>

    <card id="services" title="Services">
    <p>
        We can help you to book film tickets, restaurants or hotel rooms, online in
the wireless world.
    </p>
    </card>
</wml>
```

Notice how this approach has removed the need for the options menu being defined in any of the cards. In addition if we need to override a menu in any one specific card, we can specify, as normal, a `<do>` element in that card. This would then take precedence. The rest of the cards would function normally, It would be only this card that would function differently.

The do Element

Before we move on and look at another way of presenting the user with a list of options we should consider the do element some more. We have now seen this element on two occasions, on the first occasion to provide a back button, and, in the second the build up a list of options. Let's clarify its function and the way this is implemented. The format for a do type element is typically:

```
<do type="sometype">
    some_action
</do>
```

This code associates the action, *some_action* with the type, *some_type*. The WAP specification defines what these types are. For example, it defines the `prev` type used in the last chapter as applying to the button, or other mechanism of user input that is used by the user to return to a previous state.

The follow table details all the types you can use:

Type	Description
accept	Acceptance; on a mobile phone this is typically the left softkey since this key is normally the OK, or Yes button.
prev	Previous; the back button if it exists, typically this is the right softkey.
help	The button pressed to request help.
reset	The reset button for the device.
options	The button request asking for more operations.
delete	The button pressed to remove an item.
unknown	This can be mapped to any key on the device.

The results of using these can be quite interesting. For example, in the code above, when items are assigned to the accept type they appear on the menu that is brought up by pressing the left softkey, this is what you might expect on a mobile phone. On a PDA however, it is more likely that each of these options will appear as an icon of button within the card as PDAs tend to treat an acceptance button somewhat like a Submit button on a web page.

On the UP.Browser the first choice appears on the left softkey and any others are available in a menu accessed through the right softkey.

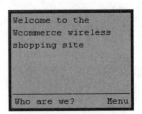

If we now press the right softkey, the menu appears. We can select an item from this list by either scrolling to it and pressing OK, or by selecting the item by number, in this case 1 or 2:

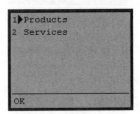

The select Element

In some cases, the option menu might not be the best place for the options. Instead, you may wish to have a list of options on a card. One way of doing this would be to simply list the items and link them to the appropriate deck or card. Another is provided by the `<select></select>` tag pair, this mechanism allows the browser to display the options in a way that groups the choices.

In the UP.Browser, for example, the options are mapped to numbers, so the user can then select a choice by simply pressing the appropriate number on the keypad. This is good for usability because it limits the number of key presses the user has to make.

The Wcommerce example's `Products` card can be extended to make use of `select` lists. Consider this new version of the products card:

```
<card id="products" title="Products">
    <p>
        Available vehicles:
        <select title="Models">
            <option>BMW Z3</option>
            <option>Audi A4</option>
s           <option>Audi A6</option>
        </select>
    </p>
</card>
```

In this example, nothing useful has been done with the `select` list, but notice the format. The entire list is enclosed in the `<select></select>` tag pair. Within this list are all the options, each enclosed in an `<option></option>` tag pair. The only attribute of the `<select>` tag that has been used here is the `title` attribute. This is optional, as it is with the `<card>` tag, and as such should also not be relied upon to inform the user what the select list contains. Depending on which browser is being used, this attribute may be ignored. On the Nokia 7110, the list is rendered a little like an options menu. The first option appears in the card in square brackets, which should alert the user that it is part of a choice. Clicking on the option brings up an options menu, and the choice the user makes is then substituted for the default value. This select list appears in the Nokia 6110 emulator as:

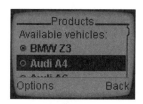

In any application, the user will need to make choices. However, it is good practice to keep these choices to a minimum. When an application has many options, things can become difficult for the user. They may well have to scroll through several screens of choices before they reach their desired item. It is advisable to keep the most common options at the top of the list and keep the options to ten at most. Another way around this is to break down the various options into subgroups. This list of subgroups could then be implemented using a list of anchor links to new cards containing the complete list of options for that subgroup.

WML also provides a simpler way of creating subgroups within a `select` list, through the use of the `<optgroup></optgroup>` tag. The above WML code could be modified so that the selection list becomes:

```
<select title="Models">
    <optgroup title="BMW">
        <option>Z3</option>
    </optgroup>
    <optgroup title="Audi">
```

```
            <option>A4</option>
            <option>A6</option>
        </optgroup>
    </select>
```

This displays as:

Selecting "Audi" then displays:

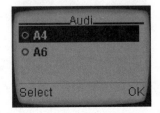

Notice that, like the `<select>` tag, the `<optgroup>` tag has a `title` attribute. In fact, the `<select>` tag has quite a few more important attributes. So far, we haven't used select lists to do anything too useful – we need to associate the choices with an action, such as navigation or changing data for example. In order to understand how to do that, however, we will first need to look at events and variables. Briefly, when an option is picked in a select list it generates an event – we can then handle that event and act upon it. Let's examine this in more detail now.

Events

Events can be used to make WAP applications dynamic. As the name suggests, an **event** is simply when something notable happens. Events are a very common concept in windows-based programs and web programming. For example, when a PC user clicks on an icon in a window, this generates an event.

The various events that you can respond to in WML are summarized below:

Event Name	Description
oneventforward	Occurs when the user navigates directly to the card, whether using the do element or by entering a URL directly.
oneventbackward	Occurs when the user navigates to the deck, using a URL retrieved from the history stack.
onpick	Occurs when the user selects, **or deselects**, an item.
ontimer	Occurs when a timer expires.

When one of these events occurs, a piece of code associated with it – called an **event handler** – is executed. There are many types of events, they can be generated by a window opening, an item being clicked on with the mouse, a set amount of time expiring or a menu being opened to name but a few. In WML, events are generated when a card is made visible, whether by navigating through to it (the onenterforward event) or by returning to it (onenterbackwards), when a set amount of time has expired (ontimer event) or when a selection is made (onpick event). Many of these events are handled using the <onevent> element, with the exception of the onpick event, which is covered later in this chapter.

The use of this element is:

```
<onevent type="eventname">
    action
</onevent>
```

We will introduce each event as the chapter progresses and we will cover the possible range of actions for each. We will see how the onenterbackward and onenterforward events can be used to alter the behavior of a card depending upon the direction in which the user is travelling through our application. We'll also look at how the timer event can be used to make our application change at a timed interval, and how to make use of select lists with the onpick event.

Overriding the Normal Navigation

When we first came across the <prev/> tag, we discussed the fact that where the back button actually takes a user, and where we would like the user to be taken, are often two different things. Take this extended version of the Wcommerce program as an example:

```
<!-- ch5_ex06.wml -->
<card id="products" title="Products">
    <do type="prev">
        <prev/>
    </do>
    <p>
    Available vehicles:
    <select title="Models">
        <optgroup title="BMW">
            <option>Z3</option>
        </optgroup>
        <optgroup title="Audi">
            <option>A4</option>
            <option>A6</option>
        </optgroup>
    </select>
<!-- when the user is ready, they can go through to the purchasing section of the
application-->
        <a href="#check">
            Buy
        </a>
    </p>
</card>
```

```
    <card id="check" title="Confirmation">
        <do type="prev">
            <prev/>
        </do>
<!-- confirm user wishes to purchase the item -->
    <p>
        Are you <b>sure</b> you wish to purchase this item:<br/>
        <a href="#buy">
            Yes
        </a>
    </p>
    </card>

    <card id="buy" title="Acknowledgement">
        <do type="prev">
            <prev/>
        </do>
<!-- Contact server to place an order here -->
    <p>
        Done.<br/>
        The product will be dispatched within 30 days
    </p>
    </card>
```

Let's examine one scenario which demonstrates a potential problem that can be solved with events. (The screenshots below are taken using the Nokia 7110 emulator.)

Suppose the user goes to the products card from the options menu:

He then selects a specific product and chooses to buy it:

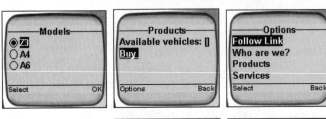

Finally, he is presented with a confirmation screen and his purchase is acknowledged:

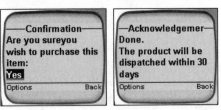

This is a very simplified example; a real application would involve some dialog with the server, and the user would probably need to enter card details, and so on. But here we are just concentrating on what happens on the UI with our WML code. This stripped down application shows you what the user might see from an m-commerce application. (Note how the browser has failed to display a space due to the use of the <b> element.)

If the user were to press the back button at this point, unless we intervene, he would see the confirmation screen again, which doesn't make a whole lot of sense. Once the user has made a final choice, they should never be able to return to the confirmation card – the order has been processed and we don't want them to be presented with a meaningless choice. At best, they have still bought a car but think they haven't; at worst, they will have two vehicles delivered to their home. So, in the event that the user tries to go back once they have confirmed their purchase, we should redirect them to another card.

This is the perfect occasion to make use of the `<onevent>` tag, and use it to handle the `onenterbackward` event. (The `onenterforward` event, is useful but not as commonly used). Here is our example again:

```
.
.
.
    <card id="check" title="Confirmation">
        <onevent type="onenterbackward">
            <prev/>
        </onevent>

        <do type="prev">
            <prev/>
        </do>
    <p>
        Are you <b>sure</b> you wish to purchase this item:<br/>
        <a href="#buy">
            Yes
        </a>
    </p>
    </card>
.
.
.
```

The change to the confirmation card means that when the user enters this card backwards, the `onenterbackward` event is generated and the `<prev/>` task is executed, taking the user back one card further. Let's take another look at our example scenario, and examine what happens when the user makes a purchase:

The user selects **Back** from the confirmation card.

And this time they are presented with the products card:

145

One other aspect of the `onenterforward` and `onenterbackward` events is that if both specify a forwarding action, we can create a card that is invisible to the user. This can be useful in dynamically generated sites that require processing. This processing can be called by an 'invisible' intermediate card.

Timers

When the concept of time is introduced into an application, it can become much more powerful. With a timer, it is possible to update information at regular intervals without user intervention. This will ensure the user is always viewing fresh, up-to-date data and allows us to consider real-time applications. Currently, the most popular use for a timer in WAP applications is to present splash screens or static advertising. When a user enters a site, or between cards; a logo or slogan can be placed onto the screen for a short period of time. On some devices we can produce simple animations by cycling through a sequence of cards at timed intervals. The usual warnings apply however, and this, like everything else, will vary from device to device.

Let's try this out in our Wcommerce site by making use of the `ontimer` event:

```
...
<!-- ch5_ex08.wml -->
<wml>
    <template>
        <do type="prev">
            <prev/>
        </do>
        <do type="accept" label="Who are we?">
            <go href="#who"/>
        </do>
        <do type="accept" label="Products">
            <go href="#products"/>
        </do>
        <do type ="accept" label="Services">
            <go href="#services"/>
        </do>
    </template>

    <card id="advert" title="Sponsor">
        <onevent type="ontimer">
            <go href="#main"/>
        </onevent>
        <timer value="40"/>
    <p>
        <img src="wroxlogo.wbmp" alt="Wrox press"/>
    </p>
    </card>

    <card id="main" title="Wcommerce">
    <p>
        Welcome to the Wcommerce wireless shopping site
    </p>
    </card>
<!-- rest of deck -->
```

Initially, this displays as:

Then after 4 seconds, it changes to:

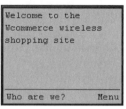

Notice that the new event, `ontimer` has been used. This event is raised whenever a timer has counted down to zero. A timer is defined by the `<timer/>` tag which takes a `value` attribute. This attribute specifies the length of time before raising an event, and is given in tenths of a second. In this example, after four seconds (since the timer has been assigned the value of 40), an `ontimer` event will occur. The WML browser then acts upon the handler for this event, which is contained between the `<onevent></onevent>` tag pair. In this case the handler has a `<go>` tag, so the browser moves to the card whose `id` has been assigned to the `href` attribute of the `<go>` tag.

Another use of the timer is in the case of an error card. If an error occurs in a WAP application, we should present the user with a card to explain that an error has occurred. While error handling on WAP devices is discussed in more detail in the next chapter, let's consider the user's position for a moment. As well as presenting the user with an error message, it is usually a good idea to return the user to a point before the error occurred, and, if possible, do something to deal with the error. We can do this by sending a deck that has as its first card, an error message that informs the user of the error, and that they will be redirected automatically back to the application. We can set a timer that displays the card for a certain amount of time before loading a new deck. Once the timer event occurs, we then direct the user to an appropriate card.

```
<card id="error" title="Error" ontimer="http://yourserver/menu.wml" >
    <timer value="30"/>
<p>
    Sorry there was an error while processing that request
    you are being redirected to our main menu
</p>
</card>
```

Note we've used a shortcut here; the code above could also be written in full as:

```
<card id="main">
    <onevent type="event">
        <go href="http://yourserver/menu.wml"/>
    </onevent>
    <p>
      Sorry there was an error while processing that request
      you are being redirected to our main menu
    </p>
</card>
```

This is a useful shortcut, particularly if you are beginning to run low on memory in the WAP device. It may be clearer what is intended in the long version, and this may be preferable if memory is not an issue.

Selections

We saw earlier how we can build up a selection list, but nothing very useful was done with it. Now that we've covered events, we can build up some code that acts upon user selection. One thing we can do is visit a different card depending on the item chosen from the select list. This is quite simple to do since the <option> tag has an onpick attribute. When the user selects an item in the select list, the card whose id is assigned to the onpick attribute is made visible. Here is the new version of the Wcommerce site:

```
<!-- ch5_ex09.wml -->
<card id="products" title="Products">
<p>
    Available phones:
    <select title="Models">
        <optgroup title="BMW">
            <option onpick="#z3">Z3</option>
        </optgroup>
        <optgroup title="Audi">
            <option onpick="#a4">A4</option>
            <option onpick="#A6">A6</option>
        </optgroup>
    </select>
    <a href="#check">
        Buy
    </a>
</p>
</card>

<card id="z3" title="Ordering a Z3">
    <onevent type="onenterbackward">
        <prev/>
    </onevent>
<p>
    This card gives the vehicle details and
    will take payment details for an Z3.
  <a href="#check">
        Done
    </a>
</p>
</card>

<card id="a4" title="Ordering an A4">
    <onevent type="onenterbackward">
        <prev/>
    </onevent>
<p>
    This card gives the vehicle details and
    will take payment details for an A4.
    <a href="#check">
        Done
```

```
            </a>
        </p>
    </card>

    <card id="a6" title="Ordering an A6">
        <onevent type="onenterbackward">
            <prev/>
        </onevent>
    <p>
        This card gives the vehicle details and
        will take payment details for an A6.
      <a href="#check">
            Done
        </a>
    </p>
    </card>
 <!-- the rest of the deck is as before ->
```

Firstly, let's have a look at a typical user session with the latest version of the Wcommerce site, that now makes use of the onpick event. First, the user selects a product group as usual and then chooses a product:

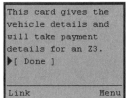

The next card takes payment details and when it is done passes the request to the confirmation card:

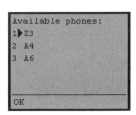

The reason that selecting a product results in a new card being shown, is that the onpick attribute of the <option> tag is being used. The important parts of the WML are highlighted in the above code extract. If the user selects the **A4** option, an onpick event is generated. In this case the selected item has "#a4" assigned to its onpick attribute, so the card with this id is found and displayed. The rules for what can be assigned to the onpick attribute are identical to those for the href attribute of the <go/> tag – a full URL can be specified if this is required.

One thing to note about the onpick event is that it may only be generated when a new selection is made. Selecting an item that has already been selected will may not generate an event. In fact, its use in this example may be misleading for the user. For example,suppose a user clicks on **A6** and they get transferred to the buy card for it. If they then reverse to the main menu and click on it again *before* clicking on any other option, they may not get sent to this card, because the event won't be generated as the option is already selected. We circumvent this problem, however, by the inclusion of the 'buy' option in the products card.

Once the subject of variables has been covered, we will look at tweaking the purchasing system to make it more robust.

149

Variables

In WML, variables are exceptionally simple; they are really just a label for a string value. Variables can be used, for example, to store data specific to a user of the application so that a more personal application can be presented to them. As they are all stored as strings they are essentially weakly typed; it is the responsibility of the programmer to enforce typing.

The scope of all variables in WML is global to the WML browser environment. What this means is that any WML deck, even decks written by other people and retrieved from a completely different location, can change and destroy your variables by using variables of the same name. In fact, any card can destroy all variables, and the entire history of the browser, using the newcontext attribute of the <card> tag. This attribute is discussed here only for the sake of completeness – it's unlikely you will find a sensible need for using it.

The only occasion when using newcontext may be acceptable is when we wish to ensure confidentiality and security of personal information. To illustrate this we will force the browser to delete all details relating to previously viewed cards and decks.

The following piece of WML uses this newcontext attribute:

```
<!-- ch5_ex10.wml -->
<?xml version="1.0"?>
<!DOCTYPE wml PUBLIC "-//WAPFORUM//DTD WML 1.1//EN"
"http://www.wapforum.org/DTD/wml_1.1.xml">

<wml>
    <card id="card1" title="First card">
    <p>
        <a href="#card2">A link</a> to the second card.
    </p>
    </card>

    <card id="card2" title="Second card" newcontext="true"><!--NEW CONTEXT-->
        <do type="prev">
            <prev/>
        </do>
    <p>
        The second card contains WML code to generate a back button.
    </p>
    </card>
</wml>
```

Let's step through a possible scenario. The browser displays the first card and the user selects the link:

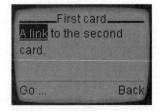

The user is presented with the second card and presses the back button:

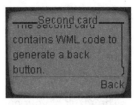

If the Back button is pressed, the browser will not do anything, and continues to display the same card:

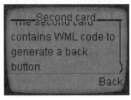

When the `newcontext` attribute is set to `true`, all the history information is lost, so when you click on the Back button, the browser doesn't know where to go. Also, all variables are cleared – so even if the user could return to previous cards, these cards wouldn't be able to rely on any data stored in variables. Obviously, we should use this attribute carefully as a Back button that doesn't work can be very frustrating!

As we have seen, variables in WML are merely labels for string values. In addition, WML does not provide a system for testing the value of the data in a variable, or manipulating it in any way. In order to do that, we would need to make use of WMLScript, which we'll be looking at in the next chapter.

In order to prevent variables being confused with other WML constructs, there are certain rules for naming them. All variable names must start with a letter or an underscore; this character can then be followed by underscores, letters or numbers.

The following are valid variable names:

❏   `a`

❏   `_variable`

❏   `variable_name`

❏   `var23`

❏   `_a2`

These names are invalid:

❏   `2variable` (variable names must start with a letter or underscore)

❏   `variable:name` (variable names cannot contain punctuation, only letters, numbers or underscores)

Using Variables

In order to make use of variables, a new tag is required. This is the `<setvar>` tag and it has two attributes: `name` and `value`. Clearly, these attributes are for the name of the variable, and the value which is to be assigned to it. To use a value stored in a variable, the variable name is prefixed with a $ (dollar sign). When the WML browser encounters a $, it simply replaces the variable name with the value stored in the variable.

Let's look at an example. Suppose we have a variable named this_variable with the value hello:

```
The result of your question is $this_variable
```

This would appear on the browser screen as:

The result of your question is hello

Note that if you wish to display a $ (dollar sign) in WML, use $$.

There are strict restrictions on where the <setvar/> tag can be used – namely, inside the <go>, <prev> or <refresh> elements only. The <refresh> tag pair is new to us, since it is only commonly used with variables. The use of this tag is very simple; the <setvar/> task inside the refresh element causes a variable assignment every time the card is displayed. Bear in mind that the refresh element can only exist inside an onevent or do element.

The following example displays these new constructs in use:

```
<?xml version="1.0"?>
<!DOCTYPE wml PUBLIC "-//WAPFORUM//DTD WML 1.1//EN"
"http://www.wapforum.org/DTD/wml_1.1.xml">

<!-- ch5_ex11.wml -->
<wml>
    <card id="main" title="Variables">
        <onevent type="onenterforward">
            <refresh>
                <setvar name="a_variable" value="Hello"/>
            </refresh>
        </onevent>
    <p>
        The variable has the value $a_variable
    </p>
    </card>
</wml>
```

Loading this into the WAP browser, it displays as:

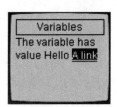

Let's step through the sequence of events as the deck is loaded into a WAP browser. If the card is not being returned to, then the onenterforward event is triggered. Since the card is being loaded into the browser, the contents of the <refresh></refresh> tag pair are executed. In this case, the <setvar/> element assigns a_variable the value Hello. The browser will now substitute every occurence of this variable, (when preceded by a $) in the text, with Hello.

Now consider the following WML:

```
<?xml version="1.0"?>
<!DOCTYPE wml PUBLIC "-//WAPFORUM//DTD WML 1.1//EN"
"http://www.wapforum.org/DTD/wml_1.1.xml">

<!-- ch5_ex12.wml -->
<wml>
    <card id="main" title="Variables">
        <onevent type="onenterforward">
            <refresh>
                <setvar name="a_variable" value="Hello"/>
            </refresh>
        </onevent>
        <onevent type="onenterbackward">
            <refresh>
                <setvar name="a_variable" value="Hello Again"/>
            </refresh>
        </onevent>
    <p>
        The variable has value $a_variable
        <a href="#link">A link</a>
    </p>
    </card>

    <card id="link" title="Variables">
    <p>
        <anchor>
            <prev/>
            Go back
        </anchor>
    </p>
    </card>
</wml>
```

This code has quite interesting behavior. The first card the user is presented with, is the same as the previous example. When they follow the link, they are presented with:

They then decide to follow the **Go back** link to the original card, which has now changed:

In this example, the value of the variable changes, depending on what direction the card is entered from. The reason for this is quite simple: when the user navigates to the card, it raises the `onenterforward` event so the following is executed:

```
<setvar name="a_variable" value="Hello"/>
```

If the user returns to the card at any point, the onenterbackward event is raised instead, and the variable value is assigned using:

```
<setvar name="a_variable" value="Goodbye"/>
```

This really begins to display the power of variables; the content of the card can change when the user enters it, depending on the direction from which it is entered. We can use this as an alternative to overloading <prev> to send the user elsewhere when they enter the card backwards – instead we can simply modify the contents of a card if the onenterbackwards event is raised.

One problem with using variables is associated with the use of quotation marks. Look at the following code:

```
The contents of the variable are "$a_variable".
```

Here, the second quote mark (") will be interpreted as being part of the variable name. Of course this isn't what is intended, and " is an invalid symbol in a variable and so will cause an error. We can get around this problem, by enclosing the variable name in brackets. We need to change the line above to:

```
The contents of the variable are "$(a_variable)".
```

This situation is so common that variable names are almost always enclosed in brackets. There is never a good reason *not* to surround a variable name in brackets, so it is good practice to always do so. Consequently, throughout the rest of this text don't be surprised if variables are surrounded by brackets, even when they would not be required. After all, a $ can be easily missed, but a $() is much easier to spot.

Escaping

Web developers may well already be familiar with the concept of URL escaping (sometimes referred to as URL encoding). It arises because there are some characters that are not valid in a URL, and so must be converted to valid symbols by **escaping** the URL. The process of converting the URL back again is called **unescaping** or URL decoding. When WML variables are used in URLs, they will also need escaping. This is done by appending the variable name with a colon (:) followed by e, E or escape.

For example, a variable named this_variable can be escaped by referring to it in one of the following ways:

- ❑ $(this_variable:e)

- ❑ $(this_variable:E)

- ❑ $(this_variable:escape)

Similarly, the variable can be unescaped using $(this_variable:u), $(this_variable:U) or $(this_variable:unesc). A WML browser should always escape variables that are being handled in URLs, so the developer should not have to worry about such things. If however, you wish to stop this escaping, then it can be prevented by using one of the following $(this_variable:n), $(this_variable:N) or $(this_variable:noesc).

Variables in Select Lists

Let's return to our Wcommerce example, and see if we can improve the user's experience by using variables in the application. We'll be looking at a few new attributes for the <select> and <option> elements to achieve this. The <select> tag can take a name attribute, which is assigned the name of a variable as the result of the selection. It can also take a value attribute, which is the default value for this variable. This is an alternative way of assigning a value to a variable.

The value of the name attribute of the select list shown below is product, so this is also the name of our variable. The default value is set to BMW. Each <option> tag can also have a value attribute, and the value of this attribute will be assigned to the product variable when the option is selected. When seen in use it is really very simple. Here's the new code:

```
<!-- ch5_ex13.wml -->
<card id="start" title="Wcommerce">
<p>
    Welcome to the Wcommerce wireless shopping site
</p>
</card>

<card id="who" title="Who are we?">
<p>
    Wcommerce is a new internet retailer ready for the wireless world.
</p>
</card>

<card id="products" title="Products">
<p>
    Available vehicles:
    <select name="product" value="BMW Z3" title="Models">
        <optgroup title="BMW">
            <option value="BMW Z3">Z3</option>
        </optgroup>
        <optgroup title="Audi">
            <option value="Audi A4">A4</option>
            <option value="Audi A6">A6</option>
        </optgroup>
    </select>
    <a href="#check">
        Buy
    </a>
</p>
</card>

<card id="services" title="Services">
<p>
    We can help you to book film tickets, restaurants or hotel rooms,
    online in the wireless world.
</p>
</card>

<card id="check" title="Confirmation">
    <onevent type="onenterbackward">
        <prev/>
    </onevent>
<p>
    Are you <b>sure</b> you wish to purchase a $(product):
```

```
        <anchor>
           Yes
        <!-- Contact the server here to place an order -->
           <go href="#buy"/>
        </anchor>
        <anchor>
           <go href="#products"/>
           No
        </anchor>
     </p>
     </card>

     <card id="buy" title="Acknowledgement">
     <p>
        Done.<br/>
        The product will be dispatched within 30 days
     </p>
     </card>
  </wml>
```

Try running through a sample purchase to see how it behaves, most of the application should be familiar by now, so we won't repeat all of it here.

Suppose the user enters the site and selects the **Products** card from the **Options** menu. If they then select an Audi A6 and go to buy the product, the confirmation card displays the name of the product which the user is trying to purchase:

 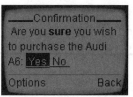

Examine how the name and value attributes have been used in the `<select>` tag:

```
<select name="product" value="BMW Z3" title="Models">
```

This creates a variable named product and gives it a default value of BMW Z3. Now look at one of the `<option>` tags:

```
<option value="Audi A4">A4</option>
```

The value attribute has been assigned the value Audi A4. So, when the user selects the **A4**, the product variable has its value changed to Audi A4. This must be a unique value because you can't have two options in the same list with the same value. Notice how the confirmation card now makes use of this variable to display the name of the product that has been selected:

```
Are you <b>sure</b> you wish to purchase a $(product):<br/>
```

Before we leave the `<select>` tag, let's just take a quick look at some other attributes first, namely, default, iname, ivalue and multiple.

The multiple attribute is straightforward; setting it to true allows multiple selections to be made. This means that when the user selects an option, it doesn't clear the currently selected option, but will allow them both. The different selections are all assigned to the variable and separated by a semi-colon. So, if we add multiple choices to our Wcommerce example, the `<select>` is modified to be:

```
<select name="product" default="BMW Z3" title="Models" multiple="true">
```

The user can now select as many products as they like. If they select all three available, the confirmation card appears as:

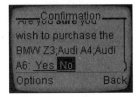

Once we have designed the user input section, we can implement the server-side code that will process the order. In the case of multiple values being sent, we can parse the values and extract each product before processing the order.

You may have noticed that at present the **BMW Z3** option is automatically selected as the default option. This is because we have given a default value in the value attribute of the <select> tag. If we do not provide a default value, the browser will normally set the first option in a select list to be the default selection. This behavior can be altered by using the ivalue attribute of the <select> tag. We simply assign it the number of the option to be set by default. For example, in order to set the Audi A4 as default, assign 2 to ivalue, since it is the second option in the list:

```
<select name="product" title="Models" ivalue="2">
```

We can set multiple default values in select lists that allow multiple selections by separating the values with semi-colons (;), in the form (1;2).

The iname attribute serves the same purpose as the ivalue attribute, that is, selecting a default option. However, it takes a variable name, not a number. The variable must hold a value that is the index number of the default value, which allows us to specify a default value dynamically. So if the variable default_val contains the value 2, the code below will have the same result as the previous example:

```
<select name="product" title="Models" iname="default_val">
```

Input and Parameter Passing

Interaction with the user can be further improved by allowing the user to enter alphanumeric data from their devices. WAP devices tend to have very limited data entry mechanisms and this needs special consideration. In this section we will discuss data entry and sending that information to the server.

Input

So far we have presented the code needed to produce links, option lists, and select lists. All these methods of user input require you to predetermine the range of possible user choices. What if the WAP application has a need for the user to actually enter some numbers or even type in some text? In order to give an input field into which a user can enter such information, WML provides the WAP developer with the <input/> element, which is very similar to that provided by HTML. The user's data is gathered in an input field and then assigned to a variable. The name of this variable is specified in the <input/> tag through its name attribute.

The example shown below asks the user for their name and then outputs a greeting:

```
<?xml version="1.0"?>
<!DOCTYPE wml PUBLIC "-//WAPFORUM//DTD WML 1.1//EN"
"http://www.wapforum.org/DTD/wml_1.1.xml">

<!-- ch5_ex16.wml -->
<wml>
    <card id="main" title="Welcome">
    <p>
        Enter name:
        <input name="person_name"/><br/>
        <a href="#card2">
            Next card
        </a>
    </p>
    </card>

    <card id="card2" title="Welcome">
    <p>
        Hello $(person_name)
    </p>
    </card>
</wml>
```

How the user enters the data is specific to the browser (as always). In the screenshots below (the Nokia 6110), a pair of square brackets is shown to indicate to the user where they should enter their name. Clicking the accept key when the brackets are highlighted brings up a card for data entry:

The user follows the link to the next card, to be greeted by name:

What has been produced here is quite straightforward – an `<input/>` tag has been used to place an input field onto the card. This is shown below:

```
<input name="person_name"/>
```

The `name` attribute specifies the name of the variable to which the user input is assigned. This variable is then used to greet the user in the WML:

```
Hello $(person_name)
```

The `<input/>` tag has many more attributes: `value`, `type`, `format`, `emptyok`, `size`, `maxlength`, and `title`. We'll spend some time looking at these now.

A default value can be specified for the input field by using the `value` attribute. This default is used if the variable named by the `name` attribute does not contain any value. So, the following could be used to prevent Rachel having to type in her name while allowing other users to enter in their names instead:

```
<input name="person_name" value="Rachel"/>
```

The default value of the `type` attribute is `text`, but it can allow us to specify the input as a `password`, for example, in which case each character is replaced with an asterisk (*), as on a PC:

```
<input name="user_password" type="password"/>
```

Use of this should be considered carefully, however. Many characters require several keystrokes, so data entry with no feedback could be a very frustrating experience. If you are targeting a Trium phone, for example, you will notice that to help with this, the entered character is displayed for a second before being replaced with an asterisk. You might decide that user discretion and the small screen size are sufficient security.

Another attribute of the `<input>` tag is `emptyok`. By default this is set to `false`, which means that the user should not be permitted to navigate further in the application, unless they have entered some data. Keeping in mind, that we wish to make the application as light as possible in terms of user input, you should set this attribute to `true` for any input that is not mandatory. In this case, you will need to inform the user that the data entry field is optional. Remember that setting a default value is an alternative to this method – setting both will simply invalidate the `emptyok` value, because there will always be some value to the input field, so it will never be empty. In practice, the current browser implementations do not support this function, so we may have to wait a while before it becomes a useful feature.

Another potentially useful attribute is `size`, which is described in the WAP specification as "the width, in characters, of the text-input area." The next sentence reads, "The user agent may ignore this attribute." Currently, every browser does just that, so this isn't really of any use!

As you have discovered by now, the amount of memory available in WAP devices is limited. What if the user decides to enter a huge amount of text into an input field? The WAP browser could fail to render your card just because the deck is too large. It is therefore sensible to restrict the amount of data the user can enter, specifying the `maxlength` attribute in characters. So, to restrict user names to 30 characters, we would modify our example like this:

```
<input value="Rachel" name="person_name" maxlength="30"/>
```

It's not over yet, the `<input/>` tag has even more attributes. One of the most useful, for the user, is the `title` attribute. At the moment, when the user selects the input field they are presented with a screen that looks something like:

Nowhere on this display does it state what the user is actually entering. We can add a title attribute to the `<input/>` tag:

```
<input title="Enter name:" value="Rachel" name="person_name" maxlength="30"
       emptyok="false" />
```

So, the input box now looks like this:

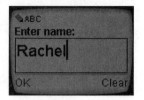

Sometimes we might want to place more restrictions on the format of the data entered by the user, other than simply on its length. Consider the situation when the user has to enter a numeric value. People will get frustrated and annoyed if they are required to press each button 4 to 5 times to access its numeric value. We can get around this by specifying the format of the input field with the `format` attribute of the `<input>` tag. In addition, this attribute can also help in data entry validation, as it will enforce the required format. Here is an example of the `format` attribute in use:

```
<?xml version="1.0"?>
<!DOCTYPE wml PUBLIC "-//WAPFORUM//DTD WML 1.1//EN"
"http://www.wapforum.org/DTD/wml_1.1.xml">

<!-- ch5_ex18.wml -->
<wml>
    <card id="main" title="Date entry">
    <p>
        Enter date (in the form mm/dd/yy):
        <input format="NN\/NN\/NN" name="the_date"/>
    </p>
    </card>
</wml>
```

Here, the format attribute has been assigned `NN\/NN\/NN`, which specifies to the user the format of the input. Each `N` denotes a single digit. The back slash indicates that the next character is to be inserted automatically by the browser, and so, once the user enters the second digit, a forward slash will be entered automatically, and similarly after the fourth digit. Note, this doesn't check that the day, month or year is valid – it just makes sure that each value consists of two numbers. (We'll examine date validation with a more sophisticated method, in the next chapter, through the use of WMLScript.) Here is what entering the sequence 123456 looks like on the browser:

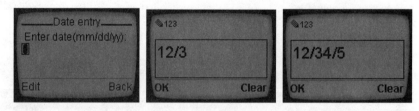

The structure of strings assigned to the `format` attribute is summarized in the table opposite.

Code	Description
A	Any uppercase alphabetical character or punctuation character.
a	Any lowercase alphabetical character or punctuation character.
N	Any numerical digit.
X	Any uppercase alphabetical character but **not** punctuation.
x	Any lowercase alphabetical character but **not** punctuation.
M	Any character, but expecting an uppercase letter.
m	Any character, but expecting a lowercase letter.
*f	Entry of an unlimited number of characters of type f, where f is one of the seven formatting codes given above. This can only be used once, and it must be at the end of the formatting string.
nf	Specifies a specific number of characters, where n is a number from 1 to 9, and f is one of the first seven formatting characters given at the start of this table. This can only be used once, and it must be at the end of the formatting string.
\c	The character c is compulsory at this position in the string.

For example, a suitable formatting string for a name would be M*m, which translates as, "There must be one letter in the name, probably a capital letter. This can be followed by any number of other letters, these will probably be lower case."

There are occasions, (the entry of a date for example), when the format attribute is not powerful enough to verify data being entered by the user. When this is encountered, the only way to successfully validate the input is to make use of scripting. Client-side scripting with WMLScript is discussed in the next chapter, and server-side processing is covered in Chapters 8 through 11.

Posting Data

Now that we know how to obtain data from the user, we need to be able to send that data back to the server for processing. The communication of user data on the Web, uses the HTTP POST and GET methods. This involves sending data to the server in an HTTP request message. POST and GET are also used in WAP, but we'll need to learn some new tag usage first. As in HTTP, GET and POST differ somewhat. When the GET method is used, the data being sent to the server is appended to the end of the URL. When the POST method is used, this data is passed in the body of the message.

POST has advantages over the GET method; we can send more data this way, since the length of URLs is be restricted on some servers and browsers, typically this may be 127 characters although it is dependent on the server, gateway or browser. Including the data in the URL of the request is less secure as it can be examined more easily. In addition some characters within a URL have special meaning and would need to be encoded. Data included in the body of a request does not require encoding.

Sending data to the server using the POST method requires only a little more work to implement than the GET method, and has the added benefits of security and unlimited data size (within reason). In that case, why would anyone ever want to use the GET method at all? Unfortunately, at the time of writing, many devices on the market don't actually support the POST method. Even when it is supported by a device, you may encounter problems with its use, namely data loss enroute.

User data is sent to the server using the <go> tag. This element has an attribute method that takes the values GET or POST. A new element is also needed, the <postfield/> tag. The <postfield/> tag is contained within the <go> element and it has two attributes, name and value. The name identifies the data that is being sent, and will be used at the server-side to process the data. The actual data being sent is assigned to the value attribute.

We now have the attributes required to send the purchases from the Wcommerce example to the server. Consider this modified confirmation card:

```
<card id="check" title="Confirmation">
   <onevent type="onenterbackward">
       <prev/>
   </onevent>
<p>
   Are you <b>sure</b> you wish to purchase a $(product):<br/>
   <anchor>
       Yes
       <go method="post" href="http://www.yourservername.com/program.asp">
          <postfield name="product" value="$(product)"/>
       </go>
   </anchor>
   <anchor>
       <go href="#products"/>
       No
   </anchor>
</p>
</card>
```

Now when the user clicks on Yes to buy the product, the name of the product is sent back to the server. In this case, nothing is done with it, but, in a real program, we could use server-side scripting to process the order. Obviously, how you handle this data on the server-side will depend very much on what platform and what kind of technology you are using. We'll be looking at such technologies in detail in Chapters 8 through 11.

Grouping Data

As you must be aware by now, differing WAP devices handle WML in very different ways. As a WAP developer, it can be very frustrating when functionality that has been described very well in our code is made completely unusable through the WAP browser's handling of it. Unfortunately, there is no way to force the WAP browser to display content in a certain form. To reduce the potential disorder, we should try and improve the appearance and usability of our WAP application by grouping relevant sections. The <fieldset></fieldset> tag pair is used to group together select lists and input fields. It has just one attribute, title. The browser may or may not display this title. It is a very simple element to use: you simply enclose the section to be grouped together within it.

The products card from the Wcommerce example can be extended to make use of this new tag:

```
<card id="products" title="Products">
<p>
   <fieldset title="Available phones:">
      <select name="product" value="BMW Z3" title="Models">
         <optgroup title="BMW">
            <option value="BMW Z3">7110</option>
         </optgroup>
         <optgroup title="Audi">
            <option value="Audi A4">A4</option>
            <option value="Audi A6">A6</option>
         </optgroup>
      </select>
      Number of items: <input name="number_of_items"
                           value="1" format="*N" title="Number of items:"/>
   </fieldset>
   <a href="#check">
      Buy
   </a>
</p>
</card>
```

Notice how a new input field has been added to allow the user to purchase multiple numbers of items. Unfortunately, this tag is so poorly supported by browsers that even the Nokia toolkit used throughout the last two chapters ignores it! We may need to wait before this feature becomes usable; for now, it may be a good idea to include it for future enhanced functionality of our applications in the next generation of devices.

Summary

The last two chapters have covered most of the Wireless Markup Language (WML). In this chapter, greater facilities for interacting with the user have been described. With our newly acquired knowledge, we can now allow users to navigate through menus, make selections from lists, and enter data into input fields. We have covered the use of events and variables. Remember that for a complete listing of all the tags introduced in this chapter and the last, you should consult the tag reference in Appendix A.

We have also covered the limitations of the current browser implementations in our code. In order to create a more professional application, we would need to add some server-side processing to it, and that's exactly what we'll be looking at later in this book. However, before we leap into the use of server-side technologies for the generation of WML applications, we should first examine how we can do some of the processing on the client-side. We have already seen some of the limitations of WML at the client-side, for example when attempting to write a formatting string to describe a date. In order to carry out more complicated processing a markup language is not sufficient. Client-side scripting of some kind could be used for this purpose – and WMLScript is the subject of the next chapter.

6

WMLScript

For all but the most basic applications, we will need to use some features of WML that require some processing. In the same way that it is possible to do client-side scripting on the Web, it is possible to script WML decks using WMLScript. As things currently stand, support for WMLScript is poor and so many developers have avoided its use at the cost of decreased performance. Throughout this chapter, we will look at WMLScript, what it has to offer, and the possible uses for it.

Devised for use on thin clients with low bandwidth communications, it is the only scripting language that can be used in a WAP device. WMLScript is based on ECMAScript, the standard scripting language for most server- and client-side scripting. However, it includes a binary specification for optimized transmission to the client. In order to achieve this, only part of the functionality of ECMAScript has been implemented.

Since ECMAScript is the standardized version of JavaScript, if you have already programmed with this, then you should pick up WMLScript very quickly. You'll probably want to skip most of the introductory parts of this chapter or just glance through them quickly, and move straight onto the sections illustrating the use of some of the standard libraries that come with WMLScript.

Currently it is expected that the use of WMLScript will be targeted at very specific applications, but with further development and the continued co-operation of the browser manufacturers, support for WMLScript should improve. With the service overload occurring already in WAP systems, we should welcome any opportunity to offload processing to the client. In addition, the introduction of access to the telephony functionality of the devices depends on WMLScript and it will therefore be essential for us to know it.

Why Do We Need WMLScript?

Unlike VBScript or JavaScript, which can be executed on the client or on the server-side, WMLScript is designed purely as a client scripting language, to be executed on the actual WAP device. WAP devices are currently small, with low processing power and very limited memory. With these limitations, the obvious question is: why do any processing on the client-side at all? Why not do all processing at the server-side? However, WAP also has the problem of limited bandwidth between the client and the server. Frequent trips back to the server to obtain the results of a new computation could be costly – this would slow down the application. If WMLScript is used, all the processing is done on the client and there is no delay caused by the limited bandwidth, enabling a much better user experience. While bandwidth will soon be improved, Frequent round-trips will mean greater load on the device. Unless battery life is improved dramatically, these additional trips will mean frequent recharging and a dissatisfied customer. Added to the server load problems, it appears that WMLScript offers us a welcome solution for improved service.

As with JavaScript and any other client-side scripting language on web browsers, WMLScript has many uses. In the previous chapter, we saw how WML lacks the power to be able to fully validate user input, but WMLScript is able to do this. You might also want to use WMLScript for any manipulation of data that is within the client. A good example of this is a currency converter. The limitations of WMLScript are more connected to the limitations of WAP devices than the language itself.

In the future WMLScript will become even more powerful. It will be able to access other facilities of a WAP device via WTA or Wireless Telephony Application. For example, in addition to access to the phone's telephony functions, it will be possible to use WMLScript to access the internal calendar and diary of a device. However, at present WMLScript is restricted. WTA will be considered in detail in Chapter 17.

A simple example

Unlike JavaScript, WMLScript is not embedded in amongst the markup. Instead, a separate file is created that contains the code and this is then called from the card on view. Whereas WML is stored in files with the `.wml` extension, WMLScript is stored in files with a `.wmls` extension. The WML file calls the script via a hyperlink. The browser then initializes an additional trip to the server to request the script file, loads it into memory and runs the code, finally ending by refreshing the WML deck.

All WMLScript is done with the use of **functions**. If you are not familiar to this concept, functions encapsulate a process. In WMLScript the function can be 'executed' or called from any deck by referencing the file name and the name of the function preceded by a #. Let's look at this in practice.

Here is an example of some WML code which calls WMLScript:

```
<?xml version="1.0"?>
<!DOCTYPE wml PUBLIC "-//WAPFORUM//DTD WML 1.1//EN"
"http://www.wapforum.org/DTD/wml_1.1.xml">

<!-- callscript.wml -->
<wml>
    <card id="main" title="WMLScript">
    <p>
        The result of the calculation "2+3" is: $(number)<br/>
        <a href="calling.wmls#calculate(2,3)">
            Calculate
        </a>
    </p>
    </card>
</wml>
```

The important concept to grasp here is how WML can call WMLScript. In fact, the WML code calls the function `calculate()` from the WMLScript code file `calling.wmls`:

```
<a href="calling.wmls#calculate(1,2)">
```

Notice that the syntax for calling WMLScript is the same as referencing another WML card. The location of the script is given using the same rules as for the location of a WML deck, and the function name is appended in the same way that a WML card would be selected with the additional brackets. So, `calculate()` is a function within a separate file called `calling.wmls`.

We now look at the file `calling.wmls` which contains the WMLScript:

```
extern function calculate(a,b)
{
    var n;
    n= a+b;

    WMLBrowser.setVar("number", n);
    WMLBrowser.refresh();
}
```

Don't worry too much about what the code means just yet – this will become clear as you work through the chapter. Running through a sample user session, a card is displayed with a link to perform a calculation which the user follows:

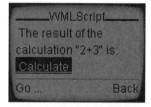

The link points the user to the WMLScript that performs a calculation, and then refreshes the browser with the result:

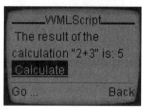

If you find that the above example does not work, there are a couple of things you should investigate. Most obviously, you need to check whether the browser you are using does support WMLScript. We recommend that you test the code from this chapter using the Nokia toolkit and the 6110 emulator, as this is the emulator with the best support for WMLScript available at the time of writing. Secondly, make sure that the MIME types have been set up on your web server and that the `.wmls` and `.wmlsc` extensions have been correctly mapped. (Check Chapter 2 for details on this.) Finally, if you are using a WAP gateway, you may well find that the gateway doesn't support WMLScript, or will only handle compiled WMLScript.

Lexical Structure

Since WMLScript is based on ECMAScript, it has a syntax very similar to JavaScript. A statement is terminated with a ; (semi-colon) and ignores whitespace except inside string literals. So:

```
This is a statement;
```

And:

```
This is also only
one statement;
```

A **block** of WMLScript is enclosed in {} (braces):

```
{
    this is
    a block;
    containing two statements;
}
```

Case Sensitivity

Like JavaScript (and indeed WML), WMLScript is case sensitive. This means that an upper case letter in the name of an identifier is recognized as being different from the same letter in lower case. For example, the two variable names `thisvariable` and `thisVariable` refer to different variables. It should be noted that variables are encoded using references tokens, so the length of the variable name will not have an affect on the resultant compiled deck.

Expressions

An expression can be defined as a combination of operations that result in a value. For example, the expression 2+4 is evaluated to give the value 6. In fact, the number 6; is an expression – it evaluates to 6.

Whitespace

The rules on whitespace in WMLScript are the same as the rules for JavaScript and many other scripting languages. Any number of tabs, spaces and new lines will be treated the same as a single whitespace character. Also the resultant compiled code size will not increase significantly with the addition of whitespace. For example, the WMLScript file `calling.wmls` previously presented could also be written as:

```
extern function calculate()
{
        var n;
    n       =       3   +    2;

    WMLBrowser.setVar("number",
                n);
        WMLBrowser.refresh();
}
```

Or even all on one line with no extra whitespace, like this:

```
extern function calculate(){var
n;n=3+2;WMLBrowser.setVar("number",n);WMLBrowser.refresh();}
```

However, it is good programming practice to lay out your code in an easily understood manner. Try to be consistent when writing the code. Generally speaking, each statement should be on a separate line and if you have several functions in a single file they should be separated with a blank line with ideally with a comment preceding the function to explain what it does. There are other ways in which we can improve the readability of the code and we will see them as we continue through the chapter; for now, anything that improves the readability of the code is good.

Comments

Text that you want to include in your script, but which should be ignored by the script engine, must be marked as a comment. There are two ways to do this, depending on the length of the comment. WMLScript follows the same rules as JavaScript for comments: you can write a single line comment starting with the characters //, and multi-line comments by including the text in a /* ... */ block. A comment using // stops at the end of the line it is on. For example, a single-line comment looks like this:

```
extern function calculate(a,b)
{
    // calculate the value of adding 2 and 3
    var n;
    n=a+b;
    WMLBrowser.setVar("number",n); // We can also place comments here
    WMLBrowser.refresh();
}
```

And a multi-line comment like this:

```
extern function calculate()
{
/* calculate the value of
    adding 2 and 3
*/
    var n;
    n=3+2;
    WMLBrowser.setVar("number",n); /* a single line 'multi-line' comment */
    WMLBrowser.refresh();
}
```

As you can see, a multi-line comment could be written on a single line, and as the */ delimits it further, code could be added on the same line following the comment, but it is best not to for readability sake.

Variables & Literals

Variables and literals can take on one of five types: Boolean, integer, float, string and invalid data.

- ❑ **Boolean** data can contain the value **true** or **false**
- ❑ **Integer**, is a whole numbers in the range **-2147483648** to **2147483647**
- ❑ **Float** which allows floating point numbers in the range **3.40282347E+38** to **1.17549435E-38**
- ❑ **String** contains character data
- ❑ **Invalid**: we will see examples of this shortly

WMLScript is a weakly typed language, which means type checking is limited. There is only one type of variable, var which means the variables are capable of holding a value of any data type, such as string, integer, float and so on. The type of calculation carried out by the operators is dependant on the data type, so adding the integer addition 2+2 will give 4, but if the variables are strings then the result of adding them will give '22'.

Variable Scope and Lifetime

The **scope** of a variable is the part of the script within which it can be used, and its **lifetime** is the time during execution of the script that the variable actually exists. Before you can use a variable in WMLScript it has to be declared. The block within which it is declared is its scope. A variable is declared through using the keyword format var *variable_name*;. For example:

```
{ // block 1
   var first_variable;
   { // block 2                        This is the      This is the scope
       var second_variable;            scope for        for block 1
   }                    block 2
}
```

Two variables have been declared: first_variable and second_variable. Since this entire piece of WMLScript is enclosed within block 1, and first_variable is declared at the start of this, its scope is the whole of the script. This means that it can be referenced from anywhere in the script. However, the scope of the variable named second_variable is block 2 since this is where it is declared, and so it can only be used within this block.

There may be occasions on which several variables are declared at the same point:

```
var x;
var y;
var z;
```

If this is the case, then they can all be declared in one line by separating the variable names with commas:

```
var x, y, z;
```

This is a useful shorthand, although some programmers have a strong objection to it as it lacks clarity.

Strings as Arrays

As well as treating strings as simple sequences of characters, WMLScript makes it possible to treat them as sequences of distinct variable length elements. This can be interpreted as equivalent to the traditional programming idea of 1-dimensional arrays.

The WMLScript method of representing 1-dimensional arrays involves the specification of a **delimiter**. This delimiter is a single character that separates the elements in a string array. Often this is a comma but it can be any character. We will look at arrays in more detail in the section on standard libraries later on in this chapter.

Operators

An **operator** is a fairly simple concept in WMLScript. Some operators have already been encountered, namely the addition operator (+) and the assignment operator (=). We'll now look at these and other operators in detail.

Assignment Operator

Assigning is the process of giving a value to a variable. The assignment operator in WMLScript is = (equals sign). In WMLScript the process is destructive: that is, a variable can change its value at any stage within its lifetime but its previous value is lost by this change. So, to give a variable x a value of 3, the only statement that is required is:

```
x = 3;
```

Remember that we always have to declare variables before using them, so x must have already been declared using:

```
var x;
```

It is also possible to assign a value to a variable when it is being declared, like this:

```
var x = 3;
```

Arithmetic Operators

The arithmetic operators perform common arithmetic calculations on variables and literals. One arithmetic operator has already been used to add two variables (x and y) which were integers, and the result was assigned to another variable (z). The line of script was:

```
z = x + y;
```

Subtraction is just as straightforward, but of course, uses a – instead of a +. Multiplication is carried out using a *. The following are all valid uses of arithmetic operators:

```
z = x + 3;
z = 3 + 4;
y = 2 * x;
x = x * y;
x = 4 - 3;
```

The division operator is a little more complicated since it comes in two forms / (forward slash) and div. The difference between them is that the result of using a / for division has the type float. Using div to perform a division gives a result with the type integer, and the fractional part of the result is simply lost:

```
x = 5 / 2;  // x has value 2.5
x = 5 div 2; // x has value 2
```

The other arithmetic operators, which are less commonly used, are:

Operator	Description
<<	Bitwise left shift
>>	Bitwise right shift with sign extension
>>>	Bitwise right shift with zero fill
%	Remainder
&	Bitwise AND
^	Bitwise XOR
|	Bitwise OR
~	Bitwise NOT

If you are familiar with programming then you will be familiar with the bitwise operations. If not, then you should consult an introductory computer science or programming text for more details. Basically, the operators perform operations on the binary representations of numbers. So the binary representations of 3 and 4 are 11 and 100. Performing a bitwise OR results in 7 which is 111.

There are also shorthand versions available for some of the arithmetic operators. For example, it is very common to want to write something in the form:

```
thisVariable += 5;
```

This is the equivalent of:

```
thisVariable = thisVariable + 5;
```

This shorthand is available for all of the arithmetic operators:

There is one more piece of shorthand that requires a little explanation: the ++ operator increments the value of variable by one. This means that the statement:

```
x = x + 1;
```

Could be replaced with either:

```
x++;
```

Or:

```
++x;
```

Similarly, the -- operator decrements the value of a number by one. Both can be used postfix and prefix as shown above. When used postfix (after the number) it will increment the number *after* it has been used in the expression it is in. If it is used prefix (before the number) it is incremented *first* and the resulting value is used to calculate the expression it is in.

To see how this works in practice, examine the following section of code:

```
// Declare variables
var x;
var y;

// Assign values
x = 3;

// Perform calculation
y = x++;   // y = 3 and x = 4
```

In this case the value of x is set to 3, which is then assigned to y before x is incremented. x now holds the value 4 and y is equal to 3. In the following script, x is incremented before its value is assigned to y, so x and y are both equal to 4:

```
// Declare variables
var x;
var y;

// Assign values
x = 3;

// Perform calculation
y = ++x;   // y= 4 and x = 4
```

Logical Operators

Whereas arithmetic operators perform calculations on numbers, logical operators perform calculations on Booleans (variables that can have value of `true` or `false`). Boolean values are used extensively for decision-making. The logical operators supported are:

WMLScript Operator	Meaning
&&	AND
||	OR
!	NOT

AND gives `true` only if both operands are equal to `true`, otherwise returns `false`. OR returns `true` if either operand is `true`, only returns `false` if both are `false`. NOT returns the logical opposite, so a `true` operand gives `false` and `false` gives `true`. Any logical operation with `invalid` operands will result in an `invalid` value.

String Concatenation

As we saw earlier, string concatenation is available through the + operator. If either one of the operands is a string and the other is not, an attempt is made to convert the non-string operand to a string. If it can be converted, it is appended to the other operand, otherwise this will return `invalid`.

Comparison Operators

All the operators introduced so far have a common property: the variables and literals they operate on are of the same type as the results they produce. Comparison operators are slightly different in that they operate on numbers or strings, but the result they produce is a Boolean. Comparison operators perform a test, the result of which is either `true` or `false`. The most simple example of this is the equality operator, ==, which tests whether or not two things are equal. For example:

```
// Declare variables
var x;
var y;
var z;

// Assign values
x = 3;
y = 4;

// Perform calculations
z = (x == y); // z has value false x is not equal to y
z = (x == 3); // z has value true x is equal to 3
z = (1 == 1); // z has value true 1 is equal to 1
```

The same operator can be used to test if the two strings have the same sequence of characters. This operation is case sensitive (x is not equal to X):

```
// Declare variables
var x;
var y;
var z;

// Assign values
x = "good";
y = "bye";

// Perform calculations
z = x == y;            // z has value false
z = x == "good";       // z has value true
z = "hello" == "hello"; // z has value true
```

This table below summarizes most of the comparison operators available in WMLScript. All comparison operators can be applied to strings, integer and float types of variables.

Comprison Operator	Description
==	Equality
!=	Not equal
>	Greater than
>=	Greater than or equal to
<	Less than
<=	Less than or equal to

Comma Operator

The comma operator is used when you wish to perform multiple evaluations in one expression. (Expressions are discussed later in this chapter.) The following example shows the comma operator in use:

```
// Declare variables
var x;
var y;
var z;

// Assign values
x = 3;
y = 4;

// Perform calculations
z = x + 12, 3 + y;
```

What is the value of z? If you're not confused, you should be! The final line of this script actually means: "add 12 to x, add y to 3 and assign the value of the last evaluation (3 + y) to z". So z has value 7. The confusion presented by this operator means that it should be avoided. It is nearly always better to write more code, and present it clearly, as this leads to fewer errors.

typeof Operator

It is possible to test for the type of a variable using the typeof operator. The typeof operator returns a number depending on the type of the variable it is operating on. The following table gives the numbers that can be produced by the typeof operator, and what types these numbers represent:

Type	Value returned by typeof
Integer	0
Float	1
String	2
Boolean	3
Invalid	4

For example:

```
// Declare variables
var w;
var x;
var y;
var z;

// Assign values
w = 3;
x = "hello";
y = 1.3432;

// Perform calculation
z = typeof w; // z has value 0
z = typeof x; // z has value 2
z = typeof y; // z has value 1
```

Note that it is possible for a variable to be invalid. An example of a situation where this happens is when a number is divided by zero. The result of dividing something by zero is undefined, so it has the `invalid` type:

```
var z;
z = typeof (1/0); // z has value 4
```

isvalid Operator

The `isvalid` function returns a Boolean result; the result is `true` for a valid variable, and `false` for an invalid variable:

```
// Declare variables
var x;
var y;
var z;

// Assign values
x = "hello";
y = 1/0;        //division by zero gives an invalid (undefined) result

// Perform calculation
z = isvalid x; // z has value true
z = isvalid y; // z has value false
```

Conditional Operator

The conditional operator syntax is as follows:

```
result = conditional_expression ? expression1 : expression2
```

The conditional expression is evaluated. If it evaluates to `true`, then `expression1` is evaluated and the result assigned to `result`. Otherwise the result of `expression2` is used.

Operator precedence

One thing to consider with expressions is the order in which they are evaluated. WMLScript follows the standard mathematical precedence for evaluating expressions like most other languages. In addition, the order in which expressions are evaluated can be forced through the use of parentheses. So in order to make the result of the above `35`, the expression can be written as:

```
z = (3+4)*5;
```

You can combine any operations as has just been shown. When we encounter functions it will be shown that these can also be combined with operations.

The following table lists the operators in order of precedence. The precedence decreases going down the table, and operators on the same row have the same precedence:

```
++ -- ~ ! + (unary) - (unary) typeof isvalid
* / div %
- +
<< >> >>>
< <= > >=
== !=
&
^
|
&&
||
?:
= *= -= /= %= div= += <<= >>= >>>= &= ^= |=
,
```

Automatic data type conversion

The way in which an expression is evaluated depends on the operands supplied with the operation. Due to the fact that WMLScript is weakly typed, it is possible to mix operand types in an expression. When the browser encounters expression with mixed types it checks whether it's possible to convert them to an equivalent type, attempt to carry out the operation and returns a value accordingly.

The order in which this is done is as follows. First the type of the operation is checked; this can be Boolean (<=, == etc), integer or float (-, /, *), string, float or integer (+) and so on. If the operands given are both of the type(s) accepted or can be converted to an acceptable type the operation is carried out, otherwise the return value is invalid.

In the case of operations that accept more than one type the order of precedence of type conversion, from lowest priority to highest, is as follows:

- ❏ Boolean
- ❏ Integer
- ❏ Float
- ❏ String
- ❏ Invalid

For example, let's take the addition operator, which accepts types integer, float and string. If either of the operands is invalid then the result is invalid. If either is a string then an attempt is made to convert the other to a string, and if the conversion is successful the expression is evaluated returning a string. If neither are strings but one is a float, then the other is converted and the result is a float. Otherwise if either is a Boolean, it is converted to an integer (1 or 0) and the expression evaluated, it will return an integer value. Given these orders of precedence it should be possible to work out what will be the result of a mixing of types.

There are also functions provided to minimize errors caused by invalid type types and we will look at these in the section called *Error Handling*.

Control Constructs

Operators have given WMLScript the power to do things that WML cannot. However, the real power of programming languages comes mainly from control constructs. Control constructs allow programs to make decisions and progress according to the results of those decisions. In WMLScript a decision is made based on the value of a Boolean. Three main control constructs exist – if, while and for.

if statement

The if statement is the most common and straightforward of the control constructs. It evaluates the expression or code block immediately following it only if a control statement evaluates to true and doesn't if it is false. The syntax of an if statement is simply:

```
if (boolean expression)
{
    statement;
}
```

If there is only one conditionally evaluate statement the braces can be omitted. Here is an example of it's use:

```
var x = 2
var y = 3
var z;
if (y > x) z = 3; // y is greater than x, z has value 3
if (x > y) z = 4; // x is not greater than y, z doesn't change its value
```

The if statement also comes in an extended form, the if-else statement:

```
if (boolean) statement1 else statement2;
```

If the Boolean expression evaluates to true, then *statement1* is executed; otherwise *statement2* is executed instead. Note that in WMLScript, there are no elseif or endif keywords, as are encountered in some other languages.

while statement

WMLScript has a couple of looping facilities, and the first of these is the while loop. The purpose of a while loop is to test a condition, and as long as that condition is met to continue to execute the code within the loop. For example:

```
var x;
x = 10;
while (x>0)
{
    x--;
}
```

The above code will loop ten times and then stop. Typically, a number of statements will be executed inside a loop, and it is uncommon for the `while` loop to be used in the form given above. For a single statement it can be used as follows:

```
var x;
x = 10;
while (x>0)
    x--;
```

The `while` loop is a powerful facility, but it does have some associated risks. There is always the potential for an infinite loop to be created. This is a loop where the condition for looping is always `true` and as a result it never terminates. For example:

```
var x = 1;
while (x >= 1)
{
    x += 1;
}
```

In the above piece of code the loop never terminates, the phone will appear to have frozen to the user and they may well have to switch it off in order to reset the phone! It is very important to prevent things like this happening, computer users may well be used to resetting their PCs but mobile phone users aren't used to having to reset their mobile phones.

for statement

It's very common to need to carry out an operation a set number of times. This was done in the above section by making use of a `while` loop. However, there is a looping structure available which is much better suited to this task, namely, the `for` loop. To use the `for` loop for looping a set number of times, use a construct like this:

```
var i;
for (i=1; i<=8; i++)
{
    // code in the loop
}
```

In this example the loop is setup to loop eight times. Notice there are three parameters to the `for` loop:

❑   Initialization of the loop variable (`i=1`) – this is executed when the loop first starts

❑   Conditional expression that causes the loop to continue (`i<=8`) – this condition is tested at the start of each loop and when it becomes `false` then the loop stops

❑   Expression that is executed during each loop (`i++`) – this is used to increment the loop variable

The above code is therefore identical to:

```
var i;
i= 1;
while (i<=8)
{
    // code in the loop
    i++;
}
```

Functions

So far, we have used functions on trust, but let us now further examine them so that we can write out own. Functions are reusable code snippets and each encapsulates a particular function or purpose. Rather than go into details on the principle and usage of functions (which is covered in many good programming books), we will focus on how they work in WMLScript. WMLScript forces all scripts to be encapsulated in functions. This forces separation of code that deals with logic and markup.

A function is defined using the following form:

```
[extern] function name_of_function()
{
    // code
    return(value);
}
```

The keyword `extern` is optional; it specifies that the function can be called from outside the containing script file. If we don't use `extern`, then only other functions in the same file can use the function. Otherwise, we can call it either from a card or from another function on a different file. The name given to the function follows the same naming convention as variables. The `return` statement is optional; we need not include it. The default return value is an empty string.

The calling function can assign the return value to a variable or use it in an operation. For example:

```
extern function calculatePIN (userNUM)
{
    var PIN = calcRandomNumber() * userNUM;   // will multiply userNUM by the
    WMLBrowser.setVar("pin", PIN);            // random number returned.
}
```

Here, we've used the `setVar()` function from the `WMLBrowser` library, which has the effect of setting the value of a WML variable. WMLScript libraries are discussed in more detail below. Note that it is impossible to create functions inside another function. For example, the following is invalid because `function2()` has been declared within `function1()`:

```
function function1()
{
    function function2()
    {
        //code
    }
    //code
}
```

Passing Parameters

Listing a parameter inside the parentheses immediately following the function name has the effect of declaring a variable of that name. When the function is called, a value for each of the parameters must be included in the function call. The variable values are passed by value. We saw this done earlier in the first example; let's review the code:

```
<a href="calling.wmls#calculate(2,3)">
```

The line of script above calls the calculate function with the parameter values 2 and 3. The function defines two variables, a and b, these are assigned the values 2 and 3 respectively. We can then go on to use those values in our code as shown below:

```
extern function calculate(a,b)
{
  var n;
  n= a+b;

  WMLBrowser.setVar("number", n);
  WMLBrowser.refresh();
}
```

We can pass by browser variables "by reference", by calling the function with the name of the variable as an argument. We can then retrieve and amend the browser variable value using setVar() and getVar(). The WML code is shown below:

```
<?xml version="1.0"?>
<!DOCTYPE wml PUBLIC "-//WAPFORUM//DTD WML 1.1//EN"
"http://www.wapforum.org/DTD/wml_1.1.xml">
<!-- hello.wml -->
<wml>
<card>
<onevent type="onenterforward">
  <refresh>
    <setvar name="Greeting" value="Hello" />
  </refresh>
</onevent>
<p>
  $(Greeting)<br/>
  <a href="greetings.wmls#addAgain('Greeting')"> // pass the variable name
    Been here before?
  </a>
</p>
</card>
</wml>
```

The code sets a variable called greeting to the value "Hello" and greets the user with it. A user who has been here previously is invited to click on the link:

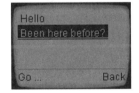

The WML card calls the function addAgain() in the greetings.wmls file, passing it the name of the browser variable "Greeting". "Greeting" is set with the value "Hello" at the top of the card:

```
extern function addAgain(strVal)
{
  var greeting = WMLBrowser.getVar(strVal);
  greeting += " Again";
  WMLBrowser.setVar(strVal, greeting);
  WMLBrowser.refresh();
}
```

This stores the browser variable name in strVal, and retrieves the stored value in greeting in this case "Hello". The function then concatenates the string "Again" to it to create the string "Hello Again", sets greeting to this value, and finally refreshes the deck:

It should be noted that the values that are passed as parameters will be escaped (special characters are converted to encoding valid in URLs). The parameters being passed can also be surrounded with ' ' (single quotes) and this should be done if only one parameter is being passed.

Using the Standard Libraries

A library is a unit containing pre-defined functions that are stored on a WAP device. These functions are called in exactly the same way as functions written by the developer, except that the library name followed by a . (period) is placed in front of the function name. So a function called refresh() inside the library called WMLBrowser can be called by using:

```
WMLBrowser.refresh();
```

In the future these libraries will be extended to allow telephony functions to be called, which means that we will be able to use WMLScript to make phone calls as well as being able to perform tasks such as accessing a device's internal calendar or phone book

The details of all the standard library functions are available in Appendix C. These libraries are part of the WAP specification and so are available from all WAP devices that support WMLScript. A few library functions have already been used in this chapter, in particular those that are stored in the WMLBrowser library. This is an especially useful library of functions since it can be used to do things that are not possible by simply writing your own functions. The WMLBrowser.refresh() function used above quite simply refreshes the present display on the browser.

Another function we've seen is the WMLBrowser.getVar() function. Remember that all WML variables are global, so WMLScript can also access them. This function takes one parameter, a string with a value that is the name of the global variable to fetch. It returns the value of this variable, which is of course a string since all WML variables are strings. For example, to get a WML variable called WMLvar and save it in a WMLScript variable called WMLSvar use:

```
WMLSvar = WMLBrowser.getVar("WMLvar");
```

Another function from the WMLBrowser library that has been used frequently is the setVar() function. Since WML variables are global they cannot just be read from everywhere, they can be changed from everywhere as well. To set the value of a WML variable WMLvar with the value of a WMLScript variable called WMLSvar use:

```
WMLBrowser.setVar("WMLvar", WMLSvar);
```

All WML variables are of type string, but the setVar() function will accept any variable as its second parameter. It performs the type conversion to a string before assigning the value to the WML variable.

Date Validation Example

In the last chapter, we learned that the only way to validate a date would be to make use of some sort of script. Now that most of WMLScript has been introduced, it is time to look at the solution to this problem. The following WML and WMLScript code prompts the user for the present date. When the user attempts to follow a link to another card some WMLScript is called to check this date. The next card will only be displayed if the user has entered a date in the valid *dd/mm/yy* form.

Here's the WML code:

```
<?xml version="1.0"?>
<!DOCTYPE wml PUBLIC "-//WAPFORUM//DTD WML 1.1//EN"
"http://www.wapforum.org/DTD/wml_1.1.xml">

<!-- dtcheck.wml -->
<wml>
  <card id="main" title="WMLScript">
    <onevent type="onenterforward">
      <refresh>
        <setvar name="greeting" value="Enter current date:" />
      </refresh>
    </onevent>
    <p>
      $(greeting)<br/>
      <input name="date" format="NN\/NN\/NN" emptyok="false" value="03/15/00"/>
      <a href="date.wmls#submit('$(date:unesc)')">
         Next card
      </a>
    </p>
    </card>
</wml>
```

The first card should be familiar since it uses the formatting for a date introduced in the last chapter. The card submits the input to the submit function in date.wmls. One thing that might look slightly strange is the way the WMLScript is called:

```
<a href="date.wmls#submit('$(date:unesc)')">
```

Remember that when a string is passed to a WMLScript function from WML it is escaped. There are / characters in the date, and to prevent these from being escaped the :unesc notation has been used.

The code first parses the submitted value for each of the day, month and year values using local functions written for that purpose. We will look at these in a moment. The code that calls them is:

```
// date.wmls
/*
  Name: submit
  Comments: provides the interface for this script
*/

extern function submit(strDate)
{
   var intMonth;
   var intDay;
   var intYear;
```

```
    intMonth = getDateVal(strDate, 0, 2);
    intDay = getDateVal(strDate, 3, 2);
    intYear = getDateVal(strDate, 6, 2);

    if (isValidDate(intMonth, intDay, intYear))
    {
        WMLBrowser.go("dtaccepted.wml");
    }
    else
        WMLBrowser.refresh();
}
```

Here is the code for getDateVal():

```
/*
  Name: getDateVal
  Comments: Returns an integer from strDate that is contained in the substring
  starting at character position startChar and eding numChars characters later
*/
function getDateVal(strDate, startChar, numChars)
{
    var strVal;
    var intVal;
    strVal = String.subString(strDate, startChars, numChars);
    intVal = Lang.parseInt(strVal);
    return(intVal);
}
```

We use this function to parse the date string (the first parameter) and extract values for the day, month and year, which are returned as integer values. Each time it's called from submit(), we pass it the same date string, but vary the starting point in the string (the second parameter) depending on whether we are after the day, the month or the year. The third parameter is used to specify the number of characters – in this case that is 2 each time, because we are expecting a date of the form *mm/dd/yy*.

All the hard work is done by the subString() function of the String library:

```
strVal = String.subString(strDate, startChars, numChars);
```

As you might expect, the String library contains functions for the manipulation and conversion of string data. The subString() function used takes a string as its first parameter, and extracts from it a string to return, starting from the position given by its second parameter with a length given by the third parameter.

The first time this code is called, we are using it to extract the month, so we are basically after the first two characters in this string, which are assigned to strVal. We then convert this to a integer value using a call to another library function:

```
intVal = Lang.parseInt(strVal);
```

The Lang library contains functions that provide core language facilities and features that are necessary in a scripting language, but are not available with the default WMLScript constructs and operators. The parseInt() function used above converts a string into an integer. It simply takes the string to be converted as its parameter and returns an integer. If the conversion from the string to an integer is not possible, then parseInt() returns invalid. For example, consider the following:

```
var intInvalid = Lang.parseInt("123z");
```

Converting the string `123z` to an integer doesn't make sense, so `intInvalid` is a variable of type `invalid`.

The final line of the `getDateVal()` function returns the integer value obtained. We get the values for the day and the year in exactly the same way, with these calls from the `submit()` function:

```
intDay = getDateVal(strDate, 3, 2);
intYear = getDateVal(strDate, 6, 2);
```

Once we've parsed the date string to obtain integer values for the month, day and year, we need to check that these are indeed valid numbers, and if they are, we accept the date:

```
if (isValidDate(intMonth, intDay, intYear))
{
    WMLBrowser.go("dtaccepted.wml");
}
```

The function `isValidDate()` takes the three integer values as parameters and checks that the date is a valid one; that is, that the day number between 1 and 28 for February, 1 and 30 for April, June and so on. The code for this function is shown below:

```
/*
  Name: isValidDate
  Comments: Returns a boolean if the given date is valid
*/
function isValidDate(intMonth, intDay, intYear)
{
   var bleReturn = false;

                // check for 31 day months
   if (intMonth==1 || intMonth==3 || intMonth==5 || intMonth==7 ||
       intMonth==8 || intMonth==10 || intMonth==12)
   {
      bleReturn=(intDay>=1 && intDay<=31);
   }
   else         //check for 30 day months
   {
      if (intMonth==4 || intMonth==6 || intMonth==9 || intMonth==11)
      {
         bleReturn=(intDay>=1 && intDay<=30);
      }
      else      //check for February
      {
         if (intMonth==2)
         {
            if (isLeapYear(intYear))
               bleReturn=(intDay>=1 && intDay<=29);
            else
               bleReturn=(intDay>=1 && intDay<=28);
         }
      }
   }

   if(bleReturn == false)
   {
      WMLBrowser.setVar("greeting", "Not valid. Please enter a valid date:");
   }
   return(bleReturn);
}
```

As you can see, this code is pretty straightforward. At the start, we assume the date is invalid and set the Boolean variable, `bleReturn` to `false`. We check whether the month value is equivalent to January, March, May, July, August, October, or December, and if it is, we set `bleReturn` to true if the integer value for the day is between 1 and 31 inclusive. Similarly, the return value is set to `true` if `intDay` is between 1 and 30 for the months of April, June, September and November. The only tricky month is February – here we need to check whether it's a leap year in order to ascertain how many days the month has:

```
if (intMonth==2)
{
    if (isLeapYear(intYear))
        bleReturn=(intDay>=1 && intDay<=29);
    else
        bleReturn=(intDay>=1 && intDay<=28);
}
```

Here is the code for `isLeapYear()`:

```
/*
   Name: isLeapYear
   Comments: Returns whether it is a leap year
*/
function isLeapYear(intYear)
{
    var bleReturn = false;

    intYear += 2000; //Y3k bug !!

    if ( ((intYear % 4)==0) && !((intYear % 100)==0) )
        bleReturn = true;
    else
        bleReturn = ((intYear%400)==0);

    return(bleReturn);
}
```

So, if the date is not validated after all this, we simply change the greeting to read "Not valid. Please enter a valid date:", and then refresh the browser. If we are happy that the date is valid, then we send the user onto the next card, contained in `date_accepted.wml`:

```
WMLBrowser.go("date_accepted.wml");
```

The `go()` function of `WMLBrowser` library means that, when the WMLScript has finished, the browser displays the card given as its parameter. The location of this card, which is a parameter to the function, has type string and the same rules apply as to the naming of a location in WML. This function could even be called with a full URL given as a string.

The file `date_accepted.wml` contains code saying that the date was accepted. Let's look at this in use. First, suppose the user selects the input field and enters an invalid date:

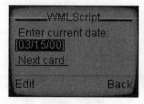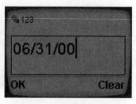

They then attempt to follow the link to the next card but it doesn't go anywhere. It merely warns them and requests a valid date:

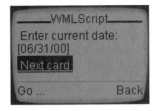 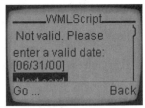

So, they edit the input to enter a valid date:

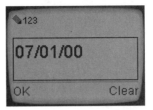 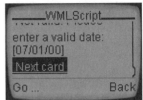

The user follows the link to the next card. This time the date is accepted and the next card is displayed.

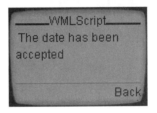

Before undertaking the task of writing some WMLScript, it is always best to check and see if a function already exists in a standard library to perform that task. If the task in question is arithmetic or involves type conversion then the required function almost certainly exists in a standard library. It is worth becoming familiar with the `String` library since string operations are incredibly common and this library contains many very useful functions.

Other libraries include `Int` and `Float`. These include various functions for manipulating integer and float values and include a random number generator. The `String` library functions include `parseInt()` as we saw above, which converts a string to an integer. We will also cover the use of the `String` libraries to simulate arrays in WMLScript. URL includes various functions to determine the context for the application such as the base URL, the function's path, port number used for access and for escaping and unescaping strings.

We have seen some of the functions available through the `WMLBrowser` library, which control the browser variables. These functions can be used to set a new context and to redirect the browser to another card from within a script. In the next couple of sections, we'll be looking more closely at the `Dialogs` and `String` libraries, for more in depth coverage on these and all the standard WMLScript libraries, you should consult Appendix C.

Dialogs Library

The `Dialogs` library, not surprisingly handles dialog with the user from within a script. The functions included are `Alert()`, `Confirm()` and `Prompt()`. `Alert()` displays a message to the user and when the user confirm the have read the message returns them to the previous menu. The syntax for this is:

```
Dialogs.alert("message");
```

Here is an example of this in action:

```
<?xml version="1.0"?>
<!DOCTYPE wml PUBLIC "-//WAPFORUM//DTD WML 1.1//EN"
"http://www.wapforum.org/DTD/wml_1.1.xml">

<wml>
  <card id="main" title="using dialog">
    <p>
      What is the capital of Turkey?<br/>
      <select name="capital" title="Models">
        <option value="A">Ankara</option>
        <option value="C">Constantinople</option>
        <option value="I">Istanbul</option>
      </select>
      <a href="alert.wmls#submit('$(capital)')">Submit guess
      </a>
    </p>
  </card>
</wml>
```

The WML code above is a multiple choice question, "What is capital of Turkey?" with possible answers, Ankara, Constantinople and Istanbul. The capital variable is assigned the value A, C and I according to the user's choice, and the user is invited to submit their answer. The value of capital is passed to the submit() function:

```
// alert.wmls
extern function submit(strCapital)
{
  if(strCapital != "A")
      Dialogs.alert("Wrong, try again!");
  else
      WMLBrowser.go("ankara.wml");
}
```

The submit() function checks if the value passed to it is A. If it is not, an alert screen is displayed with the message "Wrong, try again!" and the user is returned to the guess menu:

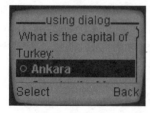  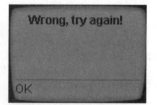

Otherwise ankara.wml is loaded as shown below:

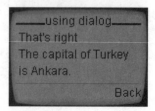

Sometimes, you want to ensure that the user to confirm an action before going ahead with it – for example, a purchase – and you can achieve this with the `confirm()` function. This takes three parameters: the confirmation message, and the alternative responses. For example:

```
Dialogs.confirm("Do you wish to continue", "yes", "more info");
```

The `prompt()` function can be used to request string input from the user from within a script. The format for using it is:

```
return_value = Dialogs.prompt(request_message, default_value);
```

The first parameter indicates to the user what input is requested, and the second can be used to give the user further information on the type of input that is required. This can be used to save the user having to type any input at all in the case where a default value may sufficient. The return value is the input from the user. For example:

```
userinput = Dialogs.prompt("Please enter your email address", "n/a");
```

The result of this code is as follows:

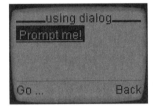 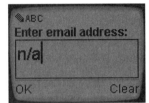

Let's now look at array handling within WMLScript.

Handling Arrays with the String Library

As we saw earlier, arrays in WMLScript are represented as strings. When you wish to extract the elements of the array, you do so by passing a library function the array and the character that delimits each array.

Look at the following string:

```
"We,are,living,in,a,yellow,submarine"
```

This contains the elements "We", "are", "living" and so on, when the delimiting character is specified as a comma. The delimiting character is specific to the application and is not hard coded in any way, so we can select one appropriate to our application. In fact, we could implement 2 dimensional arrays in principle, although it is doubtful whether there is a need for that. In this section, we'll look at the functions provided for manipulating array data.

The `String` library contains five string-array access functions, listed below:

- ❏ `String.elements()`
- ❏ `String.elementAt()`
- ❏ `String.removeAt()`
- ❏ `String.replaceAt()`
- ❏ `String.insertAt()`

We'll look at each of these in turn.

String.elements()

This function simply returns the number of elements in a given string, using the separator specified. The syntax of this function is:

```
String.elements(<array>, <separator>)
```

The two parameters supply the name of the array in question and the separator to be used. The return value of the function is an integer specifying how many elements there are in the array. If the separator supplied does not occur in the string then the return value will be 1. (The start and end of the string are treated as array terminators, and in this case these terminators will enclose a single element.)

String.elementAt()

This allows you to get the value of a specified element. The syntax is:

```
String.elementAt(<array>, <position>, <separator>)
```

`<array>` and `<separator>` have the same meaning as above, and `<position>` is the index of the element to return as the return value of the function (where 0 is the index of the first element).s

String.removeAt()

`String.removeAt()` returns the string with the specified element removed. The syntax is:

```
String.removeAt(<array>, <position>, <separator>)
```

`<array>`, `<separator>`, and `<position>` have the same meaning as before.

String.replaceAt()

This function allows you to replace an element with a new value, and has the syntax:

```
String.replaceAt(<array>, <newElement>, <position>, <separator>)
```

`<newElement>` replaces the element specified by the other 3 parameters, which have their usual meaning.

String.insertAt()

Finally, you can add elements to a string array using `String.insertAt()`. This time the syntax is:

```
String.insertAt(<array>, <newElement>, <position>, <separator>)
```

Where `<newElement>` is inserted into the array in the position specified by the other parameters.

Note

If a value of less than 0 is supplied as position the first element is returned, and if a value greater than that of the last element is supplied then the last element is returned preventing array out-of-bounds errors. Also, there is no library function to return the index of a given element. Of course, this is fairly easy to implement using the functions that do exist

Array handling in practice

One way that we can amend our earlier date-validation program is to parse the date using the string-array access functions. Our earlier example now becomes:

```
// datearray.wmls
/*
  Name: submit
  Comments: provides the interface for this script
*/

extern function submit(strDate)
{
    var intDay;
    var intMonth;
    var intYear;

    intMonth = getDateVal(strDate, 0);
    intDay = getDateVal(strDate, 1);
    intYear = getDateVal(strDate, 2);

    if (isValidDate(intDay, intMonth, intYear))
    {
        WMLBrowser.go("dtaccepted.wml");
    }
    else
        WMLBrowser.refresh();
}

/*
  Name: getDateVal
  Comments: Returns an integer from strDate that is contained in the substring
  starting at character position startChar and eding numChars characters later
*/
function getDateVal(strDate, elemNum)
{
    var strVal;
    var intVal;
    strVal = String.elementAt(strDate, elemNum, "/");
    intVal = Lang.parseInt(strVal);
    return(intVal);
}
```

The only changes are that rather than extracting the substrings, we are now extracting the date values by specifying the '/' character as an element delimiter. This makes the code much easier to understand, as it should be clearer what the first, second and third elements of the date are rather than two characters from positions 0, 3 and 6. In addition, if the format of the date changes (setting a 4 digit year, for example) the only amendment that will need to be done is rewriting the input form. The parse and validation section will still work.

Pragmas

A **pragma** is another type of command, but it is unique in that it does not make up part of a function. Pragmas control part of the interpretation of the script, or the way it's handled by the content server. All pragmas appear at the very top of a script before any function has been declared and all begin with the use keyword. A pragma is declared by using the use statement. For example:

```
use this_pragma pragma_parameter1 pragma_parameter2;
```

External Files

When a lot of WMLScript is required, maintaining it all in one file can become difficult. This is particularly the case when a group of developers are working together – even the date validation code that we saw in the last example was quite large. What is needed is some way of breaking the code down into separate files. Now, if a function calls a function in an external file, the external file must be declared. This is done using the `url` pragma. This pragma takes two parameters:

❑ The name that the external WMLScript file will be known by in this file

❑ The location of the external script – this can be a full URL or a relative path

Consider this modified version of `date.wmls`:

```
use url DateCheck "isValidDate.wmls";

/*
  Name: submit
  Comments: provides the interface for this script
*/

extern function submit(strDate)
{
    var intMonth;
    var intDay;
    var intYear;

    intMonth = getDateVal(strDate, 0);
    intDay = getDateVal(strDate, 1);
    intYear = getDateVal(strDate, 2);

    if (DateCheck#isValidDate(intMonth, intDay, intYear))
    {
        WMLBrowser.go("dtaccepted.wml");
    }
    else
    {
        WMLBrowser.setVar("greeting", "Not valid. Please enter a valid date:");
        WMLBrowser.refresh();
    }
}

/*
  Name: getDateVal
  Comments: Returns an integer from strDate that is contained in the substring
    starting at character position startChar and eding numChars characters later
*/
function getDateVal(strDate, elemNum)
{
    var strVal;
    var intVal;
    strVal = String.elementAt(strDate, elemNum, "/");
    intVal = Lang.parseInt(strVal);
    return(intVal);
}
```

Firstly note that this script is shorter than it was before, yet it behaves in the same way. The reason for this is that some of the functions have been moved into a separate file called `isValidDate.wmls`. The `isValidDate.wmls` file is included within the above script by referring to it using the `url` pragma:

```
use url DateCheck "idValidDate.wmls";
```

Two parameters have been given to this pragma. The first is the friendly-name and this will be used to refer to the file being included throughout the rest of the script. The second is the location of the script, in this case it is in the same directory so all that needs to be given is the filename. In order to use functions from this script all that needs to be done now is to give the name of the script, and the name of an external function preceded by a #. In the above script this is used in the line:

```
if (DateCheck#isValidDate(intDay, intMonth, intYear))
```

isValidDate.wmls contains all the functions that were removed from the previous script, but if they are to be called from outside this file, they do need to be declared as extern:

```
extern function isValidDate(intDay, intMonth, intYear)
```

This is necessary since it is no longer in the same script file as where it is called. The use url pragma can only be used to make functions available if they are declared as being extern; local functions will always remain local to the script in which they are defined. For example, the isLeapYear() function does not need to be declared as extern as it is only called from within the file. However, you may want to consider making a function like this external, as it is so useful and may be called from other scripts.

Breaking down a script into separate scripts is good programming practice – it makes sure that only functions that need to be made available are, and that local functions can be hidden within the separate scripts, so that problems such as naming clashes are less likely to appear. In addition, we can more closely group functions within files.

Access Control

In the future WMLScript will be used to access the internal elements of the WAP device, using WTA (discussed in Chapter 18). This could possibly include such features as accessing the internal calendar or even charging a purchase to a user's phone bill. It is obvious that with these potential applications of WMLScript some sort of control over who can use the scripts needs to be put in place – and the mechanism for this is the access pragma. This pragma is used to restrict the domain and path from which WMLScript can be called. Its use is as follows:

```
use access domain "company.com" path "/directory/path";
```

Take for example the date.wmls script. Suppose that the WML that calls it sits on the website www.wrox.com in a directory called wml. In order to restrict the functions in the WMLScript so that they are only available to this site, the following pragma would be placed at the top of the script:

```
use access domain "wrox.com" path "/wml";
```

Meta Information

The final pragma that is available in WMLScript is for passing metadata to the compiler. We have already seen metadata in WML in Chapter 4. This metadata is generic data which is be used by one of three systems. It can be used by the web server, the WAP device or written to the HTTP data. The qualifiers for specifying the system are name, user agent and http equiv respectively. The syntax for this is:

```
use meta <qualifier> <property> <content> <scheme>
```

Here, <property> is the property to set, which might be the HTTP header name, <content> is the value of the property and <scheme> relates to the formatting or treatment of the data. Its use with the user agent context qualifier is left up to the vendor.

So, to send some generic data to the WAP device use:

```
use meta user agent "some-property" "some-value"
```

Dealing with Errors

The user of a WAP device is not expecting anything to go wrong. People may be used to errors in Internet browsers and computer software generally, and it's accepted that computers do frequently have errors and need restarting. Generally, a computer is the only electrical device which a user will tolerate a fault with – if a video recorder or microwave has an malfunction it gets taken back to where it was purchased. The same is true for mobile phones; a strange symbol appears on the display or the phone behaves in an unexpected manner, or if the user feels out of his depth in operating the device, and he might return the phone. You might also consider that as this technology is so new, there are no accepted standards for usability and the users have no expectations from applications. Consequently the user of a mobile phone accessing Internet facilities with a WAP browser will not be so tolerant as typical Internet users

Unfortunately this is not the case and WMLScript is not strong in the area of error handling. While syntax errors will be picked up by the encoder, and logic errors should be flushed out by a good test regime, this leaves other unexpected errors. We will first look at how to avoid type errors and then at the specifications for run-time error handling.

Error checking

One of the best ways of checking for errors in WMLScript is to check that functions are returning the expected data type. One way to do this is to use the typeof operator, as was discussed earlier. The Lang library also includes the isInt() and isFloat() functions to test if a variable value is, or can be converted to, a valid integer or float value. Both these function return a Boolean. For example, assuming a function called calculate() is supposed to return an integer – we can check that it does so before using the return value, as follows:

```
var x = calculate();
if Lang.isInt(x)
{
    // code using x
}
else
{
    // error code
}
```

Another method of error detection that can be used is range checking. When a function returns a value, this value should be checked to make sure it isn't too small or too large. For example, assume the calculate() function is supposed to return an integer in the range 1 to 10. The following is a potential way of deal with potential errors:

```
var x = calculate();
if ( (x>=1) && (x<=10)
{
    // code using x
}
else
{
    // error code
}
```

Error handling

Error handling refers to dealing with runtime errors. WMLScript does not define exception handling logic but does require the handling of errors. What this practically means to us as developers is that the code must be as reliable as possible as there is no system for dealing with fatal errors. Common issues to watch out for include:

- ❑ Do not nest functions to deeply – the stack has limited resources
- ❑ Excessive use of variables can cause a stack overflow error – usually the result of declaring a variable within a recursively called function or within a `while` or `for` loop

Some runtime errors cannot be avoided. These include system calls to abort (due to low battery power or similar), user requested abort (pressing a stop or abort button) while other relate to site management, such as missing resources.

Non-fatal errors largely relate to mathematical operations, division by zero, integer overflow and so on. These should be handled by testing the result as indicated above. Any non-fatal runtime error should result in an error message but the application would still be running so the user should be able to press the back button and try again.

Summary

This chapter has covered the scripting language of WAP known as WMLScript. The important points from this chapter are summarized below:

- ❑ WMLScript is a client-side scripting language based on ECMAScript and has much more powerful computing constructs than WML. It is a weakly typed language, so it is important to monitor the use of variables. WMLScript contains all the basic constructs required for any computer language, such as selection and repetition.
- ❑ WMLScript has a set of standard libraries with many useful functions that perform common tasks, saving developer time. Another plus to this is the saved download time – library functions are provided as part of the interpreter and reside on the browser. They can be used to manipulate the microbrowser and in the future they will allow telephony applications to be carried out using WMLScript. (These functions are all listed in Appendices C.)
- ❑ WMLScript has particularly poor error handling facilities but, by using type and range checking on the values returned from functions, some small degree of error handling can be introduced.

All this combines to give us powerful tools for writing application, especially with further standardization of microbrowsers and WML and WMLScript support. However this power needs to be managed carefully and designed with the end-user in mind. It is easy to create confusing and frustrating applications and if we wish to avoid this we need to consider the usability of our applications, which is the subject of the next chapter.

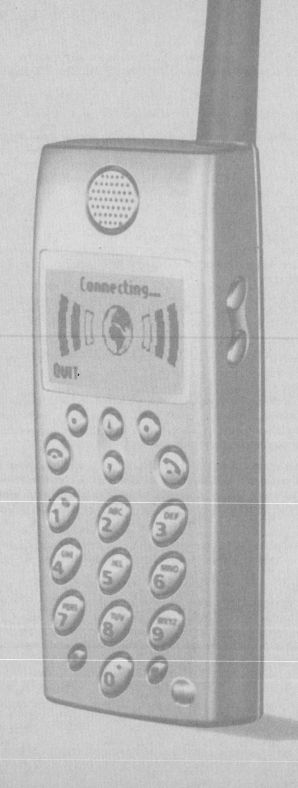

7

Usability

Usability is a term that indicates the degree of user-friendliness of a system. A usable system is one that lets its users complete tasks in a reasonably easy way. Assessing the value of a system's user interface has become increasingly important with the growth of computer use, so much so that there is now a field of computer science, Human-Computer Interaction (HCI), which deals specifically with building usable systems.

Over the past decade, we have witnessed the proliferation of increasingly more powerful applications. Advanced graphical user interfaces have become the norm in today's world, causing WAP developers to find themselves in an awkward situation. They are not developing PC applications, but applications for devices that have extremely limited input and display capabilities. To add to that, they are developing for a plethora of devices that will render their code in totally different ways. If you are a web developer, you might think that this situation resembles closely the browser war we are still witnessing on the Web. There is also the problem that WAP applications are to be developed for an audience that is not necessarily computer literate.

In this chapter, we'll take a close look at the problems that the above considerations cause. We'll examine some general usability design guidelines, as well as some that apply specifically to two of the most common devices currently available: the browser of the Nokia 7110 and the UP.Browser. Hopefully, you will be able to apply usability principles learned from these environments to the devices that will ship in the future.

Usability is very often the victim of projects that run out of budget. A usable application is more difficult and more expensive to develop. However, this chapter will explain the importance of thinking about the issues of usability and why it should never be left out of the equation when applications are under development.

Why is Usability Necessary?

While the term usability may sound intuitive to most of us, we need to refer to a more concrete definition of the concept. In order to assess how usable a WAP application is you should think in terms of:

❑ The intellectual skills required to learn to use the system

❑ The time required to learn to use the system

❑ How intuitive the system is

❑ The level of frustration involved in using the system

If the typical user perceives our WAP application as easy to use, straightforward and forgiving, then we can say it is a usable application. These aspects will be illustrated in detail later in this chapter. First, however, we'll take a look at the problems that developers must bear in mind alongside usability guidelines.

Limitations of Wireless Devices

By now you should be aware of the fact that WAP devices have several limitations when compared to personal computers. Let's recap them here:

❑ Small screens

❑ Limited input capabilities

❑ Limited processor power and RAM

❑ Limited bandwidth

❑ Limited support for graphics

❑ Limited deck size

These limitations have serious implications for the way you should design your WAP system. Let's take them one by one and examine them in more detail.

Small screens

The displays of mobile devices are small. If you are accustomed to web browsers, you'll find navigating with a WAP phone a real pain. As a general rule, plan your user interface for the lowest common denominator in terms of display capabilities. Think in terms of 4 lines of 15-18 characters. If you do this, you will not only be targeting your applications for the majority of your users, but you should find that your applications are also usable on devices with larger displays, such as some PDAs. Applications developed for big displays, on the other hand, tend to display badly on a small screen.

Limited Input Capabilities

Currently, the majority of mobile devices are phones, which have a phone keypad. While this is sufficient for dialing phone numbers, entering text with it is torture compared to a traditional QWERTY PC keyboard. The longer the URL, the longer it will take to enter. This increases the likelihood of users navigating with the use of portals alone, including Yahoo-type lists and even personalized portals in which you can specify minutely the type of content you wish to have access to.

Limited Processor Power

Phones are made to let you talk. In most cases, they don't have PDA-like functionality. WAP is a technology that is designed to 'scale down' well on such 'dumb' devices. Although some WAP-enabled devices are more powerful than others, remember that the majority of them will be mobile phones with very limited power.

Limited Bandwidth

Currently, WAP devices have very little bandwidth available when compared with PCs on the Internet. At the time of writing, users (in Europe) can expect a speed of 9600 bps. However, the introduction of GPRS should improve the situation slightly by the end of 2000. (For more detail on this, see Chapter 20.) Even in the future, when telecommunications will support high-bandwidth wireless carriers, people may continue to use less expensive low-bandwidth solutions. Therefore it is best to assume that data comes across in small chunks to the user. This is the reality awaiting us for the next two or three years.

Limited Graphics and Limited Deck Size

You have come across these limitations in the previous part of the book. The implication is that providing users with timely graphic or textual hints while they use the application is more difficult than on a PC.

All of the limitations described here are real and should be kept in mind constantly during all the phases of the development process. Unfortunately, there is another major hindrance to the development of usable WAP applications – interoperability between the different WAP-enabled devices that exist.

WML Interoperability Issues

WML delivers content and user interfaces to a wide variety of devices. However well the different devices support the WAP specifications, in practice the implementations for rendering WML between the different browser types vary greatly. This obviously affects the usability of WAP applications.

Ideally, we want to develop easy, intuitive applications in which users can find the most obvious operations one click away. Unfortunately, 'one click away' on one particular device may be two or more clicks on another device. Just to give you a simple example, the easiest way for a user to move around an application on the browser of a Nokia 7110 is via hyperlinks, but on a phone with the UP.Browser, <do> elements are to be favored for ease of use.

This situation is not simple to solve. Implementing multiple versions of an application (one for each family of browsers) may be the best option you have, and using something like XML hand-in-hand with XSLT is one way to implement this (covered in Chapter 9). There are other ways around this problem, however. One important point to stress is that WAP is not the Web. While a web site can potentially appeal to an international audience, WAP services are more often built for subscribers to a specific telecommunications network in a specific country. This means that developers can usually make assumptions about the target audience, which microbrowsers they might be using, and the gateways that provision them.

About Different Devices

From the above discussion, it is easy to see that any detailed practical discussion of usability issues needs to take place in the context of specific devices. This is not an easy task, since a plethora of new phones and PDAs are hitting the market now, and more will be released in the near future.

Later in this chapter, we will be concentrating mainly on two microbrowsers:

❑ The UP.Browser from Phone.com. (This ships on phones from many different vendors like Motorola, Siemens, Alcatel, Philips, Samsung and more. You can see the list at: `http://updev.phone.com/dev/ts/up/phones.html`.)

❑ The browser of the Nokia 7110.

The reason that we have chosen to focus on these two browsers in this chapter is that (at the time of writing) the Nokia 7110 has a large share of the market in Europe due to its early release, and the UP.Browser has the largest share of the US market.

There are other browsers hitting the market in spring 2000 that also merit thinking about. Most are discussed in Chapter 2, but see their documentation for more information. Always consider carefully which user agents you want your applications to support, since this choice may have a significant impact on your application development.

Typical Users

Whenever you are building an application of any kind, not only WAP, you should ask yourself the question, "Who is the typical user of my application?" This is very important, since the first step of building easy and intuitive applications is to enter the mind of the typical user.

Programmers are never 'average users' of applications. They know how the application works internally and they are never taken by surprise. This is hardly the case with the majority of users of the application. Most tend to think in terms of the problems they have to solve and tasks they want to achieve. On the other hand, programmers tend to think in terms of how to use the tool to solve a problem. The average application user is not as skillful as a programmer when dealing with PCs. We have to build applications that are friendlier than we programmers expect.

Let's look at a couple of examples to illustrate the point:

❑ If I am using an application and I click on a button and nothing happens for 5 seconds or so, I don't panic. I know that this might be due to a database connection or to the application trying to hit the file system, so why worry – give your PC a chance. However, when someone who does not deal with computers interacts with the same application, they will likely start clicking furiously on the same apparently inactive button. All of a sudden, a rush of unintelligible operations makes their screen flash repeatedly. This is a pretty frustrating experience for inexperienced users.

❑ Imagine that users are given a tool to create, delete and modify documents in a database through a web interface. They also have the ability to create attachments associated with a document. When a user starts creating a new document, the document does not exist in the database – it will be created when the user fills in some content and commits the operation (save, create, store or whatever you decide to call it). Sometimes users will want to create an attachment for the document they are creating, before they create the document itself. Supporting such functionality is certainly possible, but it requires a certain amount of extra work for the developer, since they have no document to build a relationship with when the user creates the attachment. Error handling makes the whole thing even more complex. In a situation like this the idea of forcing the user to save a new document first and come back for the attachment later on is often far too tempting. This is an example of forcing your users to think in terms of how to use the tool to solve the problems, rather than letting them think in terms of the problems they have to solve. Ideally, the tool should be transparent to the user.

While these examples refer to PC applications, the same principles apply to creating WAP applications. In fact, as we see in the next section, when working with WAP you really need to think even more carefully about your typical users, what experience they have and what they are expecting from your application.

Users of WAP applications

WAP users are not sitting in front of a PC. They are on the move, on their way to a meeting, in a bar or in a crowded train. Our goal when we build a WAP application should be making it *as simple to use as possible*. While this is true for any application, this is an absolute must in the context of WAP. WAP users are subject to many distracting events in the environment that surrounds them.

To add to that, there is an extra issue that you should consider carefully:

> **WAP users are not necessarily PC users.**

It has been estimated that in five years there will be over a billion mobile devices, and that over 50% of Internet access will be from a device other than a PC. The implication of this is that you cannot assume that the users of your application are also PC users. This is why WAP applications should be as intuitive as possible and should always present users with the most obvious choice just one click away. Using PC jargon does not count as intuitive.

Understanding who your users are is an important step in application design. Try to profile your users where possible, and understand their motivations. This should help you to structure your application and decide which features should be included and which may be discarded.

Where do we go from here?

So, where do we go from here? To start with, we'll examine some general-purpose usability guidelines that apply to all phones. For best performance, however, you must fine-tune your application for the specific devices you intend to support. As we said above, in this chapter we'll be focusing on usability issues for the Nokia 7110 browser and the UP.Browser. Finally, we'll look at one possible approach for building cross-browser applications for the UP.Browser and the Nokia 7110 browser.

General Guidelines

In this section, we will look in detail at our objectives for the development of an application that users will find pleasing to use, and examine some general guidelines for developing usable applications for WAP-enabled devices.

When talking about usability, there is always a difficulty in moving from abstract concepts to concrete guidelines. We need a methodology for designing usable applications. The first step is to define the term usability by means of less abstract goals.

> *It should be clear by now that the design phase is more important than the development phase in WAP applications, since bad design is guaranteed to compromise the success of the whole operation.*

Application Goals

If you are a programmer, thinking about usability is not simple. We want to achieve our goals as quickly and efficiently as possible, but unfortunately user friendliness and optimal efficiency are – if not mutually exclusive – a compromise.

Here are the questions you should ask yourself:

- ❑ Do you understand your target user?
- ❑ Is the application easy to learn? Is it intuitive?
- ❑ Is the application efficient to use? Do we have minimum user input for the best results?
- ❑ Are unusual operations easy to remember?
- ❑ Does the application lead to errors?
- ❑ Is the application pleasing (and not frustrating) for the user?

If you can answer in the affirmative to the above questions, you are on the right track.

We've already spent some time talking about typical users, so let's see how the rest of the questions above map to concrete concepts.

Intuitive Applications

Whenever the user has to stop to figure out how to use the tool, they lose focus and become frustrated. Intuitive interfaces are easier to sell, easier for users to get up-and-running and more likely to attract the user back again to a pleasant interactive experience. Your users do not want to read a manual before they use your application. They should be able to find their way autonomously. Always remember that your users are not programmers and are not power users.

Users tend to only use a small fraction of the functionality of an application. Sometimes though, they try to perform slightly less usual operations, and they should be able to do this without external help from manuals and other users – in other words, give your users a chance to discover what they still don't know.

Efficient Applications

Most people are inherently impatient to some degree. For this reason (among others) it is important to make an application that is as quick to use as possible. While this may be difficult in many situations, a balance must be made between the amount of user input and the results of the application – the application must be as efficient as possible.

Memorability

While a user may have to hunt around a little to figure out how to perform an unusual operation, it is important that once they have figured it out, they won't have to go through the same effort again when they want to perform the same operation two weeks later. They should be able to remember the process easily. If an action is only performed rarely, it is best omitted altogether.

Tolerance

Users should never find themselves one click away from a destructive action. WAP applications should be forgiving. Ask for confirmation for every destructive action. For example, if a user is about to cancel an order, you should ask them something like, "Are you sure you want to cancel your order?" This question might just prevent them from losing those 10 minutes they spent finding the CD and entering their name, address, telephone number, and credit card number.

How To Achieve The Goals

Now that the intermediate goals are clear, we'll take a look at a set of general rules that will help us achieve them:

- ❏ **Top 20% of functionality**: When porting an existing desktop or web application to WAP, you should identify only the main activities that users are interested in using on a mobile device.

- ❏ **Rate user activities**: Try to identify the main activities that the majority of the users will perform and build your application in a way that will let users perform these activities in the fastest possible way.

- ❏ **Design as a tree structure**: Lay out a hierarchical tree of activities that your application should contain.

- ❏ **Minimize data entry**: Since most phones only have a phone keypad, your application should require textual data entry only when absolutely necessary. In addition, the input mode of the terminal should be set to support the expected format for the data that users insert.

- ❏ **Personalization**: Try to enable your applications to remember data that has been input by your users.

- ❏ **Text should be terse**: Short, polished and informative text is vital to guide users.

- ❏ **Always implement a *back* functionality**: All users like to explore when confronted with a new application. Hence, you should provide a back functionality at all times.

- ❏ **Consistency is very important**: Applications can often require users to perform the same activity (or very similar activities) in different parts of the application. Consistency in how these activities are implemented is likely to make the interactive experience of your users much more pleasant. This also reduces development effort.

- ❏ **Push**: Real-time information is a key functionality to give extra value to WAP.

- ❏ **Be prepared to test**: If you are deploying a WAP application that is even moderately complex, you should be ready to build prototypes as early as possible in the development process.

One final note concerns **redundancy**. This term indicates the ability that some desktop applications have to let users do the same thing in multiple ways. For example, you can delete an e-mail by clicking on the delete button while viewing the message, choosing the delete menu item while viewing the message, hitting the delete key when viewing the list of messages, or dragging the message into your deleted item folder, and so on. In the case of WAP applications, however, redundancy has its disadvantages. Adding power-user shortcuts can be handy, but is not advantageous for the typical user because it adds complexity to your applications, which can cause confusion. For instance, if the same operation is found in two different places then many users will assume that these are two different operations.

We'll now take a look at some of the above ideas in a little more detail.

Top 20% of Functionality

Desktop and web applications can be pretty sophisticated these days. When you are confronted with the task of porting an application to WAP, you should consider which functions you should keep and which you should discard completely. Porting all functionality will probably have several negative implications. Firstly, it is going to be expensive, but this is not the biggest problem. If you have a lot of features, you are going to make your users' lives miserable while they wander through a forest of menus and submenus. They will doubtless abandon your application.

Imagine, for example, that your application lets users check their e-mail through a WAP phone. Letting users play with the settings of their spam filters through their mobile phones is an activity that you probably don't want to support, since the extra menus you introduce would increase the complexity of the application. In addition, it's possible that the amount of use would not justify the cost of development.

Many people still dispute which types of services are suitable for WAP; only time will tell which are the killer applications. Reading e-mail and looking at the price of stocks are typical examples of the kinds of activities that users will perform via WAP. Replying to e-mail, however, is much less likely, even though it makes sense in those cases where a short answer is enough. Reading news headlines also make sense in a mobile context. When trying to determine which kinds of applications you should port to WAP, one possible approach is to look at:

- ❑   Information that people want specifically when they are mobile
- ❑   Information that people want all the time

Typical examples of the first kind of application are services providing information on traffic, transport, accommodation, restaurants, entertainments and so on, which are specific to the location of the user. General examples of the second kind are more difficult to find since they vary in different regions of the world. Italians may use a WAP service to discover which beach is less crowded at that very moment, while the English might want to look at a weather forecast, and we all want to check our stocks and shares.

Also remember that users who wish access to more advanced services are likely to be the users with access to the Web from the comfort of their homes and offices. Providing a web-based interface for the most complex type of activity may be a good alternative for users and developers. Consider the possibility of providing access to an application's configuration through the Web. While not all mobile users will also access advanced features through the Web, many will appreciate this feature. This will ultimately contribute to the overall success of your application.

You might wonder when and how it makes sense to build a web interface to support your WAP application. First off, you should never *force* users to go through the web before they can use a WAP application. Remember that not all users will have access to a PC, much less want access to a PC. While the existence of a web site that supports so-called 'required-activities' won't hurt, you should make sure that this is not a requirement, or you will be losing a tremendous number of users before you start. Another aspect of the web interface concerns the kind of users the system is targeted at. For example, corporate mobile users who intend to follow the ups and downs of a portfolio of shares might very well appreciate the possibility of configuring the WAP applications they use daily through the Web.

Rate User Activities

According to MobileThink, you may lose as many as half of your users for every click they have to make. Furthermore, if you require text entry, studies have shown that 7 out of 8 users simply stop using the application there.

In order to avoid this, user activities need to be thought about very carefully. When thinking about the main functionality of your application, start by trying to rate the user activities into one of the following three categories:

❑ Activities that most users perform most of the time

❑ Activities most users perform occasionally

❑ Activities that specialized users perform once in a while

Identifying these activities is the basis for breaking down the navigation flow and optimizing the navigation path required to perform the main activities.

Let's go back to our example of the e-mail application. Suppose, for the sake of argument, that this is an application that gives users a WAP interface to their regular e-mail account. Reading e-mail is a high-use activity, so you should make sure that an e-mail message can be read in the fastest possible way, ideally by clicking on a softkey or a hyperlink. Remember that minimizing the number of operations necessary for frequent activities has capital importance. An example of an activity that is performed less often is deleting e-mail messages through a WAP phone. Some users will do that. Some won't. Most will prefer to wait until they have access to their desktops. It is important that support for the delete functionality does not make the application more difficult to use for those that do not employ the functionality. On the other hand, you want to make sure that users who do want to delete their e-mails from their WAP interface can do so reasonably easily.

The methodology recommended by Phone.com requires that you identify a profile of the average user of your application and break down the application into groups of activities your users are likely to perform more or less frequently.

For each activity you should understand how users expect to perform them according to models that users are familiar with. This could mean similarity with corresponding PC functions or with the way users perform the activity in their daily life.

Next you should classify activities into the following groups:

❑ **Required Activities** (compulsory activities for all users): these are activities that all of the application users will have to perform. One typical such activity is configuring their e-mail address and POP server when using an e-mail application for the first time. Configuring access to a different gateway is another example. It goes without saying that user-friendliness degrades unacceptably if operations like this are requested each time an application is used.

> **Avoid required activities or minimize them as much as possible.**

❑ **Main Path Activities** (high use activities): these are the activities that 80% or more of your users are likely to perform. Such activities should be easily and intuitively available, without any learning curve or unnatural interaction path for the inexperienced user. Reading an e-mail message is a typical example of main path activity. It makes sense to design your application in order to have a single main path activity, since this tends to produce a very natural interaction flow.

> **Performing main path activities should be as easy as possible.**

❑ **Semi Main Path Activities** (high use by a large segment of, but not all, users): these are activities that many users (but not the majority) perform often. For example, according to Phone.com, something like 50% of an e-mail application's users delete 80% of their e-mail after they have read it. This is a semi main path activity.

> **Keep access to semi main path activities as simple as possible, but make sure that they are not an impediment for users who do not perform them.**

❑ **Side Path Activities** (activities used occasionally by most users): these are activities that 80% of the users will use 20% of the time they use your application. Replying to an e-mail is an example of one such activity.

> **It makes sense to implement access to side path activities in a menu that is not immediately accessible.**

❑ **Rare Path Activities** (activities never used by most users): these activities are there to support power users. When you identify a rare path activity, you might want to consider the extent to which removing support for that particular activity diminishes the value of your application. It's better to have a simple system than one with a lot of obscure options.

> **Consider removing rare path activities entirely from your application.**

The classification of activities into main path, semi main and rare path gives developers an indication of how they should implement navigation to the different kinds of activities. Once a user is *inside* an activity however – no matter whether or not it's a frequent operation – you should support that activity like a main path activity, that is, you should make it easy and intuitive for the user to perform the activity.

Design a Tree Structure

Common activities should be performed through the shortest possible interaction path, while less common operations may take longer to access. To do this, you should organize the cards and decks of your application in a hierarchy and make the root of this hierarchy the application entry point. Make sure that each level of your tree is sorted based on the likely amount of usage for each activity. Starting with the most important activities, design the user interface to ensure that the higher priority activities are always available with the fewest keystrokes possible.

The tree structure of a typical application is illustrated in the diagram below:

In addition, the tree structure works well in connection with backwards navigation (shown by dashed lines), since users are able to move back towards the root very quickly. It can also be a good idea to provide users with a mechanism to return to the root (or home page) of an application in one click.

It is good practice to consistently use one method of navigation for each group of activities. For example, if you are developing for the UP.Browser, you could associate a main path activity with the **Accept** key (`<do type="accept">`) while a semi main path activity could consistently be represented with `<do type="options">`. Side path activities could be accessed through an extra level of menus. In the screenshots below, the main path activity view is shown as an **Accept** key, while the semi main path activities buy and sell are found under the **Menu** button:

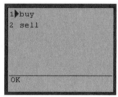

Minimize Data Entry

A golden rule in WAP development is to do whatever you can to minimize data entry. Textual data entry is the worst kind. As we discussed earlier, entering text with a phone keypad is a difficult, frustrating and error-prone operation. However, minimizing textual data entry is not simple, so in this section, we'll examine a few techniques we can employ to achieve this.

Firstly, we need to avoid data entry altogether unless absolutely necessary. If you have a mechanism for recognizing users, then you have all you need to avoid unnecessary data entry (see the next section on *Personalization*). Always make sure that there is an alternative to entering data directly – use an option list if you can, and allow the user to make choices and interact with your application that way.

In some situations data entry is necessary, for example, when inputting the URL for your WAP site. In such a situation, you should keep the URL as short as possible.

However, if you have no alternative and need to add other data entry to your application, you will need to think carefully about the design of your data entry forms. Forms with multiple input or select elements are often referred to as optional (or elective) forms, since users can choose which data they can insert and in which order. Another type of form is a wizard. Wizards are a set of cards each containing an input or select element and some clear text guiding the user. Users are required to go through each card in a specified sequence, focus on what they are doing at each step and insert the data. It might be worth giving a progress report in the wizard so users don't get disheartened. Something like 'step 1 of 3', 'step 2 of 3' and 'last step'. Wizards are better than elective forms to minimize user mistakes, since the user is forced to focus on one input at a time. Even though this method involves more button clicks, this is still preferable since more scrolling is necessary on an elective form.

Validation

Remember that textual data entry is an error-prone operation, and you might need to perform validation on the user input. Let users know as soon as possible that they have entered data incorrectly. Always remember what they have entered and let them edit it rather than sending them back to an empty text box and making them start over again. This is simple, since the nature of WML variables enforces this by default. This kind of validation can be achieved client-side, but you will usually need the server to intervene.

WAP 1.1 offers two ways to do client-side validation: WMLScript and input masks. However, when considering using WMLScript, you should bear in mind the following facts:

❑   Many telephones in the US and Asia are equipped with the UP.Browser 3.1, which does not support WMLScript.

❑   Mitsubishi Trium handsets allow the user to disable WMLScript. Your application must handle this, which is non-trivial.

❑   WMLScript cannot be nested into WML code – it needs to be contained in its own deck. The implication of this is that the phone will need to download the script from the server anyway, even when a user enters the values correctly. In the best-case scenario, you still have one return trip to the server, and, in the worst case, you end up using more time and bandwidth than you are trying to save.

UP.Browser is a remarkable exception to the above problem when used in conjunction with the UP.Link gateway. Decks and WMLScript code can be packed into a single digest and shipped to the phone in one fell swoop.

❑   At present, some gateways have problems handling WMLScript correctly, although this shouldn't be a problem in the long term.

Input masks can be useful in a few cases, but they are not powerful enough for many kinds of validation. They allow you to specify the format of user input to some extent, but you should use them with caution. Some devices have problems validating complex patterns required by input masks, and also tend to do a bad job at providing users with the correct feedback when matching against a mask. This can lead to confusion for the end-user.

Input masks are most useful for setting the keypad into number mode, and other fairly simple cases. The rest of the time, though, you can help your users much more if you tell them what they are supposed to type, rather than just enforcing it with a mask. For example, you might want to do something like:

```
<p>
    Date (mmyyyy): <!-- tell the user what to write -->
    <input name="exp" value="" format="NNNNNN"/>
</p>
```

This tells the user the format of the date that is required (a double digit month followed by a four digit year) as well as enforcing the user to only enter numbers.

To conclude, when it comes to validating user input, you need to weigh up your options and decide between the extra trips to the server, and the greater power that server-side processing gives you. However, no matter how much scripting code you use on the client, server-side validation does a better job in most cases. The reason is simple: the server is better informed. Not only can the server perform syntax checks on the input, but it can also hit the database to validate the date against a variety of application specific conditions. In terms of usability, the server gives you more flexibility, because it allows you to produce cards dynamically and thus react in a more meaningful way to user input, and give the users messages they will understand and find helpful.

Personalization

Applications that are personalized will be more usable for a number of reasons. Firstly, information about the user, such as their name and e-mail address, can be stored so that the user does not have to input this information more than once. Secondly, you might consider ordering the hyperlinks or menu items by their relevance to the particular user. The links a user follows more often, for example, might automatically come first making them more accessible. (Note that this may have the disadvantage of renumbering the short cuts for links on the UP.Browser – see later in the chapter.)

The easiest way of achieving personalization is through the use of cookies. Unfortunately, lack of cookie support by all the different gateways makes recognizing previous users difficult in the general case. You may be wondering why we need to worry about gateway support, rather than microbrowser support, but the analogy between web browsers and WAP microbrowsers is misleading in the case of cookies. Most mobile devices are not suitable for storing cookies, because cookies require a significant amount of non-volatile storage. In addition, cookies are usually set to expire in the distant future. For this reason, cookies will be supported through the gateway, rather than the microbrowser. In other words, no wireless device supports cookies. Gateways implement cookies on behalf of the devices they are provisioning.

Although many gateways, such as the Nokia gateway, do not support cookies, there are others that provide some other unique cookie (MSISDN cookie in the Ericsson gateway) on which you can build some form of personalization and session management. In practice, you have a chance to hit the database and spare the user from writing all of the data it took so much time to write the first time.

Yet other gateways, such as Phone.com's UP.Link, have full cookie support. (The phrase 'standard cookies' refers to those specified in RFC 2109 which can be found at `http://www.cis.ohio-state.edu/htbin/rfc/rfc2109.html`.) In this case not only can you recognize old users, but supporting personalization of your service also becomes a piece of a cake. If you know that your users rely on such a gateway, this is going to make your life significantly simpler.

Since the UP.Link gateway supports cookies, every mobile device automatically acquires cookie-capabilities when provisioned by the UP.Link. As well as cookies, UP.Link will also return a globally unique value for each user in an HTTP header called `HTTP_X_UP_SUBNO`.

The Ericsson gateway, on the other hand, does not provide support for RFC 2109 cookies at the time of writing, but it always provides a cookie that is unique for each provisioned device. The cookie has a format like this:

```
User-Identity-Forward-msisdn=<Unique 10 octet hex string>
```

The 10 octet hex string is a function of many different things. How to decode this is not publicly available information, in order to preserve privacy. You can exploit this cookie, though, since this is a unique key for every mobile device.

Another method for personalization is to require users to log in, and you will need to weigh up whether the benefits of personalization outweigh the problems of enforcing a login procedure. Usually this is not the case – remember the rule about never requiring your users to enter text unless absolutely necessary. The only time you should require your users to log in is if it is part of an authentication mechanism.

Text should be terse

Because WAP devices have small displays, text should be short, clear and informative. Some devices clip long text in certain situations, rather than wrapping it, which can have dire consequences for usability, so try to avoid clipping in the first place. One additional problem is that different devices clip text differently in different situations.

You should name different operations and activities in an intuitive way using verbs that identify actions, for example, Cancel, Show, Delete and so on. Deploy the language of the users that the application is aimed at. Avoid foreign words, jargon and non-obvious abbreviations. Be consistent in the use of terms – the use of a variety of synonyms for the same activity is very likely to confuse your users. You may want to use emphasis elements (bold type, for example) to point out important information. Don't depend on it though, as the majority of WAP devices currently available simply ignore these.

Implement a Back Functionality

One of the most frustrating things you can do in your application is preventing the user from navigating backwards, changing their mind. In a way, if the user follows a link and loses the current context, the impossibility of going back is perceived as having fallen into a trap. Users feel less apprehensive using an application that supports solid backward navigation.

There are pitfalls to watch out for, however. While most of the time a back button is best implemented with a `<prev />` task associated with the previous card, there are cases in which you need to identify a different card. One typical case is when you define a card to protect users from errors before a destructive action. In that case going back to the warning card does not make sense. In general you should go back to a place where it makes sense to go back to – that is, where the user expects to end up.

Push

In Europe, we are accustomed to SMS messages, which enable us to push short messages directly to our friends' mobile phones. In the US, pagers are also pretty common. Although push was not included in the 1.1 specifications for WAP, the good news is that the infrastructure is now in place and you may already have a way to push information to a WAP phone. Admittedly, there is not a standard way to do it, but there are opportunities to use push to give your application extra value.

For example, UP.Link already supports WAP push and alerts. If you visit `http://updev.phone.com`, you will find some useful libraries in Perl and C++ to start a push session directly from your server. The Ericsson gateway also supports push to WAP telephone in the form of SMS messages. Unfortunately, exploiting this possibility is not possible for the general public yet, nor has any API been publicly released.

Mobile phones follow users everywhere. A mobile phone gives developers a unique possibility to provide real time information to a specific user. Most applications could leverage push capabilities by alerting users of important events in real time. You can find out more about push in Chapter 16.

Try to exploit them if it is appropriate for your application. Don't give up on the extra value your application can acquire through push, but remember that your application should never rely on something that not all your users will have.

Be Prepared to Test

The final step is to find users and let them use your application. This will tell you how intuitive your interface is. If they have lots of problems, your interface has not been designed well and you'll need to iterate parts of the development cycle.

The main rule here is: don't skip testing. It's tremendously important. The people who road test your application should always represent typical users – don't get your grandmother to test an application aimed at mobile corporate users.

You should capture all kinds of feedback that users provide. No help should be provided to the users, nor should they have any training in advance. Use at least five different users separately. In reality, people will use real phones. It therefore goes without saying that phones should employ during the test, not emulators!

Finally, the fact we have discussed this phase as the last one in the methodology does not imply that this should be the last step in the development process. First off, you might want to involve users during the design phase to provide precious feedback about what they perceive as a natural way to break down activities. Secondly, having a test phase necessarily implies that you might have to change parts of your application. Very often, you can build static prototypes of your application in plain WML very early in the development cycle, and receive good feedback about the design before real development starts.

Guidelines for Specific Browsers

In this section, we'll take a look at usability optimization for Nokia 7110 browsers and the UP.Browser. These browsers tend to differ greatly in their implementation of WML. As a simple example, consider that the title attribute of a WML card is not automatically reflected anywhere on the display of a UP.Browser, while it is always displayed as the title of the page on the Nokia 7110 browser.

We'll now take a look at these two devices in more detail.

Guidelines for Nokia 7110

Before we delve into the details of usability optimization for the Nokia 7110, let's look at a picture that provides an overview of the interface for that particular device:

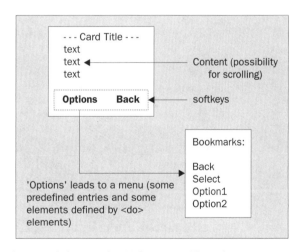

We'll use this diagram as a reference for talking about usability on the Nokia 7110. Note that:

❑ The right softkey can only be mapped to the back function through the `<do type="prev">` element.

❑ The 'navi-roller' can be pressed. Until the user navigates to another link, the function of the 'navi-roller' is mapped to the `<do type="accept">` action but it is not labeled as such. All of the other `<do>` elements (option1, option2, ...) end up in a menu triggered by the left softkey, where they will be presented as menu items. Note that there is a set of predefined menu items (Back, Select) available by default in the same menu.

Because of the above considerations, it is more natural to use hyperlinks (<anchor> elements) for navigation in the Nokia 7110 rather than <do> elements, since the hyperlinks are easier to find. Understanding this point is key to optimizing usability on the 7110.

Entering Data on the 7110

If you have an <input> or a <select> element in your code for the user to enter data, you need to make it clear to the user how they can submit the data in order to move on to the next logical step.

If you use <do> elements, the 7110 browser will interpret it by adding an extra element in the menu triggered by the left softkey. Unfortunately, pressing the left softkey and looking for an item called 'move on' (or whatever you decided to call it) is very unnatural. Users will be at a loss about what to do after they entered the data.

The only sensible thing to do in these cases is to provide a hyperlink that will keep users going with one click:

> **Always provide a link to the following card after an <input> or <select> element (or after the last input-element in the case of elective forms).**

The following code snippet gives an example of using such an approach:

```
<p>
    Name please:
        <input type="text" name="searchkey" value="" />
        <a href="search.asp">Submit data</a>
</p>
```

The 7110 will render this code like this:

Note that the link shouldn't be too long, since links on multiple lines tend to be confusing.

Menu Navigation for the 7110

As we discussed earlier, designing your application as a tree structure is the best way to allow users to keep track of where they are. Menu navigation is a straightforward way to let your users access all of the different parts of your application laid out in a tree structure. An example of this is a list of e-mail messages, each leading to a card that displays the actual body of the message. Another typical example might be a list of operations (for example, read, send, delete and so on) that the user can trigger.

The best way to implement this for a Nokia 7110 is by building a menu as a list of anchors:

```
<a href="#band" title="find">Artist/Band</a>
<a href="#song" title="songs">Title/Song</a>
<a href="#top" title="top">Top 20</a>
<a href="#new" title="new">New Releases</a>
<a href="#conc" title="live">Concerts</a>
```

And this is how the card appears to the user:

Note that forcing users to do a lot of scrolling is not a good idea. If you need to display more than 9 or 10 items, you should add a link called 'more' as the last element in the list. In other words, you should split your links over several cards.

If you look at the code above, you will notice that no `<br />` tag is inserted at the end of each anchor. This is due to the particular behavior of the Nokia 7110, which displays anchors on a line by themselves. In other words, an anchor will break your WML flow, no matter what you do to avoid it. In the case of a navigation menu, this is not much of a problem.

If you want to support the Ericsson phones however, this might be a real showstopper for you. The Ericsson R320 and the R380 do not break the WML visual flow when they display anchors. You'll have to break lines explicitly, if you want to get a navigation item effect. This means that a navigation menu optimized for the 7110 won't be so usable on the Ericsson telephones, since all of the anchors will appear in a single long wrapped line.

Backward Navigation

The right softkey of the 7110 can only be used as a back button, and labeled as such. By default it has no action at all. However, if a `<do type="prev">` is defined for a card (or at the deck level, in a template) and no label is defined for it, then the right softkey will assume that action and the key will be labeled Back. You can override the behavior of the `prev` task by providing a different URL:

```
<do type="prev">
  <go href="home.wml" />
</do>
```

What you should never do, though, is to provide a label for the `<do>` element. In such a situation, the 7110 will remove the Back label from the right softkey and will create a new entry in the menu accessed through the left softkey. This is very confusing for the user, since they are accustomed to finding a back option on this menu at all times.

Guidelines for UP.Browser

As we saw above, `<do>` elements tend to have a marginal role on the Nokia 7110 browser and should only be used for rare path activities at most. However, on the UP.Browser `<do>` elements are the most important UI constructs, since they make sure that main path activities and semi main path activities are never more than one-click away.

The following diagram gives you an abstract view of the interface offered by the UP.Browser:

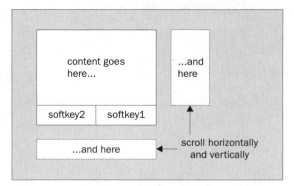

`<do type="accept">` elements are normally used to support main path activities and are mapped to softkey1. They are also called ACCEPT elements. Note that you should only have one ACCEPT task in each card. The WAP specification leaves rendering of multiple ACCEPT tasks up to the implementation of each device, so use multiple ACCEPTs with great caution. In the case of the UP.Browser they will be mapped to the available softkeys.

Other activities are supported through `<do type="options">` elements (OPTION elements) which are mapped to softkey2. If there are multiple OPTION elements, softkey2 will not be mapped onto a specific OPTION task, but will lead the user to a menu of all the existing OPTION elements.

Note that some UP.Browser phones support three softkeys. In that case, you can afford an ACCEPT task and two OPTION tasks without the need to go through an extra menu.

One final important note concerns the position of the softkeys. In the diagram above, softkey1 is represented on the right and softkey2 on the left. This is not always the case. Softkeys occupy different positions in different implementations of the UP.Browser, which is particularly important to note if you find yourself writing documentation for your application. Writing things like "Press the right button" might not be correct in all cases.

Hyperlinks shadow `<do type="accept">` elements momentarily. Suppose you have a link like the one shown below:

```
<a href="new.wml" title="New">Jump to new</a>
```

If the user scrolls to it, then the label of softkey1 becomes the same as the title of the link. The rationale behind this is always the same: let users do the most natural thing with one click. If the user moves focus to a link, then clicking on that link is the activity the user most likely wants to perform.

This will be a lot clearer if we look at a concrete example:

```
<do type="accept" label="Key1">
  <go href="key1.wml" />
</do>

<do type="option" label="Key2">
  <go href="key2.wml" />
</do>
<p>
Some text...
```

```
      <a href="new.wml" title="New">Jump to new</a>
   More text...
   </p>
   </card>
```

The screenshot shows how this appears to the user:

The Phone.com user interface guidelines for the UP.Browser recommend that no more than a couple of hyperlinks per card are used for navigation. Navigation is normally performed with <do> elements or with <select> elements, as you'll see shortly. Providing additional navigation by inserting extra links at the end of the card is confusing, since users will have to scroll back to have the softkey1 point at the main path activity again. Of course, this is in sharp contrast to how you do things on the 7110, where links are used for just about everything.

Entering Data on UP.Browser

When it comes to entering data, the UP.Browser does not require the presence of a link to be usable. A <do> element is usually the best bet:

```
<do type="accept" label="Send">
   <go href="receive.asp" />
</do>
<p>
   name please:
   <input type="text" name="username" value="" />
</p>
```

This code will produce:

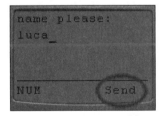

If you insert a navigation link after the input element, as you should do with the 7110, the mechanism will still work, but will not be nearly as usable:

```
<p>
   name please:
   <input type="text" name="username" value="" />
   <a href="receive.asp" title="Send">Submit data</a>
</p>
```

In fact, this construct will require no less than three clicks to post the data with the above code (remember that no link is selected by default, otherwise the accept key would not be visible):

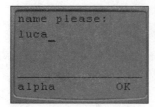 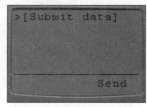

Menu Navigation for UP.Browser

If you implement menu navigation the same way as you would on the 7110 (using links), the UP.Browser will work satisfactorily. However, you would also lose a feature that UP.Browser supports to facilitate navigation for slightly more advanced users.

The code below implements menu navigation in the optimal way for the UP.Browser:

```
<select>
    <option onpick="#band" title="find">Artist/Band</option>
    <option onpick="#song" title="songs">Title/Song</option>
    <option onpick="#top" title="top">Top 20</option>
    <option onpick="#new" title="new">New Releases</option>
    <option onpick="#conc" title="live">Concerts</option>
</select>
```

Here is how UP.Browser will render this:

The numbers on the left are shortcuts. If you implement navigation menus in this way, UP.Browser users will not be required to scroll to the menu item of their choice, since they can press the relevant number on their keypads and trigger the onpick event for the corresponding menu choice.

Since this is standard WML, you might wonder what this looks like on the 7110. In principle it works, but since users are first taken to a new pseudo-card that implements the menu and the onpick event makes the flow hop from the pseudo-card directly into a new card, the result for the end-user is very confusing.

The general rule of avoiding having more than 9 or 10 menu items in a card is valid also for the UP.Browser, with the additional reasoning that menu choices above 9 do not have a shortcut number associated with them.

Backward Navigation

Phones that deploy the UP.Browser always have a physical key mapped to *Back* functionality – a hard wired back button.

The Generic Approach

Usability is one of the biggest challenges WAP developers have to tackle. What we see today is that the two major WAP browsers on the market interpret WML in very different ways, yet both browsers roughly comply with the core WAP 1.1 specifications.

The question now concerns the best approach for the development of cross-browser applications that work well enough on most of the current mobile phones. One possibility is, of course, to develop multiple versions of an application or to rely on XSL transformations (see Chapter 9). Another way to address this issue is to write WML code that is generic enough to work well and still be usable in the different implementations.

The basic idea behind this generic approach is to identify a subset of WML that both browsers interpret in a more or less usable way. In this section, we will look at which WML constructs deliver usable interface elements on both the Nokia 7110 browser and the UP.Browser.

To what extent this solution is really usable will be up to you (and the users of your application) to decide. It probably depends on the nature and the complexity of your application. A mixed solution is also possible. You can build an application that implements some modules according to the generic browser paradigm, while other modules are customized for each browser. For your convenience, we have included some routines for browser detection at the end of the chapter.

Guidelines for the Generic Approach

The generic approach is an attempt at defining the lowest common denominator features of WML that work acceptably well on the two main browsers. In this final section of the chapter, we will step through some of the constructs described for each specific browser and look at those that can satisfy the usability requirement of both browsers at the same time.

Entering data

As we have seen, the 7110 requires the use of hyperlinks, whereas, it is more straightforward to use a <do> element on the UP.Browser. Using <do> elements on the Nokia 7110 is not acceptable. On the other hand, a link introduces two extra steps on the UP.Browser. However, nothing prevents you from using both a link and a <do> element in the same card. The example we saw earlier can be modified as follows to support both:

```
<card id="card1" title="mycard">
   <do type="accept" label="Send">
      <go href="receive.asp" />
   </do>
   <p>
      name please:
      <input type="text" name="username" value="" />
      <a href="receive.asp" title="Send">Submit data</a>
   </p>
</card>
```

In the UP.Browser, users will be able to navigate with the Accept button after they have acknowledged the text they wrote in the form. As far as the Nokia is concerned, users will get a link after the input form. So it is business as usual for them.

Menu Navigation

No matter how useful the shortcuts supported by the onpick attribute of the <option> element on the UP.Browser are, the lack of support for this feature on the 7110 means that you should implement menu navigation with a list of links. The list of links works well on the UP.Browser, after all. The problem for those who intend to support the Ericsson R320 remains, though.

Activities Of Different Kinds

Since <do> elements produce interfaces with bad usability on the 7110, one big problem for complex cross-browser applications is how to map the different kinds of activities we may have specified during design onto a usable interface for the 7110. Giving guidelines in the area is not simple, and it could probably be a branch of research by itself. You will have to work out a solution according to your project and its aims. Hopefully, this chapter has given you the framework to analyze the situation.

User Agent Recognition Techniques

The last part of this chapter illustrates some generic server-side code to facilitate user agent detection. This is the base for building separate applications for different browsers. In practice, you can use any server-side web technology to identify requests coming from different kind of devices. This means that rather than feeding generic WML code to each device, you will have a chance to send different versions of the code, each customized for a family of WAP devices. This is an excellent way to map the same start URL to the different versions of the application.

There are several classes of web clients in the world that could potentially access your site. Here are the client families that we focus on in this section:

❑ HTML clients

❑ A Nokia 7110

❑ A device with the UP.Browser v3.1 or 4.x which supports WML 1.1

In the future, you may want to customize these routines to recognize different user agents as well, and we'll be seeing more about this in Chapter 9.

The following code snippets show how you can perform user agent identification in three commonly deployed server development platforms: Perl, Java servlets and ASP.

To identify which client is accessing your site, we consider two different HTTP headers: the HTTP_ACCEPT and HTTP_USER_AGENT. While neither of these are part of the WAP specifications, they are both standard HTTP headers and are defined in RFC1945. The first step when trying to identify the client is to look at the HTTP_ACCEPT header, and search for the inclusion of a WML string.

In Perl, we have:

```
#!/usr/local/bin/perl

$acc = $ENV{"HTTP_ACCEPT"}; #read the list of accepted MIME-types
$ua = $ENV{"HTTP_USER_AGENT"}; #read the User Agent ID string

if ($acc =~ "wml"){
```

```
#is "wml" among the list of accepted types?
#deliver wml
}
else{
    print' Location: http://mysite.com/index.html'."\n\n";
}
```

And in Java:

```java
public void doGet (HttpServletRequest req, HttpServletResponse res)
    throws ServletException, IOException{
        String acc = req.getHeader("Accept");
        //read the list of accepted MIME-types
        String ua = req.getHeader("User-Agent");
        // read the User Agent ID string
        ServletOutputStream out = res.getOutputStream();

        if (acc.indexOf("wml") != -1){
        // is "wml" among the list of accepted types?
        //deliver wml
        }
        else {
            res.setHeader(res.SC_MOVED_TEMPORARILY);
            res.setHeader("Location", "http://mysite.com/index.html");
        }
```

And in ASP:

```asp
<%response.buffer="true"

    Dim accstring
    Dim uastring
    'read the User Agent ID string
    uastring = request.ServerVariables("HTTP_USER_AGENT")
    'read the list of accepted MIME-types
    accstring = request.ServerVariables("HTTP_ACCEPT")

    If (InStr(accstring,"wml")) Then
        'is "wml" among the list of accepted types?
        'Deliver wml
    Else
        Response.Redirect("/index.html")
%>
```

In all of these cases, it has been established that the client sends WML using the HTTP_ACCEPT header, and we can thus assume that WML should be delivered. If WML is not found in the ACCEPT list, HTML will be delivered. This will ensure that HTML is delivered to web browsers and spiders/crawlers/site indexers. Another browser, Opera, also provides "wml" as an accepted MIME-type. Chances are that more and more of such strange creatures will be around in the future. This means that you might want to build more complex user agent analysis in your specific case.

Once a WML device is found, it is possible to see exactly which device is accessing the site. Three possibilities are accounted for in this code: the UP.Browser from Phone.com, a Nokia 7110, and any other device.

In Perl:

```
if ($ua =~"UP"){
    Print "Location: /phonecom/index.wml \n\n";
}
elseif($ua =~"Nokia"){
    print "Location: /nokia/index.wml \n\n";
}
else{
    print "Location: /generic/index.wml \n\n";
}
```

And in Java:

```
if (ua.indexOf("UP") != -1){
    res.setHeader(res.SC_MOVED_TEMPORARILY);
    res.setHeader("Location", "/phonecom/index.wml");
}
else if(ua.indexOf("Nokia") != -1){
    res.setHeader(res.SC_MOVED_TEMPORARILY);
    res.setHeader("Location", "/nokia/index.wml");
}
else{
    res.setHeader(res.SC_MOVED_TEMPORARILY);
    res.setHeader("Location", "/generic/index.wml");
}
```

ASP:

```
If(InStr(uastring, "UP")) Then
    Response.Redirect("/phonecom/index.wml")
ElsIf(InStr(uastring, "Nokia"))
    Response.Redirect("/nokia/index.wml")
Else
    Response.Redirect("/generic/index.wml")
End If
```

Summary

In this chapter we have looked at what usability is, and how to implement good usability in our applications.

While cross-browser usability is hard to achieve, general principles for good WAP design do exist, and we have covered these here. We then moved on to specific usability guidelines for the Nokia 7110 and the UP.Browser. Finally, we looked at how we might apply some of these ideas in a more generic approach, in order to create usable applications that are targeted at more than one user agent type.

Here is a quick summary of the top 5 usability tips you should always remember:

❑ Identify and implement the top 20% of functionality of existing applications

❑ Build a map of the most common user activities

❑ Minimize data entry for the user

❑ Make any displayed text terse

❑ Test with real users as much as possible and as soon as possible

Part Three

Generating Dynamic WAP Content

So far in this book, we have only seen how to write static WML pages, but as with web development, we can use any existing server-side technology to implement our WAP services. Many web sites can provide valuable content by means of static HTML files, but dynamic content goes a long way in providing precious extra functionalities, and greater interactivity for the end-user. While wireless technologies will never compete in functionality and usability with their web counterparts, dynamic sites are still very important. There are two main reasons for this:

❑   The value of wireless services is 'on the road' access. WAP users are looking for specific information, rather than surfing, so it's very important that the information is as up-to-date as possible; static WML has very limited use in the WAP world.

❑   Frequently, we will want to take the same information from a data store and display it via WAP, a traditional web browser, or any other device that comes along. To achieve this, we need a data-centric design, with our WAP decks created along side our web pages, from the same data store, using a server-side technology.

In this part of the book, we'll take a look at some diverse server-side technologies that can be utilized for dynamic generation of WAP content. We'll start with ASP (Microsoft's Active Server Pages) in Chapter 8. Chapter 9 focuses on XML, and how we can use this, at the center of a design that allows access to a site from multiple client device types. Along the way, we'll incorporate some of the strategies proposed by the W3C for mobile Internet access. In Chapter 10, we move across to the world of Java, and examine the use of JSPs for generating WML decks. This method is compared with the use of XSLT for transforming data into the final output format. Finally, in Chapter 11, we take a look at ColdFusion, find out some of the advantages that this tool provides for WAP development, and learn some tricks and techniques for developing WAP applications using ColdFusion.

Some of these technologies may interest you more than others, so you may pick and mix among these chapters as you please. There are brief introductions to the subject area in each chapter, so you should be able to understand all the examples that follow, even if you are not familiar with the technology.

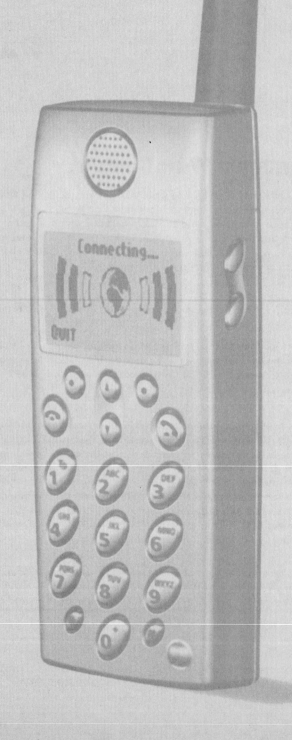

8

ASP and WAP

ASP is a server-side technology from Microsoft for the dynamic generation of web content. By allowing you to embed script in HTML or WML code, ASP makes it possible to keep the content that the application will ship to the client clear – and therefore eases maintenance. This has the advantage of speeding up prototyping and development of applications.

We will see that, while it is simple to learn, ASP allows us to build enterprise level applications with comparative eases and that those applications, if designed well, are flexible and scalable.

In this chapter, we will take a brief tour of ASP and find out how ASP can be used to access data through ADO (ActiveX Data Objects). From there, we will discover how we can use the power of ASP in WAP development.

Finally, we'll demonstrate these principles in practice by examining an application based around a fictitious radio station, which offers a WAP service where a listener can choose a song from the play list and dedicate it to someone.

Active Server Pages

This section will serve as a whistle-stop tour of ASP. If you are already familiar with this technology, you may want to skip this part of the chapter and move straight on to the example. If you are new to ASP, you should find enough information in this chapter to get you started, and to follow the example included at the end. Along the way, you should see the potential for ASP as a web and WAP development tool. If you want to find out more about it, try *Professional ASP 3.0* from Wrox Press.

ASP is Microsoft's alternative to CGI scripts and Java servlets. Just like those technologies, ASP lets a web server, (usually IIS, which we will assume is the case for the purposes of this chapter), interact with databases and other systems, including e-mail, file systems, and others.

There are third-party ports of ASP to UNIX platforms by a company called Chili!Soft
(http://www.chilisoft.com/). In spite of this, ASP is most closely associated with
Windows NT and IIS.

ASP was initially shipped with version 3.0 of Microsoft's Internet Information Server (IIS). When IIS
receives a request for a page with a .asp extension the following sequence of events occurs:

❑ Any server-side code that is embedded in the WML or HTML markup is executed (this may
result in the addition of dynamic content).

❑ The resultant file is forwarded to the browser.

This two-stage process, where the server executes nested scripting code, allows us to create pages on the
fly. This enables us to add content to the page that is time- or user-specific.

The power of ASP lies in three extremely important aspects:

❑ It makes building dynamic applications easy.

❑ It is simple, so developers can move over to ASP with ease and absolute beginners can pick
up the concepts quickly.

❑ It lets developers make use of **components** to build complex web-based services.

Components are reusable objects that provide a consistent access method from multiple development
environments. These objects include those that are part of the OS, those that are shipped with other
proprietary products, and those that you create yourself (in languages such as Visual Basic or C++).
Components often include simple and elegant access to a set of complex functions, allowing code re-use
and reducing maintenance cost. (More about this later.)

Another useful aspect of ASP is its flexibility. You can use different scripting languages to implement
your pages, for example VBScript, JScript, and even a creature called PerlScript
(http://www.activestate.com/). In spite of this, the scripting language that's most commonly used
by ASP programmers is VBScript – and this is what we'll use for the remainder of this chapter. (Much of
the ASP terminology is influenced by Visual Basic.)

As far as VBScript syntax is concerned, you won't need to be an expert to follow the examples in this
chapter – as long as you are familiar with basic programming concepts, the code presented here won't
require specific VBScript knowledge.

Installation

ASP ships with Microsoft Internet Information Server. Windows 2000 contains the latest release of IIS,
(version 5.0). This means that if you have Windows 2000 you already possess all you need to start
playing around with ASP. In Windows 2000 Server it is installed as standard, but Professional Edition
requires you to install IIS separately. If you have Windows NT 4.0, all you need to do is install Option
Pack 4 for NT. This will install IIS version 4.0 on your PC, which will be more than sufficient to run
these examples.

While ASP 1.0 pretty much belongs to the past, you might have to deal with ASP 2.0 on WinNT 4
for some time. The examples presented in this chapter will run on ASP 2.0 as well as ASP 3.0, but
you should be aware of the existence of the different versions of ASP once you go looking for
other resources.

The examples provided here use Microsoft Access 2000 as a database backend, but the concepts introduced apply to every common database. Since we're using ADO, it would be easy enough to substitute another database, for example, SQL Server – for reasons that will become apparent when we discuss this technology in a little while.

Creating Dynamic Pages with ASP

HTML pages can be turned into Active Server Pages simply by changing their file extensions to `.asp`. If you then point your browser at one of these pages you should notice... nothing different at all. Without adding any extra ASP code there will be almost no effect regarding how the page looks or functions. Almost, but not quite – there will be a slight performance hit, because the server needs to process the page. However, the latest version of ASP (version 3.0) makes this performance hit negligible, so there is a definite argument for using the `.asp` extension for all of your files, making it easier to add ASP specific code at a later date to enhance your applications.

What about WML? Well, the principle is exactly the same. However, in addition to changing the extension of WML files to `.asp` there is one more thing to do. By default, IIS will forward the contents of an ASP file to the browser using the MIME type for HTML, which will be rejected by a WAP device. So, we just need to tell the server to use the MIME type for WML (`text/vnd.wap.wml`). Let's take a simple example and see how we do this.

We'll start off with a plain WML file:

```
<!DOCTYPE wml PUBLIC "-//WAPFORUM//DTD WML 1.1//EN"
"http://www.wapforum.org/DTD/wml_1.1.xml">
<wml>
   <card title="My WAP Site">
      <p>
         Welcome to my site.
      </p>
   </card>
</wml>
```

To turn this into an ASP file we just need to give it a `.asp` extension and add the following line of code:

```
<% Response.ContentType = "text/vnd.wap.wml" %>
<!DOCTYPE wml PUBLIC "-//WAPFORUM//DTD WML 1.1//EN"
"http://www.wapforum.org/DTD/wml_1.1.xml">
<wml>
   <card title="My WAP Site">
      <p>
         Welcome to my site.
      </p>
   </card>
</wml>
```

The `<%` and `%>` characters delimit sections of script in an ASP file, and within these delimiters we are setting the MIME type (with a command that we'll look at in more detail later).

We can insert scripting code in more than one place in the file, even embedding it inside the WML content. For example, we could add the following:

```
<% Response.ContentType = "text/vnd.wap.wml" %>
<!DOCTYPE wml PUBLIC "-//WAPFORUM//DTD WML 1.1//EN"
"http://www.wapforum.org/DTD/wml_1.1.xml">
```

```
<wml>
   <card title="My WAP Site">
      <p>
         Welcome to my site.
         The time is now <%=Now()%>
      </p>
   </card>
</wml>
```

This would insert a string representing the current time (the result of a call to the VBScript Now()
function), resulting in text along the lines of:

Welcome to my site. The time is now 5/24/2000 9:36:50 PM.

Behind the scenes, IIS forwards the static part of the ASP page to the browser, but takes care of running
the server-side code, replacing any <%-%> blocks with the output produced by the code they contain (if
any). Note that the '<%-%>' notation is a short form for:

```
<SCRIPT LANGUAGE="...." RUNAT="SERVER">
   :
</SCRIPT>
```

This specifies the language used, and that the code should be run at the server. If the RUNAT attribute is
not specified, the script is sent to the client for execution. The default language for IIS is VBScript,
although many developers prefer to use JavaScript. As a result, if you are coding in VBScript, you need
not specify the language used. It is possible to change this default using:

```
<%@LANGUAGE="language"%>
```

where language is the language to be used.

ASP Object Model

Before the advent of ASP, programmers using Perl and CGI required in-depth knowledge of HTTP. For
example, it was necessary to know exactly how parameters were passed to scripts, and what HTTP
headers scripts were supposed to produce. ASP simplifies this significantly. While an understanding of
low-level details won't hurt, the learning curve for web (and WAP) application development is much
shallower with ASP.

ASP defines a set of **objects** that encapsulate many of the low-level details. These take the grunt work
away from the developer. What traditionally took many lines of CGI programming can often be
handled by a single call to an ASP object. ASP programmers are presented with familiar programming
concepts, such as objects, methods, collections and variables. These concepts are applied to what is
known as the **ASP object model**.

> *An object model is a description of the details of the object structure, relationships between objects,
> and other object-oriented features and functions. In short, an object model is the object-oriented
> version of what was once called an API (Application Programming Interface).*

Note that the ASP object model and the scripting language used to access it are independent of one
another. As we saw earlier, you can use many scripting languages in your ASP development.

The main ASP objects you need to be aware of to get started are Request, Response, Application, Session, and Server. ASP 3.0 also introduces a new object: ASPError. Let's take a look at each of these intrinsic ASP objects.

Request Object

The Request object encapsulates all the information that a user agent sends to the web server. In this section we'll look at a few of the more commonly used aspects of this object – for a more comprehensive overview you should check out an ASP reference guide.

We have already seen that in WAP (like the Web) data entered by a user in an application can be sent back to the server using HTTP GET or POST. If GET is used, then the parameters are piggybacked on the URL as a query string, and are accessible in ASP via the Request object as a collection called (sensibly enough) QueryString. Parameters sent back to the server using POST are available as the Form collection of the Request object. We can access the QueryString collection by typing Request.QueryString. To put this into an easier to understand context, we could get the value of yourname in the URL above using the following statement:

```
Request.QueryString("yourname")
```

And we can output this into a WML page using, for example:

```
<b>Welcome <% =Request.QueryString("yourname") %>!</b>
```

In addition to these parameters, cookies are also available – if they are supported (more on this later). You can get to these cookies through the Request.Cookies collection.

> *Briefly, cookies are a way of storing information on the user agent using an application. This information is often used for identifying the user in subsequent visits and forms the basis for personalized services. We'll discuss cookies, and personalization in general, in more detail later in this chapter.*

Finally, Request.ServerVariables is a collection that contains all of the traditional info about HTTP request coming from the client, such as IP address, user agent identification string, and the HTTP header content.

Response Object

The Response object can be regarded as a server response 'launching pad' to the client's request. Basically, our ASP application builds the response message, by means of the Response object, one piece at a time and sends it back to the client when it's ready. You can add custom HTTP headers, set cookies for your domain, and add content via this object.

One of the most often used methods of the Response object is Write. This method allows us to output text directly into our HTML or WML files. For example, we could replace the code from the last section:

```
<b>Welcome <% =Request.QueryString("yourname") %>!</b>
```

with:

```
Response.Write "<b>Welcome " & Request.QueryString("yourname") & "!</b>"
```

Here, the & operator is used to concatenate strings, and get exactly the same effect. The choice of which approach we take when outputting this kind of text is largely arbitrary.

Buffering

There are two strategies to building a page or deck in response to user request. One possibility is to buffer the output of your page and send sections, when the buffer is full, at appropriate places through the deck or when the ASP page terminates. This can lead to better performance for the server, but in the case of long pages, users might perceive the system as slow. In fact, buffering is on by default in IIS 3.0. In IIS 2.0 it was off by default. Buffering can be useful in those special cases when you need to reserve the possibility of aborting the execution of a page.

If buffering is disabled, then each line of markup language your page produces will be flushed to the user agent as soon as it is sent to the Response object.

The Response object can be used to control this buffering, using the code shown below:

```
<%
    Response.Buffer = True    'or False, if you wish to disable buffering
%>
```

Note that VBScript uses the ' character to specify that the rest of a line of code is a comment, which will be ignored when the script is executed.

If buffering is on, you can also flush sections of content by means of the Response.Flush method. Let's look at an example use of the Response object. The snippet of code below shows how cache control for WAP devices can be effectively achieved in ASP:

```
<%
    Response.ContentType = "text/vnd.wap.wml"

    'disable caching of this deck
    Response.Expires = -1
    Response.AddHeader "Pragma", "no-cache"
    Response.AddHeader "Cache-Control", "no-cache, must-revalidate"
%>
```

A deck containing this code will be refreshed each time it is accessed – the WAP device will not keep a cached copy.

Session Object

In any moderately advanced web application, you may wish to collect information about the users who are currently using your application. Initially, this was not simple to do because of the inherently stateless nature of HTTP. This changed with the introduction of **cookies** – which are small pieces of text data. ASP goes one step further and defines Session objects, which are capable of maintaining context information for each user accessing your site. In fact, these objects are themselves implemented through cookies – you just don't see this going on. All this implies two things:

❑ You can't use the Session object if cookies aren't supported (see the *Cookies* section below for more details on this).

❑ If you have cookies, the Session object represents a very useful abstraction to track your users without needing to build such a system using low-level cookie management.

Different Session objects are normally active on a web server – one for each user connected to the web site. Each Session object is discarded if the associated client does not request a page within a predefined amount of time – to save on server resources. Web clients do not tell web servers when they are done; this makes the automatic disposal necessary.

In the example below, you see the code used to measure how many times a user hits the same page. For each user, a variable named hits is instantiated within that user's Session object:

```
Session("hits") = Session("hits") + 1
```

The code would typically go in the top of the page and accumulates the number of times that the user has viewed a certain page by adding 1 to the hits variable each time the code page is requested.

Application Object

The Application object is created as soon as the first ASP on your web server is requested. It stores variables and object references that must be available for all of the pages on your site. These values are global to the application. They do not contain user specific information and any amendments to it, as a result of code execution, will be reflected across the whole application. This object is often used to execute initialization code for the whole web application.

Server Object

The Server object has methods for handling interaction with the scripting environment. Most notable is the Server.CreateObject method to instantiate other (COM) objects.

ASPError Object

The ASPError object is new in ASP 3.0. It contains information about the last error that occurred in the application. Error handling is not renowned for being particularly simple in ASP 2.0 and this is Microsoft's answer to it. While this object becomes pretty important when building large applications, it won't be necessary in the simple application presented later in this chapter.

Cookies

Cookies, and session management in general, deserve a big aside. Strictly speaking cookies are not part of the WAP 1.1 specification, and it is currently very rare for a WAP device to support them. However, many gateways (most notably the UP.Link) can store cookies on behalf of devices. The main reason for cookies not to exist on a WAP device is that they are costly (in terms of processing power and memory) to implement.

Cookies, where available, allow us to create personalized applications with ease. We can store information about the user in cookies, retrieving them when necessary to speed access to our applications – a user need not, for example, enter their name every time they come to a site where names are important.

Unfortunately, we cannot currently rely on the availability of cookies. One possible alternative may be to emulate the hidden field functionality of the Web. Before the emergence of cookies, developers used fields that were not visible on the web page to store information about the user. The same effect can be achieved in WML by using postfield elements. This would normally be done by providing a login form for your user, and once the user has logged in, the user name and any other data required can be passed from deck to deck.

Between sessions, the information is held in a database that is linked with the user's name and password or PIN number. This solution requires a heavier infrastructure and will increase both development time and load on the server. It may console you to know that cookie support is part of the WAP 1.2 spec.

One thing to remember is that while many applications will be aimed at the international arena, often services are developed for a specific set of users whether grouped by locality or by company. In this case, the environment the application is deployed in is much more predictable and will often determine whether you will use cookies or not.

A Simple Example

To illustrate some of the more important points from the discussion above, let's look at a simple example. Imagine we want to get some user feedback for your WAP site, in the form of a simple rating system where users can give our site a mark out of 5. The input required for this uses standard WML – a list box where the user can choose one to five stars. We'll take this input and use the `<postfield>` element to send it to an ASP page that will frame an appropriate response to the submission (we won't worry about storing responses for now).

As we discussed earlier, we might as well make all of our files ASP files, this won't affect performance noticeably, and would make our life easier if we wanted to add functionality later (we wouldn't have to change all the references to the filename). So, the 5-star rating card will be contained in the following file, `send.asp`:

```
<% Response.ContentType = "text/vnd.wap.wml" %>
<?xml version="1.0"?>
<!DOCTYPE wml PUBLIC "-//WAPFORUM//DTD WML 1.1//EN"
"http://www.wapforum.org/DTD/wml_1.1.xml">
<wml>
    <card id="rating" title="Rating">
        <p>
            How do you rate our site?<br/>
            <select iname="R" title="Rating">
                <option>*</option>
                <option>**</option>
                <option>***</option>
                <option>****</option>
                <option>*****</option>
            </select>
            <anchor>Submit
                <go href="receive.asp">
                    <postfield name="Rating" value="$(R)"/>
                </go>
            </anchor>
        </p>
    </card>
</wml>
```

The file that accepts the rating submission, `receive.asp`, is more interesting. In the first section of this file, we set the content type, extract the rating from the query string, and start composing our deck:

```
<%
    Response.ContentType = "text/vnd.wap.wml"
    Rating = Request.QueryString("Rating")
%>
<?xml version="1.0"?>
```

```
<!DOCTYPE wml PUBLIC "-//WAPFORUM//DTD WML 1.1//EN"
"http://www.wapforum.org/DTD/wml_1.1.xml">
<wml>
    <card id="respond" title="Thanks!">
        <do type="prev">
            <prev/>
        </do>
        <p>
            You gave our site <%=Rating%> star(s).
```

We place the value of the parameter into a variable, which we'll call `Rating` for simplicity, and output this value to confirm it with the user. Next, we use some more script to see if the rating given was any good (we'll assume here that 3 or more stars is good, and less is bad). We can conditionally output text based on this comparison and finish the deck:

```
<%
    If Rating >= 3 Then
%>
            Nice one! Come back anytime!
<%
    Else
%>
            Ah well. We tried.
<%
    End If
%>
        </p>
    </card>
</wml>
```

The way in which script can be broken up like this allows you to create quite complex dynamic content.

ADO (ActiveX Data Objects)

You are only really scraping the surface of ASP if you don't make use of its data access capabilities. Once we have a database behind our application, we can deploy ASP and ADO components to make the data in your database available through the Internet. ADO is the object model provided by Microsoft for general data access.

Before we begin, let's examine the reasons for using a database, or some other form of data repository, to build your WAP applications.

Database-centric Web Applications

Most web applications that offer some moderately advanced service are **database-centric** (or database-driven). This means that a database is located at the center of the system architecture and most (if not all) of the content is located in it. There are two typical motivations for database-centric applications:

❑   You already have a database full of valuable data, and the Internet gives us an excellent way to expose that data.

❑   You need to implement a dynamic web or WAP service.

In any moderately complex application there is a need to separate content and presentation. By centralizing the source of data, synchronization of data is simplified. To give one example: if the company logo changes, how many places do we have to modify code to make it appear? Keeping this kind of information together in one place makes such modifications simple. With a centralized data source, it is also possible to apply several interfaces to the data source thus allowing various levels of access to the data (for security reasons, perhaps). We can upgrade the interface independently to the data and maintenance of the data is more efficient.

No matter how skillful you become with web or WAP programming, the lack of a data repository is going to be a severe bottleneck for application's scalability. Any moderately complex Internet service is built around some form of dynamic data. This means that we'll need to update the content of a complex site quite often, in order to provide a constant flow of valuable information with which to attract users.

Another requirement, of course, is to provide the data in a form that is easy to access and functional. The key design consideration here is the separation of your valuable data and the way it is presented to end-users. The emergence of alternate data access devices such as WAP devices, PDA's and others yet to come, have made this need even more pressing. Each type of device, and even model, requires a different interface, and various levels of data. On top of this, each device has different requirements for the format of the data.

Traditional data stores are, of course, relational databases, but the nature of the Internet is changing this to some extent. Increasingly, data is not stored in RDBMS (Relational Database Management System) sources. E-mails, faxes, XML data, and web pages are just a few examples of valuable information we need to access in our daily life. For the rest of chapter, though, we will focus on database use as it remains the most widely used data storage system.

To summarize, the advantages of possessing a database-centric system are:

❑ **It's easier to keep your information up to date**. Data synchronization and maintenance is made easier.

❑ **You can base site navigation on content**. By using dynamic data discovery, we are able to base the site navigation on the available content. Inserting new content to the database would automatically add that content to the site. It also means that we do not need to update links in the site when moving content.

❑ **Users interactive experience is enhanced.** Databases are optimized for quick retrieval of information. This means that we can make large amounts of information available with a minimum performance hit.

Hopefully, this will have convinced you that databases are necessary for any moderately complex web and WAP site.

UDA

UDA **(Universal Data Access)** is a term used by Microsoft to identify its combined set of standards for data access. The latest trend in data access is to both view and access data in a consistent way. This stands in sharp contrast with the old view of data grouped in different categories. The traditional approach for controlling access to such a varied mass of information was to import the data into a relational database and then access it from there. The UDA approach is to leave information where it is, while the tools to access the information are enhanced to analyze and manipulate the information. ADO applies the UDA concept by exposing information in standard ways.

ActiveX Data Objects (ADO) 2.5

ADO is complex, and so explaining all of it here is not feasible. You can find more information in *Professional ADO 2.5 Programming* from Wrox Press. However, we will cover enough of ADO here to follow the example later on.

Before we can explain ADO we will first need to look at OLE DB, an access method that abstracts data sources. OLE DB is a set of interfaces that allows uniform access to data stored in diverse data sources. If you are familiar with database programming, OLE DB (Open Linking and Embedding DataBases) is a post-web alternative to ODBC (Open Database Connectivity), a database programming interface from Microsoft that provides a common language for Windows applications to access databases on a network. The problem with ODBC was that it revolved around a pre-web view of data access. In that view, applications were better served by maintaining an open connection to the database. In today's web world in which hundreds of users access the same database simultaneously, that approach is not scalable.

The diagram below shows the relationship between the data sources, various data access technologies, and the languages used:

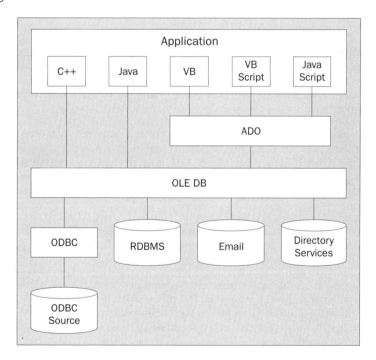

ADO is a further layer on top of OLE DB. ADO simplifies the use of OLE DB by providing the functionality of the default interface. The goal of ADO is to implement a consistent, language independent object model to allow applications access to data regardless of the specific data source containing them. ADO is responsible for providing a common object model that is available to multiple programming languages. Scripting languages and Visual Basic, for example, can use ADO, but cannot use OLE DB directly. To add to this, there is an OLE DB provider for ODBC. This means that ADO with OLE DB can access virtually any data source around.

The ADO 2.5 Object Model

All of the concepts above should be useful to us now that we come to look at the conceptual framework around ADO. In this section, we'll focus on the ADO object model and look at some code examples. Before delving into the code, let's look at the main logical steps to connect to a database with ADO:

❑ First of all, you need to create an object that will manage all the aspects of connecting to the database.

❑ The second step is to provide the object with all of the information it needs to connect to the database.

❑ The last step is to invoke the command that will open the connection.

ADO offers several ways to perform these operations. Connecting to a database with ADO is made simple by the fact that ADO creates some objects for you implicitly. If the configuration of the default object is good enough for you, then you are can write very compact code. On the other hand, if there are aspects of the connection that you need to control, you can still declare those objects explicitly and assign a non-default configuration to them.

The three main ADO objects are the Connection object, the Command object and the Recordset object.

The Connection object manages the connection to a data store. Through the Connection object, we can specify which OLE DB provider we wish to use. We can connect to a database without explicitly creating this object. If you create a Recordset or a Command object, then a Connection object is created automatically when a connection is needed, as long as the other objects have been told about the details of the connection.

If we need to optimize the system if is often better to create Connection objects explicitly. If you run several commands against a provider, then explicitly creating a connection is more efficient, since ADO won't need to create a new Connection object each time you run a command as it does when you delegate the connection to the recordset. A Connection object can also execute commands (SQL Commands or stored procedures) against the data source, and automatically create Recordset objects to hold the results.

The Command object is used to run commands against the data source. It is used when we need to give parameters to stored procedures, pre-written queries that are tailored to specific users by the inclusion of parameters.

The Recordset object is probably the most often used object in ADO, since this is the object that contains the data we extract from the database (or, more generally, the data store) when running a query on it. You can think of a recordset as a super-array. When you obtain a Recordset object as a result of a query, you can view that data in different ways, either by iterating through it or by requesting specific fields to view.

There are two other ADO objects: the Record object and the Stream object. However, they are not relevant to this chapter, and so will not be discussed here

Connecting to a Database

In order to keep things relatively simple, we will be connecting to the database, running queries, and closing the connection in the ASP page itself. In a real life scenario it would be worth considering writing a component that would take care of this. This would keep database specific information apart from the presentation part of the application.

We first create a `Connection` object, using the `Server.CreateObject` method:

```
Dim conn
Set conn = Server.CreateObject("ADODB.Connection")
```

This object encapsulates all of the properties we need to set to establish a connection with the database. The next part is specifying a `ConnectionString`, containing all of the data ADO needs to connect to a database: server address, DSN (Data Source Name), username, password, and whatever else the database requires in order to accept a connection.

If you are wondering whether to use a DSN or the full connection string you should bear it in mind that there is a negligible delay in using DSNs. On the other hand, DSNs keep connection details out of our code and allow us to change the data source without amending code.

As a final note, it is worth using the native OLE DB provider rather than going through ODBC as is the default for access. Doing this will give an improvement is performance.

For your information, here is what the connection string to MS SQL server through the native OLE DB provider looks like:

```
Conn.ConnectionString = "Provider=SQLOLEDB;Data Source = ServerName;Initial
Catalog = wap; User Id=luca;Password=wap"
```

Once you have a suitable connection string in place, connecting to the database is simple:

```
conn.Open
```

Not too difficult, is it? From this moment on, you can pass the `conn` object to any other ADO object in need of a connection.

Querying the Database

Opening connections to a database is not particularly useful until you submit a query. In order to talk to a database, you need to build a query, execute the query against the database, and create a recordset to store the result of your query.

Here is the code to run a basic query against a database, which for now we'll assume contains a list of songs along with their performers:

```
Dim rs
Set rs = Server.CreateObject("ADODB.Recordset")    ' create a Recordset

Dim SQLString
SQLString = "SELECT song_id,title FROM songs WHERE artist = ""Eurythmics"";"
rs.Open SQLString, conn
Response.Write rs("title") & " by Eurythmics"
```

The `Recordset` object is now ready to store the result of a query.

```
Dim SQLString
SQLString = "SELECT song_id,title FROM songs WHERE artist = ""Eurythmics"";"
```

The query above will return the id and title of every Eurythmics song stored in the database. Now we run the query against the database:

```
rs.Open SQLString, conn
```

Let's suppose that our database contains one Eurythmics track, with an id of 18 and a title of *I Saved The World Today*. In this case, the recordset will contain a single record with these values. We can now use these values – the last line of code writes the title of the track to the client:

```
Response.Write rs("title") & " by Eurythmics"
```

In other words, we have published content on the Internet using data contained in a database. Of course, in the general case, our recordset will contain multiple records and we will wish to loop through the entire recordset:

```
'Loop until you hit EOF (End Of File)
Do While Not rs.EOF
   Response.Write rs("title") &_" by Eurythmics <br />"& vbCrlf
   'move the cursor to point to the next Record
   rs.MoveNext
Loop
```

In the example above, we explicitly created a `Recordset` object, which is not strictly necessary since we can run a query directly through the Connection object and implicitly create a Recordset object:

```
SQLString = "SELECT song_id,title FROM songs WHERE artist = ""Eurythmics"";"
set rs = conn.Execute(SQLstring)
```

The advantage of this approach is its simplicity. The disadvantage is that we don't have much control over non-default properties of the recordset. For example, the recordsets we created in the two examples are **forward-only**. This means that we can only read it in a forward direction but improves on speed of access. It is also possible to create other kinds of recordsets that are more flexible but in order to do that, we would need to create them explicitly and set the various attributes available for that purpose.

Closing the Connection and Recordset

At the end of each ASP page, you should explicitly close all of the recordset and all of the connections you have opened:

```
rs.Close            'close the Recordset object
Set rs = Nothing    'release the Recordset object

conn.Close          'close the Connection with the database
Set conn = Nothing  'release the Connection object
```

Connection Pooling

Because the overheads of establishing a connection with a database are high, OLE DB takes care of **connection pooling** for us. What this means is that, in order to improve efficiency, OLE DB keeps connections open for a specified length of time. If, within that time, a connection is requested with exactly the same details, including the user name and password, the connection is handed to the page requesting that connection. Otherwise the connection is dropped.

Continuing from this thread, another optimization trick is to open your connections and create the recordsets as late as possible and to release them as soon as you can. This approach will allow OLE DB to recycle connections out of a relatively small connection pool. Another is never to store connections or any other ADO objects in session scope, as this will mean a new connection will be established for every user and the server will quickly grind to a halt.

An ASP application in practice

The time has come to move from words to action and use ASP to build a meaningful WAP application, involving a number of different aspects of WAP system development. WAP-Radio is a fictitious radio station. They have an excellent web site, but it is still not good enough! Many listeners are on the move. Others are working. Very few are sitting in front of a PC. A WAP site is an excellent way to let listeners interact with the radio without the need for handling hundreds of telephone calls. For example, people can participate in a quiz or an opinion poll. The latest news is always available. Information about the current radio program is displayed in real time. These are only a few of the possibilities offered by WAP in this scenario. Implementing this kind of mechanism with ASP is not difficult.

Dedicated to you

From 10pm until midnight WAP-Radio plays the songs that listeners from around the country have been choosing during the day. Anyone can search for their favorite songs from WAP-Radio's database and pick one. Once a song has been chosen, the listener can dedicate it to someone and submit it to the radio's playing system, which will put it on air.

A good place to start when designing a, WAP service is to use a piece of paper and a pencil to draw the different stages a user will have to go through in order to use the application. Start by drawing a map of the decks that compose the application. A diagram illustrating this for our WAP application is shown overleaf. The white boxes represent decks, and the arrows between each pair of boxes represent the possible navigation paths the user can take from one deck to another. There are also "local" arrows from one card to another inside the same deck.

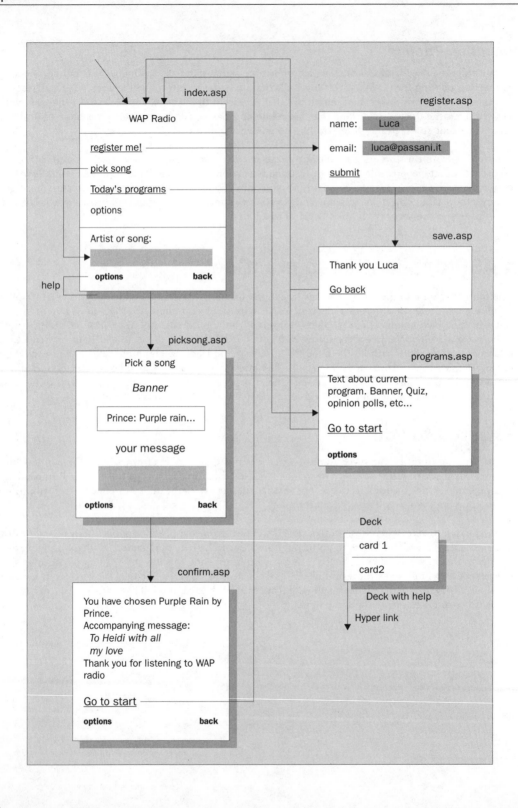

Each box represents a deck in the WAP application. If you are writing static WML, you probably think in terms of display units, that is, cards. In the case of static WML files, it is not so important to know whether two cards are part of the same deck or belong to different ones. However, the situation is different with ASP (and indeed any server-side technology).

When we send a deck containing multiple cards to a mobile phone, all the cards except one are being kept hidden by the browser. While this is useful for improving system responsiveness, an obvious implication is that such 'hidden' cards cannot contain information produced by the server as a response to the input the user provides through a card in the same deck. The hidden card is in fact already in the microbrowser while the user is composing their request. In order to produce dynamic information we need a round trip to the web server. This implies that the server must generate a brand new deck and send it to the phone whenever we wish to display some dynamic information.

When we're designing a WAP service, we need to think about these interactions with the server side of the application. Whenever the system needs to display content that depends on both user input and information residing on the server, a new deck must be delivered. Of course, this does not mean that a dynamically generated deck cannot contain multiple cards. In the diagram above, the horizontal lines inside the deck boxes delimit the boundary between cards belonging to the same deck.

The shadow decks we see in the background represent the help decks (or cards) we should associate with each function in order to build a context-sensitive help system. Remember that a WAP device is not Internet Explorer 5 on a 21-inch screen. Everything is tiny and the text is often cryptic. But most of all we need to support new (non-computer-literate) users.

Finally, we can see on the diagram that option/back 'buttons' are included at the bottom of each box. This is inspired by the way that soft keys look on the Nokia 7110, the links represent those available by pressing the appropriate button.

Let's start by looking at the first deck in the application:

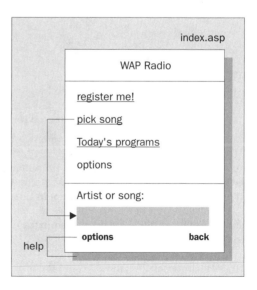

The deck contains three cards. The first card is a splash screen that contains the name and the logo of the radio. Such introductory screens are quite popular these days, and it is likely these screens will become quite standard in the future.

The second card is a kind of mini-portal. It contains links to the rest of the system, of which "Register me!" is dynamically generated (it appears for new users, not existing ones – see the section on *personalization* notes below). For the purpose of clarity, the rest of the links in this card are static. If this were a real project, you might think of having those links generated dynamically according to the current program, music, or sponsor. ASP lets you do such things in a relatively simple way. We could also include a banner – one line of advertisement. The registration link leads to a form that allows users to register some personal user information (name and e-mail). This information can be used to customize the page the next time the same user visits the service. One of the links points to the music search form, which is a card in the same deck.

The third card is the music search form. Note that no card depends on previous user input so we can put all three cards into one deck.

The second deck consists of just one card, which represents the query result. The system receives a search key from the user (through the music search form in the previous deck) and builds a query for the database. Assuming the presence of more than one resulting hit from the query the user has entered, they should see their results displayed in a list selection field:

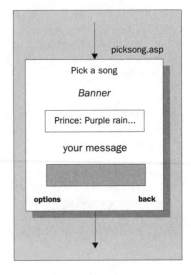

The list selection field in the middle of the card lets users pick one song out of the hit list generated by the query. The application must also handle different situations that may arise, including:

❏ What happens when no database record matches the original query?

❏ What happens when one and only one song matches the query?

In the first case, the user should be presented with a new search form. The previous search key should be reproduced in this form – it is likely that the user will most wish to edit that, rather than having to type everything again. Users are kept in this loop as long as they do not type a successful search key. When a successful key is entered, we are back in the normal flow of the application. Of course, you should always provide a way to jump back to the front door of your service if the user gets tired of the loop, but this is another issue.

In the second case, we should route the flow of the application so that it merely sends the single item rather than embedding it within a list selection field. These assume the presence of multiple items to choose from, and you never know how some devices will behave when presented with an unnatural object like a 'one-item' list. In any case, the list could be confusing to many users.

If you are new to ASP you may wish to draw a more detailed figure that describes how the above situations should be handled:

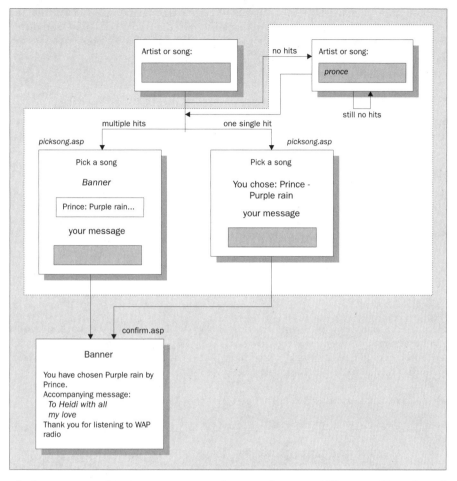

The three decks are grouped into a common area because the same ASP page will produce them all. The user agent submits a request and the ASP page will respond with one of these three possible decks. This implies that the application must know how to produce a set of different pages depending on the data it just received from the user.

An application that handles a user login is a typical example of this. If the credentials provided by the user are not accepted, a new login screen is presented; otherwise the first page of the application is shown. We can assume that upon entering the third deck, a song identifier and a dedication are passed to our ASP page:

The implementation of this deck is quite simple. We have a song and we have a string of characters representing the dedication. We save this information into the Radio's database and display a confirmation message for the user. Never forget to provide a link back to the start page (in addition to the fact that a consistent way to go back to the start page should be available in every card).

Personalization

This application will be personalized for the user – we will register basic user information (name and e-mail address), store it in a database, and retrieve it when the user returns. Not only does this sort of thing save the user from entering such details again (we all know what entering text on a phone is like), but it will allow us to personalize the application, hopefully making it more attractive to the user.

The approach taken in this application is, unfortunately, environment specific – it uses unique user IDs as automatically provided by the Ericsson gateway. Hopefully this is a system that will catch on, but you should remember that there are always alternatives. If a gateway allows you to set cookies then you could use a slightly different method – in effect storing your own version of these unique IDs. Failing that, you can always resort to a manual login procedure, although you would not want to make this mandatory, as that may turn away many of your users.

The Database

The code supplied as part of the download for this book is Access 2000 database. Obviously, in a serious WAP service, you would want to use something like SQL Server or Oracle instead, but for the purposes of this example, Access will suit us fine. Before we delve into the code, it's wise to take a look at the database. It is actually a very simple one, made of just three tables: songs, users and playlist.

The table called songs contains the full range of songs listeners can dedicate. A section of this table is shown below:

	song_id	artist	title
	63	Moloko	Sing It Back
	64	Tom Jones & The Cardigan	Burning Down The House
	65	Ace Of Base	C'est La Vie (Always 21)
	66	Pop-Englene 99	Till Christmas
	67	Scooter	Fuck The Millennium
	68	Antique	Opa Opa
	69	Pacific Blue	Ocean
	70	Blank & Jones	After Love
	71	Signum feat. Scott Mac	Comin' On Strong
	72	Balearic Bill	Destination Sunshine
	73	Dj Josè Vs. G-Spott	Wrong = Right
	74	J&R Project	Keep It Up
	75	Des Mitchell	Welcome To The Dance
	76	Roxette	It must have been love
	77	A-ha	Crying in the rain
	78	Sinéad O'Connor	Nothing compares 2 u
	79	Enigma	Sadness part 1
	80	Prince	Get off

Record: 63 of 112

User info is stored in a separate table called `users`. The `user_id` column in this table is the one we get from the Ericsson gateway:

Once a user chooses a song, the song ID, user ID, and dedication message are inserted in the `playlist` table:

pl_id	song_id	user_id	message
43	39	646467464	For Heidi
54	42	240488432	Come on the blues!
55	1	646467464	ci vediamo domani

Record: 2 of 3

The Code

We'll now turn to the code for this application. All the code is provided here, but it can also be downloaded from the Wrox site, along with the database tables and all other code for this book.

conn.asp

`conn.asp` is a short, but pretty important, file. It is responsible for opening the connection to the database. It makes sense to put this connection in a separate file, as it is code we will need to access from several of our other files – we can **include** this code in those files using the following line of code:

```
<!--#include file="conn.asp" -->
```

This will be required in each of the ASP pages that access our database.

Isolating the connection operations in its own file in this way is an alternative to encapsulating the connection code in a custom made component – if for some reason the database connection configuration changes, you don't need to modify all of the files that use the database.

`conn.asp` begins with a line of code that prevents the use of variable names that have not been previously declared using the `Dim` statement:

```
<%
    Option Explicit
```

Including the `Option Explicit` statement is considered good programming practice, since it highlights errors that are merely caused by misspelled variable names thus keeping debugging to errors in logic.

We then create a `Connection` object and open a connection to a database, bringing us to the end of this rather short piece of code:

```
Dim conn    'connection to access database
Set conn = Server.CreateObject("ADODB.Connection")
'DSN-less Connection to access
conn.open "Provider=Microsoft.Jet.OLEDB.4.0;Data Source=" & _
          Server.Mappath("wapasp.mdb")
%>
```

Note that VBScript uses an underscore character ("_") to break single lines of code across multiple lines of text.

unconn.asp

Since we have a separate file to connect to the database, it makes sense to have one to disconnect. We can include this at the end of files that use `conn.asp`.

This file is short and simple:

```
<%
    conn.close
    Set conn = Nothing
%>
```

index.asp

Let's take a look at how the code in `index.asp`, the first deck the user will see, works. The first part of the code looks like this:

```
<!--#include file="conn.asp" -->
<%
    'send the right MIME type
    Response.ContentType = "text/vnd.wap.wml"

    'disable caching of this deck
    Response.Expires = -1
    Response.AddHeader "Pragma", "no-cache"
    Response.AddHeader "Cache-Control", "no-cache, must-revalidate"
```

First we open a connection to the database (we'll need that to check if the user is new or existing), Next, we insert the HTTP headers required, to tell the device that the present deck should not be cached. (This is the standard way to achieve this effect though ASP.) We request non-caching from the browser because the response from the server varies from the first visit to the site and consequent visits. These HTTP headers can also be added automatically by IIS (4 or 5) using the HTTP headers tab of the management console. If we then need to override the default header (no cache) we can do so at deck level.

Next we initialize some variables and get the unique user ID from the gateway:

```
Dim SQLquery, uniqueid, username
Dim rsUser
```

```
uniqueid = Request.Cookies("User-Identity-Forward-msisdn")
'for testing when not going through the gateway, use this:
'uniqueid = 646467464
```

As the comment states, if our gateway does not support a unique user ID, in the cookie User-Identity-Forward-msisdn, or we are testing this code without a gateway, we can manually specify an ID. Alternatively, this is the place to add alternative methods of personalization.

Next we check to see if the user is returning to the WAP site by looking up the ID in our users database:

```
SQLquery = "SELECT user_name FROM users WHERE user_id = " & uniqueid
Set rsUser = conn.Execute(SQLquery)

If rsUser.EOF then
   username = ""
Else
   username = rsUser("user_name")
End If

rsUser.Close
Set rsUser = Nothing
%>
```

If the user is a new one, we temporarily assign an empty string to username. The last section of this code tidies up for us, by getting rid of the recordset obtained from users – we've got all the information we need from it.

The next bit of code deserves some attention:

```
<?xml version="1.0"?>
<!DOCTYPE wml PUBLIC "-//WAPFORUM//DTD WML 1.1//EN"
"http://www.wapforum.org/DTD/wml_1.1.xml">
<wml>

<%
   'give old users a chance to change their settings
   if username <> "" then
%>
   <template>
      <do type="option" label="Settings">
         <go href="register.asp"/>
      </do>
   </template>
<%
   end if
```

Here, we have an extra do element for users that are already registered. They will get an extra menu that will let them jump to the registration page. This way they'll be able to change their personal data. As we'll see shortly, users that are not registered, will be provided with a link in the main card to allow them to register. For registered users an entry in the options menu will suffice.

The current trend for flash screens does nothing for our users experience of the application, but will probably prevail nonetheless; we should make sure that our timers go off within 2 seconds or users will find the application annoying. The code that follows illustrates this.

```
    if username = "" then
%>
   <card id="logo" title="WAP Radio" ontimer="#frontpage">
      <timer value="20"/>
      <do type="accept" label="Skip">
         <go href="#frontpage"/>
      </do>
      <p>
         Welcome to
         <img src="pix/radio.wbmp" alt="WAP Radio"/>
      </p>
   </card>
<%
   end if
%>
```

If a user has registered, then they are likely to have seen the splash screen before. This means that we may want to save them some time by removing the card altogether, as shown in the above code. This splash screen look like this:

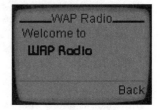

The code for the next card should come as no surprise. New users get a link to the registration facility prominently placed at the top of the card. Old users receive a personalized welcome message:

```
   <card id="frontpage" title="Choose a song">
      <do type="accept" label="Song">
         <go href="#picksong"/>
      </do>
      <do type="option" label="Prog">
         <go href="programs.asp"/>
      </do>
      <p>
<%
   'old users get a personalized welcome msg
   'new users are given a chance to register
   if username = "" then
%>
         <anchor title="Reg.">Register!
            <go href="register.asp"/>
         </anchor><br/>
<%
   else 'recognize old user
      Response.Write("Hello " & username & ", nice to see you!<br/>")
   end if
%>
         <anchor title="Song">Pick a song
            <go href="#picksong"/>
         </anchor><br/>
         <anchor title="Prog">What's on
            <go href="programs.asp"/>
         </anchor>
      </p>
   </card>
```

Note that in this card, navigation may be achieved via links or <do> softkeys, enhancing usability on multiple devices. This will be a common feature of the decks in this application.

This menu will look something like this:

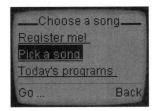

The final card lets users type a search key that will be matched against song titles and artist names available in the database. We have allowed the user to enter part names to attempt to reduce the amount of required data entry:

```
<card id="picksong" title="Pick up a song">
    <do type="accept" label="Search">
        <go href="picksong.asp" method="get">
            <postfield name="searchkey" value="$(searchkey)"/>
        </go>
    </do>
    <do type="prev">
        <prev/>
    </do>
    <p>
        Artist or song title (3 or more chars):
        <input type="text" name="searchkey" value=""/>
        <anchor title="Search">Search
            <go href="picksong.asp" method="get">
                <postfield name="searchkey" value="$(searchkey)"/>
            </go>
        </anchor>
    </p>
</card>
</wml>
```

This code is pretty standard. The GET method is used here, as currently there are problems with data loss associated with using the POST method on certain devices used in conjunction with some gateways.

Finally, we close the database connection:

```
<!--#include file="unconn.asp" -->
```

register.asp

Before we move to the card that retrieves the song, let's take a look at the registration form. It begins in a very similar way to the last piece of code:

```
<!--#include file="conn.asp" -->
<%
    'send the right MIME type
    Response.ContentType = "text/vnd.wap.wml"
```

```
    Dim SQLquery, uniqueid, username, email
    Dim rsUser

    ' see comments index.asp

    uniqueid = Request.Cookies("User-Identity-Forward-msisdn")
    'for testing when I'm not going through use this:
    'uniqueid = 646467464

    SQLquery = "SELECT user_name,email FROM users WHERE user_id = " & uniqueid
    Set rsUser = conn.Execute(SQLquery)

    If rsUser.EOF then
        username = ""
        email = ""
    Else
        username = rsUser("name")
        email = rsUser("email")
    End If

    rsUser.Close
    Set rsUser = Nothing
%>
```

Next we provide a form for user detail input, and close the database:

```
<?xml version="1.0"?>
<!DOCTYPE wml PUBLIC "-//WAPFORUM//DTD WML 1.1//EN"
"http://www.wapforum.org/DTD/wml_1.1.xml">
<wml>
    <card id="register" title="Register me">
        <do type="accept" label="Next">
            <go href="save.asp"  method="get">
                <postfield name="username" value="$(username)"/>
                <postfield name="email" value="$(email)"/>
            </go>
        </do>
        <p>
            Hello, would you please tell us your name and e-mail?<br/>
            Name: <input type="text" value="<%=username%>" name="username"
                    size="20"/><br/>
            E-mail: <input type="text" value="<%=email%>" name="email"
                    size="20"/><br/>
            <anchor title="Next">Next
                <go href="save.asp" method="get">
                    <postfield name="username" value="$(username)"/>
                    <postfield name="email" value="$(email)"/>
                </go>
            </anchor>
        </p>
    </card>
</wml>

<!--#include file="unconn.asp" -->
```

This deck is used by new users to register, as well as registered users who intend to change their personal data. If the user has previously registered, the fields will be populated with the known values, as is shown here:

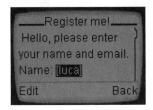

save.asp

`save.asp` updates the database. This may involve adding a user or changing the details for a user. The first, script only, section of the file performs this database access in the standard way:

```
<!--#include file="conn.asp" -->
<%
    Response.buffer = True

    'send the right MIME type
    Response.ContentType = "text/vnd.wap.wml"

    Dim SQLquery, uniqueid, username, email, newuser
    Dim rsUser

    uniqueid = Request.Cookies("User-Identity-Forward-msisdn")
    'for testing when I'm not going through use this:
    'uniqueid = 646467464

    'first, we have to identify if we are dealing with an old user or not
    SQLquery = "SELECT user_name FROM users WHERE user_id = " & uniqueid
    Set rsUser = conn.Execute(SQLquery)

    If rsUser.EOF then
        newuser = True
    Else
        newuser = False
    End If
    rsUser.Close
    Set rsUser = Nothing

    'new user data
    username =  Request("username")
    email = Request("email")

    If newuser Then  'Insert new user
        SQLQuery = "INSERT INTO users (user_id, user_name, email) values (" & _
                uniqueid & "," & _
                "'" & username & "', " & _
                "'" & email & "')"
    Else    'Update existing user
        SQLQuery = "UPDATE users SET " & _
                "user_name = '" & username & "', " & _
                "email = '" & email & "'  " & _
                "WHERE user_id = " & uniqueid
    End If
    conn.execute(SQLQuery)
%>
```

Note that in order to update the database we must set the correct permissions for the file. Specifically, we should allow the interactive guest Internet user write access to the access database file.

At this point, we display a thank you message, and give the user a link back to the front page. We could also insert an advert here if we were in the mood:

```
<?xml version="1.0"?>
<!DOCTYPE wml PUBLIC "-//WAPFORUM//DTD WML 1.1//EN"
"http://www.wapforum.org/DTD/wml_1.1.xml">
<wml>
    <card id="card1" title="Thank you">
        <do type="accept" label="Front">
            <go href="index.asp"/>
        </do>
        <p>
            Thank you <%=username%>. You will receive a regular e-mail newsletter
            with special offers and a list of all the new songs we have added to
            the song list.<br/>
            <a href="index.asp">WAPRadio Home</a><br/>
            What about some WAP
            <a href="http://wap.favouritesoftdrink.com">Advertisement here?</a>
        </p>
    </card>
</wml>
<!--#include file="unconn.asp" -->
```

picksong.asp

This file involves some slightly more involved database access than previous files, so we'll look at it in more detail. To start with, there is an extra include at the top of the file:

```
<!--#include file="conn.asp" -->
<!--#include file="Adovbs.inc" -->
```

The second included file is Adovbs.inc. This file contains the constant definitions, or type library, used by ADO that we need for advanced use of ADO. We will see why we need this shortly. Adovbs.inc is shipped with ASP, so we will find it somewhere on your system. (You may find it easiest to copy it to the same directory as the files that need it.)

The include statements are followed by the standard prolog to the deck; notice we have used the <template> element to implement the back function in each card in the deck:

```
<%
    'send the right MIME type
    Response.ContentType = "text/vnd.wap.wml"
%>
<?xml version="1.0"?>
<!DOCTYPE wml PUBLIC "-//WAPFORUM//DTD WML 1.1//EN"
"http://www.wapforum.org/DTD/wml_1.1.xml">
```

```
<wml>
   <template>
      <do type="prev" label="Back">
         <prev/>
      </do>
   </template>
</template>
```

The code that follows reads the input data the user has inserted in the previous card:

```
<%
   Dim ok, searchkey, SQLQuery
   Dim rsResult

   ok = False
   searchkey = Trim(Request("searchkey"))
```

Remember that `Request.QueryString` contains the collection of all the parameters sent with the GET method, while `Request.Form` is the collection of the parameters sent with the POST method. However, `Request()` is the collection of all the parameters, no matter what the method used is. This is a useful collection to have, since it is independent of the method used.

```
'check search key is greater than two characters
If Len(searchkey) > 2 then
```

The line above makes sure that the search key is not ridiculously short. It must contain 3 characters or more. A key that's less than 3 characters long could produce an extremely long hit list, which would be virtually unusable in a WAP device, and may even crash the browser. Note that entries such as 'the' are guaranteed to generate a large number of matching cases. We will need to cater for this situation. The usual approach is to identify the case when the database returns too many matches and paginate them over several decks, or tell users to insert a better search key depending on set criteria.

Here, we build the SQL query to extract the relevant information from the database:

```
SQLQuery = "SELECT * FROM songs WHERE title LIKE '%" & searchkey & _
             "%' OR artist LIKE '%" & searchkey & "%'"
```

LIKE returns all the values in `title` or `artist` columns of the `songs` table that contain the sequence of characters passed as an argument in their values. This means that users can search using the first three letters of the artist's name or a keyword in the song title.

ADO offers several ways to perform a query. In the example given earlier, we used the `Connection.Execute()` method, which creates a recordset object automatically for us, if necessary. In this case, though, the default configuration of the implicitly created recordset is not sufficient for our needs. We need to ask the recordset how many records it contains, which we can discover through the `Recordset.RecordCount` property.

This means that if we want to get the `RecordCount` property correctly set we need to explicitly create a recordset and give it a non-default configuration. Our best option is a **static** recordset, which is still quite efficient and counts how many records it has onboard. A static recordset can be seen as a kind of snapshot – a static copy of the records is delivered to the application, which is left free to move around the recordset and read all of the properties and information contained in them.

```
        Set rsResult = Server.CreateObject("ADODB.Recordset")
        rsResult.ActiveConnection = conn
        'we need this for the RecordCount property. Still efficient
        rsResult.CursorType = adOpenStatic
```

The last line above specifies that our recordset is static. Note that the adOpenStatic variable comes from the Adovbs.inc file we imported at the beginning.

```
        rsResult.Open SQLQuery
        If NOT rsResult.EOF Then
            ok = True
        End If
    End If
```

The rsResult.Open line actually performs the query. Immediately after the query, it is important to check that at least one record, has been found. The ok variable is only a flag. If ok has value False at the end of the query, a new search form will be produced.

As long as there is at least one record we proceed. If there is more than one option, we list the choices in a list field and allow the user to choose one. The user then enters their dedication and an acknowledgement is given. If there is only one choice, we fast-forward to the dedication entry.

Let's look at the first case first:

```
    If ok Then
        'if there are multiple hits, user should choose one
        If rsResult.RecordCount > 1 Then
%>
    <card id="pickup" title="Choose from hitlist">
        <do type="accept" label="Next">
            <go href="confirm.asp" method="get">
                <postfield name="song" value="$(song)"/>
                <postfield name="message" value="$(message)"/>
            </go>
        </do>
        <p>
            Pick song:
            <select name='song'>
<%
            Do While Not rsResult.EOF
                Response.Write "<option value='" & rsResult("song_id") & "'>" & _
                            rsResult("title") & " - " & rsResult("artist") & _
                            "</option>" & vbcrlf
                rsResult.MoveNext
            loop
%>
            </select>
```

We have coded plain WML all the way, and only used a few lines of server-side code to loop through a recordset to build a customized user interface that faithfully reflects the values in the database. The line above builds a combo box dynamically. Artist and song title compose the human readable text for each item, while the value is a system readable song ID.

In the case where the query matches one single song, the user does not have to make a choice. The `else` branch below matches the `if rsResult.RecordCount > 1 then` command above:

```
<%
    Else    'only one hit, selected by default
%>
    <card id="pickup" title="Found">
        <do type="accept" label="Next">
            <go href="confirm.asp" method="get">
                <postfield name="song" value="<%=rsResult("song_id")%>"/>
                <postfield name="message" value="$(message)"/>
            </go>
        </do>
        <p>
<%
        Response.Write rsResult("artist") & ":" & rsResult("title") & _
                        "<br />" & vbcrlf
        End If
%>
```

We just tell the user which song they have selected. The form that lets users write a dedication is the same in both cases:

```
        your message:
        <input type="text" name="message"/>
        <anchor title="Next">Next
            <go href="confirm.asp" method="get">
<%
    'if there are multiple entries, use the one selected
    'by the user. Otherwise, use the only hit available
    If rsResult.RecordCount > 1 Then
        Response.Write "<postfield name=""song"" value=""$(song)""/>" & vbcrlf
    Else
        Response.Write "<postfield name=""song"" value='" & _
                        rsResult("song_id")&"'/>" & vbcrlf
    End If
%>
                <postfield name="message" value="$(message)"/>
            </go>
        </anchor>
    </p>
</card>
```

In the case of a single match, we set the value of the song parameter with ASP; otherwise we use the value of the WML variable associated with the `<select>` (`$song`).

What remains to be seen, is the case when no match has been found, the following `Else` matches the previous `If ok Then`. We need to rebuild a search form and make sure that users will be able to edit the search key that they typed previously. We can do this using ASP, but this is not strictly necessary, because of the scoping rules of WML variables. The `<%=variable%>` syntax is a pretty smart shorthand for `<% Response.Write(variable)%>`.

Here's the rest of the code:

```
<%
    Else  'no match, try again
%>
    <card id="sorry" title="No song found">
        <p>
<%
        If len(searchkey) > 2 Then  'there was no match
            Response.Write "No match. Try with a different search key:"
        Else
            Response.Write "Search key is too short. Try with a longer search key:"
        End If
%>
            <input type="text" name="searchkey" value="<%=searchkey%>"/>
            <anchor title="Search">Search
                <go href="picksong.asp" method="get">
                    <postfield name="searchkey" value="$(searchkey)"/>
                    <postfield name="message" value="$(message)"/>
                </go>
            </anchor>
        </p>
    </card>
<%
    End If

    If Len(searchkey) > 2 Then   'in this case, recordset doesn't exist
        rsResult.Close
        Set rsResult = Nothing
    End If
%>
</wml>

<!--#include file="unconn.asp" -->
```

Closing the recordset and the connection is a good programming practice, since it helps IIS save memory and other system resources:

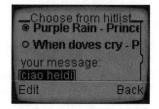

confirm.asp

The last deck acknowledges the user request and saves the song request to the database table called `playlist`. We start by assembling all the data we will need to do this:

```
<!--#include file="conn.asp" -->
<%
    'send the right MIME type
    Response.ContentType = "text/vnd.wap.wml"

    Dim uniqueid
    uniqueid = Request.Cookies("User-Identity-Forward-msisdn")
    'for testing when I'm not going through use this:
    'uniqueid = 646467464
```

```
    Dim songID, message, title, artist, SQLQuery
    Dim rsResult

    songID = Trim(Request("song"))
    message = Trim(Request("message"))

    SQLQuery = "SELECT song_id,artist,title FROM songs WHERE song_id = " & songID

    set rsResult = conn.Execute(SQLquery)
%>
```

This is the simplest way of accessing the database with the default recordset created by the Execute method. Using the name of the columns rather than the wildcard (*) in the SQL SELECT statement makes the code slightly more efficient. The wildcard forces ADO to make a preliminary query to learn about the name of the available columns, whereas if we specify the name of the columns you need in advance, this is not necessary.

Next we display a confirmation to the user:

```
<?xml version="1.0"?>
<!DOCTYPE wml PUBLIC "-//WAPFORUM//DTD WML 1.1//EN"
"http://www.wapforum.org/DTD/wml_1.1.xml">
<wml>
    <template>
        <do type="prev" label="Back">
            <prev/>
        </do>
    </template>
    <card id="confirm" title="Thank you!">
        <p>
            You are dedicating <%=rsResult("title")%> by
            <%=rsResult("artist")%><br/>
            Your message:<br/>
            <%=message%><br/>
```

and replace each occurrence of single-quote characters with two:

```
<%
    message = replace(message,"'","''")
    artist = replace(rsResult("artist"),"'","''")
    title = replace(rsResult("title"),"'","''")
```

If you have done some programming in the past, chances are that you have come across character escaping issues before. Single quotes are reserved characters inside an SQL statement, since they are used to delimit the values inserted in the database. In those cases in which the values also contain a single quote, the effect is disruptive, since the result is a failure of the SQL statement. In SQL two single quote signs (' ') are used to signify a single quote character as part of an inserted value.

For example, imagine a user message like "I'm in love". This would result in a query like the following:

```
INSERT INTO playlist (song_id, user_id, message)
    VALUES (4, 646467464, 'I'm in Love')
```

A database error message is the natural result of such a query.

In order to prevent problems with quotes, all we need to do is to replace all of the single quote characters inside our values with two quote characters, before they are used to build an SQL statement. This way the query will look like:

```
INSERT INTO playlist (song_id, user_id, message)
    VALUES (4, 646467464, 'I''m in Love')
```

This query is interpreted correctly by the database. The Replace function turns single quote characters into two single-quote characters.

Also note that different databases may have different conventions for delimiting values and escaping specific characters. In short, you will have to be aware of the specific needs of your database when coding.

At this point, we can safely insert the data into the playlist table:

```
    'let's insert the data in the playlist table
    SQLQuery = "INSERT INTO playlist (song_id, user_id, message) VALUES (" & _
            rsResult("song_id") & ", " & uniqueid & ", '" & message &"')"
    conn.Execute(SQLquery)
    rsResult.Close
    set rsResult = nothing
%>
        Thank you for listening to WAP Radio 105 FM.<br/>
        <a href="index.asp">Go to front page</a>
    </p>
    </card>
</wml>
<!--#include file="unconn.asp" -->
```

Adding a link to the front page is good usability. While most of the devices support a built-in home link (sometimes configurable), not all users are aware of it. The lack of a link to the front page can cause your users to feel abandoned, and obviously should be avoided.

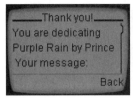 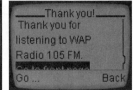

At this point, our simple application is finished. While ASP lets programmers get up to speed quickly, mastering every aspect of ASP development requires a lot of time and effort. Developing large and scalable application with ASP requires programmers to master a variety of concepts about ASP optimization, COM and COM+ programming, and database experience.

Summary

In this chapter, we have covered some of the basic concepts underlying WAP development with ASP. Like virtually any other technique to support server-side web application, ASP can be used to produce advanced WAP services.

The aim of this chapter was not to turn you into an ASP expert – which can only be achieved through experience and hard work – but rather to show how server-side code and WML can be mixed to implement dynamic WAP services. Many of the concepts illustrated here are not limited to ASP, but are general to WAP development. Building selection menus dynamically, accessing the database and passing data from one deck to the next are basic operations that you will have to implement regardless of the server-side technique you deploy.

Multiple Device Types using XML and XSLT

In previous chapters, we've discussed the issues that arise when you need to produce output for WML-enabled devices such as mobile phones. By now, you will now have a good grasp of the syntax and techniques for creating the cards and decks, but it's very easy to overlook the wider issues. OK, so it's not hard to create content that is usable on a phone, but they aren't going to be any use to other visitors using different devices. The traditional web browser is unlikely to be able to render WML, and even if it does the result certainly won't look much like a traditional web page.

Does this matter? Surely you are going to build the whole site purely to suit your WAP phone equipped visitors. Is that a realistic option? What about other types of client that might want to access your site, such as visitors using a TV set-top box, or a Sony PlayStation? And maybe that visitor, who just left your site in frustration, was trying to view your page on their refrigerator? Don't laugh; these kinds of consumer devices are going to be web-enabled any day now.

This chapter looks at two broad topic areas. The first is designed to make you think about the fundamental way you approach building a web site that has to cope with multiple disparate clients. The second topic area is that described in the chapter title – **XML** or **eXtensible Markup Language** and its associated technologies. The two topics are related, because the latter provides probably the best way to approach solving the problems raised by the former. We'll be covering:

- ❏ How we need to think about web site design at the fundamental level
- ❏ The current initiatives that are under way, which might help us achieve our goals
- ❏ How these initiatives can describe the various client devices or user agents
- ❏ How and why we might consider using XML as the base data store for a web site
- ❏ Ways that we can transform XML data into a whole range of appropriate output formats
- ❏ A simple server-based example using Microsoft's Active Server Pages

We'll start with a look at the kind of impact the various different types of new client will make, and the design issues that we will have to face and overcome in the future.

The Fundamental Design Issues

In Chapter 7, we looked in depth at some of the design issues associated with creating content and services for small screen, low power and low bandwidth devices with limited input capabilities. It is clear that a page designed to run the latest version of the standard releases of Internet Explorer or Navigator is never going to work on such a device. Instead, we need to provide content that is written in such a way as to take maximum advantage of the capabilities of the device, while removing all unnecessary content that cannot be displayed. And, more to the point, we need to provide this content in a form that is **usable** on that client.

So, we need to design our pages to suit specific devices. There is no one size that fits all solutions here. For example, this is how a list of books might be displayed in IE5 – each image is a clickable link that allows visitors to read more about each book and place an order:

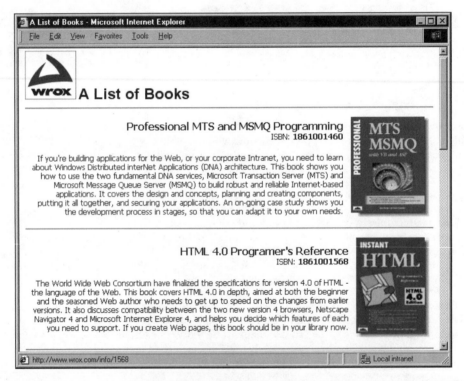

Obviously, this requires a fair amount of screen real estate to be usable. If we wanted to provide the same kind of information for a PDA, for instance, we need to use smaller graphics and less text content to suit the limited screen size. The next screenshot shows a format aimed at the latest PDAs that have a color screen. We're displaying it in Internet Explorer, but you can easily see how it is instantly more suited to this kind of device. The hyperlinks provide access to the description of the product, and ordering information:

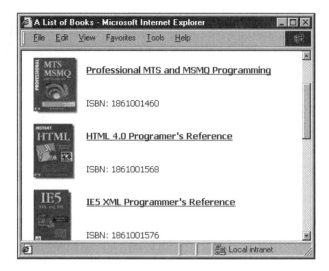

Neither of the previous two formats is really suitable for the newer types of device that are just becoming available. For example, the text and images are not suited to viewing from a distance, as would be the case for a TV set-top box. In this situation, a more suitable format requires larger images and text, and a simplified navigation system that is compatible with a remote control handset. So, we might decide to display each book on a page of its own, and allow users to scroll through them. Again, we've used Internet Explorer to display the page, in the absence of any other suitable device:

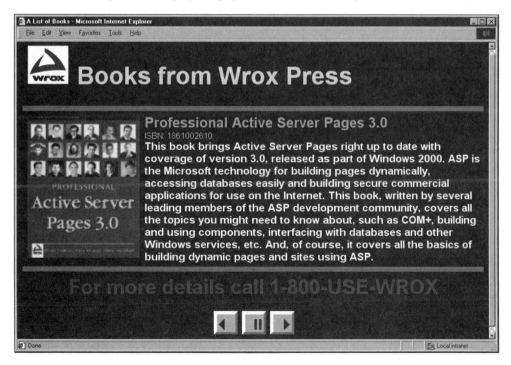

We have seen that we can provide the same content to our users in different formats. However, even the above simplified formats will only be suitable for phones that have a reasonably large display – as is the case with the hybrid phone/PDA devices that are in use now. For the more limited display of a 'normal' mobile phone, we need to simplify it even more. Perhaps something like that shown here would be suitable:

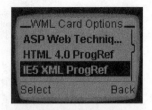

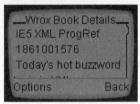

This provides ways for users to view the list of books, read a short description of each one, and (not shown) place an order or get more information.

If we are going to aim to satisfy all the different types of client, then we need to provide all the above different formats of content. More and more people will be accessing our sites using a cellular phone, PDA, TV set-top box, microwave cooker or refrigerator than will be using a traditional web browser running on a PC. Yes, it's a horrifying prospect. And it's not far away either. How on earth are we going to cope with providing four, five or more different formats of information for each web page on every site we host or manage?

In the next section, we'll discuss some of the initiatives that are under way to help us out. These will then be described in more detail before we finally return to the above situation, looking for a solution.

W3C Initiatives for Disparate Client Compatibility

For some time, the **World Wide Web Consortium** (W3C) has been looking at the issues involved in providing content to different types of client, without the need to create many different copies of each page. Under the banner of the **Mobile Access Group**, many of the new standards, proposals and working drafts – such as eXtensible Markup Language (XML), stylesheets and the Resource Description Framework (RDF) – are coming together to provide a coherent platform that will support multiple disparate types of client.

Before we look any deeper at these topics, it's worth taking a quick overview of them, so as to understand what they are designed to achieve:

❑ **XML (eXtensible Markup Language)** allows us to store information in a structured or semi-structured way, and access it using a variety of techniques. It is also ideal for providing platform independent data interchange.

❑ **XSLT** (The 'Transformations' part of the **XML Stylesheet Language** specification) provides techniques for transforming the structure or content of XML documents into almost anything else. It can be used to 'style' XML for display (by transforming it into WML, for example), or just to change the XML document into another format. At the time of writing, the XSL design committee at the W3C are working on a new display language that is intended to be platform independent. This is called **XSL Formatting Objects**, or XSL-FO. We won't be discussing this here.

❑ **XPointer** describes ways to provide links between XML documents by selecting one or more fragments. It removes the requirement for HTML <A> or <LINK> elements to be used to load other pages, and extends the possibilities for linking information from different sources in a far more comprehensive manner than is possible at present. Again, we aren't using XPointer in this chapter, as no devices support it at the moment.

❑ **XPath** defines ways to select or address specific parts of an XML document for use with XSL or XPointer. It is basically a syntax for specifying single or multiple sections of an XML document.

❑ **XHTML (eXtensible Hypertext Markup Language)** defines a document format that is XML-compliant, yet will display in a traditional web browser. It also specifies a series of modules that identify subsets of the complete language, making it easier to identify the particular features that a device supports.

❑ **RDF (Resource Description Framework)**, like XSL, XPath and XPointer, is an XML-based language for describing the content of documents, or providing other data and/or information about a document, device or resource. For example, it can be used to give more comprehensive descriptions of web pages or other resources, including the ability to use hierarchical descriptions that inherit from other documents.

We'll be using a mixture of these standards throughout the remainder of this chapter. However, we don't have room to provide full tutorials for them, so this chapter provides mainly overviews and brief descriptions of how they can be used. You can obtain the specifications and other documentation from the W3C web site at http://www.w3.org/. There is also a section devoted to their Mobile Access Group at http://www.w3.org/Mobile, and an 'Activity' statement that describes the initiative in detail. It includes this pertinent quote:

> *"W3C's Mobile Access Activity is working to ensure that the protocols and data formats of the Web provide an effective fit for all mobile devices. The Consortium is working towards world-wide standards for the technology involved, to the benefit of Web users and content providers alike."*

You'll also find a range of Wrox books covering the various technologies, such as *Professional XML*, *XSLT Programmer's Reference* and *Beginning XHTML*.

Using XML to Define Data

XML was introduced in Chapter 4 as the language that is used to define WML, and we have talked about it above in the setting of the Mobile Access Group. However, XML is used for all kinds of applications, and is a core part of many new technologies. It's unlikely that you haven't come across XML in some form or another, as it is fast becoming the hottest topic in the computing world as a whole. In this section, we'll take a quick look at what XML is, what an XML document is, and some of the practical situations in which we can make use of XML.

What is XML?

In effect, XML is simply text delimited with special characters – much like HTML and WML. The difference is that languages like HTML and WML use elements that have a pre-defined meaning. HTML is an **application** of the **Structured Generalized Markup Language** or **SGML**, while WML is an **application** of **XML**.

SGML is a highly complex language that is used to define other markup languages such as HTML, as well as many hundreds of others that you've probably never heard of. It allows the syntax of the language to be specified accurately and completely. However, it doesn't specify what the elements actually *mean*. In other words, it doesn't say how elements should be handled in a device that supports that language. For HTML and WML, the meaning of each element is laid down in the relevant specification of that language. As an example, SGML provides a way to specify that a `<table>` element will contain `<tr>` and `<td>` elements, while the HTML specification tells us that the visual result when displayed in a web browser will be a table. If HTML didn't specify the *meaning* of each element, the web browser wouldn't know what to do with it.

XML elements, however, have no intrinsic meaning. This is where the power of XML comes into its own. XML is a **subset** of SGML (rather than an **application** of SGML), and can be used both to hold information, and as a basis for applications that use XML. As we'll see later, the **XML Stylesheet Language** (XSL) – like WML - is actually an *application* of XML.

You can create an XML document that can contain information, using your own elements that mean exactly what you want them to mean. While this might seem a rather strange concept, it has a major advantage. As long as both the sender and the recipient know what the elements mean, an XML document can be used to store and transfer information in a completely platform-independent, operating system-independent and device-independent way. And, as it's pure text, it can be transmitted easily over any kind of network, including HTTP over the Internet.

XML Document Structure

As we learned back in Chapter 4, XML documents must follow a standard set of rules. Let's have a quick recap on those now.

Documents should contain the `<?xml...?>` prolog that identifies them as being XML – as in this example of a WML document:

```
<?xml version="1.0" encoding="UTF-8"?>
<!DOCTYPE wml PUBLIC "-//WAPFORUM//DTD WML 1.1//EN"
          "http://www.wapforum.org/DTD/wml_1.1.xml">
<wml>
   ...content goes here...
</wml>
```

Documents must be **well-formed**, with no 'overlapping' elements:

```
<b>This is some <i>BOLD</b> text</i>          <-- Wrong!
<b>This is some <i>BOLD</i></b><i> text</i>   <-- Correct
```

All element and attribute names should be in lower-case (always lower-case for WML), with attributes *always* in single or double quotes – even if they represent a 'numeric' value:

```
<card id="18" title="Wrox Book Details">
```

All elements must have a closing tag or use the equivalent shorthand syntax:

```
<img src="mypic.wbmp" alt="My Picture" />
<br />
```

'Minimized' attributes like those we regularly see in HTML are not permitted:

```
<option value="option1" selected />              <-- Wrong!
<option value="option1" selected="SELECTED" />   <-- Correct
```

All characters that are not legal in XML must be 'escaped' by using the entity equivalent:

```
Ben &amp; Jerry&apos;s Ice Cream
```

Or by enclosing them in a CDATA element:

```
<![CDATA[Ben & Jerry's Ice Cream]]>
```

This includes characters like the ampersand, when used in a hyperlink:

```
<a href="newpage.asp?v1=this&amp;v2=that">Click here to do this and that</a>
```

WML-specific information should be included as well as normal 'meta' information, for example the encoding of the document should be specified in both ways (note the closing slash character in the `<meta>` element):

```
<?xml version="1.0" encoding="UTF-8"?>
<meta http-equiv="ContentType" content="application/vnd-wap;charset=UTF-8" />
```

Use an `id` attribute as well as a `name` attribute, with the same values, and which are unique for the document. This will allow XPath and XPointer to access elements and content more accurately:

```
<do label="More information" id="doitem_12">
```

If the device supports style sheets, use the `<link>` element to attach the stylesheet, so clients that don't support styling do not have to download the stylesheet information:

```
<link rel="stylesheet" href="mystyle.css" type="text/css" />
```

XML documents also have to comply with a few other requirements:

❑ They must have a single root element, which encloses all the content of the document. In an XML document this root element can be anything.

❑ Other than processing instructions, only comments and document type definitions or document schemas can appear outside the root element.

For example, below is an XML document that describes some furniture. To reinforce the fact that XML elements have no intrinsic 'meaning', you can see that we've used the `<table>` element to identify the kind of table you sit round.

Notice the first three lines which include the two processing instructions (one to identify the document as XML and one to specify the stylesheet that is linked to it), and the comment element that describes the document. The content of the document is fully enclosed within the root `<tables>` element, which uses an `xmlns` attribute to specify the document schema (`tables_schema.xml`) that defines the actual structure of the document (we'll look at this topic in more detail in the next section of this chapter):

```
<?xml version="1.0" ?>

<tables xmlns="x-schema:tables_schema.xml">

<table>
  <table-name>Conference</table-name>
  <number-of-legs>4</number-of-legs>
  <table-top-material type="laminate">Ash</table-top-material>
  <table-shape>Oblong</table-shape>
  <retail-price currency="USD">1485</retail-price>
</table>

<table>
  <table-name>Windsor</table-name>
  <number-of-legs>8</number-of-legs>
  <table-top-material type="laminate">Beech</table-top-material>
  <table-shape>Oval</table-shape>
  <retail-price currency="USD">1975</retail-price>
</table>

<table>
  <table-name>Modern</table-name>
  <number-of-legs>4</number-of-legs>
  <table-top-material type="laminate">Natural</table-top-material>
  <table-shape>Round</table-shape>
  <retail-price currency="USD">1295</retail-price>
</table>

</tables>
```

You can see how flexible XML is in allowing hierarchical content to be stored.

Data Definitions for XML Documents

The XML rules we've been discussing earlier define whether an XML document is **well-formed**. While an XML document can contain any elements and attributes you like, as long as these rules are adhered to, the document is well formed and an XML parser (or a device that supports XML) will be able to read it.

However, this freedom means that it isn't possible to tell if the document is **valid** for a particular purpose. The only way we can validate the structure of an XML document is if we know what structure is acceptable for the specific task. For example, what are the names of the elements and attributes that can be used, and how can they be nested and repeated?

To define the rules that allow us to check an XML document for validity, we need to have a way of describing the structure of the document. There are currently two ways to do this, **Data Type Definitions** (DTDs) and **XML Schemas**. We'll briefly review these next, although we don't actually use them in this chapter.

Data Type Definitions

The original technique for defining the structure of an XML document was through the use of a **Document Type Definition**, or **DTD**. These are written using the syntax of SGML (discussed earlier), and so they don't look much like the WML, HTML or XML syntax we are more used to.

This is a DTD that could define the XML document we saw earlier:

```
<!DOCTYPE tables [
  <!ELEMENT tables (table+)>
  <!ELEMENT table (table-name, number-of-legs, table-top-material,
                   table-shape, retail-price+)>
  <!ELEMENT table-name (#PCDATA)>
  <!ELEMENT number-of-legs (#PCDATA)>
  <!ELEMENT table-top-material (#PCDATA)>
  <!ATTLIST table-top-material type CDATA #IMPLIED>
  <!ELEMENT table-shape (#PCDATA)>
  <!ELEMENT retail-price (#PCDATA)>
  <!ATTLIST retail-price currency (USD | GBP | EURO | YEN) "USD">
]>
```

This uses SGML `<!ELEMENT>` and `<!ATTLIST>` elements to specify which element and attribute names are acceptable. The plus sign '+' indicates that an element can be repeated one or more times, and so our XML document can contain one or more `<table>` elements within the root `<tables>` element (`table+`).

Each `<table>` element can contain one, and only one, `<table-name>`, `<number-of-legs>`, `<table-top-material>` and `<table-shape>` elements, and one or more `<retail-price>` elements. Each of these elements is of data-type #PCDATA, meaning that the content will be parsed in accordance with the rules of SGML (PCDATA means 'parsed character data'). In other words, their content will be text plus any other special characters such as & or < that are required – these are converted to the actual character when the content is displayed.

The `<table-top-material>` element also has an attribute specified by the `<!ATTLIST>` element in the DTD. This says that the attribute name is `type`, and it is CDATA or 'character data'. The content or value of the attribute is not parsed like the content of elements.

Finally, the `<retail-price>` element has an attribute named currency. The only acceptable values for this attribute are those that are listed, i.e. "USD", "GBP", "EURO" and "YEN". If no value is provided in the XML, the default value of "USD" will be assumed.

The Problems with DTDs

So, DTDs are nice and easy to work with, but they have a couple of major drawbacks. Firstly, they are inflexible and cannot provide much control over the structure or acceptable values for the elements and attributes, and there is no concept of data types – everything is character data or parsed character data.

Secondly, they are not written in an XML-compliant format. So they can't be read or processed using the techniques that work with XML documents. This means that we can't easily generate them automatically, or extract parts of the DTD to use in custom routines.

Other disadvantages include the fact that you can't define elements and attributes that have local scope (that is, apply to only one element), and you can't inherit from other schemas that define elements and attributes that are common to several documents.

XML Schemas

In response to the problems with DTDs, a second way of specifying the structure of an XML document is slowly taking over as the preferred technique. This is through a **schema** that is written in an XML format, and which is extensible and comprehensive enough to specify all the extra things we might want to know about what makes a particular XML document valid.

The following listing shows a Microsoft-specific **XML Schema** for the same table list XML document that we saw earlier. It is certainly longer, but you can see that it contains far more information about each element and attribute:

```xml
<?xml version="1.0"?>
<!-- the document prolog indicates this to be an XML-compliant document -->

<Schema name="tablesSchema" xmlns="urn:schemas-microsoft-com:xml-data"
        xmlns:dt="urn:schemas-microsoft-com:datatypes">

    <ElementType name="table-name" content="textOnly"
                 model="closed" dt:type="string">
        <description>The product name of the table</description>
    </ElementType>

    <ElementType name="number-of-legs" content="textOnly" model="closed">
        <datatype dt:type="i4">
            <dt:maxInclusive>12</dt:maxInclusive>
            <dt:min>3</dt:min>
        </datatype>
        <description>The number of legs on the table</description>
    </ElementType>

    <ElementType name="table-top-material" content="textOnly"
                 model="closed" dt:type="string">
        <AttributeType name="type" dt:type="string" />
        <attribute type="type" />
        <description>Describes the type of surface of the table top</description>
    </ElementType>

    <ElementType name="table-shape" content="textOnly" model="closed">
        <description>Specifies the shape of the table</description>
        <datatype dt:type="enumeration">
            <dt:values>round oval oblong square other</dt:values>
        </datatype>
    </ElementType>

    <AttributeType name="currency" dt:type="enumeration"
                   dt:values="USD GBP EURO YEN" default="USD" />

    <ElementType name="retail-price"
                 content="mixed" model="closed">
        <description>Specifies the current retail price of the table</description>
        <attribute type="currency" />
    </ElementType>

    <ElementType name="table" content="eltOnly" model="closed">
        <description>Repeated element that describes each table</description>
        <group order="seq">
            <element type="table-name" />
            <element type="number-of-legs" />
            <element type="table-top-material"  minOccurs="0"/>
            <element type="table-shape" />
            <element type="retail-price" minOccurs="1" maxOccurs="*"/>
        </group>
    </ElementType>

    <ElementType name="tables" content="eltOnly" model="closed">
        <description>The root element of the tables list</description>
        <element type="table" minOccurs="0" maxOccurs="*" />
    </ElementType>

</Schema>
```

Inside a schema, we use the `<ElementType>` and `<AttributeType>` elements to define the elements and attributes that we will use in the XML document. However, the structure of the document (i.e. the way that elements can nest and repeat) is defined using the `<element>` and `<attribute>` elements. This provides the disconnection between the element/attribute definition and the way that it's used in this specific document that we need to provide local scope and inheritance.

You can also see from each element definition that we can define the data type. For example `"i4"` denotes a 4-byte integer, while `"enumeration"` allows us to provide a list of acceptable values. There is also a way to add descriptions to elements and attributes that will be useful to others that read the schema, and in tools that build or manipulate schemas.

More important in many cases is the fact that this is an XML-compliant document. It can be created, parsed and modified using the same techniques that work with the XML documents that contain our data.

Processing XML Documents

To be able to process an XML document, we need some application or device that can read it and make sense of the content, in the same way as a WAP-enabled phone or other device reads and **parses** a WML document. An **XML parser** is a program that takes an XML document as input and makes its components (the elements and attributes) available for processing by other programs. For example, a Java XML parser usually makes the components of an XML document available to a Java program. The components that most programs are interested in are elements and attributes, but some parsers also make processing instructions and comments available as well.

There are many XML parsers to choose from. Sun, IBM, Microsoft, Oracle and a number of smaller companies have ongoing XML parser projects, with stable releases and regular upgrades. The reason there are so many parsers is because XML is increasingly viewed as the best format for data interchange between applications and components of applications (including data interchange between a web server and a web browser). In order to use XML that way, you need a parser.

There are two standard ways in which a parser makes the components of an XML document available to another application: one processes the document in time, the other in space. The **Simple API for XML (SAX)** associates an event with each tag (opening or closing) and with each block of text. You just write the event handlers and sit back to watch the events as the components in the document pass by. The **Document Object Model (DOM)** describes the document as a complete tree of objects. You can traverse it, edit it, do what you please with it, as long as you can keep it all in memory at once.

XML parsers can be validating or non-validating. Non-validating parsers only check for the general XML "well-formedness" of the document: all start tags must have matching end tags, the same attribute cannot have two different values within the same element, and so on. Non-validating parsers can work without a DTD or an XML schema; if one is present they only consult it in limited ways. Validating parsers, by contrast, require a DTD or an XML schema, and they check the document against its rules. There are many more non-validating parsers than validating ones.

Note that we use the Microsoft MSXML parser in our example, and it does not remove excess white space characters automatically. Therefore, when you look at the code files we provide from our web site, you'll find that they are not indented like those shown here. However, the indented format will make it easier to see how it works. You can download the latest version of this parser from: http://msdn.microsoft.com/downloads/webtechnology/xml/msxml.asp.

Transforming XML into Other Formats

The **XML Stylesheet Language** (XSL) provides a way for us to transform the content of any XML document into another format, and apply style information to it at the same time. XSL stylesheets are written in an XML-compliant format, but we use a series of elements that do have a pre-defined meaning in terms of the actions they define for the transformation (otherwise how would we know which ones to use?). The meaning is, of course, defined by the XSL processor itself, which should follow the standards created by the W3C. Hence, as we saw earlier, XSL is an **application** of XML. And, because it is XML-compliant, it means that we can process XSL stylesheets in exactly the same way as we process XML documents. You'll see why this is useful later on in this chapter.

Originally, XSL was a single proposal that specified both the way that XML transformations would be defined, and the way that a platform-independent styling grammar could be used. However, the 'transformations' part of the proposal advanced quickly and proved incredibly useful early on, while there are no real applications that use the 'styling' part of the proposal (and, many would say, little real-world use for it anyway).

The two parts of XSL have been cleaved from the original proposal into two different recommendations. The 'transformations' part is now called **XSLT** (XSL Transformation Language), while the 'styling' part is officially termed XSL Formatting Objects, or **XSL-FO**. We won't be concerning ourselves with the formatting objects part here, as we're only going to be transforming our XML into new formats and structures. So, we need to understand how XSLT works, because this is now the major tool (some would say weapon) in our arsenal when working with XML.

The XSL Transformation Language (XSLT)

XSLT is a version 1.0 recommendation from the W3C. It defines a set of XML elements that can be used to create stylesheets that transform XML documents into *any* other format. Currently, a common use is to transform XML content into HTML suitable for display in a traditional web browser. However, as you'll see later in this chapter, we can use it equally well to transform XML into WML, as well as into other formats such as another XSL stylesheet.

All we do is take an XML document and a suitable XSL stylesheet, and perform the transformation to create the output document. Depending on the content and instructions within the stylesheet, we can create any output format we like. The following diagram shows some of the possibilities:

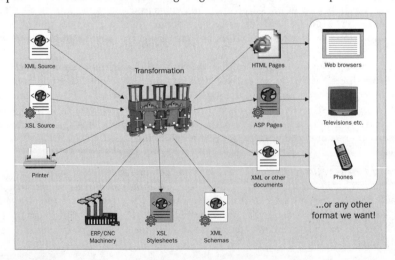

Of course, the trick is to provide the appropriate XSL stylesheet. We won't be covering the intricacies of XSLT here, though we will look at an example of an XSL stylesheet and see how it works. But before we do this, we will take a look at how XPath is related to XSLT, and also what we need to know about how XSL stylesheets are processed.

What is XPath?

An essential feature of a transformation language is the ability to refer to elements and attributes that are stored in a 'tree' within an XML parser using a **path**, both in absolute terms (starting from the root) and in relative terms (according to the current position in the tree). This includes being able to specify paths that satisfy certain conditions, or match certain patterns. As work on XSLT unfolded, this 'path language' was naturally growing in size and sophistication: it was becoming more and more like a "regular expression language for tree paths".

At some point, it was realized that exactly the same path language is needed for XLink and XPointer (two other specifications for hypertext links between XML documents and parts of XML documents). The result was that the path language became separated from both XSLT and XLink/XPointer, and assumed independent existence under the name of **XPath**. XPath was brought to a swift completion, on the same date as XSLT. The combination of XSLT and XPath creates an extremely powerful and easy-to-use tool; if there is one thing a non-programmer should learn these days, it's probably XSLT.

XSLT Processing

There are basically two scenarios for processing XSLT stylesheets. The first is for a browser to come equipped with both an XML parser and an XSLT processor working together. Such a parser would process an XML document directly, using an XSL stylesheet attached to the document. As of this writing (June 2000), only Internet Explorer 5 and Navigator 6 can do this, and IE5 uses a limited version of XSLT. However, we do use IE5 in the following examples, as it is easy to set up and use.

In the second scenario, an XML parser and an XSLT processor, working together somewhere in the background (perhaps on the server or another client machine), produce a transformed XML document – or any kind of document – and send it to another piece of software to do something with it. As we'll see later, the output can be, for example, an HTML or WML file and the receiving application may well be a web browser or WAP microbrowser.

In both of these scenarios, it is the XSLT processor that drives the process: it invokes the XML parser, and receives and transforms the parser output. A parser, as we saw earlier, expects an input that is a valid XML document.

How Does XSLT Work?

Here's part of the simple XML `<tables>` document we saw earlier:

```
<?xml version="1.0" ?>
<tables>
  <table>
    <table-name>Conference</table-name>
    <number-of-legs>4</number-of-legs>
    <table-top-material type="laminate">Ash</table-top-material>
    <table-shape>Oblong</table-shape>
    <retail-price currency="USD">1485</retail-price>
```

```
    </table>
    ...
    ... { more <table> elements go here }
    ...
</tables>
```

Next, here's an extract from an XSL stylesheet designed to perform a transformation on this XML document:

```
<?xml version="1.0" ?>
<xsl:stylesheet xmlns:xsl="http://www.w3.org/TR/WD-xsl">

  <xsl:template match="/">
    <xsl:apply-templates select="//table" />
  </xsl:template>

  <xsl:template match="table">
    <xsl:apply-templates select="table-name" />
  </xsl:template>

  <xsl:template match="table-name">
   <xsl:value-of />
  </xsl:template>

</xsl:stylesheet>
```

When we apply this stylesheet to the XML document shown earlier, the XML processor (or **parser**) goes through an iterative process of matching **templates** in the stylesheet to elements in the XML document. As it finds a match, it carries out the instructions within that template.

So, in our example above, the first step is to look for a template that matches the root element of the XML document. This is identified in the stylesheet with match="/", so the parser then executes the instruction:

```
<xsl:apply-templates select="//table" />
```

This extracts the elements that match the pattern (or **XPath**) of "//table – it matches <table> elements anywhere within the hierarchy of the document (the double slash means 'any descendant'). This set of elements becomes the **current context**. At the same time, the instruction tells it to look for any templates that match <table> elements.

The template that matches the pattern "//table" is next in the stylesheet, with match="table". So, the instruction(s) within it are executed next. The parser carries out the instruction:

```
<xsl:apply-templates select="table-name" />
```

As before, this causes it to extract from the current context of the XML document any elements matching table-name (which then become the new current context) and at the same time look for a suitable template to match this XPath. This is found in the third template.

Within this third template, the instruction is:

```
<xsl:value-of />
```

This tells the parser or XSL processor to output the value of the elements within the current context. So, the result is just a list of table names:

```
Conference
Modern
Dining
Meeting
```

Adding Output Content

Of course, this is just a simple example. In reality, we would add some extra content to the output as we create it using the stylesheet. For example, if we want to create a WML card deck listing the table names, we can add some content to the stylesheet:

```
<?xml version="1.0" ?>
<xsl:stylesheet xmlns:xsl="http://www.w3.org/TR/WD-xsl">

  <xsl:template match="/">
    <xsl:pi name="xml">version="1.0"</xsl:pi>
    <![CDATA[
      <!DOCTYPE wml PUBLIC "-//WAPFORUM//DTD WML 1.1//EN"
                    "http://www.wapforum.org/DTD/wml_1.1.xml">
    ]]>
    <wml>
      <card id="main" title="A List of Tables">
        <p>Select a table from the list of Options:</p>
        <xsl:apply-templates select="//table" />
      </card>
    </wml>
  </xsl:template>

  <xsl:template match="table">
    <xsl:apply-templates select="table-name" />
  </xsl:template>

  <xsl:template match="table-name">
    <xsl:element name="do">
      <xsl:attribute name="label"><xsl:value-of /></xsl:attribute>
      <xsl:attribute name="type">show</xsl:attribute>
      <xsl:element name="go">
        <xsl:attribute name="href">#table-<xsl:value-of /></xsl:attribute>
      </xsl:element>
    </xsl:element>
  </xsl:template>

</xsl:stylesheet>
```

In this case, we're adding WML elements and text within the XSL stylesheet template. Anything that isn't an XSL instruction (does not start with xsl:) is simply copied to the output verbatim. So, the effect of processing the root template will be to output first the opening xml processing instruction element (created by the <xsl:pi> instruction) followed by the contents of the CDATA section that provides the <!DOCTYPE> element. After this come the opening <wml> and <card> elements, and some introductory text.

Next, we execute a template that matches each <table> element, and this causes the execution of another template that matches the <table-name> elements. So, for each table name, this third template creates a WML <do> element (using an xsl:element element) and adds the label and type attributes to it using the xsl:attribute element.

Within this <do> element, it then creates a WML <go> element, and sets the value of the href attribute to "#table-" plus the name of the table (using the xsl:value-of element). So, the result of performing this transformation is:

```
<?xml version="1.0" ?>
<!DOCTYPE wml PUBLIC "-//WAPFORUM//DTD WML 1.1//EN"
          "http://www.wapforum.org/DTD/wml_1.1.xml">
<wml>
  <card id="main" title="A List of Tables">
    <p>Select a table from the list of Options:</p>
    <do label="Conference" type="show">
      <go href="#table-Conference" />
    </do>
    <do label="Modern" type="show">
      <go href="#table-Modern" />
    </do>
    <do label="Dining" type="show">
      <go href="#table-Dining" />
    </do>
    <do label="Meeting" type="show">
      <go href="#table-Meeting" />
    </do>
  </card>
</wml>
```

The result is shown in the next two screenshots:

So What's XHTML All About?

This book is about WML and WAP, and predominantly about access to Internet content and services from mobile phones. However, most existing web pages are written in HTML, and this already carries a huge amount of baggage that we've accumulated over the relatively few years that HTML has been in use.

Existing HTML pages are generally not **well-formed**, so they cannot be parsed and processed by tools designed to work with XML. However, the lax syntax requirements of most browsers mean that even HTML pages that are not valid HTML will usually be displayed – missing off the closing `</TD>` or `</OPTION>` tags doesn't matter, and even overlapping elements (such as `<B>This is some <I>italic</B> text</I>`) are accepted.

So, most HTML pages won't load into an XML parser, or (of course) into a device that expects to receive WML. There is the suspicion that, in the long term, browsers will all support the same markup language – maybe the mess we're in now with non-compatible HTML pages and devices will prompt some more effective action with WML. For example, there is a proposal called XHTML that is gaining popularity in the HTML world. The hope is that it might help us to bridge the gap that currently exists between XML, WML and HTML.

The danger is that we are going to end up with a completely different markup language for each type of device. Instead, the modularization of XHTML allows all markup languages to be just some subset of XHTML. Instead of having a markup language for low-power small screen devices, we would have devices that support the minimum number of XHTML modules, allowing us to grade functionality with the capabilities of the device – while keeping a single markup language.

What is XHTML?

In essence, XHTML is simply a reformulation of HTML into a format that is XML compliant. Why? Well, this allows tools that are designed to work with XML to operate with XHTML documents. And, as XHTML is designed to work in a traditional web browser, it means that your web pages can be processed in the same way as XML documents.

In detail, XHTML does three things designed to promote compatibility and interoperability:

❑ It aims at providing all the required display effects using a **reduced set of standard HTML elements**. This makes it easier for device manufacturers, code developers and users to build applications that are fully compatible with the XHTML standard.

❑ It lays down a **strict set of rules for the syntax of XHTML documents**, based on the standards for XML. This removes the need for a device to cope with documents that are not well-formed, and which are not XML compliant. So devices and applications are easier to develop.

❑ Version 1.1 of the specification **divides the set of available HTML elements into groups**, or **modules**. All devices must support a standard set of 'base' modules, and other modules are optional. However, devices must fully support all of an optional module that they do include. This modularization makes it easier for developers and device manufacturers to specify or discover the exact capabilities of a device.

The modularization of XHTML into a set of predefined sets of elements allows device manufacturers and developers to more easily identify the capabilities of any device. At the moment, the standards just define modules for devices that support HTML. The set of modules defined in XHTML version 1.0 is shown below:

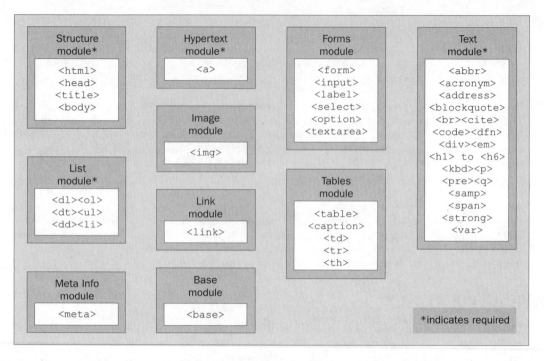

As you can see, this provides all of the standard elements in common use – including the usual HTML form controls such as `<input>` and `<select>`. What are missing are things like `<applet>` and `<object>`, as well as the more esoteric display elements such as `<marquee>` and `<blink>`. However, it's unlikely that many new browsers or any other web devices will support these types of element, and so they are not implemented in the current specifications.

So, a device now only has to specify that it supports the four standard modules – those marked with an asterisk – and indicate which optional ones it also supports. From this information, the developer or web server software can deduce the elements that can be used when serving content to this device.

XHTML and WML?

If cellular phones and mobile devices only support WML, and not HTML, what's the point of talking about XHTML here? Well, as we suggested earlier, nothing in this world is fixed – especially in the computing industry. The Worldwide Web Consortium is working away very hard to provide techniques for generating output from a web site that can be used on all the various types of client that might visit the site.

The proportion of your visitors that are sitting at a normal PC with a web browser decreases in comparison to the other types of 'Internet device' that are rapidly appearing (and the WAP-enabled phone is only one of many such devices). If you are trying to sell something to visitors, be it content, software or some physical object – a CD, a book, a new sports car or a skyscraper – you don't really want to turn potential buyers away just because they aren't using a PC and Internet Explorer 5.

Instead, you need to think about how you can satisfy all these visitors, and XHTML might just provide the key to linking all the parts of what is a complex process together. We'll see how next.

Providing Client-Specific Content

When a device sends a request to a content server, it is easy to detect the type of device by looking for the user agent (UA) string that is sent in the HTTP headers of the request. See Chapter 7 for more details on how we do this. From the UA string, we can redirect the device to a suitable set of pages, optimized for that client:

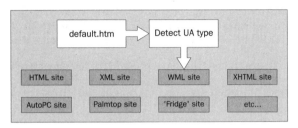

But this still leaves us with the requirement to build multiple sites to suit the various types of client. A better option would be to have some kind of system that can dynamically create the multiple versions of the site we need from a single set of source documents. Each time we change one of the source documents we simply run the update procedure to recreate the files for each version of the site:

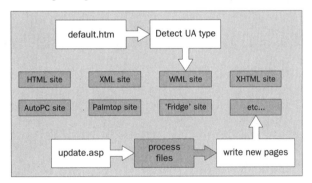

Now, when a client hits the site, they will still be redirected to the appropriate set of pages, but we don't have to spend valuable development time (and money) updating each set of pages individually. Of course, the obvious next question is how do we create the multiple versions of the site automatically from a single set of source documents? This is where the work of the W3C Mobile Access Group comes in.

Document and Device Profiles

One of the main initiatives of the W3C Mobile Access Group is to provide ways for a source document to be used to create multiple versions of a web page, each one suited to a specific set of devices. It depends on three main techniques:

❑ The use of XML to store the information content for a web page document. This is quite possible now.

❑ The use of XSL to merge and transform XML-format documents into new formats. Again, this is quite possible today.

❑ The use of RDF or some other technique to store profiles of the web page document and the device capabilities. Unfortunately, this part of the jigsaw is the one that is still missing.

The principle is that, when a device requests a document, the HTTP headers will include both the traditional user agent string that uniquely identifies the device, and a URL where a **device profile** can be found. This device profile is an RDF or other format document that describes the capabilities of the device in detail (we'll look at an example shortly). The web server will probably cache this document for a specific period, to avoid having to reference the original site on each request.

The device also adds information to the HTTP headers that indicate user-specific settings, such as whether the sound is turned on, whether the user has disabled the display of graphics or (in the case of a PDA for instance) how much extra memory the device has installed. This can be combined with the manufacturer's device profile to give a complete picture of the device's capabilities for this specific user.

The content creator, in the meantime, will have provided a **document profile**. This describes the structure of the page that the user requests, and may include information that doesn't change – such as meta information on keywords, the description, the author, etc. They will also provide a **content document** that contains just the actual information for the page. Both the document profile and the content document will probably be written in an XML format (perhaps RDF, though there is no absolute requirement for this).

The process that takes place when a request for that web page is received is shown below in outline. The device profile and the document profile are combined in such a way as to produce an XSL stylesheet that suits the specific client to the specific document. This stylesheet is then used to transform the XML content into a web page for that client:

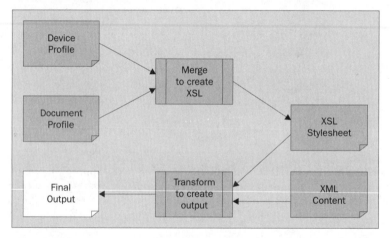

While this process is quite resource-intensive, requiring more processing than a normal HTML page, it does solve the problem we face with multiple disparate clients. In time, it's likely that the web server software and the development environments we use will provide features to automate much of the process.

However, we might decide to reduce the processing requirements by ignoring the user-specific information in the device profile, and simply concentrate on the device information that is standard for the device itself. This allows us to send the same page in response to all requests for that specific device type rather than processing the document for each individual user of that device type.

This is the process we've followed in the example that we describe next in the chapter. It lets us batch-process the documents to create the various sets of pages for each device.

A Multiple Client Compatibility Example

At the start of this chapter, we showed some pages that provided a list and details of a selection of Wrox books. To finish off the chapter, we'll see how these pages can be created from a single source XML document, using the techniques we've been describing in this chapter.

The Structure of the Site

The next diagram shows the structure of the site that we're building. The main directory (named Code) contains the base scripts that perform the processing of the pages for each client. There are also separate subdirectories for:

❑ The device profiles (one for each device, with a name based on its user agent string)

❑ The document profiles that describe each final page's appearance on the various types of device

❑ The XML files that contain the content for each document

❑ The XSL style sheets that create the intermediate output format

❑ The final output files, which are created on demand the first time a client hits the site, and then stored for future use (as described earlier)

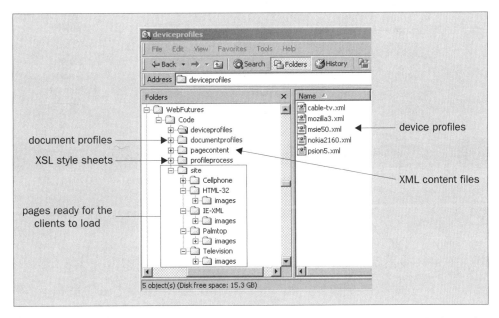

Notice that we only provide an output folder in the main suite directory for each of the basic device types, and not one for each device. We're going to build pages that are broadly suitable for each of the five types of device – cellular phones, basic browsers that support HTML 3.2, Internet Explorer 5.0 and above (sending the client the source XML for them to do the processing), palm-top and hand-held PDAs, and TV set-top boxes.

The Overall Process

The next diagram describes the complete overall process. When we get a request from a client, we detect what kind of device it is from the user agent string that it sends to us. From this, we can deduce which category of device we are dealing with (is it a cellular phone, a TV set-top box or a PDA, for example). Once we know this, we can see if there is a suitable page already available.

If there is, we simply redirect the client to that page. If not, we need to create a suitable page this time. Because the client does not (at present) send the URL of a device profile, we instead use one of our own stored device profiles, matching it to the device details in its user agent string. Then we can collect the document profile for the page that the client requested:

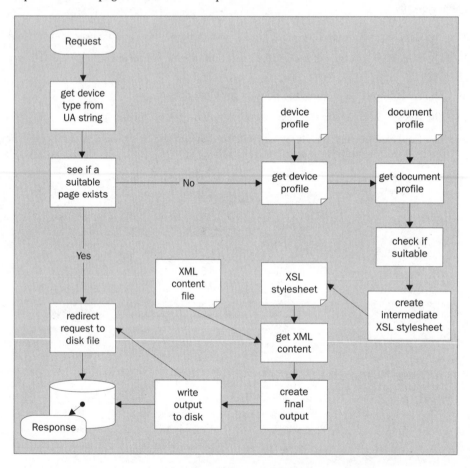

The next step is to see if the client is capable of using this document, based on information in the document profile and device profile. This is where XHTML comes in. We compare the list of XHTML modules that are required to display the final output (listed in the document profile) with the modules that the device actually supports (listed in the device profile). If all is well, this part of the process will also tell us which general type of device we are dealing with, so that we can use the appropriate section of the document profile to generate the output. We'll look at the document and device profiles in more detail shortly.

Although some devices do not support HTML or XHTML, for example cellular phones, this is not what's important here. What the XHTML modules do is give an *indication* of the *capabilities* of the device, so a device that supports images and tables will contain an indication in its device profile of this. In our example, we've modified the device profile to include the XHTML module names, as this is the standard that is most likely to be used.

Now that we know which category this device fits into, we can then use an XSL *profile* stylesheet specific to that device category (from our `profileprocess` directory) to transform the document profile. This transformation creates another XSL stylesheet (the *intermediate* stylesheet), which is specific to this device category and the requested document profile.

Using this newly-created intermediate XSL stylesheet, we can then perform another transformation that converts the information content for the requested document from the XML source file into the final output. We write this output to disk, and then redirect the client to it. Thus, when the next request from that category of device is received, we can send back the disk file we've just created.

Our XML Content Document

The XML document that contains the actual page content (the information) is shown next. You can see that it's a simple list of books, with the full title, a 'short' title, a description, the ISBN code, the path to an image of the cover, and a URL where more information about the book can be obtained:

```
<?xml version="1.0" encoding="UTF-8"?>
<booklist>
   <book>
      <title>Professional Active Server Pages 3.0</title>
      <short-title>Prof. ASP 3.0</short-title>
      <description>
      This book brings <b>Active Server Pages</b> right up to date with ... etc.
      </description>
      <isbn>1861002610</isbn>
      <cover-image>images/2610.gif</cover-image>
      <info-url>http://www.wrox.com/info/2610</info-url>
   </book>
   ...
   ...{ more books listed here }
   ...
</booklist>
```

While we've provided this as an XML-format text document, it could equally well be created using ASP (as described in the last chapter) or any other data access technology. All we have to do is extract the data from a database, wrap it up in the appropriate tags, and add the xml processing instruction to the beginning of it. You might even consider batch-processing the data – creating the XML document as a text file on disk each time the original information changes.

The RDF Device Profile Documents

To be able to discover the capabilities of each client that hits our site, we need to be able to access information about that client. We've provided some 'dummy' RDF files, based on early proposals from the W3C with some custom elements of our own added. The next listing shows the device profile we created for an imaginary Nokia cellular phone:

```xml
<?xml version="1.0"?>
<rdf:RDF xmlns:rdf="http://www.w3.org/1999/02/22-rdf-syntax-ns#"
         xmlns:prf="http://www.w3.org/TR/WD-profile-vocabulary#"
         xmlns:xhtml="http://www.w3.org/1999/xhtml">
   <rdf:Description about="HardwarePlatform">
      <prf:Defaults>
         <rdf:li resource="http://www.nokia.com/profiles/2160" />
      </prf:Defaults>
      <prf:Modifications Memory="2mB" />
   </rdf:Description>
   <rdf:Description about="SoftwarePlatform">
      <prf:Defaults>
         <rdf:li resource="http://www.symbian.com/profiles"/>
      </prf:Defaults>
      <prf:Modifications Sound="Off" Images="Off" />
   </rdf:Description>
   <rdf:Description Vendor="Nokia" Model="2160" Type="PDA" screenSize="24x3x2"
      CPU="PPC" Keyboard="No" Memory="4mB" Bluetooth="Yes" Speaker="Yes" />
   <rdf:Description oS="EPOC1.0" WMLVersion="1.1" WMLScript="1.1" />
   <rdf:Description about="XHTML-modules">
      <xhtml:accept-format>Cellphone</xhtml:accept-format>
      <xhtml:structure />
      <xhtml:text />
      <xhtml:hypertext />
      <xhtml:list />
   </rdf:Description>
</rdf:RDF>
```

You can see that the file is an XML-format document, and uses elements that are part of the RDF proposals. (So, like XSL, RDF is an **application** of XML). The `<rdf:Description>` elements contain information about various features of the device, such as the hardware and software platforms and the vendor and model details. Note that the descriptions also contain `<prf:Modifications>` elements that show user-specific information about this client, such as the fact that sound and image display are both turned off.

The final `<rdf:Description>` element is one we added ourselves. It shows the category that this device fits into `<xhtml:accept-format>`, and a list of the XHTML modules for which this device has support. Remember that this is just an *indication* of the device's abilities. Even if this device doesn't support XHTML, as is the case with current cellular phones, the list of modules will still provide an indication of its actual capabilities – in whatever native markup language it supports. In this particular case, you can see that it is limited to the four required modules.

The XML Document Profile

The next thing we need is a document profile that describes how the page should appear for each of our five chosen device categories. We're using an XML-format document, which has the following basic structure:

```xml
<?xml version="1.0"?>
<page-structure>
   <page-title>A List of Books</page-title>
   <page-url-name>booklist</page-url-name>
   <page-author>Alex Homer</page-author>
   <last-updated>2000-02-26</last-updated>
```

```
    <device-category device-type="IE-XML">
      ...
    </device-category>

    <device-category device-type="HTML-32">
      ...
    </device-category>

    <device-category device-type="Television">
      ...
    </device-category>

    <device-category device-type="Palmtop">
      ...
    </device-category>

    <device-category device-type="Cellphone">
      ...
    </device-category>

  </page-structure>
```

The first section within the root `<page-structure>` element contains details of the document profile itself, such as the page title, name, author and the date it was last updated. Next come the five `<device-category>` elements, one for each of the five device categories.

Our Custom Document Profile Language

At the moment, there is no proposed standard for document profiles. However, in line with the ideals of XML, we've just invented our own. Again, this is an **application** of XML, because we're assigning our own meanings to our own custom elements. You can see some of them in the outline of the document profile shown earlier.

Each `<device-category>` section of the document profile describes the appearance of the final page for one of the specific categories of client device – as described in the `device-type` attribute, which matches the `<xhtml:accept-format>` element values in the RDF device profiles. Earlier, we saw that the device profile for our imaginary Nokia phone has the entry:

```
<xhtml:accept-format>Cellphone</xhtml:accept-format>
```

So the device will be categorized as a cellular phone, and the contents of the `<device-category device-type="Cellphone">` element in the document profile will be used to create the intermediate stylesheet for it.

The 'Cellphone' Document Profile Section

Here is the content of that element in the document profile:

```
    ...
    <device-category device-type="Cellphone">
      <description>
        List for use with text-only small-screen phones and similar devices
      </description>
      <layout-style>
        <page-body>
          <layout-block>
            <card-deck>
```

285

```
                <main-card id="main" title="Books from Wrox">
                  <text content="Select a book from the list of Options:" />
                  <dolist repeat-for-xpath="/booklist/book"
                          sort-by-xpath="./short-title"
                          label-xpath="./short-title" href-xpath="./isbn" />
                </main-card>
                <card-list repeat-for-xpath="/booklist/book" id-xpath="./isbn"
                           title="Wrox Book Details">
                  <element-value element-xpath="./short-title" />
                  <element-value element-xpath="./isbn" />
                  <element-value element-xpath="./description" />
                  <do-item href="http://www.wrox.com/wml/bookinfo.wml"
                           label="More information" />
                  <do-item href="http://www.amazon.com/wml/order.wml"
                           label="Order this book" />
                  <do-item href="#main" label="Return to book list" />
                </card-list>
              </card-deck>
            </layout-block>
          </page-body>
        </layout-style>
      </device-category>
    . . .
```

You can see a range of 'home-made' elements here, which specify the structure of the page we're going to send to all cellular phones. Most are self-explanatory. The section that defines the layout style for the page or output is enclosed within a `</layout-style>` element. Within this, the `<page-body>` is made up of a single `<layout-block>`, which in turn specifies a single WML card deck. The main card includes the introductory text and a `<dolist>` that creates the initial menu.

> *Remember that we are aiming to create a generic format for these documents that will support all kinds of clients, so some of the elements may seem superfluous when we are dealing with simple clients like cellular phones.*

This custom `<dolist>` element specifies a list of WML `<do>` elements that will contain an entry for each item matching the XPath "/booklist/book" (that is, one item for each `<book>` element in the source XML), and that the list will be sorted by the short title of each book. The label for each `<do>` item in the menu is the short title, and the `href` for the `<go>` element it contains (for use when that item is selected) is the ISBN code:

```
<dolist repeat-for-xpath="/booklist/book"
        sort-by-xpath="./short-title"
        label-xpath="./short-title" href-xpath="./isbn" />
```

This is followed by a custom `<card-list>` element that indicates that we want to include in the deck a list of cards. The XPath in the `repeat-for-xpath` attribute specifies that there should be a card for each book in the source XML document, having the ISBN code for the `id` attribute and the `title` attribute "Wrox Book Details". Each card contains the value of the source XML document's `<short-title>`, `<isbn>` and `<description>` elements, so that our visitor can read about the book.

This is followed in each card by three `<do>` items that provide another menu list where the user can obtain more information from our web site, order the book, or return to the main book list. Each of the `<do-item>` elements that create these menu options provides the `label` text for the list, and the URL for the `href` of the `<go>` element it contains.

The Other Document Profile Sections

The other `<device-category>` elements in the document profile use a similar process to describe the output for the other four device categories. We won't be examining them all here, as they are not really concerned with the main focus of this book. However, we'll briefly look at a couple of them. You can examine the complete document to see the remainder – we've included all the code for this application with the rest of the samples for this book, which can be downloaded from our web site.

The next listing shows the `<device-category>` section for Internet Explorer 5 and higher. In this case, the browser can perform the XSL transformation itself, so all we need to send it is a page that instructs it to perform this transformation client-side. This is generally more efficient where the device supports it, and it saves us doing the processing on the server – with the associated use of resources. We make the client do the transformation itself by specifying the two documents it will need – the XML source document and the XSL stylesheet:

```
...
<device-category device-type="IE-XML">
  <require-module>TABLES</require-module>
  <require-module>IMAGE</require-module>
  <require-module>LINK</require-module>
  <description>
    Internet Explorer 5 and higher using client-side XSL transformation
  </description>
  <stylesheet-url>booklist.css</stylesheet-url>
  <layout-style>
    <load-as-xml>
      <xml-document>../../pagecontent/booklist.xml</xml-document>
      <xml-stylesheet>booklist.xsl</xml-stylesheet>
    </load-as-xml>
  </layout-style>
</device-category>
...
```

Notice that in this case, we need the client to support three of the optional XHTML modules, listed in the `<require-module>` elements (we assume that all clients will support the three standard modules, and this is why there were no `<require-module>` elements in the 'Cellphone' section of the file). As we discussed earlier, we use this information in conjunction with the RDF device profile to ensure that the final output page is suitable for this device.

For a client of device category `"Palmtop"`, we are outputting a final page that contains a simple HTML table. The section of the document profile for this device is shown next. You can see that it requires the client to support the XHTML `TABLES` and `IMAGE` modules:

```
...
<device-category device-type="Palmtop">
  <require-module>TABLES</require-module>
  <require-module>IMAGE</require-module>
  <description>
    Table for palm-tops and small-screen devices with graphic capability
  </description>
  <stylesheet-url>booklist.css</stylesheet-url>
  <layout-style>
    <page-head>
```

```
            <layout-block>
              <graphic src="images/wrox.gif" alt="Wrox Press Inc" />
              <text content="A List of Books" styleclass="mainheading" />
            </layout-block>
            <horizontal-rule />
          </page-head>
          <page-body>
            <layout-block>
              <table repeat-for-xpath="/booklist/book" sort-by-xpath="./isbn">
                <table-row>
                  <table-cell row-span="2" styleclass="tablecell">
                    <hyperlink-value href-xpath="info-url">
                      <graphic-value src-xpath="cover-image" alt-xpath="title" />
                    </hyperlink-value>
                  </table-cell>
                  <table-cell align="left" styleclass="tablecellbold">
                    <hyperlink-value href-xpath="info-url">
                      <element-value element-xpath="title" />
                    </hyperlink-value>
                  </table-cell>
                </table-row>
                <table-row>
                  <table-cell styleclass="tablecell">
                    <text content="ISBN: " />
                    <element-value element-xpath="isbn" />
                  </table-cell>
                </table-row>
              </table>
            </layout-block>
          </page-body>
          <page-foot>
            <horizontal-rule />
            <layout-block styleclass="copyright">
              <text content="&#169;2000 " />
              <hyperlink href="http://www.stonebroom.com/" title="Stonebroom" >
                <text content="Stonebroom Software" />
              </hyperlink>
              <text content=", UK" />
            </layout-block>
          </page-foot>
        </layout-style>
      </device-category>
  ...
```

The remainder of this more complex section of the document profile specifies the `<page-head>` (an image and a page heading), a `<page-body>` containing the elements to build an XHTML `<table>`, and a `<page-foot>` with a copyright notice. The rows in the table in the body section are repeated for each book in the source XML content document, and contain the cover image, a hyperlink to a page describing the book, and the ISBN code.

Processing the Document Profile

When a client hits our site, we need to convert the appropriate section of the document profile into a suitable XSL stylesheet. We'll then use this stylesheet (the *intermediate* stylesheet) to create the final output. However, how do we create this intermediate stylesheet from the document profile? The answer is simple – we use another *profile* XSL stylesheet that performs a transformation of the document profile into an XSL stylesheet (yes – we can use an XSL transformation to create a new and different XSL stylesheet). Then we'll use this new intermediate XSL stylesheet to perform the transformation of our source XML content document into the appropriate output format.

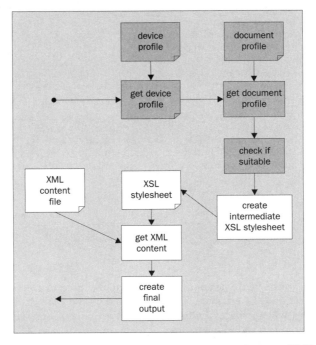

Theoretically, transforming XML into XSL is just the same as transforming XML into HTML, WML or any other format. It just requires a bit more concentration, as the process requires you to think 'two jumps' ahead. You have to decide what the final output will be, figure out what XSL elements are required to create this output, then write the XSL elements that will create these new XSL elements. Make sure you've got a big jug of black coffee and some aspirins close at hand before you start.

The XSL stylesheets that perform this first level of processing are stored in the `profileprocess` directory of our application, and there is one for each device category. We'll just look at the one for a cellular phone here. You can examine the others at your leisure to see how they work.

The 'Cellphone' ProfileProcess XSL File

The first step in our intermediate stylesheet is to provide a template that matches the root element in our document profile. From this template, we first create the `xml` 'version' processing instruction that will start off the final XSL stylesheet, as we saw done in our earlier examples. This is followed by an `<xsl:element>` instruction that creates the opening `<xsl:stylesheet>` element. To this we add the xmlns attribute using an `<xsl:attribute>` instruction. Then we have to create the template that will match the root element of the XML content document that we'll be transforming with our new stylesheet:

```
<xsl:stylesheet xmlns:xsl="http://www.w3.org/TR/WD-xsl">
<!-- stylesheet to merge data with structure for devicetype='Cellphone' -->

  <xsl:template match="/">
    <xsl:pi name="xml">
      <xsl:attribute name="version">1.0</xsl:attribute>
    </xsl:pi>
    <xsl:element name="xsl:stylesheet">
      <xsl:attribute name="xmlns:xsl">
      http://www.w3.org/TR/WD-xsl</xsl:attribute>
```

```
        <!-- create root template -->
        <xsl:element name="xsl:template">
          <xsl:attribute name="match">/</xsl:attribute>
          <![CDATA[
          <?xml version="1.0" ?>
          <!DOCTYPE wml PUBLIC "-//WAPFORUM//DTD WML 1.1//EN"
                        "http://www.wapforum.org/DTD/wml_1.1.xml">
          ]]>
          <wml>
            <!-- apply templates to create the other element templates -->
            <xsl:apply-templates
             select="/page-structure/device-category[./@device-type='Cellphone']"
             />
          </wml>
        </xsl:element>

      </xsl:element>
    </xsl:template>
    ...
```

The `<xsl:element name="xsl:template">` instruction is used to create a template element, and within it we add the `match="/"` attribute. This is followed by the `<!DOCTYPE>` instruction, and then the `<wml>` element that will appear in the final output. Within the `<wml>` element, we simply apply the templates defined later in this stylesheet to create the deck content. The XPath we've used in the `<apply-templates>` instruction selects only the contents of the `<device-category>` element of the document profile that has a `device-type` attribute '@' with the value `"Cellphone"`, so only this part of the document will be processed:

```
select="/page-structure/device-category[./@device-type='Cellphone']"
```

The result of processing this part of the stylesheet gives us:

```
<?xml version="1.0" ?>
<xsl:stylesheet xmlns:xsl="http://www.w3.org/TR/WD-xsl">

  <xsl:template match="/">
    <?xml version="1.0" ?>
    <!DOCTYPE wml PUBLIC "-//WAPFORUM//DTD WML 1.1//EN"
                  "http://www.wapforum.org/DTD/wml_1.1.xml">
    <wml>
        ...
        ... rest of output will go here
        ...
    </wml>
  </xsl:template>
</xsl:stylesheet>
```

There is one minor problem here at the moment, in that the MSXML processor we use to perform the transformations replaces characters in a CDATA section with their XML **character entity equivalents**. This means that we get the output:

```
&lt;?xml version="1.0" ?&gt;
&lt;!DOCTYPE wml PUBLIC "-//WAPFORUM//DTD WML 1.1//EN"
                  "http://www.wapforum.org/DTD/wml_1.1.xml"&gt;
```

In our example application, we solve the problem by replacing these entity equivalents with the original angle brackets just before we send back the file. You'll see this later on.

Next come the templates that are used to create the remainder of the new stylesheet content. There are three templates that match, in turn, the `<device-category>`, `<page-body>` and `<layout-block>` elements in the document profile. Each simply calls the next template in the 'chain', passing it the appropriate set of child elements by using `select="./*"`:

```
...
<!-- end of the stylesheet we are creating dynamically. -->
<!-- following templates used only in dynamic creation -->
<!-- of this stylesheet, and do not appear within it.  -->

<xsl:template match="device-category">
  <xsl:apply-templates select="layout-style/page-body" />
</xsl:template>

<xsl:template match="page-body">
  <xsl:apply-templates select="./*" />
</xsl:template>

<xsl:template match="layout-block">
  <xsl:apply-templates select="./*" />
</xsl:template>
...
```

The 'Card Deck' Template

The template that matches the `<card-deck>` element in our document profile does two things. First it applies a template to the `<main-card>` element, and then uses an `<xsl:for-each>` instruction to apply another template to each `<card-list>` element:

```
...
<xsl:template match="card-deck">
  <xsl:apply-templates select="./main-card" />
  <xsl:for-each select="./card-list">
    <xsl:apply-templates select="." />
  </xsl:for-each>
</xsl:template>
...
```

This will enable us to create the main card first, and then add any other cards that we need for our final output.

The 'Main Card' Template

The template for the main card – the one seen when the page is first loaded – is shown next. It creates a WML `<card>` element and adds to it two attributes:

❑ An id attribute with the value contained in the id attribute of the `<main-card>` element in the document profile

❑ A title attribute with the value contained in the title attribute of the `<main-card>` element in the document profile

291

In other words, it basically just copies the attributes from the <main-card> element in the document profile to the WML <card> element in our final XSL stylesheet. Then, within the <card> element, it applies any templates that match the child elements within the <main-card> element:

```
...
<xsl:template match="main-card">
  <xsl:element name="card">
    <xsl:attribute name="id">
      <xsl:value-of select="./@id" />
    </xsl:attribute>
    <xsl:attribute name="title">
      <xsl:value-of select="./@title" />
    </xsl:attribute>
    <xsl:apply-templates select="./*" />
  </xsl:element>
</xsl:template>
...
```

If you look back at the document profile, you'll see that the only two elements we have within the <main-card> element are a <text> element and a <dolist> element. We'll see how these are processed next.

The 'Text' Template

The template that's processed for each <text> element is simple. It just copies the value from the content attribute of the <text> element in the document profile into the new stylesheet, placing it into a <p> element:

```
...
<xsl:template match="text">
  <p><xsl:value-of select="@content" /></p>
</xsl:template>
...
```

The 'Do List' Template

The template that's processed for each <dolist> element, however, is considerably more complex. It has to create a section of the new stylesheet that will generate the list of <do> elements and their individual <go> elements. This is what we want to end up with for the first <card> element in our stylesheet:

```
...
<card id="main" title="Books from Wrox">
  <p>Select a book from the list of Options:</p>
  <xsl:for-each select="/booklist/book" order-by="./short-title">
    <xsl:element name="do">
      <xsl:attribute name="label">
        <xsl:value-of select="./short-title" />
      </xsl:attribute>
      <xsl:attribute name="type">show</xsl:attribute>
      <xsl:element name="go">
        <xsl:attribute name="href">
          #book_
          <xsl:value-of select="./isbn" />
        </xsl:attribute>
      </xsl:element>
    </xsl:element>
  </xsl:for-each>
</card>
...
```

The <card> and <p> elements have already been created by the two previous templates, so we only need to create the <xsl:for-each> element in this template. The code to do it is shown in the next listing. By comparing it to the output it generates, you should be able to see how it works:

```
...
<xsl:template match="dolist">
  <xsl:element name="xsl:for-each">
    <xsl:attribute name="select">
      <xsl:value-of select="@repeat-for-xpath" />
    </xsl:attribute>
    <xsl:attribute name="order-by">
      <xsl:value-of select="@sort-by-xpath" />
    </xsl:attribute>
    <xsl:element name="xsl:element">
      <xsl:attribute name="name">do</xsl:attribute>
      <xsl:element name="xsl:attribute">
        <xsl:attribute name="name">label</xsl:attribute>
        <xsl:element name="xsl:value-of">
          <xsl:attribute name="select">
            <xsl:value-of select="@label-xpath" />
          </xsl:attribute>
        </xsl:element>
      </xsl:element>
      <xsl:element name="xsl:attribute">
        <xsl:attribute name="name">type</xsl:attribute>
        show
      </xsl:element>
      <xsl:element name="xsl:element">
        <xsl:attribute name="name">go</xsl:attribute>
        <xsl:element name="xsl:attribute">
          <xsl:attribute name="name">href</xsl:attribute>
          #book_
          <xsl:element name="xsl:value-of">
          <xsl:attribute name="select">
            <xsl:value-of select="@href-xpath" />
          </xsl:attribute>
        </xsl:element>
        </xsl:element>
      </xsl:element>
    </xsl:element>
  </xsl:element>
</xsl:template>
...
```

The 'Card List' Template

The remaining templates are reasonably simple compared to the one you've just seen. When we meet a <card-list> element in our document profile, we need to create a set of WML card elements that describe each book. What we're aiming to create in our new stylesheet is something like this:

```
<xsl:for-each select="/booklist/book">
  <xsl:element name="card">
    <xsl:attribute name="id">
      book_
      <xsl:value-of select="./isbn" />
    </xsl:attribute>
    <xsl:attribute name="title">
      Wrox Book Details
    </xsl:attribute>
```

```
      <p><xsl:value-of select="./short-title" /></p>
      <p><xsl:value-of select="./isbn" /></p>
      <p><xsl:value-of select="./description" /></p>
      <do label="More information" type="show">
        <go href="http://www.wrox.com/wml/bookinfo.wml" />
      </do>
      <do label="Order this book" type="show">
        <go href="http://www.amazon.com/wml/order.wml" />
      </do>
      <do label="Return to book list" type="show">
        <go href="#main" />
      </do>
    </xsl:element>
  </xsl:for-each>
```

The template that creates the `<xsl:for-each>` element is shown in the next listing. You can see that it copies the value of the `repeat-for-xpath` attribute from the `<card-list>` element in the document profile into the `select` attribute of the `<xsl:for-each>` element. Then it creates the `<xsl:element>` instruction that will create each WML `<card>` in the new stylesheet. To this it adds the `<xsl:attribute>` instruction to create the `id` attribute in the new stylesheet, and sets its value to an XPath (copied from the `id-xpath` attribute in the document profile) that will select the ISBN code for each book. This is followed by another `<xsl:attribute>` instruction that creates the `title` attribute in the new stylesheet, and sets its value to an XPath that will select the title for each book:

```
    ...
    <xsl:template match="card-list">
      <xsl:element name="xsl:for-each">
        <xsl:attribute name="select">
          <xsl:value-of select="@repeat-for-xpath" />
        </xsl:attribute>
        <xsl:element name="xsl:element">
          <xsl:attribute name="name">card</xsl:attribute>
          <xsl:element name="xsl:attribute">
            <xsl:attribute name="name">id</xsl:attribute>
            book_
            <xsl:element name="xsl:value-of">
              <xsl:attribute name="select">
                <xsl:value-of select="@id-xpath" />
              </xsl:attribute>
            </xsl:element>
          </xsl:element>
          <xsl:element name="xsl:attribute">
            <xsl:attribute name="name">title</xsl:attribute>
            <xsl:value-of select="@title" />
          </xsl:element>
          <xsl:apply-templates select="./*" />
        </xsl:element>
      </xsl:element>
    </xsl:template>
    ...
```

Finally, this template uses an `<xsl:apply-templates>` instruction to execute any templates that match child elements (`select="./*"`) of the `<card-list>` element in the document profile. These child elements are the `<element-value>` and `<do-item>` elements. These will create the final sections of our new stylesheet – the following, which is part of the listing shown right at the start of the section about this template:

```
...
<p><xsl:value-of select="./short-title" /></p>
<p><xsl:value-of select="./isbn" /></p>
<p><xsl:value-of select="./description" /></p>
<do label="More information" type="show">
  <go href="http://www.wrox.com/wml/bookinfo.wml" />
</do>
<do label="Order this book" type="show">
  <go href="http://www.amazon.com/wml/order.wml" />
</do>
<do label="Return to book list" type="show">
  <go href="#main" />
</do>
...
```

The 'Element Value' Template

Each <element-value> element in the document profile describes an element whose value we want to appear in the final output (not in the XSL stylesheet we're creating). For this to happen, we have to create an <xsl:value-of> instruction in our new stylesheet, which specifies the appropriate element in the source XML content document. This is how it's done:

```
...
<xsl:template match="element-value">
  <p>
    <xsl:element name="xsl:value-of">
      <xsl:attribute name="select">
        <xsl:value-of select="@element-xpath" />
      </xsl:attribute>
    </xsl:element>
  </p>
</xsl:template>
...
```

This simply creates an instruction, like the following, in the new stylesheet:

```
<p><xsl:value-of select="./short-title" /></p>
```

As this template is executed three times in our sample document profile with different values for the element-xpath attribute, we get the three <xsl:value-of> elements shown earlier.

The 'Do Item' Template

Finally, we need to create the output for the <do-item> elements in the document profile. For each one, we execute this template:

```
...
<xsl:template match="do-item">
  <do>
    <xsl:attribute name="label">
      <xsl:value-of select="@label" />
    </xsl:attribute>
```

```
      <xsl:attribute name="type">show</xsl:attribute>
      <go>
        <xsl:attribute name="href">
          <xsl:value-of select="@href" />
        </xsl:attribute>
      </go>
    </do>
  </xsl:template>
  ...
```

All it does for each `<do-item>` element in the document profile is to create a WML `<do>` element, and add to it the `label` and `type` attributes. The value for the `label` attribute is copied from the value of the `label` attribute in the document profile, while the `type` attribute is always set to `"show"`. Within each of the `<do>` elements it creates, the template also creates a WML `<go>` element, setting the value of its `href` attribute to the value in the `href` attribute of the document profile's `<do-item>` element.

Re-usability of the XSL Stylesheet

So, that's all there is to it. Yes, it is tough to create these intermediate stylesheets, but remember that all they are doing is transforming our custom document profile language elements into 'real' XSL stylesheet instructions that will transform the source XML content into the final output.

When we create other document profiles and other source XML content documents, we don't have to provide a new 'profile process' stylesheet like that we've just been describing. We just need one 'profile process' stylesheet per device category, and this can be used to process any document profile that contains the same custom elements as our example. It will produce the appropriate XSL stylesheet for the final output transformation.

All it is doing is allowing us to write document profiles in a 'short-hand' language, which is easier than having to design the final XSL stylesheet each time. For example, we used the custom element:

```
<dolist repeat-for-xpath="/booklist/book" sort-by-xpath="./short-title"
        label-xpath="./short-title" href-xpath="./isbn" />
```

in our document profile, and this was automatically transformed into:

```
<xsl:for-each select="/booklist/book" order-by="./short-title">
  <xsl:element name="do">
    <xsl:attribute name="label">
      <xsl:value-of select="./short-title" />
    </xsl:attribute>
    <xsl:attribute name="type">show</xsl:attribute>
    <xsl:element name="go">
      <xsl:attribute name="href">
        #book_
        <xsl:value-of select="./isbn" />
      </xsl:attribute>
    </xsl:element>
  </xsl:element>
</xsl:for-each>
```

When we want a similar list in another page, we just use a `<dolist>` element in our document profile.

The 'process.asp' Main Processing Script

The processing you've seen so far is generic in that it uses the standard XSLT techniques to perform the transformations. However, to drive the whole application, we need some script that actually carries out the mechanics of the process – loading the files, executing the transformations, and writing the results to disk. This is done in our sample application by an Active Server Pages script, which uses the Microsoft MSXML parser.

To remind you of the process, here's the detail diagram again:

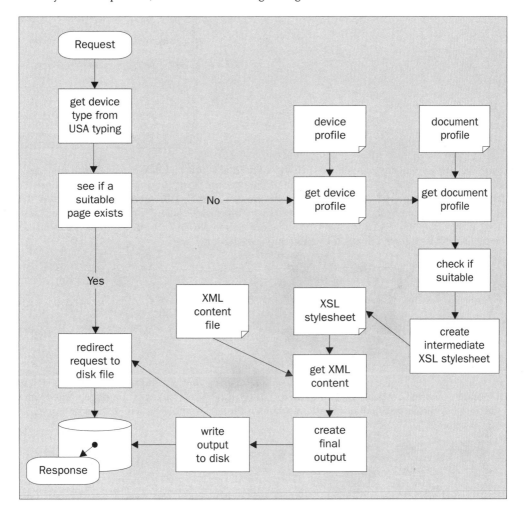

Detecting the Device Type

As this is just a demonstration of a concept, we built the
application to run in a normal web browser. The main
page, `process.asp`, is called from a default page named
`default.htm`. This page contains controls that allow you
to select which type of device you want to be, and also
view some of the intermediate results. You can see the five
different device categories that we've implemented. The
page that is loaded is always `booklist.htm` – we're
displaying the result in the browser, so we are creating
HTML as the final output in each case except for the
cellular phone where we create WML.

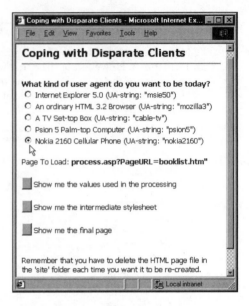

So, having chosen our device type, we can view the final result by clicking the third button to execute
the page `process.asp`, passing it the name of the page we want (`booklist.htm`) appended to the
URL. In our ASP page, we use a #include statement to insert a file named `xml_procedures.inc`,
which contains some useful functions that will make our task easier. We originally created this library of
procedures to help build various XML applications. It's included with the samples, and you can use this
in your own ASP pages if you wish by inserting it in the same way:

```
<%@LANGUAGE="VBScript"%>
<%
Response.Buffer = True
%>

<!-- #include file="xml_procedures.inc" -->
...
```

Now we can get the device type, using the user agent string that we chose in the default page as the
value of the selected `<RADIO>` button named `UAString`. We also extract the page name from the URL
as the value of the `PageURL` name/value pair (even though we know it will always be `booklist.htm`
in our example):

```
...
<%
'-- get the device profile name
'-- this would be processed from the user-agent string
strDeviceName = LCase(Request("UAString"))

'-- get the URL of the structure page
strPageName = Request("PageURL")    'the page to return to the client
...
```

Providing that we got a device name in the user agent string, we can load the appropriate RDF device profile document into an instance of the MSXML parser. To do this, we use a custom function included in the `xml_procedures.inc` file named `LoadAndParseXML`. It returns a reference to the parser object if it succeeds in loading and parsing the document. If not, it returns `Nothing`, and the second parameter will then contain the error message generated by the parser:

```
...
If Len(strDeviceName) > 0 Then

  Dim strError   'to hold error text
  '-- load the specified device profile RDF file
  strDeviceProfile = "deviceprofiles/" & strDeviceName & ".xml"
  Set objDevProp = LoadAndParseXML(strDeviceProfile, strError)
  ...
```

If we did manage to load the document without an error, we can now extract the device category from it, using another method of working with XML documents. The XML parser exposes the document it loads as a tree structure called the **XML Document Object Model**, or **XML DOM**. By using standard methods and properties of the DOM, we can get at the values that the XML document contains, and even change them while it's loaded into the parser:

```
...
If Not objDevProp Is Nothing Then
  Set objRoot = objDevProp.documentElement

  '-- get the preferred 'accept format' or 'device type'
  Set colNodeList = objRoot.getElementsByTagname("xhtml:accept-format")
  strDeviceType = "html-32"
  If colNodeList.length > 0 Then strDeviceType = colNodeList(0).text
  ...
```

In the code above, we're getting a reference to the root element of the document, and then creating a list of all the elements (or **nodes** in XML-speak) named `"xhtml:accept-format"`. The text-type child node of the `<xhtml:accept-format>` element contains the value of this element, and we use this as our device category. By presetting the value to `"html-32"`, we'll use this as the default in case we don't find a value in the device profile.

Redirecting the Client to the Appropriate Page

Now we can see if we already have a suitable page for clients of this device category by looking in the appropriate subdirectory of the main site directory. We create a URL that points to the file that was requested. However, if we are serving to a cellular phone, we need to replace the `.htm` part with `.wml`, as this is the format we'll be creating in this case:

```
...
'-- set the name of the final output file
strPageURL = "site/" & strDeviceType & "/" & strPageName
'-- see if we are creating a WML file for a Cellphone
If LCase(strDeviceType) = "cellphone" Then
  '-- if so, need to save the output page as 'xxxxxxx.wml'
  strPageURL = Replace(strPageURL, ".htm", ".wml")
End If
...
```

Then we can use another of our custom functions in the xml_procedures.inc file to convert this to an absolute file path and see if the page exists. If it does, we just redirect the client to it. If not, we need to create the file now, and so we use the name of the file to build up the paths to the document profile and XML content document that we'll be using:

```
...
'-- see if a suitable page has already been created
Dim strPhysicalPath   'to hold return value
If GetAbsoluteFilePath(strPageURL, True, strPhysicalPath) Then
  '-- page exists so return it to the client
  Response.Clear
  Response.Redirect strPageURL
  Response.End
End If

'-- not created already, so need to create it now
'-- get the path to the document profile and the XML content files
strNameOnly = Left(strPageName, InStrRev(strPageName, ".") - 1)
strStructureURL = "documentprofiles/" & strNameOnly & ".xml"
strContentURL = "pagecontent/" & strNameOnly & ".xml"
...
```

Checking the Device Capabilities

Before we start creating the page, we check to see if the particular device we're dealing with can support all the XHTML modules we specify in our document profile. We already have the device profile loaded into an instance of the MSXML parser, so we can go through it collecting a list of the optional XHTML modules that this device supports as Boolean values:

```
...
'-- get the list of XHTML modules this device supports
Set colNodeList = objRoot.getElementsByTagname("xhtml:tables")
blnTables = (colNodeList.length > 0)
Set colNodeList = objRoot.getElementsByTagname("xhtml:image")
blnImages = (colNodeList.length > 0)
Set colNodeList = objRoot.getElementsByTagname("xhtml:link")
blnLink = (colNodeList.length > 0)
Set colNodeList = objRoot.getElementsByTagname("xhtml:forms")
blnForms = (colNodeList.length > 0)
Set colNodeList = objRoot.getElementsByTagname("xhtml:metainfo")
blnMeta = (colNodeList.length > 0)
Set colNodeList = objRoot.getElementsByTagname("xhtml:base")
blnBase = (colNodeList.length > 0)
...
```

Next, we need to compare these values to the document profile contents. We load the document profile into another instance of the MSXML parser, and get a list of all the <require-module> elements from the appropriate <device-category> element. This is done by using the SelectNodes method with an XPath that specifies the current device category. For a cellular phone, for example, this will be:

```
"/page-structure/device-category[./@device-type = 'Cellphone']"
```

Having got a reference to the correct <device-category> element, we can use the getElementsByTagname method of the XML DOM to get a collection of all the <require-module> elements:

```
   ...
'-- compare these with the page structure requirements
'-- using the page structure XML file
Set objPgStruct = LoadAndParseXML(strStructureURL, strError)
If Not objPgStruct Is Nothing Then
   Set objRoot = objPgStruct.documentElement
   '-- select the appropriate device category
   strSelect = "/page-structure/device-category[./@device-type = '" _
           & strDeviceType & "']"
   Set colNodeList = objRoot.selectNodes(strSelect)
   If colNodeList.length = 1 Then
      Set colNodeList = colNodeList(0).getElementsByTagname("require-module")
      ...
```

Now we can step through the collection extracting the value from the text node of each one, and checking that the Boolean values we saved earlier for the modules that the device supports agree with our requirements. If not, we stop with an error message:

```
   ...
blnError = False
For Each objNode In colNodeList
  Select Case objNode.text
    Case "STRUCTURE"   '-- do nothing
    Case "LIST"        '-- do nothing
    Case "HYPERTEXT"   '-- do nothing
    Case "TEXT"        '-- do nothing
    Case "TABLES"
       If Not blnTables Then blnError = True
    Case "IMAGE"
       If Not blnImages Then blnError = True
    Case "LINK"
       If Not blnLink Then blnError = True
    Case "FORMS"
       If Not blnForms Then blnError = True
    Case "BASE"
       If Not blnBase Then blnError = True
    Case "METAINFO"
       If Not blnMeta Then blnError = True
    Case Else
       blnError = True
  End Select
Next
If blnError Then
   Response.Write "<p>Page structure file '" & strStructureURL _
      & "' is not valid for device profile '" & strDeviceName & "'</p>"
Else
   ...
```

Creating the Intermediate XSL Stylesheet

We're now in a position to create the intermediate stylesheet from the document profile and the profile XSL stylesheet that matches this device category. We already have the document profile loaded into a parser instance referenced by objPgStruct, so we just need to load the correct stylesheet:

```
      ...
   '-- OK to create document based on this structure and device profile
   '-- process specified structure document to create the XSL stylesheet
   strProcessXSLFile = "profileprocess/" & strNameOnly & "_" _
                   & LCase(strDeviceType) & ".xsl"
```

301

```
Set objXSLFile = LoadAndParseXML(strProcessXSLFile, strError)
If Not objXSLFile Is Nothing Then
  '-- perform tranformation to get final XSL stylesheet
  strResult = objPgStruct.transformNode(objXSLFile)
  ...
```

The final line of code above then performs the transformation, and returns the new stylesheet as a string in the variable `strResult`. Before we go any further, we check to see if the user clicked the button to display the intermediate processing values:

```
...
'-- show the values being used if required for debugging
If Len(Request.Form("showvalues")) Then
    '-- user clicked 'Show Intermediate Values' button
    Response.Write "<pre>Device Name: <b>" & strDeviceName & "</b>"
    Response.Write "Device Type: <b>" & strDeviceType & "</b>"
    ... { output other values output here } ...
    Response.End
End If
...
```

Here's the result of clicking the Show Intermediate Values button when the device category is `"Cellphone"`:

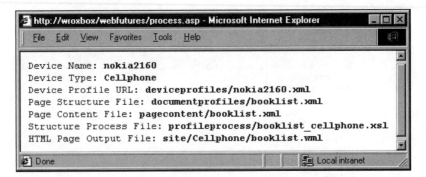

We also check to see if they clicked the button to show the intermediate stylesheet (as held in the variable `strResult`):

```
...
'-- display this stylesheet if required for debugging
If Len(Request.Form("showdevicexsl")) Then
    '-- user clicked 'Show Intermediate Stylesheet' button
    Response.Clear
    Response.ContentType ="text/xml"
    Response.Write strResult
    Response.End
End If
...
```

Here's the result of clicking the Show Intermediate Stylesheet button when the device category is `"Cellphone"`, seen in Internet Explorer 5:

```
http://wroxbox/webfutures/process.asp - Microsoft Internet Explorer

File   Edit   View   Favorites   Tools   Help

<?xml version="1.0" ?>
- <xsl:stylesheet xmlns:xsl="http://www.w3.org/TR/WD-xsl">
  - <xsl:template match="/">
      <?xml version="1.0" ?> <!DOCTYPE wml PUBLIC "-//WAPFORUM//DTD
      WML 1.1//EN" "http://www.wapforum.org/DTD/wml_1.1.xml">
    - <wml>
      - <card id="main" title="Books from Wrox">
          <p>Select a book from the list of Options:</p>
        - <xsl:for-each select="/booklist/book" order-by="./short-title">
          - <xsl:element name="do">
            - <xsl:attribute name="label">
                <xsl:value-of select="./short-title" />
              </xsl:attribute>
              <xsl:attribute name="type">show</xsl:attribute>
            - <xsl:element name="go">
              - <xsl:attribute name="href">
                  #book_
                  <xsl:value-of select="./isbn" />
                </xsl:attribute>
              </xsl:element>
            </xsl:element>
          </xsl:for-each>
      </card>
    - <xsl:for-each select="/booklist/book">
      - <xsl:element name="card">
        - <xsl:attribute name="id">
            book_
            <xsl:value-of select="./isbn" />
          </xsl:attribute>

Done                                                     Local intranet
```

You can clearly see here how the relevant section of our document profile has been transformed into a new XSL stylesheet aimed at creating the final WML output for our cellular phone clients.

Creating the Final Output

So, we've got our intermediate stylesheet, and (providing that the 'Show the Final Page' button was clicked), we can go ahead and use it to transform the source XML content document into the final output. We load the intermediate stylesheet string `strResult` into a new instance of the MSXML parser, and the source XML document into another new instance. Then we perform the transformation:

```
...
'-- otherwise, perform the transformation to create the final output
'-- page using the content document and the newly created stylesheet
Set objXSLFile = LoadAndParseXML(strResult, strError)
If Not objXSLFile Is Nothing Then
   '-- load the appropriate XML content data file
   Set objXMLFile = LoadAndParseXML(strContentURL, strError)
   If Not objXMLFile Is Nothing Then
      '-- perform tranformation to get final output document
      strResult = objXMLFile.transformNode(objXSLFile)
   ...
```

Now the variable `strResult` holds the final output that we need to send to the client. We first use our custom function to get the absolute physical path to the directory where we'll be placing the file (one of the subdirectories within the site directory). However, if we have created the WML version of the page, we have a minor task to complete before we can write the file to disk. As mentioned earlier, we have to convert the XML character entities for the open and close angle brackets (< and >) back into the 'proper' characters. We do this using the VBScript `Replace` function:

```
        ...
        blnOK = GetAbsoluteFilePath(strPageURL, False, strPhysicalPath)
        If blnOK Then
            '-- see if we are creating a WML file for a Cellphone
            If LCase(strDeviceType) = "cellphone" Then
                '-- if so, need to modify the file contents because
                '-- output from XSL has HTMLEncoded element delimiters, so:
                strResult = Replace(strResult, "&lt;", "<")
                strResult = Replace(strResult, "&gt;", ">")
            End If
        ...
```

Finally, we can write the newly created output document to disk, and redirect our visitor to it:

```
        ...
        blnOK = WriteToFile(strPhysicalPath, strResult, strError)
        If blnOK Then
            Response.Clear
            Response.Redirect strPageURL
            Response.End
        ...
```

The remainder of the page is simply the error handling code for each of the `If...Then` constructs that we started in our code, and we haven't listed it here. You can examine and try out the code yourself, as it is included in the samples of code that can be downloaded from our web site. And the final result? When we execute the application with the 'Nokia cellular phone' option selected, this is what we get in IE5:

You can see that IE5 recognizes and parses WML quite happily, even adding in the optional attributes such as `newcontent` and `ordered` that we missed out in our code. You can also expand and collapse the various parts of the XML document to make it easier to see what it contains. To see the result in your WML editor or WML development environment, simply load the page `booklist.wml` from the `Cellphone` subdirectory of the main site directory:

Summary

In this chapter, we've discussed the issues that arise when you need to produce output for WAP-enabled devices such as mobile phones. We started with a look at the kind of impact the various different types of new client will make, and the design issues that we will have to face and overcome in the future. We tried to make you think about the fundamental way you approach building a web site that has to cope with multiple, disparate clients.

Then we moved on to look at the eXtensible Markup Language and its associated technologies such as XSLT, XPath and XHTML. Together with some server-side scripting, these provided us with one solution to the problem of coping with those multiple, disparate clients.

Finally, we saw how all this worked in practice with an example using ASP. In the next chapter, we'll be seeing some similar tricks – but on a different platform. We'll be finding out how to use JSP to produce web and WAP output, and compare this technique with the use of XSLT.

10

Java, XML and WAP

In this chapter, we show how to generate WML content using Java Server Pages (JSP) and XML. We use as a specific focus for the chapter the development of an application that uses a database as its data source. This application is a Ride Board, and may be familiar to many students across the world. It enables people to either post or look for rides (or lifts) from one place to another.

In this chapter, we will think of the actual WML content of the decks that are sent to the user as the tip of a large application iceberg, or the icing on a big application cake. Most of the work is done elsewhere, in processing the user request and obtaining the data the user wants. Once this is done, we just need a general-purpose output component that wraps the data into WML, but can also wrap it into other formats. This output component is our main interest, and we will present two versions of it, a JSP version and an XSLT version. After we present both of them, you will be able to decide for yourself which of these technologies works better for you. We believe that both have a great potential and both should be in the toolkit of a WAP and web programmer.

This chapter may be approached in two halves. In the first half, we consider using JSP as the output component. In order to do this, we start the chapter with an introduction firstly to servlets, and then JSP. If these technologies are already common knowledge to you, then of course you may move forward to the following sections where we first discuss the strategies of developing the application, and then go on to explain the application in full.

In the second half of this chapter we will be considering using XSLT as the output component for the application. Since XSLT was discussed in detail in Chapter 9, we quickly move onto an example, and then redevelop the Ride Board application in this perspective.

In order to work through this chapter, you need to have a little background knowledge of Java and XML. In Java, you just need to know the basics of the language, as we will introduce the necessary background in servlets and JSP. In XML, you need to know about XML documents, DTDs, what it means for a document to be well formed and valid, and the details of the XSLT language. This, together with material on XML parsing and XSLT processing, was discussed in Chapter 9 of this book. We also assume that you know how a SAX parser works. We will be using some SAX classes and interfaces, such as `InputSource` *and* `DocumentHandler`.

After you finish the chapter, you will have learnt two important technologies: servlets and JSP, and obtained a deeper understanding of XSLT. Our main focus will be JSP and XSLT but, as you will see, an understanding of servlets is necessary because they are actively involved with the other two technologies: JSP are just servlets in disguise, and an XSLT processor is most commonly used within a servlet. In addition to learning about those technologies, you will, more importantly, learn how to use them within a 3-tier application with Java middleware.

The Ride Board Application

The application is fairly small but it goes much further than generating WAP content from an XML file: it is a complete 3-tier application, in the sense that it has a dedicated component that retrieves data from a database and makes it available for either web or WAP output. The database component is robust (it provides for security and connection pooling), so the application can be scaled up easily.

Our application is developed within a generic framework that is quite flexible both on its data end and on its output end. On the data end, it is quite easy to change the content of the application – just replace the database and the queries. Alternatively, you can replace the database with a different data source altogether, as long as it contains the same kind of metadata that a database does – the names of data fields and their data types. (For instance, it would be easy to use a mail folder and retrieve summary information from it.)

On the output end, it is quite easy to retarget the output from the WAP microbrowser to a different program, for example, a web browser, so our framework will allow you to generate both WAP and web content from the same database, using a number of shared components. In general, you can output any XML content. (Remember that both WML and XHTML are XML applications.)

The main components of our application are shown in the diagram below. Using this diagram, it will be easy to see what you need to know to work through this chapter, how this chapter is organized, and what you will have learned by the time the chapter is over:

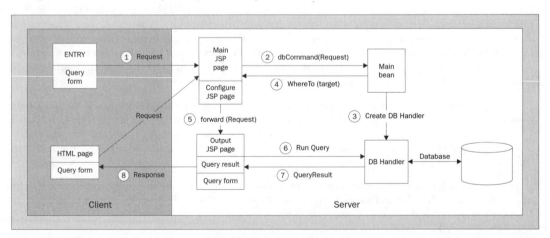

In this diagram, the Main servlet or a Java Server Page (JSP) sits between the web server and the Java application. The central point of the application is a bean, a Java class that analyzes the request coming from the client and instructs the Main servlet where that request should be forwarded. The recipient of the forwarded request is another servlet or JSP page that is customized for one particular kind of request.

It sends the query embedded into the request to the Main bean, and the Main bean dispatches it to the data handler component. The data handler submits the query to the data source, obtains the result, and sends it to the output component. That component uses the query result to create an XML document and sends it back to the client.

In terms of this diagram, our framework has the following options or 'degrees of freedom':

❑   We can use either a servlet or a JSP page for the Main servlet. We will use a JSP page to illustrate the way JSP works; there's no strong advantage to JSP over a simple servlet for this component of the system.

❑   Our data source can be a relational database or any other source of structured data, as long as the data comes together with the names and data types of its fields. We will use a database.

❑   The output component that incorporates query results into the output documents can be a JSP page or an XSLT processor. As discussed above, we will use a JSP page in the first half of the chapter, and then replace it with XSLT.

❑   Finally, the output can be any kind of XML; in fact, if the output component is a JSP page then output can be literally anything, as we will see later. We will mostly be outputting WML, but will also show how to create a similar web (XHTML) application.

Most of the technologies mentioned above should be familiar to you if you have read through the preceding chapters. You may wonder why we would show a web application in a book on WAP. However, we remark that a very common situation will be that you will need to send the same information (at a different level of detail and differently formatted) both to the wired and the wireless web. At the present stage of tool development, we actually find it easier to debug the wired (XHTML) version as a stage in developing the WML; the tools are more mature.

Try Out the Ride Board Application

Before we get involved in the technicalities of servlets and JSP, you may want to try out the Ride Board application. All the code for the application can be downloaded from our web site. Point your WAP device at wml/top.jsp and you will see the following screen:

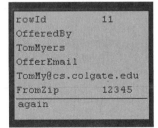

The operation of the program is completely straightforward. As distributed, the database doesn't have a lot to offer; we suggest that you offer several rides yourself before asking for one of them. Upon a successful operation (whether search, offer or accept), the page will display the response followed by the same form as in the initial screen. For instance, if you offer a ride, you will see a screen like this:

Note that in the code available for download there is an extra option available from the main page for checking ride details. This has not been included in the code description for the sake of simplicity.

Introduction to Servlets

Servlets are Java programs that perform the same function as CGI scripts or Active Server Pages (ASP): they receive a request that has been sent by a client to the web server, do some computations, and produce a response to be sent back to the client. In other words, they sit between the web server and the Java middle tier that implements the business logic of the application:

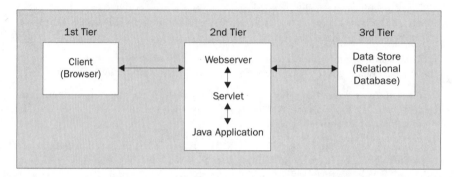

In order to run servlets, you need either a web server that understands servlets (such as Apache with Tomcat), or a self-standing servlet engine that communicates with the web server (such as JRun from Allaire). In either case, there is a specific directory where you place compiled servlets. In order to run a servlet, you do exactly the same thing you would do to run a CGI script or an ASP page: either enter the servlet's location as a URL, make it the value of the action attribute of an HTML form, or make it the value of the `href` attribute of a `<go>` element of a WML deck.

An Overview

A servlet's lifetime consists of these stages: initialization `init()`, the service stage `doGet()`/`doPost()`, and destruction `destroy()`. These are 'callback methods' that are not called by the servlet itself but rather by the servlet engine, in response to certain events. The lifetime of a servlet unfolds as follows. When a request addressed to the servlet arrives at the server, the servlet engine calls its custom-designed class loader. The class loader checks to see whether the servlet class is already loaded and whether the loaded version has the same time stamp as the `.class` file. If the servlet class is not loaded or is older than the disk file, the engine loads the class into the special Java Virtual Machine (JVM) provided for that purpose and creates an instance of it. At this point the servlet is ready for initialization. Initialization and destruction occur once per lifetime, while the service methods are repeated in response to every request.

> *Servlets are, in some ways, like applets. They are not self-standing applications and do not have a* `main()` *method. Also, they are not called by the user or programmer, but by another application (the web server).*

Programming a servlet is very much like programming any other Java class that depends on a Java API: you import the necessary packages and extend one of the classes in them. Here are the minimal imports:

```
import java.io.*;
import javax.servlet.*;
import javax.servlet.http.*;
```

Most servlets extend the `HttpServlet` class:

```
public class MyServlet extends HttpServlet
```

Everything you need in order to process a request and send back a response is declared in two interfaces, `HttpServletRequest` and `HttpServletResponse`, within the `javax.servlet.http` package. Two objects implementing these interfaces are provided as arguments to the main workhorses of a servlet: the `doGet()` and `doPost()` methods:

```
public void doGet (HttpServletRequest req, HttpServletResponse res)
        throws ServletException, IOException
```

The declaration for `doPost()` is similar.

We need to implement `doGet()` or `doPost()` depending on whether you expect to handle a GET or a POST request. Frequently (or even, always), a sensible thing to do is to implement both, one doing all the work, the other one calling the first. You will see an example shortly.

In outline, a `doGet()` or `doPost()` method has to go through these steps:

❑ Set the content type of the `Response`

❑ Get a `PrintWriter` to send the `Response` to

❑ Extract information from the `Request`

❑ Use the extracted information to perform some computation – for example, a database query and retrieval

❑ Compose WML (or HTML or ...) text and send it back down the response stream

A Simple Example

As a simple example, consider a servlet that separates the last three stages into separate methods:

```
// servlet Query0 as first 3tier example

import java.io.*;
import javax.servlet.*;
import javax.servlet.http.*;

public class Query0
extends HttpServlet
{
    String userProfile="";

    public void init() throws ServletException
    {
        userProfile=getInitParameter("userProfile");
    }

    public void doGet (HttpServletRequest req, HttpServletResponse res)
        throws ServletException, IOException
    {
        res.setContentType("text/vnd.wap.wml;charset=ISO-8859-1");
        PrintWriter out = res.getWriter();
        String key = req.getParameter("theKey");
```

```
        //'theKey' is the NAME attribute of input field in submitting form

        String result = doSomething(key);        // does some computation

        String title = "Report";
        wrapInWMLPage(out,result,title);   // does all output WML work
    }

    public void doPost (HttpServletRequest req, HttpServletResponse res)
        throws ServletException, IOException
    {
        doGet(req,res);
    }

    public void wrapInWMLPage(PrintWriter out, String queryResult, String title)
            throws IOException
    {
        out.println("<?xml version=\"1.0\"?>");
        out.println("<!DOCTYPE wml PUBLIC \"-//WAPFORUM//DTD WML 1.1//EN\"");
        out.println("   \"http://www.wapforum.org/DTD/wml_1.1.xml\">");
        out.println("<wml>");
        out.println("  <card id=\"" +title+ "\">");
        out.println("    <p align=\"center\"> ");
        out.println(queryResult);
        out.println("</p></card></wml>");
    }

    public String doSomething(String key)
    {
        return userProfile + key;
    }
}
```

We place Query0.java in Tomcat's webapps\examples\WEB-INF\classes directory to be on the classpath at the right time. Then we put a servlet declaration (including a value of ABCD for the userProfile init parameter) and a servlet mapping in the conf\web.xml file, to look like this:

```
<servlet>
  <servlet-name>Query0</servlet-name>
  <servlet-class>Query0</servlet-class>
  <init-param>
    <param-name>userProfile</param-name>
    <param-value>ABCD</param-value>
  </init-param>
</servlet>
<servlet-mapping>
  <servlet-name>Query0</servlet-name>
  <url-pattern>/Query0</url-pattern>
</servlet-mapping>
```

Then we can use

```
http://localhost:8080/examples/Query0?theKey=keyVal
```

This generates the WML output:

```
<?xml version="1.0"?>
<!DOCTYPE wml PUBLIC "-//WAPFORUM//DTD WML 1.1//EN"
  "http://www.wapforum.org/DTD/wml_1.1.xml">
<wml>
   <card id="Report">
      <p align="center">
         ABCDkeyVal
      </p>
   </card>
</wml>
```

This then appears on a cell phone simulator as:

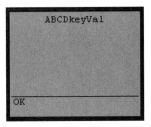

Obviously, this servlet is not doing anything useful, but it shows the kind of things servlets ordinarily do: they use information in the `Request` object; they do some computation, and they send the response down the output stream that they obtain from the `Response` object. In this example, it is all done within the servlet object itself. Much more commonly, you would create a 'worker' object that does the computation and another object for handling output. (You will probably want those objects to be beans, as we'll go on to explain in the section on JSP. Using a JSP instead of a servlet greatly simplifies the task of putting the response together, because you don't have to use `out.println()` statements and quote the output.)

In the remainder of this section, we will cover these common tasks:

- ❏ Servlet initialization
- ❏ Getting information out of a `Request` object and putting information into it
- ❏ Including a servlet and forwarding to another servlet
- ❏ Session handling

Servlet Initialization

All initialization is performed in the `init()` method. This is a good place to initialize request-independent resources. You can either hard-code those initializations into the `init()` method as we did in the example above, or you can provide them as initialization parameters, stored in the 'properties' files of your servlet engine. In Servlet 2.0 API and earlier, you retrieve an initialization parameter, such as a username, like this:

```
public void init(ServletConfig config) throws ServletException
{
    super.init(config);
    String usrProfile = getInitParameter("usrName"); // a ServletConfig method
```

In Servlet API 2.1 and later, this is simplified to the following (but the old code also still works):

```
public void init() throws ServletException
{
    String usrProfile = getInitParameter("usrName");
```

As you can see, initialization parameters are name-value pairs where both the names and values are strings. They are stored in a `.properties` file, which is just a text file whose location is specific to the servlet engine. Usually, you can manipulate that file through one of the dialog boxes of your servlet engine's administration utility, or you can edit it directly in an editor.

If you have long-term, request-independent information that you as the web site administrator want to make available to your servlets, initialization parameters are good for storing it. The `ServletConfig` interface declares two methods for obtaining initialization parameters:

```
public String getInitParameter(String name);
public Enumeration getInitParameterNames();
```

The Service Stage

After initialization, the servlet advances to its service stage. At this point, it acquires a `ServletContext`, a `Request` object and a `Response` object.

ServletContext, include() and forward()

The `ServletContext` object implements the `ServletContext` interface, and is available throughout the service stage. There is one instance of `ServletContext` for each servlet running on a server. It provides information about the server and its attributes, other loaded servlets, the MIME types of files on the server, and real file system paths of any virtual path, including the servlet root.

Perhaps the most interesting thing you can get out of `ServletContext` is a `RequestDispatcher`:

```
public RequestDispatcher getRequestDispatcher(String uripath);
```

`RequestDispatcher`, new in 2.1 API, is an object that can dispatch the `Request` object to another resource for processing. The resource is specified by the `uripath`, which can refer to any resource that the servlet engine knows about, for example another servlet, a Java Server Page, or a CGI script.

`RequestDispatcher()` has two methods: `forward()` and `include()`.

`include()` is used when you want some other program (that can be referred to by a URI) to generate some content and include it in the body of your servlet's response. This method enables server-side includes that are not static files, but generated by a program.

`forward()` is used when you want your servlet to do some processing and then forward the current request from your servlet to another resource on the web server. This method is useful when one servlet does preliminary processing of a request and wants to let another object generate the response. For instance, you may want to do the computation tasks in the servlet, but forward the results of the computation to a JSP page because it can handle output much better. You would then proceed as follows.

Your servlet would have some code like this:

```
MyBean myBean = new MyBean(....);      // Set up a bean, perform computations
request.setAttribute("myBean", myBean);
RequestDispatcher rd =
        getServletContext().getRequestDispatcher("/templatepage.jsp");
rd.forward(request, response);
return;
```

The page `templatepage.jsp` will handle the output. We will return to this example in the later section on JSP.

Requests and Responses

A servlet's main purpose in life is to receive a request and send back a response. In order to process requests and responses, the servlet needs to be able to:

- ❑ Get request parameters out of a request
- ❑ Get environment variables information out of a request
- ❑ Store Java objects in a request before forwarding it to another 'computational resource'
- ❑ Obtain a stream to write a response to
- ❑ Serve multiple requests and responses within a single session

Much of this functionality is wrapped into the request and response interfaces that come on two levels: the more general `ServletRequest-ServletResponse` pair, and the more specific `HttpServletRequest-HttpServletResponse` pair. The `HttpServlet` interfaces extend the more general Servlet interfaces. The interfaces are implemented in two objects, a `Request` and a `Response`, that the servlet engine passes as arguments to the `service()` method.

Request parameters are accessed by one of the following methods:

```
public String getParameter(String name);
public Enumeration getParameterNames();
public String[] getParameterValues(String name);
```

The last method is for those parameters that have multiple values, such as multiple selections in a `<select>` element in either WML or HTML.

Request parameters are gettable but not settable; there is no `setParameter()` method. If you want to store information in the `Request` object, you have to use its attributes (name-value pairs). Attribute names are `Strings`, but the attribute values are `Objects`, so you may have to cast them after you retrieve them. There are three methods for working with attributes associated with the `Request` object:

```
public Object getAttribute(String name);
public Enumeration getAttributeNames();
public void setAttribute(String name, Object object);
```

Session Tracking

A session is a series of request-response exchanges with the same client. Since HTTP is a stateless protocol, identifying the client as 'the same' is not a trivial task. Over the many years of CGI programming, several approaches to this task have been developed, using cookies, hidden form fields and so on. When you work with servlets, you don't have to be aware of them because the Servlet API has higher-level session tracking facilities that hide these details from the programmer.

Session management depends on a 'session ID', usually a number; when the server creates and stores a session, it sends the session ID to the client (browser) which echoes that ID so that the server knows what session to retrieve. The session ID can be made part of the URL itself (this is called 'URL rewriting'), but is more usually stored as a 'cookie', a small file on the client represented by an object of class `javax.servlet.http.Cookie`. However, not all browsers will accept cookies; when this becomes a problem, we fall back on the `HttpServletResponse.encodeURL(String uri)` method to generate the 'ACTION=' target which is to be rewritten (for example, within the two `ridesInc.jsp` files which you will see later).

Methods for session tracking are declared in the `HttpSession` interface. An object implementing that interface is associated with every visitor to the site, and you can store, retrieve and delete arbitrary name-value pairs in that object. The association between a visitor and a session is established by giving each visiting client a unique session ID, typically a very long string created and maintained by the server. Every time a new request comes in, the client is checked to see whether it has a 'valid' ID. If the answer is no, the session is considered to be 'new.' If the answer is yes, then the client is in the middle of an ongoing session.

To obtain an existing or a new `HttpSession` object use the `getSession()` method:

```
public HttpSession getSession();
```

Or:

```
public HttpSession getSession(boolean create);
```

If the Boolean `create` is `true` and there is no current session, then a new `HttpSession` object is created and given an ID. If the Boolean is `false` then a new session object is not returned, only an existing one if it does indeed exist. The default value of the Boolean is `true`.

Once you have a session object you can inquire whether or not its ID is saved using a cookie or URL rewriting:

```
public boolean isRequestedSessionIdFromCookie();
```

Or:

```
public boolean isRequestedSessionIdFromURL();
```

More importantly, you can ask for the ID itself, and whether or not it is valid:

```
public String getRequestedSessionId();
```

Or:

```
public boolean isRequestedSessionIdValid();
```

In summary, the session object goes through these stages: new, valid, invalid. Once it is invalid, it is removed from memory, and its session ID on the client becomes invalid. All this is taken care of by the servlet engine; the servlet programmer can sit back and relax.

The actual methods of HttpSession fall into two groups. One has to do with values: getting, putting and removing them. The other has to do with various properties of a session, such as its newness and validity. First off, there is:

```
public boolean isNew();
```

A session is considered new if it has been created by the server and not received from the client as part of the current request. In a situation where you require the user to go through a login procedure, this method should be used to check whether the client has indeed logged in or has arrived at your page in some illegitimate way.

If the session is not new but is not valid either, then trying to do anything with it, including asking whether or not it is new, will result in an IllegalStateException. If the session is valid, then you can get its ID and ask it various questions about its age and what it's been doing lately:

```
public String getId();
public long getCreationTime();
public long getLastAccessedTime();
public int getMaxInactiveInterval();
```

A session with an ID remains valid until it is invalidated, either by an explicit call on HttpSession's invalidate() or if the session remains inactive for a specified period of time. There is usually a default value of about 20-30 minutes for that period. You can find out what that maximum period of inactivity is by getMaxInactiveInterval(), and you can change it by setMaxInactiveInterval().

You can associate any number of name-value pairs with a session object, depending on what you want to do. The name is a String and the value is an Object. You manipulate them using these methods:

```
public Object getValue(String name);
public String[] getValueNames();
public void putValue(String name, Object value);
public void removeValue(String name);
```

A common example of using a session object is when your users do multiple database access and you want the database connection (or a hook into a connection pool containing it) to last for the duration of the session. In this case, you store the Connection object or the hook in the session object and pass the Session object to the code that handles database queries. A more general example is security information, such as the username and password to be associated with database activity. You will see examples of this usage later in the chapter.

Temporal Scopes of Servlet Objects

To summarize, an object within a servlet can have one of three possible durations or temporal "scopes":

❑   The shortest duration is local scope within a servlet's method.

❑   The next duration is the duration of a single request-response cycle. Everything you store as an attribute in the Request object will have this duration.

❑   The next duration is a series of requests from the same client within a session. Everything you store as a value in the Session object will have this duration.

You will see that these scopes, and much else from the servlet world, reappear in the JSP world because JSP builds upon servlets, and deep down inside, JSPs are servlets.

Introduction to JSP

JSP (Java Server Pages) are an alternative to servlets. They are also similar to ASP (Active Server Pages), the difference being that they use Java rather than a scripting language such as VBScript. If you are familiar with ASP, you'll find JSP very easy to get used to. Some people argue that JSP is a superior technology because Java is a more powerful language than the scripting languages of ASP, because of better security, better exception-handling, and better type structure; some of this is a matter of personal style, but some may not be. Another argument to consider is this: at its first use, the JSP page gets compiled into a Java servlet class, and after that the compiled code is used every time the page is invoked. This makes JSP more efficient than ASP, which uses an interpreted scripting language.

What is a JSP?

A JSP is an HTML, XML or WML page that may contain JSP elements, which will be discussed below. Even with no JSP elements, it is still a legitimate JSP page (just change the extension, for example from .wml to .jsp) and it will be displayed as normal. In processing a JSP page, the JSP processor leaves markup material untouched, but processes any JSP elements. JSP elements can contain Java code: either Java expressions or Java statements. Java expressions get evaluated and any value is inserted into the markup page in place of the Java expression. On the other hand, Java statements can control the page content; for example, a stretch of markup material can either be repeated, if it is inside a Java loop, or included conditionally, if it is placed inside a Java conditional statement.

JSP elements are delimited by JSP tags. Some of these tags have standard XML+Namespaces syntax, within the jsp: namespace. Other JSP tags have JSP-specific syntax that is different from XML. However, beginning with version 1.0, all non-XML tags have equivalent XML tags defined in the JSP Document Type Definition (DTD), so that a JSP page can now be a valid XML page. Beginning with version 1.1 (which is the current version as of this writing, May 2000) JSP processors are required to accept and validate JSP pages in purely XML syntax. In effect, JSP 1.1 processors contain a validating XML parser.

The purpose of JSP tags is to include Java code in the page and to perform servlet-related tasks, such as request processing and forwarding, session maintenance, and communication with the middleware application. Describing these tasks within elements that have XML syntax can be awkward, because Java code often contains characters that have to be escaped in XML (such as "<"). As a result, you have to use CDATA sections a lot. In a manually composed JSP, it is common to use non-XML tags, but XML tags are expected to be very useful when JSP editors become available.

JSP Applications and Beans

JSP syntax is compact and uses the familiar format of tags and attributes, so learning JSP on the level of syntactic correctness is easy. The challenge is to find good ways of using JSP in the overall system: the technology is very young and good practices have not yet been established. Paradoxically, the versatility of JSP may hinder, rather than promote, good system design. There is a natural temptation to use a JSP page simultaneously as a servlet, a backend processor, and a template file for output, simply because you can. This can easily result in long monolithic JSP pages that are difficult to understand, debug and maintain. A better approach is to break such a page into several pages that do different things. We usually have a 'main' page that functions as a servlet and has little or no static output in it, and several output pages, one for each different type of output.

Beans can be a big help in structuring JSP-based applications. Instead of mixing web content with unstructured stretches of Java code, a JSP page can isolate its procedures into a compiled bean, and use its JSP elements to create and manipulate an instance of such a bean.

At this point, some of you may ask, "What's a bean?" The answer is very simple: a bean is any Java class that satisfies these simple conditions:

❑   A bean must have a default no-argument constructor

❑   A bean must be serializable (implement the `Serializable` interface)

❑   A bean must follow standard naming conventions for its get and set methods

What are these standard naming conventions? Suppose your bean has a variable called `beanVar` that is an object of class `SomeClass`. To make it accessible you define a get method like this:

```
public SomeClass getBeanVar(){return beanVar;}
```

If you want that variable to be modifiable, you define a set method like this:

```
public void setBeanVar(SomeClass arg){beanVar=arg;}
```

And that's all there is to being a bean, as far as JSP is concerned. These two properties make it very easy for a JSP page to create an instance of a bean and to initialize its variables from user input (whether that input comes from a WML `<go>` element or an HTML form). You will see examples of this when we return to design considerations and start making more specific suggestions. However, our first example given below doesn't need design: it is just a short page whose purpose is to introduce the syntax and function of JSP elements.

A simple JSP Example

Here is a short 'kitchen-sink' example, `HelloJSPWML.jsp`, put together from examples in the JSP 1.0 distribution and together with our own embellishments. Note that you can use standard XML comments (`<!-- comment -->`) within the XML sections of a JSP page, and standard Java comments (`// comment`) within Java code in the page:

```
<?xml version="1.0"?>
<!DOCTYPE wml PUBLIC "-//WAPFORUM//DTD WML 1.1//EN"
   "http://www.wapforum.org/DTD/wml_1.1.xml">
    <%@ page contentType="text/vnd.wap.wml;charset=ISO-8859-1" %>
    <%@ page import="java.util.Date" %>            <!-- directives -->
    <%! int i=5,j=2; %>                            <!-- a declaration -->
    <%! String s=" Wireless World!"; %>            <!-- a declaration -->
<wml>
  <card id="start">
    <p align="center" >
      <big><strong>
      <br/>Hello <%= s %>
      <br/>It's <%= new java.util.Date() %>
      <br/> trial <%= ++i %>
      </strong></big>
    </p>
```

```
            <do type="accept" label="Go!">
               <go href="http://www.wapforum.com" />
            </do>
            <do type="accept" label="help" >
               <go href="#help" />
            </do>
         </card>
         <card id="help">
            <p align="center">
               <% if(i<=12){ %>                        <!-- code fragment; -->
               <big>How can I help you?</big>          <!-- template appears if i<= 12  -->
               <% }else { %>                           <!-- else clause  -->
               <small> More than a dozen </small> <!-- template for i > 12 -->
               <% } %>
            </p>
         </card></wml>
```

If you have this document served to you by a JSP-enabled server (a server that has a JSP engine, which is discussed below) then this is what you will see:

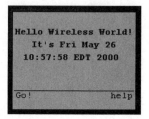

(You would click on the left button below the screen to **Go!**, and on the right button below the screen to see the **help** card.) The WML source for this page will be something like that shown below. Note how all JSP elements have disappeared but the comments remain:

```
<?xml version="1.0"?>
<!DOCTYPE wml PUBLIC "-//WAPFORUM//DTD WML 1.1//EN"
   "http://www.wapforum.org/DTD/wml_1.1.xml">

                  <!-- directives -->
                              <!-- a declaration -->
                  <!-- a declaration -->
<wml>
   <card id="start">
      <p align="center" >
         <big><strong>
         <br/>Hello  Wireless World!
         <br/>It's Fri May 26 11:30:21 EDT 2000
         <br/> trial 6
         </strong></big>
      </p>
      <do type="accept" label="Go!">
         <go href="http://www.wapforum.com" />
      </do>
      <do type="accept" label="help" >
         <go href="#help" />
      </do>
   </card>
   <card id="help">
      <p align="center">
                        <!-- code fragment; -->
         <big>How can I help you?</big>       <!-- template appears if i<= 12  -->

      </p>
   </card>
</wml>
```

Click the **Reload/Refresh** button several times. If your device is caching the page, you'll just see it again and again. If your device is actually asking the server each time, you will see that the integer value and eventually the help card that follows it change. Our next task is to understand how this comes about. Note that a JSP file consists of template data, which is just XML or other markup and JSP elements of various kinds. The file above shows a declaration, a directive, and several code fragments and expressions; these will be explained in the next section. Each is indicated by a specific JSP tag.

We will now summarize the syntax and meaning of JSP tags, before going on to explain how the above example is processed.

Overview of JSP Element Syntax

JSP syntax is quite straightforward and compact: it all fits on a double-page syntax card available from Sun (http://java.sun.com/products/jsp/syntax.pdf). As we have seen, a JSP page consists of template data and JSP elements. Template data is just HTML or XML; the JSP processor passes it on to the output untouched. The JSP elements fall into the following groups:

❑ Directives

❑ Scripting elements (consisting of declarations, expressions and code fragments, or scriptlets)

❑ Comments

❑ Actions

The first three groups of elements have always been part of JSP and have non-XML syntax, as well as alternative XML+Namespace syntax. However, the actions group is more recent and has only XML+Namespace syntax.

Non-XML Elements

The non-XML syntax of directives, scripting elements (declarations, expressions and code fragments) and comments is summarized in the table below. You have seen all of them used in our simple example above.

Type of element	Syntax description	Example
Directives	`<%@ directive %>`	`<%@ page language="java" %>`
Declarations	`<%! declarations %>`	`<%! int i=0, j=5; %>`
Expressions	`<%= expression %>`	`<%= i+7 %>`
Code fragments	`<% code fragment %>`	`<% if(i < j-4 { %>`
Comments	`<%-- comment --%>`	`<%-- not for the client --%>`

XML Elements

A JSP page that is also a valid XML document opens with the following declarations:

```
<! DOCTYPE root
   PUBLIC "-//Sun Microsystems Inc.//DTD JavaServer Pages Version 1.0//EN"
   "http://java.sun.com/products/jsp/dtd/jspcore_1_0.dtd">
<jsp:root xmlns:jsp="http://java.sun.com/products/jsp/dtd/jsp_1_0.dtd">
```

XML alternatives to older non-XML syntax, and the XML syntax of newer action elements are summarized in the following table:

Type of element	XML tag
Directive	`<jsp:directive.page ... />` `<jsp:directive.include ... />`
Declarations	`<jsp:declaration>...</jsp:declaration>`
Expressions	`<jsp:expression>...</jsp:expression>`
Code fragments	`<jsp:scriptlet>...</jsp:scriptlet>`
Comments	`<%-- not for the client --%>`
Actions	`<jsp:useBean>` etc.

What They All Mean

❑ Directives are addressed to the JSP engine. They do not produce any output. They are EMPTY elements – they have no content, but take a number of attributes.

❑ Scripting elements (declarations, expressions or code fragments) have no attributes, and only PCDATA content. That content will often contain special characters, such as <, & and quotes. These have to be escaped, or else the entire body of the scripting element has to be made into a CDATA section. To us, writing extensive scripting elements seems like an error-prone process in precisely the complex cases where it really matters. It is possible that good 'lint'-style tools will appear that will catch a forgotten closing bracket. A better approach is never to write a scripting element that is longer than a line or two, but to use beans instead.

❑ Declarations are exactly that: Java declarations and, perhaps, initializations. Declarations do not produce any output.

❑ Expressions are Java expressions; they are evaluated and their values are inserted into the output stream.

❑ Code fragments or scriptlets are pieces of Java code. They don't have to be complete statements or valid expressions.

❑ Comments are not sent to the client; they are strictly for documenting code. You can also use standard XML comments in a JSP page and they will be treated like regular XML comments. You can even include non-XML JSP content in XML-style comments, and it will be treated as part of comments, that is, ignored.

❑ Action elements, like scripting elements, often contain special characters, which have to be escaped.

The semantics of scripting elements are easy to understand; it's just Java code. Comments, similarly, are quite simple. However, directives and their attributes require a bit more discussion, as do action elements.

JSP Directives

There are three JSP directives:

❑ `include`

❑ `page`

❑ `taglib`

Since `taglib` is new in version 1.1; we only use `include` and `page` directives here.

include Directive

The syntax of this directive is as follows: `<%@ include file=... %>`. This directive is simply used to include files into a page. The included file does not have to be a complete page; its text is included verbatim in the page that contains the directive. (This occurs before the page is compiled into a servlet – see later in this chapter.) The `include` directive is very useful for structuring JSP applications, as you will see in the examples later in the chapter.

page Directive

The `page` directive sets up a number of attributes; we will go through them in order.

Attribute	Description
`language`	Specifies the language of the scripting elements; currently only Java is supported.
`extends`	Allows you to specify a parent class for the servlet that is automatically generated from the JSP page. It is rarely used because it prevents the engine from doing some optimizations.
`contentType`	Specifies the MIME type and encoding; one per page.
`import`	Specifies Java packages and classes to be imported.
`session`	If `true` then the implicit variable named `session` of type `javax.servlet.http.HttpSession` is available to the code of the page; it references the current/new session for the page. If `false` (the default), that variable is unavailable.
`buffer`	Controls the size of the buffer associated with the `JspWriter`. If you want unbuffered output, set it to `none`.
`autoFlush`	Specifies whether the buffered output should be flushed automatically (`true`) when the buffer is filled, or whether an exception should be raised (`false`) to indicate buffer overflow.
`isThreadSafe`	If `false`, the JSP page implementation will implement `javax.servlet.SingleThreadModel`, so that all requests sent to that instance will be delivered serially to the `service()` method of the page implementation class. Synchronization issues are complex; consult the specification for a detailed discussion.
`info`	Provides an information message about your JSP page; it becomes the return value of the `Servlet.getServletInfo()` method of the implementation class.
`errorPage`	Specifies a relative URL of the local page to which any Java programming language `Throwable` object(s) that is thrown but not caught by the page implementation is forwarded for error processing.
`isErrorPage`	Specifies whether this is or is not an error page.

Here is an example of using a page directive that imports two packages and sets up an error page:

```
<%@ page import="java.util.*, MyNa.utils.*" errorPage="errorpage.jsp" %>
```

Action Elements

Action elements fall into three groups as follows:

❑ Actions having to do with beans: useBean, getProperty, setProperty

❑ The include and forward actions, corresponding to the include() and forward() methods of the RequestDispatcher interface in the javax.servlet package (see the earlier section on servlets)

❑ The plugin action, for downloading a plugin to the client (not used in this book)

All action tags appear with the jsp: namespace prefix, i.e. they are XML type elements. Some action elements are EMPTY, with a number of attributes; others have content. When action elements appear in a JSP page that is intended to be a well-formed and valid XML document, their content frequently has to be wrapped in a CDATA section.

Beans and Properties

Here is an example of using the useBean action element:

```
<jsp:useBean id="mbean" scope="session" class="rideboard.MainBean" />
```

The id attribute of useBean (which is required by the DTD) specifies the name of the bean within the application. The scope attribute can have one of the values we discuss later: page, request, session, or application. Finally, the class attribute (which is also required by the DTD) gives the fully qualified class name of the bean.

The DTD also specifies useBean as having %jsp.body; content. That content can be empty, as in our example, but it may not be. If there is content, it is usually setProperty elements that customize the bean. Alternatively, setProperty elements may follow the useBean element.

Here is an example of using setProperty:

```
<jsp:setProperty name="bbean" property="*" />
```

To set a property, one needs a property name and a value. There are two ways of specifying values. One is as an attribute of a setProperty element:

```
<jsp:setProperty name="abean" property="prop1" value="value1" />
```

More often, the values come from request parameters, ultimately, from form inputs on the client. In this case, instead of value, you specify the name of the parameter whose value is to be used:

```
<jsp:setProperty name="abean" property="prop" param="param1" />
```

If the name of the bean property is the same as the name of the request parameter, then you don't have to specify the parameter name. If you want all request parameters copied to bean properties of the same name, you code property="*", as in the first example we looked at, above.

The Include Action

Here's an example that illustrates the include action. The including deck sets up a request attribute and calls the include action.

The `include` action inserts the included page:

```
<?xml version="1.0"?>
<!DOCTYPE wml PUBLIC "-//WAPFORUM//DTD WML 1.1//EN"
   "http://www.wapforum.org/DTD/wml_1.1.xml">
    <%@ page contentType="text/vnd.wap.wml;charset=ISO-8859-1" %>
<wml>
<!-- the including deck -->
  <card id="includeSample">
    <p align="center">
        including page
    </p>
    <% request.setAttribute("uid","TEST"); %>
    <jsp:include page="tstInc2.jsp" flush="true" />
    <p>
        <br />It's easy.
    </p>
  </card>
</wml>
```

The included page, among other things, retrieves the value of the attribute set up in the including page, to demonstrate how information can be passed between them:

```
<!-- the included page -->

<p>
    included page: "uid" =
    <%= request.getAttribute("uid") %>
    <br />which ought to be "TEST".
</p>
```

The output, as shown in View|Source, comes out like this (some whitespace has been removed):

```
<?xml version="1.0"?>
<!DOCTYPE wml PUBLIC "-//WAPFORUM//DTD WML 1.1//EN"
   "http://www.wapforum.org/DTD/wml_1.1.xml">

<wml>
<!-- the including deck -->
  <card id="includeSample">
    <p align="center">
        including page
    </p>
<!-- the included page -->
<p>
included page: "uid" =
TEST
<br />which ought to be "TEST".
</p>
<p>
    <br />It's easy.
</p>
</card>
</wml>
```

On the phone, it looks like this:

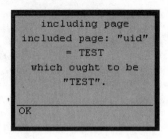

Two include Mechanisms

We have now seen two mechanisms for including material in a page, namely a directive and an action. The table below summarizes their properties:

Type of element	Syntax	Phase	Parsed?
directive	`<%@ include file=... %>`	translation-time	yes
action	`<jsp:include page=... />`	request-time	no

You may find the following analogy helpful: the `include` directive is like a `static` method in Java that is executed before an instance of the page is created to process a request. On the other hand, the `include` action is like an instance method that is executed 'at run time', in response to a specific request.

How does JSP Work?

Now that we have seen a discussion of the types of JSP elements, we return to our "Hello Wireless World!" example, and explain how it is processed.

In order to display JSP pages, you need a server that has a JSP engine. The engine can be a separate piece of software or it can be integrated with the server. An example of an integrated servlet engine is Tomcat, an open-source project within the Apache family of projects (`http://jakarta.apache.org/tomcat`). Tomcat has been developed with considerable help from Sun and serves as the reference implementation of Servlet API 2.2 and JSP 1.1. While it comes with a small server of its own, on larger sites Tomcat should be used only as a JSP engine working together with a full-featured server such as Apache. You can find details of a basic installation of Apache with Tomcat in Appendix F. An example of a self-standing JSP engine is JRun (2.3 and later) from `www.allaire.com/Products/JRun/`.

JSP pages work within a request-response, client-server protocol, such as HTTP. Although the JSP specification talks about JSP engines implementing other protocols, at present JSP engines only support HTTP, so when we say 'request' or 'response', we mean the HTTP versions.

When a request for a JSP page comes from a client to a JSP-enabled server (whether as a URL to load or a form action to execute), the server passes it on to its JSP engine. The JSP engine delivers requests from the client to the JSP page and delivers responses from the JSP page to the client. Theoretically, JSP engines are free to implement 'request' as they wish, but in practice, this is what happens: deep down inside, a JSP page is translated into a servlet, requests are sent to that servlet as `HttpServletRequest` objects, and responses from the servlet are received as `HttpServletResponse` objects. (Frequently, we just refer to these as `Request` and `Response` object.)

How and when does a JSP page become a servlet? This is an optimization trick that is not codified in a definitive way: the translation of JSP text into servlet code can happen at any time before or during the processing of the first request for the target JSP page. Typically, during the "receipt and processing" of the first request, the servlet class is compiled and loaded, so subsequent requests return much faster than the first one. The class is not recompiled until changes to the JSP pages are made. This may be a problem for pages that dynamically load beans because if a bean is changed and recompiled, the system won't notice unless you also 'touch' the JSP page to force recompilation of the servlet.

We are not going to cover the translation process in detail here, but will just give an overview of the process. If you are interested in further details, it can be found in *Professional Java XML Programming*, from Wrox. We do recommend that you locate the "working" directory where the JSP engine puts the code of the automatically generated servlet, and read the code. (This directory is called `work` in the Tomcat installation.)

In addition to code that comes from the specific page, the generated servlet contains code that is common to all such servlets. For instance, here is a complete list of import statements in the servlet generated for our "Hello" example:

```
import javax.servlet.*;
import javax.servlet.http.*;
import javax.servlet.jsp.*;
import com.sun.jsp.runtime.*;
import com.sun.jsp.JspException;

import java.io.PrintWriter;
import java.io.IOException;
import java.io.FileInputStream;
import java.io.ObjectInputStream;
import java.util.Vector;
import java.beans.*;

import java.util.Date; // generated from a page directive
```

Implicit Objects and Scope

As you can see from the list of imports, a JSP page has some implicit objects associated with it. They are: `Request`, `Response`, a `Writer`, a `PageContext`, a `Session`, a `ServletConfig`, and an `application`, which is a `ServletContext` object. In addition, if an exception is thrown but not caught by the implementing class of a JSP page, and a special error page is specified by a page directive (see above), that exception becomes an implicit object in the error page, referred to by the name `exception`.

In addition to implicit objects, JSP code can create other objects as needed, or dynamically load objects; loading beans is particularly easy. Each object has a specific scope associated with it (the tag has a scope attribute). The following scopes are supported:

❑   page – Objects with page scope are accessible only within the page where they are created. This is the most limited scope for strictly local processing; once the page is processed the object is gone, even if the response has not yet been sent in. Use this scope for computations local to a page.

❑   request – Objects with request scope are accessible from pages processing the same request where the objects were created. Once the request is processed, the object is gone, but if the request is forwarded, you can still reference the object. References to objects with request scope are stored in the request object. Use this scope for computations whose lifetime is a single request-response cycle.

❑ session – Objects with session scope are accessible from pages processing requests that are in the same session as the one in which they were created. You can only create these in pages that are 'session-aware'. (See above about the page directive.) References to objects with session scope are stored in the session object associated with the page activation.

❑ application – Objects with application scope are accessible from all pages that are in the same application as the page in which they were created. References to objects with application scope are stored in the application object associated with a page activation. Use this scope for global variables.

And That's All There is to it

We hope you agree that, with the possible exception of synchronization issues, the syntax and semantics of JSP pages are quite clear and intuitive. (This does not mean that the current generation of JSP engines always behave in clear and intuitive ways.) The main challenge is in large-scale structuring of JSP applications. This is what we are going to work on now. In the next section we present two possible approaches. We then go on to illustrate one of them in a large example application: the Ride Board.

Design Considerations

As we said before, the biggest challenge of JSP is to find a good way to structure the application into components. The main two approaches to a good structure are:

❑ Separate a main JSP page, which functions as a servlet, from the JSP pages for output. Perhaps even use a servlet rather than a JSP page for that purpose.

❑ Isolate Java code into a compiled bean, and use JSP elements mainly to create and manipulate an instance of such a bean.

The subject of structuring JSP applications has received a lot of attention on the JSP-INTEREST list. We summarize one of the suggestions below, and present one of our own.

Servlet for Entry, JSP for Output

Servlets and JSP are so closely related that you can forward from a servlet to a JSP. This makes the following strategy possible. Use a servlet as the main entry point of your server-side application. Have the servlet create instances of Java classes that do all the work in the application, but forward to a JSP for output. Since the entry point servlet does not produce any output, there would not be any advantages for using a JSP in its place, while Java code is easier to read in a servlet as it is more logically structured according to function.

The servlet would have some code like this:

```
// Set up a bean with the results of the processing
MyBean myBean = new MyBean(....);
request.setAttribute("myBean", myBean);
RequestDispatcher rd =
    getServletContext().getRequestDispatcher("/nextpage.jsp");
rd.forward(request, response);
return;
```

To access the bean from within the JSP page, the useBean directive is then invoked:

```
<jsp:useBean id="myBean" scope="request" class="MyBean" />
```

Note that the bean is passed from the servlet to the JSP as an attribute of the `request` object, and, in the JSP, is declared as having `request` scope. If you need the information for a longer period of time, then you can have your servlet store objects into the user's session (with `session.putValue()`) instead, and use `scope="session"` instead of `scope="request"` in the useBean directive.

Separate the Servlet from Output Given in JSP

The strategy described above is a neat scheme, because it implements different functionalities as slightly different entities: servlets and JSP. However, keeping two slightly different syntaxes in sync may be confusing. Another approach would be to keep everything in JSP (and beans, of course) but have a very clear distinction between the main page and the output template pages:

❑ The main page is the target of the action attribute of the HTML form or the WML <go> element.

❑ The main page produces little or no output.

❑ The main page may contain some Java code, but mostly it instantiates the main bean and perhaps other classes that do the business logic of the application.

❑ The main page may include, or forward to, different output pages depending on the values computed by the main bean.

❑ Output pages have little or no Java code. They contain mostly template material and Java expressions to be evaluated. If they have shared material, it can be placed into a file that all of them include.

Dialog with the Client

In the example application presented in this chapter, we will be using a version of the last approach, with an additional twist that allows for a very compact and elegant conversation between the JSP page and the client. The idea is that the main JSP page, functioning as a servlet, uses `include` or `forward` directives to specify output template pages, while each output template page contains either an HTML form whose action attribute is the main JSP page or a WML <go> element whose `href` attribute is the main JSP page.

In more detail and specific to our application, the main JSP page interacts with the main bean using two string variables: `beanCmd` and `jspCmd`. The `beanCmd` variable, set from the JSP page, determines the kind of action that the bean executes. The `jspCmd` variable, set in the bean, determines the output template that the main JSP page selects for sending back the response:

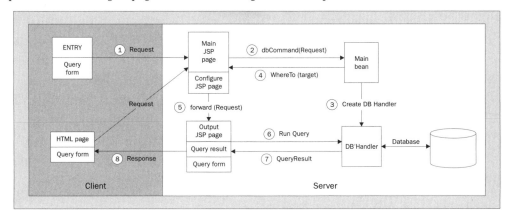

The Ride Board Application

The subject matter of our application is a Ride Board of the kind you frequently find on college campuses. If you are traveling across the country and have room in the car to give other people a ride or a lift, you can use the Ride Board to advertise this fact. If on the other hand, you need a ride or a lift to another part of the country, you can use the Ride Board to look for rides, and sign up for a ride when you find one. This application was developed using the UP.Browser, some browsers may have difficulties with the implicit call to the `onpick` event handler as mentioned in Chapter 7.

The Strategy

In the Ride Board application, we will use the design discussed in the previous section *Dialog with the Client* and illustrated in the diagram above. We will have a main JSP page forwarding the user to different output pages depending on what kind of query has been received from the client and whether the client is a web browser or a WAP microbrowser. We now describe how this works in the case of WML.

The opening URL of the application is a JSP page, `top.jsp`, which has no content of its own: all it does is include another JSP page, `ridesInc.jsp`. That page is also included in all the output pages. It has no Java content whatsoever, only a few cards. The first card has a select element that allows the user to select a query: this can be to Find Ride, Accept ride, or Offer ride:

```
1▶find ride
2 Accept ride
3 Offer ride



OK
```

Whichever query is selected, the user is taken to an appropriate card that has one or more `<input>` elements and a `<go>` element. For example, here is the card for the 'find a ride' query:

```
<card id="find">
  <do type="accept" label="Go!" >
    <go href="/examples/jsp/rides/core.jsp">
        <postfield name="query" value="findByZip" />
        <postfield name="QP1" value="$toZip" />
        <postfield name="target" value="wml-findByZip" />
    </go>
  </do>
  <p align="center">Rides to Zip </p>
  <p>
    Zip? <input name="toZip" format="*N" maxlength="5" /><br />
  </p>
</card>
```

As you can see, the `<go>` element of the card sends the query to `core.jsp`. This is the main page of the application that functions as the servlet. It instantiates a bean and forwards the action to the output page for, in this case, the `findByZip` query. The output page contacts the database that holds all the data on posted rides, gets the result and incorporates it into the output. The last thing it does is to include the same `ridesInc.jsp` page, so that the user can submit another query.

This was a barebones skeleton of the application. The web version is very similar to the WAP version; the only difference is in the output JSP pages. To emphasize how little the two versions differ, we will first present the WAP version. It will take the next fifteen pages or so. After that, we'll need only a page or two to retarget the application to a web device.

We will present the Ride Board application in the following order:

- ❑ The database
- ❑ The entry page: `top.jsp` and `ridesInc.jsp`
- ❑ The main JSP page (which is Java code only): `core.jsp`
- ❑ The configuration page, `configure.jsp`, and two back-end utility classes called `DBHandler` and `Dict`
- ❑ The main bean: `qBean`
- ❑ The output JSP pages: `wml-findByZip.jsp`, `wml-acceptZip.jsp` and `wml-offer.jsp`

Before we go on, note that the application is fairly generic: in order to change the subject matter from a Ride Board to, for instance, a weather report, all you would need to do is:

- ❑ Provide a different database
- ❑ Replace the configuration file
- ❑ Provide appropriate WML decks for input and output

The Database

We assume that we have a database whose ODBC name is `MyNaWap`, with a table called `Rides`. Each row in the table has the following fields (all of type `TEXT`, except `rowID` which is `INT` and `Day` which is `DATE`):

- ❑ rowID (the primary key)
- ❑ OfferedBy
- ❑ email contact for offerer
- ❑ FromZip
- ❑ ToZip
- ❑ Day of Ride
- ❑ AcceptedBy (initially empty)
- ❑ email contact for accepter

As distributed, the database doesn't have a lot to offer; we suggest that you offer several rides yourself before asking for one of them.

The Entry Page: top.jsp and ridesInc.jsp

The application's entry page `top.jsp` is deliberately simple, being reduced to just the essentials. Most of its material is in the included `ridesInc.jsp`:

```
<%@ page contentType="text/vnd.wap.wml;charset=ISO-8859-1" %>
<?xml version="1.0"?>
<!DOCTYPE wml PUBLIC "-//WAPFORUM//DTD WML 1.1//EN"
    "http://www.wapforum.org/DTD/wml_1.1.xml">
```

```
<wml>
<%@ page errorPage="../wmlerrorpage.jsp" %>
<jsp:useBean id="qBean" scope="session" class="MyNa.jspUtil.QBean" />

<head>
  <meta http-equiv="Cache-Control" content="no-cache" forua="true"/>
</head>

<%@ include file="ridesInc.jsp" %>
</wml>
```

Note the use of the <meta> element, to control caching. Since WAP microbrowsers cache very aggressively to reduce traffic, it is essential to turn caching off when you want fresh updates.

The included file, ridesInc.jsp, consists of four cards: the first card is used to select a query and the three other cards are used for the three different queries. It has no JSP-specific elements at all; the only reason it's a JSP file is because this way it can be included in other JSP files and easily extended to include some computed material, for example the last values entered by the user. (We don't do this here for reasons of simplicity, but would of course do so in a real application.)

Here is the entire page.

```
<card id="start">
  <p>
  <select>
    <option onpick="#find">Find ride </option>
    <option onpick="#accept">Accept ride </option>
    <option onpick="#offer">Offer ride </option>
  </select>
  </p>
</card>

<card id="find">
  <do type="accept" label="Go!">
    <go href="/examples/jsp/rides/core.jsp">
      <postfield name="query" value="findByZip" />
      <postfield name="QP1" value="$QP1" />
      <postfield name="target" value="wml-findByZip" />
    </go>
  </do>
<p align="center">
  Rides to
</p>
<p>
  Zip? <input name="QP1" format="*N" maxlength="5" /><br />
</p>
</card>

<card id="accept">
  <do type="accept" label="Go!">
    <go href="/examples/jsp/rides/core.jsp">
      <postfield name="query" value="acceptZip" />
      <postfield name="QP1" value="$QP1" />
      <postfield name="QP2" value="$QP2" />
      <postfield name="QP3" value="$QP3" />
      <postfield name="QP4" value="$QP4" />
      <postfield name="target" value="wml-acceptZip" />
    </go>
  </do>
```

```
  <p align="center">
    Accept a ride
  </p>
  <p>
    Name? <input name="QP1" format="*m" maxlength="8" /><br />
    eMail? <input name="QP2" format="*m" maxlength="20" /><br />
    Date? <input name="QP3" format="NN\/NN\/*N" maxlength="10" /><br />
    toZip? <input name="QP4" format="*N" maxlength="5" /><br />
  </p>
  </card>

  <card id="offer">
    <do type="accept" label="Go!">
      <go href="/examples/jsp/rides/core.jsp">
        <postfield name="query" value="offer" />
        <postfield name="QP1" value="$QP1" />
        <postfield name="QP2" value="$QP2" />
        <postfield name="QP3" value="$QP3" />
        <postfield name="QP4" value="$QP4" />
        <postfield name="QP5" value="$QP5" />
        <postfield name="target" value="wml-offer" />
      </go>
    </do>
  <p align="center">
    Offer a ride
  </p>
  <p>
    Name? <input name="QP1" format="*m" maxlength="8" /><br />
    eMail? <input name="QP2" format="*m" maxlength="20" /><br />
    fromZip? <input name="QP3" format="*N" maxlength="5" /><br />
    toZip? <input name="QP4" format="*N" maxlength="5" /><br />
    Date? <input name="QP5" format="NN\/NN\/*N" maxlength="10" /><br />
  </p>
  </card>
```

All three of the query cards are structured in the same way: they have a <do> element that submits the query and a <p> element that contains input fields. We pre-format the date field so that the user doesn't have to type non-alphabetic characters.

You will see this page again when we get to the JSP pages for output. As was discussed in the design section, all three output pages end with the same forms that produce them allowing the user to 'continue the conversation' with the database. Rather than repeating that material, we put it into ridesInc.jsp, which can be included in the end of each output page.

The nature of the queries and the process of specifying a query will be discussed shortly. For now, just note two details. First, each form has a hidden field, query, whose value is the name of the query: findByZip, acceptZip and offer. Second, query parameters are the values of input fields with names like QP1, QP2, and so on.

When submitted, the form goes to the main JSP page, core.jsp.

The Main JSP: core.jsp

This page has no output elements, only directives, action elements and Java code. Since it produces no output, the main page does not need a header, whether HTML or XML, or WML. It carries out the following tasks:

❑   Instantiate the main bean, qBean

❑ Configure the bean using the `configure.jsp` file, which we will see shortly, that is included into `core.jsp`

❑ Call the bean's `doCommand()` method with the `request` object as argument

❑ Forward the `request` to the output file determined by the bean's `whereTo()` method

In this example, the destination is the output file corresponding to the submitted query. Later in the chapter, the number of destinations will double to include JSP pages that produce output for web browsers as well as WAP microbrowsers:

```
<!-- database fields are as follows:
    rowId,OfferedBy,OfferEmail,FromZip,ToZip,Day,AcceptedBy,AcceptedEmail
of types:
    INT,TEXT,TEXT,TEXT,TEXT,DATE,TEXT,TEXT -->

<%@ page  errorPage="errorpage.jsp" %>
<jsp:useBean id="qBean" class="MyNa.jspUtil.QBean" scope="session"/>

<%@ include file="configure.jsp" %>
<%
  qBean.doCommand(request);
    if(true){
      out.clear();
      pageContext.forward(qBean.whereTo());
      return;
    }
%>
```

The curious notation `if(true)` is needed because JSP inserts Java scriptlets (code fragments) into the larger body of the generated servlet code, and the code is then compiled. If you simply insert a line that says `return` in the middle of other code, the compiler will complain that subsequent code is unreachable. In this case we do want the remaining code to be unreachable, but the compiler doesn't understand that, and needs to be pacified.

Two larger items mentioned in this page that require an explanation are the configuration page and the bean. We move onto these next.

The Configuration Page: configure.jsp

The `configure.jsp` page contains nothing but Java code – it consists of a single scriptlet. Within it, there are three sections, corresponding to three kinds of information that are needed for setting up a session. First, once per session, the user has to connect to the database. Second, within a session the user submits query requests, and depending on the query, the request is forwarded to one of several JSP pages for output. The first part of `configure.jsp` contains the information for setting up the database connection; the second part specifies the queries available to the user, and the third part specifies the output page for each query, and an error page.

The configuration page concludes with the call on `qBean.configure()`. The task of `configure()` is to set up an object of our `DBHandler` class (presented in the next section) which handles all the interactions with the database. Although `configure()` is called once per request, it will have no effect after the first call, when the session is set up and a `DBHandler` object is stored in it. (The method starts with an `if` statement that checks to see whether the `DBHandler` is null or not.)

This is not the ideal way to handle configuration, and in our own practice we usually do it differently: we instantiate and configure the main bean, including a DBHandler from an XML configuration file. However, this would require a lot more background machinery to explain here. The method used in this chapter allows a system administrator to configure the database access and alter the target files, without introducing too many new concepts.

Here is the entire page; the explanation that follows is divided into three subsections corresponding to the divisions in the page:

```
<%
    // Part1: information for connecting to the database
String[][]dbParams=new String[][]{
  {"dbDriver", "sun.jdbc.odbc.JdbcOdbcDriver"},
  {"dbName", "jdbc:odbc:MyNaWap"},
  {"dbUser","userName"},
  {"dbPwd",""},   {"dbDateFormat","yyyy-MM-dd"} // sets input format;
          // in this version, date output format is fixed
};

    // Part2: queries available to the client
String[][]dbQueries=new String[][]{
  {"findByZip",
    "SELECT * FROM Rides WHERE ToZip=?",
    "TEXT"},
  {"acceptZip",
    "UPDATE Rides SET AcceptedBy=?,AcceptedEmail=? "+
    "WHERE rowId=(SELECT Min(rowID) FROM Rides "+
    "WHERE Day=? AND ToZip=? AND AcceptedBy='-')",
    "TEXT,TEXT,DATE,TEXT"},
  {"offer",
    "INSERT INTO Rides SELECT 1+Max(r.rowId) as rowId,"+
    "? as OfferedBy,? as OfferedEmail,? as FromZip,? as ToZip,"+
    "? as Day,'-' as AcceptedBy,'-' as AcceptedEmail FROM Rides r",
    "TEXT,TEXT,TEXT,TEXT,DATE"}
};

    // Part3: output JSP files for queries (and an error page)
String[][]responseTargets=new String[][]{
  {"error","/jsp/rides/errorpage.jsp"}
  {"wml-findByZip","/jsp/rides/wml/findByZip.jsp"},
  {"wml-acceptZip","/jsp/rides/wml/acceptZip.jsp"},
  {"wml-offer","/jsp/rides/wml/offer.jsp"}
};

  qBean.configure(dbParams,dbQueries,responseTargets); // once per session
%>
```

Connecting to the Database

In order to connect a user to a database, we need information about the user and information about the database. In the **Java Database Connectivity** (JDBC) framework, a database is specified by two items: a JDBC driver that connects Java code to the database, and the name by which the database can be found. On the basis of these two pieces of information, the program can construct a Connection object that handles the connection details.

The user information consists of a user name and a password. A simple approach to security is to send the initial request encrypted and have the database itself handle user authentication. Our DBHandler assigns each user (each username-password pair) a separate connection pool, so that different users don't mix.

Query Specification

The second section has to do with running queries. In our framework, queries have names and values, where the value is a SQL string with question marks used as place holders for the parameters of the query. (See the example below.) In JDBC, you use such strings to create a PreparedStatement object that has an executeQuery() method. Once the database connection is established, the PreparedStatement object can be used to run a query, with parameters supplied by the Request object.

When the user submits a query, the submitted values of the WML input elements replace the question marks in the SQL string. The values of the input elements are, of course, text strings that have to be converted to the appropriate SQL data types. In the case of DATEs, this conversion is not trivial because dates are formatted differently in different parts of the world. In order to make sure that the conversion process works correctly, we provide a string that lists the data types of the parameters. For instance, the acceptZip query is like this:

```
{"acceptZip",
  "UPDATE Rides SET AcceptedBy=?,AcceptedEmail=? " +
    "WHERE rowId=" +
    "(SELECT Min(rowID) FROM Rides " +  // accept the first match
    "WHERE Day=? AND ToZip=? AND AcceptedBy='-')",
  "TEXT,TEXT,DATE,TEXT"},
```

Here, the first string is the name of the query, the second is a SQL string with four place holders in it, and the third a list of four data types for the four query parameters. You will see how it works in the section on the DBHandler, coming up soon.

The SQL strings are stored in a dictionary-like object, indexed by the corresponding names. In order to run a query, the user only has to use the appropriate form and provide the values for the parameters of the PreparedStatement. Since these parameters are ordered, the input elements for entering query parameters must have such names as QueryParameter1, QueryParameter2, and so on. For the Wireless Web, where every byte counts, we shorten them to QP1, QP2, and so on. You saw these names in the entry page.

The SQL query for offering rides is a bit more involved. We'll take a brief detour to go through it before resuming the overview of the configure.jsp page.

The Offer Query

The tricky part about this query is that we want new offers to go to the end of the Rides table so they are listed in the order in which they are submitted. In order to find the end of the table we have to refer to it in the inner SELECT query as well as in the outer INSERT query. It is easy to send SQL into an infinite loop here; the way to stay out of trouble is to provide an alias for 'Rides' and use it in the inner query:

```
{"offer",
  "INSERT INTO Rides SELECT 1+Max(r.rowId) as rowId,"+
  "? as OfferedBy,? as OfferedEmail,? as FromZip,? as ToZip,"+
  "? as Day,'-' as AcceptedBy,'-' as AcceptedEmail FROM Rides r",
  "TEXT,TEXT,TEXT,TEXT,DATE"}
```

Output Templates

The third and final section of the configuration page specifies an output template for each type of query. It also consists of name-value pairs where the names are the names of queries, and the values are the names of JSP files to forward the request to. In addition to the error page, there are three forward destinations, which correspond to the three available queries. Later in the chapter, to produce web-based output, we'll add three more forward destinations for JSP pages whose template material is XHTML rather than WML.

A Look at the Back End

The centerpiece of the back end processing is the main bean, QBean.java, which dispatches queries from the main JSP page to an appropriate handler and forwards the result to the appropriate page for output. It uses two custom classes to do its job: DBHandler and Dict. While the details are a bit involved, the main ideas behind these two classes can be summarized compactly. We do it here, to take the mystery out of it and also to explain how the application gets initialized from the request data.

DBHandler

Our main tool for database processing is the DBHandler class. There is a DBHandler object for each database that is used by the application within a user session. This means that a DBHandler object needs three kinds of information:

❑   Information about the database: the JDBC driver and the database URL

❑   Information about the user: username and password

❑   Information about the applications: what queries does the application make available to the user?

The first two items on this list are just Strings, and you have seen them specified in the configuration file. But how does one represent queries? DBHandler contains an inner class called Query that implements the 'named query' abstraction: a Query object is, in effect, a query string for a PreparedStatement (in the JDBC sense) with a name given to it. DBHandler contains a Hashtable of such Query objects, indexed by their names. The configuration file you have just seen results in a DBHandler object whose queries Hashtable contains three Query objects, named findByZip, acceptZip and offer.

A DBHandler is created once per session. Once it is created, it connects to the database (through a 'connection pool' – reusing existing connections as much as possible). Next, it creates its PreparedStatement objects. After that, the program is ready to accept queries from the query entry page. Let us walk through an example of a query. The entry page for our Ride Board application contains the following card, among others:

```
<card id="accept">
  <do type="accept" label="Go!">
    <go href="/examples/jsp/rides/core.jsp">
      <postfield name="query" value="acceptZip" />
      <postfield name="QP1" value="$QP1" />
      <postfield name="QP2" value="$QP2" />
      <postfield name="QP3" value="$QP3" />
      <postfield name="QP4" value="$QP4" />
      <postfield name="target" value="wml-acceptZip" />
    </go>
```

```
     </do>
  <p align="center">
    Accept a ride
  </p>
  <p>
    Name? <input name="QP1" format="*m" maxlength="8" /><br />
    eMail? <input name="QP2" format="*m" maxlength="20" /><br />
    Date? <input name="QP3" format="NN\/NN\/*N" maxlength="10" /><br />
    toZip? <input name="QP4" format="*N" maxlength="5" /><br />
  </p>
  </card>
```

To run this query, the user fills in the entry fields for query parameters (named QP1, QP2, and so on). This information gets to the DBHandler via the Request object and the main bean. The DBHandler retrieves the PreparedStatement using the name given, replaces its question marks with the values of the QP parameters, and runs the query.

This is an outline. It will be fleshed out to a certain extent as we go through the code of the main bean. For the complete detail, including the connection pooling mechanism that is built into the DBHandler, you should consult the code, which is available with the rest of the code for this book.

The Dict class

The Dict class is a convenience class for storing and retrieving Strings. It is derived from java.util.Properties (itself derived from Hashtable). The reason we extend Properties rather than use the class directly is because we want a couple of additional features, as follows:

❑   Dict is used for configuration by system administrators, so we make the keys case-insensitive: "Key", "key" and "KEY" all map to the same value.

❑   We make it possible to place a limit on how long the total length of the output can be, set by the outLimit variable. This is useful for HTML, and crucial for WML.

❑   We define a setDef() method, overloaded so that in addition to a single name-value pair, it can take an array of such pairs (a 2-dimensional array of Strings), or two parallel arrays of names and values, or, indeed, a Request object arriving from a servlet or a JSP page.

❑   Finally, we define a getDef() method that is like the getProperty() method of Properties, except it makes the retrieval case-insensitive and it keeps track of outLimit. This latter feature can be useful for WML output where the maximal page size is on the order of 1.5K.

The entire class is shown below:

```
package MyNa.jspUtil;
package MyNa.jspUtil;

import java.util.Properties;
import javax.servlet.http.HttpServletRequest;

  public class Dict extends Properties {
     int outLimit; // controls amount of output

     // two basic constructors that create an empty Dict
     public Dict(int outLimit){
       this.outLimit=outLimit;
```

```java
  }
  public Dict(){this(-1);} // there is no limit

  // the remaining constructors all use setDef() method
  public Dict(String[][]pairs){
    this(-1);
    setDef(pairs);
  }
  public Dict(String[]names,String[] vals){
    this(-1);
    setDef(names,vals);
  }
  public Dict(HttpServletRequest req){
    this(-1);
    setDef(req);
  }

  // setter and getter for outLimit
  public void setOutLimit(int outLimit){
    this.outLimit=outLimit;
  }
  public int getOutLimit(){
    return outLimit;
  }

// several versions of setDef
  public void setDef(String name,String val){
    setProperty(name.toUpperCase(),val);
  }

  public void setDef(String[][]pairs){
    for(int i=0;i<pairs.length;i++)
      setDef(pairs[i][0],pairs[i][1]);
  }
  public void setDef(String[]names,String[]vals){
    int len=names.length; if(len>vals.length)len=vals.length;
    for(int i=0;i<len;i++)
      setDef(names[i],vals[i]);
  }
  public  void setDef(HttpServletRequest req){
    java.util.Enumeration enum=req.getParameterNames();
    while(enum.hasMoreElements()){
      String name=(String)enum.nextElement();
      String val=req.getParameter(name);
      setDef(name,val);
    }
  }

// several versions of getDef
  public String getDef(String name){
    return getDef(name,"");
  }

  public String getDef(String name,String dflt){
    String val=getProperty(name.toUpperCase(),dflt);
    if(val==null)val="";
    if(outLimit<0)return val;
    int len=val.length();
    if(len>outLimit){
      val=val.substring(0,outLimit);
      outLimit=0;
    } else outLimit-=len;
```

```
    return val;
  }

  public String[]getDef(String[]names,String[]dflt){
    String[]vals=new String[names.length];
    for(int i=0;i<vals.length;i++){
      vals[i]=getDef(names[i],dflt[i]);
    }
    return vals;
  }

  public String[]getDef(String[]names,String dflt){
    String[]vals=new String[names.length];
    for(int i=0;i<vals.length;i++){
      vals[i]=getDef(names[i],dflt);
    }
    return vals;
  }
  public String[]getDef(String[]names){
    return getDef(names,"");
  }

} // end of Dict class
```

Most of this code is completely straightforward, except perhaps the second version of `getDef()`. Remember that `outLimit` sets the allowed length of output, so every time we output a string we subtract its length from `outLimit`. If the length of the string is greater than the remaining quota of characters, we output as much as we can and set `outLimit` to 0.

The Main Bean: qBean

With the supporting classes cleared, it is now time to look inside the main bean. The most important tasks of the main bean are to set up a DBHandler and to forward the request to the right target. All the pertinent information has to be extracted from the Request object. It follows that the bean needs three variables: a DBHandler, a Dict to hold the request object information, and a Dict to hold the targets after they are extracted from the request. Here is the beginning of the bean's code:

```
package MyNa.jspUtil;
import java.sql.SQLException;
import javax.servlet.http.HttpServletRequest;

public class QBean {

  DBHandler dbH=null;
  Dict targets=null;
  Dict requestDict=null;

  public QBean(){}

  public Dict getTargets(){
    return targets;
  }
  public Dict getRequestDict(){
    return requestDict;
  }
```

configure()

The first thing that the bean does is configure(), which is called from configure.jsp. The call, as you may remember, looks like this:

```
qBean.configure(dbParams,dbQueries,responseTargets);
```

Here, dbParams is an array of strings that contains database connection information, and the other two arguments are two-dimensional arrays of strings in which each row is a name-value pair. Not surprisingly, they end up as Dict objects:

```
public void doConfigure(
    String[]dbParams,          // dbName,jdbc driver name,username and password
    String[][]dbQueries,       // query name,sql string for PreparedStatement
    String[][]responseTargets)// query name,output JSP page
            throws SQLException{
    if(dbH!=null)return;       // we only do this once per session
    targets=new Dict();
    targets.setDef(responseTargets); // store response targets in the Dict
    dbH=makeDBHandler(dbParams,dbQueries);
}
```

Now, how do you make a DBHandler? Actually, it's quite easy:

```
private DBHandler makeDBHandler(
    String[]dbParams,
    String[][]dbQueries)
        throws SQLException{
  String dbDriver=dbParams[0];
  String dbName=dbParams[1];

//set dbUser, dbPwd or leave as null if not provided
  String dbUser, dbPwd;
  if(dbParams.length<3)dbUser=null; else dbUser=dbParams[2];
  if(dbParams.length<4)dbPwd=null; else dbPwd=dbParams[3];

// Misc.column() is a utility that returns a column of a 2-d array
  String []qNames=Misc.column(0,dbQueries);
  String []qSqlStrings=Misc.column(1,dbQueries);
  return new DBHandler(dbDriver,dbName,
                    dbUser,dbPwd,
                    qNames,qSqlStrings);
}// DBHandler is created, ready to run queries
```

This concludes the configure() part, executed from configure.jsp that is included in the main JSP page, core.jsp. As you can see, although configure() is called on every request, its code gets executed only once, when the session is first created.

doCommand() and whereTo()

The main JSP page, core.jsp, calls doCommand() and whereTo() which get executed on every request. doCommand() does not do much at all: it just wraps the request object into a Dict object and calls setupRequest(), a placeholder method that can be used, as needed, to validate the request information; we leave it empty of content:

```
public void doCommand(HttpServletRequest request){
  requestDict=new Dict();
  requestDict.setDef(request);
  setupRequestDict();  // check through parameter name assumptions
}
private void setupRequestDict(){
  // here we can check the request and complain if we don't like it
}
```

The business of identifying the page to forward to is dispatched by whereTo(). By now, all request information is in the requestDict, and all targets are in the targets Dict, so we use getDef() often.

```
public String whereTo(){
  String targetType=requestDict.getDef("target","");
  if(0==targetType.length())targetType=requestDict.getDef("query","");
  if(0==targetType.length())targetType="error";
  return targets.getDef(targetType,"");
}
```

To give an example, if the query is findByZip, then requestDict.getDef("target") will return wml-findByZip, and targets.getDef("wml-findByZip") will return "wml/findByZip.jsp", the name of the JSP page to forward the request to.

What about the query?

The main bean does include a method for executing the query, queryResult(), but it is not called from any of the JSP pages that you have seen: it is called from the target page to which the request is forwarded. The queryResult() method, in turn, calls an output method of the DBHandler. The DBHandler has several such methods that differ in how the result set is packaged: it can be a two-dimensional array of Strings, or a lazily evaluated sequence. Whatever the format, the result of the query is returned as a variable within an object that implements our QueryResult interface. QueryResult extends the XmlOb interface, both within the MyNa.jspUtil package:

```
public interface XmlOb {
  public String toXmlString();
}

public interface QueryResult extends XmlOb {
  public String[] getColumnHeaders();
  public String[] getColumnTypes();
  public String[][]getRows();
}
```

As you can see, an object that implements XmlOb knows how to write itself out to an XML string. An object that implements QueryResult, in addition, can provide two String arrays of equal size that specify the names and data types of record fields. The fields themselves are returned, as a String matrix, by the getRows() method.

Here is the queryResult() method that calls the DBHandler's getQueryResult. Note that the argument to getQueryResult() is a Dict, not a Request object. There is no dependence on the specific servlet/JSP context: DBHandler doesn't know or care where the Dict object comes from. It can, for instance, come from an XML file or from a socket stream:

```
public QueryResult queryResult()throws SQLException{
  // called from receiving page, not forwarding page.
  return dbH.getQueryResult(requestDict);
}
```

And that's all there is to the main bean. It is now time to move on downstream to the output pages.

JSP for Output

There are three WML output pages corresponding to the three queries: findByZip, acceptZip and offer. The names of the output files are the same as the names of the queries, with .jsp added on the end; they will be stored in a wml directory, so that the findByZip query with wml-findByZip target is the wml/findByZip.jsp file. There will also be an xhtml directory with files of the same names which respond to the same queries; the whereTo() method in the bean must direct these requests appropriately. As described in the section on design considerations and in the section on the entry page, all three output pages end with the same forms that produce them, allowing the user to 'continue the conversation' with the database. The repeated material is in ridesInc.jsp, which gets included in the end of each output page. You saw that page in the entry page section, so we won't repeat it here.

The material that precedes this input file varies depending on the query. Let's start with the natural first query, wml-findByZip.jsp.

findByZip.jsp

Like all output pages, this page starts out by creating an instance of the main bean and asking it to run a query. The query returns a QueryResult object, from which we extract a two-dimensional array of Strings. The rest of the page is a typical example of how a JSP page would display the result of a database query as a WML table. Although the page is fairly long, we don't break it into pieces but provide a running commentary:

```
<%@ page contentType="text/vnd.wap.wml;charset=ISO-8859-1" %><?xml version="1.0"?>
<!DOCTYPE wml PUBLIC "-//WAPFORUM//DTD WML 1.1//EN"
  "http://www.wapforum.org/DTD/wml_1.1.xml">
<wml>
<%@ page errorPage="../wmlerrorpage.jsp" %>
<jsp:useBean id="qBean" scope="session" class="MyNa.jspUtil.QBean" />

<head>
  <meta http-equiv="Cache-Control" content="no-cache" forua="true"/>
</head>

<card id="output" title="findByZip">
  <do type="accept" label="again" > <go href="#start" />   </do>

<%
  MyNa.jspUtil.QueryResult qR=qBean.queryResult();
    // QueryResult has an array of headers and a 2-d array of records
  String[][]rows=(null==qR)?null:qR.getRows();
  if(null==rows || rows.length<1){ // no matches found?
%>
  <p>Sorry, no rides to your zip-code.</p>

<% }else{ String[]headers=qR.getColumnHeaders();  %>
```

```
      <p>
      <table columns="2">
<%  // we use only rows[0] to generate a 2-column table of fields
      for(int j=0;j<headers.length;j++){
%>
      <tr>
         <td><%= headers[j] %></td><td><%= rows[0][j] %></td>
      </tr>
<%      }                                                    %>
    </table>
    </p>
<% } %>
</card>

<%@ include file="ridesInc.jsp" %>

</wml>
```

acceptZip.jsp

The beginning and the end of this page are the same as the preceding one; only the display of the query result is different:

```
<%@ page contentType="text/vnd.wap.wml;charset=ISO-8859-1" %><?xml version="1.0"?>
<!DOCTYPE wml PUBLIC "-//WAPFORUM//DTD WML 1.1//EN"
    "http://www.wapforum.org/DTD/wml_1.1.xml">
<wml>
<%@ page errorPage="../wmlerrorpage.jsp" %>
<jsp:useBean id="qBean" scope="session" class="MyNa.jspUtil.QBean" />

<head>
   <meta http-equiv="Cache-Control" content="no-cache" forua="true"/>
</head>

<card id="output" title="acceptByZip">
   <do type="accept" label="again" > <go href="#start" />  </do>

<%
   MyNa.jspUtil.QueryResult qR=qBean.queryResult();
   String[][]rows=(null==qR)?null:qR.getRows();
   if(null==rows || rows.length<1 || rows[0].length<1){
%>
   <p>Sorry, no ride; please try again.</p>
<%
   }else{
       int numberAffected=Integer.parseInt(rows[0][0]);
       if(numberAffected==0){
%>
   <p>Sorry, no ride available.</p>
<%      } else {     %>
   <p>Okay, you've got a ride!</p>
<% } } %>
</card>
<%@ include file="ridesInc.jsp" %>

</wml>
```

In this case, the result of the query is just an integer – the number of rows affected. (It is still returned inside a two-dimensional array of strings that has one row and one column.) The same is true for the next query; the only difference is that in acceptZip we modify an existing row of the database table, while in offer we add a new one, or several new ones if more than one seat is added.

offer.jsp

Since this output page is very similar to the preceding one, we'll only repeat the middle part, until the `include` directive:

```
<card id="output" title="offer">
  <do type="accept" label="again" > <go href="#start" />  </do>

<%
  MyNa.jspUtil.QueryResult qR=qBean.queryResult();
  String[][]rows=(null==qR)?null:qR.getRows();
  if(null==rows || rows.length<1 || rows[0].length<1){
%>
  <p>Sorry, your offer went wrong; please try again.</p>
<%
  }else{
      int numberAffected=Integer.parseInt(rows[0][0]);
      if(numberAffected==0){
%>
  <p>Sorry, your offer failed. Please report this problem
  to our Friendly Support Staff. (or try again).</p>
<%       } else {       %>
  <p>Thanks; now we'll see who accepts it.</p>

<% } } %>
</card>
```

Adding a New Query to the Program

In conclusion to the application, let's consider how we could modify the application to add a new type of query. For instance, a reasonable addition to the program would be to allow offering, searching and accepting rides by state rather than a zip code. The point of this exercise is, that in order to add a query you don't need any new Java code.

First, let us assume that the database, in addition to the Rides table has a States table that has these two columns (in addition to the others): Zip and Abbrev. The table lists all the zip codes in the USA and provides an abbreviated state name for each, such as NY for 13346 and MA for 02138.

We want the user to be able to say, "I want a ride to CA (California)" and get a listing of all the available rides to that state, including the zip codes. Given such a listing, the user can decide whether any of those rides are close enough to where they want to go.

The only files that need to be changed to achieve this are configure.jsp and ridesInc.jsp. We also need to provide a new output page. Here's what needs to be done.

Changes in configure.jsp

First, we add the following item to the query list:

```
{"findByState",
    "SELECT R.* FROM Rides R, States S "+
      "WHERE R.ToZip=S.Zip AND S.Abbrev=?",
    "TEXT"}
```

This says: list all those rows from the `Rides` and `States` tables that have the same `Zip` values, with the additional condition that the value of `Abbrev` must be the same as the value specified by the user. Recall that the `?` is a place holder for a field value.

Second, we add a new response target to the target list in the same file:

```
{"wml-findByState","/jsp/rides/wml/findByState.jsp"},
```

This is all we need to do in `configure.jsp`.

Changes in ridesInc.jsp

In `ridesInc.jsp`, we need to add one more card. It is very similar to the card for `findByZip`, because we again have a single parameter of type `TEXT`:

```
Enter = the two-letter abbreviation for your destination state:<br/>
<input name="QP1" type="TEXT" size="2" value="WY" />
<input name="query" type="HIDDEN" value="findByState" />
<input type="submit" value="findByState" />
</form>
```

What about the Output Page?

Yes, we do need an output page, but it's virtually identical to the output page for the `findByZip` query. The only modifications will be in the name of the query and the accompanying prose. We are going to leave these modifications as an exercise. Meanwhile, you can test it with a copy of the `wml-findByZip` output page: the prose will be wrong, but it will show the right data.

Summary: How to Add a Query

In summary, this is what needs to be done in order to add a new query

❑   Write the query in SQL, with question marks for parameters to be entered by the user

❑   Give the query a name

❑   Add a new card to `ridesInc.jsp`. Provide an input element for each parameter of the query. Name those elements `QP1`, `QP2`, and so on

❑   Modify `configure.jsp`, in two ways:

   ❑   Add a new item to the query list (query name, query SQL string, and list of data types)

   ❑   Add a new item to the list of output JSP pages

❑   Create an output JSP page for the new query

The new query is then ready for use. As we said, in the 'real' framework instead of modifying `configure.jsp`, you would edit an XML configuration file, but editing `configure.jsp` works fine here. Here are a few queries that would be easy to add to the application:

```
{"findByState", // implemented in the text of preceding section
  "SELECT R.* FROM Rides R, States S "+
    "WHERE R.ToZip=S.Zip AND S.Abbrev=?",
  "TEXT"},
{"reportAll",   // not implemented
  "SELECT * FROM Rides",
  ""},
```

```
{"deleteRow",  // not implemented
  "DELETE FROM Rides WHERE rowID=?",
  "INT"},
{"findByDate", // not implemented
  "SELECT * FROM Rides WHERE Day BETWEEN ? AND ?",
  "DATE,DATE"}
```

The point of this section was not simply to show how easy it is to add new functionality to our WAP application. Adding new targets is just as easy as adding new queries, which is what is needed to re-target our output from WAP to the Web. The flexibility of the framework works both ways: deeper into the back end, towards the database, and in the user interface, towards the output targets.

Changing to a Web Application

We are ready to move on to the Web. Let us summarize what needs to be done. To add web output, we need to:

❑   Add material to configure.jsp to show more targets.

❑   Write new versions of ridesInc.jsp and top.jsp.

❑   Add output pages that produce XHTML rather than WML. This may involve changes in the JSP Java code sections, to adapt the output to web display conditions.

The result, when we are done, will look as follows (we show the initial screen that you see upon connecting to the site, and the result of the findByZip query). To see the initial screen, point your browser at http://localhost:8080/examples/jsp/rides/xhtml/top.jsp:

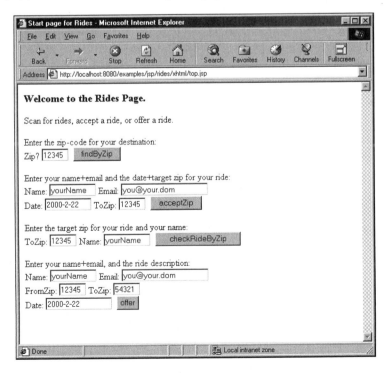

Choose findByZip, fill in the zip field and send the query. If a ride to that zip is available, the result will look somewhat like this:

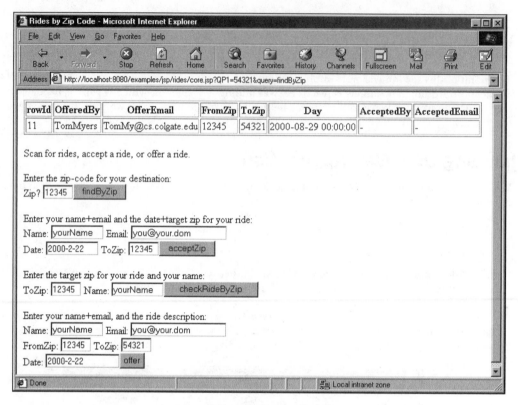

We are not going to show many screen shots because the logic of the XHTML application is exactly the same as that of the WML application, which has already been debugged and explained. Instead, we'll have a quick look at the parts of the code that will need some changes.

configure.jsp

The changes in `configure.jsp` are trivial: we just add three more output targets for our three queries, putting the corresponding files in a separate directory. The output targets section of the configuration file now looks like this:

```
String[][]responseTargets=new String[][]{
  {"error","/jsp/rides/errorpage.jsp"},
  {"findByZip","/jsp/rides/xhtml/findByZip.jsp"},
  {"acceptZip","/jsp/rides/xhtml/acceptZip.jsp"},
  {"offer","/jsp/rides/xhtml/offer.jsp"},
  {"wml-findByZip","/jsp/rides/wml/findByZip.jsp"},
  {"wml-acceptZip","/jsp/rides/wml/acceptZip.jsp"},
  {"wml-offer","/jsp/rides/wml/offer.jsp"}
};
```

`top.jsp` and `ridesInc.jsp` get rewritten to output XHTML and to show different query names.

top.jsp

Here too, the changes are trivial: we just replace the WML declarations with XHTML declarations and output XHTML:

```
<?xml version="1.0" encoding="UTF-8"?>
<!DOCTYPE html PUBLIC "-//W3C//DTD XHTML 1.0 Strict//EN"
    "http://www.w3.org/TR/xhtml1/DTD/strict.dtd">
<html xmlns="http://www.w3.org/TR/xhtml1/strict" xml:lang="en" lang="en">

<head><title> Start page for Rides </title></head>

<body>
  <h3>Welcome to the Rides Page.</h3>
  <%@ include file="ridesInc.jsp" %>
</body>
</html>
```

ridesInc.jsp

ridesInc.jsp within the xhtml directory is completely rewritten and now contains nothing but XHTML code:

```
Scan for rides, accept a ride, or offer a ride.

<form method="GET" action="/examples/jsp/rides/core.jsp" >
Enter the zip-code for your destination:<br/>
Zip?
  <input name="QP1" type="TEXT" size="10" value="12345" />
  <input name="query" type="HIDDEN" value="findByZip" />
  <input type="submit" value="findByZip" />
</form>

<form method="GET" action="/examples/jsp/rides/core.jsp" >
Enter your name+email, and the date and target zip for your ride:<br/>
Name:
  <input name="QP1" type="TEXT" size="10" value="yourName" />
Email:
  <input name="QP2" type="TEXT" size="20" value="you@your.dom" /><br />
Date:
  <input name="QP3" type="TEXT" size="10" value="2/22/2000" />
ToZip:
  <input name="QP4" type="TEXT" size="5" value="12345" />
  <input name="query" type="HIDDEN" value="acceptZip" />
  <input type="submit" value="acceptZip" />
</form>

<form method="GET" action="/examples/jsp/rides/core.jsp" >
Enter your name+email, and the ride description:<br/>
Name:
  <input name="QP1" type="TEXT" size="10" value="yourName" />
Email:
  <input name="QP2" type="TEXT" size="20" value="you@your.dom" /><br />
FromZip:
  <input name="QP3" type="TEXT" size="5" value="12345" />
ToZip:
  <input name="QP4" type="TEXT" size="5" value="54321"/><br />
Date:
  <input name="QP5" type="TEXT" size="15" value="2/22/2000" />
  <input name="query" type="HIDDEN" value="offer" />
  <input type="submit" value="offer" />
</form>
```

349

As we saw before with the WAP application, adding a query is fairly straightforward: you just need to add an option to the ridesInc.jsp and add a form to submit the new query. Changes in configure.jsp are the same as in the WAP case.

findByZip.jsp

The new output file is as follows:

```
<?xml version="1.0" encoding="UTF-8"?>
<!DOCTYPE html PUBLIC "-//W3C//DTD XHTML 1.0 Strict//EN"
    "http://www.w3.org/TR/xhtml1/DTD/strict.dtd">
<html xmlns="http://www.w3.org/TR/xhtml1/strict" xml:lang="en" lang="en">
<head><title>Rides by Zip Code </title></head>
<body>

<%@ page errorPage="../errorpage.jsp" %>
<jsp:useBean id="qBean" scope="session" class="MyNa.jspUtil.QBean" />

<%
  MyNa.jspUtil.QueryResult qR=qBean.queryResult();
  // QueryResult has an array of headers and a 2-d array of records
  String[][]rows;
  if(null==qR)         // validity check: make sure query result is there
    rows=null;
  else
    rows=qR.getRows(); // extract the rows
  if(null==rows || rows.length<1){ // check to make sure there are matches
%>
  Sorry, no rides for this zip-code.

<% }else{ String[]headers=qR.getColumnHeaders(); // get headers          %>

    Get ready to ride...<br />
    <table border="1"> // start outputting an HTML table
      <tr>
<%
    for(int j=0;j<headers.length;j++){ // a loop to output headers
%>
        <th><%= headers[j] %></th>
<%      }                                                                 %>
    </tr>
<%    for(int i=0;i<rows.length;i++){// outer loop to output records        %>
      <tr>
<%
    String[] row=rows[i];
    for(int j=0;j<row.length;j++){ // inner loop to output fields
%>
        <td><%= row[j] %></td> <!-- put each value into a td -->
<%      }                                                                 %>
    </tr>
<% }                                                                      %>
    </table>
<% } %>
<%@ include file="/jsp/rides/xhtml/ridesInc.jsp" %>

</body></html>
```

Note how this page gets the result set from the DBHandler as a string matrix and dumps it directly to output, without any regard for its size. This is OK for a web application, but a risky thing to do in a WAP application.

acceptZip.jsp

The beginning and the end of this output page are the same as for `findByZip.jsp`. Only the display of the query result is different:

```
<?xml version="1.0" encoding="UTF-8"?>
<!DOCTYPE html PUBLIC "-//W3C//DTD XHTML 1.0 Strict//EN"
    "http://www.w3.org/TR/xhtml1/DTD/strict.dtd">
<html xmlns="http://www.w3.org/TR/xhtml1/strict" xml:lang="en" lang="en">
<head><title>response to accepted Zip Code </title></head>
<body>

<%@ page errorPage="../errorpage.jsp" %>
<jsp:useBean id="qBean" scope="session" class="MyNa.jspUtil.QBean" />

<%
  MyNa.jspUtil.QueryResult qR=qBean.queryResult();
  String[][]rows;
  if(null==qR)
    rows=null;
  else
    rows=qR.getRows();
  if(null==rows || rows.length<1){
%>
  Sorry, your ride went wrong; please try again.
<%
  }else{
      int numberAffected=Integer.parseInt(rows[0][0]);
      if(numberAffected==0){
%>
  Sorry, your ride was taken before you signed up.
<%  } else {    %>
  Okay, you've got a ride!

<% } } %>
<%@ include file="/jsp/rides/xhtml/ridesInc.jsp" %>
</body></html>
```

offer.jsp

Again this output page is much the same as the others. We only give the middle part concerning the query:

```
<%
  MyNa.jspUtil.QueryResult qR=qBean.queryResult();
  String[][]rows=(null==qR)?null:qR.getRows();
  if(null==rows || rows.length<1 || rows[0].length<1){
%>
  Sorry, your offer went wrong; please try again.

<%
  }else{
      int numberAffected=Integer.parseInt(rows[0][0]);
      if(numberAffected==0){
%>
  Sorry, your offer failed. Please report this problem
  to our Friendly Support Staff. (or try again).
<%      } else {    %>
  Thanks; now we'll see who accepts it.
```

A Pause before Changing Direction

We are about to shift gears in a major way, so it might be a good idea to pause and review what we have accomplished. We started this chapter with a very general picture of a distributed application framework with several degrees of freedom. We narrowed our choices to an application that has the following options:

❑ It can receive requests either from a WAP microbrowser or a web browser

❑ The requests contain database queries

❑ Queries are dispatched to a database

❑ The result of the query can be incorporated into either a WML deck or a web page

At two critical junctures, the application uses JSP: as a Main servlet that configures the application and processes the incoming requests, and as output templates that incorporate the results of the queries. We gave an overview of the JSP technology and presented design ideas for their effective use.

The role of output JSP pages in our Ride Board application can be described as follows: they function as a transformer between the output of a database query and the response sent to the user agent. Whether the user agent is WAP or web, the input to JSP pages is the same, a two-dimensional array of strings, itself generated from a query result set. The output is, at some level of generality, also the same: an XML document of a specific document type (XHTML or WML). The task of the JSP pages in the middle is to generate an XML document from a two-dimensional array of strings. JSP, as you can see, can carry out the task easily, but as often with JSP, there is a concern that a system administrator who is not a programmer will find it hard to maintain a JSP page that mixes Java code with XML tags. And in any event, at this early stage in the development of XML technologies, it is important to explore the alternatives.

One alternative is to use another general-purpose tool for generating or transforming XML documents. It is called **XSLT: eXtensible Stylesheet Language for Transformations**, and was introduced in Chapter 9. In the remainder of this chapter, we will re-implement the Ride Board application using XSLT. Except for the output component and a few few lines that will need to be added to the main bean, the rest of the application will remain unchanged. A major implementation effort has gone into the background task of converting a two-dimensional array of strings into something that an XSL processor can handle, but this task and the new component that implements it are not specific to this application, or even to the entire WAP-web problem. The new component, consisting of the XmlStringDoc and XmlQueryStringDoc classes, will be of use every time an XML document needs to be generated from a non-XML object in memory.

In order to work your way through the rest of this chapter, you will need some background in XML parsing and XSLT. If a refresher is needed, review the corresponding sections in Chapter 9 of this book. They introduce all the concepts that are necessary for understanding our XSL-based WAP application (except for its 'virtual document' component discussed in this chapter). For more detail, see many existing books on the subject, including *Professional XML* and *XSLT Programmer's Reference* from Wrox Press.

In outline, the rest of the chapter will proceed as follows:

❑ A simple WML XSLT example

❑ The revised Ride Board application

We start with a quick tour of XSLT.

XSLT

As was discussed in Chapter 9, XSLT is a language used for writing stylesheets, which can be used to transform XML documents into virtually any other format. An XSLT stylesheet resembles a JSP page in that it has some constant material that the processor just passes through to output, and some material that gets transformed and recombined before being sent to output.

To try the code in this part of the chapter, you'll need both an XSLT processor and an XML parser:

- ❏ For the XSLT processor, we use James Clark's XT, downloadable from `http://www.jclark.com/xml`. (James Clark is the editor of the XSLT Recommendation and a co-editor of the XPath Recommendation.)

- ❏ For the XML parser, we use Sun's Java API for XML Parsing (JAXP) package, available from `http://java.sun.com/products/xml/index.html`.

- ❏ You will also need the Java Development Kit, version 1.2 or later, available from `http://java.sun.com/products/jdk/1.2/`.

When installing, make sure that `jaxp.jar` from Sun and `xt.jar` from James Clark are in the classpath. To run, give this command (wrapped here for readability):

```
java -Dcom.jclark.xsl.sax.parser=com.sun.xml.parser.Parser
     com.jclark.xsl.sax.Driver <xml-file> <xsl-stylesheet> <output-file>
```

The `-D` option tells the `Driver` which XML parser to use. Instead of a command-line option, you can specify the parser in the `System.properties` file. For more detail, see `xt.htm` in the XT distribution.

XT can also be run as a servlet called `XSLServlet`. We explain how to configure the servlet/JSP engine for that after we go through our first XSLT example.

An XSLT and WML Example

For an example of using XSLT, consider an XML file, rows.xml, which describes the contents of a database table, such as the rides table used in our Ride Board application:

```
<table>
  <row>
    <field name='rowId'>1</field>
    <field name='OfferedBy'>Sandy Weston</field>
    <field name='OfferEmail'>sweston@btu.edu</field>
    <field name='FromZip'>12345</field>
    <field name='ToZip'>54321</field>
    <field name='Day'>2/20/2000</field>
    <field name='AcceptedBy'>Trish Cooper</field>
    <field name='AcceptedEmail'>tcooper@btu.edu</field>
  </row>
  <row>
    <field name='rowId'>2</field>
    <field name='OfferedBy'>Sandy Weston</field>
    <field name='OfferEmail'>sweston@btu.edu</field>
    <field name='FromZip'>12345</field>
    <field name='ToZip'>54321</field>
    <field name='Day'>2/20/2000</field>
    <field name='AcceptedBy'>-</field>
    <field name='AcceptedEmail'>-</field>
  </row>
</table>
```

The corresponding database table would have two rows of data.

In this example, we will pretend that this table is the result of us having done a search by zip on the databse table `Rides`. From this table, we want to output a single record, the first record that satisfies the conditions of the search. We will therefore design an XSL stylesheet, called `findByZipFile.xsl` (within `rides/wml`), to convert this XML file into a WML deck. The final stylesheet will be `findByZip.xsl`, and will work directly from database output rather than from a file. (There will also be an XHTML version within `rides/xhtml`, and it will generate all matching rows rather than just the first, because this version assumes that you have more space to work in.)

As an extra feature that will take us a step closer to the real application code, we will output the query entry cards at the end of this generated deck. Since these are included in every output page, we place them in a separate stylesheet, `ridesInc.xsl`, and include it in each of the stylesheets which generate query responses. Unlike JSP, including a stylesheet really means including some template definitions; to include the material produced by those templates, you need to call them using the `<xsl:call-template>` element.

Specifying the WML content type is considerably more involved than specifying XHTML content type, and requires a change within the XT code. The problem is that although WML is an XML language, its content type is not `text/xml`, but `text/vnd.wap.wml`. This is not a type that XT is aware of, and so we had to invent something of a kluge to get it right. We come back to this point later.

rides\wml\findByZipFile.xsl

Here is the stylesheet, broken into pieces for ease of discussion. After the piecemeal presentation we'll bring it all together.

The Declaration

An XSL stylesheet is an XML document whose root element is `<xsl:stylesheet>`. The `xsl:` namespace that it uses is defined in the beginning of the stylesheet. (A word of warning here: IE5.00 XSL also uses the `xsl:` prefix but associates it with a different URI, the URI for the Working Draft that was current when IE5 was released.)

```
<xsl:stylesheet version="1.0"
    xmlns:xsl="http://www.w3.org/1999/XSL/Transform"

    <!-- new namespace for Java code that does WML output-->
    xmlns:javaout="http://www.jclark.com/xt/java"
    exclude-result-prefixes="javaout"><!-- do not show namespace on output -->
```

The last line is added to make sure that the namespace attribute is not generated. This is essential for WAP microbrowsers: the namespace declaration is not one of the optional attributes for the `<wml>` element, and our microbrowser blows up rather than ignoring it. You will see this line in the upcoming stylesheets where there will be several additional namespaces, most of them to be excluded from the output.

Top-level Elements

There is a single top-level element in this stylesheet, `<xsl:output>`. Its method attribute specifies that WML output will be produced. Its indent attribute says that the processor can add whitespace to give output a little formatting:

```
<xsl:output <!-- custom output element for WML; uses our XMLOutputHandler -->
    method="javaout:MyNa.jspUtil.XMLOutputHandler"
    indent="yes"
    encoding="UTF-8"
    media-type="text/vnd.wap.wml" <!-- becomes content-type -->
    omit-xml-declaration="no"
    doctype-public="-//WAPFORUM//DTD WML 1.1//EN"
    doctype-system="http://www.wapforum.org/DTD/wml_1.1.xml"
 />

<xsl:include href="ridesInc.xsl" />
<!-- makes the rides-forms template defined in ridesInc.xsl available;
     it gets called in the end of the deck -->
```

As we mentioned above, the only difficult part of the stylesheet is this <xsl:output> element. We will return to its contents later in the chapter when we discuss our extensions to XT code.

The Rest of the Stylesheet in Outline

In this particular stylesheet, there is a single <xsl:template> element whose match attribute matches the root node. All processing takes place inside that element; more precisely, it takes place inside an <xsl:choose> element within the <xsl:template> element. In outline, the rest of the stylesheet looks like this:

```
<xsl:template match="/"> <!-- matches the root of the XML document tree -->

<!-- first block of WML material to pass through to output -->

<xsl:variable ... /> <!-- declares and initializes a variable -->

<xsl:choose>
 <!-- checks to see if there is output;
      if not, outputs a message; otherwise outputs a table -->
</xsl:choose>

<!-- second block of WML material for output -->

</xsl:template>
</xsl:stylesheet>
```

Fixed WML Material

The first block of WML material is just the beginning of a WML document, and a <go> element pointing towards a card called start (within the ridesInc.xsl code):

```
<head>
  <meta http-equiv="Cache-Control" content="no-cache" forua="true"/>
</head>

<card id="output" title="findByZipTst">
  <do type="accept" label="again">
    <go href="#start" />
  </do>
```

The second block of WML material consists simply of the closing tags:

```
</card>
</wml>
```

In between is the interesting part.

A Little XSLT: Declare a Variable

First we declare a variable that would refer to all the `<row>` elements. A detail to note is that the root of the document tree that XSLT is working on is not the root element, but its parent. If the XML document had, for instance, processing instructions as siblings to the root element, they would also be children of the root of the tree.

Since our `<xsl:template>` element selected the root, we want to refer to its child by the name `<table>` and select all the children of `<table>` who are `<row>`s:

```
<xsl:variable name="rows" select="table/row" />
```

Since `<table>` in our simple example of this section only has `<row>` children, we would achieve the same result by saying, "select all children of `<table>`":

```
<xsl:variable name="rows" select="table/*" />
```

The expressions that appear in quotes as values of `match` or `select` attributes are XPath expressions. You have seen several here: `"/"` refers to the root; `"table"` refers to those children of the current element whose name is `"table"`; `"table/*"` refers to all children of `<table>`. As you will see in a moment, XPath also has functional expressions.

More XSLT: Output a Table

Here is the rest of the stylesheet, mostly self-explanatory and quite readable:

```
<xsl:choose>
   <xsl:when test="count($rows)=0">
     Sorry, no rides to your zip-code.
   </xsl:when>
   <xsl:otherwise>
     <table columns="2"><!-- output two-column table -->
       <xsl:for-each select="$rows[1]/field" >
         <tr>
            <td> <xsl:value-of select="@name" /> </td>
            <td> <xsl:value-of select="text()" /> </td>
         </tr>
       </xsl:for-each>
     </table>
   </xsl:otherwise>
</xsl:choose>
```

The XPath expression that is the value of test contains both a variable reference ($rows) and a function call. The variable refers to an array, and we can refer to its first element as $rows[1]. (XSLT arrays are *not* zero-based because XSLT is primarily addressed to people who do not know C or Java.) The XPath expression @name refers to the name attribute.

There are several `<xsl:value-of>` elements in this stylesheet. The value of an attribute is its "normalized" value, after all the entities have been replaced and white space normalized. The value of an XML element is the concatenation of the text values of all its children. So, for instance, if you say:

```
<xsl:template match="/">
   <xsl:value-of select="."/>
</xsl:template>
```

you will get the entire text of the document run together, without any markup. As you may have guessed, the XPath expression " . " refers to the currently selected node.

```
<xsl:call-template name="rides-forms"/><!-- template within ridesInc.xsl -->
```

The Whole Stylesheet

Here is the entire text of our first stylesheet:

```
<xsl:stylesheet version="1.0"
  xmlns:xsl="http://www.w3.org/1999/XSL/Transform"

  <!-- new namespace for Java code that does WML output-->
  xmlns:javaout="http://www.jclark.com/xt/java"
  exclude-result-prefixes="javaout"><!-- do not show namespace on output -->

<xsl:output <!-- custom output element for WML; uses our XMLOutputHandler -->
    method="javaout:MyNa.jspUtil.XMLOutputHandler"
    indent="yes"
    encoding="UTF-8"
    media-type="text/vnd.wap.wml" <!-- becomes content-type -->
    omit-xml-declaration="no"
    doctype-public="-//WAPFORUM//DTD WML 1.1//EN"
    doctype-system="http://www.wapforum.org/DTD/wml_1.1.xml"
/>

<xsl:include href="ridesInc.xsl" />
<!-- defines a template that gets called in the end of the deck -->

<xsl:template match="/">

<wml> <!-- First block of WML content -->
<head>
  <meta http-equiv="Cache-Control" content="no-cache" forua="true"/>
</head>

<card id="output" title="findByZipTst">
 <do type="accept" label="again" >
   <go href="#start" />
 </do>

<xsl:variable name="rows" select="table/row" />

<p> <!-- tables are within <p>'s in WML -->

<xsl:choose>
  <xsl:when test="count($rows)=0">
    Sorry, no rides to your zip-code.
  </xsl:when>
  <xsl:otherwise>
    <table columns="2"><!-- output two-column table -->
```

```
      <xsl:for-each select="$rows[1]/field" >
        <tr>
          <td> <xsl:value-of select="@name" /> </td>
          <td> <xsl:value-of select="text()" /> </td>
        </tr>
      </xsl:for-each>
    </table>
  </xsl:otherwise>
</xsl:choose>

</p></card>

<xsl:call-template name="rides-forms"/><!-- template within ridesInc.xsl -->

</wml>
</xsl:template>
</xsl:stylesheet>
```

ridesInc.xsl

The included stylesheet, `ridesInc.xsl`, consists of the top declarations and a single template. The opening part of the stylesheet is the same as in the stylesheet above. The template, called `rides-forms`, produces exactly the same cards that were produced by `ridesInc.jsp` in the earlier part of the chapter. It consists of a single large block of WML material that the template spits out when called. We show only the first card, since they are exactly same as in `ridesInc.jsp`:

```
<xsl:stylesheet version="1.0"
  xmlns:xsl="http://www.w3.org/1999/XSL/Transform"
  xmlns:javaout="http://www.jclark.com/xt/java"
  exclude-result-prefixes="javaout" >

<xsl:output    method="javaout:MyNa.jspUtil.XMLOutputHandler"
  indent="yes" encoding="UTF-8"
  media-type="text/vnd.wap.wml" omit-xml-declaration="no"
  doctype-public="-//WAPFORUM//DTD WML 1.1//EN"
  doctype-system="http://www.wapforum.org/DTD/wml_1.1.xml"
/>
```

```
<xsl:template name="rides-forms">
<!-- begin a large block of WML material: all forms -->
<card id="start" >
  <p>
  <select>
    <option onpick="#find">Find ride </option>
    <option onpick="#accept">Accept ride </option>
    <option onpick="#check">Check ride </option>
    <option onpick="#offer">Offer ride </option>
  </select>
  </p>
</card>
<!-- many more cards, as in ridesInc.jsp -->
</xsl:template>
</xsl:stylesheet>
```

Results of the Stylesheet

When we use XT to apply `findByZipFile.xsl` to `rows.xml`, we get the following WML page (somewhat reformatted for readability):

```
<?xml version="1.0" encoding="utf-8"?>
<!DOCTYPE wml PUBLIC "-//WAPFORUM//DTD WML 1.1//EN"
    "http://www.wapforum.org/DTD/wml_1.1.xml">
<wml>
<head>
 <meta http-equiv="Cache-Control" content="no-cache" forua="true"/>
</head>
<card id="output" title="findByZipTst">
 <do type="accept" label="again">
  <go href="#start"/>
 </do>
 <p>
  <table columns="2">
   <tr> <td>rowId</td>          <td>1</td> </tr>
   <tr> <td>OfferedBy</td>      <td>Sandy Weston</td> </tr>
   <tr> <td>OfferEmail</td>     <td>sweston@btu.edu</td> </tr>
   <tr> <td>FromZip</td>        <td>12345</td> </tr>
   <tr> <td>ToZip</td>          <td>54321</td> </tr>
   <tr> <td>Day</td>            <td>2/20/2000</td> </tr>
   <tr> <td>AcceptedBy</td>     <td>Trish Cooper</td> </tr>
   <tr> <td>AcceptedEmail</td>  <td>tcooper@btu.edu</td> </tr>
  </table>
 </p>
</card>
<card id="start">
 <p>
  <select>
   <option onpick="#find">find ride </option>
   <option onpick="#accept">Accept ride </option>
   <option onpick="#check">Check ride </option>
   <option onpick="#offer">Offer ride </option>
  </select>
 </p>
</card>
<card id="find">
 <do type="accept" label="Go!">
  <go href="/examples/jsp/rides/core.jsp">
   <postfield name="query" value="findByZip"/>
   <postfield name="QP1" value="$toZip"/>
   <postfield name="target" value="wml-findByZip"/>
  </go>
 </do>
 <p align="center">Rides to Zip </p>
 <p>
  Zip? <input name="toZip" format="*N" maxlength="5"/>
  <br/>
 </p>
</card>
<card id="accept">
 <do type="accept" label="Go!">
  <go href="/examples/jsp/rides/core.jsp">
   <postfield name="query" value="acceptZip"/>
   <postfield name="QP1" value="$uName"/>
   <postfield name="QP2" value="$uEmail"/>
   <postfield name="QP3" value="$rDate"/>
```

```
      <postfield name="QP4" value="$toZip"/>
      <postfield name="target" value="wml-acceptZip"/>
    </go>
  </do>
  <p align="center">Accept ride [by zip] </p>
  <p>
   Name? <input name="uName" format="*m" maxlength="8"/> <br/>
   eMail? <input name="uEmail" format="*m" maxlength="20"/> <br/>
   Date? <input name="rDate" format="NNNN\-NN\-NN" maxlength="10"
        value="2000-02-22"/> <br/>
   toZip? <input name="toZip" format="*N" maxlength="5"/> <br/>
  </p>
 </card>
 <card id="check">
  <do type="accept" label="Go!">
   <go href="/examples/jsp/rides/core.jsp">
     <postfield name="query" value="checkRideByZip"/>
     <postfield name="QP1" value="$toZip"/>
     <postfield name="QP2" value="$uName"/>
     <postfield name="target" value="wml-checkRideByZip"/>
   </go>
  </do>
  <p align="center">check ride [by zip] </p>
  <p>
   Name? <input name="uName" format="*m" maxlength="8"/> <br/>
   toZip? <input name="toZip" format="*N" maxlength="5"/> <br/>
  </p>
 </card>
 <card id="offer">
  <do type="accept" label="Go!">
   <go href="/examples/jsp/rides/core.jsp">
     <postfield name="query" value="offer"/>
     <postfield name="QP1" value="$uName"/>
     <postfield name="QP2" value="$uEmail"/>
     <postfield name="QP3" value="$frZip"/>
     <postfield name="QP4" value="$toZip"/>
     <postfield name="QP5" value="$rDate"/>
     <postfield name="target" value="wml-offer"/>
   </go>
  </do>
  <p align="center">Offer ride</p>
  <p>
   Name? <input name="uName" format="*m" maxlength="8"/> <br/>
   eMail? <input name="uEmail" format="*M" maxlength="20"/> <br/>
   fromZip? <input name="frZip" format="*N" maxlength="5"/> <br/>
   toZip? <input name="toZip" format="*N" maxlength="5"/> <br/>
   Date? <input name="rDate" format="NNNN\-NN\-NN" maxlength="10"
        value="2000-02-22"/> <br/>
  </p>
 </card>
</wml>
```

Running the Example with XSLServlet

Clark's XT can be run either from the command line or as a servlet, XSLServlet. We have already shown the command line, but what we did not add is that following the arguments you can have any number of parameter settings, in the form param-name=param-value; these parameters are then available to the stylesheet:

```
java -Dcom.jclark.xsl.sax.parser=com.sun.xml.parser.Parser
     com.jclark.xsl.sax.Driver rows.xml findByZipFile.xsl findByZipFile.wml
     paramName=paramVal moreParamsIfWanted=MoreValues
```

It is common to have a .bat file (or an equivalent UNIX shell script) that looks like this:

```
java -Dcom.jclark.xsl.sax.parser=com.sun.xml.parser.Parser
     com.jclark.xsl.sax.Driver %1 %2 %3
```

In this section we will now show how to configure the JSP engine Tomcat 3.1 to run XSLT stylesheets using XSLServlet, or rather a slightly modified form of XSLServlet, which we call XSLSessionServlet. The primary modification is simply to make the servlet aware of its own SessionID. This section is, in effect, a conceptual overview of configuration instructions for the rest of the chapter. The overview is accurate but incomplete; you must consult the readme.txt file that comes with the code in the zip file for this chapter.

Configuring Tomcat and XSLServlet

There are two issues involved in configuring the XSLServlet:

❑   How to specify the parser

❑   How to make the servlet known to the server

For the parser, go into startserver.bat (or the equivalent Unix file) in the Tomcat root directory. The classpath is specified in that file, and the Java processor is called explicitly. Put the same -D option in that file that you use on the command line.

Regarding the servlet-server connection, the *Servlet Usage* section of xt.htm that comes with the XT distribution, describes it so:

"XT can be used as a servlet. This requires a servlet engine that implements at least version 2.1 of the Java Servlet API. The servlet class is com.jclark.xsl.sax.XSLServlet. The servlet requires an init parameter stylesheet; the value is the path of the stylesheet in a form suitable to be passed to ServletContext.getResource. The translated path gives the XML document to be transformed. An extension of .xml will be automatically added to the translated path if necessary. (Some browsers assume that a URL ending in .xml is an XML document.) Parameters from the query part of the URL are passed in as parameters to the stylesheet. The stylesheet is cached on initialization."

This is how it works out in the case of Tomcat. We have an XML file rows.xml and a stylesheet to go with it, findByZip.xsl. (This a version of findByZipFile.xsl, structured to be used as a servlet.) You want to be able to invoke the stylesheet on the XML file from a browser by saying:

```
http://localhost:8080/findByZip/xslrules/rows
```

Here, findByZip is a virtual path, xslrules is a real directory, and rows.xml is a file in that directory. (Note that you don't want to put .xml at the end because – quoting from the quote above – "some browsers" will then assume that you just want the XML file with the browser's default stylesheet rather than the result of the servlet running your stylesheet on it.)

In order to have this usage available, the following steps need to be taken:

❑ Create an `xslrules` subdirectory of the default directory for web pages, such as
`C:\jakarta-tomcat\webapps\examples`; put the XML file and the stylesheet into that
directory.

❑ Modify Tomcat's `C:\Jakarta-tomcat\conf\web.xml` file to add servlet-mapping and
servlet elements, one for each stylesheet. The two additions are described below.

*Note that we have already performed those steps for you by modifying the Tomcat installation; all
you need to do is expand our zip file into your Tomcat distribution directory. However, remember
that you must consult the readme.txt file for complete installation instructions.*

Within `<servlet-mapping>` elements, add the following:

```
<servlet-mapping>
  <servlet-name>xslRidesFindByZip</servlet-name>
  <url-pattern>/xslRidesFindByZip/*</url-pattern>
</servlet-mapping>
<servlet-mapping>
  <servlet-name>xslRidesAcceptZip</servlet-name>
  <url-pattern>/xslRidesAcceptZip/*</url-pattern>
</servlet-mapping>
<servlet-mapping>
  <servlet-name>xslRidesOffer</servlet-name>
  <url-pattern>/xslRidesOffer/*</url-pattern>
</servlet-mapping>
<servlet-mapping>
  <servlet-name>wmlXslRidesFindByZip</servlet-name>
  <url-pattern>/wmlXslRidesFindByZip/*</url-pattern>
</servlet-mapping>
<servlet-mapping>
  <servlet-name>wmlXslRidesAcceptZip</servlet-name>
  <url-pattern>/wmlXslRidesAcceptZip/*</url-pattern>
</servlet-mapping>
<servlet-mapping>
  <servlet-name>wmlXslRidesOffer</servlet-name>
  <url-pattern>/wmlXslRidesOffer/*</url-pattern>
</servlet-mapping>
```

Within `<servlet>` elements, add the following:

```
<servlet>
  <servlet-name>xslRidesFindByZip</servlet-name>
  <servlet-class>MyNa.jspUtil.XSLSessionServlet</servlet-class>
  <init-param>
    <param-name>stylesheet</param-name>
    <param-value>/jsp/rides/xhtml/findByZip.xsl</param-value>
  </init-param>
</servlet>
<servlet>
  <servlet-name>xslRidesAcceptZip</servlet-name>
  <servlet-class>MyNa.jspUtil.XSLSessionServlet</servlet-class>
  <init-param>
    <param-name>stylesheet</param-name>
```

```
        <param-value>/jsp/rides/xhtml/acceptZip.xsl</param-value>
      </init-param>
    </servlet>
  <servlet>
    <servlet-name>xslRidesOffer</servlet-name>
    <servlet-class>MyNa.jspUtil.XSLSessionServlet</servlet-class>
    <init-param>
      <param-name>stylesheet</param-name>
      <param-value>/jsp/rides/xhtml/offer.xsl</param-value>
    </init-param>
  </servlet>
  <servlet>
    <servlet-name>wmlXslRidesFindByZip</servlet-name>
    <servlet-class>MyNa.jspUtil.XSLSessionServlet</servlet-class>
    <init-param>
      <param-name>stylesheet</param-name>
      <param-value>/jsp/rides/wml/findByZip.xsl</param-value>
    </init-param>
  </servlet>
  <servlet>
    <servlet-name>wmlXslRidesAcceptZip</servlet-name>
    <servlet-class>MyNa.jspUtil.XSLSessionServlet</servlet-class>
    <init-param>
      <param-name>stylesheet</param-name>
      <param-value>/jsp/rides/wml/acceptZip.xsl</param-value>
    </init-param>
  </servlet>
  <servlet>
    <servlet-name>wmlXslRidesOffer</servlet-name>
    <servlet-class>MyNa.jspUtil.XSLSessionServlet</servlet-class>
    <init-param>
      <param-name>stylesheet</param-name>
      <param-value>/jsp/rides/wml/offer.xsl</param-value>
    </init-param>
  </servlet>
```

With these additions in place, you should be all set. As we mentioned, we have performed all these steps for you, so all you have to do is expand our zip file into your Tomcat distribution directory. However, remember that you must consult the readme.txt file for complete installation instructions.

Adding Another Stylesheet

To use a different stylesheet, say innerloop.xsl, on the same XML file, you would add another <servlet-mapping> element and another <servlet> element. Furthermore, if innerloop.xsl has a top-level parameter called tablesize then you can set this parameter to 8 from the browser by typing in the location window:

```
http://localhost:8080/xslnest/xslrules/rows.xml?tablesize=8
```

This is really quite convenient. The only problem is that, as xt.htm tells us, "[t]he stylesheet is cached on initialization", and so this setup is not good for debugging. We recommend that you do most of your debugging on the command line with dummy data files and dummy parameters; there should be very few XSLT bugs left in your stylesheet by the time you're running it as a servlet.

XSLT with Database Queries

Once you learn XSLT and XPath, running XSLT stylesheets on XML files to produce WML (or any other XML language) is no big deal: this is what XSLT is designed for. It is also quite common to run a database query and save the results in an XML file similar to our file `rides.xml`. Putting the two actions together, we have a solution of sorts for the task of generating WML from a database query:

❑   Run the query

❑   Save the result as an XML file

❑   Run an XSLT stylesheet on that file to produce desired output

However, this is not the solution we want. We want to be able to run the query from within the stylesheet, obtain the result as an object in memory (such as a two-dimensional array of strings), and run the stylesheet on that object as argument.

There are two issues involved here. One is running the query – some Java code – from within an XSLT stylesheet. The other is running a stylesheet on an object in memory that is not an XML stream at all. Once we learn how to do those two things, we can produce a complete XSL solution to the web-WAP problem. It will still be using JSP, but not for the output templates. Instead of forwarding the request to an output JSP file, we will be forwarding it to `XSLServlet`, to run an XSL stylesheet on the result of the query. Some people will argue that this has major advantages because XSLT is a more congenial tool for non-programmers. It is probably too early to make such assertions with any certainty, especially since both XSLT and JSP are rapidly moving targets. Our goal here is to provide a framework within which both can be used and compared to each other.

The Ride Board Application Revisited

The revised XSLT-based system for web-WAP generation is described by the following diagram:

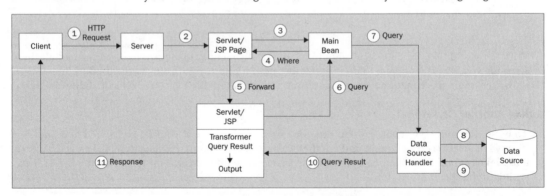

The main addition to the previous design is the 'conversion module' in the middle that converts the result of the query into something that an XML parser can parse and deliver to the XSLT processor. Apart from that, the changes that need to be made are as follows:

❑   The entry pages `top.jsp` (XHTML and WML versions) will remain the same. (These entry pages are in the `rides/xhtml` and `rides/wml` directories, whereas the shared files, `core.jsp` and `configure.jsp`, are in the parent directory.)

❑   The main JSP page `core.jsp` will remain the same.

- The configuration page, `configure.jsp`, will show more targets.

- The main bean will have three more lines added to its `doCommand()` method. They take care of making the `session` and `sessionID` available to the stylesheet.

- There is one more new line in the `doCommand()` method: a call on `XSLPrune.reset()`, a new mechanism for controlling the size of the output. The `getDef()` method is no longer helpful because the stylesheet will be getting its information from parsed XML nodes rather than from a `Dict`. We do not use `XSLPrune` in this chapter, but if your WML pages can grow unpredictably beyond 1.5K, then you may find XSLPrune a simple but useful mechanism for preventing microbrowser blowups.

- We provide two classes that are minor revisions of classes provided within XT. In both cases, our classes contain small but crucial additions. One class is `XSLSessionServlet`, a modified copy of `XSLServlet` that passes the `sessionID` to the stylesheet as a stylesheet parameter. The other is `XMLOutputHandler`, a copy of the XT class of the same name, with a few lines added to provide an XSLT 'mode' for any content-type specified by the application. In our case here, the mode is WML, of course.

- Within the stylesheet, a major addition is the mechanism for running Java methods from within XSLT. (It is the stylesheet, not a JSP page, that calls `qBean.queryResult()` in this version of the framework.)

We will present the changes in the order they are listed here, saving the 'conversion module' till the end. If you just want to see the XSLT code, jump to the `findByZip.xsl` section.

The Configuration Page: configure.jsp

The configuration page, as you recall, is for a system administrator to edit in order to configure and maintain the system. We thought the task would be easier if, instead of doubling the names of possible targets again, we would provide a single binary switch between the JSP-based system and an XSLT-based one. The assumption is that at any given time only one of the two systems will be in use, and that switching between them will be infrequent.

It is because of the switch in the configuration page that we could leave the entry pages (both XHTML and WML versions) unchanged, ignorant of whether the request will be processed using JSP or XSLT. The alternative would be to double the number of targets again, forcing the user to make decisions about the inner workings of the framework.

We only show a segment of the code here, since the only changes are within the 'targets' section:

```
    "DATE,DATE"}
};

String sendTo="XSL"; // "XSL" or "JSP".
String[][]responseTargets;

if(sendTo.equalsIgnoreCase("JSP"))responseTargets=new String[][]{
  {"error","/jsp/rides/errorpage.jsp"},
  {"reportAll","/jsp/rides/xhtml/findByZip.jsp"},
  {"deleteRow","/jsp/rides/xhtml/acceptZip.jsp"},
  {"findByZip","/jsp/rides/xhtml/findByZip.jsp"},
  {"checkRideByZip","/jsp/rides/xhtml/findByZip.jsp"},
  {"acceptZip","/jsp/rides/xhtml/acceptZip.jsp"},
```

```
    {"offer","/jsp/rides/xhtml/offer.jsp"},
    {"wml-findByZip","/jsp/rides/wml/findByZip.jsp"},
    {"wml-checkRideByZip","/jsp/rides/wml/findByZip.jsp"},
    {"wml-acceptZip","/jsp/rides/wml/acceptZip.jsp"},
    {"wml-offer","/jsp/rides/wml/offer.jsp"}
  }; else responseTargets=new String[][]{
    {"error","/jsp/rides/errorpage.jsp"},
    {"reportAll","/xslRidesFindByZip/xslrules/rides"},
    {"deleteRow","/xslRidesAcceptZip/xslrules/rides"},
    {"findByZip","/xslRidesFindByZip/xslrules/rides"},
    {"checkRideByZip","/xslRidesFindByZip/xslrules/rides"},
    {"acceptZip","/xslRidesAcceptZip/xslrules/rides"},
    {"offer","/xslRidesOffer/xslrules/rides"},
    {"wml-findByZip","/wmlXslRidesFindByZip/xslrules/rides"},
    {"wml-checkRideByZip","/wmlXslRidesFindByZip/xslrules/rides"},
    {"wml-acceptZip","/wmlXslRidesAcceptZip/xslrules/rides"},
    {"wml-offer","/wmlXslRidesOffer/xslrules/rides"}
  };

    qBean.configure(dbParams,dbQueries,responseTargets); // once per session
%>
```

The new targets mean that there are six stylesheets, in the `rides` directories, pointed at by the servlet configuration file `conf/web.xml`. `xslRidesAcceptZip` is actually the stylesheet `xhtml/accept.xsl`, while `wmlXslRidesFindByZip` is the stylesheet `wml/findByZip.xsl`. In the `webapps/examples/xslrules` directory is an XML file, `rides.xml`. In a framework that uses XML more (either for configuration or data interchange or both), this file could contain useful information. In our toy example, it is simply ignored, as the stylesheet synthesizes its output from the result of the query.

doCommand() in the Main Bean

The expanded `doCommand()` looks like this:

```
public void doCommand(HttpServletRequest request){
  requestDict=new Dict();
  requestDict.setDef(request);
  setupRequestDict();  // check through parameter name assumptions

// the following lines are for use with XSLSessionServlet;
// they are irrelevant but harmless for jsp output

  javax.servlet.http.HttpSession session=request.getSession(true);
  String sessionId=session.getId();

  SessionCache.getInstance().put(sessionId,session);
}
```

The first two lines of the addition extract the `session` object and its `sessionID` out of `Request`. The third line stores it in `SessionCache`, indexed by its ID. This is needed for the task of constructing a `NodeIterator` object that XT can work on. This is described in the final part of this section. The `SessionCache` is a subclass of our `Cache` class that is also used in connection pooling. (It's a `Singleton` class, which automatically has application scope, and we use it for caching objects of all kinds, in nested `Hashtables`, whenever we take the notion.)

XSLSessionServlet and XMLOutputHandler

In this section we present modified versions of two classes within James Clark's XT package. The two new classes are named in the title of this section; they are both in the `MyNa.jspUtil` package. We'll start with more extensive changes to `XMLOutputHandler`.

The `XMLOutputHandler` class has an `init()` method, declared as:

```
public DocumentHandler init(Destination dest, AttributeList atts)
        throws IOException {
```

The task of the method is to produce a `DocumentHandler` for output with all its properties set up on the basis of attributes in the `AttributeList` argument. One of the main things to configure is the output stream, `this.out`. The original XT code sets the stream's content type to `application/xml`:

```
this.out = dest.getOutputStream("application/xml", null);
```

Even though WML is an XML language, WAP expects a special content-type, `text/vnd.wap.wml`. We pass it to `init()` as a media-type attribute. Here is the modified code:

```
public DocumentHandler init(Destination dest, AttributeList atts)
        throws IOException {
// start modifications
  String mediaType = atts.getValue("media-type");
  if (mediaType == null){
      mediaType = "application/xml";
  encoding = atts.getValue("encoding");
  }
  if (encoding == null) {
      // not all Java implementations support ASCII
      writer = dest.getWriter(mediaType, "iso-8859-1");
      // use character references for non-ASCII characters
      maxRepresentableChar = '\u007F';
  }
  else {
    writer = dest.getWriter(mediaType, encoding);
    this.out = dest.getWriter(mediaType, null);
// end modifications; the rest is James Clark's original code
    this.keepOpen = dest.keepOpen();
    if ("yes".equals(atts.getValue("omit-xml-declaration")))
      omitXmlDeclaration = true;
    this.standalone = atts.getValue("standalone");
    this.doctypeSystem = atts.getValue("doctype-system");
    this.doctypePublic = atts.getValue("doctype-public");
    if (this.doctypeSystem != null || this.doctypePublic != null)
      outputDoctype = true;
    if ("yes".equals(atts.getValue("indent")))
      return new Indenter(this, this);
    return this;
  }
```

XSLSessionServlet

The `MyNa.jspUtil.XSLSessionServlet` class is a copy of James Clark's `XSLServlet` as distributed with XT, except for two changes. First, there is a 'new' one-line `doPost()` function, consisting of a call on `doGet()`.

Second, the two lines below have been added to `doGet()`:

```
String sessionID=request.getSession(true).getId();
xsl.setParameter("theSessionID",sessionID);
```

This is how our stylesheets get the `sessionID`. Recall that our `QBean` has an additional line that stores the session itself in the `SessionCache`, indexed by its ID. Since the stylesheet is now in possession of the ID, it can pass it to a Java method that can use it to retrieve the `session` object itself. Since the `session` has the main bean (qBean) stored in it, the stylesheet can, indirectly, call qBean's `queryResult()` method, just as our output JSP pages did. We just have to make sure that the stylesheet gets a top-level parameter called `"theSessionID"`:

```
<xsl:param name="theSessionID" select="NoHttpSessionIDProvided"/>
```

It is now time to open up a stylesheet.

findByZip.xsl

As with the simpler versions, we will start with a presentation in small chunks, with comments, before displaying it all together.

Declarations and Top-level Elements

Some of this will be familiar from the earlier simple example, but note how two special namespaces are declared to correspond to Java classes in addition to our `XMLOutputHandler`:

```
<xsl:stylesheet version="1.0"
  xmlns:xsl="http://www.w3.org/1999/XSL/Transform"
  xmlns:javaout="http://www.jclark.com/xt/java"

  xmlns:xt="http://www.jclark.com/xt"
  xmlns:xqd="http://www.jclark.com/xt/java/MyNa.jspUtil.XmlQueryStringDoc"
  exclude-result-prefixes="javaout xqd"
>
<xsl:output   method="javaout:MyNa.jspUtil.XMLOutputHandler"
  indent="yes" encoding="UTF-8"
  media-type="text/vnd.wap.wml" omit-xml-declaration="no"
  doctype-public="-//WAPFORUM//DTD WML 1.1//EN"
  doctype-system="http://www.wapforum.org/DTD/wml_1.1.xml"
 />
<xsl:param name="theSessionID" select="NoHttpSessionIDProvided"/>

<xsl:include href="ridesInc.xsl" /><!-- include the forms at the bottom -->
```

The `xt:` namespace corresponds to XT itself: we apply its `nodeSet()` method to 'tree fragments' that are produced by our `queryResult()` method. The difference between a tree fragment and a node-set is technical and a bit controversial: some people would argue that there should be no such difference. In any event, it is a node-set that XT expects from a matching operation.

The `xqd:` namespace is declared to be associated with the `XmlQueryStringDoc` class in the `MyNa.jspUtil` package. This is the class that runs the query, converts its `QueryResult` to an XML string and passes it on to an XML parser. This is all done by a static `queryResult()` method that returns a `NodeIterator` object, which is the kind of object that XT expects from its parser.

We are going to use the `queryResult()` method within the stylesheet. Java methods are one particular kind of what are called 'extension functions' in the XSLT Recommendation. The Recommendation says that although the 1.0 version of XSLT does not define a standard mechanism for implementing such extensions, the "XSL W[orking] G[roup] intends to define such a mechanism in a future version of this specification or in a separate specification." According to Steve Muench, who is a member of the XSL Working Group, standardizing the extension functions mechanism for Java is very high on the group's agenda. Since James Clark is the editor of the current version and is likely to be involved in producing the next one, it makes sense to see how extension functions are implemented in XT.

The first step, as you can see, is to associate a namespace prefix with a Java class. The class must be identified by its fully qualified name appended to `http://www.jclark.com/xt/java/`. Since you don't want extension namespace prefixes to appear on output, you list them within the value of the exclude-result-prefixes attribute of `xsl:stylesheet`. (There is also an extension-element-prefixes attribute that has the same effect.)

Overview of the Rest

The rest of the stylesheet is structured exactly as the stylesheet of the preceding section. We repeat the outline highlighting the new elements:

```
<xsl:template match="/"><!-- matches the root of the XML document tree -->

<!-- first block of WML material to pass through to output -->

<xsl:variable ... >
  <!-- declares and initializes a tree fragment variable -->
<xsl:variable/>
<xsl:variable ... /><!-- converts tree fragment to node set 'rows' -->

<xsl:choose>
<!--
  checks to see if there are rows of output;
  if not, outputs a message; otherwise outputs a table
-->
</xsl:choose>

<!-- second block of WML material for output -->

</xsl:template>
</xsl:stylesheet>
```

An Extension-function Call

The first block of WML material is exactly the same as before, but the 'rows' variable is initialized differently. In the simple examples above, we initialized it by a simple match operation:

```
<xsl:variable name="rows" select="table/row" />
```

This time, it is initialized in two steps, each involving a Java method call:

```
<xsl:variable name="tree-frag">
  <xsl:copy-of select="xt:node-set(xqd:query-result($theSessionID))" />
</xsl:variable>
<xsl:variable name="rows" select="xt:node-set($tree-frag)//row" />
```

The first thing to notice is the convention for calling static Java methods. If the name of the class is associated with the xqd: namespace prefix then a call on the queryResult() method of that class becomes "xqd:query-result(...)". Second, notice that the session ID, stored as a parameter of the stylesheet, is passed to the method as a stylesheet variable, $theSessionID.

The query-result() method, as we said, returns a NodeIterator object that points to the root of the tree that the stylesheet is going to process. However, the NodeIterator object returned by our code is in some ways different from the NodeIterator that XT expects. So, we pass it through the <xsl:copy-of> operation that returns a tree fragment; the resulting tree fragment is then passed through xt:node-set() (which is another Java method call, this time on James Clark's method within XT code). The final result is a rows variable that behaves exactly the same way as its namesake in simple versions obtained by XT directly from a parsing operation followed by a matching operation. As a result, the rest of the stylesheet is identical to what you have already seen.

The Entire Stylesheet

We can now show the entire stylesheet. All the work is done, as before, within an xsl:choose element that checks the number of rows, and, if there are any, outputs the first row as a table. In the end, we call the template from the included stylesheet in order to include all the input forms:

```
<xsl:stylesheet version="1.0"
  xmlns:xsl="http://www.w3.org/1999/XSL/Transform"
  xmlns:javaout="http://www.jclark.com/xt/java"
  xmlns:xt="http://www.jclark.com/xt"
  xmlns:xqd="http://www.jclark.com/xt/java/MyNa.jspUtil.XmlQueryStringDoc"
  exclude-result-prefixes="javaout xqd">
<xsl:output   method="javaout:MyNa.jspUtil.XMLOutputHandler"
  indent="yes" encoding="UTF-8"
    media-type="text/vnd.wap.wml" omit-xml-declaration="no"
    doctype-public="-//WAPFORUM//DTD WML 1.1//EN"
    doctype-system="http://www.wapforum.org/DTD/wml_1.1.xml"
 />

<xsl:param name="theSessionID" select="NoHttpSessionIDProvided"/>

<xsl:include href="ridesInc.xsl" />
<xsl:template match="/">
<wml>
<head>
  <meta http-equiv="Cache-Control" content="no-cache" forua="true"/>
</head>

<card id="output" title="findByZip">
  <do type="accept" label="again" > <go href="#start" />  </do>
  <xsl:variable name="tree-frag">
    <xsl:copy-of select="xt:node-set(xqd:query-result($theSessionID))" />
  </xsl:variable>
  <xsl:variable name="rows" select="xt:node-set($tree-frag)//row" />
  <p>
  <xsl:choose>
  <xsl:when test="count($rows)=0">
    Sorry, no rides to your zip-code.
  </xsl:when>
  <xsl:otherwise>
    <table columns="2">
```

```
       <xsl:for-each select="$rows[1]/field" >
        <tr>
         <td> <xsl:value-of select="@name" /> </td>
         <td> <xsl:value-of select="text()" /> </td>
        </tr>
       </xsl:for-each>
     </table>
   </xsl:otherwise>
  </xsl:choose>
  </p>
  </card>
  <xsl:call-template name="rides-forms"/>
  </wml>
  </xsl:template>

  </xsl:stylesheet>
```

A findByZip Stylesheet for XHTML

Before presenting the underside of the system (extending XT's classes), we complete the system with an XSLT stylesheet that produces HTML output from a database query. At this point, it consists almost entirely of elements you have already seen, either in the JSP XHTML version or in the WML XSL stylesheet, and is actually slightly simpler than the WML stylesheet because it doesn't need a special OutputHandler class. We show the changes highlighted:

```
<xsl:stylesheet version="1.0"
   xmlns:xsl="http://www.w3.org/1999/XSL/Transform"
   xmlns="http://www.w3.org/TR/xhtml1/strict"
   xmlns:xt="http://www.jclark.com/xt"
   xmlns:xqd="http://www.jclark.com/xt/java/MyNa.jspUtil.XmlQueryStringDoc"
   exclude-result-prefixes="xqd xt #default"
>
<xsl:output method="html" indent="yes"    />

<xsl:param name="theSessionID" select="NoHttpSessionIDProvided"/>
<xsl:include href="ridesInc.xsl" />

<xsl:template match="/">
<html>
<head><title>Rides by Zip Code </title></head>
<body>
 <xsl:variable name="tree-frag">
  <xsl:copy-of select="xt:node-set(xqd:query-result($theSessionID))" />
 </xsl:variable>
 <xsl:variable name="rows" select="xt:node-set($tree-frag)//row" />
 <xsl:choose>
 <xsl:when test="count($rows)=0">
  Sorry, no rides for this zip-code.
 </xsl:when>
 <xsl:otherwise>
   <p>
    <table border="1">
     <tr>
       <xsl:for-each select="$rows[1]/field" >
        <th> <xsl:value-of select="@name" /> </th>
       </xsl:for-each>
     </tr>
```

```
      <xsl:for-each select="$rows" >
    <tr>
      <xsl:for-each select="field" >
        <td> <xsl:value-of select="." /> </td>
      </xsl:for-each>
    </tr>
    </xsl:for-each>
    </table>
  </p>
 </xsl:otherwise>
</xsl:choose>
<xsl:call-template name="rides-forms"/>
</body>
</html>
 </xsl:template>

</xsl:stylesheet>
```

The stylesheet logic is more complex in one way: since XHTML pages have more room for data, we show all the matches rather than just the first, so the xsl:for-each structure is nested with an HTML table row for each matched row of database data, and a column for each field. The result looks like this:

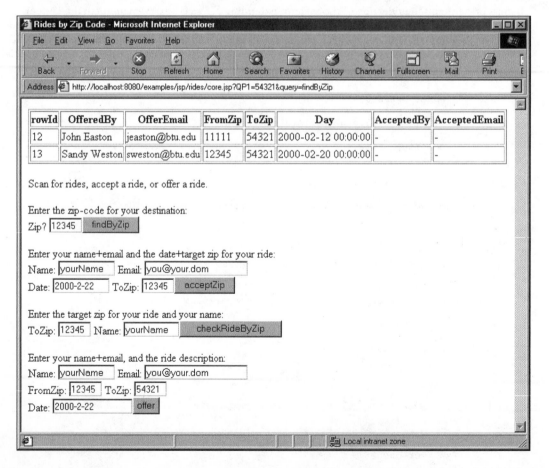

This concludes our discussion of XSLT stylesheets for WML and HTML output. As you can see, most of the extra work for database query processing is offloaded to embedded Java method calls. The remainder of this section looks inside those calls to present the technical detail of how query output is fed into the XML parser for XSLT processing. After that, we will compare the pure JSP and the JSP+XSLT frameworks that we have seen in this chapter.

Feeding a NodeIterator into XT

This section describes the background machinery that makes these XSLT lines possible:

```
<xsl:variable name="tree-frag">
  <xsl:copy-of select="xt:node-set(xqd:query-result($theSessionID))" />
</xsl:variable>
```

We can rewrite this with one extra line, to focus on our topic more precisely:

```
<xsl:variable name="root" select="xqd:query-result($theSessionID)" />
<xsl:variable name="tree-frag">
  <xsl:copy-of select="xt:node-set($root)" />
</xsl:variable>
```

It is the first of these lines that we are interested in: it calls a Java method that returns the root of a tree that XT can copy, traverse and transform. What's in that method?

XmlQueryStringDoc

The XPath expression shown below means that the xqd namespace prefix is associated with a Java class that has a static queryResult() method:

```
xqd:query-result($theSessionID)
```

The class, if you look it up in the XSLT declarations, is XmlQueryStringDoc, within MyNa.jspUtil. Here is its code:

```
import org.xml.sax.*;
import org.xml.sax.helpers.*;
import com.jclark.xsl.om.*;
import com.jclark.xsl.sax.*;

import java.sql.SQLException;
import javax.servlet.http.HttpSession;

public class XmlQueryStringDoc extends XmlStringDoc {
  public static NodeIterator queryResult(String sID)throws SQLException{
      HttpSession hS=(HttpSession)(SessionCache.getInstance().get(sID));
      if(null==hS)return null;
      QBean qB=(QBean)hS.getValue("qBean");  // the bean's name here
      if(null==qB)return null;
      QueryResult qResult=qB.queryResult();
      return stringToNodeList(qResult.toXmlString());
  }
}
```

The queryResult() method spends most of its time getting to qBean; once qBean is obtained, the method packs a lot of action into its last line that actually produces the NodeIterator. In order to get to qBean, we proceed as follows:

❑ From the sessionCache we request the session via sessionID

❑ From the session we request the bean

❑ From the bean we request the QueryResult

❑ From the QueryResult we request an xmlString

Reminder: QueryResult and QueryResultTable

As discussed earlier in the chapter, QueryResult is an interface that extends the XmlOb interface, from which it inherits the method toXmlString(). Otherwise, QueryResult expects its implementing classes to be able to produce two string arrays, columnHeaders and columnTypes, and a string matrix named rows.

The actual object that is returned by qBean.queryResult() is a QueryResultTable. That class implements toXmlString() by assuming a generic DTD for database tables, dbdata.dtd. Using the given column headers, column types and the rows matrix, the method constructs an XML document that looks like this:

```
<table name=Rides>
<headers>
  <header name='rowId' fieldType='INT'/>
  <header name='OfferedBy' fieldType='TEXT'/>
  <header name='OfferEmail' fieldType='TEXT'/>
  ...
</headers>
<row>
  <field name='rowId'>1</field>
  <field name='OfferedBy'>Sandy Weston</field>
  <field name='OfferEmail'>sweston@btu.edu</field>
  <field name='FromZip'>12345</field>
  <field name='ToZip'>54321</field>
  <field name='Day'>2/20/2000</field>
  <field name='AcceptedBy'>Trish Cooper</field>
  <field name='AcceptedEmail'>tcooper@btu.edu</field>
</row>
  ...
</table>
```

The document (without the formatting white space) is constructed in a StringBuffer and returned as one long String. At this point, we are in the last line of the XmlQueryStringDoc.queryResult() that says:

```
return stringToNodeList(qResult.toXmlString());
```

What happens there?

Reminder: the InputSource

XmlQueryStringDoc extends XmlStringDoc where stringToNodeList() is defined. Before we look inside, recall the section on XML parsing and the setup steps that are needed before the parser can get to work. For parsing to happen, you need two things, a parser and something to parse: an InputSource. XT has a parser, specified by the -D command option. It only needs an input source. The InputSource class (defined in org.xml.sax) has three constructors. One of them takes a file name argument, another an InputStream, and the third a Reader. This last option is the one we exploit. Here is XmlStringDoc:

```
import org.xml.sax.*;
import org.xml.sax.helpers.*;
import com.jclark.xsl.tr.LoadContext;
import com.jclark.xsl.om.*;
import com.jclark.xsl.sax.*;

public class XmlStringDoc {

  public static NodeIterator stringToNodeList(String xmlString){
    try{
      Parser parser=ParserFactory.makeParser("com.sun.xml.parser.Parser");
      XMLProcessorEx proc=new XMLProcessorImpl(parser);
      // create an input source from xmlString
      InputSource in=new InputSource(new java.io.StringReader(xmlString));
      LoadContext lC=new LoadContextImpl();

      // we now have everything to get to the root
      Node root=proc.load(in,0,lC,new NameTableImpl());
      return root.getChildren();
      }catch (Exception e){
        e.printStackTrace();
        return null;}
    }
  }

  private static class LoadContextImpl implements LoadContext {
    public boolean getStripSource(Name name){return false;}
    public boolean getIncludeComments(){return true;}
    public boolean getIncludeProcessingInstructions(){return true;}
  } // end of LoadContextImpl
} // end of XmlStringDoc
```

Parts of this code will have to remain a little mysterious, but the main outline should be clear. The first two lines create a parser and an XMLProcessorEx, an XT interface that declares a load() method. That's the method we need. It takes four parameters, the first of which is an InputSource. We create an InputSource by wrapping our xmlString into a StringReader and giving it as an argument to the input source constructor.

The remaining three arguments of load() would take us too deeply into XT code; what matters is that a call on load() returns a Node (com.jclark.xsl.om.Node, to be precise), and its getChildren() method returns a NodeIterator that we need. NodeIterator itself is an interface that simply declares a next() method, but that's all XT needs in order to do its work.

Summary

This chapter has been a long journey that took us to several places:

- Servlets and JSP
- Architectures for JSP applications
- Generating WML (and other XML) content from database queries using JSP
- Channeling query output through the XSLT processor
- Generating WML (and other XML) content from the same data source using XSLT for output

We are hoping that the chapter has been useful in bringing up several quite general design ideas. Their main point has been to create a framework for generating both WML and XHTML content from the same data source. In the actual application of the chapter, the data source is a relational database, but it doesn't have to be: the framework is general enough so that anything wrapped in a `Dict` object or described by an XML document can be a source of data. We did not have time in this chapter to explore that data connection in depth because our task has been to explore and compare the output methods. We have done quite a bit of exploring; it is now time for a comparison between JSP and XSLT.

However, in truth, we don't feel that there is enough accumulated experience as yet to pass definitive judgments. Both JSP and XSLT are extremely powerful tools that can certainly do the job. For applications that are maintained by programmers, JSP is probably a better choice, if only because they are needed anyway, and why bring in yet another set of tools? However, XSLT enables non-programmers to do very impressive things, and so in an organizational context in which extensibility by non-programmers is important, the XSLT may prove preferable.

Let's pass a preliminary judgment, anyway: we like both. We intend to provide combinations of JSP and XSLT for our own clients, structured in somewhat the same way as this chapter (but with more XML used for configuration).

In the meantime, the framework developed in this chapter should provide a useful test bed for more exploring and experimentation. Enjoy!

11

ColdFusion and WAP

ColdFusion is a powerful web application development environment from Allaire. Designed originally to create HTML applications for web browsers, it can just as easily be used to create WML applications for wireless devices.

ColdFusion is exceptionally well suited to wireless application development. It's easy to use–and just as important–it's easy to understand someone else's code that you have to support. It's scalable, works in multiple environments, and is widely supported.

If you're looking to take your WAP applications to the next stage, including dynamically generated, database-driven output, as well as data entry applications, scheduled content (reminders and notifications), and more, ColdFusion is a great place to start.

Topics covered in this chapter include:

❑　A brief introduction to ColdFusion and it's features

❑　Key issues when developing WAP applications with ColdFusion

❑　ColdFusion Studio/HomeSite features useful for WAP development

❑　Techniques, tricks and traps

If you're an experienced ColdFusion coder, you'll most likely want to skip the next section, and move straight onto *WAP and ColdFusion*, but whether you're new to ColdFusion or experienced, this chapter will give you the jump-start you need to begin creating wireless applications in ColdFusion.

ColdFusion – A Brief Introduction

ColdFusion (CF) is the leading cross-platform web application server. It can be used on Windows as well as UNIX platforms, and it works with nearly all web servers and databases. CF's core strength has been its ability to make it easy to integrate databases with web applications. By web applications, we mean web sites that are driven by programs that generate web pages. These pages are often generated from database data, though web applications are also the key to creating interactive, two-way web pages, such as forms, search interfaces, data entry applications, and more.

While ColdFusion was designed to generate web pages that send HTML to web browsers, it can just as easily be used to generate WML pages sent to microbrowsers. This chapter describes how to do that, and it describes how ColdFusion programming works, for those new to it. There are some introductory facets that should be discussed first.

How ColdFusion Works

ColdFusion works in tandem with your web server to serve web pages to your site visitors. ColdFusion is not a web page design tool, like Microsoft FrontPage, Macromedia DreamWeaver, or NetObjects Fusion. It's more akin to Active Server Pages. In fact, CF and ASP can do pretty much the same things.

ColdFusion's programming language, CFML, is tag-oriented and can be learned very easily whereas ASP is script-oriented and typically leverages Visual Basic programming skills. (Another benefit of ColdFusion over something like ASP is that a ColdFusion program written for a Windows server can run virtually unchanged on a UNIX or Linux box.)

Whereas tools like FrontPage and DreamWeaver help you design and layout static web pages that you then place on the server for the user to see, with web application servers like ColdFusion and ASP you instead place a program on the web server. When a visitor enters a web address (URL) for that program, the program is executed on the server. The following picture depicts the process of how ColdFusion processing works:

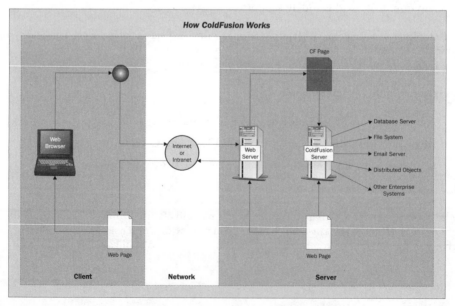

In the case of ColdFusion, the web server receives the request to execute the page and tasks the ColdFusion server, generally running on the same box, to run the program. The program (often referred to generically in CF as a "template") creates HTML or WML as a result, which is sent back to the end user by way of the web server.

Keep in mind that the ColdFusion tags will NOT be sent to the browser or microbrowser. The browsers understand only HTML or WML elements. ColdFusion templates are evaluated by the ColdFusion Server software, and any resulting HTML or WML code is sent to the browser with the ColdFusion tags stripped and their result displayed instead.

The end user needs nothing but a normal browser. When they request a page from a ColdFusion server (whether from a web or WAP browser), the result they see is just a web or WAP page like any other that they would browse. They have no clear indication that the page has been served by ColdFusion. The result of executing a ColdFusion page is just HTML or WML (whichever the ColdFusion page was designed to create), though that code can be generated from a database, can show the result of a search, and more, as described previously.

As for ColdFusion code itself, CFML is very straightforward. The following is a classic Hello World example as would be used for an HTML web page:

```
<html>
<head>
    <title>Hello World</title>
</head>
<body>
    <h2>Hello World</h2>
    <CFSET location="World">
    <CFOUTPUT>
        Hello #location#.
    </CFOUTPUT>
</body>
</html>
```

This is a trivial example, but it demonstrates two key points. ColdFusion is a programming language, and as such it supports creating and processing variables. Here we have created a location variable using the ColdFusion tag CFSET, assigning it the value "World". Then we have displayed the result of that variable to the user by way of the ColdFusion tag CFOUTPUT. Obviously, there's much more that ColdFusion can do. There are more substantial examples offered in the remainder of this chapter and in the example source code available for this chapter.

CFML supports more than 70 server-side tags, 200 functions, and 800 third-party components – making it the most productive environment available for creating advanced Web applications.

ColdFusion offers capabilities that can extend your wireless applications to much broader horizons, including the ability to query and update virtually any database (including SQL Server, Sybase, Oracle, Access, and many more), integration with other objects on your server (including COM, CORBA, and Java, to name a few), portability among multiple operating systems and web servers (on both UNIX and Windows), and support for state management, error handling, load balancing, failover, and much more. See the Allaire web site for more information on ColdFusion (http://www.allaire.com/Products/coldfusion/).

About ColdFusion Studio and HomeSite

We explained that ColdFusion is a server application, as compared to tools like FrontPage and DreamWeaver, which are web page design and editing tools. The ColdFusion programs (or templates) that you create are simple text files that include tags that describe how the program is to be executed. While you can use a tool like DreamWeaver or NetObjects Fusion (but not FrontPage) to create ColdFusion templates, it's generally more suitable to create them in a text editor.

Allaire has created a powerful text editor that not only makes it easy to create HTML (and now WML) pages but also adds various features to make it easy to create ColdFusion pages. ColdFusion Studio is that editor. It's actually based on another Allaire HTML editor, called HomeSite. This award-winning editor is highly regarded for its ease of use and powerful web page editing features. In fact, it's included with DreamWeaver and NetObjects Fusion as the text editor of choice for those web page design tools.

You can use either Studio or HomeSite, both available for purchase at Allaire's site, to develop ColdFusion programs generating either HTML or WML, but Studio has a few more features (database tools, remote development tools, and an interactive debugger for HTML page testing) than HomeSite.

Another benefit of ColdFusion Studio is that it includes a single-user version of ColdFusion Server. This is great for developers who test their programs, locally but ultimately place them on a remote server.

It's important to remember the difference between ColdFusion Studio (the editor used by developers to create CF templates) and ColdFusion Server (the web application server that works in tandem with a web server to serve web pages to visitors).

Later in this chapter, we'll explain how Studio and its cousin HomeSite have been modified in their latest versions to support WML tags.

Obtaining ColdFusion Server and Studio

It's not necessary to download and install ColdFusion server to benefit from the information provided in this chapter, but to run the examples you will need to have access to a server running ColdFusion.

ColdFusion Server, as well as the web page editors ColdFusion Studio and HomeSite, can be purchased from Allaire at http://www.allaire.com.

ColdFusion Server is available in three versions. The first, ColdFusion Express is a free, limited functionality version of ColdFusion. Designed to give web developers an easy entry into ColdFusion programming, it unfortunately cannot currently be used to serve WML pages (see the discussion later in this chapter).

ColdFusion Professional is the minimum configuration needed to serve WML sites. ColdFusion Enterprise, the third configuration, adds technology specifically suited to large-volume, transaction-intensive web applications such as load balancing, failover, native database drivers, CORBA support, and more. Thirty-day evaluation versions of each product are available for download at the Allaire site.

Using ColdFusion on a Commercial Hosting Provider

To serve your own ColdFusion programs, it is not necessary to purchase and install ColdFusion Server. There are hundreds of commercial web hosting providers, advertised in nearly every PC and web developer-oriented magazine. Many, if not most of them, offer ColdFusion as one of their services. In that case, you develop your applications on your local workstation and then send them (generally via FTP) to the remote server to be accessed by your visitors.

Setting Up a Web Server for ColdFusion

Unfortunately, we really don't have the space in this chapter to explain setting up ColdFusion. The excellent ColdFusion manuals provide ample explanation and the best recommendation is to read those carefully if you want to run ColdFusion before proceeding with this chapter.

Keep in mind as well that the intent is to make your ColdFusion pages available to external WAP visitors. Unless you have a full-time Internet connection on your workstation, it really doesn't make sense to install ColdFusion Server there (except for testing or development purposes).

You should install ColdFusion on a machine intended to be used as a dedicated web server. Then you can either do your development directly on that server, or perhaps more appropriate, develop your ColdFusion templates on a local workstation (running the single-user version that comes with ColdFusion Studio) and then move them to the production server.

Remember, as we mentioned previously, that ColdFusion works in tandem with web server software. You will first need a web server installed and running before installing ColdFusion. There are several free ones, for both Windows and UNIX platforms.

Configuring ColdFusion Server for WML Development

Configuration of the web server for WML development has been discussed in previous chapters, where you learned to associate MIME types with specific file extensions, such as .wml and .wmls.

ColdFusion pages (or, again, programs or templates as they may be referred to) always have an extension of .cfm (or, less often, .cfml). As such, there is no specific WAP configuration to be done for the web server to support ColdFusion pages that create WML output.

WAP and ColdFusion

Developing WAP applications in ColdFusion means using ColdFusion's many powerful features in the creation of WML decks sent to a microbrowser. It's important to approach this chapter with a firm foundation in WML. Please be sure to read previous chapters about using WML, especially matters regarding user interface design, limited information presentation, etc.

For those with existing ColdFusion applications generating HTML, it's not really appropriate to expect to port these to applications generating WML. As has been said before in this book, you really need to rethink your applications when building for WML.

In this section, we'll learn the key to creating WML applications in ColdFusion—the CFCONTENT tag. We'll also show a basic example, as well as how to create and execute such CF code, and even how to use this approach to support different wireless programming languages.

Beyond that, we'll cover the detail of creating real WAP applications, including processing form submissions, performing database query and update processing, creating enhanced displays, and much more.

The Key to the Kingdom: CFCONTENT

The key to developing WAP applications in ColdFusion comes down to a single tag, <CFCONTENT>. Just add the following CFCONTENT tag to the top of your ColdFusion template (.cfm file), coded otherwise with normal WML:

```
<CFCONTENT TYPE="text/vnd.wap.wml">
```

To generate WMLScript decks, use:

```
<CFCONTENT TYPE="text/vnd.wap.wmlscript">
```

What these tags do is change the MIME type for the page being generated – remember this was first discussed back in Chapter 2. The <CFCONTENT> tag 'tells' the file to send its output using the appropriate MIME type. (Of course, you can still have static, non-ColdFusion WML and WMLScript pages on your server, served as .wml and .wmls files as described in previous chapters. Refer to those for more information on configuring your web server to serve those sorts of files. What we're saying here is that for .cfm files, the CFCONTENT tag indicates the type of page being sent to the browser.)

This will allow you to enter (or have ColdFusion generate) any valid WML (or WMLScript) code, and that code will be sent to the browser in a format that a wireless browser (or emulator) will expect. (Of course, you should cause only valid WML to be sent to the microbrowser. Some CF tags build HTML or JavaScript, and they should be avoided. See more on this matter in *Techniques, Tips, And Traps*.)

A Basic ColdFusion WAP Example

Let's take a quick look at a simple WML example to see how this works in practice. Enter the following code as a .cfm file called wml_hello.cfm:

```
<CFCONTENT TYPE="text/vnd.wap.wml"><?xml version="1.0"?>
<!DOCTYPE wml PUBLIC "-//WAPFORUM//DTD WML 1.1//EN"
"http://www.wapforum.org/DTD/wml_1.1.xml">

<wml>
<card>
   <p>
      <CFSET fname="Bob">
      <CFOUTPUT>
         Hi there, #fname#
      </CFOUTPUT>
   </p>
</card>
</wml>
```

When executed (as described below), this simple ColdFusion program assigns the name "Bob" to a variable we've decided to call fname, and then displays a message using a string (Hi there,) and that variable. The <CFSET> tag creates the variable to be displayed, and the <CFOUTPUT> tags surround the text that will display such variable values. Within the <CFOUTPUT> tags, we use # signs to denote ColdFusion variables to be evaluated. Because # signs have special meaning in WML – as anchors, similar to their use in HTML – you need to be careful if you plan to use one for that purpose within <CFOUTPUT>. See *Techniques, Tricks, and Traps* for further discussion.

The observant reader may have noticed that the first line of code has the <?xml> tag appearing on the same line as the CFCONTENT tag. That's not a mistake. There have been reports of some browsers and WAP servers failing to read a page as valid WML if a carriage return is sent to the browser prior to that <?xml> tag.

Saving and Calling the Sample Code

If you save the code above as `wml_hello.cfm` in a directory on your web server, you can then test it in any WML-compliant browser via the address: `http://yourserverdomain/wml_hello.cfm`.

Though it's not necessary, it would be best to create a new directory in your web server in which to put your WML files. It will facilitate handling errors that may arise, as discussed later in the chapter.

The page will be rendered and will display Hi there, Bob on the browser. We can now expand upon this by adding any ColdFusion code we'd like to generate dynamic WML.

If you receive an error, running this simple example, it's possible that you've tripped over one of a few other possible problems that may have to do with the configuration of your ColdFusion server to properly handle certain aspects of processing for creating WML files. We address several of these configuration issues later in *Techniques, Tricks, and Traps*.

Supporting Other WAP Language Variants

You may have noticed that in the example above we used WAP Forum's specification for the WML DTD. Another specification is that of Phone.com (see Chapter 2), and to use this instead, you need to code the DOCTYPE line as:

```
<!DOCTYPE wml PUBLIC "-//PHONE.COM//DTD WML 1.1//EN"
"http://www.phone.com/dtd/wml11.dtd" >
```

Note that the code in this chapter has been tested on the UP.Simulator and a Sprint Touchpoint phone with the UP.Browser embedded, but it worked fine with the WAP Forum DTD.

Using Other Features of ColdFusion

There are some useful features of ColdFusion that make life easier for the WAP developer, or make your applications more capable. This section will examine some of the more interesting ones.

Processing Form Submissions

Fortunately, some things in WML are very similar to HTML processing, and the ColdFusion support for these is equally straightforward. Form field (and query string) processing is a great example – that is, processing data entered by a user on a form. If you want to store it in a database, or e-mail it, or do any sort of thing on the server with that data, you'll need to pass it from the browser to the server, using either POST or GET methods. We saw how to do this with static WML back in Chapter 4.

The WML for creating a simple form follows:

```
<CFCONTENT TYPE="text/vnd.wap.wml"><?xml version="1.0"?>
<!DOCTYPE wml PUBLIC "-//WAPFORUM//DTD WML 1.1//EN"
"http://www.wapforum.org/DTD/wml_1.1.xml">

<wml>
<card>
```

```
    <do type="accept">
        <go href="wml_action.cfm" method="post">
            <postfield name="symbol" value="$(symbol)"/>
        </go>
    </do>
    <p>
        Enter stock symbol:
        <input name="symbol" format="4A"/>
    </p>
</card>
</wml>
```

The user is prompted to enter a stock symbol (i.e. a symbol representing a stock that, for example, you may have shares in). Here's what it looks like in the Phone.com UP.Browser emulator:

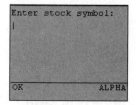

When the user enters a symbol and clicks the OK or Accept button, this page passes control (via the `<go href>` element) to a ColdFusion page (`wml_action.cfm`) that can process the form. We'll see more on that in a moment.

Most of the WML code should be familiar to you by now, but especially for coders more familiar with HTML form processing, some things should be pointed out. Notice first that there is no `<FORM>` tag as in HTML. And we are submitting the form via an HREF, not an "action". We repeat the field to be submitted, first in the `<input>` and then in the `<formfield>` elements, and there is a useful `format` attribute for the `<input>` element. WML form processing is indeed quite different. Be sure to read the previous chapters on WML programming!

You may also observe that this file has no ColdFusion code in it at all! We could have left out the `<CFCONTENT>` tag and coded the example as a plain WML file. There are two reasons not to do this:

❑ Doing it this way makes the form extensible. We could add ColdFusion code to it very easily and would not need to change the file name and any links pointing to it. (In fact, we'll be changing it shortly to present a list of stock symbols to the user customized for them.)

❑ Leaving this non-ColdFusion WML file as a ColdFusion template solves the problem of a web server that has not yet been configured to support WML files – the code will still work. (Remember, the web server is not telling the browser that the file is a WML MIME type, the CFCONTENT tag is.)

When the user submits the form, the form field `symbol` will be passed to the "action" page. In this case, `wml_action.cfm` will process the form. There are many things that this action page can do (which we will show in a moment). For now, let's focus on just a very simple example:

```
<CFCONTENT TYPE="text/vnd.wap.wml"><?xml version="1.0"?>
<!DOCTYPE wml PUBLIC "-//WAPFORUM//DTD WML 1.1//EN"
"http://www.wapforum.org/DTD/wml_1.1.xml">

<wml>
<card>
    <p>
```

```
      The stock symbol selected was:
      <CFOUTPUT>#form.symbol#</CFOUTPUT>
   </p>
   </card>
   </wml>
```

If the user enters the symbol ALLR (the symbol for Allaire, makers of ColdFusion), on the form, then they should see something that looks like this:

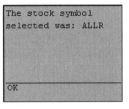

Let's talk about the code. The challenge in some server programming languages is that they use rather clumsy or verbose mechanisms for identifying the form data passed in to this action page. As you can see, it's quite straightforward in ColdFusion. We simply refer to the field name that was given when the form field was created on the <postfield> element, which was named symbol. More specifically, we refer to the field by its type as well, which being a form field is form and is specified as form.symbol. This is called a **prefix** in ColdFusion, and we'll see some more as we go along. We could have had any number of form fields passed in from the form, and they would all be accessible using the syntax form.*fieldname*.

Before moving on, there's one other way to process a form and/or pass data to a ColdFusion page, and it involves another type of variable prefix: the url prefix. This is the easy way that ColdFusion allows you to refer to data passed as a query string on a URL when calling one page from another. An example of such passing of data is:

```
<go href="wml_action.cfm?symbol=($symbol)" method="get"/>
```

This is just as an alternative to using the "post" method of form processing and using the <postfield> element for passing data from a form. The choice is really yours as a WML programmer.

The good news is that such data is just as easy to process in ColdFusion as form data. In the example given, we could (in wml_action.cfm) refer to the data passed in as #url.symbol#. In that respect, you can use it in just the same way you use form fields. (In fact, ColdFusion doesn't really even require that you specify the prefix for these two types of variables, so in the ColdFusion code in wml_action.cfm, you could refer in both examples to just #symbol#.)

You should be aware, however, that passing multiple variables on the query string has unique challenges in WML processing. Be sure to read the *Techniques, Tricks, and Traps* section for more information.

So far, we've seen only how to print back to the user information that they have already entered. But this is just the beginning.

Query Processing

Of course, we could do much more on the action or "backend" page than simply repeat the user's input back to them. (In fact, unlike in HTML forms, we could use straight WML to do that sort of confirmation page on the client, simply by forwarding the user to another card devoted to that purpose. It would refer to the WML variables.) The previous example was just a chance to see how easily form fields are processed in ColdFusion. Let's look at a more realistic example, building on what we've learned.

More typically, we will take the user's input and use it either to query a database, or perhaps to insert or update a record in a database. You just need to have a database (available from the web server) and know a little SQL (which is really not that hard).

> *To learn more about SQL, especially as used with ColdFusion, check out "Teach Yourself SQL in 10 Minutes", from Sams, by Ben Forta—a noted ColdFusion expert. Also see Instant SQL Programming by Wrox Press, ISBN 1874416508.*

To be clearer, the database and database server need to be available to the ColdFusion page. ColdFusion, when installed, includes support for communicating with Microsoft Access files and any other ODBC-compliant database (which includes even enterprise class DBMSs, such as SQL Server, Oracle, Sybase, DB2, etc.) Such a database needs merely to be defined as a "datasource" to the ColdFusion server administrator and accessible to the CF server (either on the same machine or on a LAN-connected machine).

In the example that follows, we are presuming that you've already defined such a datasource named "portfolios". (The subject of defining databases and datasources is beyond the scope of this book. See the ColdFusion documentation from Allaire for further explanations. If you're new to ColdFusion, you just need to know that defining such a datasource is very simple and it simply creates an alias to refer to the database. This way, our code doesn't really need to know the physical location of the database nor even the DBMS under which it's defined. We need only refer to the datasource name and use proper SQL to refer to its table and column names. Communicating with databases easily is clearly ColdFusion's strength. This chapter is not meant to be a tutorial on all aspects of using ColdFusion, so we leave it to you to refer to the CF documentation, which clearly explains this fundamental process in its very first chapters.)

Getting back to the previous example, let's say that we had wanted to take that stock symbol entered by the user and look up the number of shares that the user holds in a database. (A later example will show how to update such a database table)

> *I'm sure some of you are thinking, "Hey, I thought you were going to look up their stock's current price". Well, that would be a neat application. In order to do it, we would need to have a means by which to lookup the current price, perhaps on a site that serves such information to licensed users of such a service. ColdFusion offers a feature to do just that, by way of the CFHTTP tag. We discuss that at the end of this section, but we cannot legally show you such an example as such services require you to have a license to reuse their information that way.*

Let's assume that among our database's many tables we have one called "ClientHoldings", which has the following columns:

- ❑ ClientHoldings
- ❑ HoldingsId (PK)
- ❑ ClientId (FK)
- ❑ Symbol (FK)
- ❑ NumShares
- ❑ PurchaseDate
- ❑ PurchasePrice

The designations PK and FK mean "primary key" and "foreign key", respectively. (Again, for further explanation, consult a good book on databases.) Note that this is a simplified design – a real database of such information would have a more complex design involving several tables.

In fact, our portfolios database does have more tables, but they're not related to the example currently being discussed. The following is the complete list of tables, columns, and their relationships:

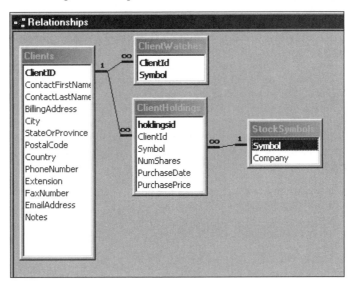

If we wanted to find the current holdings in a given stock (for example, ALLR), for a given client (for example, with ClientId of 1), we might code the following SQL query:

```
SELECT * FROM ClientHoldings
WHERE ClientId=1
AND Symbol='ALLR'
```

To execute this query within ColdFusion, we simply wrap the statements within a set of CFQUERY tags, pointing to the datasource holding the table, and giving the query a name so that we could refer to it later. This would look like the following:

```
<CFQUERY DATASOURCE="Portfolios" NAME="GetHoldings">
    SELECT * FROM ClientHoldings
    WHERE ClientId=1
    AND Symbol='ALLR'
</CFQUERY>
```

The name of the query, GetHoldings, allows us refer to the query results later on. Now, to make this useful for our Stock request form above, we'd need to make the Stock Symbol that we search for be driven by the user's input, rather than be hard-coded as it is in the above SQL query. The next example shows how easy that is.

Before we show that, however, the ClientId represents an entirely different challenge. Here we've hard-coded it as a 1, just to show how the SQL would work with hard-coded values. But we'd want that to be a variable as well. It would not, typically, be entered by the user. Instead, it would be known by the ColdFusion server as the id for this user. The question is how the CF server would know it, and how it would be available on this form processing page.

There are several approaches. One way would be for the ColdFusion page that generated the form (wml_form.cfm, above) form to have placed an additional <postfield> element on the page holding the value of this user's ClientId. If we did that, then the ClientId would be available on the action page as form.clientid. This approach will work, but it has a security risk as someone could call the action page from a modified version of the form that they could create, having put a different value in for the ClientId. There are ways to detect that the calling page is not one that we expect, but that's beyond the scope of this chapter.

Yet another approach would be to have the user authenticated by some previous login page (not demonstrated in this chapter) and then have that process store the value of the current user's ClientId in what's called a "session" variable. Sessions are another topic beyond the scope of this chapter to discuss, but they're an important part of web application development in any platform (ColdFusion or otherwise). Unfortunately, most session processing approaches (including ColdFusion's) rely on use of browser cookies to carry unique identifying information regarding each user. Not all WML browsers and gateways support cookies, so session variable processing may not work for all WML applications. We will proceed with the examples assuming that session variables are properly configured and supported in your environment. The sample applications included with this chapter use a feature to set a hard-coded value for session.clientid.

So now let's turn our attention back to executing the query used above on a form's action page, using form and session variables. It could look as follows:

```
<CFQUERY DATASOURCE="Portfolios" NAME="GetHoldings">
    SELECT * FROM ClientHoldings
    WHERE ClientId=#session.clientid#
    AND Symbol='#form.symbol#'
</CFQUERY>
```

Notice that we have substituted the hard-coded values for ClientId and Symbol to use the values of the corresponding variables instead. Note, too, that we have respected the SQL requirement to put quotes around variables, whose values are being used to search a column that expects a string.

> *Remember that when we wanted to show the value of a ColdFusion variable within a CFOUTPUT tag, we wrapped it in # signs. When doing a query where the SQL will be driven by variables (form, session, or otherwise), we also wrap those variables in # signs.*

ColdFusion allows us even further flexibility than this in building a SQL statement dynamically – we could also use conditional statements, such as CFIF or CFSWITCH, to modify the SQL before it's passed to the database for processing. When the </CFQUERY> tag is reached, the resulting SQL is executed.

Displaying and Using Query Results

When the query above is executed on the form action page, it will result in finding 0 or more records. The results of the query are held in the memory of the ColdFusion server ready for use. This is where the name given to the query becomes handy.

Let's assume that one or more records were found by the query. If we want to display the result of the query, we simply use the QUERY attribute of the CFOUTPUT tag – this turns the CFOUTPUT into a loop that executes code once per record found:

```
<CFOUTPUT>
    <p>
        Holdings for #form.symbol#:
    </p>
```

```
  </CFOUTPUT>
  <p mode="nowrap">
     <CFOUTPUT QUERY="GetHoldings">
        #NumShares# on #PurchaseDate# at #PurchasePrice#<br/>
     </CFOUTPUT>
  </p>
```

Notice that we have simply referred to the query's columns as variables. This is another example of how easily ColdFusion works with database processing. In some situations, it may be necessary to prefix the three column variable references above with the name of the query, as in `GetHoldings.NumShares`. However, it was not necessary in this case.

The code offered above could give an output like this:

```
Holdings for ALLR:
▷100 on 1999-04-23 at
 200 on 1999-06-14 at
 100 on 2000-02-01 at



OK
```

Notice also that, from a WML perspective, we are wrapping the output lines with a <p> element using the `mode=nowrap` attribute. In the UP.Browser this causes lines wider than the screen to be horizontally scrolled automatically in the browser when the cursor is placed on such a line (though this feature is not supported in all WML browsers):

```
Holdings for ALLR:
45
 200 on 1999-06-14 at
 100 on 2000-02-01 at


OK
```

A nice feature to add to this application would be a message reporting that no records were found for the search criteria provided. ColdFusion provides some special variables after any query that indicate such things as the number of records found (*queryname*`.recordcount`), and the columns returned by the query (*queryname*`.columnlist`). And within a loop, we can also refer to *queryname*`.currentrow`, which indicates the relative position in the result set of the record being processed.

Here is an example that adds the method for doing this:

```
<CFQUERY DATASOURCE="Portfolios" NAME="GetHoldings">
   SELECT * FROM ClientHoldings
   WHERE ClientId=#session.clientid#
   AND Symbol='#form.symbol#'
</CFQUERY>

<CFIF getholdings.recordcount is 0>
   <CFOUTPUT>
      <p>You have no holdings for #form.symbol#</p>
   </CFOUTPUT>
<CFELSE>
   <CFOUTPUT>
      <p>Holdings for #form.symbol#:</p>
   </CFOUTPUT>
   <p mode="nowrap">
      <CFOUTPUT QUERY="GetHoldings">
         #NumShares# on #PurchaseDate# at #PurchasePrice#<br/>
      </CFOUTPUT>
   </p>
</CFIF>
```

We will alter this form soon to allow the user only to make choices for the stocks they do hold.

Table Formatting: Challenges for both ColdFusion and WML Developers

The output shown above is acceptable, but we could manipulate the displayed data to take up less space. Also, we might prefer to show the data in columns. Just as in HTML, an easy way to achieve columnar display is to format the information in a table, as in the following:

```
<CFOUTPUT>
    <p>Holdings for #form.symbol#:</p>
</CFOUTPUT>
<p mode="nowrap">
    <table columns="3">
        <tr><td>Shrs</td><td>BuyDt</td><td>Price</td></tr>
        <CFOUTPUT QUERY="GetHoldings">
            <tr>
            <td>#NumberFormat(NumShares)#</td>
            <td>#DateFormat(PurchaseDate,"m/d/yy")#</td>
            <td># PurchasePrice#</td>
            </tr>
        </CFOUTPUT>
    </table>
</p>
```

It is possible that some WML browsers may not support tables. Be sure to investigate this further before relying on this feature to format your output. However, this could create the following much more attractive display:

Holdings for ALLR:		
Shrs	BuyDt	Price
100	4/23/99	45
200	6/14/99	75 3/8
100	2/1/00	95 1/4
OK		

We define the rows of the table containing data from the query within the <CFOUTPUT QUERY ...> loop, but *not* the table element or column header line, else they'll be repeated multiple times. Our goal usually is to have a <tr> element defined just at the start of the loop, and to close it with </tr> just at the end of the loop, to create a single row per record. Of course, you could choose to show multiple rows of table data per record, given the limited screen real estate. Just be sure to properly format the table.

Adding ColdFusion Functions

We saw a couple of useful ColdFusion functions in the table example above. The numberformat() and dateformat() functions are used to modify the display of the data within the data cells. The first formats the numeric output to use commas to separate hundreds and thousands, etc, and the second causes the date display to follow the most concise format for display on the small screen (it has other options for changing the date presentation layout, as discussed in the CF manuals). The use of functions like these can make the application more user-friendly.

There is also a dollarformat() function to format the display of price (it takes a number, such as 25, and shows it as $25.00). There are two reasons for avoiding this. Firstly, stock prices aren't generally shown with dollar ($) signs and decimals. Instead, they're shown in fractional amounts, such as 100 1/2 or 25 7/8.

More important, the dollarformat() function is a potential trap for WAP developers, even if you *do* want to show real dollar formats. WML browsers use the $ sign as a reserved character to mean a local variable. So, if you send something like $25.00 for display to the browser, you'll get an error. You can solve the problem, though, if you really want to show a dollar sign, by escaping it, which in CF means we repeat it. In the case of displaying it before the output of the dollarformat() function, the $ sign would precede the function call.

An example might be:

```
$#dollarformat(price)#
```

Performing Database Updates

So far, we've just been producing query output on the form's action page. Let's move on to something more compelling. Just as we can use the form variables as part of the SELECT statement, we can also perform SQL INSERT, UPDATE, and DELETE processing. Again, we'll leave it to you to learn more about these SQL statements, if needed. We'll show some rather basic examples.

Let's assume that the purpose of the form and action page is instead to prompt the user for a stock symbol that they want to add to a 'watch list'. By this we mean that we will have a part of the application that watches for changes to this stock. (We will not develop the 'watching' part of the application. We'll just focus on how we could add to the list of stocks to be watched.)

Assume we have a table called "ClientWatches", which has just the following columns:

❑   ClientWatches

❑   ClientId (PK, FK)

❑   Symbol (PK, FK)

With the form field being available in the page as form.symbol, and a session variable tracking the ClientId, we can easily insert the data for them into a new record. The query, placed on the form's action page, looks as follows:

```
<CFQUERY DATASOURCE="Portfolios" >
    INSERT INTO ClientWatches (ClientId, Symbol)
    VALUES ('#session.clientid#', '#form.symbol#')
</CFQUERY>
```

We don't need to name the query, since INSERT queries generally return no result.

Of course, if the database insert failed, the user would get an error. Unfortunately, ColdFusion's error processing will create an HTML page by default.

Later, in the *Techniques, Tricks, and Traps* section, we explain how we can trap any ColdFusion error so as to prevent the user getting that default HTML-formatted error page from ColdFusion.

There is yet another way to detect the failure of a CFQUERY action. ColdFusion supports a CFTRY/CFCATCH approach as of Release 4.0. It's powerful, and solves the problem of being able to detect and control the display of errors coming from some particular statement or set of statements. It's beyond the scope of this chapter to explain that, but an example is shown below (from insert_action.cfm in the source code for this chapter). See the Allaire manuals for more information.

Before showing that example, note that we also would not want to allow the user to insert a new stock into the ClientWatches if they already had a watch active for that symbol. One way to handle this would be to simply perform a query to see if the record already exists, and if so, generate an error. This approach is demonstrated in the example below (and in insert_action.cfm). There are a couple of other new features introduced, which are discussed momentarily.

```
<CFQUERY DATASOURCE="Portfolios" NAME="GetWatches">
   SELECT count(*) as reccount
   FROM ClientWatches
   WHERE ClientId=#session.clientid#
   AND Symbol='#form.symbol#'
</CFQUERY>

<CFIF getwatches.reccount is not 0>
   <p>
      <CFOUTPUT>
         Watch already set for #form.symbol#.
      </CFOUTPUT>
   </p>
<CFELSE>
   <CFTRY>
      <CFQUERY DATASOURCE="Portfolios" >
         INSERT INTO  ClientWatches (ClientId, Symbol)
         VALUES (#session.clientid#, '#form.symbol#')
      </CFQUERY>
      <CFCATCH>
         <p>
            Error inserting watch:<br/>
<!--- Can't view real error message (in CFCATCH.detail) because it's formatted as
HTML without formatting it for display. Can use xmlformat in 4.5. --->
            <CFOUTPUT>
               #CFCATCH.SQLSTATE#<br/>
               #XMLFormat(CFCATCH.detail)#
            </CFOUTPUT>
         </p>
<!--- Notice that we must abort this program, because the catch otherwise falls
through and reports success. Notice too that we must put in the closing page tags
before aborting, lest we send incomplete WML to the browser--->
         </card>
         </wml>
         <CFABORT>
      </CFCATCH>
   </CFTRY>
   <CFOUTPUT>
      <p>
         Watch added for #form.symbol#
      </p>
   </CFOUTPUT>
</CFIF>
```

Some additional notes on this example: note the use of the ColdFusion comment tags <!--- --->. These tags will be stripped out before being sent to the browser. The comments are useful for CF developers viewing your source program on the server. Also, the code discusses using the <CFABORT> tag, which is discussed later under *Techniques, Tricks, and Traps*.

The comments are pointing out that within the <CFCATCH> tag we have access to a variable called cfcatch.detail, which holds the details of the error. Unfortunately, ColdFusion (or the database server) may include in that error message characters that are not proper for display on the microbrowser. One way to handle that problem is to use the XMLFormat() function. It's not perfect (it escapes special XML characters, such as the less than (<) and greater than (>) signs, and it still may cause text invalid for WML browsers to be sent to the screen), but it's better than nothing. Note that this function is new in version 4.5 of ColdFusion. Prior to that, the HTMLEditFormat() function could be used as a reasonable alternative. See the Allaire documentation for more information on both.

A more efficient way of detecting the duplicate record is to use the TRY/CATCH method described in the code above, testing if an error occurs that indicates an attempt was made to insert a duplicate record. The specific test will depend on the database and again it's beyond the scope of this chapter to go into the details. See your database reference manuals for the error code returned when a duplicate record is inserted, and see the example applications reference to the `cfcatch.sqlstate` variable, which could prove useful in developing this sort of approach. An example for doing it for an Access database is shown in the example `insert_action2.cfm` in the source code provided.

Using Queries to Build Select Lists

So far we've used a query only on the action page, but there's certainly no reason we couldn't use it on the form itself. Consider our example where we prompted the user to enter the stock symbol. Rather than make them type in the symbol, why not let them pick from a list of their currently held stocks? It makes perfect sense for that application.

In fact, this raises a point that's critical when programming for wireless devices. Making the user enter any text input should be avoided when possible. It's very difficult to enter text in most phones, so this opportunity to present the user a list of choices is very important for WML programming. (See also Chapter 7.) The previous example was simplified so we could focus on just the basics of passing data from forms to action pages. Whenever possible, provide the user a pick list. (Of course, with a list being generated from a database table, we also have to be careful about not sending too much information to the browser. You can use the *queryname*.`recordcount` variable mentioned before, as well as multi-deck programming techniques discussed in previous chapters, to break up the output into more manageable chunks or to simply stop sending choices above a certain limit—being sure to tell the user that you've done so.)

So we want to present a list of choices to the user. We need to build the WML for creating pick lists. Doing this is really no different than the approach we used to build the table from the query result. We create a form with the current stock holdings by first running a query (to get the data to be shown) and then building the `<select>` `<option>` elements in a `<CFOUTPUT QUERY>` loop:

```
<CFQUERY datasource="portfolios" name="getstocks">
   SELECT distinct symbol FROM clientholdings
   WHERE ClientId=#session.clientid#
</CFQUERY>

<card>
<CFIF getstocks.recordcount is 0>
   <p>You have no stocks to view</p>
<CFELSE>
   <do type="accept">
      <go href="getholdings_action.cfm" method="post">
         <postfield name="symbol" value="$(symbol)"/>
      </go>
   </do>
   <p>
      Choose one of your stocks to view:
      <select name='symbol'>
         <CFOUTPUT query="getstocks">
            <option value="#symbol#">#symbol#</option>
         </CFOUTPUT>
      </select>
   </p>
</CFIF>
</card>
```

You should find the <select> control very familiar, but notice that you must specify the value attribute of the <option> element even though (as in this case) the value shown to the user (the string between the tags) and that passed to the action page (identified by the value keyword) are identical.

Note how we wrap the <OPTION> element in <CFOUTPUT QUERY...> tags, but not the <SELECT> element. As with creating tables, we want only one <SELECT> control, but as many <OPTIONS> as there are records.

We used a special SQL SELECT statement keyword (distinct) in that query to get only a non-repeated list of the client's holdings (they may have made multiple purchases of a given stock). This code also shows how to test for the case where no records are found. If the user has no current stock holdings, there's no point showing them the select control with no choices available.

The result of running the code appears as:

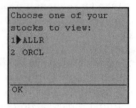

The user can use their phone's "cursor control" or equivalent buttons to make a choice.

Recall that the select control offers a multiple-choice option (multiple="true"), so the user can select multiple values. Note that they're sent to the action page as semi-colon separated values (rather than as comma-separated values, as in HTML). We'll see how to deal with this later, in the section, *Techniques, Tricks and Traps*.

Also, note that the <option> element offers the onpick option that causes the user's choice to launch a URL. See the index.cfm file in the attached sample code, which uses this feature to let you run any of the sample programs.

Other Important ColdFusion Features to Remember

We obviously can't get into all of the features of ColdFusion Server here (whole books have been written on the subject!), but some of them are particularly well suited or important to remember when doing WAP development. Among them are the following:

❑ <CFMAIL> is a very easy to use (yet powerful) tag for sending mail from a ColdFusion page. The mail can be sent to one person, or to all e-mail addresses found in a query. The body as well as the subject can contain variables, including query columns when using a query.

❑ <CFSCHEDULE> allows you to schedule a ColdFusion page to be executed on a set schedule, either just once or on a recurring basis. Imagine using it to have a process monitor some event and warn you via a WML notification.

❑ <CFSEARCH> allows users to search against large bodies of text. Whether this is an HTML file, Word document, or even Adobe Acrobat PDF, <CFSEARCH> makes quick work of the task. Used in conjunction with <CFCOLLECTION> and <CFINDEX>, it uses the built-in Verity Indexing engine, which is provided free with ColdFusion.

❑ Client, Application, Server, Cookie, and CGI variables (in addition to the form, url, and session variables mentioned previously): these are additional prefixes you may use when creating and referring to variables. Each has a different purpose, and some require additional setup to use.

While session variables are stored in the web server's memory, and typically are used only for short-term storage (the life of the user's visit to the site), client variables are typically used to track an individual user's values over multiple visits. They're generally stored on the server, in your choice of the registry or a database. In either case however, they, too, leverage cookies for their way of connecting the user's browser to their client variable values and so they may not be useful in all WAP applications. Note that the client variables and values themselves can also be stored in cookies. Support for client variables must be enabled by way of the <CFAPPLICATION> tag.

Application and server variables can be thought of as global variables. The first are variables available to all users of an application, i.e. the users of all templates under control of a given <CFAPPLICATION> tag. Server variables are available to all users on the entire ColdFusion server, without any setup required. Both those are available without need for cookie support.

Cookies themselves are an interesting possibility for WML browsers that do support them, and ColdFusion makes them very easy to use by way of the "cookie." prefix.

Finally, the "CGI." prefix can be used to refer to a whole host of variables passed to the CF page from either the browser/gateway or the web server. There are variables that identify the IP address of the user, or in the case of WML browsers all sorts of information about the browser. You owe it to yourself to look into these available variables. The sample source code files for this chapter includes a show_cgi_vars.cfm that lists those available from your phone/browser/gateway and web server.

❑ Query caching: By way of additional attributes on the <CFQUERY> tag, called CACHEDWITHIN and CACHEDAFTER, you can specify that a query's result be held in memory on the ColdFusion server for longer than the life of the template doing the query (normally, query results are lost at the end of a template's execution). If you have queries whose results don't change much or often during the day, you can gain substantial performance improvements by using caching. It can also be useful when you're creating an interface where the user looks at a search result over several pages (showing only a few records at a time). Why not cache the query results, at least for the few minutes that they'll need to look at the sets of results?

❑ <CFHTTP> is a wonderful feature that many wireless developers will cherish. It allows you to have your ColdFusion file execute a request to browse a remote web page (HTML or WML). The value is that you can then parse that web page's results and show some portion of it to your wireless visitors. The ColdFusion server visits the site on your behalf (acting as an agent) and returns the web page contents as a variable. Then you can use CF functions such as Left, Right, RemoveChars, Find, and so on, to strip out the portion that you want. It can even be setup to pass form data to form processing pages, and more. It's been used to gather cities from the post office based on zip code, books from Amazon.com that meet criteria passed in by your visitors, and more.

❑ The <CFOUTPUT> tag's GROUP attribute allows you to create what are known in traditional reporting tools as "control breaks" when displaying query output. By this we mean grouping output so that repeating data is not displayed redundantly but rather a break in the report, with a new heading, signals a new grouping of data. An example is offered in the source code example in the pair of files, getholdings_list_form_multiple.cfm and getholdings_action_multiple.cfm.

Next, we'll see the many ways that ColdFusion Studio and its close cousin HomeSite have been modified in Release 4.5 to facilitate WML coding. Then, we'll look at lots of tricks and traps that you'll likely trip over in doing WML-based ColdFusion development.

ColdFusion Studio/HomeSite Editing Features for WAP Development

ColdFusion Studio is Allaire's development tool for creating ColdFusion code. If you're confused about the difference between ColdFusion Server and ColdFusion Studio, refer to the opening section of the chapter. ColdFusion Server resides on a web server and serves your CF templates to visiting users. ColdFusion Studio is a development tool used by CF programmers to create CF templates. We've been describing to this point how to use CF Server to serve dynamically generated WML. Now we're going to discuss some features of the Studio editor that have been bolstered to support WML development (dynamic or static).

As mentioned in the opening of the chapter, Allaire has based Studio on another product in their line, called HomeSite. Studio adds many features for CF development (a visual database query tool, interactive debugger, and much more), but for the purpose of this section, the features we're discussing are found in either Studio or its less-powerful (and less expensive) cousin.

ColdFusion code, like WML, is simply plain text so it can technically be created in any text editor, including lowly NotePad. But Studio/HomeSite is a much more powerful tool for creating ColdFusion code than a simple editor like NotePad. Developed primarily as an HTML editing tool, it has been extended in the recent Release 4.5 revisions to add features for creating WML code.

> *For simplicity, I will refer from now on to just Studio, but unless otherwise specifically stated, the features described apply to HomeSite as well as Studio.*

Among the features that make ColdFusion Studio so useful for HTML editing are such features as tag attribute insight, tag editors, a tag chooser, tag help and more. Experienced Studio users may notice that tag completion and tag validation features are not mentioned. Unfortunately, testing in 4.51 shows that these features are not yet working for WML tags.

Tag Attribute Insight

Tag insight shows you all the attributes available for a given tag, making it very easy to enter or edit WML tags. When you're typing in a tag, and you press the space bar to enter the first attribute, Studio pops up a list of the available attributes. For instance, consider we are entering a <go> element into our program. As we type in "<go" and then press space to enter the first attribute for that element, if we wait one second, ColdFusion will pop up a list of the valid attributes of the <go>element, such as href and method. This is illustrated in the screenshot on the following page.

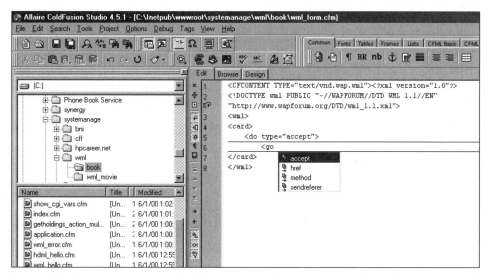

Note that you don't even have to wait for that one-second delay to have the attributes pop up. You can configure Studio to respond more quickly. To set Tag Insight to pop up the choices instantly, use the Studio Options command on the menu and choose the Settings|Tag Insight and then slide the control for delay before displaying tag insight to zero seconds. (The steps are only slightly different in previous releases of Studio.)

But the pop up list of tag attributes is not all that's great about this feature. Once you've selected an attribute, Studio then proceeds to pop up a list of the available values for that attribute, if there are any pre-existing ones. So, had we selected the method attribute instead via tag insight, Studio would have popped up in a similar manner the choices post and get, which we could select the same way.

This feature isn't reserved only to inserting new tags. It also works when you're editing a tag later. All you need to do is place your cursor within a tag, and enter a space after the tag or an existing attribute/value pair. All the attributes for that tag are shown again for your selection.

There are three potential problems to be aware of:

❏ Studio can't tell that you're coding WML, so if you're entering a tag that has an HTML counterpart (such as <input> or <select>), it will present the attributes for both WML and HTML. Currently there's no way to avoid that problem.

❏ The choices offered are not generic, standard WML attributes but are instead based on the Phone.com specification for WML. Therefore, there may be attributes or values offered that are specific to Phone.com browsers and not all WML browsers. (See Appendix A.)

❏ Finally, when these attributes are entered by Studio on your behalf, they may be entered in upper case which would be unfortunate, because WML tags/elements as well as their attributes and values must be entered in lowercase. There is a Studio option that controls this, and you need to ensure it's set properly. See the Studio Options command on the menu and choose the Settings option, then from the list of areas to control choose Html, and then turn ON the option listed first, namely lowercase all inserted tags.

These challenges are a bit troubling, but the benefits of tag insight far outweigh these minor problems.

Tag Editors

Another useful feature built into Studio is the notion of Tag Editors, which is yet another approach allowing you to see the available attributes for a tag. To edit a tag using the tag editor, you can place the cursor on a tag and right-click, choosing Edit tag. You're then shown a dialogue window like this:

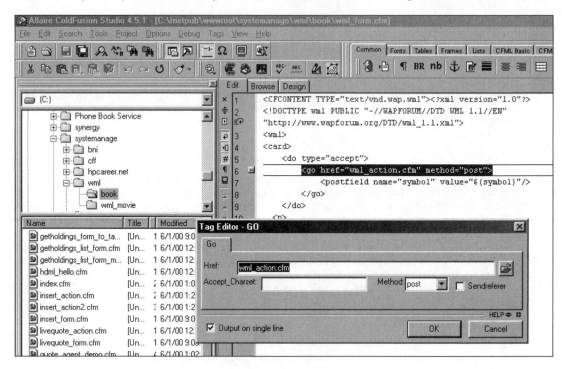

In tag editors with many attributes, a significant benefit is that they show a tabbed interface presenting the most important, commonly used attributes on the first tab's display. Note also that the editor also makes intelligent use of input controls, so true/false options are presented as checkboxes, multiple choice options are presented as drop-downs, and so on. One last thing: those of you who prefer keyboard shortcuts should note that the tag editor can also be called up by clicking on a tag and pressing *CTRL-F4*.

Tag Chooser

Another great time saver is Studio's Tag Chooser. Accessible anytime using the menu command Tools|Tag Chooser (or the shortcut CTRL-E), this presents a categorized list of tags. It starts out (generally) showing available ColdFusion tags, but you can use the interface to change it to list WML tags, as shown opposite:

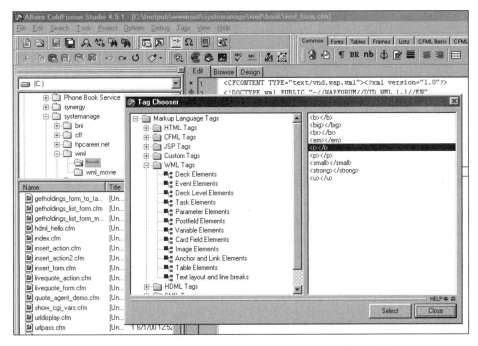

The display shows all WML tags listed, but if you moved the cursor to one of the categories, such as **Task Elements**, the list on the right would be reduced to only the tags in that category. Notice also that when you do select a tag from the tag chooser, you're taken to that tag's tag editor (unless it's a very simple tag, in which case it simply enters the tag or tag pair for you).

Tag Help

You can obtain help for any tag – even for WML tags – by pressing the F1 key while the cursor is on a tag (WML, CFML, HTML, or other) or function. To return to the edit mode once the help is displayed, press the **Edit** tab listed just above the code editing area of the display.

Another way to access help is within the Tag Editor feature described above. Though you could easily miss them, there is a pair of "help" buttons in the lower right corner of every tag editor (see the screen shot for the tag editor feature, above). Clicking one of these help buttons will either show the help in an embedded pane of the tag editor window, or it will show the help in an entirely new window.

Tag Completion and Tag Validation

We should mention that Studio also offers a couple of other very useful tag editing features: tag completion and tag validation. With the first, Studio creates a tag's "closing" tag for you when you type the "opening" tag's closing bracket (>). With the second, it validates the entered attributes and values for the given tag (as well as a valid tag) when you enter the closing bracket for a tag.

Unfortunately, Studio doesn't currently support either of these features for WML tags. It doesn't close WML tags and the validation capability doesn't recognize them. Even more troublesome, some tags that are valid in both WML and HTML will not be closed – for example entering a <p> tag does not lead to a closing </p> tag being created.

Perhaps Allaire will address this in future releases, but for now, just be careful. Also, if you want to, you can add to the list of auto-completed tags, using Options|Settings|Editor|Tag Completion|Add.

Another problem with tag completion (when it does work for tags that are valid in both WML and HTML, such as <select>) is that it may create tags in upper case, similar to the problem described earlier. See the section, *Tag Attribute Insight*, to find out how to correctly set this Studio option.

New Page Wizard

Finally, another useful enhancement in version 4.5 for WML development is the inclusion of a new page wizard for WML files. All this is, really, is a mechanism to create a single, new, untitled WML page within Studio, but it does save you typing all the basic tags that every page should have (the <?xml>, <!DOCTYPE>, <wml>, and <card> tags, and their closing counterparts.)

The feature is accessible by choosing File from the command line (Alt-F), then choosing New. A window will open showing the available wizards for HTML development. Click on the WML tab listed at the top right of that dialogue window, to see the two WML wizards:

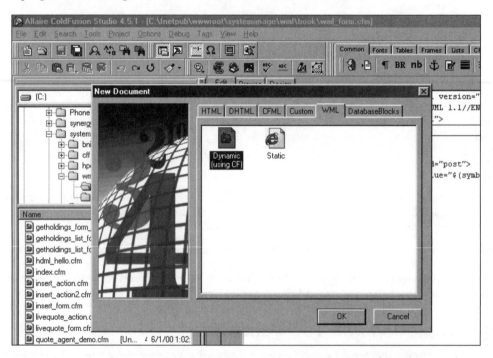

By choosing one of these wizards, you'll create a new untitled document with the basic, skeletal tags needed for creating a WML page. The difference between the two is that the "dynamic" page will place the CFCONTENT tag at the top of the page, while the "static" one will not.

A word of caution here, however: the WML-oriented new page wizards in Studio create a page using the Phone.com DTD. You can modify this by modifying the file from which it's created, which is in your Studio installation directory (typically Program Files/Allaire/ColdFusion Studio 4.5/Wizards/WML). You can even use Studio to edit the file.

There is another reason you may want to tweak the new page wizard. You may remember we mentioned that some WML browsers and gateways complain if there are carriage returns before the initial <?xml> tag. Unfortunately, Studio's "dynamic" new page wizard creates a page not only with the <?xml> tag on its own line but with a blank line between that and the preceding CFCONTENT line. If your testing shows it best to put the CFCONTENT on the same line as the initial <?xml> tag, you can use the approach mentioned above to correct the Studio wizard file(s).

Techniques, Tricks and Traps in ColdFusion/WAP Development

Let's get down to brass tacks and talk about some of the real challenging issues that may rear their ugly heads in your first forays into WAP programming in ColdFusion. If you're ready to start programming, you can just go to work with the things we've described so far. You'll have a great head start given that there is no documentation in the Allaire manuals on WML development, especially the specifics of doing it with ColdFusion. The rest of this book gives you a great resource for working with WML in general.

But once you begin coding WML applications, you learn that there's really a lot more to doing WML programming than just knowing WML and ColdFusion tags. As we saw in the last section, because ColdFusion was originally designed for the development of "traditional" web applications, some Studio features may not work as you would expect.

The same is true with respect to some ColdFusion programming features. You'll inevitably trip over them, and you can get around most of these problems with the right solutions. They're just not always obvious, so you need to know what to look out for. Some may feel that this section reads like a reference. If you prefer, you can use it that way. If you want to avoid the problems up front, read on.

The topics include:

- ❑ Error handling
- ❑ ColdFusion environment configuration
- ❑ Browser detection and redirection
- ❑ Form processing

We also conclude with a handful of miscellaneous concerns that don't fit into any category but are just as important (potential problems using <CFABORT>, processing URL parameters, and more).

Along the way, we include solutions to a handful of potential errors that will prevent your code from working, even if the code seems correct.

Error Handling

Let's start with the first big challenge – viewing errors themselves. Here's one rule that you must always remember:

> **ColdFusion error messages are *not* WML-compliant by default.**

In your first attempts to use ColdFusion-driven WML templates, one major challenge is simply being able to discern the cause of the error. When your code has an error in the ColdFusion code itself, ColdFusion will indeed generate an error message that is sent to the browser for display. Sadly, ColdFusion formats the message in HTML. That's always been fine (indeed, useful), until WML development came along. The problem is that a WML browser will choke on an HTML error message as being malformed WML.

Not only can you not see the error that is causing a problem – it might instead appear that the problem is with your code coming to the browser, or with the browser or network.

The problem is exacerbated by the fact that most WML browsers don't give you much assistance in the way of showing you what has caused an error. Some try, but most leave a lot to be desired. We'll most likely have to wait for a new generation of WAP browsers before we see a solution to that particular problem – but in the mean time, how do we manage?

Trapping and Reporting Errors with CFERROR

There is a way to make most ColdFusion template errors become more usefully reported to you and your users. You can change some (but only some) of the ColdFusion errors that arise to be viewable in WML, so that you can see them in the browser, using a feature of the <CFERROR> tag that is new in version 4.5 of ColdFusion.

First let me explain the overall use of the feature, which has been around in previous versions.

<CFERROR> has always been available to allow you to direct ColdFusion to send your users to a different – customized – error display page when an error occurred. Again, the default is to just show a plain error to the user, but <CFERROR>, when used, allowed you to modify the error display page to use your site's background colors and images, and even offer contact information for your help desk or support staff.

Unfortunately, prior to 4.5 this custom error page did *not* allow you to do any ColdFusion processing. It offered a pre-defined set of error information variables indicating the error detail, time, browser address, and so on which you could show to the user. But you couldn't do much else on the page: you couldn't use <CFMAIL> to send the message to your administrator; you couldn't use <CFQUERY> to log the error.

Worse for WML developers, there is no way with this approach to have the error page send the user a WML formatted message. Even though you can control what's sent to the user, it's still sent as HTML by default, and there's currently no way to change that. And since you can't put the <CFCONTENT> (or any other CF) tag on the page, you can't override that default. Things would seem hopeless.

In ColdFusion 4.5, however, Allaire has extended <CFERROR> with a new TYPE="exception" option. When there is an execution error, this feature can direct the user to a page with the full power and capability of ColdFusion. As such, a WML error page with the CFCONTENT tag would be a good thing to create.

Here is an example of a custom WML error page that could work in version 4.5:

```
<CFCONTENT TYPE="text/vnd.wap.wml"><?xml version="1.0"?>
<!DOCTYPE wml PUBLIC "-//WAPFORUM//DTD WML 1.1//EN"
"http://www.wapforum.org/DTD/wml_1.1.xml">

<wml>
<card>
```

```
    <CFOUTPUT>
        <p><b>An error has occurred in this application. Please share this
diagnostic information with the system administrator<CFIF cferror.mailto is not
"">  at #cferror.mailto#</CFIF>.</b></p>
        <p><b>Error Text:</b> #xmlformat(cferror.diagnostics)#</p>
        <p><b>DateTime:</b> #cferror.datetime#</p>
        <p>
            <b>Error Template:</b>
            <CFIF cferror.Template is "">
                (unavailable)
            <CFELSE>
                #cferror.Template#
            </CFIF>
        </p>
        <p>
            <b>Referrer: </b>
            <CFIF cferror.httppreferer is "">
                (unavailable)
            <CFELSE>
                #cferror.httppreferer#
            </CFIF>
        </p>
        <p>
            <b>Query String:</b>
            <CFIF cferror.querystring is "">
                (unavailable)
            <CFELSE>
                #cferror.querystring#
            </CFIF>
        </p>
        <p>
            <b>Browser: </b>
            <CFIF cferror.browser is "">
                (unavailable)
            <CFELSE>
                #cferror.browser#
            </CFIF>
        </p>
    </CFOUTPUT>
</card>
</wml>
```

Now, this is not perfect. The <CFERROR TYPE="execution"> tag doesn't catch *every* error occurring in ColdFusion (it doesn't catch errors due to CF compilation, or "file not found" errors, to name just a couple).

Also, the detail of the error message itself, available in the variable CFERROR.DIAGNOSTICS, is itself formatted as HTML. The best we can do is use the XMLFORMAT function (or the HTMLEDITFORMAT function prior to 4.5) to cause the HTML to be rendered appropriately, such as with > and < tags. Using either function is a kludge, since some WML browsers still may not support all the code that may be sent, but it's the best we can do.

Finally, another thing to consider is that if you don't limit what's sent to the browser in the error message displayed, it could send so much information to the browser as to choke it.

Still, doing something so that most errors are properly formatted is better than doing nothing and having none of them properly formatted.

And, of course, this error handling solution won't help if the problem isn't a ColdFusion error but instead a problem of badly formatted WML. In that case, the browser will reject it as well. How to tell the difference? It does get thorny. Just learn how to use all available error diagnostic tools, and test, test, test.

The way to use the error page shown above is to create it as a file called (for example) wml_error.cfm, saving it in your directory of WML files. This is one reason why it's a good idea to keep all your WML files separately in one directory – we don't want this page to be used when HTML files get an error. (We'll see shortly how to set up browser detection to direct pages appropriately)

To call upon this newly created error page, we'd want to direct our templates to execute the following tag at their initiation:

```
<CFERROR TYPE="exception" TEMPLATE="wml_error.cfm" >
```

This would cause any exception errors to direct the browser to our newfangled wml_error.cfm file, which would show a nice (well, acceptable) WML formatted error message. Notice that we said that we need this command executed for every page. Before you start putting that statement in each file, you should know about an available solution: the application.cfm file. Let's have a quick look at that now.

Using the application.cfm File

The application.cfm file is another special file (and the name is indeed specific). If this file exists in a directory, then any pages in that directory will first execute the code in that file before executing themselves. This is a useful and powerful way to cause some command to take effect for all files, without having to put the command itself into every file.

This is just what we want for our <CFERROR> command. If you create an application.cfm file in your WML directory with the following code fragment, things will be improved:

```
<!--- Setup to test the version of ColdFusion server currently running. --->
<CFSET version= ListGetAt(Server.ColdFusion.ProductVersion,1) & "." &
ListGetAt(Server.ColdFusion.ProductVersion,2)>

<!---
Turn on use of the wml_error.cfm with new CFERROR TYPE="exception"
Before 4.5, the CFERROR TYPE="Exception" was not allowed, and won't compile.
The trick below gets it to work indirectly (if >= 4.5), while still allowing this
code to be used in a 4.0 server--->
<CFIF version GE 4.5>
    <CFSET type="exception">
    <CFERROR TYPE="#type#" TEMPLATE="wml_error.cfm" >
</CFIF>

<!--- More tags will be offered in a later figure --->
```

There's actually more going on here than just the use of the <CFERROR> tag, as we have to deal with the fact that this code may be run in both 4.5 or in earlier versions.

ColdFusion / WML Environment Configuration

The error-handling feature above is one example of code that should be made a part of all ColdFusion-generated WML programs. If you leave things at their default configuration, it can wreak havoc. There are a few other configuration issues that could cause trouble.

Server-Side Debugging

Server-side debugging information (turned on in the administrator) is used by experienced ColdFusion developers to show all manner of information about the status of the execution of a page. This isn't usually something you let end-users see, but as a developer it can be very valuable. You can see variables passed to the page (for example, form, url, cookie, and CGI variables), queries executed on the page, and more. As with the case of error handling, however, there is another important fact to remember:

> **Server-side debugging information is not WML-compliant**

Unfortunately, Allaire sends the debugging information in HTML format, which will cause errors on the WML browser. Fortunately, there is a solution that will prevent this error. Of course, one solution would be to turn off debugging in the administrator (see the Allaire manuals for how to do that), but if your site serves HTML pages as well, this may be an unacceptable solution.

A better approach is to handle the problem on a program-by-program basis, since there is a way to disable debugging in a given CF program. As a developer, you won't be able to see the debugging info, but at least you won't cause errors in the browser when you view the page. The tag to use is:

```
<CFSETTING SHOWDEBUGOUTPUT="no">
```

When doing WML development, you'd really want to issue this tag on all CF-generated WML pages (again, it's best placed in the application.cfm file). As this particular attribute of <CFSETTING> came out in Release 4.0, it will cause an error if used in the application.cfm file on a server running an earlier version of ColdFusion. If so, just remove it. You'll have to then turn off debugging in the administrator in order to avoid every page failing in the WML browser.

Using <CFCONTENT>

As we saw at the start of the chapter, the <CFCONTENT> tag is key to WML programming, as it's this tag that allows us to set the correct MIME type. Perhaps the greatest indignity after reading this far is that you may try even the simplest example of a ColdFusion template doing WML processing only to have it fail through no fault of your own. There are two instances when the <CFCONTENT> tag itself cannot be used.

One is a problem that you simply can't get around if you're using the free, limited functionality version of ColdFusion Server, called ColdFusion Express:

> **ColdFusion Express does not support the <CFCONTENT> tag.**

This is a real shame, as the developers who would like to experiment with ColdFusion and WAP programming are therefore precluded from trying it using this version.

The second problem can occur even in environments with a full-featured ColdFusion Server. The ColdFusion administrator may have chosen to restrict access to the <CFCONTENT> command:

> **The CFCONTENT tag can be disabled by the CF administrator**

As a security precaution, Allaire has enabled ColdFusion administrators to selectively disable any of a handful of tags that might be used in an inappropriate way, potentially violating security on the server. <CFCONTENT>, sadly, is one of those tags (only because it has an available FILE attribute that can be used for entirely unrelated purposes to its use described in this chapter).

Many CF administrators choose to follow the general recommendation to lock down all the tags that can be restricted, and WML developers will suffer as a result.

What makes this error even more pernicious is that it will also cause the wml_error.cfm template (that we saw earlier) to fail, since it starts with a <CFCONTENT> tag. So you may be really hard-pressed to discover what's causing the problem if your administrator has disabled the tag.

At least in the UP.Simulator, you can see the actual code (and error message) being sent to the browser. The error will be formatted in HTML, so you have to wade through the diagnostic tool. If you could display it in HTML, it would show the following:

```
Error Diagnostic Information
The CFContent tag is disabled.
The administrator has chosen to disable this functionality on this server unless
executed from a specified directory.
```

There would seem to be no hope short of getting the administrator to make sure that <CFCONTENT> is turned on. However, if you look again at the last sentence in the above error message, you can see that there could be another solution. What it's saying it that (as of Release 4.5) the disabling of the restricted tags is lifted if the code executing the tag is in a directory specified by the ColdFusion administrator as being allowed to execute these restricted tags. (See the bottom of the page offered under the "Basic Security" link in the administrator.)

We may be able to take advantage of this new feature on servers that have otherwise restricted the <CFCONTENT> tag.

By default, the directory that is allowed to execute such templates using such otherwise restricted tags is the directory where the administrator files themselves are stored. Assuming the administrator code's directory has not been moved for security reasons, and your web server's root is C:\INETPUB\WWWROOT\, then the directory allowing such templates is C:\INETPUB\WWWROOT\CFIDE\Administrator.

This directory is typically (and should be) secured so as to be accessible only by someone with administrator privileges (more on that in a moment). If we can work with such a person to place a file in that directory, we can work around the restriction of <CFCONTENT> (for our particular needs only). This is not a security hack, it's an intentional use of a new feature designed specifically for this sort of problem.

What we'd want to do is place a file in that location. The file, which we'll call do_cfcontent.cfm, would need only one line of code, our needed <CFCONTENT> tag:

```
<CFCONTENT TYPE="text/vnd.wap.wml">
```

We can then call upon that code from any CF template on our server using a special tag:

```
<CFINCLUDE TEMPLATE="\CFIDE\Administrator\DO_CFCONTENT.CFM">
```

The <CFINCLUDE> tag pulls the code in from the named file in the named directory. Because the CF administrator by default has what's known as a "mapping" pointing to the web server's root, the tag finds the named file in the named directory. (Some may wonder if we could or should execute the template using the <CFMODULE> tag instead, but it's not necessary to do so.)

Now wherever we would have used <CFCONTENT>, we simply use the <CFINCLUDE> command instead, as in:

```
<CFINCLUDE TEMPLATE="\CFIDE\Administrator\DO_CFCONTENT.CFM"><?xml version="1.0"?>
<!DOCTYPE wml PUBLIC "-//WAPFORUM//DTD WML 1.1//EN"
"http://www.wapforum.org/DTD/wml_1.1.xml">

<wml>
<!--- rest of template would follow --->
```

As mentioned previously, this directory where the administrator allows unsecured access to tags to be executed should definitely be locked down and protected to keep people from putting just these sorts of files there without authorization. Allaire security documents do recommend that the administrator directory should be locked down.

If the directory is not locked down, see to it that this is done straight away. If it is locked down, and you're not authorized to write to it, simply explain your need to the administrator and show him/her the code that will be executed. They should have no problem placing it there for you, and you'll have solved this thorny problem.

Adding These Solutions in a Directory with HTML Files

While we're on the subject of using <CFCONTENT>, or the <CFINCLUDE> approach described above when it's needed, you may be able to make your coding just a little bit easier if you put the <CFCONTENT> tag into the application.cfm file. This way, it will be present on all CF-generated WML pages, and if there is ever a need to change it, you can change it in just one place.

One trap that you need to be aware of, if you're using <CFCONTENT> in application.cfm, is that if you have any CF templates intended to generate HTML output in the same directory, then they will no longer be viewable in your HTML browser. The <CFCONTENT> tag in the application.cfm will be sending the wrong MIME type. The HTML browser will prompt you to either save or execute the pages, since it doesn't know what to do with a file with a WML MIME type.

There is a similar problem that occurs even if you don't set <CFCONTENT> in your application.cfm. If you've used the <CFERROR> solution mentioned above, any pages located in that directory that are intended to be run in an HTML browser will—if they have an error—try to use this <CFERROR> directive. Since *that* error-processing file uses the <CFCONTENT> tag to send error output in WML, the HTML browser will again not know what to do with it.

One solution is:

> **Put CF/WML files in a directory separate from any with CF/HTML files**

Another possibility is to make the <CFERROR> (and even the application.cfm) detect what sort of browser is requesting the page, and then execute tags appropriate to each type of browser (HTML versus WML). We'll see how to do that shortly.

Controlling application.cfm Output

Another risk of using application.cfm, especially adding the tags above to an existing one used to serve HTML files, is that you need to be sure that such a file doesn't send any non-WML output to the browser.

One way to ensure this is to use a <CFSETTING> option called ENABLECFOUTPUTONLY="yes". This tag has existed for some time to ensure that pages didn't send needless amounts of white space and carriage returns to the server, where ColdFusion tags had existed on the page before rendering it for sending to the browser. We can take advantage of it to avoid the very problem above. You'd want to turn the option on at the start of the application.cfm, so that no text from that file is sent to the browser, and turn it off at the end, so that any text created by subsequent pages is indeed sent to the browser.

Creating An Optimal WAP Development Configuration

Given everything we've covered so far, it may be worth examining an optimal development configuration for doing WML coding in ColdFusion, including an expanded application.cfm file. The recommendations are:

❑ Create and serve CF-generated WML files from their own directory.

❑ In that directory have an application.cfm file that prevents the file itself from inadvertently sending any non-WML text to the browser, sets up the WML error handling, turns off server-side debugging, and perhaps sets the <CFCONTENT> tag on for every page.

❑ If you're working in an environment where <CFCONTENT> is disabled, create and use the do_cfcontent.cfm file described above.

Here is an example of a standard application.cfm file that you could use:

```
<CFSETTING ENABLECFOUTPUTONLY="Yes">
<!--- the line above prevents this file from sending any code to the browser until
the end. I have placed the comment after it to prevent even a needless carriage
return being sent to the browser--->


<!--- You can choose to set the CFCONTENT here, saving the need to do it in each
template. If you do so, be sure to remove it from the templates under this file's
control. We've placed it at the top so that it might affect any errors arising on
this page not caught by the CFERROR later.

<CFCONTENT TYPE="text/vnd.wap.wml">

If you want to use the tag here, move it out from within this comment. If you are
forced to use the DO_CFCONTENT approach, move this line instead:

<CFINCLUDE TEMPLATE="\CFIDE\Administrator\DO_CFCONTENT.CFM">

The path may change in your environment. It should be wherever you placed the
do_cfcontent.cfm file in the "unsecured tags directory".
--->

<!--- following tag needed only if session or application variables will be used -
-->
<CFAPPLICATION NAME="wml_demo" SESSIONMANAGEMENT="Yes"
SESSIONTIMEOUT="#CreateTimeSpan(0,0,20,0)#">
```

```
<!--- Setup to test the version of ColdFusion server currently running. --->
<CFSET version = ListGetAt(Server.ColdFusion.ProductVersion,1) & "." &
ListGetAt(Server.ColdFusion.ProductVersion,2)>

<!---
Turn on use of the wml_error.cfm with new CFERROR TYPE="exception"

Before 4.5, the CFERROR TYPE="Exception" option was not allowed. The tags and
attribute existed, but the options did not. We can't even list the option if
before 4.5, as the compiler will generate an error. But we can play a trick to get
it to work if at least version 4.5, while still allowing this code to compile
successfully in a 4.0 server
--->

<CFIF version GE 4.5>
   <CFSET TYPE="exception">
   <CFERROR TYPE="#type#" TEMPLATE="wml_error.cfm" >
</CFIF>

<!--- Use CFSETTING to turn off ColdFusion server-side debugging, if turned on,
since it, too, is HTML that will choke a WML browser.

Before 4.0, the CFSETTING SHOWDEBUGOUTPUT attribute was not allowed, but there's
no way to trick the server with this one since you can't use variables for either
tags or their attributes. If you're running a release older than 4.0, simply
remove the following line
--->

<CFSETTING SHOWDEBUGOUTPUT="no">

<!--- restore the setting that prevented this file sending any text to the
browser.  Must be done or subsequent pages will send no output to the browser
unless it's enclosed in CFOUTPUT. Generally not desirable
--->

<CFSETTING ENABLECFOUTPUTONLY="no">
```

Browser Detection and Redirection

A common situation you'll find yourself in is when you need to create a site that serves *both* WML and HTML clients. The challenge is to detect the type of browser that is making a request, and serve up content appropriate for it. In this section, we describe techniques regarding browser detection and redirection.

Detecting the Browser Requesting the Page

Fortunately, browser detection is quite easy with ColdFusion. We mentioned previously that ColdFusion provides access to several CGI variables that indicate information provided by the browser to the server. And one of the things the browser reports is the file MIME types it's capable of accepting. This is reported in the variable CGI.http_accept.

Some people recommend using the CGI variable http_user_agent instead, which reports the browser type. If you could know what sort of browser types are most common to your users, you could try to trap that and send WML browsers to a WML page and HTML browsers to an HTML page. The problem is that there are so many browsers out there, of both types, and each reports a different name in the user_agent variable! So, this is really not the best approach.

Instead, it would be more effective to use the variable CGI.http_accept. In HTML browsers, it generally looks like this:

```
HTTP_ACCEPT=image/gif, image/x-xbitmap, image/jpeg, image/pjpeg,
application/vnd.ms-excel, application/msword, application/vnd.ms-powerpoint, */*
```

In WML browsers, it looks like this:

```
text/vnd.wap.wml, text/vnd.wap.wmlscript, application/vnd.wap.wmlc,
application/vnd.wap.wmlscriptc, image/vnd.wap.wbmp
```

While they may appear to be very similar, there is at least one difference: the value in WML browsers includes the very MIME type we've been referring to all along: text/vnd.wap.wml. Fortunately, it's quite easy to test whether this variable contains that string. The test uses the ColdFusion contains evaluation operator, and is specified as:

```
<CFIF CGI.http_accept CONTAINS "text/vnd.wap.wml">
   <!--- do something --->
</CFIF>
```

Now we just need to decide what to do when we detect the user is coming from a WML browser.

The Risk of Creating All-in-One HTML/WML Pages

It's tempting to want to serve both HTML and WML users in a given CFM page, testing the kind of browser and sending either HTML or WML as needed on that page. If you have a site that's already built for HTML and you just want to convert it to WML processing, you might be especially tempted to do this. However, this could be challenging on a number of fronts. Not only would the programs become more complex, it's also possible that the templates you'd create for WML display will be quite different in other ways from their HTML counterparts, in terms of the kind of processing you'd do, how many records you can show to the user (and how you'd handle that), and many other possible issues. (See Chapter 7 for more details.)

Instead, it's usually better simply to redirect WML visitors right from the front of your site to the WML directory recommended above and its pages designed just for them, as described next.

Redirection using <CFLOCATION>

If you want to transfer control from one page to another, known as "redirection", the trick is to use the <CFLOCATION> tag. The syntax for this tag is <CFLOCATION URL="some_url">, where some_url can either be a complete URL (domain, path, and file) or any valid subset of that (with an important caveat when working with WML code).

Continuing with our detection code from above, if we want to direct users to a file called wml_index.cfm, we could use the following code:

```
<CFIF CGI.http_accept CONTAINS "text/vnd.wap.wml">
   <CFLOCATION URL="/wml/wml_index.cfm">
  </CFIF>
```

This code looks for the file `wml_index.cfm` in a directory called `wml`, just below our web server root (`inetpub\wwwroot\wml`, for instance). One potential trap to be aware of when performing redirection with WML processing is when the file you're redirecting to is in the same directory or even on the same server. In that case it's typical to use just the file name in the URL of a `<CFLOCATION>`, leaving off both the domain and the path. But, the experience of many WML developers suggests that it's better to always use a directory path as well, even in that case. More to the point, it seems that it's best to use a path relative to the web server root. Notice how we have done that in the example above.

You could specify a full path, with the domain as well, but if the files are on the same server as each other, that's not only unnecessary but also takes up valuable space in the limited size available for WML code to be sent to the browser.

Mapping

Some ColdFusion developers may be under the impression that attempting to use the directory name in the URL of the `<CFLOCATION>` tag will require the creation of a "mapping" in the ColdFusion administrator for that WML directory. As we mentioned earlier under using the CFINCLUDE of `do_cfcontent.cfm`, there is already a mapping in the administrator for the web server root directory ("/"), created by default at the installation of ColdFusion server. So, as long as you specify the directory as a complete reference from the root directory, you don't need to create a mapping. If there's a chance that the directory may move, and you may have many `<CFLOCATION>` tags referring to it, then creating a mapping may be wise. See the Allaire documentation for more information.

Loss of Text

When `<CFLOCATION>` sends the user to the next page, it flushes any output that was being created prior to that tag. Although ColdFusion does *execute* any tags in the page prior to the `<CFLOCATION>` tag, it will not *send* any WML (or HTML, for that matter) to the browser. (Actually, there's one tag that will not execute as expected. If you use the `<CFCOOKIE>` tag to set a cookie – where cookies are supported – and then do a CFLOCATION on the same page, the cookie will not be set, for the same reasons. The tag actually creates an http header that never reaches the browser.)

Some developers are under the impression that `<CFLOCATION>` does some sort of client redirection, as can be done with a META "refresh" tag. It doesn't. It sends an HTTP header that causes the redirection. Any other data sent to the page prior to the `<CFLOCATION>` is simply never shown to the user, not even for a split second.

Browser History and Caching

Finally, there may be other ramifications of using `<CFLOCATION>` with respect to its impact on the WML browser's history list as well as caching of the page in the browser. These aren't facets unique to ColdFusion but crop up whenever we use redirection on WML decks.

Changing Your Front Door to Do Browser Detection

The approach described above for detecting the browser is useful, and you may consider using it on the front page of your web site so that users are directed to the appropriate page for their browser. One caveat is that the code we offered is ColdFusion code and therefore must be executed within a .cfm file. This is a dilemma if you currently have your front page being served as, say, `index.html`. You can't put this code in that page, unless you rename it as `index.cfm`.

That can be problematic in a number of ways. First, if a .cfm file has a little ColdFusion code at the top but then the rest is entirely HTML, there is a slight performance hit as the ColdFusion server does unnecessary work looking for any other ColdFusion code on the page. This may be only a minor concern, however, since ColdFusion actually caches the compilation of templates the first time they're executed (re-compiling and re-caching them whenever they're modified).

A bigger problem with renaming your index.htm to index.cfm occurs if anyone has bookmarked the page pointing at the index.htm name.

> *You may wonder if you could use JavaScript to do the detection and redirection instead. Sadly, WML browsers don't know how to interpret JavaScript, and WMLScript really can't be used to solve this problem.*

Form Processing

There are a few generic form processing problems that WML developers are encountering which you should keep in mind, such as form fields not being passed to action pages. There are also some specific tricks and traps for ColdFusion developers, as well, such as how to process "multiple-value" form fields and performing form validation.

When Form Fields Are Not Found

One generic form processing problem is that on some WAP gateways (and possibly some phones) form submission happens with a transcoding process where data arrives at the server encoded as: application/x-www-form-urlencoded;charset=UTF-8 – a format not currently recognized by ColdFusion. The upshot is that ColdFusion may not (again, on some browsers) convert the form fields to form prefixed variables, so you won't be able to access data posted from a WML deck back to the server. (The same thing is reported to be happening in ASP programs and Java servlets, as discussed in the bugs' page at Phone.com, at http://developer.phone.com/dev/ts/up/bugs.html.)

If this problem occurs, you can solve it by changing the form method to "get", and then the referring to the form fields not with the "form" prefix but with "url", as discussed earlier in this chapter. Some have even argued that you should just pass all form fields using method="get". The choice is yours.

Multiple Form Fields

We saw earlier that it's possible to allow the user to choose multiple options on a select control, by setting the multiple attribute of the <select> element to true. In this case, the choices are not passed as comma-separated values (as in HTML) but rather as semi-colon separated values. If you're not prepared for this, it can cause problems. However, before we look at the problems (and how to solve them in ColdFusion), let's see a multiple select control in action. We'll return to our earlier stock check application.

Assume the stock symbol field is a multiple select field. All we'd need to do is change the <select> element as shown below:

```
<CFQUERY datasource="portfolios" name="getstocks">
   SELECT distinct symbol FROM clientholdings
   WHERE ClientId=#session.clientid#
</CFQUERY>
```

```
<card>
   <CFIF getstocks.recordcount is 0>
      <p>You have no stocks to view</p>
   <CFELSE>
      <do type="accept">
         <go href="getholdings_action.cfm" method="post">
            <postfield name="symbol" value="$(symbol)"/>
         </go>
      </do>
      <p>
         Choose one of your stocks to view:
         <select name="symbol" multiple="true">
            <CFOUTPUT query="getstocks">
               <option value="#symbol#">#symbol#</option>
            </CFOUTPUT>
         </select>
      </p>
   </CFIF>
</card>
```

When you run code with this sort of select control, the display appears as in:

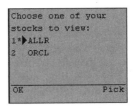

Most regular Internet users will know how to select multiple options by holding down the *CTRL* or *Shift* keys while clicking values. In wireless browsers it's generally more straightforward. Notice the Pick option listed for the right button.

In the case of HTML, where multiple results are returned as comma-separated values, developers can pass these directly to SQL statements that support comma-separated values, such as the SELECT ... WHERE ... IN () clause. Also, there are several useful ColdFusion "list" functions that work on such comma-separated lists.

But if a WML browser presents multiple values as a semi-colon separated list, that won't work, as usual. So how do we get around these problems? We'll look at three handy solutions in this section:

❑ Tell the list functions to work with any separator, such as the semi-colon

❑ Change the list to be comma-separated instead of semi-colon-separated before processing it in SQL

There is one final problem, however – string data that is passed to SQL also needs quotes around *each* value. We can get around this using a relatively new and little known function, which solves that very problem – the ListQualify() function.

These three techniques are discussed in the next three sections.

Using ColdFusion List Functions

ColdFusion provides a number of useful list processing functions for dealing with any sort of multi-valued list of values. These include functions to find things within the list, count items in the list, return elements from the list, add things to the list, sort the list, and more. While the default list separator is the comma, nearly all those list functions provide an option to select a *different* list separator, so you can also work with a semi-colon separated list of values, as is this case with a multi-valued WML form control.

Converting to Comma Separated List

We mentioned previously that in order to pass multiple values to a SQL SELECT statement using the IN clause, we need it to be a comma separated list of values. If a WML browser sends multiple values as semi-colon separated list, we can't use it. Or so it would seem. Fortunately, ColdFusion provides us with a function, ListChangeDelims(), which can convert a list from having one separator into another list separated with any other string. So, to convert our list from semi-colons to commas, we could use:

```
<CFSET SymbolList = ListChangeDelims(form.symbol,",",";")>
```

This creates a new list, which we've called SymbolList in this example, which is now a legal string to pass to the SQL statement, as in:

```
<CFQUERY datasource="portfolios" name="getstocks">
    SELECT * FROM clientholdings
    WHERE Symbol IN (#SymbolList#)
</CFQUERY>
```

String Lists, SQL, and Adding Quotes

If the values being passed from our form are numeric values, then the technique described above is all we need. But, if the values are strings, we have yet another problem.

Consider again the stock list example offered above. When submitted, it passes the stock symbols themselves (string values) as the values to be looked up on the action page. If we want to use these in a SQL IN clause, there is a problem.

If the user selects multiple values (say, ALLR and ORCL), they arrive as ALLR;ORCL. We can convert this to comma-separated values easily enough using the ListChangeDelims() function, then we'd end up with a result like this: ALLR,ORCL

Unfortunately, we can't pass this list, as is, to a SQL SELECT statement with an IN clause, for example:

```
SELECT * FROM ClientHoldings
WHERE ClientId=#session.clientid#
AND Symbol IN ('#SymbolList#')
```

The problem is that the values need to be quoted. While we do have quotes around the variable holding the list to be used for the search, we'll get a failure (or invalid result) because we'd be trying to do a search for any records with Symbol having literally the value 'ALLR,ORCL'. Instead, we need a comma-separated list of values with quotes around each string, as in:

```
'ALLR','ORCL'
```

Again, ColdFusion's list functions come to the rescue – with ListQualify(). New in 4.01 of ColdFusion Server, it can convert the list to have quotes (or whatever we choose) around each value:

```
<CFSET SymbolList = ListQualify(SymbolList,"'",",","all")>
```

The function takes 4 parameters:

❑ The list to be converted

❑ The "qualifier" that we want to use to surround each value, which in our case is the single quote (but surrounded with double quotes as function parameters usually are)

❑ The "delimiter" that currently separates the items in the list (a comma, in our case, again enclosed in quotes)

❑ The "all" parameter, which says to convert all the items in the list

Now the resulting SymbolList will look like this:

```
'ALLR','ORCL'
```

which is just what the SELECT ... IN clause needs.

But, sadly, we're still not done. There is actually a little problem of ColdFusion trying to help us in a way we don't need. Assume we pass the new SymbolList variable to the SELECT statement like this:

```
SELECT * FROM ClientHoldings
WHERE ClientId=#session.clientid#
AND Symbol IN (#SymbolList#)
```

There is an unexpected conversion that ColdFusion does on the string before passing it to the database. It actually converts our single quotes to a pair of double quotes. This is clearly intended to solve some unrelated problem, but it's a behavior, which produces an unintended result in this example. The statement as sent to SQL ends up looking like:

```
SELECT * FROM ClientHoldings
WHERE ClientId=#session.clientid#
AND Symbol IN (''ALLR'',''ORCL'')
```

That's not what we want either (escaped quotes, that is, two pairs of single quotes around each value). Fortunately, there is still another function that solves our problem – preservesinglequotes(). It prevents ColdFusion from "escaping" those single quotes. So our SELECT statement ends up as:

```
SELECT * FROM ClientHoldings
WHERE ClientId=#session.clientid#
AND Symbol IN (#preservesinglequotes(SymbolList)#)
```

Phew! Again, none of this would be a problem if we were passing multiple numeric values. This certainly argues for thinking twice about using strings as the values in a multiple SELECT list.

Field Validation

Users familiar with ColdFusion's support of "hidden field validation" will find yet another sore spot when it comes to WAP development. We can't use this approach for validating WML forms because the error page that ColdFusion creates is pure HTML. There's no way to change that, even by using <CFERROR type="validation"> to override the default validation error display. (This is a variation of the <CFERROR> tag we described earlier in the chapter.) Such an error page cannot use the <CFCONTENT> (or any other CF tag), so we can't cause CF to send any validation errors as a WML MIME type.

Now, we could *almost* solve the problem by using <CFCONTENT> in the application.cfm (as we mentioned earlier). But there's yet another problem – even if we setup such an error page to refer to the validation message variable available on this page (Error.InvalidFields), that variable has HTML embedded in it. (The message lines are formed as an HTML list, with <UL> and <LI> tags, which are not valid WML and therefore choke the browser.)

And we can't even use ColdFusion functions to strip those out because, again, no ColdFusion tags or functions are allowed on these limited, old style templates as pointed to by `<CFERROR TYPE="Request">` and `<CFERROR TYPE="Validation">`. There's also no way to direct these hidden field validation error messages to the new-style `<CFERROR TYPE="exception">` page. That form of `<CFERROR>` simply doesn't trap validation errors.

> **ColdFusion's hidden field validation doesn't work with WML decks: don't use it.**

Along the same lines, another form processing feature that experienced ColdFusion developers may try, but won't work with WML browsing, is `<CFFORM>`. This tag can create JavaScript validation code, as well as optionally send some Java applets to a form to provide some alternative interface features. Keeping in mind that WML doesn't support either JavaScript or Java, using `<CFFORM>` is inappropriate.

> **Don't use `<CFFORM>` in WAP development.**

Miscellaneous Concerns

The rest of these tricks and traps are just various ones to be aware of, especially for experienced ColdFusion developers coming into WML.

Using `<CFABORT>`

If you use a `<CFABORT>` tag to terminate the execution of a ColdFusion page, such as when a logical error has been detected and you want to stop processing the page, be careful that you don't leave the page being sent to the browser with incomplete WML. Consider the following page fragment, which we might use as a test on our example form action page (from above) to see if the user's input of the stock symbol form field was blank:

```
<wml>
<card>
   <CFIF form.symbol is "">
       <p>You must enter a stock symbol</p>
       <CFABORT>
   </CFIF>
<!--- code to be executed if they give us a symbol would follow --->
</card>
</wml>
```

The theory is that we don't want to execute the code following the test if the test fails. Fair enough, but the problem is we end up sending to the browser an incomplete WML page. In this example, if the test failed we'd end sending to the browser a page comprised of:

```
<wml>
<card>
<p>You must enter a stock symbol</p>
```

Notice that there are no closing `</card>` or `</wml>` elements. When `<CFABORT>` is executed, the template stops dead in its tracks. It doesn't just stop doing ColdFusion tags. So the closing elements, which are indeed available at the bottom of the template, are simply never sent to the browser.

The solution is to include whatever WML elements would be needed to close the page in a syntactically correct and complete way just before any <CFABORT> tag. For example, the fragment above would be more effectively written as:

```
<wml>
<card>
    <CFIF form.symbol is "">
        <p>You must enter a stock symbol</p>
        </card>
        </wml>
        <CFABORT>
    </CFIF>
<!--- code to be executed if they give us a symbol would follow --->
</card>
</wml>
```

While it's true that this gives the impression, on first viewing, that the closing </card> and </wml> elements are offered twice, the truth is that unless the IF condition is true, the code within it will not be executed or sent to the browser.

This is a problem that actually plagues many ColdFusion/HTML pages. However, even experienced developers don't pay much attention to it because HTML browsers are more forgiving about leaving a page with incomplete tag pairs.

Using Cookies

Cookies are a useful feature, and between ColdFusion's tag for creating them, <CFCOOKIE>, and the easy way to refer to them (the cookie prefix), it's a great way to store and track information about the client. Unfortunately, many WML browsers and gateways don't support cookies.

> **If you need to support a wide range of browsers, it's best to avoid cookies.**

Creating Multiple URL Variables with &: Must Use &

Another problem that might rear its ugly head, if you're not prepared, is that if you intend to pass multiple field=value pairs on a URL, you must separate them with the special character & (the trailing semi-colon is important), rather than & as in HTML. This is a WML issue, not a ColdFusion one, and it may not be true in all browsers. But if the problem arises, you should be aware of it.

Suppose we create a <go> element that passes data to a ColdFusion page:

```
<go href="wml_display.cfm?fname=Joe&Lname=Smith">
```

(This is presuming a method of GET, the default if none is specified.)

This could generate an error in the browser when the page is loaded (not when the action specified by the <go> tag is performed, but when the page showing this code is itself loaded in the browser). The solution (again not a ColdFusion one) is to use the special character & to represent the ampersand character legally:

```
<go href="wml_display.cfm?fname=Joe&amp;lname=Smith">
```

This will cause the browser to render the ampersand properly when the code is sent to the browser. Therefore, when the result is passed to the next page (wml_display.cfm in this example), it will arrive properly as a normal pair of URL variables.

Linking to Card ID's within CFOUTPUT

As we learned way back in Chapter 4, there is a form of the <go> element that can be used to hyperlink to a card by referring to that card's id value. Recall that this form of the href attribute uses # signs:

```
<go href="#card2"/>
```

Unfortunately, if you happen to wrap <CFOUTPUT> tags around that element, the ColdFusion interpreter will throw an error thinking the # sign is the beginning of a ColdFusion variable. The solution is to escape the # signs; that is, repeat them. This way, the ColdFusion interpreter ignores them and knows you mean for the # sign to be sent to the browser. So, the example above might be coded as:

```
<CFOUTPUT>
...
<go href="##card2"/>
...
</CFOUTPUT>
```

When this is sent to the WML browser, the double # signs will revert back to a single # sign.

Using dollarformat()

A similar but reverse problem will arise if you try to send to the WML browser characters that it uses for its own purposes. For example, the dollar sign character. This is used by WML to refer to its own variables. So if you try to use ColdFusion's dollarformat() function, which formats a numeric value to have a leading dollar sign and embedded commas, you'll generate a WML browser error when the page is rendered on the browser.

In this case, you need a solution whereby the WML browser will ignore the special character and simply display it. And it again involves "escaping" the character, though this time it's for the WML browser to ignore. So you could code a line such as:

```
<CFOUTPUT>
...
$#dollarformat(1234)#
...
</CFOUTPUT>
```

Notice that we have placed the $ outside the reference to the dollarformat() function (and the # signs, which are needed so the function can be evaluated within the <CFOUTPUT> tag). The leads to $$1,234.00 being sent to the WML browser, which may look strange, but when it's rendered on the WML browser, it will display as expected, as $1,234.00.

Debugging

Studio contains an interactive debugger that can be used to step through the execution of ColdFusion code. Unfortunately, it's designed specifically to work with the "internal browser" feature of Studio (which is always a HTML browser) and therefore cannot be used to debug WML pages (since they cannot be executed by way of the internal browser).

While you can't use the interactive debugger, it is useful to consider that you can apply other debugging techniques to determine why a WML application is not working. For one thing, when you get errors, it may be useful to remove all but the most minimal code from the application. Sometimes you'll find that the problem isn't with the CF code you've entered but some other matter (such as failing to specify the `<wml>`, `<card>`, or `<p>` elements.)

You may also find it useful sometimes to run code through an HTML browser first, especially when it's being dynamically generated like we've been doing. Of course, you can't always do this since much of WML simply can't be represented with HTML equivalents. And you'd need to remove the three header tags (`<CFCONTENT>`, `<?xml>`, and `<!DOCTYPE>`) to keep the HTML browser from choking. But it can be very useful.

An example is when trying to debug query-driven tables, since HTML tables are very close to WML tables. You can remove the WML-specific attributes during the testing, and then add them back when things seem correct in the HTML browser. Or, you could leave the WML in and not bother trying to view the output in the browser. Just use your browser's View Source or equivalent command to look at the source code rendered. At least then, you could see what's been generated for you by ColdFusion.

Summary

In this chapter, we've seen that there's a lot of potential for creating WML applications with ColdFusion. It's a powerful environment, with even more features that we simply couldn't address. (After all, this is a book on WAP/WML programming, not ColdFusion programming).

We learned a bit about ColdFusion in general, for those new to the environment. Then we spent a good bit of time learning about the most basic types of processing we might do (forms, queries, reports, updates) and how to do that using WML generated by ColdFusion. Along the way, we offered lots of tips and solutions to commonly encountered problems.

We also covered the features of ColdFusion Studio that have been enhanced in version 4.5. You don't need to use Studio to do ColdFusion development (in fact, you don't even need to use version 4.5 of ColdFusion Server to generate WML pages). But the new Studio features (such as tag insight, tag help, tag editors, and more) can help make it much easier to enter WML (and CF and HTML) code.

Finally, we concluded with a substantial section on *Techniques, Tricks, and Traps*. We covered many different topics there including creating an optimal environment for error handling and dealing with various limitations that may be imposed by your ColdFusion environment configuration. We showed how to do browser detection as well as some vagaries of form processing, and a host of other miscellaneous issues.

> **Each of the features described in this chapter is also demonstrated in an associated set of annotated example programs. The starting point for executing these is `index.cfm`, which presents a scrollable list (to be run from a WML browser, of course) of each of the demonstration programs. These programs can be downloaded from the Wrox site and can be found in the `chapter11` folder. The example programs offer many comments, especially features were introduced that were beyond the scope of this chapter.**

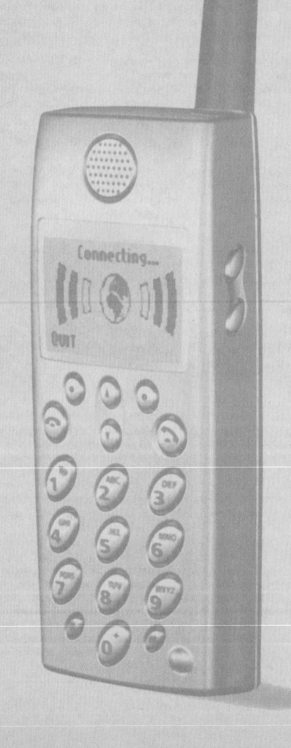

Part Four

Developing Advanced WAP Applications

One of the most frequently asked questions about WAP is, "What will be the killer app?" As you will have figured out by now, WAP is not the same as the Web, and the types of services that are popular over WAP are likely to be different. There is much expectation and excitement about the advantages that m-commerce may bring, but until we have seen it in action in the marketplace, it is hard to predict what will work and what won't. So, we won't be defining the definitive WAP application in this book – that will be left as an exercise for the reader! But, the fourth part of this book will focus on some advanced techniques that should help you on your way towards developing fully-fledged professional WAP services and m-commerce applications.

As we have seen time and again, there is a lot more to WAP than simply porting all your web content to another browser platform – we need to think carefully about the types of content and services that people will find useful over WAP. However, there will obviously be scenarios where you have the same data that you want to make available over web and WAP. We saw some examples of how this might be achieved in the last section. In business terms, though, you may not be ready (or have the time or money) to redesign your site around XML from the ground up, so Chapter 12 looks at some alternatives. It examines some existing tools that allow you to convert existing HTML content to WAP, and then presents a working example of such a tool, including the Java source code.

Chapters 13 and 14 examine how we can incorporate into WAP applications, e-mail and directory services respectively. You may, for example, want to be able to check your e-mail remotely from your WAP phone. By storing and maintaining your data centrally in a directory server, you make it easily accessible and updateable from a number of client devices, including WAP phones. We'll see how to do this with Netscape Directory Server in Chapter 14, along with an example illustrating the use of LDAP for authentication.

Finally, Chapter 15 discusses the subject of security, examining some of the basic concepts, and comparing the WAP security model with that of the Internet. We cover in detail some of the issues specific to WAP and wireless devices, and examine WTLS, Wireless Transaction Layer Security.

12

Converting Existing Web Sites to WAP

This chapter discusses the conversion of existing web content to WAP. More strictly, we mean the conversion of HTML to WML, HTML being the most common form of text content on the web. While some gateways do this automatically – notably that of Phone.com – they are quite brittle implementations as they attempt to be generic in an area that is far from predictable.

We will investigate this aspect later, but before we get into the technicalities, we examine the reasons why we might convert a site rather than develop from scratch, and what type of site is suitable for conversion. We'll take a look at what advantages and disadvantages conversion has compared to new development, and review some existing commercial conversion tools.

A simple Java HTML to WML converter is presented, based on Apache's Cocoon publishing framework, which can be used as the basis for a platform-independent tool, with suggestions for extensions and improvements.

To make best use of the example application in this chapter, you will need knowledge of the following:

- ❑ Java and servlets (see Chapter 10 for a brief introduction to servlets)
- ❑ Basic WML principles (Chapters 4 and 5)
- ❑ Basic HTML principles
- ❑ Basic XML principles (Chapter 9)
- ❑ Access to a servlet-enabled web server (refer to Appendix F for help)
- ❑ Access to a WAP client simulator for testing (Nokia or Phone.com toolkits, for example)

Why convert an existing site?

According to the www.inktomi.com press release, as of April 2000 there are an estimated 1 billion HTML pages/services available on the Web. In contrast, it is estimated that there are between 50,000 – 1,500,000 pages in WML (the latter figure is a somewhat optimistic figure from a search engine vendor boasting its capabilities). In a straw poll, using AltaVista, we obtained the following search results:

❑   Pages containing the word 'HTML'.   10,631,094

❑   Pages containing the word 'XML'.   604,240

❑   Pages containing the word 'WML'.   59,650

These two estimates of WML usage reflect the immaturity of the mobile Internet, not only in content, but also in the paucity of devices and open WAP gateways. Yet, as we have already seen, the predictions are that mobile access to the Internet will exceed that of fixed access within the next 3 years. How will the development world solve the problem of having to produce the same range and quality of mobile web sites as there are fixed sites, and yet produce them in a shorter time?

There are two possible scenarios for short-term WAP development in light of this:

❑   Only a limited subset of WAP sites will develop when compared with WAP's potential.

❑   WAP sites will proliferate quickly because they will not all be developed from scratch.

The first scenario is a distinct possibility, if only due to the fact that URLs and WAP gateway settings are awkward to enter on a WAP phone, and gateway owners (usually mobile operators) will naturally want to 'wall in' their WAP customers to increase revenue, although a work around may be over-the-air configuration. Customers may passively accept the limited variety of services offered by their particular operator. Mobile operators are also reluctant to be seen to support sites outside their 'walled garden' because they have no control over content and quality, and yet, the first place for complaint by a user is quite likely to be the mobile operator's support center.

The second scenario is where conversion tools come in. In order to satisfy the massive predicted growth in WAP phones, companies will use conversion tools, just to get their services out there first, or to pilot them to gauge interest. If this conversion is done well, companies will have an added bonus. As much of the work is done by the conversion utility, maintenance of output to multiple client types is reduced. The danger of this second scenario is that the content is not of guaranteed quality. Problems such as missing pages, or pages suitable for one type of WAP device but not another, may damage WAP acceptance in the first year or two.

Realistically, there will be a mix of both these scenarios over time. At the time of writing, there were very few operators offering access outside their 'walled garden', and the majority of WAP site access is to a small number of 'closed' services. However, as more 'open' services appear, and are publicized, the mobile operators will, one by one, open their gateways to give access outside of their own services, and many of these external sites will use converted HTML services. This will probably happen in the medium term, say, 6-12 months. In addition to public services, individual corporations are buying their own gateways for private access (intranet/extranet), and these will also be making use of conversion tools as a swift route to their existing backend data services.

Over the longer term, optimal design methods for multi-device access will prevail, such as the XML-to-WML / XHTML techniques as discussed in Chapter 9, and conversion of existing sites will become less attractive as pure XML/WML sites compete with them. In this future solution, backend data will be presented as XML, and possibly stored as XML too, which will then be converted to HTML, WML and any other flavor of markup language you care to name or invent. Because the XML data is in presentation-neutral format, the utilities to convert the XML will be the standard tools built into servers, operating systems and even clients, such as IE5's and Netscape 6's XML capabilities. Some sites are already moving this way, but it is not a decision to be taken lightly, since in place of a single HTML file, you will now need an XML file plus *n* XSL files – one per protocol, and possibly even one per type of client device. (Remember that even if you're dealing with just WAP content, you still need to think about the different implementations of WML provided by the different devices.) Such a design requires careful planning, but your overall effort will eventually be less, even if it doesn't feel like it in the first few months!

In addition to the relative speed of WAP development using a conversion tool, there are other advantages, related to the way conversion tools work. The tools can access an existing HTML site from anywhere, remotely, and thus allow development where:

❑ You don't know the details of the original web site design.

❑ You don't have direct access to the server site.

In the first case, this can be useful if a different company or developer did the development. In the second case, the site owner may not wish to give you direct access to their backend database, if they consider their APIs to be valuable property.

Example sites using conversion techniques are given at the end of this chapter.

How do converters work?

Simply put, converters work by extracting text from a source page, in our case an HTML page, and then reformatting that text into the target markup language, in this case, WML.

Here's a very simple example:

In the best traditions of n-tier design, the converter is performing the conversion of formatted data to pure data, so we, as the conversion author, can decide the format we wish to apply to it. The intermediate data can be manipulated without backend and front-end processes affecting that manipulation.

There are two possible routes here. We can either:

❑ Extract all possible content in the page such as title, welcome message, links, and so on.

❑ Extract specific parts of the page, say just the news headlines, or just the stock prices.

We have defined these two types of conversion as *fully automated* and *configurable* respectively.

In addition to converting text elements of the page, navigation from page to page needs to be taken into account, as does user input. In a good fully automated converter, both the links and input forms in the converted page will still be available to the user. For the configurable converter, the choice of what is presented is down to the developer, since a configurable converter needs to be told which parts of the page to convert. Finally, it is worth mentioning that content converters are also known as 'transcoders'.

427

What makes suitable content for conversion?

When deciding why we might consider converting an existing site rather than developing it from new, there was an implication that all sites could be candidates for conversion. This is patently untrue. However, there are still plenty of possible sites out there to consider for conversion rather than fresh development. So, how do we decide?

In general, the main feature that makes existing web sites a suitable target for conversion to WAP is that they provide **small amounts of timely text-based information**. Let's step back from this and briefly define what we mean by a good WAP service – one that **delivers the maximum pertinent information with the minimum user input**. 'Maximum pertinent information' means the site supplies the user only the information they are interested in, with an absolute minimum of padding. 'Minimum user input' means the less navigation and typing required to get at the desired information, the more likely the user is to use the service.

Using our definition of a good WAP service, let's now apply it to see how it can focus our decision when selecting conversion or fresh development for our new WAP site.

The questions we need to ask ourselves are:

❑ Can I extract from the HTML site, snippets of text that are suitable for display on approximately 4 or 5 lines of 15 characters, with a maximum of two or three screens of information?

❑ Can I navigate to each piece of text within four or less hyperlinks?

❑ Is the text changing often enough to make this site 'dynamic', or can I just afford to write the WML by hand and update it when required?

❑ If there is more than one piece of text information per page that I wish to extract, is each piece a repetition in terms of format?

An example of a site that might fit the bill here is one with automatically generated HTML pages, driven by some back-end database. Ideally the application would then access the data source directly. However, if time is of the essence, we can leave the web application to process the information, and then extract it from the resultant HTML. News items, weather, stock prices, sports results, music and video charts, prices, and price comparisons are all examples of small pieces of text which make suitable WAP content.

Having described what makes a suitable conversion site, you will find many types of sites are not suitable for conversion. Examples of these are graphical and audio-based sites – for example, weather images, navigation that uses image maps, color-coded data, and similar design techniques. Graphical content is fine as long as there is the text equivalent somewhere on the page too. Of course, if an image map leads to 6 pages of distinct text information, part of the conversion process can include replacing the 6 links with textual ones. Other sites to be avoided are those with reams of text content, especially if heavily formatted content; converter or no converter, WAP is not the medium for such sites yet. Resist!

What are the advantages?

The major advantages of conversion over building new sites from the ground up are:

❑ Speed to market
❑ Cost
❑ Independence from the original design or actual site

Speed to market and cost are both due to the fact that conversion of existing sites takes less programmer time than starting from scratch. Another advantage is that the user converting the site does not have to be a code guru – a web designer with reasonable understanding of markup languages can master a converter application. In the current market of significant demand for WAP developers, this could be quite an advantage.

Also, and possibly more significantly, the content extracted from the original page can be held in a format-independent manner, so formats other than WML can be applied to serve other client types. This is an area of great interest with the increase of non-PC devices on the Web. A converter can be written that delivers content to PCs, WAP phones, PDAs, Internet screen-phones, TV set-top boxes, and any other Internet device that appears along the way.

The target markup language doesn't have to be WML – XML and Compact HTML, HDML, and XHTML are also ideal targets, as is HTML itself, and any future formats. Of course; it would be a simple addition to generate 'reduced' HTML from HTML, in addition to WML, which may become an important area with the Microsoft dual WML/HTML browser imminent.

Another advantage is that the ability to create a WAP 'mirror' site means we don't need access to the backend data sources. Imagine approaching a company saying, "We want to give all your content to WAP users, you can have some of the advertising revenue." They don't have to lift a finger to get this revenue, while you raise the company's profile and their revenues. It also means the original hosting company is not compromising their security.

One final issue is that you will rapidly learn what makes a good WAP site, and which elements of your existing site are the real 'nuggets' of information. Assuming your conversion tool is XML-based, you will also have learnt XML without sacrificing the whole site to a new technology.

What are the disadvantages?

There are also several disadvantages that we must bear in mind, however. Possibly one of the most irritating is that if the original source page changes format (which the converter may depend upon to recognize the vital pieces of text to extract), the converter may fail to convert that page.

Therefore, it is important that you both:

- ❏ Ask the site owner/customer to inform you prior to any changes.
- ❏ Allow some small amount of time in your development effort for continued support of the converted pages.

There are two ways of looking at this – a nice revenue stream if you're charging a customer, or a pain if your customer is internal and expects the earth!

A small legal note on site conversion: it should be obvious that you cannot extract data from other sites without either prior permission or acknowledgement, since the copyright is not yours. There are various landmark cases related to this area, known as 'deep-linking'. The current situation is that it is legal to 'deep-link' – to avoid a site's original home page and go direct to the relevant data – as long as you do not pass the data off as your own, but there is no guarantee that this will be true in the future. If in doubt, consult a lawyer. Better still, get written permission to do so from the copyright owner.

Another potential problem, which might put you at a disadvantage to a competitor, is performance. There are two aspects here:

❑   The additional processing power required for converting content, rather than just generating and serving WML pages from a backend database. This may be only minor, but if you have 10,000 users hitting your site at once, this may well cause your server to overload, and you will find yourself buying additional hardware.

❑   The original HTML document may be significantly larger than the WML equivalent. A site built specifically for WML would avoid processing of data that will not be used.

Cost of development tools is another disadvantage. Although we present a simple converter here, the full commercial conversion development tools available can be prohibitively expensive, especially for characteristically small WAP development houses. Having convinced your boss of the need to buy a $50K conversion tool for your existing site, he may not be that open to the "Let's do it properly in XML, now" argument. Make sure he/she understands it's often not a permanent solution – just a year or so stop-gap.

Finally, another factor that we have not yet examined, is the fact that, aside from all these disadvantages, some sites are not even suitable for conversion. As a general rule, you should consider if the site in question provides information, or a service, that would be useful to mobile users, whether or not it already exists in HTML form. Given enough time, money, and resources, would it be worth creating this as a WAP application from the start? If the answer to this is "no", then you should not even consider trying to convert the site. Remember that whatever the similarities are, WAP is not the Web, and porting the entire content of Internet to WAP is neither desirable nor useful.

Methods of Converting Existing Sites

Several diverse vendors are already offering conversion tools to generate WML, and more. In this section, we will cover the most prevalent tools currently available, and identify their pros and cons. The tools are split into *fully automated* and *configurable* converters. Then we will move on to consider how you might create your own converter, depending on your needs.

Fully automated converters

Fully automated converters are 'dumb' in that they take no user configuration, and thus are extremely useful for converting *any* HTML page. There is no attempt to customize individual pages, every page is treated using the same built-in conversion rules, but this is not to say the rules themselves – or the tool – are really dumb. Rather the reverse – any tool that can get something readable onto a WAP phone without developer intervention definitely has its place!

There are inherent problems with fully automated converters, in that they have no control over the original content. They can only make their best attempt at extracting useful information, and if that doesn't produce a reasonable result, then the user will not have a satisfying experience. When all else fails, these can offer a good fall-back position: that is, where you can use original WAP content or a configurable converter you should do so, and for all other sites your user might want to visit, offer an automated converter as the 'sweeper'. However, any auto-converting tool should come with a 'health' warning to temper the user's expectations.

All the converters described, here, and in the *configurable converters* section, are dynamic converters. In other words they convert the original HTML on the fly, ensuring you always get WAP pages which are as up-to-date as their HTML source.

We'll look at two fully automated converters in this section:

❑ Phone.com

❑ Argo Actigate

Phone.com WAP Gateway

Phone.com includes an automated content converter with their WAP gateway that extracts the HTML title, and all text and links, and presents the result to a WAP device. If the text is greater than a deck can handle (~1400 bytes) then the converter splits the resulting WML into multiple decks, and links them with More buttons. You also have the option to just display the links of an HTML page, for swifter navigation. The converter supports input forms, but does not support frame conversion, or dynamic conversion of images.

The gateway also allows shortened URLs to be entered, so entering yahoo causes the gateway to prefix http://www. and postfix .com to create the full correct URL of http://www.yahoo.com. Although this is not strictly a converter function, it is a simple feature that all auto-converters should aspire to (as are any improvements in usability).

> *Note that this functionality of the gateway is not limited to phones with a Phone.com browser, such as Alcatel, Motorola, and Siemens – all WAP-compliant browsers can use this feature of the Phone.com gateway.*

Unfortunately, this converter is not available separately from the gateway, and the gateway is an expensive piece of software, certainly more than you want to pay just to obtain the converter.

From the user's, and a business point of view, the Phone.com offering is both good and bad: it's great if you are served by a Phone.com gateway, it's of no use whatsoever if you use another manufacturer's gateway. One more complication is that it is possible for gateway owners to switch off the converter, so even if you are served by a Phone.com WAP gateway, there's no guarantee the converter will be available to you. In summary, if you're in the market for an enterprise-quality gateway, and you want auto-conversion, then consider the Phone.com gateway.

Argo ActiGate

ActiGate is not just a WAP converter – it converts from HTML to WML, HDML, and XML, for PDAs with limited screens and processing power. ActiGate goes a few steps further than Phone.com, and converts images to monochrome, JPEG files to GIF, and re-samples images at different scales, and at different color depths, all of which can increase overall download speeds. If a device cannot display images, then the image title replaces it. It does not appear to currently support the WBMP format.

Obscure link names are translated to be the title of the target page, making them readable. An example is a link which has no associated text description, such as '../subscribe/index.html'. In this case, ActiGate reads the subscribe/index.html page and uses its title as the link text in place of the ugly '../subscribe/index.html'. JavaScript links are also converted (but not the JavaScript itself), and any duplicate links found are removed.

Large pages are split into WAP-manageable chunks (as expected) with navigation added between the resulting smaller pages, and converted documents are cached for improved performance. Frame conversion is also supported.

Because it supports HTML to HTML, it also has a 'clean-up' function to correct any errors found in HTML web pages, such as nested structures that are opened and not closed, or are closed in the wrong order, making sure that the HTML is well-formed, like XHTML and XML.

Configurable converters

Configurable converters, the subject of the majority of this chapter, rely on developer input in order to customize the conversion results into something that is indistinguishable from a 'standard' WML page. In this section, we'll be looking in detail at:

- ❑ Oracle's Portal-to-Go
- ❑ Spyglass' Prism
- ❑ Orchid's Webshaper

Oracle's Portal-to-Go

Portal-to-Go, originally called Project Panama, does not limit itself to just HTML input and WML output. Rather, it has multiple possible input streams (SQL, PLSQL and HTML as default), and multiple output streams via the use of JSP and XSL with XML being the intermediate data language. WML, HTML, Compact HTML, and VoxML are example output formats. Not only does it offer excellent flexibility, but also it allows the addition of your own input transformers ('adapters' in Oracle-speak) and output transformers. Portal-to-Go can be found at
http://www.oracle.com/html/portaltogo.html.

To convert a page, you simply type in its URL, and the parser returns the content of the page split into its constituent parts, such as title, paragraph, anchors, images, inputs, tables, and so on. You can then choose to remove, or modify these elements, and create a new input form (if there was input), and a new output format. You can hide extracted input fields from the user, and have them set to default values. This can be very useful if there are, say, 10 input fields, yet only 3 are mandatory, and you don't want to clutter the WML input card.

From the basic services you have defined (**master services**), Portal-to-Go allows you to build a **service tree** – a set of services that the user can navigate around, and which can be chained together to create a complete end-to-end converted set of WML (or other format) pages. The chaining can be conditional depending on the result returned from the backend web server. Although this is not a function of the converter part of the tool, such capabilities are vital to create a unified WML site.

If you don't like the automated content retrieval, you can dig into the raw HTML by hand, and mark areas of interest, known as 'regions'. This is a simple 'start' and 'end' text delimiter way of extracting data, and can be extremely useful where HTML tags cannot be used as delimiters, such as large paragraphs with partially auto-generated content that you would like to extract and display in WAP. We cover this method of converting content in our code example later.

For formatting output, Portal-to-Go comes complete with example XSL style sheets that can be applied to the extracted data for all the common WAP phones and PDAs. You can also chain together the resulting XML, so it's possible to combine the content of multiple pages together.

Page splitting, like Phone.com's gateway and Spyglass, is not standard, but you can programmatically define how many bytes of data each deck will contain, and add splits in the XSL.

Portal-to-Go runs on Solaris, H-P, and Windows NT currently, with other platforms being added in the future. The tools are tied to the Oracle database, but you can access other vendor's databases using gateway technologies. On the portal side, it supports the normal access permissions you might expect, such as users, user groups, and access per service or service group. Portal-to-Go also offers the capability to fully customize each user's service and store their preferences in a repository, so that each user gets a personalized site. It does not attempt to convert images.

With XML as the intermediate language, it also offers an ideal future-proof route to 'correct' web site design. Any existing HTML-only pages can slowly be converted over to be database-XML driven, and used to generate HTML or XHTML, WML, or any other format that appears in the future. In addition, Portal-to-Go also offers user preferences, and customization.

Portal-to-Go was developed with Telia in Sweden and is currently deployed in the UK as part of BT Cellnet's Genie mobile website. In addition Motorola have announced an alliance with Oracle and they will be using it in their MIX platform.

Spyglass' Prism

Spyglass' Prism supports automated conversion, including images (using your browser type to decide which is the best format conversion to apply), as well as custom conversion, so it spans both types of converter that we have defined. Spyglass have a mobile portal which demonstrates Prism's capabilities, and it supports dozens of devices, including Windows CE handhelds, Pocket-sized PCs, 3COM Palm Pilots, and WAP simulators and phones.

Prism performs four types of content conversion:

- ❑ Automated text and image conversion
- ❑ Content extraction
- ❑ Markup language conversion
- ❑ Custom conversion

Automated text and image conversion is the translation of existing content to another format – the equivalent to our fully automated converter. Currently, Prism only outputs WML and HTML. On the image conversion side, Prism can perform color depth changes, resolution reduction, JPEG quality, and other graphical functions, and in addition it can convert other image formats to WBMP.

Content extraction removes portions of a source document and delivers only that subset of content. This requires the developer to have detailed knowledge of the document's content and structure. This is useful when a site contains large amounts of graphic content and text not applicable to WAP, and equates to our definition of a configurable converter.

Markup language conversion converts a document from one markup language to another. An example is to replace HTML tags with the appropriate WML tag where necessary, or just remove the tag if there is no WML equivalent.

Lastly, Prism's architecture allows for the creation of custom conversions. These custom conversions can be written in either C or C++. This would allow you to create XML content, for example.

Prism has a distributed architecture, hooked together using CORBA, which allows good scalability. Server platforms include Microsoft IIS, Netscape Enterprise Server, on Solaris and NT. Spyglass uses Inktomi Traffic Server to implement caching for superior performance. Only HTML and WML output formats are currently supported.

Orchid WebShaper

Orchid has similar features to the other converters, but also includes conversion by 'screen-scraping' – obtaining data from, typically, a mainframe text console. This gives WAP devices access to legacy mainframe applications with minimal development effort. Output formats include WML, XML, VoxML, Motorola's Flex and the Bellcore microbrowser. It does not support automated conversion of 'unknown' sites. Beneath the covers, WebShaper is CGI-based and runs on Apache, Netscape Enterprise Server, and Microsoft's IIS.

Conversion by Source Modification

There is one more route to HTML-to-WML conversion that we've ignored so far, and that is conversion by modification of the HTML document. By this we mean the addition of 'helper' tags, which mark up the areas of interest for a converter to use as a place marker when extracting data. This initially seems an attractive and simple approach, but if you have to resort to modifying the HTML, then why not just go the whole hog and generate the WML in the first place, alongside the HTML? To be fair, in its favor is the reduced processing power required to extract the data, and the ease with which a converter can be written. An example of this type of converter, called TRANSWAP, can be found at: `http://amaro.g-art.nl/info.html`.

TRANSWAP

TRANSWAP requires only two comment tags to be added to your existing HTML:

```
<!-- WAP_START -->
    this is the part of the HTML-document you want to display
<!-- WAP_END -->
```

The application searches for the tagged text in a HTML-document and imports it in a WML skeleton. A demonstration server is located at `http://amaro.g-art.nl/wap/?u=<your homepage>.html`, where `<your homepage>` is the location of your modified HTML page. The tool appears to make no effort to display anything other than plain text, but for very simple sites, it may be of use.

Other Tools

In addition to the above, there are also other more generic conversion tools available, such as OmniMark (`http://www.omnimark.com/`). OmniMark is similar to an XML SAX parser, in that it is an event-based language – it traverses through a file or data stream looking for specific characters or strings, and when it finds them, it fires off an event to do something, such as extract the text, or maybe modify it. From OmniMark's online documentation, is this useful definition:

> *"An OmniMark program consists of rules that define data events, and actions that take place when data events occur. Suppose you wanted to count the words in the text "Mary had a little lamb." You would write an OmniMark rule that defined the occurrence of a word as an event:*
>
> *find letter+*

This is an OmniMark find rule. Find rules attempt to match patterns that occur in a data stream, and if they match something completely, they detect an event. This rule matches letters. The "+" sign after the keyword letter *stands for "one or more", so this rule will go on matching letters until it comes to something that is not a letter, such as punctuation or a space. Having run out of letters, it will see if it needs to match anything else. Since it doesn't, the pattern is complete and the rule is fired. Any actions following the rule are then executed. This rule will fire once for every word in the data, so all that remains to do is increment a counter each time the rule is fired."*

For data extraction from a data source, such as an HTML file, OmniMark uses what is known as a pattern processor, which looks for patterns in the input stream, and fires an event when the is matched. On the output side, OmniMark has built-in parsers for XML and SGML, so you don't need to code all the element matching rules – they're there ready for you, which is good news for XML conversion/publishing if you don't want to use an existing XML publishing package such as Cocoon. OmniMark also has a library for HTTP requests, to handle connection and any error handling. Command-line OmniMark is free and well documented, and comes with several relevant examples, such as XML conversion and fetching and extracting text from an HTML page.

If you don't want to learn Java or ASP/COM but you are keen on content translation, OmniMark could be the solution. It's designed specifically for parsing and converting content, with the only downsides being its relative obscurity to, and its lesser flexibility than, the more common general programming languages. The OmniMark compiler runs on both Windows and Unix platforms.

Conclusion

In conclusion, the ideal tool is XML-based, performs both automated and configurable conversion, and for future-proofing, contains image conversion, in anticipation of improved image handling of mobile devices, not necessarily WAP-driven. Our preference in terms of functionality is Oracle's Portal-to-Go, but this must be tempered with the understanding that to obtain such a tool, there is a significant cost not only in time but training time, and this needs to be balanced against the time and money of re-designing a site to use XML from the ground up. The short answer is that if you can generate extra business that is of greater value than the cost of the tool, and the time to learn it, then you must seriously consider it.

Simple Conversion Tool

Having examined the advantages and disadvantages of conversion, and seen some of the existing tools, let's dip into some simple HTML conversion ourselves. We will create a simple 3-tier converter – but with no logic in the middle tier. This will allow you to get used to the framework that is needed to support any conversion tool, such as servlets, properties files, publishing tools, and so on.

Our example converter is a configurable converter that – having been configured – will allow us to pick multiple sections of text out of an existing HTML page. This extraction is performed live by fetching the page from the Web, so the resulting WML is as current as the HTML page it was created from. The data extracted is held in a tree of XML elements, which we will transform with XSL stylesheets, to create the resulting WML. As a demonstration of multi-device output, we also output the selected text as HTML – in effect, a summary of the original page – which could be used for a Palm HTML browser or similar limited screen HTML-browsing device.

This 3-tier approach will get you started quickly on the conversion route, and also potentially gives better performance because of its simplicity. The three tiers are:

1. Data extraction from HTML, into XML

2. XML manipulation (not implemented)

3. WML generation (or HTML, etc)

To generate WML from XML in Step 3, we use a publishing framework called **Cocoon**. Before we dive into the detail of tier 1 above, its worth describing again why we're using XML, and how we will generate WML from that XML.

WML is an XML-conformant markup language. This fact alone should guide our choice of publishing tools. Since we will create an XML document from our HTML source, we can pass this into a publishing tool that in turn will, with the help of an XSL stylesheet, output WML for us. XSL, in effect, turns raw data – the XML – into formatted content that can be made specific to a device or particular markup language. XML and XSL fundamentals are covered in more depth in Chapter 9.

There are several publishing frameworks available. For example, the majority of database vendors such as Oracle, ObjectStore, and Informix offer XML publishing tools. For platform simplicity, and vendor independence, we have chosen an open source framework from the Apache Software Foundation named Cocoon. The good news is that not only will it generate WML, but also any other XML-conformant languages, such as XHTML, Compact HTML and even HTML itself. Generating HTML from HTML may sound like a waste of time, but it could be a very useful solution for small screen HTML browsers such as Palms and Psions, where you need to modify the content and layout of a document that was designed for PC.

Apache Cocoon Features

Apache's Cocoon is succinctly described on their web site as "a 100% pure Java publishing framework that relies on new W3C technologies (such as DOM, XML, and XSL) to provide web content." Rather than just create HTML and publish that HTML direct to the Web, Cocoon supports the creation of XML, which is then converted to HTML, XHTML, WML, or any other XML-compliant format you wish to supply. In doing this, Cocoon supports the separation of content, logic and style from each other, which XML was designed to enable.

Cocoon is 100% Java and servlet-based, which is excellent for portability, not only across platforms, but also across tools. We can pick and choose operating systems, web servers, JVMs, parsers, and so on. Cocoon supports both static generation – from XML documents resident on a file system or other fixed store – and also dynamic generation, where a tool has generated the XML document on the fly. We are specifically interested in the dynamic generation of content, since we cannot predict the content of our HTML source document – we need to extract our data every time a user asks for it.

Cocoon also has a sophisticated caching system to increase page-serving performance. XML processing can be resource-hungry because of the potentially large number of objects needed to represent a document, which requires processing time for creation, and also memory allocation, and management overheads. The caching system copes with both static and dynamic pages, but you need to give hints to the cache as to whether your dynamic page has changed.

Now we understand the three tiers, we can start by defining an extraction algorithm, which is the meat of tier 1 above. We'll then code and test the algorithm.

Simple Extraction Algorithm

Before we dive into the source code, let's first describe how we will identify and extract text from the original HTML page. We can identify areas of interest in a page by defining the strings of text that delimit them. In other words, we're looking for unique strings at the start and end of the text we want to extract, so we can use them as start/stop tags. As an example, we have chosen to extract details from the Wrox international distributor page below (go to `http://www.wrox.com/` and follow the link right at the bottom of the page to see the page online):

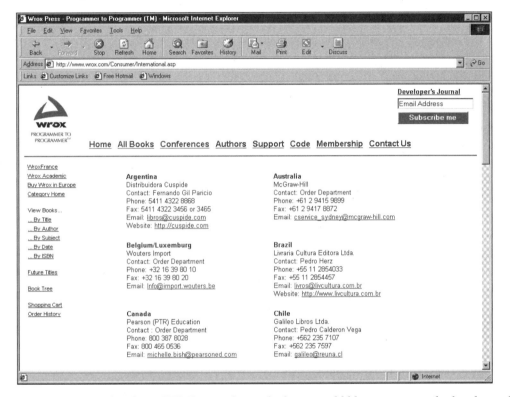

Listed below is part of the above HTML page from which we would like to extract only the phone, fax and email details for our WAP equivalent page. We don't want any of the other items like HTML tags, or links, and so on:

```
. . .

<td VALIGN="top">
<b>Australia</b><br>
McGraw-Hill<br>
Contact: Order Department<br>
Phone: +61 2 9415 9899<br>
Fax: +61 2 9417 8872<br>
Email: <a HREF="mailto:cservice_sydney@mcgraw-hill.com">cservice_sydney@mcgraw-
hill.com</a><br><p>
</td>
</tr><tr>
```

```
<td VALIGN="top">
<b>Belgium/Luxemburg</b><br>
Wouters Import<br>
Contact: Order Department<br>
Phone: +32 16 39 80 10<br>
Fax: +32 16 39 80 20<br>
Email: <a HREF="mailto:Info@import.wouters.be">Info@import.wouters.be</a><br><p>
</td>
...
```

To extract the country, for example, we need to get the string delimited by b> and <:

```
b>Belgium/Luxemburg<
```

To extract the phone number, we need to get the string delimited by Phone: and <:

```
Phone: +32 16 39 80 10<
```

To extract the fax number, we need to get the string delimited by Fax: and <:

```
Fax: +32 16 39 80 20<
```

And to extract the e-mail address, we need to get the string delimited by Email: <a HREF="mailto: and ":

```
Email: <a HREF="mailto:Info@import.wouters.be"
```

For other pages, we might need to use other delimiting text strings, and this example converter lets you define the strings, as you will see later.

Note that were we to just parse the whole of the HTML document using the four delimiting string pairs, we might be returned more than just country, phone, fax and e-mail. (As it happens, this distributor page doesn't actually have very much additional source after the country details, but many web pages you may wish to convert will have much more data following the bit you're actually interested in). We need to do two things:

❑ To avoid wasting time extracting areas of HTML that we're not interested in, we set an overall start delimiter and an overall end delimiter. These aren't visible in the small HTML extract above, but for this particular page, they happen to be Order History and Mission.asp respectively.

❑ We must assume that the country, phone, fax and e-mail are always grouped together as a set of information; we can search for a country, phone, fax, and e-mail, followed by another country, phone, fax, e-mail and so on, until we find the overall end delimiting text string.

More generically, rather than limit ourselves to four extractions, we will design to allow for unlimited extracts, and use a configuration file to specify how many items are grouped together.

Here's the relevant part of the configuration file for the HTML shown above. Firstly, there is the definition of the overall start and stop delimiters, a count of the number of items in the extraction group, and then finally, the extract delimiters:

```
distributors.overall.start=Order History
distributors.overall.end=Mission.asp

distributors.extract.count=4
distributors.extract0.name=country
distributors.extract0.start=b>
distributors.extract0.end=<
distributors.extract1.name=phone
distributors.extract1.start=Phone:
distributors.extract1.end=<
distributors.extract2.name=fax
distributors.extract2.start=Fax:
distributors.extract2.end=<
distributors.extract3.name=email
distributors.extract3.start=Email: <a HREF="mailto:
distributors.extract3.end="
```

In order to perform the extraction, we start at the `overall.start` string and stop when at the `overall.end` string. We search for the first string, namely the `distributors.extract0.start` string defined in our example above. When we find it, we then search for its matching end string, `distributors.extract0.end`. Then we search for `distributors.extract1.start`, followed by `distributors.extract1.end`, and so on, until we have found all the start /end tags in the group (in our case 4, since `distributors.extract.count=4`, so there are four lots of start/end strings to find). Then, assuming we still haven't reached the very end string, `distributors.overall.end`, we continue searching. Here is some of the pseudo-code that searches for the groups of extracts:

```
Find overall.start
While overall.end not reached
{
  for n=1 to number of extract items
  {
    find extract[n].start
    find extract[n].end
    extract string between extract[n].start and extract[n].end
    move to end of extract[n].end string
  }
}
```

Example Java Extraction Application

Having described the algorithm for finding the relevant data, let's see the extraction algorithm in action by creating a stand-alone Java application, which we can debug, before plugging it into the Cocoon framework, to wrap the algorithm up with a little functionality. This includes reading in the configuration file, inputting the target URL to fetching the data from the URL, and finally saving the extracted data in some form, in this case XML DOM.

Here is the functionality we cover in data extraction:

❑ Reading in the properties file which holds the definition of our services

❑ Initialization of the extractor with the content of the properties file

❑ The extraction method

❑ Storage of the extracted data in an XML Document Object Model (DOM)

439

Initialization & Properties

The application is named HTMLExtractor, and takes two arguments; the first defines the conversion service to be run, and the second defines the name and path of the extractor properties file. It creates an XML Document in the form of a Document Object Model (DOM), but as yet does nothing with it, other than print the content out, if you wish.

The command line to run HTMLExtractor looks like this:

```
java HTMLExtractor distributors extractor.properties
```

We'll not include the full code listing here for the sake of space, but note that it is available with the rest of the code from this book.

> Note that this code, and all the code in this chapter, is released under the *GNU Public License*, the details of which are available with the code download from the Wrox web site.

The main() method of the HTMLExtractor class is shown below. This checks that both arguments are present on the command line, creates an instance of HTMLExtractor, creates an instance of the Service class (described below) and requests the XML Document from the Service instance. Here is the detail:

```
//Main method for testing from command line, or IDE
  public static void main(String[] args) throws IOException
  {
    //Check both args have been specified on command line
    if (args.length < 2)
    {
      System.err.println("Usage: java HTMLExtractor serviceName " +
                          "extractorPropertiesFileName");
      return;
    }
    //Create the HTMLExtractor
    HTMLExtractor mHTMLExtractor = new HTMLExtractor(args[1]);

    //Create the Service via the HTMLExtractor
    Service mService = mHTMLExtractor.getService(args[0]);

    //If everything went well, then get the XML document
    if (mService != null)
    {
      Document mDoc = mService.getDocument();
      //If XML document was created successfully,
      //print a line to System.out for confirmation
      if (mDoc != null)
      {
        System.out.println("XML Document created successfully - " +
                "uncomment the lines in Service.createDOM to see raw result.");
      }
    }
  }
```

The `HTMLExtractor` constructor reads the properties file in:

```
//Constructor
  public HTMLExtractor(String propertiesFile)
  {
    //Read the extractor properties file
    try
    {
      FileInputStream sf = new FileInputStream(propertiesFile);
      try
      {
        properties.load(sf);
      }
      catch(IOException ioe)
      {
        System.err.println("Constructor: IOException reading " +
                           "the properties file '" + propertiesFile + "'");
        return;
      }
    }
    catch(FileNotFoundException fnfe)
    {
      System.err.println("Constructor: Properties file \"" +
                         propertiesFile + "\" could not be found");
      return;
    }
  }
```

We then check that the service name actually has an entry in the extractor properties file. If it does, then we create the appropriate `Service` object; otherwise we return `null`:

```
//Methods
  public Service getService(String serviceName) throws IOException
  {
    Service mService= null;
    //Make sure our service is defined in the extractor properties file
    if (properties.getProperty(serviceName) == null)
    {
      System.err.println("The service \"" + serviceName +
                         "\" was not found in the extractor properties file");
      return null;
    }
    else
    {
      //Our service is defined, so create a Service object, and populate it
      mService = new Service(serviceName, properties);
    }
    return mService;
  }
```

The `Service` object holds all the property values, populated laboriously from the contents of the properties file, and so describes each service that we have defined, such as the distributor list shown above.

In addition to the start/end delimiters we need to define:

- ❑   A unique service name
- ❑   The source URL (of the HTML document)
- ❑   The maximum number of items to extract (because of WML's ~1400 byte limitation)
- ❑   Processing instructions for XSL (covered later)

A `Service`'s full set of properties looks like this:

```
distributors=Wrox Distributors

distributors.url=file:///c:/wrox/distributors.html
distributors.overall.start=Order History

distributors.overall.end=Mission.asp
distributors.extract.count=4
distributors.extract0.name=country
distributors.extract0.start=b>
distributors.extract0.end =<
distributors.extract1.name=phone
distributors.extract1.start=Phone:
distributors.extract1.end =<
distributors.extract2.name=fax
distributors.extract2.start=Fax:
distributors.extract2.end =<
distributors.extract3.name=email
distributors.extract3.start=Email: <a HREF="mailto:
distributors.extract3.end ="
distributors.max.items=10

distributors.pi.count=4
distributors.pi0.target=xml-stylesheet
distributors.pi0.data=href="file:///C:/wrox/Cocoon/samples/wap/contact-html.xsl"
type="text/xsl"
distributors.pi1.target=xml-stylesheet
distributors.pi1.data=href="file:///C:/wrox/Cocoon/samples/wap/contact-wml.xsl"
type="text/xsl" media="wap"
distributors.pi2.target=xml-stylesheet
distributors.pi2.data=href="file:///C:/wrox/Cocoon/samples/wap/contact-
phonecom.xsl" type="text/xsl" media="phonecom"
distributors.pi3.target=cocoon-process
distributors.pi3.data=type="xslt"
```

Here is the code that reads all these properties in:

```
//Constructor
  public Service(String serviceName, Properties properties)
  {
    //Populate all our variables from the values
    // in the extractor properties file
    serviceTitle = properties.getProperty(serviceName);
    serviceURL = properties.getProperty(serviceName+".url");
    overallStart = properties.getProperty(serviceName+".overall.start");
    overallEnd = properties.getProperty(serviceName+".overall.end");
    extractCount =
        Integer.parseInt(properties.getProperty(serviceName+".extract.count"));
    extractItem = new ExtractItem[extractCount];
```

```
    //get details of each item to extract, i.e. country, phone, fax, email
    for (int i = 0; i < extractCount; i++)
    {
      extractItem[i] = new ExtractItem();
      extractItem[i].name =
                  properties.getProperty(serviceName+".extract"+i+".name");
      extractItem[i].start =
                  properties.getProperty(serviceName+".extract"+i+".start");
      extractItem[i].end =
                  properties.getProperty(serviceName+".extract"+i+".end");
    }
    piCount = Integer.parseInt(properties.getProperty(serviceName+".pi.count"));
    piItem = new ProcInstruct[piCount];

    //For each Processing Instruction - get its details
    for (int i = 0; i < piCount; i++)
    {
      piItem[i] = new ProcInstruct();
      piItem[i].target = properties.getProperty(serviceName+".pi"+i+".target");
      piItem[i].data = properties.getProperty(serviceName+".pi"+i+".data");
    }
    maxItems =
            Integer.parseInt(properties.getProperty(serviceName+".max.items"));

    //Initialize the array that we will hold our extracted data in
    for (int i = 0; i < extractCount; i++)
    {
      extractItem[i].data = new String[maxItems];
    }
  }
```

There is no limit to the length of delimiting text strings. We have chosen to use a standard Java properties file, since we do not intend to convert many different pages at once for this simple example, making the file quite short. You may wish to replace this with a database of configuration information. In a real-world application, plenty of error checking needs to be added here for typos in the properties file, and for missing properties.

Service Object Initialization

The Service object holds all these parameters ready for when a user request arrives at the web server. In our final design, the Cocoon servlet receives requests via the doGet() method. However, for the time being, we will fake the user request by entering the service and properties file on the command line.

Having obtained a Service object, we call its getDocument() method, to obtain the XML document:

```
    //Initiate the HTML reading, and if successful, return the XML document
    public Document getDocument() throws IOException
    {
      if (readHTML())
      {
        extract();
        return createDOM();
      }
      return null;
    }
```

There are three steps here:

- ❏ Read the HTML into a buffer, readHTML()
- ❏ Extract the specific sections from that buffer using our extraction algorithm, extract()
- ❏ Create an XML document from the extracted strings, createDOM()

If the HTML document is read in without error, then extraction and document creation occur, otherwise a null Document is returned, signifying failure.

Reading the HTML Document

ReadHTML() just requires the use of a URL object to access the HTML document and read the content in line by line into a large StringBuffer. The StringBuffer is then converted back to a String object afterwards, so we can use the indexOf() method later. There is some simple error checking, so if anything fails, a Boolean false is returned:

```
//Read the HTML file into a buffer.
//Return true if successful, otherwise false
private boolean readHTML()
{
  BufferedReader reader;
  String line;
  try
  {
    //Create the URL object from the xxx.url string specified
    //in the properties file
    URL mURL = new URL(serviceURL); ;
    StringBuffer wholeFile = new StringBuffer();

    try
    {
      //Read the HTML into a StringBuffer, a line at a time
      //Use a StringBuffer, because String appends are slower
      reader = new BufferedReader(new InputStreamReader(mURL.openStream()));
      while ((line = reader.readLine()) != null)
      {
        wholeFile.append(line);
      }
      reader.close();
    }
    catch(IOException ioe)
    {
      System.err.println("Service: the source document " +
                         serviceURL + " could not be found or read.");
      return false;
    }
    //Finally convert StringBuffer to a plainString
    html = wholeFile.toString();
    return true;
  }
  catch(MalformedURLException mue)
  {
    System.err.println("Service: the source URL " + serviceURL
                       + " is malformed.");
    return false;
  }
}
```

Extraction Method

Once we have the HTML page contents in the `String` html, we can apply our extraction algorithm introduced earlier:

```
//Having read the HTML source file into a buffer, we can extract the pertinent
//data, as directed by the values read in from the extractor properties file.
  private void extract()
  {
    //Overall start point in the HTML
    int startIndex = html.indexOf(overallStart) + overallStart.length();

    //Overall end point in the HTML
    int endIndex = html.indexOf(overallEnd, startIndex);

    //Our current position in the HTML
    int currentIndex = startIndex;

    //The number of sets of information found in the HTML
    items = 0;

    while ((currentIndex < endIndex) && (items < maxItems))
    {
      //Loop for as many things as there are to be extracted
      //(i.e. country,phone,fax,email)
      for (int i = 0; i < extractCount; i++)
      {
        //Find start delimiter
        int extractStartIndex = html.indexOf(extractItem[i].start,
                                              currentIndex);
        //Find end delimiter
        int extractEndIndex = html.indexOf(extractItem[i].end,
                       extractStartIndex + extractItem[i].start.length());
        //Take text between the start and end delimiters,
        //allowing for the length of the start delimiter
        extractItem[i].data[items] = html.substring(extractStartIndex +
                          extractItem[i].start.length(), extractEndIndex);
        //Move on through HTML
        currentIndex = extractEndIndex + extractItem[i].end.length();
      }
      items++;
    }
  }
```

An `ExtractItem` exists for each type of item to be extracted; in this case the country, phone, fax and e-mail. `ExtractItem` also holds the n arrays of extracted data, up a maximum of `maxItems`.

The final piece of the jigsaw is to create an XML document from the extracted data.

Create the Document Object Model (DOM)

Now we have our extracted data in a 'pure' form, with no formatting information mixed in with it, all we need to do is create an XML `Document` from it. To do this, we can use one of the many XML parsers freely available. In this example, we'll use Apache's Xerces, because Cocoon uses it anyway, and also, because of its superior 'pretty-printing' support. We'll also demonstrate Sun's XML parser that comes with JAXP 1.0. (Note that JAXP 1.0 should only be used with JDK 1.2.x or 1.3.)

Here is how we fill the DOM with our extracted data:

```
//Create the XML DOM from the extracted data
  private Document createDOM() throws IOException
  {
     //Xerces method of creating an initially empty XML Document
     DocumentImpl mDoc = new DocumentImpl();

     //Sun method of creating an initially empty XML Document
     //(Uncomment to see Sun pretty-print)
     //XmlDocument mDoc = new XmlDocument();

     //The root element of our XML document
     Element eb = mDoc.createElement("extractbody");
     mDoc.appendChild(eb);

     //Add the processing instructions, as specified in the
     //extractor properties file
     for (int i = 0; i < piCount; i++)
     {
       ProcessingInstruction pi =
           mDoc.createProcessingInstruction(piItem[i].target, piItem[i].data);
       mDoc.appendChild(pi);
     }

     //Add a title element, using the title given in the
     //extractor properties file
     Element title = mDoc.createElement("title");
     title.appendChild(mDoc.createTextNode(serviceTitle));
     eb.appendChild(title);

     //Add all the text extracted from the HTML
     for (int j = 0; j < items; j++)
     {
       Element ei = mDoc.createElement("extractitem");
       ei.setAttribute("id", Integer.toString(j));
       eb.appendChild(ei);
       //Loop for each element to be displayed, i.e. country, phone, fax, email
       for (int i = 0; i < extractCount; i++)
       {
         //If extract name is dummy, then ignore it.
         //This gives us some flexibility when it's difficult to uniquely identify
         //the text we want to extract.
         if (extractItem[i].name.equals(dummy))
         {
           continue;
         }
         Element e = mDoc.createElement(extractItem[i].name);
         e.appendChild(mDoc.createTextNode(extractItem[i].data[j]));

         ei.appendChild(e);
       }
     }

     //Uncomment these lines to see the raw document printed out,
     //complete with null elements.
     //Useful for debugging in the early stages, when running HTMLExtractor.
/*
     NodeIteratorImpl ni =
         (NodeIteratorImpl)mDoc.createNodeIterator(mDoc.getDocumentElement(),
                                                   255, null, true);
```

```
        Node node = ni.nextNode();
        while (node != null)
        {
          System.out.println(node.getNodeName() + "=" + node.getNodeValue());
          node = ni.nextNode();
        }
*/

        //Uncomment to see pretty-print Sun document output
/*
        Writer out = new OutputStreamWriter(System.out);
        mDoc.write(out);
        out.flush();
*/
        return mDoc;
    }
```

A brand new Document is created first, and then elements are added to it. There are three elements added which have fixed names:

❏ extractbody

❏ title

❏ extractItem

The element extractbody wraps up the whole of the extracted data, and is therefore the parent element. title we simply added because one is usually needed on any page you are likely to display. The title is derived from the property distributors=Wrox Distributors. The element extractItem wraps each group of extractItems together. Each extractItem element has a unique identifier as an attribute, which we use later in our XSL to make sure each WML card created has a unique name. Within each extractItem we use the name of the extract to define the element name, that is, country, phone, fax and email.

There are two loops of processing, one to add XML processing instruction elements and one to add our extracted text. For our command line, the processing instructions make no difference, and aren't visible on the console, but they are in the XML document. Cocoon will make use of them later.

The dummy extract (comparison against the string dummy) is a useful cheat to avoid missing extract strings that have non-unique delimiters around them. A more sophisticated approach would be to use regular expressions and search for the string (numeric char)-->, and this would match 1-->, 2-->, 3-->, and so on. We didn't actually need to use it in the distributor list example, but you may need it in your conversions.

If you uncomment the last few lines above and run HTMLExtractor from the command line, you will get something rather raw, like this:

```
...
#text=Australia
phone=null
#text=+61 2 9415 9899
fax=null
#text=+61 2 9417 8872
email=null
#text=cservice_sydney@mcgraw-hill.com
```

```
extractitem=null
country=null
#text=Belgium/Luxemburg
phone=null
#text=+32 16 39 80 10
fax=null
#text=+32 16 39 80 20
email=null
#text=Info@import.wouters.be
extractitem=null
country=null
#text=Brazil
phone=null
#text=+55 11 2854033
fax=null
#text=+55 11 2854457
email=null
#text=livros@livcultura.com.br
...
```

Below is listed the result if you use Sun's XML parser, which gives a human-readable XML output. Note that the DOM it creates is identical to that of Xerces or any other parser, its just that Sun have supplied a printing method, which adds indentation and carriage returns, to please the eye when the DOM is sent to an output stream:

```
<?xml version="1.0" encoding="ISO-8859-1"?>
<extractbody>
  <title>Wrox Distributors</title>
  <extractitem id="0">
    <country>Argentina</country>
    <phone>5411 4322 8868</phone>
    <fax>5411 4322 3456 or 3465</fax>
    <email>libros@cuspide.com</email>
  </extractitem>
  <extractitem id="1">
    <country>Australia</country>
    <phone>+61 2 9415 9899</phone>
    <fax>+61 2 9417 8872</fax>
    <email>cservice_sydney@mcgraw-hill.com</email>
  </extractitem>
  <extractitem id="2">
    <country>Belgium/Luxemburg</country>
    <phone>+32 16 39 80 10</phone>
    <fax>+32 16 39 80 20</fax>
    <email>Info@import.wouters.be</email>
  </extractitem>
  <extractitem id="3">
    <country>Brazil</country>

  </extractitem>
</extractbody>
<?xml-stylesheet href="file:///C:/wrox/Cocoon/samples/wap/contact-html.xsl"
type="text/xsl"?>
<?xml-stylesheet href="file:///C:/wrox/Cocoon/samples/wap/contact-wml.xsl"
type="text/xsl" media="wap"?>
<?xml-stylesheet href="file:///C:/wrox/Cocoon/samples/wap/contact-phonecom.xsl"
type="text/xsl" media="phonecom"?>
<?cocoon-process type="xslt"?>
```

If you wish to use the Sun parser instead of Apache's Xerces, you must first import the Sun classes:

```
import com.sun.xml.tree.*;
```

Then, in `Service.createDOM()`, replace the standard Xerces `DocumentImpl` with the Sun `XmlDocument` class:

```
// DocumentImpl mDoc = new DocumentImpl();
XmlDocument mDoc = new XmlDocument();
```

And print out the document with these lines, after the `XmlDocument` has been populated. These are currently commented out in the listing:

```
Writer out = new OutputStreamWriter(System.out);
mDoc.write(out);
out.flush();
```

One last note on the design: we separated out the `Service` object so that in future designs we can just read the properties file once, create all the appropriate `Service` objects, and then sit there waiting for requests to arrive. We don't actually implement it in this way, but the ability is there. To avoid the overhead of repeatedly reading the properties file, we must create the `Service` once, and read the properties once. In the case of Cocoon, this can be done by creating and initializing the `Service` object from within what is known as the `Producer`, as described below.

Now we have an XML DOM full of useful extracted data, let's see how to convert that into actual WML, by hooking together our extraction code with Cocoon.

WML Generation

As described earlier, our WML generation from XML will be performed by Apache's Cocoon. Cocoon is Java and servlet-based, so to run Cocoon, you merely add the Cocoon servlet to your servlet-enabled web server, and fire HTTP requests at it. It then takes those requests and processes them, returning a result page, which, amongst other factors, is dependent on your browser type.

Apache Cocoon Detailed Features

Cocoon is modular, and reflects the content/logic/style split with three components:

- ❑ Producers
- ❑ Processors
- ❑ Formatters

The **Producer** 'produces' the XML document, where an XML document is supplied to the Cocoon engine. Our HTMLExtractor can be considered to be a producer, but we must, of course, match Cocoon's Producer API. There are default Producers supplied with Cocoon – `ProducerFromFile`, and `ProducerFromRequest` amongst others. `ProducerFromFile` supplies Cocoon with an XML document from a file. The file name is specified in a standard `HttpServletRequest` class that is passed in as a parameter to all Producers. `ProducerFromRequest` expects the XML to be embedded within the `HttpServletRequest` itself. Whilst these are useful examples, we will need to create our own Producer, since Cocoon does not know how we wish to extract data from HTML. We will cover how to create a new Producer later. Producers are specified in the actual HTTP request to the Cocoon servlet. Here is an example:

```
http://<hostname:port>/dummy.xml?producer=dummy
```

This effectively instructs Cocoon to use the dummy Producer to handle this HTTP request. dummy is an example Cocoon Producer. It is up to the dummy Producer to decide how to interpret the rest of the URL, that is, the dummy.xml part. In the dummy Producer's case, it actually ignores it, but we could use this part of the URL to specify which conversion service to invoke. The Cocoon authors advocate using a Producer interface to pass the XML into Cocoon, rather than say, piping the output of a servlet into Cocoon's servlet (known as servlet-chaining).

The **Processor** allows the processing of the DOM tree that was created from our XML document, brought in by a Producer. There are several Processors supplied as standard with Cocoon, including a SQL processor. The Processor to use, per page, is specified by an XML Processing Instruction. For example, this line specifies the XSLT processor:

```
<?cocoon-process type="xslt"?>
```

We will use the standard XSL Processor supplied with Cocoon; Xalan. To use this, we need to create the above line when we generate our XML document. In addition, we must also specify the actual XSL stylesheet(s) we want the XSLT processor to use:

```
<?xml-stylesheet href="portfolio-wml.xsl" type="text/xsl" media="wap"?>
```

The XSL document is portfolio-wml.xsl. Recall that in the Service.createDOM() method there was a loop to read in these Processing Instructions from the HTMLExtractor properties file. Here is an extract of relevant parts of that properties file, which shows one of the stylesheet definitions, and also the Processor definition:

```
...
distributors.pi1.target=xml-stylesheet
distributors.pi1.data=href="file:///C:/wrox/Cocoon/samples/wap/contact-wml.xsl"
type="text/xsl" media="wap"
...
distributors.pi3.target=cocoon-process
distributors.pi3.data=type="xslt"
```

The media attribute is "wap". This attribute tells Cocoon how to match XSL stylesheets to HTTP user agents. These mappings are specified in a Cocoon configuration file, conf.properties, which we shall revisit later. In Cocoon's case, "wap" maps to the User-Agent HTTP header of value "Nokia-WAP-Toolkit", so beware: "wap" is not a particularly good description, and we will define our own additional media type later!

The **Formatter** formats the document. In our case we do not need to use this, since an XSL stylesheet, specified by the XSLT Processor above, will do all the necessary work. However, there are options for outputting PDF, and other formats if required. Here is the now familiar format of the Processing instruction:

```
<?cocoon-format type="yyy"?> for formatting
```

The Formatter is optional in the XML, since the default is text/html. To produce WML output, we specified the following in our WML stylesheet, contact-wml.xsl:

```
<xsl:processing-instruction name="cocoon-format">type="text/wml"</xsl:processing-
instruction>
```

Cocoon comes with several examples of each of these components, but you are encouraged to add your own, especially where you have your own dynamic generation engine, such as we have created in `HTMLExtractor`.

Installation of Cocoon

The best advice, before embarking on implementing this step, is to make sure your web server is working as you expect, by testing a simple `HelloWorld` servlet, before diving into this installation. Once you're happy your current environment is stable and working as expected, download the Cocoon binaries from `http://xml.apache.org`. To support Cocoon, you also need an XML parser and an XSLT Processor. It makes sense to use the Apache offerings here, respectively Xerces and Xalan. Both are bundled with Cocoon 1.7.3 & 1.7.4. You may use other XML parsers and XSLT processors, a selection of suggestions are listed in the Cocoon installation instructions.

Note that versions 1.7.2 and earlier releases require manual tweaks and fixes, which we do not go into here, suffice to say, that the later versions should install with almost no modifications to Cocoon settings, only to your web server in order for it to find and load the Cocoon servlet. All versions of Cocoon come with extensive documentation, both for installation and development, so we have not attempted to reproduce that here, other than the salient points.

To install the Cocoon servlet into your web server, the `org.apache.cocoon.Cocoon` servlet needs adding to the server's list of servlets, and you need to map the desired HTTP requests to the Cocoon servlet. For simplicity we assume that you have a development environment with the following attributes:

- ❑ Cocoon was installed into the directory `<install-dir>`
- ❑ `cocoon.jar` is in your classpath, or your web server's servlet search path, so that it can find the Cocoon servlet code
- ❑ In your web server, you map any URLs starting with 'cocoon' to the Cocoon servlet (alternatively, map all requests for `.xml` pages to the Cocoon servlet)
- ❑ In your web server, you have mapped the document root to `<install-dir>/Cocoon/samples`

In your web server, for the Cocoon servlet, you need to create a property named `properties` and give it the value `<install-dir>\Cocoon\conf\cocoon.properties`. This allows the Cocoon servlet to find its properties file, and initialize itself.

Start your web server, checking that the Cocoon servlet initialized without error, and load the page:

```
http://<webserver:port>/index.xml
```

Modify this URL if you chose to map your root web directory elsewhere. You should be served the 'Cocoon Live Show' example page. This is an XML page, so if you can see a result, you have successfully exercised both Cocoon's own `ProducerFromFile` class and the Xalan XSLT processor, (or your choice of XSLT processor), when you requested the page.

Having successfully tested the installation, let's make sure we can output some WML from some XML input. Start up your WAP simulator and load the example WAP XML page to generate some example WAP output:

```
http://<webserver:port>/wap/example-portfolio.xml
```

Now load exactly the same page using your PC browser (Netscape, Internet Explorer, etc) to see the same data output in HTML. Here we see the beauty of XML – two different languages and styles delivered from a single XML document.

Here are the results. Note that it takes three screens to get specific stock values on the WAP device, but only one screen of HTML:

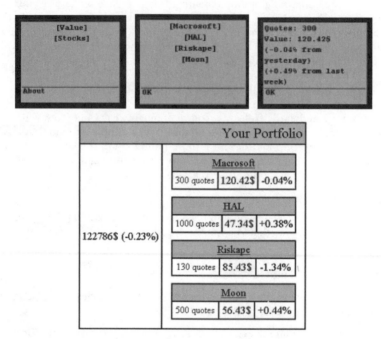

Here is the original XML code, i.e. the raw data for the above screens:

```
<?xml version="1.0"?>
<?xml-stylesheet href="portfolio-html.xsl" type="text/xsl"?>
<?xml-stylesheet href="portfolio-wml.xsl" type="text/xsl" media="wap"?>
<?cocoon-process type="xslt"?>

<!-- Written by Stefano Mazzocchi "stefano@apache.org" -->

<!-- Let us suppose this page has been dynamically generated  -->
<!-- against a stock quotes database.                         -->

<portfolio>
 <total>122786</total>
 <variations>
  <!-- these are not calculated, only to show off -->
  <day rate="-">0.23</day>
  <week rate="+">1.82</week>
  <month rate="+">1.32</month>
  <ever rate="+">45.00</ever>
 </variations>
 <stocks company="Macrosoft" url="http://www.macrosoft.com">
```

```
    <quotes>300</quotes>
    <value>120.42</value>
    <total>36126.00</total>
    <variations>
     <day rate="-">0.04</day>
     <week rate="+">0.49</week>
     <month rate="-">3.89</month>
     <ever rate="+">459.58</ever>
    </variations>
   </stocks>
   <stocks company="HAL" url="http://www.hal.com">
    <quotes>1000</quotes>
    <value>47.34</value>
    <total>47340.00</total>
    <variations>
     <day rate="+">0.38</day>
     <week rate="+">0.59</week>
     <month rate="-">1.34</month>
     <ever rate="-">34.53</ever>
    </variations>
   </stocks>
   <stocks company="Riskape" url="http://www.riskape.com">
    <quotes>130</quotes>
    <value>85.43</value>
    <total>11105.00</total>
    <variations>
     <day rate="-">1.34</day>
     <week rate="-">10.49</week>
     <month rate="+">4.89</month>
     <ever rate="+">50.58</ever>
    </variations>
   </stocks>
   <stocks company="Moon" url="http://www.moon.com">
    <quotes>500</quotes>
    <value>56.43</value>
    <total>28215.00</total>
    <variations>
     <day rate="+">0.44</day>
     <week rate="+">2.38</week>
     <month rate="-">0.2</month>
     <ever rate="+">87.03</ever>
    </variations>
   </stocks>
  </portfolio>
```

If you examine the `example-portfolio.xml` file above, you will see at the top of the file the XSL processing instructions that caused the HTML and WML generation to be different. They are:

```
<?xml-stylesheet href="portfolio-html.xsl" type="text/xsl"?>
<?xml-stylesheet href="portfolio-wml.xsl" type="text/xsl" media="wap"?>
```

In the second processing instruction, it states that if the media is `"wap"`, (which translates to a User-Agent value of `"Nokia-WAP-Toolkit"` in the Cocoon properties files), then use the stylesheet, `portfolio-wml.xsl`. Otherwise, the processing will default to `portfolio-html.xsl`.

And here are those XSL stylesheets referred to, that formatted the data into WAP and HTML respectively. First the WAP-generating XSL:

```
<?xml version="1.0"?>

<!-- Written by Stefano Mazzocchi "stefano@apache.org" -->

<xsl:stylesheet version="1.0" xmlns:xsl="http://www.w3.org/1999/XSL/Transform">

 <xsl:template match="portfolio">
  <xsl:processing-instruction name="cocoon-
format">type="text/wml"</xsl:processing-instruction>

  <wml>
   <card id="index" title="Your Portfolio">
    <p align="center">
     <a href="#value">Value</a><br/>
     <a href="#stocks">Stocks</a><br/>
    </p>
    <do type="accept" label="About">
     <go href="#About"/>
    </do>
   </card>

   <card id="about" title="About">
    <onevent type="ontimer">
     <prev/>
    </onevent>
    <timer value="25"/>
    <p align="center">
     <br/>
     <br/>
     <small>
      Copyright &#xA9; 1999<br/>
      Apache Software Foundation.<br/>
      All rights reserved.
     </small>
    </p>
   </card>

   <card id="value" title="Portfolio Value">
    <p>
     Total value: <b>$$<xsl:value-of select="total"/></b><br/>
     <small>(<b><xsl:value-of select="variations/day/@rate"/>
       <xsl:value-of select="variations/day"/>&#x25;</b> from yesterday)
     </small><br/>
     <small>(<b><xsl:value-of select="variations/week/@rate"/>
       <xsl:value-of select="variations/week"/>&#x25;</b>
         from last week)
     </small><br/>
     <small>(<b><xsl:value-of select="variations/month/@rate"/>
       <xsl:value-of select="variations/month"/>&#x25;</b>
       from last month)
     </small><br/>
     <small>(<b><xsl:value-of select="variations/ever/@rate"/>
       <xsl:value-of select="variations/ever"/>&#x25;</b> ever)
     </small><br/>
    </p>
     <do type="prev" label="Back">
       <prev/>
     </do>
   </card>
```

```
    <card id="stocks" title="Your Current Stocks">
     <p align="center">
      <xsl:for-each select="stocks">
       <a href="#{@company}"><xsl:value-of select="@company"/></a><br/>
      </xsl:for-each>
     </p>
       <do type="prev" label="Back">
         <prev/>
       </do>
    </card>

    <xsl:apply-templates select="stocks"/>
   </wml>
  </xsl:template>

  <xsl:template match="stocks">
   <card id="{@company}" title="{@company}">
    <p>
     Quotes: <xsl:value-of select="quotes"/>
     <br/>
     Value: <xsl:value-of select="value"/>$$<br/>
     <small>(<b><xsl:value-of select="variations/day/@rate"/>
        <xsl:value-of select="variations/day"/>&#x25;</b>
        from yesterday)
     </small><br/>
     <small>(<b><xsl:value-of select="variations/week/@rate"/>
        <xsl:value-of select="variations/week"/>&#x25;</b>
        from last week)
     </small><br/>
     <small>(<b><xsl:value-of select="variations/month/@rate"/>
        <xsl:value-of select="variations/month"/>&#x25;</b>
        from last month)
     </small><br/>
     <small>(<b><xsl:value-of select="variations/ever/@rate"/>
        <xsl:value-of select="variations/ever"/>&#x25;</b> ever)
     </small><br/>
    </p>
    <do type="prev" label="Back">
      <prev/>
    </do>
   </card>
  </xsl:template>
 </xsl:stylesheet>
```

And then the HTML-generating XSL:

```
<?xml version="1.0"?>

<!-- Written by Stefano Mazzocchi "stefano@apache.org" -->

<xsl:stylesheet version="1.0" xmlns:xsl="http://www.w3.org/1999/XSL/Transform">

  <xsl:template match="portfolio">
   <xsl:processing-instruction name=
   "cocoon-format">type="text/html"</xsl:processing-instruction>
   <html>

    <head>
     <title>Your Portfolio</title>
    </head>
```

```
    <body BGCOLOR="#FFFFFF">
     <center>
      <table border="0" cellspacing="0" cellpadding="3">
       <tr>
        <td width="100%" align="center">
         <table border="0" width="100%" bgcolor="#000000"
          cellspacing="0" cellpadding="0">
          <tr>
           <td width="100%">
            <table border="0" cellpadding="4">
             <tr>
              <td bgcolor="#C0C0C0" align="right" colspan="2">
               <big><big>Your Portfolio</big></big>
              </td>
             </tr>
             <tr>
              <td bgcolor="#FFFFFF" align="center">
               <big>
                <xsl:value-of select="total"/>
                <xsl:text>$ (</xsl:text>
                <xsl:value-of select="variations/day/@rate"/>
                <xsl:value-of select="variations/day"/>
                <xsl:text>%)</xsl:text>
               </big>
              </td>
              <td bgcolor="#FFFFFF" align="center">
               <table border="0" width="100%" cellspacing="10">
               <xsl:apply-templates select="stocks"/>
               </table>
              </td>
             </tr>
            </table>
           </td>
          </tr>
         </table>
        </td>
       </tr>
      </table>
     </center>
    </body>
   </html>
</xsl:template>

<xsl:template match="stocks">
 <tr>
   <td valign="top">
    <table border="0" width="100%" bgcolor="#000000"
     cellspacing="0" cellpadding="0">
     <tr>
      <td width="100%">
       <table border="0" cellpadding="4" width="100%">
        <tr>
         <td bgcolor="#C0C0C0" align="center" colspan="3">
           <a href="{@url}">
            <big>
             <xsl:value-of select="@company"/>
```

```
            </big>
          </a>
        </td>
      </tr>
      <tr>
        <td bgcolor="#FFFFFF" align="center">
         <xsl:value-of select="quotes"/>
         <xsl:text> quotes</xsl:text>
        </td>
        <td bgcolor="#FFFFFF" align="center">
         <font color="#0000FF"><big>
          <xsl:value-of select="value"/>
          <xsl:text>$</xsl:text>
         </big></font>
        </td>
        <td bgcolor="#FFFFFF" align="center">
         <big>
          <xsl:value-of select="variations/day/@rate"/>
          <xsl:value-of select="variations/day"/>
          <xsl:text>%</xsl:text>
         </big>
        </td>
      </tr>
     </table>
    </td>
   </tr>
  </table>
 </td>
</tr>
</xsl:template>
</xsl:stylesheet>
```

If you're not clear on how this transformation process works, refer back to Chapter 9, which discusses this in more detail.

As a last step in introducing Cocoon and static XML serving, let us add a new media device – that of a Phone.com browser.

Adding a New Media Device

Phone.com's User-Agent value is "UP". Let's assume you did have the Nokia toolkit installed, and you would like to try out the Phone.com simulator. (Reverse all this if you had Phone.com and you want to try the Nokia simulator!)

You need to add a new browser type to the Cocoon properties file. Also, assuming you want to take advantage of the Phone.com implementation of WML functions, then you need to add a new stylesheet just for Phone.com browsers. A trivial example might be the mode ="nowrap" feature of paragraphs, which is standard WML but not supported by the ubiquitous Nokia 7110. We could add that to our Phone.com XSL file, so that any long lines scrolled across the phone's display, rather than taking up valuable screen space.

The first step is to edit <install-dir>\Cocoon\conf\cocoon.properties and add the new browser:

```
browser.6 = phonecom=UP
```

If you are using Cocoon 1.7.3 or higher, you will see there is already an entry for the browser "UP". Modify this so that its media type is "phonecom", as above, instead of plain old "wap". Then edit `<install-dir>\Cocoon\samples\wap\example-portfolio.xml` and add the following line:

```
<?xml-stylesheet href="portfolio-phonecom.xsl" type="text/xsl" media="phonecom"?>
```

Lastly, copy the `portfolio-wml.xsl` file to `portfolio-phonecom.xsl`, and modify `portfolio-phonecom.xsl` to have `nowrap` enabled. Change the lines in the `value` card from:

```
<card id="value" title="Portfolio Value">
    <p>
```

to:

```
<card id="value" title="Portfolio Value">
    <p mode="nowrap">
```

Then restart your web server so the Cocoon servlet reads in the new properties file, and reload the page:

```
http://<hostname:port>/wap/example-portfolio.xml
```

When you click on the [Value] link, you can see all the percentages without needing to scroll down. We could continue and convert all the cards <p> statements to be `nowrap`.

Here are the two results, both viewed via the UP.Simulator to show the difference:

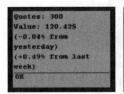 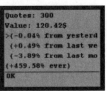

In the second image, the `nowrap` function of the Phone.com browser has allowed us to see two more lines, with little loss in information. Whichever line currently has the '>' scrolls sideways about once a second to display the rest of the line, so it's always readable by the user. This is just a small demonstration of a simple change that can take advantage of different browser capabilities, and why XSL should be applied not only per markup language, but also per device type, wherever possible.

Now we have a route to WML generation from XML, let's connect together the data extraction and the WML generation. We need some way of firing off the HTML data extraction from within Cocoon, and the way to do this is using a Producer.

Cocoon Producers Revisited

Cocoon's Producer class has two possible routes to deliver our data into Cocoon, getStream() and getDocument(). getStream() accepts a stream of XML as the input parameter, which is useful, except for the fact that we don't want to expend effort converting our DOM into an XML stream only to convert it back. GetDocument() accepts a DOM as the input parameter, so this is one we will use. Note that getStream() maps onto getDocument(), and you may find this useful in other projects, where some pages are already in XML, and you just want to convert them into WML, or some other format.

So, we need to create our own Producer class, which we have called `ProducerFromHTML`, and define the appropriate `getDocument()` method which will call our HTML extraction routine.

Creating and Testing a New Producer

This is required if you are to avoid wrapping the Cocoon servlet within your own, which is somewhat inelegant. The following steps are a simple test to demonstrate a new Producer, by copying the `DummyProducer` example code:

1. Copy `<install-dir>\Cocoon\src\org\apache\cocoon\example\DummyProducer.java` to `ProducerFromHTML.java`

2. Customize `ProducerFromHTML.java` (do whatever extra/different that you want to achieve, like change the dummy string)

3. Compile `ProducerFromHTML.java`

4. Add the resulting `ProducerFromHTML.class` to your classpath, if it's not already in it

5. Edit `<install-dir>\Cocoon\conf\cocoon.properties` and add the following line in the Producer section:

```
producer.type.ProducerFromHTML = <packagename>.ProducerFromHTML
```

6. Restart your web server (if need be) to force Cocoon to read the new properties file

7. On your PC, enter the URL:

```
http://<hostname:port>/cocoon?producer=ProducerFromHTML
```

The dummy text within `ProducerFromHTML.java` should be generated. Note that you will not get a result on your WAP simulator from the same URL at this point in the test, because HTML is the default output format. You would have to specify the XSL and Cocoon Processor type of 'xslt' to generate the equivalent WML.

Calling HTMLExtractor from Cocoon

Now we have both a working extractor that generates XML, and our own example Producer, all we need to do to complete the simple conversion tool is make our `ProducerFromHTML` obtain the service name and extractor properties file from the URL entered, and then instantiate and use `HTMLExtractor`. An example URL to drive the conversion tool, with the additional parameters, is:

```
http://<hostname:port>/cocoon?service=distributors&extractorprops=extractor.proper
ties&producer=ProducerFromHTML
```

Briefly, the parameters in the URL are:

❏   `service` – the name of the service in the properties file (this allows us to define many services in a single properties file).

❏   `extractorprops` – the properties file name containing all the start/end strings.

❏   `producer` – the name of the Cocoon producer (for use by Cocoon servlet, not ourselves).

The only other change we need to make is to use the `Producer.getDocument()` method instead of `Producer.getStream()`, because we have already created a DOM. Were we to create an XML stream and use `getStream()`, not only would it cost us processing time to create the stream from our DOM, but we would also cause Cocoon to waste time parsing that stream.

When the Cocoon engine calls `getDocument()` in our `ProducerFromHTML` code, we read our two parameters from the URL:

❑   service

❑   extractorprops

The third parameter specified, producer, has already been used by Cocoon to direct it to use our Producer, `ProducerFromHTML`.

Having extracted the two parameters, we then call `HTMLExtractor` to read in the properties file, and create our `Service` object which duly returns the XML, instead of pushing out the example dummy XML string.

Here is the amended `ProducerFromHTML` code to handle the URL request above:

```
public class ProducerFromHTML extends AbstractProducer implements Status
{
  //Methods

  //Never called - just here to satisfy AbstractProducer implementation
  public Reader getStream(HttpServletRequest request) throws IOException
  {
    return new StringReader(null);
  }

  //This is the method that Cocoon calls when directed to use
  //the ProducerFromHTML producer in a URL.
  public Document getDocument(HttpServletRequest request) throws IOException
  {
    //Read the parameters specified in the URL
    String serviceName = request.getParameter("service");
    String propertiesFile = request.getParameter("extractorprops");

    //Create the HTMLExtractor, passing in the properties filename from the URL
    HTMLExtractor mHTMLExtractor = new HTMLExtractor(propertiesFile);

    //Create the Service via the HTMLExtractor
    Service mService = mHTMLExtractor.getService(serviceName);

    //Finally get the XML document, and return it to Cocoon for XSLT processing
    return mService.getDocument();
  }

  public String getPath(HttpServletRequest request)
  {
    return "";
  }

  //For information only
  public String getStatus()
  {
    return "ProducerFromHTML";
  }
}
```

Note the null `getStream()` is just there to satisfy its abstract definition in the `AbstractProducer` class – it never actually gets called, because we never deliver a `Reader`, only a nice ready-to-use DOM.

Here is the result we get from all our hard work. First the WAP output, which firstly gives a list of countries to select from, and then displays the selected countries details:

And here is the HTML equivalent, which displays all the details in one long HTML file:

One final test is to change the URL in the `extractor.properties` file to point to the real web address of the Wrox distributor page (`http://www.wrox.com/Consumer/International.asp`), and run the converter again. Don't forget, by the time you read this book, the layout of that page may have changed. If so, then you will have to modify the start/end delimiter strings accordingly.

Limitations of Simple Conversion Tool

Before we leave the conversion tool, there are a few limitations to note:

❑ To create different output formats, you need to not just define output data in the properties file, but you must add the supporting code to create the matching DOM.

❑ The extractor properties file and the basic XSL files are inextricably linked, and should be abstracted out into a single file of properties/information.

❑ The properties file is needlessly read in every time a conversion takes place. We can remedy this by loading the properties file once, during Cocoon initialization.

❑ Error handling is minimal. In particular, there is no attempt to check whether the WML deck size is too large for a device.

❑ Distributor contact details isn't exactly a 'compelling' WAP service. However, for the Wrox employees themselves this could be a useful service. Maybe your company has a similar contact list or office location list just ripe for conversion.

Suggested Extensions to the Simple Conversion Tool

Our simple conversion tool only handles text, and in a limited layout at that, and so offers plenty of room for improvement and extension. Although we don't have room to expand on these in detail, here are some suggestions for improvement. We have split these suggestions into three areas:

❑ Additional features

❑ Flexibility

❑ Performance

Additional Features

The most obvious features missing are to be able to link pages together, and to allow the user to input data. You need to support both hyperlink extraction and input form extraction. Rather than code up to extract all the possible HTML input fields, there are some tools out there ready to help you. For example, Swing comes with an HTML parser that will let you extract input fields from HTML forms (javax.swing.text.html), but will not cope with poorly authored HTML. Another HTML parser can be found at H-P: http://www-uk.hpl.hp.com/, but this is not for commercial use. You can also use non-Java parsers, such as the IE5 one, of course, using ASP and COM objects as your interfaces.

To cope with potentially badly structured HTML, use Tidy from the W3C, and the Java implementation, JTidy. This wonderful tool cleans up all those nasty missing tags from HTML, sorts out incorrectly nested tags, and other life-savings tricks. Although JTidy cannot clean up all HTML errors, it will warn of problems and errors during generation, so you can write handler to cope with these exceptions. Combine JTidy and your choice of HTML parser together and you will save a lot of coding effort.

Once you have implemented support for input forms, and feel comfortable with handling them, you will eventually meet the mega-form – the one with 25 radio buttons, and 10 entry fields. A WAP user will not thank you for presenting that on their five-line phone. The ideal is to be able to cut the number of fields delivered to the phone right down to the bare minimum. An example might be a plane flight search, where the equivalent HTML page offers 10 input fields, but the backend engine only mandates 'From', 'To' and 'Date'. In such a case, you should present only the three that matter, but allow for the fact that you may need to force some default values onto some of the other fields. You can either handle these at the server side, or you can push the defaulted input fields up to the phone, so when the users hit the 'Find' button, the values all get sent to the backend engine.

Other useful features would be support for SSL, so you could decode, extract, and re-encode, on behalf of the user. Note this has the same security gap as current WAP gateways, and so needs careful thought not only on how to secure your server, but also whether users will even accept such a service.

Many sites require cookie support for navigation, and session handling. This is not easy with current WAP devices, since support for cookies is not widespread. You will need to implement the cookie handling yourself, to get these sites to function correctly.

Lastly, dynamic image conversion can already be performed, with current tools, to produce WBMP output from various input formats. As yet there is only one online WBMP converter, from Teraflops New Media. It converts GIF, JPEG and BMP online into WBMP.

Flexibility

Flexibility in this case means the ease of converting new sites, without resorting to changing the Java source code. All changes should be to properties files and XSL files only. As we saw earlier, abstracting out the extract properties and XML should help make the tool more flexible.

Another enhancement would be to allow the order content to be altered on the output, compared to the input – both the fields within each ExtractItem, and the ExtractItems themselves (maybe offer choices such as alphabetic, ascending numerical, and so on).

To avoid having to create any raw WML at all, we could use the extract properties file to build an initial tree of links to all conversion services, specifying the order in that tree within the extract properties file itself.

One level of flexibility, certainly from your user's point of view, would be the ability to enter any URL and have your converter return the best WML it can from the unknown HTML in a similar manner to the fully automatic converter tools reviewed earlier in the chapter. Again Tidy/JTidy potentially comes to the rescue because it offers an additional benefit of XHTML generation from HTML, delivering a DOM as the result. Feeding JTidy's XHTML output into your Cocoon Producer and manipulating the content before delivering to the WAP device should be a good way to do this, but be aware that JTidy's DOM implementation was not complete as of the time of writing. Functionality for handling large pages by splitting them into multiple decks would need to be added, and ideally, this would be linked to the user agent, since different WAP devices have different deck size limitations.

Performance

The converter presented here is not high performance. Rather, it shows the 'clean' way to convert content, and deliver to multiple platforms. If performance is a major consideration, then consider the following revisions.

Cocoon's caching algorithm takes hints from the hasChanged() method within the Producer class to tell it whether your document has changed. You could check the last-modified HTTP header returned from a HEAD HTTP request on your source HTML. You would of course have to save that last-modified value, per service that we create. Using the HEAD request gives two savings assuming the HTML hasn't changed. Firstly you don't need to read the whole of the HMTL document to find whether its changed, and secondly you don't need to perform any extraction if it the HTML hasn't changed, because Cocoon has already cached our original generated WML for us.

If your production web server is 'dumb' (if it doesn't support servlets), or if once-a-day updates are sufficient, then you can simply run Cocoon overnight and just upload the generated WML to the site, along with the HTML.

Finally, and more drastically, if you can guarantee your target format is always WML and you believe its layout will rarely change, then code directly from the parsed data straight to WML within your Java code. This will save the considerable overhead of XML and XSL. However, beware that the downside is that you will have to create custom code for each target output – both device and language, should your guess turn out to be wrong! It probably best to cover both possibilities – have an XML-based solution for the majority of your work, and then any specific sites that require high performance can be tuned to generate WML directly in your Java code.

Also, as a final thought on improvements, it is worth mentioning that we have only covered Java solutions here. There are plenty of non-Java solutions out there, just waiting for you to try, such Microsoft's IE5 HTML parser and OmniMark, which may well fit the bill better than the solution presented here. The same theories of extraction apply, even though the environment may be different. If you concentrate on creating intermediate data described using XML there is no reason why you should not mix these technologies with success. That's the beauty of open standards.

Future Trends

The future of conversion software – and document production in general – is obviously XML-based. In fact, the standards fight is now moving from XML itself to XML definitions – my way of describing a Customer is better than yours. For this reason, we can expect conversion technologies to be eventually eclipsed by pure XML-generated web sites. However, this sort of wholesale change is not a one-week project for the large corporate, and it's going to take several years before the web is transformed. There is probably a 1-3 year window for developers to use conversion tools whilst they plan how to re-work their backend and web delivery systems.

In the near future, before the end of 2000, Cocoon 2 will be available, which threatens to be faster and offer more comprehensive site management Cocoon 1. Because of the memory-hungry nature of the DOM – it stores the whole object tree in memory – Cocoon 2 will be moving to a SAX-based parser. In our example we created our own DOM, not Cocoon, and furthermore, because we're limited by the ~1400 byte WAP default deck size, this is not quite so critical to us. Also for improved performance, Cocoon 2 will pre-compile as much content as possible.

On the publishing front, Cocoon 2 offers some significant improvements for handling a complete web site, which Cocoon 1 cannot currently manage. The Cocoon authors have tried to disentangle the different parts of a web site from each other, to make the site more manageable. An example of the problem they are trying to overcome is that to modify the styling behavior of a document, you currently need to change the document itself. (In our code example above, we needed to add a new/modified processing instructions to our generated XML, for example). The ideal would be to have the XML and XSL totally separate. The Cocoon 2 solution to this is called a 'sitemap'. From the Cocoon web site:

> *"A sitemap is the collection of pipeline matching information that allows the Cocoon engine to associate the requested URI to the proper response-producing pipeline. The sitemap physically represents the central repository for web site administration, where the URI space and its handling is maintained."*

This is still in the throes of being defined, so we will not elaborate any further, other than to suggest you visit the Cocoon website.

As a final look to the future of improved XML handling, as opposed to just conversion technology, look out for the following technologies:

❑   JDOM from Jason Hunter and Brett McLaughlin, (http://www.jdom.org/). JDOM offers reduced complexity for Java developers who wish to manipulate DOMs without having to use the clunky W3C APIs.

❑   Apache's XSP (http://www.apache.org/). XSP stands for eXtensible Server Pages, and is Cocoon's technology for building web applications based on dynamic XML content. XSP is similar to JSP, since the XSP instructions, embedded within the XML page, are used to create a Cocoon producer (as opposed to a generic servlet), which then generates the dynamic content in the page.

Summary

In summary, here are some checkpoints for deciding whether to convert or build from scratch. Answering 'yes' to several of these, suggests that you should consider conversion for your development:

- ❑ Is my idea/site suitable for WML, regardless of how I choose to create it? Is it a compelling service?

- ❑ Is my existing HTML suitable for conversion to WML, rather than fresh creation? Is it uniformly formatted small amounts of text?

- ❑ Is time to market a problem?

- ❑ Is performance a minor issue?

- ❑ Are skilled development resources scarce?

- ❑ Am I remote from (not allowed access to) the backend database/data source?

- ❑ Am I remote from (not allowed access to) the existing HTML-generating code?

- ❑ Is the existing HTML-generating code written using a tool I am not familiar with?

13

WAP and E-Mail

Generally acknowledged as being the 'killer app' of the Internet, e-mail is more frequently used than even the Web. As more and more people rush online, e-mail will become, even more, the ubiquitous means of communication between individuals, for all sorts of purposes, in many different spheres of activity.

E-mail has achieved a phenomenally wide user base over the last few years, which is due in part to the power and design of the Internet mail protocols that we will be examining later in this chapter. Programming with those e-mail protocols is, however, a subject that has received surprisingly little attention from the mainstream programming textbooks.

One of the secrets of e-mail's amazing success with the general public is that it hides the underlying complexities and details of transmitting and retrieving electronic mail from the end user, allowing for low maintenance and ease of use. Mobile phones and PDAs have also been tremendously successful because, like e-mail, they provide a user-friendly interface to a powerful communication paradigm. These wireless consumer devices are likely to be far more quickly and widely adopted by the largely non-technical general public in the next few years, overtaking the more powerful and complex personal computer.

The market penetration of WAP-enabled mobile phone technology will bring with it greater demand for more flexible, and powerful, mobile computing applications. Wireless e-mail functionality will be at the core of this revolution.

> **E-mail and WAP are fast becoming the most demanded combinations of technology by both corporations and general consumers.**

Within today's e-commerce computing systems, the ability to exchange messages is an important feature, and one which will be demanded far more frequently as the functionality provided by e-mail becomes a de-facto standard, replacing the outdated fax technology for most businesses, and being fully integrated with corporate voice mail systems.

In fact, the ultimate goal for messaging technology for many organizations is a *universal* inbox in which voice, fax, and e-mail can be viewed in any format by a mobile communicator device. For example voice mail, e-mail and faxes should be viewable as e-mail, audible like a voice mail, or sent to a nearby fax machine or printer.

In this chapter we will:

❏   Review the history of e-mail and the current e-mail protocol standards

❏   Look at Sun's JavaMail API

❏   Build server-side Java programs to deliver e-mail messaging features for WAP-enabled devices

❏   Briefly examine how to use CDO and ASP to incorporate e-mail into web applications on the Microsoft platform

Build an e-mail application that uses all three technologies, WAP, CDO and ASP.

Introduction to E-Mail

E-mail is an asynchronous message exchange technology. This simply means that when you send an e-mail message the recipient(s) does not have to be available at that instant to receive the mail, but may collect the message at his or her own leisure.

E-mail was one of the first applications to be used on the Internet and has shown a remarkable amount of tenacity. The protocols used to transmit and deliver e-mail have been evolving and changing over the years, and we have seen a wide variety of proprietary protocols come and go. Most of these proprietary solutions are now either obsolete or have been adapted to the open standards adopted on the Internet at large.

> **The idea of proprietary e-mail systems is no longer feasible in the Internet computing world – systems *must* interconnect to benefit from the huge installed base of Personal Computers, Macs and workstations, interactive TVs and mobile devices, linked to the Internet.**

The History of Internet E-Mail

The ARPANET (Advanced Research Projects Agency Network) was created in 1969 as an experimental project to enable communication between participants in the DARPA (Defence Advanced Research Projects Agency) community. Ray Tomlinson wrote SNDMSG, the first ARPANET e-mail system, in 1972, and e-mail protocols and systems have snowballed since then.

To gain an idea of the worldwide adoption of this technology, here are some figures detailing e-mail usage (taken from NUA Internet Surveys):

❑ In the early 1990s, there were only 15 million e-mail accounts in the world

❑ There were 569 million e-mail accounts globally at year-end 1999; this figure is up 83% on the previous year

❑ It is predicted that there will be in excess of one billion e-mail accounts worldwide by 2002

The Decline of X.400 and the Rise of Internet Mail Protocols

The International Standards Organization (ISO) spent many years working on the vast and complete X.400 protocol as the de-facto standard for electronic mail.

However, whilst waiting for the final published specification, many vendors developed proprietary e-mail systems that achieved a wide deployment. The ISO e-mail standard, along with X.500, its sister standard for directory services, was simply released too late to achieve market dominance. The PC revolution was in full swing, and other, less expensive implementations such as MS Mail, Lotus Notes and cc:Mail had achieved a critical market share. Despite the vast reach of the ISO and the comprehensiveness of the enterprise (the brief was to design a complete mail specification), the standard was unable to displace the mass of e-mail systems already firmly established.

Acceptance of X.400 was further hampered by the fact that the ISO had missed some fairly vital pieces of functionality, such as the ability to asynchronously access mail messages without a permanent connection to the Internet in a way we will discuss later using the Post Office Protocol (POP3).

Nevertheless, X.400 may see some sort of renaissance as a mail backbone to transfer mail messages between mail servers, and is actually being used as a standard mail backbone protocol by several of the major vendors, including Lotus, Microsoft, IBM, and HP.

X.400 does provide:

❑ Good support for Binary Large Objects (BLOBS)

❑ Support for Electronic Data Interchange (EDI)

❑ Security via X.509 certificates

❑ Well designed connectivity of mail functionality with the X.500 Directory Service specification

WAP and E-Mail

We are now seeing the emergence of devices that integrate the more traditional capabilities of e-mail with the telephony features available to mobile phones, and other wireless devices. These devices are able to leverage the functionality, and familiarity, of both e-mail and wireless technologies. They are also truly portable, unlike most mail-enabled devices that have been used previously.

Short Messaging Service (SMS)

Short Messaging Service (SMS) messages, currently available on most modern mobile phones, have now reached over one billion messages exchanged a month in the European market alone, despite relatively light marketing of the feature by network operators and handset manufacturers.

However, sending an SMS message is unwieldy; you can only send messages in 160 character chunks of text. The editing of SMS messages is usually a cumbersome and laborious process and the user typically receives no warning when the character limit is about to be reached. Furthermore, to use SMS you need to know the mobile number of the person you wish to contact.

What E-Mail and WAP Can Offer

The popularity achieved by the very limited SMS technology indicates that demand for messaging via mobile phones certainly exists, and giving mobile phones all the functionality of e-mail seems to be the next logical step.

E-mail is a substantially more advanced technology than SMS, even if it is only used for simple SMS-like text messages. Message recipients are not limited in how they receive the message when using e-mail. Rather than only being able to access the message from a single mobile phone, the user can choose to access it from whatever client e-mail software he or she prefers, whether that is another WAP phone, a home PC, laptop, or even a UNIX workstation. E-mail, unlike SMS, allows for the recipient to have an address that is more like 'natural-language' than a phone number, and is thus easier to remember. Furthermore, e-mail provides the ability to mail 'group' addresses; for example, all@wapbook.org. As we will see later in the chapter, e-mail also has substantial multi-media functionality, and can use a variety of security protocols.

WAP devices and e-mail capabilities seem to be an ideal technological fit since they allow for a useful synergy of personal communication technology: delivering the convenience of portability from mobile phones, whilst allowing instant access to e-mail, providing asynchronous access to written messages.

It is interesting to supplement the figures on e-mail usage listed above, with some corresponding figures on mobile and WAP usage, in order to assess the scale of the potential market that WAP e-mail functionality may reach (source: Durlacher Research Ltd):

❑   There are currently 300 million mobile subscribers, growing at 50% per annum (PC growth globally is now only about 20% p.a. and falling).

❑   WAP penetration into the mobile phone market is predicted to be 8% in 2000, 22% in 2001, 50% in 2002 and 85% in 2003.

❑   It is predicted that the m-commerce market in Europe will be worth 5 billion euros during 2000, rising to over 20 billion euros by 2003. E-mail will play a vital part in this boom.

❑   By 2003, over 50% of Internet access will be by non-PC devices (Meta Group).

❑   By 2005, 1 billion mobile devices will be used worldwide (Gartner Group).

The convergence of technology between the established e-mail protocols and WAP devices provides an immediate and interesting challenge to the entrepreneurs and programmers of the next few years.

Key Elements of E-Mail

To help us understand the issues we will discuss later in the chapter concerning JavaMail, CDO and programming e-mail systems, we must first explore the key elements of an e-mail system.

There are essentially two types of protocol used in the e-mail process: transport protocols, and storage and retrieval protocols. We will look at these protocols and the overall mail process in some detail, before moving onto programming e-mail in the next section.

The Mail Process

The sender of an e-mail message uses a program to create and send mail; this program is known as the Mail User Agent (MUA). Once created, the message must be moved to the recipient's mail server over a transport medium – the Internet or a company's intranet for example – using a Mail Transfer Agent (MTA). The message is then delivered to the recipient using a Mail Delivery Agent (MDA) and stored until the recipient chooses to read it using his or her MUA.

So, the most important mechanisms in the mail transport system are:

❏ **Mail User Agent** (MUA) – A program used to create and receive mail messages

❏ **Mail Transfer Agent** (MTA) –The means by which mail messages are transferred between machines over the Internet

❏ **Mail Delivery Agent** (MDA) – The mechanism that delivers the mail message to the recipient's mailbox when mail is delivered via an MTA to the mail server

The Protocols of Internet Mail

To understand how to code applications using e-mail functionality, it is unfortunately necessary to understand the large number of acronyms that come with the territory! Some of these acronyms are associated with e-mail protocols, which have evolved into sophisticated messaging tools. Thus, we will now take a look at the following questions:

❏ What are RFC 822 and MIME?

❏ What are S/MIME and OpenPGP?

❏ What is SMTP/E-SMTP, how does it work?

❏ What are POP and IMAP?

❏ How does LDAP fit into mail systems?

❏ How does ACAP fit into mail systems?

Programming WAP applications with e-mail capabilities will involve some or all of these protocols.

Mail format and transport protocols

In this section we will look at the mail protocols associated with formatting and transportation of messages. This will in effect answer the first three questions asked above.

On the Internet, Mail User Agents (MUAs) typically send messages in a MIME encoded format to Mail Transfer Agents (MTAs), which transport messages using SMTP/ESMTP protocols.

RFC 822

In the past, e-mails were sent in a standard format, specified in RFC (Request For Comment) 822, entitled 'Standard for the format of ARPA Internet text messages'. This encoded the mail as plain text in a US-ASCII 7-bit character set format with no multi-part structure to the message body. The need for the inclusion of other language's character sets, and multi-media attachments led to a need for a more complex message structure, which was solved by the creation of MIME.

MIME

MIME (Multipurpose Internet Mail Extensions) defines the necessary message structure (see RFC 2045-2049) needed to work with different 8-bit character sets and multi-part messages. MIME was constructed as an extension to RFC 822, allowing older MUAs to continue to work, ignoring the new features, formats and extensions. MIME specifies a `Content-Type` header that can be used to specify a character set or media type for the e-mail message, for example:

```
Content-Type: text/plain; charset=us-ascii
```

This indicates that the message is in plain text using the traditional US-ASCII character set. However, it also has the ability to specify more exciting types, such as images and other binary attachments.

In a typical e-mail message, you may see several attachments indicated by MIME type boundaries. For example the following e-mail header snippet indicates that the e-mail it came from contains a simple text section, followed by a Microsoft Word document (`Content-Type: application/msword`) as an attachment:

```
------_=_NextPart_000_01BFA0AF.11763546
Content-Type: text/plain;
    charset="iso-8859-1"

------_=_NextPart_000_01BFA0AF.11763546
Content-Type: application/msword;
    name="Speaker FAQ.doc"
Content-Transfer-Encoding: base64
Content-Disposition: attachment;
    filename="Speaker FAQ.doc"

------_=_NextPart_000_01BFA0AF.11763546--
```

It is the responsibility of the receiving MUA to correctly interpret and display the message based on the specified type(s).

End-to-End Security

Security services can be added to each step of the communication path, for example by using Transaction Layer Security (TLS), also known as Secure Socket Layer (SSL). Alternatively, the security can be 'wrapped around' the data being transmitted, making it independent from the transport mechanism. This second type of security is known as 'end-to-end' security. S/MIME (Secure MIME) and OpenPGP (Open Pretty Good Privacy) are two competing protocols that provide 'end-to-end' security for e-mail messages.

S/MIME and OpenPGP provide all the functionality of MIME but, in addition, allow you to sign e-mail, and send it in a secure 'envelope'. LDAP (a directory service which is discussed in the next chapter) and X.509 certificates can also be used to secure Internet mail.

Work is currently being done by the IMC (Internet Mail Consortium), and the IETF (Internet Engineering Task Force), to resolve S/MIME and OpenPGP, which represent two incompatible standards for mail encryption and security, into a single standard.

S/MIME

S/MIME was originally developed by RSA Data Security Inc. and is based on the Public-Key Cryptography Standards (PKCS) #7 Cryptographic Message Syntax (RFC 2315), and the X.509v3 certificate format. S/MIME creates a message digest, which is encrypted to ensure the message cannot be tampered with in transit. In order to 'seal the message envelope', S/MIME encrypts all the contents using a triple-DES key algorithm.

OpenPGP

OpenPGP, which has superseded the PGP/MIME format, is based on the Pretty Good Privacy (PGP) data encryption standard.

SMTP

A transfer protocol is the language spoken by Mail Transfer Agents (MTAs). There are many such protocols in existence, such as X.400, UUCP (Unix to Unix Copy), and SMTP (Simple Mail Transfer Protocol). SMTP is by far the most commonly used and is the standard message interchange protocol on the Internet.

SMTP uses an *envelope* and *body* metaphor to structure a mail transfer. The envelope is used to transfer messages and contains information about the message sender and the destination address. The originating address is used to notify the sender of the message when a delivery failure occurs. The SMTP body contains the entire message including the body and header information.

E-SMTP

Extended Simple Mail Transfer Protocol (E-SMTP), which is described in RFC 1869, is an extension of SMTP to allow for an 8-bit character set. The 7-bit US-ASCII character set, which SMTP used, needed to be extended to allow for other European and Asian characters and to cope with multi-media message bodies. This is very much in line with the MIME extensions to RFC 822.

Storage and Retrieval protocols

When a user retrieves mail from his Internet Service Provider (ISP) he will almost certainly be using POP3 or IMAP4, as the retrieval protocol.

POP

The Post Office Protocol (POP3) would not be necessary if users had a permanent connection to the Internet and received SMTP messages directly. Historically, users would dial into such a permanently connected machine to read their e-mail remotely; this mail server would be constantly connected to the transport medium of the Internet, allowing it to receive mail continuously.

With the growth in personal computing, there was increased demand for e-mail to be stored locally, with only sporadic connections to the Internet. This led to the development of POP3 as a protocol to retrieve mail from a remote mailbox, via the user's MUA, allowing the mail to be read and stored locally.

IMAP

The most commonly used mail retrieval mechanism is still the Internet's POP3. However, the Interactive Mail Access Protocol (IMAP4) is gaining ground fast.

While POP3 stores all messages in a single message queue, IMAP4 allows for a more flexible mail storage metaphor, using a hierarchical folder concept in which to store messages, and providing a richer set of mail manipulation functions.

IMAP was designed with the following goals in mind:

- ❑ To provide the ability to store mail in folders besides your own inbox

- ❑ To provide a richer set of functionality for manipulating mail folders

- ❑ To provide better access to a mailbox in *online and disconnected* access modes than the simple *offline* access offered by POP3

- ❑ To facilitate access to a user's e-mail from more than one client computer (for example, from a mobile device and an office PC)

- ❑ To be fully compatible with the open standards of Internet messaging such as RFC822, MIME, and E-SMTP

As people access their mailboxes from a wider and wider variety of different locations and devices, IMAP4 will come into its own as a more comprehensive mail storage protocol than the traditional POP3. IMAP4 will continue to grow in popularity, replacing POP3, as the requirement for more flexible and powerful e-mail storage increases.

However, as POP3 is still the dominant protocol in use on the Internet, and as it is slightly easier to program and conceptualize, the examples using mail retrieval in this chapter will use POP3.

E-Mail's Relationship with LDAP

Ever since the development of X.400 and X.500, e-mail services and directory services have been functionally linked. Lightweight Directory Access Protocol (LDAP), which is the subject of the next chapter, is by far the most commonly deployed directory service for storing corporate address book information, and can be used to deliver address book functionality to MUAs. This is particularly useful to mobile users: there is little benefit in storing globally-administered information locally when it can be efficiently accessed from a single central source, thereby eliminating duplication and the need for synchronization.

E-Mail's Relationship with ACAP

The Application Configuration Access Protocol (ACAP) was conceived at Carnegie Mellon University as part of an ongoing project to enhance the university's e-mail and message exchange systems, known as Project Cyrus. ACAP has been proposed as an Internet standard as defined in RFC 2244.

ACAP covers a lot of the same functionality as LDAP in that it aims to store attributes (name/value pairs) relating to a user on a centrally accessible server. ACAP's focus is to allow highly mobile users the ability to retain configuration information and preferences specific to an individual user – for example, implementing a personal address book – and has been used by some MUAs for this purpose. ACAP client software is also designed to work offline, unlike LDAP.

Work has been done to closely integrate ACAP and the IMAP mail protocol, and if these services achieve a wide market penetration, they may provide substantial benefits to mobile users. However, ACAP suffers from not being as broad in its approach as LDAP, which is ahead in terms of both the maturity of the protocol, and its market share.

A Typical E-Mail System

To summarize, it might be helpful to look at some diagrams of a typical mail system using the Internet protocols. From a user's point of view e-mail is sent via SMTP, collected from their mailbox using POP3 or IMAP, and any address book information is searched for using LDAP (or ACAP):

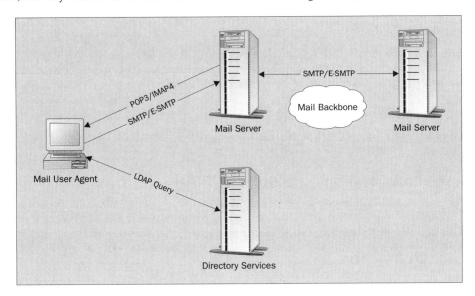

In terms of the flow of a message (either a RFC822, or a MIME, formatted message) from sender to recipient, the transmission path looks like this:

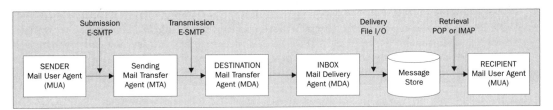

You should now understand how a mail system is structured. We have looked at how a Mail User Agent talks to a Mail Transfer Agent to send e-mail across a mail backbone, how mail is retrieved from a store and how LDAP is accessed for address book information.

Our next task is to look at how we can incorporate this mail functionality into our mobile applications, using WAP and e-mail to deliver real business value.

Programming E-Mail

There are a number of messaging APIs (Application Programming Interfaces) on the market that enable developers to write simple and 'generic' mail functionality into their programs. Before we look at some specific code examples, and consider how to construct applications that make use of messaging functionality, we will now look at the major API sets, which are:

❑   Common Mail Calls

❑   Vendor Independent Messaging

❑   CDO and CDONTS

❑   JavaMail

Common Mail Calls

Common Mail Calls (CMC) is the X.400 standard mail API set developed by the X.400 API Association (XAPIA), and as such, has a limited application to this chapter since we are dealing with the Internet mail standards – SMTP, POP3, and so on – rather than X.400.

Vendor Independent Messaging

Developed by Lotus, Vendor Independent Messaging (VIM) provides a simple set of API calls that provide platform-independent access support for mail systems.

Microsoft's Collaboration Data Objects (CDO)

CDO is an extremely simple-to-use API that is based on COM objects. What this means in practice is that it's the API you will want to use if you are coding in Visual Basic, Visual C++, or scripting languages on Microsoft platforms – which will be the case if you are using ASP to generate WML pages dynamically – we'll look an example of how to do this later in the chapter. CDO comes in two variants, CDO and CDONTS (CDO for NTServer).

CDO is designed to run against Microsoft's Exchange Server – a sophisticated mail server that can send and receive mail and organize all users' mail accounts for a large organization. Exchange Server's functionality is considerable and is accessible practically in its entirety from CDO. That means that although CDO is still relatively simple to use, it is more complex than you might want for very basic send/receive e-mail functionality. For this reason Microsoft developed CDONTS as an alternative. CDONTS can run either against Exchange Server or against the simple SMTP service that is shipped with Internet Information Server (IIS). CDONTS can't do much beyond sending and receiving e-mails, but that means it is incredibly easy to use – as we'll see later on when we look at an example using CDONTS to programmatically send an e-mail with just three lines of VBScript code.

Using CDO, complex messaging functionality can be pulled together with other related COM based programming models such as ActiveX Data Objects (ADO) and the Active Directory Service Interface (ADSI). This linkage will provide mechanisms to manipulate mail, and easily extend CDO applications, to include other areas of personal information management functionality, such as contact and calendar management.

JavaMail

Released by Sun in August 1998, JavaMail aims to revolutionize access to mail systems in the way that Java Database Connectivity (JDBC) revolutionized access to databases. We will be dealing with this at length in the next section. The advantages of using JavaMail include:

❑   It is available on the majority of current operating systems

❑   It offers an e-mail API that is both flexible and easy to use

❑   It offers excellent networking capabilities as standard

In the public imagination, Java and the Internet are inextricably linked, and to the programmer Java continues to offer the simplest and most elegant language with which to implement network-centered applications. The wealth of networking APIs and server-side solutions offered by Java makes it an obvious choice for implementing the distributed backend systems needed for our WAP applications.

We can make use of Java on the server-side to effectively scale and efficiently partition our WAP applications. With JavaMail, Sun has provided an essential API that will enable us to give WAP advanced mail functionality, adding value to our m-commerce solutions.

Introduction to the JavaMail API

The JavaMail API offers a clean object-oriented framework of classes that model a theoretical mail system. JavaMail is platform-independent and protocol-independent, and therefore presents an ideal way to build e-mail and messaging solutions that will work with WAP technology.

Many applications can benefit from e-mail support; using JavaMail, developers can rapidly construct messaging functionality whilst abstracting the underlying vendor's implementation in a similar way to the abstraction achieved from relational databases with JDBC.

In many ways the JavaMail service providers act in a similar way to those that provide JDBC drivers, doing for SMTP, Lotus Notes etc, what JDBC does for Oracle and Sybase. In our examples, we use the SMTP and POP3 drivers provided by Sun.

> **JavaMail models an abstract messaging service and any vendor specific mail system that provides a JavaMail interface implementation can be accessed with minimal – (ideally no) – recoding.**

Next we are going to take a look at some examples that make use of e-mail capabilities using JavaMail. The first example will show how an m-commerce application can use SMTP to send an e-mail confirming to the customers that their order has been placed, and the second example will utilize SMTP and POP3 to code a WAP based web mail application.

The following sections assume a basic working knowledge of Java Servlets. These were introduced in Chapter 10, but for more detailed information, see Java Server Programming by Andrew Patzer et al, published by Wrox.

Installation of tools

All the examples in this chapter were tested under Microsoft Windows NT version 4.0, service pack 5, and Windows 98 and Windows 2000. You will need to download and install the following software to compile and run the examples in the rest of this chapter:

❑ JDK (Java Development Kit) 1.2.2. Download from `http://java.sun.com/jdk/`

❑ JSDK (Java Servlet Development Kit) 2.1. Download from `http://java.sun.com/products/` (This is also available in the JSWDK download)

❑ JAF (Java Activation Framework). Download from `http://java.sun.com/beans/glasgow/jaf.html`

❑ Java Mail 1.1.3, which includes an SMTP service provider. Download from
`http://java.sun.com/products/javamail`

❑ Java Mail POP3 provider. Separate download from
`http://java.sun.com/products/javamail/pop3.html`

You will also need to have access to a web server, in which to deploy the Java servlets we will write, and a WAP browser emulator, to test the code. In this chapter we used:

❑ Gefion Web Server Lite (`http://www.gefionsoftware.com/LiteWebServer/`)

❑ Phone.com UP.SDK 4.0 beta 2 Simulator (`http://www.phone.com`)

Access to a SMTP server and a POP3 server is also needed. You can find out your POP3 and SMTP host names by contacting your Internet Service Provider or network administrator. They will be similar to the following:

❑ `pop.yourISP.net`

❑ `smtp.yourISP.net`

Classpath

You will need to add the following jar files to your Java environment's CLASSPATH variable in order to compile the example.

Under Windows 95/98 the relevant CLASSPATH amendments can be made in your autoexec.bat:

```
CLASSPATH = C:\jaf-1.0.1\activation.jar;
CLASSPATH = %CLASSPATH%;c:\jsdk2.1\servlet.jar;
CLASSPATH = %CLASSPATH%;c:\pop3-1.1.1\pop3.jar;
CLASSPATH = %CLASSPATH%;c:\javamail-1.1.3\mail.jar;
CLASSPATH = %CLASSPATH%;c:\jdk1.2.2\lib\WML.jar;
```

Under Windows NT, you can make the necessary changes by right-mouse clicking on the **My Computer** icon on your desktop and choosing **Properties**, or opening the **System** icon in the Control Panel. The Classpath environment variable can then be added or modified in the **Environment** tab:

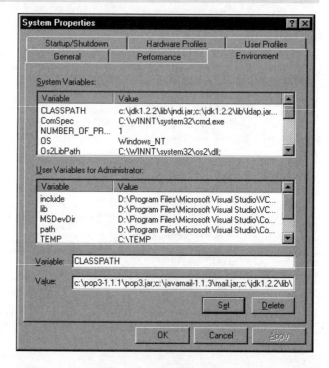

Configuring your web server to talk WAP

To configure your web server to work with the WAP MIME types you must add the WAP MIME types to the web server's configuration files, as was discussed in Chapter 2.

Java Activation Framework (JAF)

The JavaMail API leverages the capabilities for dealing with complex data types from the Java Activation Framework (JAF), which is part of the *Glasgow* JavaBeans specification. JAF provides Java with similar capabilities that plug-ins provide for web browsers. The Java Activation Framework allows for the querying and handling of multi-media data types, although this is of limited use on the current generation of WAP-enabled phones.

As more advanced and richer featured devices become available, JAF will provide the programming framework needed to integrate our e-mail application with the functionality of MIME. Enhancing the next generation of wireless devices to utilize complex mail attachments will be a trivial step using JAF, but will be a critical step in making WAP devices a *must have* commodity item.

The most important JavaMail classes

We will now introduce some of the most important JavaMail classes that we will see used in later examples.

javax.mail.Session

The `javax.mail.Session` class (not to be confused with the `javax.servlet.http.HttpSession` class) is used to control access to the implementations of the other mail classes that represent the services offered by the mail system, for instance `javax.mail.Store`.

javax.mail.Transport

This class is used for sending mail messages via a specific protocol such as SMTP, as implemented by the service provider.

javax.mail.Store

This class is implemented by the service provider. It aims to allow access to read, write, monitor, and search activities for a particular mail protocol such as POP3, or IMAP4. A reference to the `javax.mail.Folder` class is obtained via this class.

javax.mail.Folder

The `javax.mail.Folder` class gives a hierarchical view of `javax.mail.Message` objects, and provides access to specific messages for read, delete and reply actions.

javax.mail.internet.MimeMessage

This class models the actual mail message. The `javax.mail.internet.MimeMessage` class holds very little information and data about the message when it is first instantiated; as successive methods retrieve more data about the message, this class is used to store that data.

This *lightweight* message structure – populating the message with data only as it is needed – is an advantage when you wish to scroll through lists of message headers in your inbox without downloading the whole of each item. If a message contains a 10Mb attachment, this need only be retrieved when it is required, which considerably increases the speed of viewing lists of messages on a first generation GSM WAP phone!

The ability to download the attributes of a message, and not its entire contents, is optional for compliance with the POP3 protocol. However, most POP3 implementations allow for this partial retrieval of message information, enabling the JavaMail implementation to take advantage of this feature.

javax.mail.internet.InternetAddress

This class models a RFC822 e-mail address, that is an address of the form `john_doe@wapbook.org`. If an incorrect address format is encountered an error occurs, and an `AddressException` is thrown, within the Java method processing the e-mail address.

We will now take a quick look at a class designed to make the generation of WML easier for the servlet to handle. We can do this by providing a class that models the creation of WML, abstracting out some routine tasks such as generating the WML header, and opening, and closing both cards and the deck itself.

Simplifying WML generation – A WML helper class

In this section, we'll look at a WML class that will make the generation of WML easier, and to separate some of the WML syntax logic from the Java servlet code. This class models the formatting and header information needed to produce a valid WML document, thus allowing our servlet code later in the chapter to concentrate on the business of being a servlet, and hides some of the underlying complexity of creating WML from our JavaMail code.

The WML class is fairly basic and could be extended to interpret more of the tags that can be used within WML cards. The abstraction and separation of this presentation code is vital, as all WAP applications will eventually need to cope with a wide variety of different device capabilities, and being able to separate our business logic from our presentation logic is the first step on the road to achieving this goal.

The maximum defined size of a WSP data unit is 1400 bytes. This means that if our decks become too large the WAP device will not be able to receive them. It is good practice to keep deck sizes to below one kilobyte; with this in mind, the size of our deck contents is specified as:

```
private static final int _deckSize = 1024;
```

This header string defines the document as being a WML deck. Beware of including unnecessary line breaks in this string – it shouldn't matter, but certain WML browsers currently have problems with linefeed characters.

```
<?xml version=\"1.0\"?>
<DOCTYPE wml PUBLIC \"-//WAPFORUM//DTD WML 1.1//EN\"
"http://www.wapforum.org/DTD/wml_1.1.xml\">
```

WML.java

Here is the WML class in full.

```java
package com.wrox.util;

import java.util.Date;
import javax.servlet.http.*;
import java.io.IOException;
import java.io.PrintWriter;

//Utility class encapsulating some basic WML
public class WML
{
   private StringBuffer _buffer;
   private static final int _deckSize = 1024;

   private void setBuffer(StringBuffer newBuffer) {
      _buffer = newBuffer;
   }

   private StringBuffer getBuffer() {
      return _buffer;
   }

   public WML() {
      setBuffer(new StringBuffer(_deckSize));
      beginDeck();
   }

   private void beginDeck () {
     getBuffer().append("<?xml version=\"1.0\"?>");
     getBuffer().append("<!DOCTYPE wml PUBLIC \"-//WAPFORUM//DTD WML 1.1//EN\"" +
                        "\"http://www.wapforum.org/DTD/wml_1.1.xml\">");
     getBuffer().append("<wml>");
   }

   private void endDeck() {
      getBuffer().append("</wml>");
   }

   public void addCard(String id) {
      getBuffer().append("<card id=\"" + id + "\">");
   }

   public void addCard(String id, String title) {
      getBuffer().append("<card id= \"" + id + "\" title=\"" + title + "\">");
   }

   public void endCard() {
      getBuffer().append("</card>");
   }

   public void println(String line) {
      getBuffer().append(line);
   }
```

```
    private String getDeck()   {
        endDeck();
        return getBuffer().toString();
    }

    public void outputWML (HttpServletResponse response, boolean disableCaching) {
        PrintWriter writer = null;
        try {
            response.setContentType("text/vnd.wap.wml");
            if (disableCaching) {
                //Send a NO CACHING instruction to the user agent
                response.setHeader("Cache-Control", "must-revalidate, no-store");
            }
            //Set the Date header to help calculate cache timeouts
            Date now = new Date();
            long timeNow = now.getTime();
            response.setDateHeader("Date", timeNow);

            writer = response.getWriter();
            writer.println(this.getDeck());
        } catch (IOException ioe) {
            ioe.printStackTrace();
        } finally {
            if (writer!=null) writer.close();
        }
    }
}
```

The WML class encapsulates the details and logic needed by the servlet to generate a correctly formed WML page to send as the response to the user's WAP browser request.

Using the WML class

To use the WML class the client code simply creates a new WML instance, and then sends it the strings that make up the content of the WML cards. In this simplistic implementation <p> paragraph and <br/> line breaks are input by the client, but a more sophisticated WML class would want to encapsulate this logic as well.

As an example of how to use the WML class, consider the following code snippet:

```
WML wml = new WML();
wml.addCard("WAPMailLogout");
wml.println("<p align=\"left\">");
wml.println("Thank you for using WAP Mail<br/>");
wml.println("<anchor>Restart E-mail");
wml.println("<go href=\"" + request.getRequestURI() + "\"/>");
wml.println("</anchor>");
wml.println("</p>");
wml.endCard();
wml.outputWML(response, true);
```

This produces a deck that contains a single card; this card in turn contains a single paragraph, which displays a message and provides a hyperlink.

Caching

Caching presents the developer of WAP applications with both benefits and problems. The benefits of caching are obvious; it reduces the need for a device to repeatedly fetch information from the server, when it is unnecessary to do so. In this sense caching is a *feature* and can drastically improve the performance of some applications.

However, this feature can also present a problem for the developer, who has to handle this caching correctly. For an application that visits the same page again and again it is sometimes necessary to convince the browser to fetch a fresh version of the page if the information contained therein has changed, and not rely on any cached version it may have tucked away in memory.

The knowledge of how to disable the caching of WAP pages is then an important item in the development of WAP applications; to disable caching our WML class contains the following boolean test:

```
if (disableCaching)
{
    //Send a NO CACHING instruction to the user agent
    response.setHeader("Cache-Control", "must-revalidate, no-store ");
}
```

The `Cache-Control` instruction we have used in the above WML class should give us the ability to disable the caching of the page by the WAP browser. However, this does not seem to be fully implemented in the Nokia and Phone.com simulators at the time of writing.

Cache-Control Header

The `Cache-Control` header can take various values, including those used in our WML class, which are summarized below:

- ❑ `no-cache`
  This indicates that the browser should not cache the WML deck.

- ❑ `no-store`
  This indicates not only that the WML deck should not be cached by the browser, but that it shouldn't even be stored by proxy servers. This setting is usually used with sensitive, or time-critical, fast-changing information.

- ❑ `max-age=seconds`
  This specifies a period of time after which the document should be considered invalid and retrieved. For example a 'clock' page might specify `max-age=60` so that it is freshly retrieved every minute.

- ❑ `must-revalidate`
  The `must-revalidate` response header instructs the browser to revalidate, and if necessary re-retrieve each page stored in the history stack even when doing a backwards fetch. It can be combined with the other `Cache-Control` instructions. For example, the following code instructs the browser to force a reload of a page, even on a `<prev>` fetch from the browser's recent history stack:

```
response.setHeader("Cache-Control", "must-revalidate, no-cache");
```

Expires Header

The `Expires` header could also be used (although it isn't in our WML class), and specifies a time after which the cached page is invalid and should be re-retrieved. For instance to set the page to expire at 11am GMT on Friday 21ˢᵗ April 2000, you would write:

```
response.setHeader("Expires", "Fri, 21 Apr 2000 11:00:00 GMT");
```

E-Mail and E-Commerce Sites

One of the most important lessons for an Internet retailer is to ensure that the online buying experience is as easy and as enjoyable for the customer as possible. It is essential that the customer feels in control of the situation and is informed and reassured every step of way. A customer who cannot easily retrace his or her steps, change or cancel their order, or is confused or uncertain as to what is happening before, during and after a transaction, is unlikely to return, or to recommend the site to their friends and colleagues.

A frequent feature of on-line ordering is an acknowledgement e-mail sent to the customer to reassure them that the order has been successfully placed, and is being dealt with; this technique is used to good effect on such sites as Amazon, with its instant order acknowledgement.

We will now look at an example of such a situation, and the code needed to ensure that a customer receives an e-mail thanking them for their order, and confirming both the goods ordered and the price ordered at, within minutes (if not seconds) of placing their order.

E-Mail for E-Commerce Order Confirmation

This example uses a Java servlet to send an automatic e-mail, acknowledging an order placed from a WAP device. But first we will take a look at the WML deck from which the order is made.

OrderConfirmation.wml

The card resulting from the code below is displayed just prior to an order being placed on our imaginary system. The customer is asked to enter his or her e-mail address and can then click to place the order:

```
<?xml version="1.0"?>
<!DOCTYPE wml PUBLIC "-//WAPFORUM//DTD WML 1.1//EN"
"http://www.wapforum.org/DTD/wml_1.1.xml">

<wml>
   <card id="OrderConfirmation" title="Place Order">
      <p>
      E-mail:<input name="email" maxlength="100" />
      <br/>
      <anchor>Place Order!
         <go href="http://localhost/servlet/WAPOrderConfirmationEmail"
            method="post">
               <postfield name="email" value="$email"/>
         </go>
      </anchor>
      </p>
   </card>
</wml>
```

Using the emulator supplied by Phone.com, the WML page above is
displayed in quite a primitive way. Input of information is via the
phone's keypad, and the input box and Place Order! link are
displayed on separate screens:

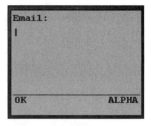

We first type in the e-mail address to
which the acknowledgement is to be sent.
Pressing the OK button enables us to then
proceed to the next screen, where we can
confirm the order by selecting the Place
Order! option:

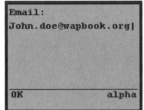 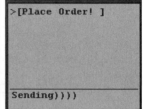

WAPOrderConfirmation.java

The Java servlet, WAPOrderConfirmation, which is invoked by the WML page above, takes the user's
e-mail address and sends a simple response. In the real world Wireless Transaction Layer Security
(WTLS) would be used to secure this order – especially if details such as credit card numbers were
being transmitted – however, for the purposes of the example, we will ignore security requirements
here. (Note that security is covered in detail in Chapter 16.)

Let's plunge straight into the code; the relevant lines will be explained afterwards.

```java
import java.io.IOException;
import java.util.Properties;
import javax.mail.*;
import javax.mail.internet.*;
import javax.servlet.*;
import javax.servlet.http.*;
import com.wrox.util.WML;

public class WAPOrderConfirmation extends HttpServlet {

    public void doPost (HttpServletRequest request, HttpServletResponse response)
        throws ServletException, IOException {

    String host = "smtp.yourISP.net";
    String from = "orders@machincorp.co.uk";
    String to = request.getParameter("email");
    String subject = "Your order with Machin Corp International";
    StringBuffer text = new StringBuffer();

    text.append("Thank you for ordering from MachinCorp International");
    text.append("\n\n");
    text.append("If you need to get in touch with us about your order ");
    text.append("please send an e-mail message to orders@machincorp.co.uk ");
    text.append("(or just reply to this message)");
    text.append("\n\n");
    text.append("Please note that you can view the status of your account and ");
    text.append("orders, cancel undispatched orders, and change the ");
    text.append("delivery or invoice information for undispatched orders at ");
```

485

```
text.append("any time through the \"My Account\" link in the side ");
text.append("panel of our Web site.");
text.append("\n\n");
text.append("MachinCorp.co.uk Customer Service");
text.append("\n\n");
text.append("orders@machincorp.co.uk \t http://www.machincorp.co.uk");
try {
    //Get system properties
    Properties props = System.getProperties();

    //Setup mail server
    props.put("mail.smtp.host", host);

    //Get session
    Session session = Session.getInstance(props, null);
    session.setDebug(false);

    //Define message
    MimeMessage message = new MimeMessage(session);
    message.setFrom(new InternetAddress(from));
    message.addRecipient(Message.RecipientType.TO, new InternetAddress(to));
    message.setSubject(subject);
    message.setText(text.toString());

    //send message
    Transport.send(message);

    WML wml = new WML();
    wml.addCard("OrderSent", "Order Sent");
    wml.println("<p align=\"center\">" +
        "Thank you for your order! " +
        "</p>");
    wml.endCard();
    wml.outputWML(response, false);

}catch (Exception e) {
    e.printStackTrace();
}
}
}
```

The first part of the above code is simply involved in setting up all the text for the e-mail to be sent. The important JavaMail section of this code occupies less than a dozen lines of code. Considering what this code is actually doing, this is really quite remarkable!

Essentially there are three steps to the process of composing and sending an e-mail using JavaMail:

1. Create a valid mail session

2. Create a message object

3. Send the message object

`java.lang.Properties` are used throughout the JavaMail API to provide a mechanism to control the behavior of many methods:

```
//Get system properties
Properties props = System.getProperties();

//Setup mail server
props.put("mail.smtp.host", host);
```

The first step in sending an e-mail is to instantiate a `Session` object.

```
//Get session
Session session = Session.getInstance(props, null);
session.setDebug(false);
```

At the core of sending mail is the creation of a MIME message object:

```
//Define message
MimeMessage message = new MimeMessage(session);
message.setFrom(new InternetAddress(from));
message.addRecipient(Message.RecipientType.TO, new InternetAddress(to));
message.setSubject(subject);
message.setText(text.toString());
```

We may then use the `send()` method of the `Transport` class, passing in this message object. This brevity in the `send()` is possible because we have specified the SMTP host in the session using the `Properties` object as shown above:

```
//send message
Transport.send(message);
```

Once the order confirmation e-mail is sent to the specified address, a quick WML response is sent back to the device. The final part of the code simply uses the WML class we saw earlier to generate the WML, which is shown here:

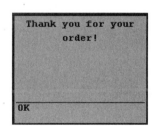

A Complete E-Mail Application

In the example given above, we have seen how to use JavaMail to send e-mail messages. We will now outline the other core operations of a mail system:

- ❑ Viewing lists of mail messages
- ❑ Reading specific messages
- ❑ Dealing with the capabilities of the device, and MIME types
- ❑ Deleting mail from a mail folder

Once we have discussed how to incorporate this essential functionality of e-mail within WAP applications, we can move on to our second WAP example, WAPMail, which will incorporate all of these features into a primitive, but functional e-mail system.

POP3 Programming Hints

Unlike the more advanced IMAP4 protocol, POP3 only supports a single queue of messages, and does not cater for multiple folders. In JavaMail, this message queue is represented by a single folder named "INBOX".

In a similar manner to the way we have created SMTP sessions, we must also open up a session to the POP3 service in order to be able to retrieve our e-mail:

```
//Get POP3 Session
Session pop3Session = Session.getInstance(System.getProperties(), null);
pop3Session.setDebug(false);
```

Once the session is created, you must connect to the POP3 message store using your username (uid) and password (pwd) to access your e-mail messages:

```
String pop3host = "pop.yourISP.net";
String username = request.getParameter("uid"); //e.g. user@wapbook.org.uk
String password = request.getParameter("pwd");

//Get POP3 Store
Store pop3Store = pop3Session.getStore("pop3");
pop3Store.connect(pop3host, username, password);
```

Viewing the INBOX

To view the INBOX – the only folder for POP3 stores – the folder must be retrieved and then opened, specifying an access permission. In the WAPMail example later in the chapter, we will see that READ_ONLY is used for viewing the INBOX and reading mail, whereas READ_WRITE is needed to remove e-mail from the inbox:

```
//Get Folder
Folder folder = pop3Store.getFolder(inboxString);
folder.open(Folder.READ_ONLY);

//Get Messages
Message message[] = folder.getMessages();

//Show messages list
. . .
```

Folder objects should be closed when you have finished performing operations on them to free up resources:

```
//Close connection
folder.close(false);
```

Determining the Number of Mail Messages

To determine the number of e-mails waiting to be read in the inbox, you can use the getMessageCount() method of the javax.mail.folder object:

```
//Get number of e-mails waiting in folder
int totalCount = folder.getMessageCount();
```

Reading a Mail Message

To read a particular message the getMesssage(int Index) method of the folder object can be used:

```
//Get a specific Message
int messageIndex = Integer.parseInt(request.getParameter("index"));
Message message = folder.getMessage(messageIndex);

//Show the message
. . .
```

How the Java Activation Framework (JAF) is used

To correctly display a MIME e-mail we must first decide what the content of the mail is. If the mail is plain text – it has a MIME type of "text/plain" – then we can display it quite simply. If, however, the MIME type is more complex – for example, the mail is an image or an acrobat file – then we cannot display it directly on a first generation WAP phone, such as the Nokia 7110.

```
// Determine Message contents data type
Object messageContent = message.getContent();

if (message.isMimeType("text/plain") && messageContent instanceof String) {
    // Show message
} else {
    //Error! WAP Mail can only read plaintext e-mails
}
```

Deleting a message from a POP3 folder

POP3 does not support the folder.expunge() method that can be used with IMAP. To delete, and expunge, messages, you must set the Flags.Flag.DELETED flag on the messages to true by closing the folder using the folder.close(true) method:

```
//Get Folder
Folder folder = pop3Store.getFolder(inboxString);
folder.open(Folder.READ_WRITE);

//Get Directory
int messageIndex = Integer.parseInt(request.getParameter("index"));
Message message = folder.getMessage(messageIndex);
```

```
message.setFlag(Flags.Flag.DELETED, true);

//close connection
folder.close(true);
```

A WAP-based E-mail Application

Web mail accounts such as the ubiquitous 'Hotmail', or 'Yahoo! Mail' are fast becoming the most popular kind of e-mail – there are almost 170 million subscribers to this type of account.

Web-based mail allows users convenient web access to their mail account without any messy machine configuration issues. Our second sample application implements a simple WAP mail system, allowing access to an SMTP/POP3-based e-mail account.

This example uses Java servlets and JavaMail to:

❑   Compose, send and reply to mail via an SMTP server

❑   View an inbox and read mail using a POP3 service

❑   Determine the number of messages waiting in the inbox

❑   Delete mail

Diagram of WAPMail's Functionality

Below is a diagram illustrating the functionality of the basic web mail system we will create in WAPMail.java. The user can logon to the system, view their POP3 inbox, read mail, reply to, compose, send, and delete e-mail:

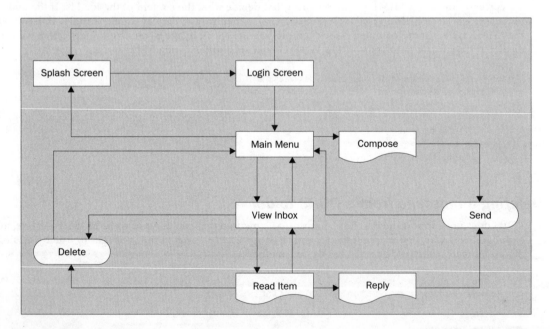

WAPMail.java

WAPMail provides all the basic functionality described above, but the code has been designed for illustration rather than deployment in a production environment. It should be noted that the code is limited in the following ways:

❑ It has minimal error checking.

❑ There is no guarantee that a WML deck of more that 1400 bytes will be accepted by the WAP browser. Large e-mails or a long list of e-mails in the inbox will cause problems.

❑ It is not implemented for maximum speed and efficiency (for example, use of `String` concatenation rather than `StringBuffers`)

❑ It can only be used by a single user – session information is held in a static class variable. We would need to use some session tracking code to make this code multi-user and scaleable.

❑ It has some problems if the browser does not correctly respond to `Cache-Control` response headers.

`WAPMail.java` is quite a long piece of code. Below, we'll step through it one piece at a time so we might clearly understand what the code is doing.

The first piece of code shows the servlet's main decision code. When the servlet receives a HTTP `POST` or `GET` request, it executes the `doPost()` or `doGet()` respectively. If the user has not logged in, and had the necessary session information created, they are shown the splash screen, which requires them to login to proceed:

```java
import java.io.*;
import java.util.*;
import javax.mail.*;
import javax.mail.internet.*;
import javax.servlet.*;
import javax.servlet.http.*;
import com.wrox.util.WML;

public class WAPMail extends HttpServlet implements SingleThreadModel
{
    private static String inboxString = "INBOX";
    private static UserSessionData _userSessionData;

    public void doGet (HttpServletRequest request,
                       HttpServletResponse response)
        throws ServletException, IOException
        {
            this.doPost(request,response);
        }

    public void doPost (HttpServletRequest request,
                        HttpServletResponse response)
        throws ServletException, IOException
        {
            UserSessionData userSessionData = getUserSessionData();
            String action = request.getParameter("action");

            //Main decision making "loop"
            try {
                //SHOW SPLASH SCREEN
```

```
           if ((action == null) ||
               ((!action.equalsIgnoreCase("login")) &&
               (userSessionData == null))) {
               this.splashScreen(request, response);
           }
           //LOGIN
           else if (action.equalsIgnoreCase("login")) {
               this.login(request, response);
           }
           //LOGOUT
           else if (action.equalsIgnoreCase("logout")) {
               this.logout(request, response);
           }
           //SHOW MAIN MENU
           else if (action.equalsIgnoreCase("mainmenu")) {
               this.mainMenu(request, response, this.getUserSessionData());
           }
           //COMPOSE
           else if (action.equalsIgnoreCase("compose")) {
               this.compose(request, response);
           }
           //SEND
           else if (action.equalsIgnoreCase("send")) {
               this.send(request, response, this.getUserSessionData());
           }
           //VIEW IN BOX
           else if (action.equalsIgnoreCase("viewinbox")) {
               this.viewInbox(request, response, this.getUserSessionData());
           }
           //READ
           else if (action.equalsIgnoreCase("read")) {
               this.read(request, response, this.getUserSessionData());
           }
           //DELETE
           else if (action.equalsIgnoreCase("delete")) {
               this.deleteMessage(request, response, this.getUserSessionData());
           }
           //REPLY
           else if (action.equalsIgnoreCase("reply")) {
               this.replyToMessage(request, response,
                                   this.getUserSessionData());
           }
       } catch (MessagingException me) {
           me.printStackTrace();
       }
   }

   public void splashScreen(HttpServletRequest request,
                            HttpServletResponse response)
       throws ServletException, IOException, MessagingException
   {
   this.splashScreen(request, response, "");
   }
}

   public void splashScreen(HttpServletRequest request,
                    HttpServletResponse response, String message)
       throws ServletException, IOException, MessagingException {

   WML wml = new WML();
   wml.addCard("WAPMailSplash");
   wml.println("<do type=\"accept\" label=\"Login\">" +
```

```
            "<go href=\"" + request.getRequestURI() + "\" method=\"post\">" +
               "<postfield name=\"action\" value=\"login\"/>" +
               "<postfield name=\"uid\" value=\"$uid\"/>" +
               "<postfield name=\"pwd\" value=\"$pwd\"/>" +
               "</go>" +
               "</do>" +
               "<p align=\"center\">" +
               "WAP E-mail" +
               "</p>");
    if (message != "") {
      wml.println("<p align=\"left\">" +
                    "<i>" + message + "</i>" +
                    "</p>");
    }
        wml.println("<p>" +
            "Username:" +
            "<input name=\"uid\" title=\"user name\"/><br/>" +
            "Password:" +
            "<input name=\"pwd\" type=\"password\" title=\"password\"/><br/>" +
            "</p>");
      wml.endCard();
      wml.outputWML(response, true);
    }
```

The user is required to log in by specifying their POP3 username (e-mail address) and password. Here is a screen shot sequence of the login process using the UP.Simulator:

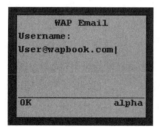 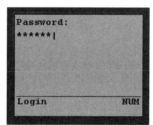

If there are any problems in the login process, for instance an incorrect password, the user is presented with this error message, and an opportunity to re-try the login:

This login process creates an SMTP and a POP3 session, storing them in an instance of UserSessionData, which models this information throughout the rest of the WAPMail code. We will see the code for this class at the end of the WAPMail listing.

It is the use of a static variable to store the UserSessionData instance that limits the use of the system to a single user. To allow multiple access to the system, WAPMail could be re-modeled to track the user's HttpSession, making use of this to provide an indexed list of these UserSessionData objects. Here, this is left as an exercise for the reader.

The next piece of code shows the login process:

```
public void login(HttpServletRequest request, HttpServletResponse response)
    throws ServletException, IOException, MessagingException {

    try {
        String pop3host = "pop.yourISP.net";
        String smtphost = "smtp.yourISP.net";
        String username = request.getParameter("uid");
        String password = request.getParameter("pwd");

        //Get SMTP Session
        Properties props = System.getProperties();
        props.put("mail.smtp.host", smtphost);
        //Get SMTP session
        Session smtpSession = Session.getInstance(props, null);
                    smtpSession.setDebug(false);
        //Get POP3 Session
        Session pop3Session = Session.getInstance(System.getProperties(), null);
        pop3Session.setDebug(false);
        //Get POP3 Store
        Store pop3Store = pop3Session.getStore("pop3");
        pop3Store.connect(pop3host, username, password);

        //Create a new UserSessionData object
        UserSessionData usd = new UserSessionData(smtpSession, pop3Session,
                                        pop3Store, username);
        this.setUserSessionData(usd);

        //if all okay show main menu
        this.mainMenu(request, response, usd);

    } catch (Exception e) {
        e.printStackTrace();
        this.splashScreen(request, response, "Error logging in!");
    }
}

public void logout(HttpServletRequest request, HttpServletResponse response)
    throws ServletException, IOException, MessagingException {

    try {
        this.getUserSessionData().destroy();
        this._userSessionData = null;

        WML wml = new WML();
        wml.addCard("WAPMailLogout");
        wml.println("<p align=\"left\">" +
                        "Thank you for using WAP Mail<br/>" +
                        "<anchor>Restart E-mail" +
                        "<go href=\"" + request.getRequestURI() + "\"/>" +
                        "</anchor>" +
                        "</p>");
        wml.endCard();
        wml.outputWML(response, true);
    } catch (Exception e) {
        e.printStackTrace();
    }
}

public void mainMenu(HttpServletRequest request,
```

```
                  HttpServletResponse response, UserSessionData userSessionData)
       throws ServletException, IOException, MessagingException {

       try {
          WML wml = new WML();
          wml.addCard("WAPMailMainMenu", "Main Menu");
          wml.println("<p align=\"left\">" +
               "<anchor>1. Read Mail " + this.getInboxCount(userSessionData) +
               "<go href=\"" + request.getRequestURI() +
               "?action=viewinbox\"/>" +
               "</anchor><br/>" +
               "<anchor>2. Compose" +
               "<go href=\"" + request.getRequestURI() + "?action=compose\"/>" +
               "</anchor><br/>" +
               "<anchor>3. Logout" +
               "<go href=\"" + request.getRequestURI() + "?action=logout\"/>" +
               "</anchor><br/>" +
               "</p>");
          wml.endCard();
          wml.outputWML(response, true);
       } catch (Exception e) {
          e.printStackTrace();
       }
   }
}
```

This code takes the user's username and password as supplied, and attempts to connect to his POP3 inbox, to enable the user to read his mail. It also creates an SMTP session in order to send mail. We can see the logout method below, and the method that constructs the main menu for the WAP mail system.

This produces the main menu of WAPMail:

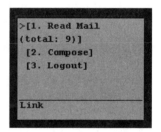

The following code shows the compose() method, which constructs a WML page that enables the user of our mail system to enter the details of an email: who it is to, what the subject is, and the text of the e-mail:

```
public void compose(HttpServletRequest request, HttpServletResponse response)
       throws ServletException, IOException, MessagingException {
    this.compose(request, response, "", "");
}

public void compose(HttpServletRequest request,
               HttpServletResponse response, String to, String subject)
       throws ServletException, IOException, MessagingException {

    WML wml = new WML();
    wml.addCard("WAPMailCompose");
    wml.println("<p>" +
       "<fieldset title=\"Compose\">" +
```

```
                "To:<input name=\"to\" maxlength=\"100\" emptyok=\"false\"" +
                " value=\"" + to + "\"/><br/>" +
                "cc:<input name=\"cc\" maxlength=\"100\" emptyok=\"true\"/><br/>" +
                "Subject:<input name=\"subject\" value=\"" + subject +
                "\" emptyok=\"true\"/><br/>" +
                "Text:<input name=\"text\" maxlength=\"500\" emptyok=\"true\"/><br/>" +
                "</fieldset>" +
                "<anchor> Send " +
                "<go href=\"" + request.getRequestURI() + "\" method=\"post\">" +
                "<postfield name=\"action\" value=\"send\"/>" +
                "<postfield name=\"to\" value=\"$to\"/>" +
                "<postfield name=\"cc\" value=\"$cc\"/>" +
                "<postfield name=\"subject\" value=\"$subject\"/>" +
                "<postfield name=\"text\" value=\"$text\"/>" +
                "</go>" +
                "</anchor>" +
                "</p>");
        wml.endCard();
        wml.outputWML(response, true);
    }
```

To compose an e-mail, the user must enter:

❏   A recipient

❏   A circulation list (optional – leave blank if not required)

❏   A subject for the message

❏   Some text for the body of the message

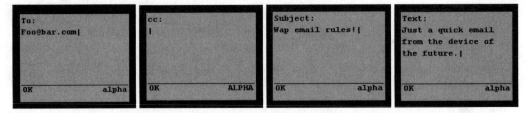

The example of constructing a message above relies on the fact that the String 'to' is a single Internet address in the form of john_doe@wapbook.org:

```
    message.addRecipient(Message.RecipientType.TO, new InternetAddress(to));
```

If you wish to give your users the ability to type in a comma delimited list of e-mail addresses then you can use the parse() method of the InternetAddress class to return an array of InternetAddress objects and use the setRecipients() of the message object:

```
    message.setRecipients(Message.RecipientType.TO, InternetAddress.parse(to));
```

If an invalid string is encountered when trying to construct an InternetAddress object, an AddressException is thrown.

Now, on with the code: The next section shows the method that sends e-mail using the same JavaMail process we encountered in our first code example. We can also see listed below the viewInbox() method that shows the e-mails waiting in our inbox:

```java
public void send(HttpServletRequest request,
            HttpServletResponse response, UserSessionData userSessionData)
    throws ServletException, IOException, MessagingException {

    try {
        String from = userSessionData.getEmailAddress();
        String to = request.getParameter("to");
        String cc = request.getParameter("cc");
        String subject = request.getParameter("subject");
        String text = request.getParameter("text");

        //Define message
        MimeMessage message = new
        MimeMessage(userSessionData.getSmtpSession());
        message.setFrom(new InternetAddress(from));
        message.addRecipient(Message.RecipientType.TO,
                        new InternetAddress(to));
        try {
            message.addRecipient(Message.RecipientType.CC,
                        new InternetAddress(cc));
        } catch (AddressException ae) {
            //Bad cc address
        }
        message.setSubject(subject);
        message.setText(text);

        //send message
        Transport.send(message);

        this.mainMenu(request, response, userSessionData);
    }catch (Exception e) {
        e.printStackTrace();
    }

}

public void viewInbox(HttpServletRequest request,
            HttpServletResponse response, UserSessionData userSessionData)
    throws ServletException, IOException, MessagingException {

    try {
        //Get Folder
        Folder folder = userSessionData.getPop3Store().getFolder(inboxString);
        folder.open(Folder.READ_ONLY);

        //Get Directory
        Message message[] = folder.getMessages();
        int n = message.length;
```

```
            WML wml = new WML();
            wml.addCard("WAPMailViewInbox");
            wml.println("<p align=\"left\">");
            wml.println("Inbox:<br/>");
            for (int i=0; i < n; i++) {
                String emailAddress =
                    ((InternetAddress)message[i].getFrom()[0]).getAddress();
                wml.println((i + 1) + ": " + emailAddress + "<br/>" +
                    message[i].getSubject() + "<br/>" +
                    "<anchor>Read" +
                    "<go href=\"" + request.getRequestURI() + "\" method=\"post\">" +
                    "<postfield name=\"action\" value=\"read\"/>" +
                    "<postfield name=\"index\" value=\"" + (i + 1) + "\"/>" +
                    "</go>" +
                    "</anchor><br/>" +
                    "<anchor>Delete" +
                    "<go href=\"" + request.getRequestURI() + "\" method=\"post\">" +
                    "<postfield name=\"action\" value=\"delete\"/>" +
                    "<postfield name=\"index\" value=\"" + (i + 1) + "\"/>" +
                    "</go>" +
                    "</anchor><br/>" +
                    "------------<br/>");
            }
            wml.println("</p>" +
                "<p>" +
                "<anchor>Main Menu" +
                "<go href=\"" + request.getRequestURI() + "?action=mainmenu\"/>" +
                "</anchor>" +
                "</p>");
            wml.endCard();
            wml.outputWML(response, true);

            //Close connection
            folder.close(false);

        } catch (Exception e) {
            e.printStackTrace();
        }
    }
}
```

We can view the inbox as follows:

The following code shows the method that reads a particular e-mail:

```
public void read(HttpServletRequest request,
        HttpServletResponse response, UserSessionData userSessionData)
    throws ServletException, IOException, MessagingException {
```

```
try {
   //Get Folder
   Folder folder = userSessionData.getPop3Store().getFolder(inboxString);
   folder.open(Folder.READ_ONLY);

   //Get Message
   String indexString = request.getParameter("index");

   int messageIndex = Integer.parseInt(indexString);
   Message message = folder.getMessage(messageIndex);
   Object messageContent = message.getContent();

   WML wml = new WML();
   wml.addCard("WAPMailReadMail");
   String emailAddress =
         ((InternetAddress)message.getFrom()[0]).getAddress();
   wml.println("<p align=\"left\">" +
         "From: " + emailAddress + "<br/>" +
         message.getSubject() + "<br/>" +
         "------------<br/>");
   if (message.isMimeType("text/plain") &&
                     messageContent instanceof String) {
      wml.println((String)messageContent);
   } else {
      wml.println("Error! WAP Mail can only read plaintext e-mails");
   }
   wml.println("------------<br/>" +
      "<anchor>Reply" +
         "<go href=\"" + request.getRequestURI() + "\" method=\"post\">" +
            "<postfield name=\"action\" value=\"reply\"/>" +
            "<postfield name=\"to\" value=\"" + emailAddress + "\"/>" +
            "<postfield name=\"subject\" value=\"Re: " +
            message.getSubject() + "\"/>" +
         "</go>" +
      "</anchor><br/>" +
      "<anchor>Delete" +
         "<go href=\"" + request.getRequestURI() + "\" method=\"post\">" +
            "<postfield name=\"action\" value=\"delete\"/>" +
            "<postfield name=\"index\" value=\"" + messageIndex + "\"/>" +
         "</go>" +
      "</anchor><br/>" +
      "------------<br/>" +
      "</p>" +
      "<p>" +
      "<anchor>Main Menu" +
      "<go href=\"" + request.getRequestURI() + "?action=mainmenu\"/>" +
      "</anchor><br/>" +
      "<anchor>Back to Inbox" +
      "<go href=\"" + request.getRequestURI() + "?action=viewinbox\"/>" +
      "</anchor>" +
      "</p>");
   wml.endCard();
   wml.outputWML(response, true);

   //Close connection
   folder.close(false);
```

```
        } catch (Exception e) {
            e.printStackTrace();
        }
    }
```

It is then possible to read an e-mail:

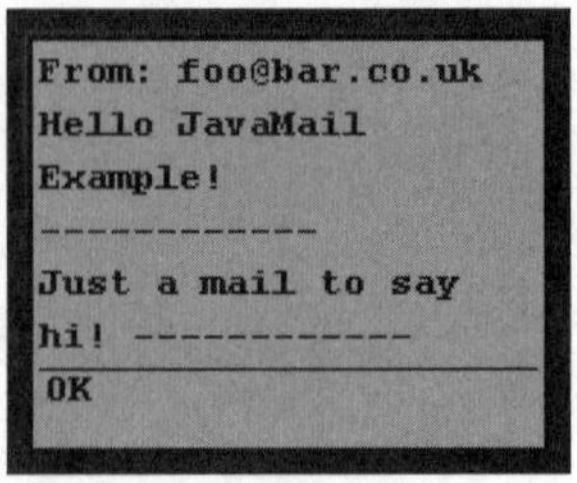

The final section of the WAPMail code shows the method that deletes e-mails from our inbox, and also some utility methods including a method that facilitates replying to a mail, and a method that determines the number of e-mails waiting in the inbox:

```
    public void deleteMessage (HttpServletRequest request,
                  HttpServletResponse response, UserSessionData userSessionData)
            throws ServletException, IOException, MessagingException {
        try {
            //Get Folder
            Folder folder = userSessionData.getPop3Store().getFolder(inboxString);
            folder.open(Folder.READ_WRITE);

            //Get Directory
            int messageIndex = Integer.parseInt(request.getParameter("index"));
            Message message = folder.getMessage(messageIndex);

            message.setFlag(Flags.Flag.DELETED, true);

            //close connection
            folder.close(true);

            this.mainMenu(request, response, userSessionData);
        } catch (Exception e) {
            e.printStackTrace();
        }
    }

    public void replyToMessage(HttpServletRequest request,
                  HttpServletResponse response, UserSessionData userSessionData)
            throws ServletException, IOException, MessagingException {
        //Not using the reply mechanism of the Message object
        String to = request.getParameter("to");
        String subject = request.getParameter("subject");
        this.compose(request, response, to, subject);
    }
```

```
    public String getInboxCount (UserSessionData userSessionData)
    throws Exception {
       //Get Folder
       Folder folder = userSessionData.getPop3Store().getFolder(inboxString);
       folder.open(Folder.READ_ONLY);

       //Get Count
       int totalCount = folder.getMessageCount();

       //Close Connection
       folder.close(false);

       return "(total: " + totalCount + ")";
    }

    private static UserSessionData getUserSessionData() {
       return _userSessionData;
    }

    private static void setUserSessionData(UserSessionData usd) {
       _userSessionData = usd;
    }

    public String getServletInfo() {
       return "A simple WAP e-mail application servlet";
    }
}
```

This class is used by WAPMail as a storage mechanism for the SMTP and POP3 sessions that are created by the login process.

By storing the user's session information in a separate class (UserSessionData) we remove some of the session logic from the rest of the servlet, which should make it easier to extend the functionality of WAPMail as the need arises:

```
// Storage class for user's session information
class UserSessionData {
    private Session _smtpSession;
    private Session _pop3Session;
    private Store _pop3store;
    private String _userEmailAddress;

    public UserSessionData(Session newSmtpSession,
                 Session newPop3Session,
                 Store newPop3Store,
                 String newUserEmailAddress) {
       setSmtpSession(newSmtpSession);
       setPop3Session(newPop3Session);
       setPop3Store(newPop3Store);
       setEmailAddress(newUserEmailAddress);
    }
```

```
public void destroy() {
    try {
        if (getPop3Store() != null) {
            getPop3Store().close();
        }
    } catch (Exception e) {
        e.printStackTrace();
    }
}

public void setEmailAddress(String newUserEmailAddress) {
    _userEmailAddress = newUserEmailAddress;
}

public String getEmailAddress() {
    return _userEmailAddress;
}

public Session getSmtpSession() {
    return _smtpSession;
}

public void setSmtpSession(Session newSmtpSession) {
    _smtpSession = newSmtpSession;
}

public Session getPop3Session() {
    return _pop3Session;
}

public void setPop3Session(Session newPop3Session) {
    _pop3Session = newPop3Session;
}

public Store getPop3Store() {
    return _pop3store;
}

public void setPop3Store(Store newPop3Store) {
    _pop3store = newPop3Store;
}
}
```

This specifies the logout screen:

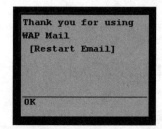

Enhancements to WAPMail

The implementation of WAPMail is designed to illustrate basic e-mail functionality and is not a very elegant example of Java servlet programming. Many things could be done to improve the design of WAPMail, for example:

❑ Use reflection to eliminate the huge `if` statement in the `doPost()` method.

❑ Use a separate JavaBean to model the mail system moving the logic out of the Java servlet, with which the Servlet would then interface.

❑ Use `HttpSession` tracking to allow multi-user access to WAPMail.

❑ Allow the user to specify the POP3 and SMTP servers; perhaps allow for multiple accounts to be read.

❑ If the e-mail contains illegal WML characters, then the e-mail text needs to be parsed to ensure that we encounter no problems. For example, the following use of '<' and '>' in the e-mail address field seen in some e-mails is an illegal character sequence in WML, and causes the generated WML response to be rejected by the browser: for example, `John Doe <John_Doe@wapbook.org>`

Sending and Receiving E-Mail using ASP

So far in this chapter, we've concentrated on using Java for incorporating e-mail into WAP applications. If you're in the Microsoft camp, however, you will most likely be using ASP to generate your WAP (and web) content. In this section we'll show how to use ASP with VBScript to generate WML pages that access e-mail functionality.

Due to space constraints we're going to keep the examples simple – if you've got this far in the book then you must already be familiar with WML, and if you're interested enough to read this section then presumably that means you're already familiar with ASP itself too! So, we're not going to stop to explain anything about ASP itself, and we're not going to waste time writing a sophisticated set of WML pages – instead we'll just demonstrate a simple page that sends an e-mail based on a couple of options, as well as another page that lets you check for incoming e-mail messages, all from your mobile phone.

In order to keep things simple, we'll also use CDONTS rather than CDO The examples here were tested with CDONTS running on Windows 2000 Professional, with IIS 5 installed. CDONTS will be default use the SMTP service that comes with IIS as its mail service. However, if you prefer, you can run CDONTS using Exchange Server.

Sending an E-Mail

Sending an e-mail with CDONTS could hardly be easier. For example, here's the VBScript code that sends an e-mail addressed to my own local account, `simon@biggybiggy.lt.local`.

```
dim objSendMail
set objSendMail = Server.CreateObject("CDONTS.NewMail")
objSendMail.Send "editors@wrox.com", "simon@biggybiggy.lt.local", _
    "Meeting!", _
    "Meeting to go over final adjustments to Pro WAP is today at 2pm."
set objSendMail = nothing
```

In other words all we need to do is create an object of type `CDONTS.NewMail` and call its `Send` method. The four parameters passed are (in order):

❑ The address of the sender (Note that no validation is performed on this: You can put in any address you want – it doesn't have to be your own address).

- ❑ The address the mail should be delivered to
- ❑ The title of the message
- ❑ The text of the message body

You can also optionally add a fifth parameter, the message importance, which can take any of the values 0 (low), 1(normal, the default value) and 2(high).

Note that the SendMail object does have somewhat more functionality than we have shown – for example it can "cc" and "bcc" e-mails, and attach files, but the above is all we need for our purposes.

So running an ASP page with the above script in it generates this e-mail message:

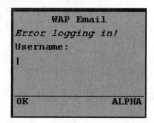

We're going to show how this could work in practice with a registration example. The example is based on a bank that has a facility to allow users to manage their accounts to a limited extent using their mobile phones. The bank has a new low-interest loan scheme, which it is heavily trying to promote. So when users have just gone online from their mobile phones to manage their bank accounts, and have just completed their transactions, they will normally be presented with a page that quickly mentions the new loan, and asks them to click on a link if they would like their branch to contact them about it. The result of clicking on the link is that an e-mail is sent to the branch to inform them of the request.

> *Strictly speaking, you could argue that a large bank may be more likely to automatically enter the request into a database for later processing – but we won't worry about that for the purposes of this example.*

We won't go into the details of the preliminary WML cards here since you've already covered all the WML you need to figure out how those might be written – we're simply going to present the ASP page that actually sends the e-mail. The page will be called MailOut.asp, and will accept the e-mail address of the user via the form variable EmailAddress. (Note that this variable name is case-insensitive.)

The address the e-mail needs to be sent to is Promotions@Internal.SuperBank.com. (The usual disclaimer applies – I've never heard of a bank called Superbank but if by chance one exists then any similarity in the name is purely coincidental.)

The ASP page looks like this:

```
<%Response.ContentType = "text/vnd.wap.wml"

Sub WriteSucceededPage
     Response.Write "<card id=" & Chr(34) & "card1" & Chr(34) & _
         " title=" & Chr(34) & "Mail Sent" & Chr(34) & ">" & vbCrLf
     Response.Write "<p>An email has been sent to your branch.</p>" & vbCrLf
     Response.Write "<p>An adviser will contact you soon about " & _
         "the LowInterest loan</p>" & vbCrLf
End Sub
```

```
Sub WriteFailedPage
    Response.Write "<card id=" & Chr(34) & "card1" & Chr(34) & _
            " title=" & Chr(34) & "SendMail Failed" & Chr(34) & ">" & vbCrLf
    Response.Write "<p>Sorry but a problem occurred " & _
            "accessing our database.</p>" & vbCrLf
    Response.Write "<p>Please try again later.</p>" & vbCrLf
End Sub

%><?xml version="1.0"?>
<!DOCTYPE wml PUBLIC "-//WAPFORUM//DTD WML 1.1//EN"
"http://www.wapforum.org/DTD/wml_1.1.xml">

<wml>

<%
On Error Resume Next
Dim bOK
bOK = True
Dim objSendMail
Set objSendMail = Server.CreateObject("CDONTS.NewMail")
If err.number <> 0 Then bOK = False
objSendMail.Send "Promotions@Internal.SuperBank.com", _
        "AutoMail@Internal.SuperBank.com", _
        "LowInterest Loan Info Request", _
        "Adviser should contact customer with email address " & _
            Request.Form("EmailAddress")
If err.number <> 0 Then bOK = False
Set objSendMail = Nothing

If (bOK = True) Then
    WriteSucceededPage
Else
    WriteFailedPage
End If
%>

</card>
</wml>
```

The code contains two subs, `WriteSucceededPage` and `WriteFailedPage`, which write out the appropriate WML depending on whether the attempt to send the e-mail succeeded or not. Of course dispatching the e-mail using CDONTS should always succeed unless there's a major systems failure at the bank, but we do need to allow for that possibility and display something reasonably gracious.

Note that the call to the `Send` method will merely stick the mail in a queue ready for Exchange Server or the SMTP service to send, then the method call returns. It is the responsibility of the mail service to actually attempt to send the mail and deal with any errors that might occur in sending it (for example, undeliverable address). By that time, of course, the `Send` method will already have returned a success – so you shouldn't rely on the return value of this method as a guarantee that the mail has been sent. SendMail will only generate an exception if a problem occurs handing the e-mail over to the mail server for processing.

If the code succeeds it will generate this WML page:

```
<?xml version="1.0"?>
<!DOCTYPE wml PUBLIC "-//WAPFORUM//DTD WML 1.1//EN"
"http://www.wapforum.org/DTD/wml_1.1.xml">

<wml>

<card id="card1" title="Mail Sent">
<p>An email has been sent to your branch.</p>
<p>An adviser will contact you soon about the LowInterest loan</p>

</card>
</wml>
```

Note that the use of Chr(34) in the VBScript to generate the quote marks around the card ID and title.

This page displays in the Nokia toolkit like this

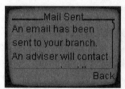 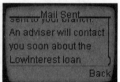

Reading E-mails

In this section we'll move on to show how you can use ASP in conjunction with CDONTS to read your e-mails and display them in WML pages.

Displaying the full text of e-mails on WAP devices can be problematic since many simply contain too much text – and there's no easy way to display attachments. But for the next example we're going to assume that you regularly need to read e-mails from your manager while you are on the move. So, you need to be able to access a WML page that checks specifically for e-mails *from* your manager and displays *only* those. We'll assume your manager knows that you read e-mails from your mobile phone and understands he needs to keep them short. We've made this assumption here to keep the code simple – in real life you'd want to be a bit more careful and perhaps have only the first few lines of each message sent to the WAP browser.

We've also designed a page that sends all the information in one go. The first card displays a list of e-mails, and subsequent cards display each e-mail. This minimizes network traffic, but in real life we'd also need to take care not to exceed the maximum size of the deck.

So, when reading the first card of the page the user should see this:

And on scrolling down...
If the user chooses the e-mail with the title "Problems at Hi Tech.."

They will then be presented with the following card:

And on scrolling down...

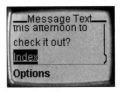

Note we use a link at the bottom to return to the list of messages. Hopefully, from this example, you can see how useful it could be to be able to access e-mails on the move from a page like this.

The ASP code to generate this page looks like this:

```
<%Option Explicit%>

<?xml version="1.0"?>
<!DOCTYPE wml PUBLIC "-//WAPFORUM//DTD WML 1.1//EN"
"http://www.wapforum.org/DTD/wml_1.1.xml">

<wml>

<%
On Error Resume Next

' set up email address of sender we are interested in
Dim sEmailFrom
sEmailFrom = "Manager@biggybiggy.lt.local"

' get to collection of messages
Dim objSession
Set objSession = CreateObject("CDONTS.Session")
objSession.LogonSMTP "Simon Robinson", "simon@biggybiggy.lt.local"
Dim objInbox
Set objInbox = objSession.Inbox
Dim colMessages
Set colMessages = objInbox.Messages

' count how many messages come from this sender
Dim i
Dim nMessages
nMessages = 0
```

```
For i=1 To colMessages.count
    If (lcase(colMessages(i).sender) = lcase(sEmailFrom)) Then _
        nMessages = nMessages+1
Next

' write main index card
Response.Write "<card id=" & Chr(34) & "index"  & Chr(34) & _
    " title=" & Chr(34) & "Inbox" & Chr(34) & ">" & vbCrLf
Response.Write "<p>" & nMessages & " Messages</p>" & vbCrLf
For i=1 To colMessages.count
    If (lcase(colMessages(i).Sender) = lcase(sEmailFrom)) Then
        Response.Write "<p><a href=" & Chr(34) & "#mail" & CStr(i) &_
                        Chr(34)& ">" & colMessages(i).Subject & "</a></p>" &_
                        vbCrLf
    End If
Next

Response.Write "</card>" & vbCrLf

' write cards with the messages on
For i=1 To colMessages.count
    If (lcase(colMessages(i).Sender) = lcase(sEmailFrom)) Then
        Response.Write "<card id=" & Chr(34) & "mail" & CStr(i)& Chr(34) & _
                " title=" & Chr(34) & "Message Text" & Chr(34) & ">" & vbCrLf
        Response.Write "<p><b>" & colMessages(i).Subject & "</b></p>" & vbCrLf
        Response.Write "<p>" & colMessages(i).Text & "</p>" & vbCrLf
        Response.Write "<p><a href=" & Chr(34) & "#index" & Chr(34)& ">" & _
                        "Index</a></p>" & vbCrLf
        Response.Write "</card>" & vbCrLf
    End If
Next

' clean up etc.
objSession.Logoff
Set objSession = Nothing
%>

</wml>




%option explicit%>
<?xml version="1.0"?>
<"http://www.wapforum.org/DTD/wml_1.1.xml">

<wml>

<%
on error resume next

in
dim sEmailFrom
sEmailFrom = "Manager@biggybiggy.lt.local"
```

```
' get to collection of messages
dim objSession
set objSession = CreateObject("CDONTS.Session")
objSession.LogonSMTP "Simon Robinson", "simon@biggybiggy.lt.local"
dim objInbox
set objInbox = objSession.Inbox
dim colMessages
set colMessages = objInbox.Messages


sender
dim i
dim nMessages
nMessages = 0
nMessages+1
next
```

The CDONTS code is slightly more complex than for reading e-mails, so we'll quickly go through the main points. We first store the address of the person we're interested in getting e-mails from in the variable sEmailFrom. In production code this might be retrieved from a database or the HTTP header information.

The next bit of code navigates through CDONTS's hierarchy of objects to get to the list of messages:

```
dim objSession
set objSession = CreateObject("CDONTS.Session")
objSession.LogonSMTP "Simon Robinson", "simon@biggybiggy.lt.local"
dim objInbox
Set objInbox = objSession.Inbox
Dim colMessages
Set colMessages = objInbox.Messages
```

We start off with a session object that represents our connection to the mail server – which depending on how we've set up CDONTS could be either the IIS SMTP service or Exchange Server. Logging on via theLogonSMTP method isn't really authenticating in the sense that there is no password supplied that could be rejected – you simply supply the e-mail address of the folder you are interested in and your preferred display name. We then use the Session object to navigate down to the inbox and the collection of your messages, each represented by CDONTS objects. Note that the Session and the Inbox are only CDONTS objects that form part of the CDONTS object model. They aren't necessarily related to – for example – any inbox stored by your mail client or server.

We now need to count how many messages there are:

```
' count how many messages come from this sender
Dim i
Dim nMessages
nMessages = 0
For i=1 To colMessages.count
   If (lcase(colMessages(i).sender) = lcase(sEmailFrom)) Then _
      nMessages = nMessages+1
Next
```

Note that CDONTS does provide a count property, which we use to loop through the messages. However this property is the number of messages in our inbox in total, from everyone. We only want to display the messages from our manager, manager@biggybiggy.lt.local, so we do need to count through to identify just these messages. We can test for the sender of each message by looking at the Sender property of the CDONTS message object. We use VBScript's Lcase function to convert the strings to lower case just to make sure we do a case-insensitive comparison.

Armed with this information we can go on to write out the WML script for the main index page, and for the pages with each message on, in each case only writing out messages from our manager.

The ASP page generates this WML:

```
<?xml version="1.0"?>
<!DOCTYPE wml PUBLIC "-//WAPFORUM//DTD WML 1.1//EN"
"http://www.wapforum.org/DTD/wml_1.1.xml">

<wml>

<card id="index" title="Inbox">
<p>2 Messages</p>
<p><a href="#mail1">Vivid meeting postponed</a></p>
<p><a href="#mail2">Problem at HiTech</a></p>
</card>
<card id="mail1" title="Message Text">
<p><b>Vivid meeting postponed</b></p>
<p>Rich from Vivid can't make it tomorrow. We're meeting Friday at 2pm instead

</p>
<p><a href="#index">Index</a></p>
</card>
<card id="mail2" title="Message Text">
<p><b>Problem at HiTech</b></p>
<p>The system we installed at HiTech has crashed. Can you call in there this
    afternoon to check it out?
</p>
<p><a href="#index">Index</a></p>
</card>

</wml>
```

Which – as you should be able to verify – gives the user output shown earlier.

Note that there is one other simplification here – we've assumed the text in the mail messages doesn't contain any characters that will be interpreted by the browser as WML tags. In real life, you'll want to WML-encode the text prior to adding it to the page. Unfortunately, as yet there are no methods available on the intrinsic ASP objects that will WML-encode, in the way that you can, for example, encode text for HTML pages using the Server.HTMLEncode method. So you'll have to write a function to do that yourself – since this function will perform textual substitutions on the relevant characters, we've left it as an exercise for you...

We've only very briefly looked at a few of the things you can do with CDONTS, to give a flavor of how you can generate WML pages with e-mail functionality on the Microsoft platform. If you want to find out more about programming with CDO, then you should check out *Professional CDO Programming*, from Wrox Press.

vCard and exchange of personal information

Wouldn't it be great if there were an easy way to use a personal data interchange format that was standard across all software and all devices, like an electronic signature or business card? This is exactly the niche vCard aims to fill. Although vCard is not a part of WAP, it is particularly relevant to the discussions we have had in this chapter about mail applications and mobile devices, so we'll just finish off with a very brief look at it here.

vCard was originally conceived by the versit Consortium, an industry body including Apple, AT&T, IBM and Siemens, as a mechanism to enable exchange of personal 'business card' data between any operating environments. The Internet Mail Consortium (IMC) took over the vCard, and also the vCalendar, specifications from the versit Consortium at the end of 1996.

vCard is not based on XML, but is constructed in a simple manner using attributes (name-value pairs). vCard information looks like this:

```
BEGIN:                    VCARD
N:                        Machin;Rob;Mr.
FN:                       Rob Machin
EMAIL;TYPE=INTERNET:      machinr@airius.com
BDAY:                     19730401
ADR;TYPE=WORK,POSTAL:     96 The Street;London;E1 123;UK;
TEL;TYPE=WORK,VOICE:      +44 (0) 1234 56789
TEL;TYPE=WORK,FAX:        +44 (0) 1234 56780
VERSION:                  3.0
END:                      VCARD
```

The IMC is currently working with the IETF to promote the use of vCard data as a standard part of the MIME message format to enable automatic signing of e-mail with a vCard, amongst other applications for the format. LDAP servers could also be used as an organization's central repository for vCards, presenting a searchable directory of contact information stored in this intelligent format. Furthermore, vCards could utilize the local storage of a WAP device, such as a mobile phone's SIM card, for 'offline' use.

As mobile devices develop multiple channels for communication, for example mail and voice, a data format such as vCard could add considerable value to the way people maintain their contact information. WAP phones and PDAs would certainly benefit from the use of this data format, which will represent a powerful, vendor-neutral way to sensibly exchange and store contact information.

Most e-mail and PIM software vendors include vCard support, and Nokia has included vCard support in their 9000i and 9110 communicator products, as have Palm and Symbian in their respective products.

However, although the WAP specification does detail support for the vCard format, it has not yet found widespread support or interest from the manufactures of WAP browsers and software. Nevertheless, the momentum behind vCard is certainly building, which should indicate that support for vCard from WAP vendors will grow in the near future.

Summary

In this chapter we have covered:

- The history and evolution of the Internet mail protocols
- How an Internet mail system is structured
- Programming Internet mail for a WAP device using JavaMail
- Programming WAP mail applications with CDO

JavaMail and CDO both provide WAP developers with an easy way to construct server-side applications that can deliver simple, and yet powerful, messaging capabilities. We have seen in this chapter how we can leverage these existing technologies in our new WAP applications, whatever platform our base is.

WAP provides an opportunity to redesign and rethink the way people communicate and utilize digital information. E-mail represents one of the most important and growing communications mechanisms. As the focus on the Internet shifts from personal computers and wired devices to a more natural mobile web of interconnected WAP devices, providing WAP-based applications with e-mail capabilities will be one of the key factors in creating successful m-commerce applications.

In the next chapter, we'll move on to see how we can use directory services in our mobile applications, by combining WAP and LDAP.

14

WAP and LDAP/ Directory Services

Today's networks run a multitude of operating and application environments, each of which requires information about users and resources. As the cost of ownership is scrutinized, and the maintenance and synchronization of multiple systems becomes critical, storing and managing information effectively has become a major source of concern to IT departments. **Directory services** aim to solve this problem by presenting a single source of information that is secure, scalable, and easy to maintain in a distributed network environment. This can be a key factor in the success of many programming projects.

Directory services can be used to store a wide range of information including personnel information, address books, user configuration data, network information – such as information on network printers – and even the storage of Enterprise JavaBeans (EJB).

Giving customers the ability to access such **directory information** efficiently via wireless devices is a challenge that must be met in order to manage the predicted growth in mobile computing. In the next few years the amount of important data accessed from wireless devices will dramatically increase. The capabilities offered by directory services to manage and facilitate this growth could be a key factor in the success of the devices in both the corporate, and consumer markets.

> The growth of wireless devices such as thin-clients to enterprise systems presents us with the challenge of delivering information efficiently to many devices with the minimum effort in terms of time to market and administration.

By far the most widely used and implemented directory service is the Lightweight Directory Access Protocol (LDAP). LDAP has become the de facto standard for accessing directory systems, and is programmable by a number of methods including Sun's JNDI and Microsoft's ADSI.

In this chapter we will be taking a look at the following:

❑ Directory services and their evolution, focusing in particular on LDAP

❑ What information can be stored effectively in an LDAP directory service

❑ How LDAP can be programmed using Sun's JNDI (Java Naming and Directory Interface) and Microsoft's ADSI (Active Directory Services Interfaces) APIs

❑ How LDAP and directory services can add value to WAP applications

Introduction to Directory Services and LDAP

In this first section we will discuss the functionality of a directory service, and how it compares to other related services. We can then move on to examine the history of directory services and, in particular, how LDAP came about.

What is a Naming Service?

A computer naming service is a service that associates a unique name to a piece of information or a resource. The most widely used distributed naming service in the world is the Fully Qualified Domain Name (FQDN) system in use on the Internet. For example, `wrox.com` is a FQDN, and as such, is guaranteed to be unique.

> **A naming service enables very efficient referencing and retrieval of unique key information.**

What is a Directory Service?

A classic example of a directory service is a company's telephone directory, which until a few years ago would almost certainly have been (and in many cases, still will be) paper-based. The purpose of the directory is to allow staff to rapidly look up telephone numbers of colleagues based on the individual's details such as a name, job title, department, and so on.

The directory services discussed in this chapter are much like a company's telephone directory service, in that they both store data indexed by a unique set of key information. A computer directory service, however, has far less limitations than a paper directory in the type and amount of information it can store. A directory service is subsequently far more powerful as a tool for accessing and controlling online information.

Computer directory services are designed for fast retrieval of information over a network – they are optimized for many reads and infrequent writes. A directory service will always contain, and is founded on, a naming service, which it uses to identify and organize the directory objects that represent the information. It is typically based on a hierarchical database, but the specifics of its implementation are less relevant than the protocol used to define how a client can access the data it contains.

An example of a directory service is the Internet's Domain Name Service (DNS), which takes a FQDN and returns an IP address. This means that all we have to remember when browsing the Internet is the domain name, for example `wrox.com`, since we can rely on DNS to inform the browser that for this FQDN, the Internet Protocol (IP) address it must search for is 204.148.170.3.

Directory applications can be grouped into three types of services:

- ❑ Management and storage of user and network resource information
- ❑ Management and storage of resources, such as Certificates, or CORBA and Java Objects
- ❑ Authentication and security services, i.e. a single sign-on service

What were the Motivations behind Creating Directory Services?

Directory services are essential in a networked world to provide:

- ❑ Rapid access to information
- ❑ Central user authentication and management

In a business environment, the same data is often used or referenced by more than one application. If this data is duplicated in different individual applications (as illustrated in the following diagram) it leads to the increased administrative burden of manually keeping records synchronized, which is both inefficient and increases the potential for error.

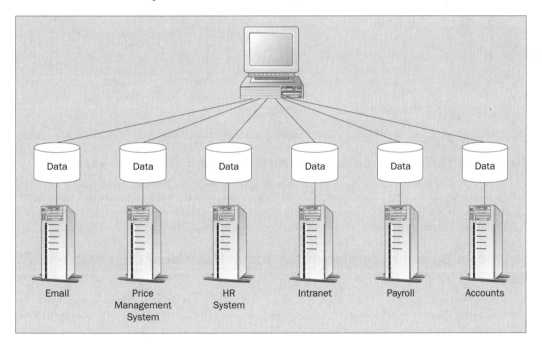

In an ideal world, when the same information is commonly accessed by different applications, it should be held in a single central source to allow for ease of maintenance and eliminate the need for duplication and synchronization. Directory services carry out this essential task.

> **A directory service provides a single repository for accessing data, which all other systems – subject to security requirements – may reference.**

By eliminating duplication of data, administration costs are reduced, and the accuracy – or at least the consistency – of the shared information is improved. This can be critical to the efficiency and success of companies working in today's information-rich business environment. This architecture is shown in the diagram below:

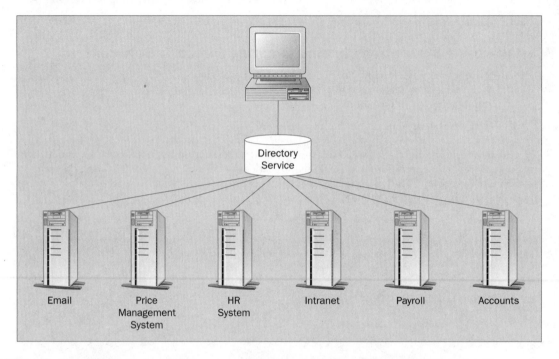

What is the Difference between a Naming and a Directory Service?

All directory services contain a naming service. A naming service identifies an object as unique. In addition to that, a directory service allows you to look up an object, and to associate objects with attributes (name/value pairs). The key distinguishing feature of a directory service, therefore, is that it maintains *attributes* of the object that it represents.

How does a Directory Service differ from a Relational Database or a File System?

So why would you want to use a directory service rather than a relational database, and where would a relational database be more suitable? Furthermore, how is a directory service different from a network file system?

Typical differences between directory services and relational databases include:

- ❑ Do not have a powerful and standard query language, like SQL
- ❑ Cannot handle transactions against multiple operations
- ❑ Do not support a two-phase commit
- ❑ Are not able to easily perform advanced relational style queries (for example, table joins)

Directory services are not a substitute for a file system since they:

❑ Are not well suited to large binary file objects

❑ Do not have a locking mechanism needed by a file system to read/write protect files

A directory service would, therefore, not be suitable in a situation where:

❑ Complex relationships exist between data elements

❑ Reporting on the data is a key requirement – the reporting capabilities of directory services are not as advanced as that of a typical RDBMS which can use a report generation tool like Brio's SQR, for instance

❑ Writing information to the data store must happen within a transaction

❑ Large binary objects must be stored

However, directory services:

❑ Are optimized for fast read access

❑ Have protocols designed for network use from the ground up

❑ Are typically widely replicated

❑ Are typically designed to be distributed/partitioned between multiple servers

❑ Are typically used with out-of-the-box schema, or modified versions of the pre-configured schema, rather than self designed table structures

❑ Are simpler to configure and maintain than a relational database

Directory Services: a Brief History

As with much modern technology, such as object-oriented programming and graphical user interfaces, directory services found their first proper home at the Xerox Palo Alto Research Center. In the early 1980s, as part of the research done on a distributed system architecture called 'Grapevine', a directory service known as 'Clearinghouse' was created. It was used to provide a personalized desktop environment, similar in concept, to the roaming profile in Windows. However, as with many of Xerox's ground breaking technological ideas, it was left to others to take the concept forward to become a marketable product.

There are a number of important naming and directory services in use across the computing landscape; here is a selection of the most important:

❑ Domain Naming Service (DNS)

❑ Common Object Service (COS) – CORBA Naming Service

❑ Sun Microsystem's Network Information Service (NIS/NIS+)

❑ Novell Directory Service (NDS)

❑ Microsoft's Active Directory Services (ADS)

❑ Netscape/iPlanet Directory Server

X.500

X.500, the Open Systems Interconnection (OSI) directory service standard, defines a relatively comprehensive set of directory architectures. These include the Directory Access Protocol (DAP), which is used by clients to access the services offered, as well as an authentication framework, an information structure model, a namespace configuration, and a functional model.

In a similar way to the X400 protocol for e-mail, the X.500 protocol failed to gain widespread deployment within the enterprise. This was because:

❑   X.500 is hard to implement, and contains a lot of non-essential bells and whistles

❑   It uses the OSI networking protocol stack, which itself is not widespread

❑   It is too resource hungry in its implementation and reliance on the OSI protocol stack

❑   It does not provide a very flexible implementation path (for example, it dictates a specific transport protocol)

The size and complexity of the X.500 implementation made it difficult to run on the average desktop PC and Macintosh client machine, which have limited computational and memory resources.

For these reasons, X.500 has been displaced by LDAP, which has become the standard for Internet-based applications to access information stored in a directory.

> **LDAP was originally developed by researchers at the University of Michigan, and members of the OSI Directory Services working group, as a universal front-end to X.500 services.**

The Road to LDAP

The LDAP protocol was initially created as a 'light' interface or gateway service to the 'heavy' X.500. It was originally designed to provide access to the X.500 Directory Access Protocol (DAP) without incurring all the resource requirements, and implementation issues, of a full X.500 and OSI system, and enables directory access from lighter, more limited client devices.

Originally LDAP functioned solely as an interface to an X.500 implementation of a directory service. However, the developers of LDAP, observing the lack of industry support for X.500 and OSI, designed SLDAP (Standalone LDAP). LDAP could now operate independently as a complete directory service, rather than merely acting as the interface to another directory service implementation.

With the creation of SLDAP, the phrase *LDAP* can now be taken to mean either the protocol used to access a directory service such as X.500, or the directory service itself.

LDAP remains quite closely aligned with X.500 and they share many conceptual similarities, including the basic information and naming models.

LDAP and its Advantages over Competing Directory Services

LDAP defines the way clients should access data on the server, but does not specify how that data should be stored internally. LDAP, therefore, offers excellent access to other directory services. As a consequence of its flexibility, LDAP has been implemented as a front-end to a multitude of data-stores, and all the major directory vendors are revising their products to incorporate, and take advantage of, LDAP.

LDAP has many advantages over DAP. For instance, LDAP:

❏ Runs over the ubiquitous TCP/IP. LDAP is not transport-protocol specific, and can be designed to run over any transport protocol; at the moment LDAP only runs on TCP/IP, but Novell do offer an LDAP front end to their IPX based NDS system.

❏ Uses a simplified functional model.

❏ Has the ability to act as an interface to a multitude of disparate directory services. This has allowed LDAP to extend the functionality of X.500 in certain areas: for instance, LDAP offers many security features not available to X.500, such as Simple Authentication and Security Layer (SASL).

❏ Has widely deployed client software; for example access to LDAP is now available as part of both Netscape's and Microsoft's web browser software. Using these clients, directory information can be accessed via an LDAP URL; we will discuss these later in the chapter.

❏ Runs over TCP/IP, and hence can make use of Transport Layer Security (TLS, also known as SSL). In the mobile world these security features will become increasingly important as the information transmitted to wireless devices becomes more sensitive, or contains a transactional element.

For further information on LDAP, see Implementing LDAP, by Mark Wilcox, from Wrox Press, or Understanding and Deploying LDAP Directory Services, by Tim Howes and Mark Smith, from Macmillan.

LDAP and WAP

We have already explored how LDAP provides access to an easily manageable and centrally configured repository for information, that can be used to store user details, personalization information, and much more besides.

LDAP provides programmers with an efficient, and functional, way to store useful information that can be used by applications, like the phone number search utility we will see later. This can be particularly useful to WAP devices.

As relatively thin devices, WAP products have more limited presentational capabilities than personal computers. This means that the issues around removing redundant functionality for each user, and the persistence of user configuration options for an application, become more important. Perhaps one of the most important uses of LDAP in developing WAP applications will be the ability LDAP gives us to easily store and retrieve configuration options, that a customer can use to mould an application into a useful and personal tool.

WAP systems will need to be able to authenticate users in order to allow privileged access to on-line applications; LDAP will provide a means to create a secure and manageable single sign-on environment. Using a directory service to store user authentication details removes the burden on individual applications of maintaining and securing their own security information, and provides a single point of maintenance and administration for the users. We will look later at a code example that demonstrates authenticating a user against a username and password stored in a directory service.

How LDAP Data is Structured

LDAP assumes a very similar information model and namespace to X.500. The conceptual model of the data is a hierarchical tree structure, referred to as the Directory Information Tree (DIT).

LDAP Information Model

- ❏ The information model is centered on **entries**, which are the equivalent of relational database rows

- ❏ Entries are composed of **attributes**

- ❏ Each attribute consists of a **type** and a **value**

- ❏ Each entry is associated with an **Object Class** which determines which attributes are required and which are allowed

- ❏ Entries are arranged into a tree-structure called the **Directory Information Tree** (DIT)

- ❏ The top level element is referred to as the **top-level domain**

- ❏ Mid-level elements are called 'sub' domains, and are often referred to as **branches** or **organizational units**

- ❏ Any entry that is not a domain, i.e. that does not have any child elements is called a **leaf**

- ❏ A **schema** is a set of rules that define the structure of the data stored in the LDAP server. Schema specify the types of data elements that can be stored by entries in the domain model

So the LDAP information model is specified by a schema, and made up of:

- ❏ A top level domain

- ❏ Sub-domains, known as branches or organizational units

- ❏ Leaves

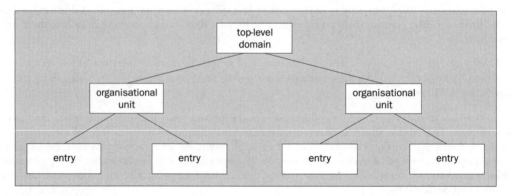

LDAP Naming Model

The LDAP naming model specifies how the information within the directory is organized and referenced. The names of individual data elements are based on a hierarchical naming model. Entries are given a **Distinguished Name** (DN) according to their position in the tree hierarchy. This DN is decided by a naming service and consists of several components. Each component of a DN is called a **Relative Distinguished Name** (RDN).

The original X.500 syntax of country, location and company name lead to a DN bloat! For example, an X.500 DN might look like:

```
dn: uid=machinr, ou=Concise Mobile, o=Concise Group Ltd, l=London, c=UK
```

To explain this unique identifier, or distinguished name, for Rob Machin at Concise software, here is what the elements mean:

- ❑   c = Country
- ❑   l = Location
- ❑   o = Organization
- ❑   ou = Organizational Unit (Department)
- ❑   uid = User ID (Typically network login name)

Using this naming scheme, a DN could reach quite a ridiculous length, before any really useful information was imparted.

The Fully Qualified Domain Name (FQDN) service, which is used to identify web sites, already represents an existing global standard to associate a company with a unique name, regardless of local company law and custom. This system was already familiar to the vast majority of users, and was therefore selected as the basis for the domain naming system for LDAP.

An example of a DN could then be:

```
dn: uid=machinr, ou=Concise Mobile, o=concise.co.uk
```

The designers of LDAP recommend that the Fully Qualified Domain Name (FQDN) of the organization be used as the top-level domain name. This was based on the assumption that any organization technologically advanced enough to be deploying LDAP would also have a web presence.

The Internet Engineering Task Force (IETF) also have a recommendation – proposed as a draft standard in RFC 2377 – for constructing a DN from a FQDN, which uses a **domain component** (dc) attribute. For example:

```
dn: uid=machinr, ou=Concise Mobile, dc=Concise, dc=co, dc=uk
```

Both of the DN schemes using the FQDN can be found in use today.

In summary, the data stored in an LDAP directory service can be viewed as a hierarchical tree, usually based on an organization, such as airius.com (the sample companies directory installed with the Netscape directory server), split into organizational units and finally into entry leaves. A typical structure might look like this:

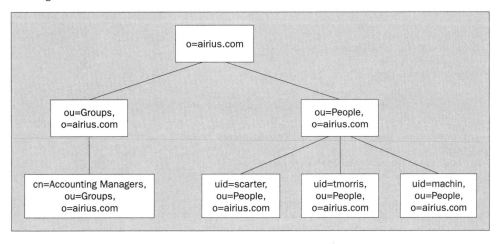

Miscellaneous LDAP Issues

The ideas and concepts we need to understand LDAP are each surrounded by layers of acronyms, terminology, and useful innovation that must be understood. So, before we go on to look at the actual protocol, and code examples using LDAP, there are a number of issues that need some explanation, and there is some vocabulary to learn.

We must consider:

❑   What is the LDIF format?

❑   What is Directory Service Markup Language?

❑   What is the LDAP URL format?

❑   What are aliases?

❑   What are Abstract Syntax Notation One (ASN.1) and the Basic Encoding Rules (BER)?

What is the LDIF Format?

LDAP Data Interchange Format (**LDIF**) is a simple ASCII format used to represent LDAP data and facilitate the exchange of that data between LDAP servers. The following is an example of an individual's record in LDIF format:

```
dn: uid=scarter, ou=People, o=airius.com
cn: Sam Carter
sn: Carter
givenname: Sam
objectclass: top
objectclass: person
objectclass: organizationalPerson
objectclass: inetOrgPerson
ou: Accounting
ou: People
l: Sunnyvale
uid: scarter
manager: uid=jvedder, ou=People, o=airius.com
title: VP, Accounting
mail: scarter@airius.com
telephonenumber: +1 408 555 4798
facsimiletelephonenumber: +1 408 555 9751
roomnumber: 4612
userpassword: sprain
```

And here is an example of an LDIF entry for a group – which is an organizational unit:

```
dn: cn=Accounting Managers,ou=groups,o=airius.com
objectclass: top
objectclass: groupOfUniqueNames
cn: Accounting Managers
ou: groups
uniquemember: uid=scarter, ou=People, o=airius.com
uniquemember: uid=tmorris, ou=People, o=airius.com
description: People who can manage accounting entries
```

What is Directory Service Markup Language?

Directory Service Markup Language (DSML) is an initiative to create an open standard, XML based markup language to describe directory information, which may eventually replace LDIF for many practical purposes.

For example, in DSML the entry for `scarter` we looked at above in LDIF would look like this:

```
<dsml:entry dn="uid=prabbit,ou=development,o=bowstreet,c=us">
<dsml:objectclass>
    <dsml:oc-value>top</dsml:oc-value>
    <dsml:oc-value>person</dsml:oc-value>
    <dsml:oc-value>organizationalPerson</dsml:oc-value>
    <dsml:oc-value>inetOrgPerson</dsml:oc-value>
</dsml:objectclass>
<dsml:attr name="sn"><dsml:value>Carter</dsml:value></dsml:attr>
<dsml:attr name="uid"><dsml:value>scarter</dsml:value></dsml:attr>
<dsml:attr name="mail"><dsml:value>scarter@airius.com</dsml:value></dsml:attr>
<dsml:attr name="givenname"><dsml:value>Sam Carter</dsml:value></dsml:attr>
<dsml:attr name="cn"><dsml:value>Sam</dsml:value></dsml:attr></dsml:entry>
. . .
```

For more information on DSML, see the DSML initiative website at `http://www.dsml.org`.

What is the LDAP URL Format?

One of the components of the LDAP specification is the LDAP URL format, which allows a query to be performed directly by a browser. It should be noted that the current generation of WAP microbrowsers do not support this URL format.

The LDAP URL takes the format:

```
ldap://domain:port/query_string
```

The default port for LDAP is port 389, as we will see in our code examples later. The query format can become quite complex, but to return details of an entry you can type the DN. For example:

```
ldap://localhost:389/uid=scarter,ou=People,o=airius.com
```

There is also a secure format for LDAP addresses where the connection to the LDAP server is encrypted. This format is only currently supported by Netscape. The URL takes the format:

```
ldaps://domain:port/query_string
```

The default port for this type of query is 636. For example:

```
ldaps://localhost:636/uid=scarter,ou=People,o=airius.com
```

What are aliases?

An **alias** entry in a directory structure performs a similar function to a *shortcut* in Windows 95/NT or a symbolic link in UNIX; it redirects the user to another entry location. Using aliases, you can overcome some of the limitations of a strictly hierarchical information structure.

Aliases present an alternative to a referral – discussed later – but the use of aliases can present certain performance problems, since the alias will be validated each time a search is performed that includes the entry containing the alias. A better approach might be to store an LDAP URL, instead of the alias, and handle chasing the entry's alias data programmatically, when it is required.

What are Abstract Syntax Notation One (ASN.1) and the Basic Encoding Rules (BER)?

Abstract Syntax Notation One (ASN.1) is defined by X.208, and generally uses the Basic Encoding Rules (BER) defined by X.209 to encode data. However, although X.208 does not specify the use of BER for ASN.1, with LDAP the BER are always used with ASN.1 to encode data (phew!).

As a programmer of WAP devices, you may never need to know more about these two subjects ever again! However, as these two terms appear in some of the literature about LDAP, you will need to know that both LDAP and X.500 use the ASN.1 specification to create a binary format for data exchange. This format is used in preference to plain ASCII text since it is both more efficient to transmit than plain text, and easier for machines to interpret.

The LDAP protocol

The LDAP protocol defines how the data and functions of an LDAP server are accessed over the transport protocol. Possible user operations on an LDAP service include:

- Binding (authenticating)
- Comparing elements
- Searching
- Adding
- Modifying
- Deleting

We will see some code examples of these operations later in the chapter.

Other protocol services

As well as providing the operations listed above, LDAP specifies – or is being developed to specify – certain other critical types of behavior needed for a directory service to function in a networked environment:

- Replication
- Chasing Referrals
- Support for Unicode Characters
- Security
- Access Control Lists

Replication

The LDAP specification does allow for the replication, or synchronization, of server information. All major vendors implement some sort of replication model, although it should be noted that there is no official standard for this process at the time of writing.

Replication can enhance the use of LDAP by:

❑ Improved performance, through local access to central data

❑ Improved reliability, through techniques such as load balancing

❑ Greater flexibility in the security model

Chasing of Referrals

A referral is a *pointer* that allows LDAP servers to link together to share an information pool. To handle this type of response does involve a little extra work as a programmer.

A referral can be returned in response to a query sent to an LDAP server, if that LDAP server is unable to service the request alone. It indicates that the involvement of another LDAP server is necessary to formulate the correct response to the original query. Long supported by X.500, LDAP introduced referrals in version 3 of the specification.

For example, imagine your organization had two LDAP servers, one in London and another in New York, each containing information relating to the staff at their offices. In the server administration, you could specify that the London server should refer any queries about New York personnel to the New York server. The result of a subsequent query to the London server for New York personnel information would result in a referral object being passed back from the query. Your client code would now have to handle this, or ignore the referral; this interaction will typically occur without the user being aware of any physical split in the data between the two offices.

Support for Unicode Characters

LDAP is a fully international standard and consequently supports the UTF-8 character encoding rules, ensuring that non-ASCII character sets – such as Japanese, Russian and Chinese – are supported within an LDAP data store.

UTF-8 is a binary-encoding standard that supports a 16-bit (2 byte) Unicode character format, with full backward compatibility with the Latin-1 ASCII set. Unicode may require some extra work if you are using a C or Perl API to write your application, but Java should handle the Unicode characters seamlessly based on the local settings of the Java Virtual Machine (JVM).

Security

LDAP is a connection-oriented protocol – to perform an operation on an LDAP server, a user must first **bind** to the server, which opens a session. Any subsequent operations the user is able to perform are executed within the scope of that session. LDAP implements a flexible security model, and can benefit from the security protocols available to the underlying network transport protocol. For TCP/IP this means TLS (SSL) can be used, and for WAP's Wireless Datagram Protocol (WDP), WTLS will be available.

Access Control Lists (ACLs)

Access Control Lists (ACLs) provide the ability to finely control the access available for users to read, modify and delete, your directory information, restricting certain tasks to particular users, or groups. At present no standards document specifies the format of the ACL attribute, and each vendor has its own format for configuring these permissions. The Internet Engineering Task Force (IETF) is currently formulating a standard syntax for expressing access control.

In the Netscape Directory Server the access control lists are specified by using the aci attribute for an entry, and can be assigned to individual leaves, or domains within a top-level domain. For an example of how to structure ACLs within the Netscape Directory Server, we can look at the top-level domain for airius.com (in the airius.ldif file that comes with the Netscape Directory Server installation):

```
dn: o=airius.com
objectclass: top
objectclass: organization
o: airius.com

aci: (target ="ldap:///o=airius.com")(targetattr !="userPassword")(version 3.0;acl
"Anonymous read-search access";allow (read, search, compare)(userdn =
"ldap:///anyone");)

aci: (target="ldap:///o=airius.com") (targetattr = "*")(version 3.0; acl "allow
all Admin group"; allow(all) groupdn = "ldap:///cn=Directory Administrators,
ou=Groups, o=airius.com";)
```

Two aci's are specified in the LDIF code above for the airius top level domain:

❑ The first allows anonymously authenticated users access to all attributes except the userpassword

❑ The second allows members of the group Directory Administrators full access to all attributes

ACLs are essential to the proper management of an LDAP directory. Fortunately, a friendlier interface is provided to edit, and tune, these control attributes than editing LDIF in a text editor. Most commercial LDAP vendors provide some sort of tool for the management of ACLs; see your server documentation for details.

Current LDAP Protocol Issues

The Internet Engineering Task Force (IETF) is developing the LDAP specification to enable LDAP to respond and perform in a way necessary for it to succeed in an enterprise environment. Amongst the most hotly debated issues in the working groups are:

❑ The LDAP Directory Update (LDUP) working out a standard for the replication of LDAP servers

❑ The LDAP Extensions (LDAP-EXT) working group evolving the capabilities of the LDAP APIs and dealing with issues such as access control lists

Major vendors of LDAP servers

From its conception, LDAP has been maintained as an open standard, and many vendors are beginning to offer LDAP access to their directory services. The major LDAP server vendors include:

❑ OpenLDAP (http://www.openldap.org/)
Derived from the code from the University of Michigan – the original implementation of LDAP.

❑ iPlanet (`http://www.iplanet.com/`)
iPlanet is an initiative bringing together the collective expertise and market share of AOL/Netscape, Innosoft and Sun Microsystems, providing, among other things, a powerful LDAP offering. This alliance, according to IDC, captured 70% of the directory service market in 1999 with over 150 million directory licenses sold worldwide.

❑ Novell (`http://www.novell.com`)
The latest version of Netware allows you to query the Novell Directory Service (NDS) via an LDAP interface. NDS, like LDAP, was based on X.500, but unlike LDAP, which runs over TCP, NDS works over the IPX transport protocol.

❑ Microsoft (`http://www.microsoft.com/`)
Microsoft, in their release of Windows 2000, has embraced the LDAP standard by incorporating Active Directory functionality into many essential system administration functions. Active Directory will see LDAP technology moved into the mainstream, and adopted by many corporations as they roll out Windows 2000.

Programming LDAP: Using LDAP APIs and SDKs

Here we will take a brief look at the packages available to make programming LDAP easier, namely:

❑ University of Michigan/openLDAP C API

❑ Netscape LDAP C SDK

❑ Microsoft's ADSI

❑ Netscape LDAP Java SDK

❑ Sun's JNDI

In later sections, we will be examining JNDI and ADSI in more detail and using them in some code examples.

University of Michigan/openLDAP C API

The University of Michigan provided the first C API for use with LDAP. This API was initially released for UNIX and Linux clients; it has now, however, been ported to DOS, Windows, and Macintosh systems. The API, like the whole of the University of Michigan LDAP system, is open source and should see a strong following from the OpenLDAP camp, which is taking forward the LDAP work of the University of Michigan. This research and development is now being funded by Novell.

A good book to buy covering this API, amongst other things, is LDAP: Programming Directory-Enabled Applications With Lightweight Directory Access Protocol published by Macmillan (ISBN 1578700000) and written by Tim Howes and Mark Smith.

Netscape LDAP C SDK

The Netscape LDAP C SDK leans heavily on the University of Michigan's original C API for inspiration, and is also open source. Netscape continues to be a leader in the IT industry using the Mozilla project, and their more recent alliance with Sun Microsystems, to reach out to developers. The Netscape Directory Server ensures that the company will continue to innovate, and maintain dominance, in the directory server market.

Netscape LDAP Java SDK

Netscape provide an LDAP API for use with their Netscape Directory Server. This Java SDK is based upon the model of their successful C SDK, which can trace its lineage back to the University of Michigan C API. Therefore the concepts and model have received a substantial amount of peer review and refactoring over the years. The Netscape API is aimed specifically at LDAP, and as such can provide optimized access to the underlying LDAP API protocol, compared to the competing Java API JNDI, which we discuss shortly. The Java SDK was released in 1997, and in 1998 the source code for the SDK was made available through the Mozilla open source project. The position of the Netscape SDK has been further strengthened by the recent alliance between Sun Microsystems (the home of Java) and AOL/Netscape (the home of the wildly successful Netscape Directory Server).

Sun Microsystems' JNDI

JNDI (Java Naming and Directory Interface) provides a unified interface to a naming or directory service. It was originally developed as part of the Enterprise JavaBean (EJB) framework to provide an interface to a directory service for EJB objects. Sun Microsystems designed JNDI to provide an abstracted interface, to allow applications written in the Java programming language to access naming and directory services. The JNDI is designed to be independent of specific vendor naming and directory services implementations. This makes it relatively easy for JNDI interfaces to be added to other naming and directory services, as they are needed. JNDI can be thought of as very similar to Java Database Connectivity (JDBC) in this respect.

Microsoft's ADSI

Microsoft's Active Directory Service Interface (ADSI) is to COM, what JNDI is to Java. To whit, it is a generic directory service API that can be used with a wide variety of directory servers, including LDAP. The reason for the similarity in design between JNDI and ADSI is that both Sun and Microsoft faced a similar dilemma when confronted by LDAP. Both companies recognized the potential of the new technology, and wanted to provide an API to allow programmers to make use of directory services. At the same time, both companies realized that their own proprietary directory services were going to be around for a long time. This led to Microsoft developing ADSI to allow any COM-enabled language, for example Visual C++, Visual Basic and Delphi, to access the power of LDAP, ADS, and any directory service that provides an ADSI interface.

Other Language APIs

Many other languages provide good LDAP APIs; perhaps the most widely used of these are the two Perl APIs, PerLDAP and Net::LDAP API. There is also a Tcl LDAP API produced by a company called NeoSoft. It is worth noting that PHP provides a very good, and in keeping with the spirit of the language, very easy to use API. Check the Internet to see if your favorite language has LDAP support; as long as it's not Snobol, you could be in luck!

JNDI and LDAP

In this section we will take a closer look at JNDI (Java Naming and Directory Interface) and the packages it contains. These will be used later in the section for two different examples of how directory services can be used.

Simplifying Access to Directory Services

JNDI provides a layered interface to directory services: it has classes that can model a simple naming service, a simple directory service and even has specialized packages for dealing with LDAP directory services.

Most widely deployed directory services provide an LDAP interface. We can access these directory services through JNDI using either their LDAP interface or, if preferred, a 'native' service provider bypassing LDAP.

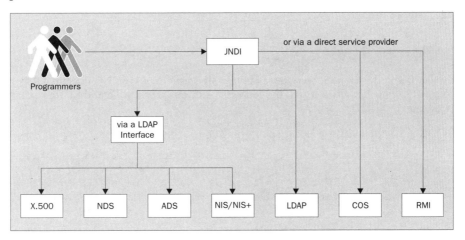

JNDI is a powerful tool for the application developer, and aims to do for LDAP, ADS etc. what JDBC has done for Oracle, DB/2, and Sybase. Using JNDI hides a lot of the complexity of interfacing with multiple directories.

The JNDI Packages

The design philosophy of the JNDI framework is grounded in the idea that as a developer you should only 'pay for what you use'. Subsequently, the packages listed below represent layers of functionality and complexity, modeling a naming and directory service that can be used or excluded as needed.

javax.naming

`javax.naming` contains the core classes and interfaces necessary for Java applications to access a naming service.

javax.naming.directory

`javax.naming.directory` models the functionality required for Java applications to access directory services, building on the `javax.naming` foundations. This package provides all the functionality needed to use all but a small proportion of the services offered by LDAP.

javax.naming.ldap

This contains the classes necessary for Java applications to access specific functionality relating to LDAP directory services, and provides support for some of the LDAP version 3 management features. These features represent advanced LDAP functionality and the majority of applications will not need this package.

javax.naming.event

The `javax.naming.event` package contains the classes and interfaces necessary for supporting event notification in naming and directory services.

javax.naming.spi

This provides the framework for creating extensions to the base JNDI classes to allow for the construction of other JNDI service providers. This package potentially enables developers and third party vendors to create access classes to other naming and directory services that do not come with 'out-of-the-box' support from Sun.

Installation of Tools

All the examples in this chapter were tested under Microsoft Windows NT version 4.0, service pack 5. You will need to download and install the following software to compile and run the examples in the rest of this chapter:

- ❑ JDK 1.2.2 (Download from `http://java.sun.com/jdk/`)
- ❑ JSDK 2.1 (Download from `http://www.java.sun.com/products/servlet/`)
- ❑ JNDI (Download from `http://java.sun.com/products/jndi/`)
- ❑ Netscape Directory Server 4.11 (Download from `http://www.iplanet.com/downloads/download/index.html`)
- ❑ Gefion Software Web Server Lite (Download from `http://www.gefionsoftware.com/LiteWebServer/`)
- ❑ Nokia WAP Gateway 1.0 (Download from `http://www.nokia.com/corporate/wap/order_prods.html`)
- ❑ Nokia WAP Toolkit 1.3 beta

The JNDI is included in the JDK v1.3, but must be downloaded separately for JDK1.1.x and 1.2.x. The JNDI base classes and various service providers can still be downloaded from Sun.

To follow the examples presented over the next few pages, you'll need a basic working knowledge of Java servlets. Servlets were introduced back in Chapter 10, but for more detailed information, you should consult *Professional Java Server Programming*, from Wrox Press, ISBN: 1861002777.

Both the examples use the `Airius.ldif` data that comes with the Netscape Directory Server.

Classpath

Your class path must be configured to include the JNDI, LDAP and servlet jar files to compile the example, as well as our WML helper class in `WML.jar` (see Chapter 13).

Under Windows 95/98 the relevant CLASSPATH amendments can be made in your `autoexec.bat`:

```
CLASSPATH = c:\jsdk2.1\servlet.jar;
CLASSPATH = %CLASSPATH%;c:\jdk1.2.2\lib\jndi.jar;
CLASSPATH = %CLASSPATH%;c:\jdk1.2.2\lib\ldap.jar
CLASSPATH = %CLASSPATH%;c:\jdk1.2.2\lib\WML.jar;
```

Under Windows NT, you can make the necessary changes by right-mouse clicking on the My Computer icon on your desktop and choosing Properties, or opening the System icon in the Control Panel. The Classpath environment variable can then be added or modified in the Environment tab.

A Simple WML Login Screen

With the rise in the number of applications demanding security over the Internet, or company intranet/extranet, it has become necessary for users to memorize a multitude of usernames and passwords. With passwords spread over multiple systems, users often choose passwords badly and record them in insecure ways.

Using LDAP, any application can pass a username and password given by the user to an LDAP server for authentication; the application will then receive a direct response indicating success or failure. The advantage of using LDAP to authenticate the user is this way, is that we can eliminate the need for individual applications to maintain, and secure, their own separate list of username and password combinations.

This concept could be extended to a single sign-on environment, by assigning the user a trusted identifier. After the user has been authenticated by the security service for the first time, the identifier can then be presented to subsequent systems in lieu of a username/password sign-on.

> *See the Netscape Documentation describing this concept at:*
> *http://developer.netscape.com/docs/manuals/security/SSO/index.htm.*

The example given here uses servlets and JNDI to authenticate a username and password, and to return confirmation of a correctly entered password. It illustrates how LDAP can be used to obtain confirmation of successful sign-on ('binding') for user authentication purposes.

Login.wml

The login process requires the user to provide their username, and password, which is sent to the directory service for authentication:

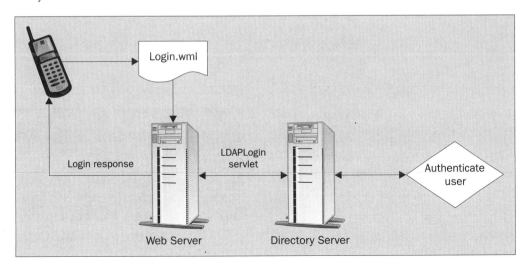

We will begin by taking a look at the initial sign-on WML page, which asks the user for a username and password:

```
<?xml version="1.0"?>
<!DOCTYPE wml PUBLIC "-//WAPFORUM//DTD WML 1.1//EN"
"http://www.wapforum.org/DTD/wml_1.1.xml">

<wml>
<card id="ldapLoginCard" title="Airius Login">
    <p>
    Username: <input name="uid" title="user name"/>
    Password: <input name="pwd" type="password" title="password"/>
    <anchor>Login
        <go href="http://127.0.0.1/servlet/LDAPLogin" method="post">
            <postfield name="uid" value="$uid"/>
            <postfield name="pwd" value="$pwd"/>
        </go>
    </anchor>
    </p>
</card>
</wml>
```

This produces the Airius Login screen, which is displayed below on the Nokia 7110 emulator:

For example, here we will log in as Sam Carter. In the section of code from the `Airius.ldif` file below, we see that Sam Carter's username is `scarter` and password is `sprain`:

```
dn: uid=scarter, ou=People, o=airius.com
cn: Sam Carter
sn: Carter
    .
    .
    .
roomnumber: 4612
userpassword: sprain
```

The Nokia 7110 does not support *in-situ* editing; to enter the username and password, the relevant field must be highlighted and selected. An editing screen like the one below will then be displayed. We enter both fields in this way:

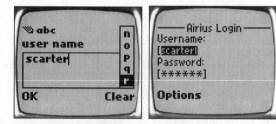

If a piece of text is highlighted as you scroll over it on the Nokia 7110, this indicates that the text represents a hyperlink.

Clicking on this Login hyperlink will invoke the LDAPLogin.java servlet's doPost() method, as we specified in the WML page, and pass the username (uid) and password (pwd) information to the servlet.

```
<anchor>Login
  <go href="http://127.0.0.1/servlet/LDAPLogin" method="post">
     <postfield name="uid" value="$uid"/>
     <postfield name="pwd" value="$pwd"/>
  </go>
</anchor>
```

LDAPLogin.java

We now come to the code that checks the username and password against data stored in a directory service:

```java
import javax.servlet.*;
import javax.servlet.http.*;
import java.io.*;
import java.util.Hashtable;
import javax.naming.*;
import javax.naming.directory.*;
import com.sun.jndi.ldap.LdapCtxFactory;
import com.wrox.util.WML;

public class LDAPLogin extends HttpServlet {

    private static String THIS_INIT_CONT_FAC="com.sun.jndi.ldap.LdapCtxFactory";
    private static String THIS_PROV_URL="ldap://localhost:389";
    private static String THIS_SEC_AUTH="simple";

    public void doPost(HttpServletRequest request,
                       HttpServletResponse response)
        throws IOException, ServletException
    {
        response.setContentType("text/html");
        PrintWriter out = response.getWriter();

        WML wml = new WML();
        wml.addCard("WAPLoginResponse");
        wml.println("<p>");

        try {
            String THIS_SEC_PRIN="uid=" + request.getParameter("uid") + ", ou=People,
o=airius.com";
            String THIS_SEC_CRED=request.getParameter("pwd");
```

```
            if ((THIS_SEC_CRED == null) || (THIS_SEC_CRED.equals("")))  {
            wml.println("Please enter a valid password");
            } else {
            Hashtable env=new Hashtable();

            env.put(Context.INITIAL_CONTEXT_FACTORY, THIS_INIT_CONT_FAC);
            env.put(Context.PROVIDER_URL, THIS_PROV_URL);
            env.put(Context.SECURITY_AUTHENTICATION,THIS_SEC_AUTH);

            env.put(Context.SECURITY_PRINCIPAL,THIS_SEC_PRIN);
            env.put(Context.SECURITY_CREDENTIALS,THIS_SEC_CRED);

            DirContext ctx = new InitialDirContext(env);

            wml.println("Login successful");
            }
        }catch(AuthenticationException ae) {
            ae.printStackTrace();
            wml.println("Incorrect user name or password<br/>Login Failed!");
        }catch(Exception e) {
            e.printStackTrace();
            wml.println("Error accessing LDAP<br/>Login Failed!");
        } finally {
            wml.println("</p>");
            wml.endCard();
            wml.outputWML(response, true);
        }
    }
}
```

If the login is successful the following screen will be displayed:

Authentication Using LDAP

The act of binding successfully to the LDAP server using the provided username and password, indicates a successful login and this result, therefore, is enough to authenticate the user.

To bind to the LDAP server, you must first populate an instance of Hashtable with the necessary environment information:

- ❑ The implementation of the DirContext to use, in this case "com.sun.jndi.ldap.LdapCtxFactory"
- ❑ The URL of the LDAP server
- ❑ The Security Mechanism to use
- ❑ The DN of the user trying to authenticate
- ❑ The password of that user

This was done in LDAPLogin.java. In our particular example, this piece of code translates to:

```
Hashtable env=new Hashtable ();
env.put(Context.INITIAL_CONTEXT_FACTORY, "com.sun.jndi.ldap.LdapCtxFactory";);
env.put(Context.PROVIDER_URL, "ldap://localhost:389");
env.put(Context.SECURITY_AUTHENTICATION, "simple");
env.put(Context.SECURITY_PRINCIPAL, "uid=scarter, ou=People, o=airius.com";);
env.put(Context.SECURITY_CREDENTIALS, "sprain");
```

Once the environment Hashtable has been correctly constructed, a new DirContext can be instantiated, creating a session for that user with the LDAP service. As we saw in the LDAPLogin.java code listing, if authentication fails, an AuthenticationException is thrown:

```
DirContext ctx = new InitialDirContext(env);
```

Many WAP applications could use this authentication mechanism to ensure a user is correctly authenticated, whilst allowing the user to remember and maintain a single user name and password.

Searching with JNDI

The main way to search an LDAP service with JNDI, is the search() method of the DirContext class. If the search is successful a NamingEnumeration object is returned containing the search results.

How to Perform a Search

We will first need to specify what our search base will be and which attributes we are interested in:

```
private static String THIS_SEARCHBASE="ou=People, o=airius.com";
private static String THIS_ATTRS[] = {"cn", "telephonenumber"};
```

We will then need to obtain a context in a similar manner to our login example (except that in the phone search we are using anonymous authentication):

```
DirContext ctx = new InitialDirContext(env);
```

The next step is to specify the scope of the search (which will be discussed below) and retrieve the results using the search() method of the context:

```
SearchControls constraints = new SearchControls();
constraints.setSearchScope(SearchControls.SUBTREE_SCOPE);

NamingEnumeration results = ctx.search(THIS_SEARCHBASE, THIS_FILTER, constraints);
```

We can then cycle through this result set in the following manner:

```
while (results != null && results.hasMore()) {
    SearchResult result = (SearchResult) results.next();
    String dn = result.getName() + ", " + THIS_SEARCHBASE;

    Attributes attrs = ctx.getAttributes(dn, THIS_ATTRS);
```

```
    if (attrs != null) {
        for (int i = 0; i < THIS_ATTRS.length; i++) {
            Attribute attr = attrs.get(THIS_ATTRS[i]);
            if (attr != null) {
                for (Enumeration e = attr.getAll(); e.hasMoreElements();) {
                    wml.println((String)e.nextElement());
                }
            }
        }
    }
}
```

This while loop cycles through results, which is a NamingEnumeration object, and for each item in that set it extracts each of the values for all of the attribute keys specified in the THIS_ATTRS array.

Remember that certain attributes can appear multiple times in an entry; for example, an individual can have many telephonenumber attributes.

The Scope of a Search

The starting point of the search is specified by a base entry as shown in the variable THIS_SEARCHBASE above.

The base entry is the highest-level DN of the search. For example a search base entry of:

```
String THIS_SEARCHBASE="ou=People, o=airius.com"
```

would search all entries in the directory starting in the People organizational unit within Airius.

There are three levels of scope:

❑ SearchControls.SUBTREE_SCOPE
Searches everything from the base entry downwards

❑ SearchControls.ONELEVEL_SCOPE
Searches only the entries directly below the base entry

❑ SearchControls.OBJECT_SCOPE
Searches only the base entry

The default scope is SUBTREE_SCOPE. So the line in the code given in the above section is actually redundant.

A Phone Book Application

LDAP is used within many organizations to maintain, and make available, the corporate phone book. A computer-based phone book is easily accessible to mobile users, and has tremendous advantages compared to an infrequently updated and paper-based phone list system.

In the next example application, we see how to create a simple phone book search facility for a WAP-enabled device. This application looks up phone numbers for individuals whose details are stored in an LDAP directory service.

The user will be presented with a search screen – using anonymous authentication – and will enter a search string. The formatted search results will then be listed with names and numbers. This simple application illustrates how simple it is to provide functional and useful applications, even via WAP devices with limited functionality.

WMLPhoneSearch.wml

We will initially take a quick look at the WML card that allows the user to search the company's phone book listing:

```
<?xml version="1.0"?>
<!DOCTYPE wml PUBLIC "-//WAPFORUM//DTD WML 1.1//EN"
"http://www.wapforum.org/DTD/wml_1.1.xml">

<wml>
    <card id="ldapLoginCard" title="Airius Phone List">
        <p>
            Search For:<input name="search" title="user name"/>
            <anchor>Find Now!
                <go href="http://127.0.0.1/servlet/WMLPhoneSearch" method="post">
                    <postfield name="search" value="$search"/>
                </go>
            </anchor>
        </p>
    </card>
</wml>
```

On the Nokia 7110 emulator, this Airius phone list search screen looks like this:

WMLPhoneSearch.java

Now we turn to the Java code that is referred to in the above WML card, which carries out the task of searching the phone book listing:

```
import java.io.*;
import java.util.*;
import javax.servlet.*;
import javax.servlet.http.*;

import javax.naming.*;
import javax.naming.directory.*;

import com.wrox.util.WML;
import com.sun.jndi.ldap.LdapCtxFactory;

public class WMLPhoneSearch extends HttpServlet {
```

```
    private static String THIS_INIT_CONT_FAC="com.sun.jndi.ldap.LdapCtxFactory";
    private static String THIS_PROV_URL="ldap://localhost:389";
    private static String THIS_SEARCHBASE="ou=People, o=airius.com";
    private static String THIS_ATTRS[] = {"cn", "telephonenumber"};

    public void doPost(HttpServletRequest request,
                       HttpServletResponse response)
        throws IOException, ServletException
    {
        String THIS_FILTER="(cn=*" + request.getParameter("search") + "*)";

        WML wml = new WML();
        wml.addCard("LDAPSearchResponse");
        wml.println("<p>");

        try {
            Hashtable env=new Hashtable();

            env.put(Context.INITIAL_CONTEXT_FACTORY, THIS_INIT_CONT_FAC);
            env.put(Context.PROVIDER_URL, THIS_PROV_URL);

            DirContext ctx = new InitialDirContext(env);

            SearchControls constraints = new SearchControls();
            constraints.setSearchScope(SearchControls.SUBTREE_SCOPE);

            NamingEnumeration results = ctx.search(THIS_SEARCHBASE, THIS_FILTER,
constraints);
            wml.println("Results: <br/>");
            while (results != null && results.hasMore()) {
                SearchResult result = (SearchResult) results.next();
                String dn = result.getName() + ", " + THIS_SEARCHBASE;

                Attributes attrs = ctx.getAttributes(dn, THIS_ATTRS);

                if (attrs == null) {
                    wml.println("Error: " + dn + " does not contain specified
attributes");
                } else {
                    for (int i = 0; i < THIS_ATTRS.length; i++) {
                        Attribute attr = attrs.get(THIS_ATTRS[i]);
                        if (attr != null) {
                            for (Enumeration e = attr.getAll(); e.hasMoreElements();) {
                                wml.println((String)e.nextElement());
                                wml.println("<br/>");
                            }
                        }
                    }
                }
                wml.println("------------<br/>");
            }
        }catch(Exception e) {
            e.printStackTrace();
            wml.println("Search Failed!");
        } finally {
            wml.println("</p>");
            wml.endCard();
            wml.outputWML(response, true);
        }
    }
}
```

The user is required to enter part of the user's 'common name', i.e. cn, attribute. This is then used to search for an individual whose name contains that string:

If more than one individual is found matching the search criteria, the search results can be scrolled through.

Search Filters and LDAP

LDAP does not have a standard query language like SQL. Instead, searching through LDAP data stores is based around a **search filter**.

In the above code we saw a simple search being performed with a search filter based on the *common name* of the *People* from *airius.com*. The search operation was performed like this:

```
String THIS_SEARCHBASE="ou=People, o=airius.com";
String THIS_FILTER="(cn=*" + request.getParameter("search") + "*)";
...
NamingEnumeration results = ctx.search(THIS_SEARCHBASE, THIS_FILTER, constraints);
```

Here are some examples of constructing search filters:

❏　All entries with Common Name (cn) equal to 'Rob Machin'.

```
(cn=Rob Machin)
```

❏　All entries with Common Name equal to 'Rob Machin' **and** (&) having Organizational Unit (ou) equal to 'IT'.

```
(&(cn=Rob Machin)(ou=IT))
```

❏　All entries with Common Name equal to 'Rob Machin' **and** (&) with Organizational Unit equal to 'IT' **or** (|) 'Sales'.

```
(&(cn=Rob Machin)( | (ou=IT)(ou=Sales)))
```

❏　All entries with Common Name ending 'Machin' but excluding 'Rob Machin'.

```
(&(cn=*Machin)( !(cn=Rob Machin)))
```

❏　All entries with Surname (sn) which *sounds like* 'Machim':

```
(sn~=Machim)
```

The Netscape directory service supports a metaphone algorithm to determine approximate 'sounds like' matches.

❏　'Greater than or equal to' and 'Less than or equal to' matches, are performed like this:

```
(sn<=Machin)
```

541

The search above looks for all entries that have a surname with a value lexicographically less than or equal to 'Machin'.

If you want to perform a 'greater than' or 'less than' search, you cannot use > or <, but must use the negative complement of >= or <=, for example, 'greater than' would not be:

```
(age>45)
```

But would be performed like this:

```
(!(age<=45))
```

❑   Search for entries which contain a particular attribute. To filter all the entries in a particular search that contain a specific attribute, you can use a **presence filter:**

```
(telephonenumber=*)
```

This will return all entries that have a telephone number.

Using the Numbers Returned by the Search

The Nokia 7110 has a rather handy Use Number feature, which scans the current card and looks for possible phone numbers – if it finds more than one possibility you are presented with a list of choices.

For example, consider the following card, shown on the Nokia 7110 emulator:

Clicking on Options gives you the ability to choose Use Number. Choosing Use Number allows the phone to search the current card and use any potential phone numbers it finds:

For a detailed discussion on the opportunities for WAP devices to make use of phone functionality directly through the **Wireless Telephony Application Interface (WTAI)**, see Chapter 17.

Further JNDI Programming Issues

JNDI can be used to maintain the information within an LDAP datastore; entries can be added, modified and deleted, using the standard JNDI API. We will now take a quick tour of the JNDI code necessary to perform some of these data maintenance tasks.

Note that in the examples used below to add, modify and delete an entry, the entry details are hardcoded. This allows us to concentrate on the JNDI code, and ignore the added complexity that passing in the parameters would generate.

Adding an Entry

Adding an item to an LDAP directory server using JNDI is slightly more cumbersome than you might expect. A separate class implementing the `DirContext` interface must be created for each highest level *Object Class* you wish to add.

For example, if you wanted to add a new `inetOrgPerson` to the Airius database, you must first create an instance of a specially designed class, which must be written to model the type of entry you wish to add. In this example we have created an InetOrgPerson class which must be instantiated and populated with the relevant data, before the `bind()` method of the context object is called to *bind* this object with a DN, thereby adding it to the directory.

The class `InetOrgPerson`, *which is listed below but not in full, is derived from the* `Drink.java` *example in the JNDI tutorial available from Sun. The Sun JNDI tutorial is available at:* `http://java.sun.com/products/jndi/tutorial/`.

```
class InetOrgPerson implements DirContext {

    String type;
    Attributes myAttrs;

    public InetOrgPerson(String uid, String givenname, String sn, String ou, String
telephonenumber) {
        type = uid;

        Attribute oc = new BasicAttribute("objectclass");
        oc.add("inetOrgPerson");
        oc.add("organizationalPerson");
        oc.add("person");
        oc.add("top");

        Attribute ouSet = new BasicAttribute("ou");
        ouSet.add("People");
        //ouSet.add("ou");

        myAttrs = new BasicAttributes(true);   // case ignore
        myAttrs.put(oc);
        myAttrs.put(ouSet);
        myAttrs.put("uid", uid);
        myAttrs.put("sn", sn);
        myAttrs.put("cn", (givenname + " " + sn));
        myAttrs.put("givenname", givenname);
        myAttrs.put("telephonenumber", telephonenumber);
    }
```

JNDIAddRobMachin.java

The following is a Java servlet which, when doGet() is invoked, adds an instance of Rob Machin to a directory server:

```java
import java.io.*;
import java.util.*;
import javax.servlet.*;
import javax.servlet.http.*;

import javax.naming.*;
import javax.naming.directory.*;

import com.wrox.util.WML;
import com.sun.jndi.ldap.LdapCtxFactory;

public class JNDIAddRobMachin extends HttpServlet {

    private static String THIS_INIT_CONT_FAC="com.sun.jndi.ldap.LdapCtxFactory";
    private static String THIS_PROV_URL="ldap://localhost:389";
    private static String THIS_MGR_DN="uid=kvaughan, ou=People, o=airius.com";
    private static String THIS_MGR_PWD="bribery";

    public void doGet(HttpServletRequest request,
                      HttpServletResponse response)
        throws IOException, ServletException
  {
    WML wml = new WML();
    wml.addCard("JNDIAddRobMachin");
    wml.println("<p>");

    try {
        Hashtable env=new Hashtable();

        env.put(Context.INITIAL_CONTEXT_FACTORY, THIS_INIT_CONT_FAC);
        env.put(Context.PROVIDER_URL, THIS_PROV_URL);
        env.put(Context.SECURITY_AUTHENTICATION, "simple");
        env.put(Context.SECURITY_PRINCIPAL, THIS_MGR_DN);
        env.put(Context.SECURITY_CREDENTIALS, THIS_MGR_PWD);

        DirContext ctx = new InitialDirContext(env);

        InetOrgPerson rm = new InetOrgPerson ("rmachin", "Rob", "Machin",
"ou=Accounting", "+44 1234 5678");

        ctx.bind("uid=rmachin, ou=People, o=airius.com", rm);

        wml.println("Rob Machin added to Airius!");

    }catch(Exception e) {
        e.printStackTrace();
        wml.println("Add Failed!");
    } finally {
        wml.println("</p>");
        wml.endCard();
        wml.outputWML(response, true);
    }
  }
}
```

Modifying an Entry's Attributes

You can use the JNDI context's `modifyAttributes()` method to modify an existing entry's attributes. Three operations are possible:

- ❑ Adding attributes
- ❑ Replacing attributes
- ❑ Removing attributes

Adding an Attribute

An attribute can be added to an LDAP entry using the `DirContext.ADD_ATTRIBUTE` flag, provided that the attribute is allowed in the schema for that Object Class.

The code below adds in a new `mail` attribute with the value `rmachin@airius.com`:

```
modifications[1] = new ModificationItem(DirContext.ADD_ATTRIBUTE,
                   new BasicAttribute("mail", "rmachin@airius.com"));
```

Replacing an Attribute

If you replace an attribute that has multiple values, without specifying which one to replace, all of the values will be removed and replaced with the single replacement.

This code replaces all the telephone number attributes for the element specified with the number +44 1234 56789:

```
modifications[0] = new ModificationItem(DirContext.REPLACE_ATTRIBUTE,
                   new BasicAttribute("telephonenumber", "+44 1234 56789"));
```

Removing an Attribute

The `REMOVE_ATTRIBUTE` flag will remove the specified attribute:

```
modifications [0] = new ModificationItem(DirContext.REMOVE_ATTRIBUTE,
                    new BasicAttribute("mail"));
```

JNDIModifyRobMachin.java

This code performs some modifications to the record in the LDAP directory for Rob Machin at Airius.com, by adding, modifying and removing attributes:

```
import java.io.*;
import java.util.*;
import javax.servlet.*;
import javax.servlet.http.*;

import javax.naming.*;
import javax.naming.directory.*;

import com.wrox.util.WML;
import com.sun.jndi.ldap.LdapCtxFactory;
```

```
public class JNDIModifyRobMachin extends HttpServlet {

    private static String THIS_INIT_CONT_FAC="com.sun.jndi.ldap.LdapCtxFactory";
    private static String THIS_PROV_URL="ldap://localhost:389";
    private static String THIS_MGR_DN="uid=kvaughan, ou=People, o=airius.com";
    private static String THIS_MGR_PWD="bribery";

    public void doGet(HttpServletRequest request,
                      HttpServletResponse response)
        throws IOException, ServletException
    {
        WML wml = new WML();
        wml.addCard("JNDIAddRobMachin");
        wml.println("<p>");

        try {
            Hashtable env=new Hashtable();

            env.put(Context.INITIAL_CONTEXT_FACTORY, THIS_INIT_CONT_FAC);
            env.put(Context.PROVIDER_URL, THIS_PROV_URL);
            env.put(Context.SECURITY_AUTHENTICATION, "simple");
            env.put(Context.SECURITY_PRINCIPAL, THIS_MGR_DN);
            env.put(Context.SECURITY_CREDENTIALS, THIS_MGR_PWD);

            DirContext ctx = new InitialDirContext(env);

            ModificationItem[] modifications = new ModificationItem[2];

            // Replace telephone number attribute with new value
            modifications[0] = new ModificationItem(DirContext.REPLACE_ATTRIBUTE,
                new BasicAttribute("telephonenumber", "+44 1234 56789"));

            // Add an e-mail address
            modifications[1] = new ModificationItem(DirContext.ADD_ATTRIBUTE,
                new BasicAttribute("mail", "rmachin@airius.com"));

            ctx.modifyAttributes("uid=rmachin, ou=People, o=airius.com",
modifications);

            wml.println("Rob Machin's details modified!");

        }catch(Exception e) {
            e.printStackTrace();
            wml.println("Modification Failed!");
        } finally {
            wml.println("</p>");
            wml.endCard();
            wml.outputWML(response, true);
        }
    }
}
```

Once an entry has been added we can view it in the Netscape Directory Server's administration console. After the above modifications, Rob Machin's entry in the Netscape Directory Server administration console looks like this:

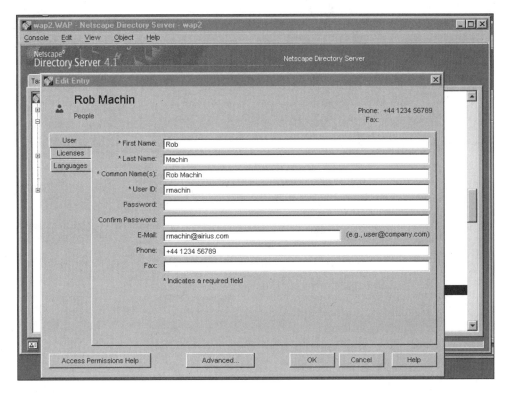

Deleting an Entry

If you wish to remove an entire entry from your directory – rather than just removing an attribute from an existing entry – you must use the `destroySubcontext()` method of the `DirContext` interface:

```
DirContext ctx = new InitialDirContext(env);
ctx.destroySubcontext("uid=rmachin, ou=People, o=airius.com");
```

Note that you must authenticate as the *Directory Manager* to remove an entry.

JNDIDeleteRobMachin.java

The following code demonstrates the deletion of an element from an LDAP directory:

```
import java.io.*;
import java.util.*;
import javax.servlet.*;
import javax.servlet.http.*;

import javax.naming.*;
import javax.naming.directory.*;

import com.wrox.util.WML;
import com.sun.jndi.ldap.LdapCtxFactory;

public class JNDIDeleteRobMachin extends HttpServlet {
```

```
        private static String THIS_INIT_CONT_FAC="com.sun.jndi.ldap.LdapCtxFactory";
        private static String THIS_PROV_URL="ldap://localhost:389";
        private static String THIS_MGR_DN="cn=Directory Manager";
        private static String THIS_MGR_PWD="wap2serv";

        public void doGet(HttpServletRequest request,
                          HttpServletResponse response)
            throws IOException, ServletException
    {
       WML wml = new WML();
       wml.addCard("JNDIDeleteRobMachin");
       wml.println("<p>");

       try {
          Hashtable env=new Hashtable();

          env.put(Context.INITIAL_CONTEXT_FACTORY, THIS_INIT_CONT_FAC);
          env.put(Context.PROVIDER_URL, THIS_PROV_URL);
          env.put(Context.SECURITY_AUTHENTICATION, "simple");
          env.put(Context.SECURITY_PRINCIPAL, THIS_MGR_DN);
          env.put(Context.SECURITY_CREDENTIALS, THIS_MGR_PWD);

          DirContext ctx = new InitialDirContext(env);

          ctx.destroySubcontext("uid=rmachin, ou=People, o=airius.com");

          wml.println("Rob Machin's details deleted!");

       }catch(Exception e) {
          e.printStackTrace();
          wml.println("Phew! Deletion of Rob Machin Failed!");
       } finally {
          wml.println("</p>");
          wml.endCard();
          wml.outputWML(response, true);
       }
    }
  }
}
```

Active Directory and ADSI

So far we have concentrated on presenting Netscape Directory Server as the directory used for examples, and on JNDI as the mechanism for accessing Netscape Directory Server. However, if you are coding on a Microsoft platform and need to dynamically generate WML pages, then you will most likely be using ASP and may need to access Active Directory. In this section we will take a look at how to use ASP to do just that.

> *First, we need to distinguish between Active Directory and ADSI: Active Directory is the directory of all domain and security information for NT domains in Windows 2000 machines. ADSI is Microsoft's COM-based API for accessing directories – which means that you can use ADSI to access Active Directory (as well as other directories).*

We will be using Microsoft's Active Directory Services Interfaces (ADSI) to actually read and write to directories. ADSI is roughly analogous to JNDI to the extent that it is a high level API that allows you to talk to LDAP directories (and also to some other directories that are not LDAP-compliant, but for which Microsoft have written ADSI providers). If you are generating WML pages using ASP (with VBScript or another scripting language for your server-side scripting), then ADSI and not JNDI will be the API you will need to use for your directory access.

Although we are going to use Active Directory for one of the examples in this section, we should emphasize that it is perfectly possible to access Active Directory using JNDI, just as it is possible to use ADSI to reach Netscape Directory Server. However, the advantage of ADSI is that you are not tied to Java – you can use ADSI from any COM-aware language, which means C++, VB, J++, Delphi and MS scripting languages.

The ability to use ADSI opens up an entire new range of possibilities for functionality you can access from WMLScript. Besides accessing generic directories, you can write WML pages that let you perform administrative tasks on your network – for example, starting and stopping NT services, managing print queues, print jobs and file shares, and managing user accounts (setting passwords and disabling or enabling accounts and so on). This means, in theory, that you could perform systems administration tasks using your mobile phone. More importantly, you can use ADSI generally to access information in any directories – this is particularly significant since in Windows 2000 Active Directory is more than just a directory of domain and security information: it can be used to add any other information that you want – for example, records of company employees. In short, it can act as a perfectly generalized directory service in the same way that Netscape Directory Server has been able to.

We are going to look at two examples in this section: a WML page that lists the users on an NT domain using ADSI, and another page that performs searches – again looking for users that satisfy certain criteria. Neither page is particularly useful in its own right, though they both might serve a purpose as part of a larger set of pages: we are presenting them here in order to give simple examples of what can be done using ADSI in conjunction with ASP to generate your WML pages. Before we present the examples, however, we need to explore how ADSI works a little more. We only have space here for a very brief outline. For more information you may want to check out *Professional ADSI*, from Wrox Press.

Inside ADSI

ADSI works using what are known as providers: you can think of an ADSI provider as the software that allows you to talk through ADSI to a particular directory service or set of directory services. Among the providers available are:

- ❑   The LDAP provider allows access to any LDAP-compliant directory service, including Active Directory and Netscape Directory Server.

- ❑   The WinNT provider allows access to network domain information, such as computer and user accounts, NT services, print queues and print jobs, and remote file shares. It works on both NT4 and Windows 2000 and has the advantage that it simulates some of the benefits of Active Directory on NT4 machines, for which Active Directory itself is not available.

- ❑   The IIS provider allows access to the IIS metabase.

- ❑   There are also providers that access Novell Netware directories.

This is illustrated in the diagram below:

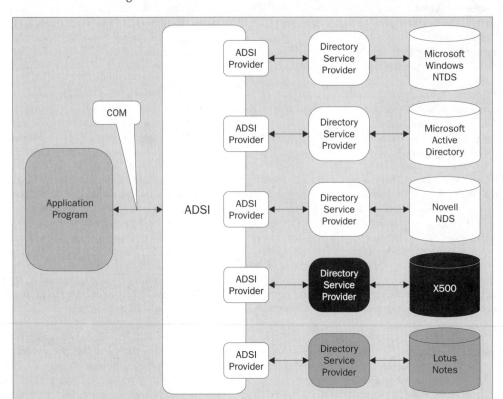

Since the Exchange Server directory and the Site Server membership directory are LDAP-compliant, you can use ADSI to access these directories using the LDAP provider.

Unlike most APIs that you can use in VBScript, you will never use VBScript's `CreateObject()` function to instantiate an ADSI object. This is because ADSI doesn't work by having a fixed set of COM objects. Rather, you name the object in the directory that you want to read from or write to, and pass the name to the `GetObject()` function. This instantiates an ADSI object that is specifically geared to wrap around the named directory object and allow access to it from VBScript.

For example, if I want to get to the object in Active Directory that represents my domain controller, named `CrashLots`, I would use the following method:

```
dim objDC
set objDC = GetObject("LDAP://CrashLots/CN=CRASHLOTS,", & _
    "OU=Domain Controllers,DC=lt,DC=local")
```

The actual string you pass to `GetObject()` is known technically as the ADsPath, and you can think of it as the full name of the object running down the directory tree. The first part of the ADsPath is the name of the provider followed by `://`, so for example LDAP objects begin `LDAP://`. The actual path of the object then follows, in whatever syntax is used by that particular provider. For Active Directory and other LDAP-compliant directories this is simply the distinguished name of the object, preceded optionally by the name of the server we expect to be able to provide the information. Since Active Directory is stored on the domain controllers, the server in this case is just the said domain controller, CrashLots. The distinguished name in the above example is for my own local (non-Internet-connected) domain, called lt.local). The CN=, OU= and DC= are just LDAP's way of identifying the type of an object. To remind you, CN stands for common name, and is a generic term used to name lots of different objects. OU stands for organizational unit, and DC for domain component (that's a term Microsoft introduced to describe levels of the Windows 2000 domain trees).

For the WinNT provider (and also incidentally for the IIS provider) the ADsPath consists of names of the objects running down the directory tree, separated by slashes. The details of the WinNT directory tree are beyond the scope of this book, but suffice to say that the objects running down it are the domain followed by any computers in the domain – so to connect to the object representing my CrashLots computer using the WinNT provider, I would use the following code:

```
dim objDC
set objDC = GetObject("LDAP://CrashLots/CN=CRASHLOTS,", & _
    "OU=Domain Controllers,DC=lt,DC=local")
```

This latter code has the advantage that it will work on NT4 domains as well as Windows 2000 domains. Conversely, using WinNT: rather than LDAP: means that on any machine you will be restricted to the domain functionality that was available in NT4, and not be able to use any of the new Active Directory features, even if your domain controller is running Windows 2000.

Once you have connected to an object, coding with ADSI is fairly intuitive. You can access a large number of named properties using the code below, where "Name" is the name of the property you want:

```
response.write objADSI.Get("Name")
```

In many cases the following simpler syntax also works, though this is not guaranteed for all properties – you'd need to check the ADSI documentation to check which ones it applies to. Here objADSI is the variable holding an ADSI directory object we have obtained using GetObject() as shown above.

```
response.write objADSI."Name"
```

You can update properties of directory objects in the following way – this example changes the user-friendly description of an object:

```
objADSI.Put("Description", "This is the new description")
objADSI.SetInfo
```

This is slightly more complex than reading a property because ADSI uses a system of locally caching properties. The call to SetInfo() is necessary to tell ADSI to propagate changes from the local cache to the directory itself.

It is not possible here to give a list of all the different properties, or to say which ones are read-only and which are writeable, because that depends on the object to which you are connecting. A computer will have a different set of properties, for example, from a PrintJob. However, every ADSI object is guaranteed to have a property called Name which stores the name of the object, and a property called ADsPath, which (surprisingly) stores the full ADsPath – the one you may have supplied to GetObject() to bind to the ADSI object in the first place!

Directories are arranged in a hierarchical structure, similar to the folders and files on a file system. This means that given an object, we often need to access all the children of that object – in directory parlance, the objects contained within the container. This is also quite intuitive in VBScript – we use a `For...Each` loop, the same technique as for any other collection of objects. So, for example, to get all the domain controllers in Active Directory:

```
dim objDC
set objDC = GetObject("LDAP://Crashlots/CN=CRASHLOTS,", & _
   "OU=Domain Controllers,DC=lt,DC=local")
dim objComputer
for each objComputer in objDC
' process the computer
next
```

Listing Users in WinNT

Now we are going to see how to put all this into practice by writing an ASP page that generates the WML page to list the users in an NT4 or W2K domain, using the WinNT provider. The page will consist of an initial card that lists the users, and subsequent cards that display the description of each one – the same structure as for the MailRead example in the Chapter 13 that displayed e-mails.

The ASP code looks like this:

```
<%option explicit%>

<?xml version="1.0"?>
<!DOCTYPE wml PUBLIC "-//WAPFORUM//DTD WML 1.1//EN"
"http://www.wapforum.org/DTD/wml_1.1.xml">

<wml>

<%
'on error resume next

' set up ADsPath of the domain controller
dim sDomain
set sDomain = GetObject("WinNT://LT/CRASHLOTS")

' bind to domain controller and set filter so we only look at users
dim objDC
set objDC = GetObject(sDomain)
objDC.Filter = Array("User")

'count how many users there are
dim objUser
dim nUsers
nUsers = 0
for each objUser in objDC
   nUsers = nUsers + 1
next

' write main index card
Response.Write "<card id=" & Chr(34) & "index"  & Chr(34) & _
   " title=" & Chr(34) & "Users" & Chr(34) & ">" & vbCrLf
Response.Write "<p><b>" & nUsers & " Users</b></p>" & vbCrLf
for each objUser in objDC
```

```
      Response.Write "<p><a href=" & Chr(34) & "#" & objUser.Name & Chr(34)& ">" & _
         objUser.Name & "</a></p>" & vbCrLf
next
Response.Write "</card>" & vbCrLf

' write cards with the user descriptions
for each objUser in objDC
   Response.Write "<card id=" & Chr(34) & objUser.Name & Chr(34) & _
      " title=" & Chr(34) & objUser.Name & "Description" & Chr(34) & ">" & vbCrLf
   Response.Write "<p><b>" & objUser.Name & "</b></p>" & vbCrLf
   Response.Write "<p>" & objUser.Description & "</p>" & vbCrLf

   Response.Write "<p><a href=" & Chr(34) & "#index" & Chr(34)& ">" & _
      "Index</a></p>" & vbCrLf
   Response.Write "</card>" & vbCrLf
next

' clean up etc.
set objDC = nothing
%>

</wml>
```

We will not go over this code in detail since we have already discussed the principles of the ADSI methods. We will note, however, that just after binding to the domain controller, we set a property called `Filter`:

```
set objDC = GetObject(sDomain)
objDC.Filter = Array("User")
```

The reason for this is that the domain controller contains many other objects in the WinNT directory – users, groups, NT services and print queues etc. We are only interested in the user accounts, so we set a filter that ensures that only these objects are returned by the following `For...Each` loops. We also manually count how many users there are so that we can display this information on the index card. Theoretically ADSI container objects have a property, `Count`, which should give this information straight away. Unfortunately in many cases this property is not actually implemented by the ADSI providers – so we have not taken the chance, but have worked out the count for ourselves manually.

The ASP code generates the following WML page:

```
<?xml version="1.0"?>
<!DOCTYPE wml PUBLIC "-//WAPFORUM//DTD WML 1.1//EN"
"http://www.wapforum.org/DTD/wml_1.1.xml">

<wml>

<card id="index" title="Users">
<p><b>7 Users</b></p>
<p><a href="#Administrator">Administrator</a></p>
<p><a href="#Guest">Guest</a></p>
<p><a href="#IUSR_CRASHLOTS">IUSR_CRASHLOTS</a></p>
<p><a href="#IWAM_CRASHLOTS">IWAM_CRASHLOTS</a></p>
<p><a href="#krbtgt">krbtgt</a></p>
<p><a href="#simon">simon</a></p>
```

```
<p><a href="#TsInternetUser">TsInternetUser</a></p>
</card>
<card id="Administrator" title="AdministratorDescription">
<p><b>Administrator</b></p>
<p>Built-in account for administering the computer/domain</p>
<p><a href="#index">Index</a></p>
</card>
<card id="Guest" title="GuestDescription">
<p><b>Guest</b></p>
<p>Built-in account for guest access to the computer/domain</p>
<p><a href="#index">Index</a></p>
</card>
<card id="IUSR_CRASHLOTS" title="IUSR_CRASHLOTSDescription">
<p><b>IUSR_CRASHLOTS</b></p>
<p>Built-in account for anonymous access to Internet Information Services</p>
<p><a href="#index">Index</a></p>
</card>
<card id="IWAM_CRASHLOTS" title="IWAM_CRASHLOTSDescription">
<p><b>IWAM_CRASHLOTS</b></p>
<p>Built-in account for Internet Information Services to start out of process
applications</p>
<p><a href="#index">Index</a></p>
</card>
<card id="krbtgt" title="krbtgtDescription">
<p><b>krbtgt</b></p>
<p>Key Distribution Center Service Account</p>
<p><a href="#index">Index</a></p>
</card>
<card id="simon" title="simonDescription">
<p><b>simon</b></p>
<p></p>
<p><a href="#index">Index</a></p>
</card>
<card id="TsInternetUser" title="TsInternetUserDescription">
<p><b>TsInternetUser</b></p>
<p>This user account is used by Terminal Services.</p>
<p><a href="#index">Index</a></p>
</card>

</wml>
```

And running it gives this page for the index:

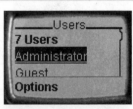

Selecting the Administrator link to view the description of the
Administrator's account yields:

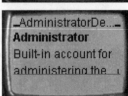

Searching Active Directory

We will finish this chapter with an example that illustrates how to perform searches using ADSI. Because of the way ADSI has been implemented, it is not possible to use ADSI directly from scripting languages to perform searches. Instead, an ADSI provider for ADO/OLE DB is available specifically for this purpose – so searching is actually performed using ADO. There is a further restriction that not all ADSI providers support searching – for the simple reason that not all directories have the underlying infrastructure needed to support it. In particular, the LDAP provider, and Active Directory do allow searching, but WinNT: does not.

> *The following discussion assumes that the reader is familiar with the basic principles of ADO programming (discussed briefly in Chapter 8) and so we will be focusing on the features specific to ADSI.*

Searches are performed by asking ADO to execute a command. The syntax of the command is based on the LDAP search filters that we studied earlier in this chapter. In detail, the command syntax is this:

```
<Base>;(Search-Filter);Properties;Scope
```

In other words, we need to supply four pieces of information, separated by semi-colons. First up *Base* is the ADsPath of the search base – the object from which we want to start the search. Depending on the value of the *scope* (see below), only objects located at or below the base in the directory hierarchy will be returned. Note that this ADsPath must be enclosed in angled brackets.

Next is the search filter – in exactly the format described earlier, and surrounded (as usual for search filters) by round brackets.

Properties is simply a comma-separated list of the properties we are interested in for the objects returned. If you want all properties returned, put a * here. Note, however, that this will clearly have performance implications since it means the directory service will have to go to the trouble of retrieving all the properties and sending them over the network. For some directories, this can mean hundreds of properties, when you are only actually interested in the values of a couple of them.

The last part of the command syntax is the *Scope*. This can have one of three values:

❑   base will search only the search base – in other words you end up with a way of getting properties back for that one object.

❑   onelevel means that only immediate children of the base will be searched.

❑   subtree means that the search base and all objects below it will be searched. This is the option you will choose most often.

To see how this works in practice, we'll look at the command text for the example we're about to present:

```
<LDAP://CrashLots/DC=lt,DC=local>;(objectCategory=Person);sAMAccountName;subtree
```

This indicates that we start the search at the top of the domain tree for the lt.local (or in LDAP parlance, dc=lt,dc=local) domain. The search filter is (objectCategory=person) and works because all objects in Active Directory have a property, objectCategory, which indicates the general type of object – Person for user accounts. We only want to retrieve one property, the name of the user accounts: in Active Directory this is known as the sAMAccountName (note the case). Finally we want to search the whole of Active Directory so we specify a scope of subtree.

Finally, in order to ask ADO to hook up to the ADSI provider, we need to specify a provider name of `ADsDSOObject`.

Armed with all this information we can now look at the ASP code to generate a list of user accounts:

```
<%option explicit%>

<?xml version="1.0"?>
<!DOCTYPE wml PUBLIC "-//WAPFORUM//DTD WML 1.1//EN"
"http://www.wapforum.org/DTD/wml_1.1.xml">

<wml>

<%
on error resume next

' set up ADO connection
dim oConnection, oCommand
set oCommand = CreateObject("ADODB.Command")
oCommand.ActiveConnection = "Provider=ADsDSOObject"

' set up command text
dim sBase, sFilter, sProperties, sScope
sScope = "subtree"
sFilter = "(objectCategory=Person)"
sProperties = "sAMAccountName"
sBase = "LDAP://CrashLots/DC=lt,DC=local"
dim sString
sString = "<" & sBase & ">;" & sFilter & ";" & sProperties & ";" & sScope

' execute search
oCommand.CommandText = sString
dim objRS
set objRS = oCommand.Execute(sString)

' display results
Response.Write "<card id=" & Chr(34) & "index"  & Chr(34) & _
    " title=" & Chr(34) & "Users" & Chr(34) & ">" & vbCrLf
dim field
do while not (objRS.EOF)
    Response.Write "<p>" & objRS("sAMAccountName") & "</p>" & vbCrLf
    objRS.MoveNext
loop
Response.Write "</card>" & vbCrLf

%>
</wml>
```

This code generates the following WML:

```
<?xml version="1.0"?>
<!DOCTYPE wml PUBLIC "-//WAPFORUM//DTD WML 1.1//EN"
"http://www.wapforum.org/DTD/wml_1.1.xml">

<wml>
<card id="index" title="Users">
<p>Administrator</p>
<p>Guest</p>
<p>TsInternetUser</p>
```

```
<p>IUSR_CRASHLOTS</p>
<p>IWAM_CRASHLOTS</p>
<p>krbtgt</p>
<p>simon</p>
</card>

</wml>
```

And when we display the WML on a microbrowser, it should look something like this:

The Application Configuration Access Protocol

A quick word is needed on a competing standard to LDAP, and the other directory services we have discussed, in their role as a repository of configuration and personalization data for an application.

The **Application Configuration Access Protocol** (**ACAP**) started life at Carnegie Mellon University as part of a project to integrate their e-mail and messaging systems, known as *Project Cyrus*. ACAP has now been proposed as an Internet standard, defined in RFC 2244. Like LDAP, ACAP is designed to store and serve general attributes (name-value pairs) from a central network server.

The focus of ACAP is the personalization of applications for highly mobile users. Its widest adoption has been by e-mail and web browser software vendors, where ACAP has been used to share address book and bookmark information, acting as a central repository for roaming users. For example, a user's home and office systems could seamlessly share configurations and address books, and additionally this information could be shared with the user's other e-mail systems, such as their WAP phone or Palm e-mail software.

ACAP benefits from a specific design focus, and may well have a part to play in the areas of application configuration, and the storage of user information. For example, ACAP differs from LDAP in that it is designed to be able to cache information at the client side, so it can work 'offline'. However, it should be noted that ACAP is *not* designed to compete with LDAP in the storage of large amounts of corporate data, such as corporate-wide phone books etc.

If the focus of the directory system is specifically in the area of personalization, then ACAP must be considered as a viable alternative to a full-blown directory service. ACAP has not yet however, found widespread implementation.

Wireless Issues

M-commerce is centered on the intrinsic value of information; LDAP and WAP show great potential as an efficient and flexible mechanism for data storage and manipulation. LDAP will enable mobile users of WAP devices to benefit from access to centrally administered information and configuration files.

Profile information collected from customers and stored in directories can be used to sculpt applications written for mobile devices, ensuring that the online experience using a WAP system is as satisfying, sleek, and efficient as possible.

It will be the enterprises that can provide useful information, and utilize data gained from customer experience, which will thrive in the new economy. This use of information will be the key differentiator between organizations that succeed, and companies that lose touch with the needs of their patrons.

As well as being used to store corporate address book information and resource information, in the future we may see LDAP commonly used for:

- Storage of vCard 'business card' information
- Users' certificates storage, for use in single sign-on systems
- Storage of CORBA, COM+, and EJB objects in distributed computing systems
- JINI and Bluetooth technologies, to determine 'local' services and networkable resources, enabling massive interconnectivity and seamless configuration of devices, enabling truly useful information exchange

LDAP will be a critical tool in establishing the information capture and exchange that is at the heart of the technological paradigm shift to WAP-enabled computing.

Summary

We have seen how LDAP evolved from the X.500 Directory Service, and have looked at the purposes and uses of directory services.

In summary, LDAP:

- Can provide rapid access to user and resource information
- Is designed from the ground up for a distributed, networked environment
- Is widely implemented and vendor-neutral

LDAP can best be used in the development of WAP applications, by using server-side technologies. In this chapter we have seen how Java servlets can be used to provide WAP-enabled devices with powerful functionality, by interfacing with LDAP and generating dynamic content in WML.

Sun's JNDI API and Microsoft's ADSI have been reviewed at a basic level, and we have seen how we can use these technologies to leverage the power of LDAP in our WAP applications. Whichever platform you are using, LDAP is a relatively easy technology to start working with and, like WAP, has an exciting future. Coupled with good application design, LDAP can satisfy a variety of business needs, and will amply repay the time and effort needed to learn it.

The growing importance of directory services within many organizations will see the use of LDAP becoming key to IT systems development in the next few years. With m-commerce set to dominate the agenda of many web-based development efforts, the combination of WAP and LDAP becomes an important, and challenging, area of technological growth. The task for us as programmers is to integrate wireless devices with existing systems, and to create new *killer-apps* that can deliver real business value.

15

WAP Security

Security has always been a hot topic. For centuries the technologies involved were fairly simple, so the steps needed to implement security were correspondingly easy to identify and implement. Commercial computing raised the stakes, both in terms of the technology – and therefore the complexity – and in terms of the damage that could be caused or power gained by breaches of security. Once computer security was only a preserve of large corporations, and very few people had to deal with its complexities. However, nowadays it is not only a concern for large corporations, but for everyone who has Internet access. As WAP expands into new markets, the context within which security becomes a consideration broadens. One day, when we all have intelligent connected appliances in our homes, you may even have a potential security issue with your fridge. Security has been, and remains, one of the biggest concerns for both users of the Internet and for the vendors and service providers who wish to use it as a channel to market.

In this chapter, we will be looking at some of the security issues that impact on the WAP applications that you will be writing and the environment in which they will be deployed and used. We will also look at some of the potential solutions and technologies that can be used to address these issues. In order to do this, we will start by reviewing some of the basics of the technologies involved. If you feel that you already know enough about the underlying technologies then you can easily skip those sections.

This chapter does not contain a 'one size fits all' solution to your security requirements, or a recipe that you can simply follow to implement a secure m-commerce application. There is no such thing. Each environment has to be looked at individually to understand the specific security exposures, and then decisions need to be made as to how best to protect the information, users and application. We'll take a high-level overview in this chapter, with the intention of highlighting the key security issues in wireless applications.

You should note that most activities involved in implementing security are tasks for the systems administrator rather than the programmer, (unless you are a developer writing security products, of course), so there is no programming in this chapter.

The Need for Security

Wherever people or organizations want to conduct commercial transactions over computer networks (wireless or otherwise), the need to protect data such as credit card numbers is obvious. But there are more complex issues as well. For example:

❑ How do I know that the web site that I am connecting to really is the vendor's web site?

❑ How can the vendor prove that the order was really placed by me?

❑ How does the vendor know that it really is my credit card, and that I haven't stolen the number?

Not so long ago, these issues would have been addressed by actually going to the store (where it would be fairly obvious if it wasn't the vendor's store), signing credit card slips, everyone having copies of documents, and so on. None of these solutions work in the connected economy, but effective security measures are still a necessary prerequisite for both e-commerce and m-commerce.

The need for security does not stop with e- or m-commerce, however. There are institutions for whom the integrity and secrecy of their data is paramount, even if no one is directly paying for it. Market-related intelligence, for example, is of significant commercial value to many major corporations and their competitors. Information has value and power in itself.

And then, of course, there is also the need to protect systems so that malicious parties cannot gain access to them and wreak havoc. Without the ability to protect themselves and their operation through appropriate levels of security, both organizations and individuals will be reluctant to provide or utilize services over a publicly accessible communications channel.

So, security has a dual role to play: it is both an enabling technology and a disabling technology. On the one hand it is intended to prevent people from doing things that they are not supposed to do, but on the other hand, it is a mechanism that enables us to participate in activities that may otherwise be too risky.

Security in Context

We all understand the need for robust security, but we need to be careful to take things in context so that we have a clear picture of exactly what can and what cannot be achieved. By its very nature, security is difficult to test. While it is true that a specification for a security product – or for the implementation of security into an environment – can be written and tested, this will not prove that the environment is invulnerable to attack. Attackers always target the 'loopholes'; they always go for the unexpected. It can never be said that an environment is 100% secure – it is only ever secure as far as can reasonably be ascertained, given a level of knowledge of different types of attacks and vulnerabilities. Similarly, no one can really, in my opinion, claim to be an expert in security, because there is always something that you haven't thought of or don't know.

Expectations, both on the part of the security architect and on the part of the client, have to be managed and kept within realistic bounds. What can be stated is that an environment is *secure enough* for a particular purpose. It can be asserted, for example, that the current fixed and mobile security standards, such as TLS (Transport Layer Security) and its wireless equivalent WTLS (Wireless Transport Layer Security), are secure enough to allow most people and organizations to perform business transactions securely over the Internet and wireless communications channels. This does not mean that these technologies are impervious – just that breaking the security is difficult enough to ensure that it is beyond the capabilities of most would-be hackers, and costly enough to outweigh the benefit that could be gained.

Security Basics

To begin with, lets investigate some of the basic concepts that lie behind the art of security. This will help us establish a vocabulary to use throughout the rest of the chapter. In this section, we'll be focusing on:

- ❏ Authentication
- ❏ Confidentiality
- ❏ Integrity
- ❏ Authorization
- ❏ Non-repudiation

You may already be familiar with many of the terms covered in this section, but it may be helpful to quickly review them anyway.

Authentication

Authentication is the process of making sure that another party is actually who they claim to be. While this sounds like a trivial undertaking, it is actually quite complex, and it is a problem that is not unique to the world of computers. In the real world, we all authenticate ourselves many times a day and in many different ways. We recognize people that we know when we see them, or by the sound of their voices. These authentication protocols come built into us as humans. Other animals have different protocols available to them that are suited to their capabilities and their environment, relying more perhaps, on their sense of smell. There are many different ways of authenticating parties to a transaction or interaction, and different mechanisms are appropriate to different types of individuals or organizations. The participants in the transaction need to agree an authentication protocol that they are capable of using and that meets their requirements.

In some situations it is necessary to authenticate people we have never seen before, in which case we typically use a token of some sort. A token has certain characteristics that make it acceptable as an **authentication token**: it is issued by a recognized **Certification Authority** (CA), for example the government, and it usually contains something that enables it to be used to prove the bearer's identity, for example, a photograph or a signature. A passport is a typical example of an authentication token. Once an immigration official is satisfied that a passport genuine, he can use it to validate the identity of the bearer. In a similar way, **digital certificates** and the **signatures** that they contain can be used to authenticate the participants in an electronic transaction.

The purpose of authentication protocols is to try to catch an activity called **spoofing**. This is occurs when one party tries to hide their true identity and assume another's – by carrying a false passport, for example. Spoofing is not just a problem that can occur at the beginning of a transaction. With long-lived transactions, it is possible for a spoofer to interpose themselves after the initial authentication has already taken place, and then pretend to be either one or both ends of the transaction. The only way to guard against this kind of problem is to periodically re-authenticate the participants during the transaction.

Confidentiality

Confidentiality is one of the most important aspects of security. While authentication may have conclusively identified the participants in a transaction, the information that the two parties are communicating may well be sensitive. It is notoriously easy to intercept digital communications – and virtually impossible to prevent it or even identify when it has happened – so it is often necessary to assume that communications will be intercepted and take steps to ensure that when the information is intercepted it cannot be understood or used. To ensure the confidentiality of information it is usually **encrypted**. Encryption is simply the process of encoding information into a different representation that cannot easily be understood. Effective encryption, however, is a very complex issue, which we will examine in a bit more detail later in the chapter. It is obviously always necessary that we have a method to decrypt the information so that we can obtain the original message.

Integrity

If it is necessary to assume that messages are going to be intercepted, it must also be assumed that messages can be interfered with along the way. Typically, this involves either changing some of the content of the message, or substituting the message with another. Either way, we need to be able to make sure that the message was not tampered with during transmission. This is what **integrity** is all about. In the world of computing, message integrity is usually assured by deriving a **hash value** for the message and transmitting that value either along with the message or independently. Basically, a **hash function** is a mathematical algorithm that is used to calculate a number (the hash value) derived from and dependent on the content of the message. If the content changes, then the hash value changes. So, by checking the original hash value of a message (sent separately to the message itself) against the hash value of the message as calculated at the receiving end, you can check whether or not the message has been tampered with. A hash value is also sometimes called **message digest** because it is a 'digested' form of the message.

Authorization

Authorization is the process of determining whether a particular party has the right to perform a particular action with respect to a particular object, in a particular situation. All of these 'particulars' need to be taken into account in order to make an authorization decision. For example, it may be the question of whether I have the right to withdraw funds from your bank account. The particular party and object are important since you are allowed access to your account, whereas I am not, but I am allowed access to my own account. The particular action is also important since I may be entitled to deposit funds in your account, but not withdraw them. The context or situation, often overlooked, is also important, since I should only be able to withdraw funds from my own account if there are sufficient funds in the account.

For authorization to be meaningful there has to be, at the very least, an effective mechanism of authentication. Authentication is therefore a necessary prerequisite for authorization.

Authorization is not directly dependent on – or related to – the channel by which communication takes place, so the issues will be the same whether the transaction takes place over the Internet, at the local branch, or using a mobile phone.

Non-repudiation

Non-repudiation means implementing some sort of mechanism so that it is impossible for the parties to a transaction to deny either that the transaction took place, or that they were party to it. One of the oldest scams in the book is to try and escape the consequences of an action by denying having actually done it, and the wired world is no exception. Like authorization, non-repudiation is also dependent on an effective means of authentication. Non-repudiation is an issue over both the Internet and wireless communications channels, and the need for effective non-repudiation mechanisms has implications for the protocols that are implemented and the types of transactions that can take place in the absence of those protocols.

Encryption Technologies

Encryption and its related technologies are the keystones of secure electronic communications. In this section we are going to briefly look at how various aspects of encryption are used in this context. None of this is unique to wireless communication and applies equally to communication over the Internet, but it is useful to understand this material as a background to the discussion on WAP security that is to follow. The subjects that we will be looking at include:

- ❑ Cryptography
- ❑ Keys
- ❑ Symmetric and Asymmetric Ciphers
- ❑ Cipher Suites
- ❑ Certificates

We are not going to cover these topics in detail since encryption is a very complex subject relying on nightmarishly complex algorithms and abstract mathematical concepts, which would require an entire book to investigate thoroughly.

> *If you are interested in the topic there are many excellent books on the subject, but be prepared to wade through some very complex mathematics. (Applied Cryptography, from John Wiley & Sons, is usually regarded as one of the best introductions to the subject, although it is possibly a little out of date now and doesn't cover Elliptic Curve Cryptography (ECC). For ECC, try Implementing Elliptic Curve Cryptography from Manning Publications.)*

Basic Principles

Encryption is the process of encoding data such that only the intended recipients can understand it. This simple concept has been somewhat extended and enhanced over the years, and today's encryption and related techniques are used in a number of ways to protect data. The original intention remains the same, however, irrespective of the specific techniques that are used or the way that they are used: it is to protect the privacy of data and prevent it from being compromised. The various techniques currently available can be used to address several of the key security issues that we identified at the start: confidentiality, integrity, authentication, and – in conjunction with other technologies – non-repudiation.

However, a sense of perspective has to be kept about the role of cryptography in security. Cryptography alone does not necessarily make an application or environment secure – it takes an entire security strategy, carefully constructed and properly implemented to achieve that.

There is a little bit of terminology that you need to be familiar with to understand the following sections: **plaintext** (also called **cleartext**) and **ciphertext**. Plaintext is text or data that has not been encoded. If it is text it will be in human readable form. Ciphertext is the result of applying a cryptographic algorithm to the plaintext.

Cryptography

Cryptography is the art of keeping messages hidden or secure, which is achieved by encoding, or enciphering data using some sort of reversible algorithm to obscure its meaning. By reversible, we mean that messages can also be decoded to derive the plaintext from the ciphertext. The algorithm that is used is referred to as a **cipher**. Cryptographic algorithms are extremely difficult to invent and prove the robustness of, so there are only a few algorithms in the world that have any level of credibility.

Note that there would be no point in using *just* an algorithm to encode data, because cracking an encrypted message would reduce to identifying the algorithm used to encode it. To get around this problem cryptographic algorithms use **keys** to control how they convert the plaintext into ciphertext. The result is that an encoded message cannot be deciphered without knowing both the key *and* the algorithm used for the encoding.

Cryptanalysis is the study of trying to break the ciphers, and therefore expose the weaknesses, of various algorithms. This is an important part of proving that a cipher is robust, and a cipher only gains credibility when it has withstood a significant amount of cryptanalysis. Some of the ciphers in common use today have withstood several decades of cryptanalysis. Many cryptographic algorithms are in the public domain, so that they can be exposed to cryptanalysis by many mathematicians over a long period. Therefore any algorithm that is not in the public domain or which has not been subjected to significant cryptanalysis should not be trusted. It has often been proven that security by obscurity doesn't work.

Keys

Keys are critical to cryptography. A key is a value used in the algorithm to influence its operation so that it is capable of producing different ciphertext for identical plaintext. You can think of it as a way to customize an algorithm, so that each time it is used with a unique key it gives a unique result. Of course, applying the same key to the same plaintext with the same algorithm gives the same result, but the key introduces an extra dimension of complexity. So, as we said above, in order to decode the message you need to know both the algorithm *and* the key.

The length of the key used is an important factor in how easy or difficult it is to break the code, because the longer the key the more possible values there are that the key could take. One of the most common methods of finding the key is simply to try every conceivable combination of values until one works. This is referred to as the **brute force method**, and in the case of a good encryption algorithm it is the only method available to an attacker. The table below lists the number of possible combinations in bits sequences for keys of various lengths:

Bits	Number of Combinations
2	4
40	1.1×10^{12}
56	7.2×10^{16}
112	8.35×10^{30}
128	4.53×10^{33}
168	1.16×10^{39}
256	1.28×10^{47}
512	6.58×10^{59}
1024	1.52×10^{72}

Note, however, that size can also actually impede your performance. Encrypting and decrypting data is quite expensive in computer terms, and longer keys make the process even more expensive.

The strength of an encryption algorithm is not merely a function of the size of the key. Keys of a similar size used in different algorithms differ in terms of the relative ease with which they can be cracked.

Symmetric and Asymmetric Ciphers

There are a couple of ways of categorizing ciphers, but we'll just look at one of them here. Ciphers can be categorized according to the number of keys that they use, and how those keys are used to encrypt and decrypt data. Using this categorization scheme there are two types of ciphers: symmetric ciphers and asymmetric ciphers, and both are used in securing electronic transactions, although in different ways. Symmetric ciphers simply use the same key for encryption and decryption, whereas asymmetric ciphers use a pair of keys – one to encrypt and one to decrypt.

Symmetric Ciphers

Using the same key for encryption and decryption of data means, of course, that both parties have to have a copy of the key. What this also means is that if anyone else gets hold of the key, then all the messages encrypted with that key can be decrypted, so the security of the entire system is dependent on keeping the key secret.

Once both parties have a copy of the key then this is not a big problem. But, we need to find a secure way to *exchange* the key in the first place. I can't just send you the key, because it is not itself encrypted, so anyone could intercept it. I could encrypt the key before I send it to you, but then I would have to get to you the key that I had used to encrypt the key that I want to use to encrypt the message. You see the problem. Of course there may be a secure way of exchanging the key such that no one else could get hold of it, but if that is the case then why don't I just give you the message in that secure way in the first place and not bother with the encryption at all?

So, exchanging the key securely is a big problem. But that doesn't mean that symmetric keys are not used; in fact, they are used for by far the majority of the encryption that takes place in the world today, including the encryption that is used on the Internet. The reason for that is because they are significantly faster than the alternative, asymmetric keys, and that counts for a lot. Besides which, there is actually a way in which we can exchange the key securely, which we'll see shortly, in the section *Key Exchange*.

Asymmetric Ciphers

Asymmetric ciphers use a matched pair of keys. One of the keys is a **public key**, which does not have to be kept secret, and the other is a **private key**, which does have to be kept secret. The public key is derived from the private key using a mathematical algorithm in such a way that the pair of keys has a peculiar and useful property. Data that is encrypted using the public key can only be decrypted using the private key that the public key was derived from. In some versions of these asymmetric key algorithms, data that is encrypted with the private key can also be decrypted with the public key; in other words they work in reverse. These reversible keys can be used for signatures and authentication as well as encryption, although there are also algorithms that are only used for generating signatures.

The basic concept behind the utilization of these asymmetric keys is that if I want to send you a secret message I would need to get hold of your public key and use it to encrypt the data. This should not be a problem, providing that you were willing to give it to me, because if it gets stolen no harm can come of it. All that could happen is that whoever stole your public key could use it to encrypt some data and send it to you as well. That may surprise you, but it is unlikely to harm you. Any of the data that anybody sends you that has been encrypted with your public key can only be decrypted using your private key, which you don't give to *anyone*. If you want to send me data then you would do exactly the same thing: you would get hold of my public key, use it to encrypt the data, and I would use my private key to decrypt it. So, although we have to exchange public keys, there is no risk in that, and private keys don't get exchanged at all, so there is no danger of them being stolen in the process.

This clever arrangement of public and private keys eliminates the problem associated with exchanging symmetric keys. Of course, this entire system is dependent on the fact that we both keep our respective private keys secret, otherwise it breaks. The disadvantage of asymmetric keys is that they take considerably more computing power than symmetric keys, so it is not really feasible to use them for encrypting each and every piece of data that is transmitted, even with fairly powerful computers. To get around this problem, but still retain the advantages afforded by asymmetric keys, they are often combined with symmetric keys in cipher suites to facilitate the exchange of keys that are then used with symmetric ciphers for encrypting data. This helps to reduce the amount of computation that is required.

Cipher Suites

Cryptography, in the real world, comes pre-packaged in suites. Cryptographic suites are collections of algorithms, which, individually or together, support one or more of the operations that are required for the secure transmission of data, namely:

- ❑ Key exchange
- ❑ Encryption
- ❑ Creating message digests using the hash function

In some cases, one algorithm may be capable of supporting more than one of these operations. In this section, we're going to look at the operations and relate them to some of the algorithms that could be used to support them. Note, however, that this list is by no means comprehensive; there are far more omissions than inclusions.

Key Exchange

Key exchange algorithms allow us to exchange symmetric keys securely. They use asymmetric keys to facilitate the exchange of a shared secret, which is used to derive a symmetric key, which can then be used with a symmetric encryption algorithm to encrypt the rest of the data in the communication. Note that what is encrypted and exchanged is not actually the secret key itself, but rather a value that is used to derive a secret key. Each party takes this value and derives the secret key independently. This allows a secret key to be established between two parties, as if it had been directly exchanged, without fear of security being compromised, even if the shared secret is intercepted. If it is intercepted it doesn't matter because it is encrypted and can only be decrypted with the private key that matches the public key that was used to encrypt the secret.

The requirement to derive the secret key from the shared secret and the public key actually makes this process even more secure, because if the value is intercepted it cannot be used as a secret key directly. Whoever intercepted it also has to have the wherewithal to generate the secret key from the exchanged value after it has been successfully decrypted. Algorithms that can be used as part of the key exchange process include Diffie-Hellman (DH), RSA (named after its creators: Rivest, Shamir and Adelman) and Elliptic Curve Cryptography (ECC). DH is the oldest of the key exchange algorithms, and therefore probably not the strongest. RSA has become the de facto standard and has been shown to be secure over decades of intensive cryptanalysis. ECC is the new kid on the block, but has some interesting properties in that it is significantly more efficient than DH and RSA, while also being less susceptible to cracking. This means that shorter keys can be used with the algorithm to achieve a similar level of security. ECC is the preferred algorithm for processor challenged devices, such as mobile phones. All three of these algorithms are included in the WAP standard.

Encryption

This is the meat of the subject – the algorithms that are actually used to encrypt the data. Even though many of the algorithms listed in the key exchange section can also be used to encrypt data, because of the performance implications of asymmetric algorithms, they are not usually used to encrypt data beyond the initial key agreement phase. Symmetric algorithms are usually used to encrypt data during communications, once an asymmetric algorithm has been used to facilitate the exchange or generation of a symmetric key.

Typical examples of the algorithms that you will find listed here are DES (data encryption standard), 3DES, IDEA, and the Rivest ciphers (RC2, RC4, RC5). DES is the oldest of the ciphers, and is the de facto standard in many cryptographic applications. For many years it has withstood cryptanalysis, but new techniques are allowing it to be cracked in ever-shorter timescales. 3DES is an implementation of DES that effectively encrypts the data either two or three times using multiple keys, which effectively increases the strength of the algorithm, but sacrifices performance in doing so. 3DES has not yet (to my knowledge) been cracked. IDEA is similar to DES in its performance, but appears to be harder to crack. The Rivest ciphers vary in their performance characteristics and their strengths.

Message Digests

As we discussed before, hash functions are used to generate a message digest, which is a value that can be used to test the integrity of the message and prove that it has not been interfered with. The basic principle of a hash function is that it takes some data as input and produces a 'digested' hash value that is dependent on the content of the input and the hash algorithm used. The correct technical term used to describe this state of events is that the hash function is **deterministic**. Even small changes in the input data should result in significant changes in the hash value that results. Thus it becomes easy to determine when the original data has been corrupted or interfered with.

To qualify as a good hash function the algorithm needs to be **collision resistant**. This means that two different input values should never produce the same hash value. Another characteristic of a robust hash function is that it must be difficult to derive the original input from the hash value and the algorithm alone. In this sense, these are one-way functions. In order to verify the integrity of the data it is necessary to re-hash it and compare the two hash values. You will also hear the term message authentication code (MAC), and a MAC is basically a message digest that has been generated using a key. A number of hash algorithms have MAC versions.

The hash functions that you are most likely to come across are MD2, MD4, MD5 and SHA-1. MD4 we can immediately disregard because it has been discredited. MD2 has been around for a while and has held up well under cryptanalytic scrutiny. MD5 is based on MD4 and seems more robust, but there are some doubts, particularly with regard to its collision resistance. SHA-1 (Secure Hash Algorithm-1) is also based on MD4, but it is very different to MD5 and, so far at least, SHA-1 doesn't appear to have MD4's weaknesses. SHA-1 is currently the hash algorithm of choice.

When a message digest is combined with reversible asymmetric encryption it can be used to generate a **signature**. To sign a message I would generate a message digest and encrypt it using my private key. You would receive the message and also generate a message digest from it. You would then take the signature that came with the message, decrypt it using my public key (hence the need for reversible ciphers), and compare the message digest that you generated with the one that came with the message. If they match, then you know that it was me that sent the message. If they don't, then you know that this is a forgery, or the message was interfered with on route. Signatures extend the usefulness of message digests to address some of the issues that we discussed about authentication and non-repudiation.

Certificates

Certificates were designed primarily for the purposes of authentication and can be regarded as an electronic equivalent of a passport. A certificate, like a passport, can be used to identify me, and is acceptable because of the recognized authority that issued it.

The certificate contains various items of information about the party being vouched for, called the subject of the certificate, including the subject's public key. In this respect, the purpose of the certificate is to vouch that the public key contained in the certificate belongs to the subject of the certificate. Thus you can feel satisfied that you can use this public key to send information securely to the subject of the certificate, and that the pubic key does not actually belong to someone else who would then have access to your information. The certificate also contains some information about the authority that is vouching for the subject, and is signed by this authority.

Certificates may expire or become invalid for some reason, but because they are widely distributed, and are held on a large number of computers, mobile phones, and in various other places, it is not feasible to try and get hold of them and physically delete them. To address this situation, certificates that are no longer valid can be revoked by being published on a certificate revocation list (CRL). Before accepting a certificate, the onus is on you to make sure that you check that the certificate has not been revoked.

Because of the large number of certificates in existence, a mechanism is required to simplify the storage and management of certificates. Certificate servers are used for this purpose, and can be accessed to retrieve the public keys of organizations that you want to deal with. Organizations can issue certificates to their employees, and in the case of a large organization they may have tens of thousands of these to deal with, so they may also run their own certification server to centralize administration of their employees certificates. This also means that each user does not have to keep everyone else's public keys. Certificate servers help to eliminate the hassle of updating your own public key. All you need to do is post your new key to the certificate server and anyone can get hold of it, rather than having to track down everyone who has your key and send them an updated version manually.

Certificate Authorities

Certificates are issued by a trusted organization called a Certification Authority (CA). In order to make the job of certification of large numbers of users feasible, certificates support a decentralized certification mechanism in which the certification authority is delegated. Certified parties can certify other parties by signing their certificates, and organizations can issue certificates for their own use.

While this hierarchical structure makes the job of issuing certificates more achievable, it also makes it harder to prove the validity of a certificate. To address this problem there is a mechanism that allows certificates to be chained, so the certificate that is presented may be certified by a certified party, whose certificate in turn is certified by another certified party, and so on. In order for the certificate to be acceptable the user has to 'walk' up the chain until the certificate of an acceptable certification authority, or a certificate that is signed by a party that is deemed to be acceptable, is encountered. This may simply be someone who you know and whose public key you have, so that you can check the signature on the certificate. If no acceptable CA is encountered then the certificate is rejected.

The CA's certificate is self-signed. You can calculate the message digest of the entire certificate, which is called a **fingerprint**, and you can use this fingerprint to verify that the certificate is genuine. The CA can use any means available to make the fingerprint of their certificate available, specifically so that people can use it to check certificates. Remember that a message digest is a reasonably small string of characters, so you could even phone the relevant CA and ask them to read their certificate fingerprint to you. These certification authorities include:

- ❏   AT&T Certificate Services
- ❏   GTE CyberTrust (http://www.baltimore.com)
- ❏   KeyWitness International
- ❏   Thawte Consulting (http://www.thawte.com)
- ❏   VeriSign (http://www.verisign.com)

Anyone can apply for a certificate, either for personal use of for a server. You can apply directly to any of the organizations listed above, although this list is not exhaustive and there are many other organizations that can issues certificates for you. Prices of certificates vary, depending on how you intend to use them, from around US$1000 to about US$100. As part of obtaining your certificate you will need to provide some documentation, which again, will depend on how you intend to use your certificate. If you are obtaining a certificate for your web site then you will need to provide proof of your organizations name, and proof of your right to use the domain name. If you want a certificate issued in your own name then you will need to provide evidence of your identity, such as a passport.

Comparing Security Models

Space in this book does not allow for a complete discussion of everything that you need to know to implement a secure environment for your wireless applications. What we will do instead is compare security in the WAP environment to the more familiar environment of the Internet. This will give you a perspective on what can be achieved with regard to the security of your WAP applications, and what you need to be aware of. Note that almost all of what has to be done to implement a secure environment will be undertaken by the administrators at your site, for example, the people who install and configure your gateways, web servers, proxies and firewalls.

If you are performing that administration role, then we'll assume that you already have most of the knowledge that you need to create a secure network environment (the protocols, the frame formats, the message sequences, understanding of firewalls and proxies, how hackers operate, intrusion detection, remote access, and so on). If you do not have a solid understanding of these issues, then you should either do some research before attempting to design and implement a corporate security policy, or obtain help from someone else.

In the next two sections, we'll examine and compare two hypothetical environments, one an Internet environment and the other a wireless environment. Bear in mind that these are for illustrative purposes and represent only one possible network security configuration. It is extremely unlikely that your environment will look exactly like this, because it will have been designed to meet the needs specific to your particular environment.

Security on the Internet

Security is provided at a number of levels and in a number of ways. Multiple protocols are involved in securing communication, many of which are not discussed in this chapter. There are many excellent books on Internet security, should you want to understand more about the areas not covered in detail as part of this discussion.

The diagram below illustrates a typical model of how communication takes place over the Internet:

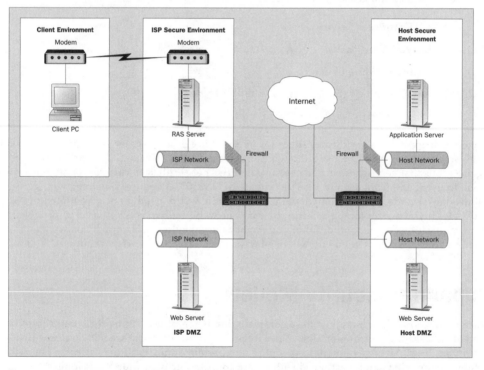

In the diagram above, it is assumed that the client device is a PC or laptop of some sort, and the connection to the Internet is via an ISP. To begin with, we can examine the connection between the client device and the ISP. The client will typically use a modem or IDSN TA to connect to the ISP, and PPP (point-to-point protocol) can be assumed to be the protocol used over this connection. PPP is the de facto standard bearer protocol for tunneling IP and higher layer protocols over serial lines. PPP uses the Link Control Protocol to negotiate the settings for the session, including the type of authentication to use. The Encryption Control Protocol can also be used to negotiate for encryption to be applied to all packets exchanged between the two peers.

It is normal for a user dialing in to be authenticated by the ISP before being allowed to use the ISP's network. There are a number of possibilities for how this may be achieved, for example opening a terminal window in which the client is expected to type in a user ID and password, or using one of the well-known authentication protocols: PAP, CHAP, SPAP, MS-CHAP or MD5-CHAP. PAP is the simplest of the authentication protocols, and actually transmits the user ID and password as clear text. The other protocols are more sophisticated and use some form of encryption to protect the user ID and password in transit.

Once the authentication is completed successfully the client device is allocated an IP address, registered on the ISP's network, and the RAS server will then act as a proxy for the client device, transmitting IP packets received from the client and collecting packets addressed to the client and forwarding them over the PPP connection. (There are a number of protocols involved in achieving this.) The ISP's network will be connected to the Internet backbone through a router or gateway of some sort, as is shown in the diagram. It is fairly normal to protect a network from Internet traffic through some sort of firewall, running either on a separate device or as part of the router. In our diagram it is shown as sitting on its own device between the router and the secure part of the ISP's network. It is also fairly normal to run a demilitarized zone (DMZ) that is not protected by a firewall or where the protection is less stringent. Typically the DMZ is on a different network segment (as shown above), with the firewall guarding the gateway between the secure part of the network and the DMZ. Although this model is quite common, it is by no means the only way to configure a network, and a lot of thought needs to go into setting up the routers and firewalls in any environment.

Once through the gateway to the Internet, data will traverse many intervening circuit-switched or packet-switched networks, being passed from router to router along the way to the destination network. How packets of information find their way across the Internet is a fascinating subject, but unfortunately beyond the scope of this book. It is sufficient to know that they will eventually arrive at the destination network, which they will enter through a router. They will then either be passed into the destination DMZ or across a firewall into the host network, where they will be processed by some application server. A fairly common scenario is illustrated in the diagram, in which the web server is hosted in the DMZ, and only traffic from the web server is allowed to access the other servers behind the firewall, but again, this is not the only possible set up.

There are a number of ways in which security can be added into this process, the most common of which is the **Transport Layer Security** protocol, **TLS**, formerly know as **SSL (Secure Sockets Layer)**, which is a transport layer protocol.

When a client requests a secure session with a server, the parameters of the session are negotiated between the client and server, and a secure session is established between them. All communication between the client and server is then encrypted using algorithms and keys that are exchanged as part of the session set up. Although it is possible for an eavesdropper to intercept or monitor the session set up packets, the key exchange suites are robust enough to ensure that the integrity of the session will not be compromised. This is achieved largely by exchanging shared secrets from which session keys are derived using a combination of public and private keys (as discussed in the section on key exchange), rather than exchanging the session keys themselves. In order to generate the session key from the shared secret the eavesdropper would need to be in possession of one of the private keys. TLS, therefore, provides an **end-to-end** secure communications channel between a client and a server, in which all data is encrypted and cannot be decrypted by any intervening nodes between the client and server.

TLS is suited to establishing secure communications on an ad hoc basis between clients and servers across the Internet. There is another technology called virtual private networks (VPNs), that allow clients to establish secure communications across the Internet, but there are some subtle differences between a VPN and a TLS session. The first, is that the client and server have to be configured to allow a tunnel to be established, and the tunnel is for a particular client to a particular server. Another, is that the VPN is established from the client device to the host network, rather than to a specific server on the network. There has to be a device at the other end of the tunnel, and this is often either a dedicated VPN server or a router. Typically VPNs are used to provide secure access for remote users to a corporate network, rather than secure public access to a server. A different set of protocols is used to set up the VPN, and the VPN will exist from the time at which the client accesses the network through to when the client logs off.

Security in WAP

Security in WAP has been implemented in such a way as to provide maximum benefit with the least amount of pain. One of the goals of the WAP Forum has been to *not* 'reinvent the wheel'. They have an objective of making use of whatever is already available, and of using Internet technologies as a model. Interoperability with the Internet and Internet protocols is an important goal, so, as on the Internet, security is explicitly implemented in WAP in the transport layer. The means of achieving this is very similar to the Internet model: the Internet model implements most of its security features in TLS, and WAP implements most of its security in **WTLS**. The name should give you a clue: WTLS is similar to, and based on TLS. The actual network configuration is subtly different, though, and these differences have important security implications.

To illustrate where these differences lie we will look at how communication takes place in the WAP environment with the aid of a similar diagram to the one we used in the discussion of the Internet communication model:

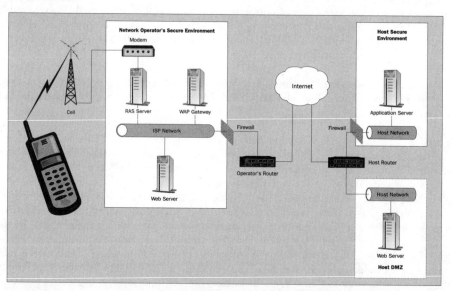

In this model, connection is still made via a phone call, but this time the connection is typically handled by the network operator rather than an ISP. This does not have to be the case, as we will discuss later, but for the purposes of this discussion we will assume that it is, simply because it is likely to be the most common model. The phone call, when the operator receives it, is routed through to one of its own modems and connects up to a RAS server, the same as in the Internet model. The WAP Forum has mandated that the mobile device should use PPP, although the PPP itself is actually tunneled through OTA (over-the-air) bearer protocols, and a number of related protocols that are involved in handling any mobile phone call. There is also a level of encryption between the phone and the base station that operates independently of anything negotiated by PPP or higher-level protocols. This encryption is specified as part of GSM. This additional security layer does make it a little more difficult for anyone trying to eavesdrop on the call, but the encryption algorithms are not very strong and do not apply beyond the base station, so it cannot be regarded as a secure connection per se.

The RAS server will perform authentication, as in the Internet model, but once the packet is through the RAS server things become slightly different. Instead of being routed over the Internet to a web server, the data is routed to the WAP gateway. The WAP gateway, as we saw in Chapter 3, is responsible for the translation of the WML and WMLScript to and from the binary format that is transmitted over the air, and also acts as a proxy for the phone, communicating with the web server on the phone's behalf, using normal HTTP 1.1 protocols to do so. The web server is not aware of the fact that it is talking to a WAP gateway; it sees the gateway as simply another client device.

Typically, the web server will be the network operator's own web server, and so the packets possibly will never leave the network operator's own network. However, you can usually access services that are provided by other organizations, should you want to, in which case the WAP gateway will simply send its HTTP packets through the firewall to a remote web server on another organization's network. The network operator could also have a DMZ in place with web servers offering WAP or Internet services to the general public, but the premium services are likely to be on a separate server that cannot be accessed by the public.

As far as security is concerned, the first thing that is apparent is that if the WAP gateway acts as a proxy for the phone and uses normal HTTP 1.1 protocols (which is what the specification mandates) then there is no reason that TLS cannot be used to secure all communication between the WAP gateway and the web server, exactly as happens on the Internet. But TLS cannot be used to secure the communications between the phone and the WAP gateway, because TLS requires a reliable transport – in particular TCP – and the phone does not use TCP to communicate with the WAP gateway. TCP/IP is suited to higher bandwidth and more reliable networks than you are likely to encounter with a mobile phone, and the typical mobile device is too processor and resource challenged to run a TCP/IP protocol stack, so the WAP Forum has designed another protocol stack which is more lightweight and better suited to the environment (see Chapter 1 for details). This protocol stack uses UDP over IP based networks, or WDP over non-IP networks.

To address the issue of security between the device and the WAP gateway the WAP Forum defined a new protocol, WTLS, which is based on TLS and provides a similar level of security. WTLS is capable of running over WDP or UDP, and is optimized for use on devices that do not have significant processing resources. What this means, however, is that there is one security mechanism in place from the device to the gateway, and another from the gateway to the web server, which implies that there must be a transition from WTLS to TLS at the gateway. This is an issue that we will discuss in more detail in the next section.

Wireless Security Issues

It is clear that the wireless communication model and the Internet communication model are very similar. There is one essential difference, however, which is the presence of the WAP gateway. A second, not so obvious issue is to do with authentication. In this section, we'll discuss these two issues and attempt to put them into context. How exactly this impacts on your applications depends on your specific environment and your security requirements. For some organizations they are not a big problem, while for other organizations they will be significant issues requiring the investment of a lot of time and money.

Device Versus User

The issue related to authentication may not be immediately obvious at first glance, but can be quite pernicious. It boils down to the question of what or who is being authenticated by the presentation of some sort of credentials, whether those are a certificate, or a user ID and password combination. When you log in to your ISP you are typically required to provide a user ID and password for the ISP to authenticate you. But stop and think a moment: when last did you actually type in your user ID and password while connecting to the Internet? Most of us store these along with our dial up settings on our computers, and they are presented on our behalf by the system.

This is all very convenient when I am the only person that has access to my computer, but what happens when someone else gains access to my system? That person can log on to the Internet as me, access my mailbox, send e-mails using my credentials, post messages to newsgroups with my reply-to address, and even use my certificates. And the more of your user ID and password combinations that you allow your computer to store on your behalf, the more access under your name a user of your system can obtain. Every time I access the Barclaycard web site to pay my Barclaycard bill the system offers to remember my user ID and password. Convenient though this may be, it does have implications from the point of view of security.

This is also true of certificates, which highlights a difference between certificates as an authentication token and something like a passport. In the case of a passport what is being certified is clear – it is the person to whom the passport was issued and whose photograph and signature appear inside. But in the case of the electronic transaction it usually ends up being the device that is certified, because it is the device that actually holds the certificate. Currently, even if the certificate is issued to me as an individual I will almost certainly keep it on my computer, and it will automatically be used from there when necessary to certify me in transactions. Certificates are large and complex enough to prohibit typing them in all the time, so if I use another computer, my certificate won't accompany me. Also, if someone manages to gain access to my system, there is nothing to prevent that person from using my certificate to pretend to be me. While these risks may be small enough to ignore in the fixed wire world, in the wireless world they present more of a problem. There is clearly a difference between authenticating the device and authenticating the user, and this difference is significant in the case of many applications.

Although this problem exists in the world of e-commerce as well as in the mobile world, it is exacerbated in the mobile world, simply because the device is just that – mobile. Last year (1999) for the first time Railtrack in the UK reported that the number of mobile phones left on trains had exceeded the number of umbrellas, which had been the most common item left on trains for most of the century. As the number of mobile phones and other mobile devices increases, the incidence of them being lost and stolen will increase as well. The implications in terms of allowing unauthorized access to systems are not the only issue. Some organizations have even abandoned the use of laptop computers by their field sales staff, because the laptops keep being lost with personal information about clients, policy holders and policy details on them.

All of this illustrates the need to ensure that your security implementation takes account of the types of applications and the environment in which the applications will be used. Some of these issues cannot simply be addressed by means of a protocol either. Many operating systems provide file level security through the use of access control lists (ACLs) and so on, but if the ACL is not stored with the file then there is a possibility that the file could be read via another system. This is not a WAP issue per se, but it certainly is a mobile issue and needs to be taken into account in your mobile security policy if it is likely that mobile devices could end up storing sensitive information.

You may want to consider implementing your applications in such a way that sensitive data is never stored on the mobile device, if that is possible in your applications. Another possibility is to look at ways to authenticate the user, as opposed to the device. One way of doing this is to use certificates as you normally would, which effectively authenticates the device and establishes a secure connection, and then, when a secure session is in place and all data being transmitted is encrypted, request the user to enter a user ID and password. You could then use any of the normal mechanisms to validate the user ID and password combination, including Kerberos, LDAP, or some other external or internal authentication product, just as you would for any other application, whether mobile, Internet or client-server based. This is exactly the same sort of solution that is used for authentication at an automated teller machine, where you type in a pin number that matches your card. Many ATM pin numbers are only between 4 and 6 digits long, so it is not necessary to go to ridiculous lengths either. All of the standard common sense rules, such as obscuring the characters of the password on the screen as they are typed with asterisks apply. Perhaps in the future, thumb print readers and retina scanners will be used.

The WAP Gateway

For most purposes, WTLS is a perfectly adequate security solution, just as TLS is on the Internet. However, there is a situation with regards to WAP that does not occur with non-WAP connections, and this situation arises because of the WAP gateway. WAP requires WML and WMLScript to be interpreted into a binary form that is suitable for transmission over bandwidth challenged networks to resource challenged devices, and the WAP gateway is responsible for performing this translation. This has two very important implications:

❑ The WTLS secure session is between the phone and the WAP gateway, not the vendor's server. This means that the data is only encrypted between the phone and the gateway, at which point it is decrypted by the gateway before being re-encrypted and sent on to the vendor's server over a TLS connection.

❑ The WAP gateway gets to see all of the data in cleartext. The gateway may well not be owned by whoever owns the server, so a third party potentially gets access to all of the data transmitted over what is supposed to be a secure connection.

In the fixed-wire world, your secure session is typically with the vendor's web server, presuming that you have a direct connection to the Internet with nothing interfering along the way. If you are accessing the Internet from a corporate network, then it is entirely possible that you are going through a proxy server to access the Internet. If this is the case, then the level of security depends on which proxy server the company is running and how it has been configured. Many ISPs also provide caching services, some of which are proxy servers at the ISP's site that you may choose to make use of to surf the Web by setting your web browser to use them, others of which are transparent proxies that your HTTP requests will be passed through without you knowing about it. This may seem analogous to the situation in which the WAP gateway interposes itself between the device and the server, but there is a fundamental difference in that the proxy server should – and all of the big name proxy servers can – tunnel SSL/TLS sessions. The proxy server acts as little more than a router, simply passing the packets on. It does not attempt to decrypt any of the data and therefore does not get to see the data.

In a similar vein, you could argue that the web server gets to see all the data because the secure session is with the web server rather than the back-end application behind it, but for most organizations with significant security requirements this is not an issue because they own their own web server as well as the network that it is on and which connects it to the back-end application. This means that they control who gets to find out where the web server is, who sees it, who has administrative privileges on it, when it is taken down for maintenance, and all of the other things that contribute to the security of the web server and the network.

But just how much of a risk is it to have the network operator host the gateway? The honest answer is that the risk is minimal, but there is still a risk. The reputable gateway vendors and network operators put a lot of effort into securing their WAP gateways. Clearly, it would be disastrous for their business to implicated in any sort of security mishap, so they ensure that unencrypted data is never written to disk, that the decryption and re-encryption takes place **in memory**, as quickly as possible, and that all memory used in the process is overwritten before being released in order to make sure that the data is as secure as possible.

All of this is very reassuring and probably meets most people's requirements. However, the skeptics among us will probably still not be convinced. We should take into account the fact that, despite the best efforts of some of the largest software vendors in the world, and some of the best programming brains in the world, security exposures are coming to light all the time in all sorts of products. Some would argue that sooner or later there will be security exposures associated with WAP gateways at network operators sites, either as a result of a weakness in the software, an error in configuration or management, or as a result of deliberate or accidental actions on the part of an employee.

The obvious solution to these security concerns is for organizations that have strenuous security requirements to run their own gateway, and this is entirely possible. There are several gateway products that are available from reputable vendors, such as Nokia, that you could host at your own site, and some web and application server vendors have also built WAP gateway capability into their products, for example BEA's WebLogic. There are some issues to think about, however, if you decide that you need to host your own WAP gateway. Depending on what your security requirements are and how you want to configure your environment, the bottom line is that if you are hosting your own gateway, you could end up becoming your own ISP. If the applications that you want mobile access to are sensitive enough that you do not want them to be accessed via the Internet, you will need to set up banks of modems and RAS servers to enable dial-up access to your network. You will need to support your users in connecting to your WAP gateway and the services behind it, and, unless you intend to allow your users to surf the Web via your network and configure an Internet gateway on your network, then users will not have access to other WAP services on the Internet. An example of what this may look like is shown below:

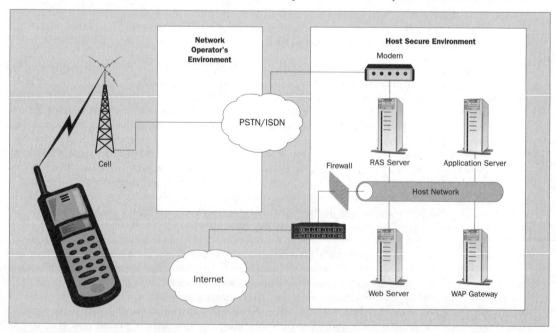

Depending on the services that you are trying to provide, these issues may not be a problem. Many of my clients do not have a problem accommodating these requirements because they already have large and complex computing environments with dial-up support, and they expressly do not want their WAP applications to be available over the Internet, or to have people accessing the Internet from their network. They are, however, large investment banks and fund managers with very stringent security requirements, and sufficient funds to allow them to build this kind of infrastructure. If you are a small dot-com start up then this solution is probably not for you.

There is another configuration that still allows you to host your own WAP gateway, but without all of the onerous costs associated with being your own ISP. Depending on your security requirements this kind of configuration may or may not be secure enough for you, largely because it means that your WAP gateway is accessible over the Internet, and therefore more vulnerable to attack than a gateway that is not. Some of the boundaries of responsibility between yourself and the ISP when users experience problems accessing the system may also not be as clear as in the previous model, but this model does have the advantage of being far more feasible for most organizations that want to provide public access to their services, but still want to own the gateway. In this model, the user would dial into an ISP, as they would for fixed wire access to the Internet, thereby using the ISP's RAS servers, and then access the WAP gateway over the Internet as they would any web server. This is still a secure model, because WTLS is used effectively as a tunneling protocol to tunnel between the phone and the WAP gateway. This scenario is illustrated in the diagram below:

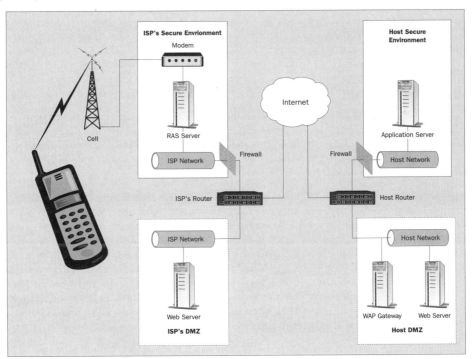

Although the WAP gateway and the web server are shown as being on the same network segment in this diagram, this does not need to be the case. In the same way that the WAP gateway and the web server are on different networks when the gateway is hosted by the network operator, the web server can be on a different network segment, or even on a different network accessed via the Internet. Because TLS is used to secure the connection between the gateway and the web server, it is as secure as any other connection between a client and server over the Internet.

It is interesting to note that some of the retail financial institutions have opted to make their services available to consumers through network operators gateways, obviously because of the need to provide easy, widespread access to their mobile banking services. It is, of course, up to consumers to decide whether they feel comfortable with the idea of putting financial transactions against their accounts through these services while there is a break in the security chain. This issue will also impact on people's willingness to use credit cards over mobile connections.

Considering the requirement for translation of WML and WMLScript into a binary form, it seems likely that an end-to-end solution will only become available when there is support at the application level for the use of certificates and data encryption. The crypto library in the WAP 1.2 specification, which is the current version as of time of writing, contains only one function, which allows a signature to be generated for a string of text, but the specification does indicate that further cryptographic functionality is a possibility in a future version of the specification. When devices start including support for **WIM** (the **WAP Identity Module**), then it will become possible to store the key used to generate the signature on a smart card. The WAP Forum are aware of the issues around end-to-end security and are working on a solution, but there is no standard solution available at the time of writing, so you will need to design your applications to work with what is available today.

TLS and WTLS

The predecessor to TLS is SSL, which is the de facto standard for most security on the Internet. SSL was created by engineers at Netscape back in 1993, with the intention of providing a mechanism for implementing security that would not require changes to existing applications and protocols. The fact that it is the most popular form of Internet security is testament to how effective their solution is. Today SSL has become an Internet standard and is under the control of the Internet Engineering Task Force (IETF). It has been renamed TLS, and the WAP Forum have based their security implementation on it.

TLS, although it sits at the transport layer, is in fact an additional layer that is interposed between the application layer and the 'real' transport layer specifically for the purpose of implementing security. WTLS also sits above the transport layer, but above it are the WTP and WSP transaction and session layers, which are not present in the Internet model. This arrangement allows them to be independent of the services that are requested by the application.

A significant difference between TLS and WTLS lies in the fact that TLS requires a reliable transport layer, in particular TCP, in order to operate. TLS, therefore cannot operate over UDP. The WAP protocol stack does not provide a reliable transport layer, and actually mandates UDP as its preferred transport layer protocol over packet based networks. It builds reliability in at higher levels of the protocol stack, through WTP and WSP. This is probably the biggest motivation for the design of yet another protocol: WTLS can operate over WDP and UDP. The WTLS frame defines a sequence number field, which is not found in TLS. This sequence number field is part of what enables WTLS to work over unreliable transports. WTLS also does not support the fragmentation and reassembly of data across multiple frames – it presumes that its underlying transport will handle that. TLS will fragment packets received from the upper layer protocols.

Both TLS and WTLS differentiate between a session and a connection. Connections are regarded as more transient than sessions and come and go. In the case of the wireless world, the lifetime of your connection could depend on the quality of the coverage wherever you are at the time, whether the train you are traveling on is about to vanish into a tunnel, and even on the weather. Sessions are more persistent than connections and may exist across multiple connections and are identified by a session ID. The security parameters associated with the session are used to secure the connection. What this means in effect, is that if a connection gets disrupted, the session can still exist and can be resumed at a later point in time.

Sessions can be resumed, which means that a session that is being established can use the same set of security parameters as another session. That session could be from the connection that is currently active, another currently active connection, or a connection that was active in the past. Resuming sessions allows for an optimized handshake in which not all of the message exchanges have to take place. It can also be used to open a number of simultaneous connections that share a common set of security parameters. It is up to the server to determine whether it is happy to permit the session to be resumed or not.

The WTLS specification allows for authentication of both clients and servers, either through the use of certificates or anonymously, that is with the client or server providing their public key in the session set up messages. To ease implementation, however, three classes of WTLS implementation are specified, which define minimum levels of functionality by marking features as mandatory, optional or excluded. Class 1 only requires support for public key exchange, encryption and MACs, with client and server certificates and shared secret handshake being optional. (A shared secret handshake is one in which both the client and the server already know the secret and it is therefore never exchanged between them.) Compression algorithms and the smart card interface are excluded from Class 1 implementations. Class 1 implementations may still choose to support both client and server authentication through certificates, but it is not required. For Class 2 implementations, support for server certificates is mandatory, and for Class 3 implementations, support for both client and server certificates is mandatory. Support for compression and smart card interface is optional in both Class 2 and 3.

The client begins the process of setting up a secure session by sending a message to the server to request negotiation of secure session settings. It is always up to the client to begin the negotiation process. There is a message that the server can send to the client to request it to begin session negotiation, but it is up to the client whether it wants to do so or not. At any time during the session, the client can also send this message to request renegotiation of the settings. Renegotiating settings helps to limit the amount of data exposed if security has been compromised through eavesdropping, by forcing a new secret key to be generated. When the client requests negotiation of a secure session, it provides a list of the security services that it can support. The client also specifies how often the security parameters have to be refreshed in terms of numbers of messages. In the extreme case the client can request that parameters must be refreshed with every message.

If the public key exchange mechanism that was agreed is not an anonymous, then the server must send the client a certificate to identify itself. The certificate sent must obviously match the key exchange algorithm agreed on. The message actually includes a certificate chain from the server's own certificate to the CA. The senders certificate must come first in the list, and each following certificate must certify the one preceding it. The root CA's certificate may be omitted from the list, on the basis that it is reasonable to assume that the root CA's certificate is freely available, and is probably already in the possession of the client. If it isn't then the client can easily get hold of it.

If the key exchange is not anonymous, then the server can also request a certificate from the client. If the client does not have a certificate, it can send a message that contains no certificates. It is up to the server to decide whether it wants to proceed without a valid certificate from the client. By sending this message, the client proves that it has the private key associated with the public key contained in the certificate that it sent to the server. The client sends this message, containing a hash of all of the previously exchanged handshake messages between the client and server, and it signed using its private key. This allows the server to perform a similar computation on its side and check the message digest that it receives as part of the signature against the one that it generates. If they match, the server knows that the client is genuine. If they don't match then something has gone wrong.

The certificates for TLS are expected to be X.509 certificates, but WTLS defines a new type of certificate specifically for use on mobile devices. While it is possible for WTLS to use X.509 certificates, most mobile devices are unlikely to support them because of their relatively large size. WTLS certificates are optimized to suit the limited storage capacity of many mobile devices. A comparison of the format of the WTLS certificate and the X.509 certificate is presented in the table below:

X.509	WTLS
Version	Version
Serial number	
Algorithm identifier	Signature algorithm
Name of issuer	Name of issuer
Period of validity	Period of validity
Name of certificate owner (subject)	Subject
Subject's public key	Subject's public key
Issuer ID	
Subject ID	
Issuer's signature	Issuer's signature

Both TLS and WTLS can fulfill the two roles that we have come across in our discussions: the roles of client and of server. In the role of client, TLS/WTLS initiates communication with the server on the remote host and proposes the security options to be used. In the role of server, it will examine the options proposed and select the options that will actually be used to secure the communications. In its simplest form any protocol, including TLS and WTLS, consists of a set of messages that are exchanged between the two hosts playing the client and server roles, and a set of rules about when these messages can and cannot be sent

Future of Wireless Security

It is always dangerous to predict what is going to be available in the future – no more so than where technology is concerned – but there are a few things the WAP Forum is currently working on that it seems likely will happen over the next couple of years. Until the specifications are ratified and published, it is not very useful to speculate too much as to how things are going to be implemented, and after the publication of the specification it will take some time for new facilities to filter through and become available in both the handsets and the gateway's. It is not really an option to develop applications today that are dependent on technology that is not going to be available for some time.

WAP 1.2

The most recent release of the WAP specification as of the time of writing is version 1.2. Although the 1.2 specification was ratified some time ago, most of the handsets and gateways are still at version 1.1. However, everything that has been said about security in this chapter applies equally in versions 1.1 and 1.2. It is unlikely there will be significant changes to WTLS itself in the near future, largely because it is based on TLS, which is already a mature protocol. This is actually good news for us as WAP developers, because it means we are working with a technology that is tried and tested. That doesn't mean that there will not be any developments in the future, but WTLS is a stable basis on which WAP security will continue to be built for the foreseeable future.

One thing that is likely to change in the future is that devices and software will implement support for Class 2 and 3 WTLS, with server and client certificate based authentication respectively. Timescales for this depend on the vendors. Another feature of WAP 1.2 that is not widely supported at the moment is the WIM, which we'll look at in the next section.

WIM

The WIM specification is new in WAP 1.2. The purpose behind WIM is to allow security functionality to be offloaded from the handset to a tamper-resistant device. What this means in reality is a smart card, or even the SIM. A smart card has its own processor, so it is feasible to have encryption and decryption algorithms and hash functions implemented on the chip in the card. This has several advantages over a software implementation in the phone, one of which is definitely performance, because the chip can be designed specifically for cryptographic functions. The smart card can also store data. What you are most likely to find stored on the card is private keys and shared secrets for use in long-lived sessions. Deriving keys from shared secrets is fairly intensive processing, so being able to have these long lived sessions that can be suspended and resumed is important from a performance perspective, but this also implies the need to store the shared secrets and keys derived from them for long periods. Storing this in a smart card means that they don't live in the phone, so if you lose your phone whoever finds it cannot simply reuse your existing sessions, and if your battery runs down you don't loose the secret key and have to regenerate it.

The specification for the WIM does not include any API and is not accessible directly from WML or WMLScript at this point in time, although this may change in the future. The specification defines the behavior of the card and the low-level interfaces to it, and is there primarily so that those vendors that provide implementations of WTLS on mobile devices can interoperate with any compliant WIM. This means that the availability of this functionality is clearly dependent on the device vendors.

The ability to separate private keys and other sensitive security information from the device could also be part of a solution to the problems raised earlier with regard to validating the person as opposed to the device, as long as the user has the discipline to keep the smart card separate from the device other than when it is actually needed. There is also the concern of loosing the smart card instead of the device, but if the phone numbers are stored in the SIM, for example, the private keys in the smart card, and the user has to enter their PIN on accessing the secure site, then we have achieved a scenario that is probably even *more* secure than anything that the fixed wire world can offer at this point in time.

Security products

Until there is an end-to-end security standard from the WAP Forum WTLS is what we have to work with. There are a number of products on the market that implement WTLS, and we'll cover a few of them here.

> *The inclusion in this section of any particular vendor is for information only and in no way implies any endorsement of their products, or any statement about the robustness of the product or its suitability for your environment.*

Before selecting a security product, you will need to conduct a proper evaluation of the available products and make a selection that is appropriate for your environment. You should also remember that WTLS has to be implemented both on the mobile device and on the gateway, and your ability to influence and control each of these will vary. As long as both of the implementations conform to the WAP standards there should not be any problems with interoperation between different vendor's products.

Different devices may present different opportunities to change the software that implements the security environment. With a device like a mobile phone you are likely to be limited (at least at this point in time) in that you may not be able to change much about the operational environment, for example the microbrowser, so you get whatever the vendor decides to implement. If your mobile device is at the higher end, in terms of capability, for example a Palm or an EPOC device, you are likely to have more options. You can realistically expect most of the devices available at the time of writing to implement a Class 1 WTLS environment, but the specific capabilities as regards to the optional parts of the Class 1 specification will vary from device to device. Keep a look out for devices in the future that implement higher levels of WTLS conformance, or which implement smartcard based security.

The other half of the WTLS implementation will be in the WAP gateway. If you use a network operator's gateway then the network operator will be responsible for implementing WTLS in their environment. This relieves you of the effort and risks associated with implementing a secure environment, but it also leaves you powerless to select products that meet your own requirements.

If you intend to run your own gateway then you will be responsible for obtaining the necessary security products, designing a security strategy, and making sure that they are properly implemented. Depending on which gateway you purchase you may be able to buy a security add-on, as is the case with the Nokia gateway, for example. But there are also a number of established security product vendors who provide wireless security solutions. Some of these vendors aim their products at network operators or at large content providers, so these products are unlikely to fit within your budget constraints if you are a small business. An example of a vendor who fits within this category is Across Wireless (http://www.acrosswireless.com). Other organizations have toolkits that are aimed at vendors building secure WAP gateways. Vendors who fit into this category include Certicom (http://www.certicom.com), Entrust (http://www.entrust.com), Baltimore (http://www.baltimore.com) and RSA (http://www.rsa.com).

The kind of vendor whose products you would be more likely to look at would be vendors of WAP gateways that have a WTLS implementation, and there are several of those. Some that are worth being aware of include:

- ❏ BEA: BEA are the world's leading provider of object transaction monitors and application servers. They have worked with Nokia to integrate a WAP gateway into their WebLogic application server. A WTLS implementation is available. WebLogic is developed in Java and therefore runs on all Java capable platforms, and supports servlets and EJB. There is an evaluation download available at http://www.beasys.com.

- ❏ Ericsson: A name that many people associate with mobile phones, but not a big player in the software world. See http://www.ericsson.se/ for more information.

- ❏ Jataayu: Jataayu offer both a carrier grade and an enterprise version of their WAP gateway. Both products includes a WTLS implementation and run on Windows 9x/NT, Linux or Solaris. They also have an embeddable client and a PC based client, as well as a personal WAP gateway. More information is available from http://www.vsellinindia.com/jataayu or http://www.integramicro.com.

- ❏ Nokia: Another name strongly associated with WAP and mobile telecommunications, although possibly not with software in most people's minds. Nokia have a WAP gateway available for evaluation download and there is a WTLS option that can be purchased. The download is available at http://www.forum.nokia.com. It is developed in Java and supports Java servlets.

❑ Silicon Automation Systems: SAS have both a WAP client and a WAP gateway. As at the time of writing the client is text only, but has a full WTLS 1.1 implementation. The WAP gateway is also new, with full support for WAP 1.1 compatibility and a WAP 1.2 version due shortly. The product gateway includes a WTLS implementation, and runs on Windows NT and a variety of Linux/Unix platforms.

❑ Infinite Technologies: Provide the WAPLite WAP gateway, available with a WTLS implementation built using Baltimore Technologies toolkit. You can download an evaluation copy at http://www.waplite.com.

Bear in mind that the majority of these products are fairly new, so not all the features that you would want are necessarily present at this point in time.

Baltimore Technology

Baltimore have a broad range of products, from corporate solutions through to development kits and security hardware. In the realm of wireless security they provide the Telepathy suite of products. Foremost among their wireless security products is the Telepathy WAP security Gateway. This is a WTLS gateway that is interposed between the mobile device and the WAP gateway and provides security though a WTLS implementation. The idea behind this configuration is to enable users to add security to an existing configuration that does not include a WTLS implementation, without the need to replace the entire WAP gateway. For this configuration to work, you need to be hosting your own WAP gateway, because the WTLS gateway communicates with the WAP gateway using unsecured UDP over IP.

In addition to their WTLS gateway offering, Baltimore can provide a complete enterprise infrastructure for securing wireless applications, as well and the entire computing environment. This product set includes the Telepathy WAP Certificate Authority that can be used to produce WTLS certificates and the Telepathy PKI registration and validation system for managing and validating certificates. Baltimore are also a root Certification Authority and can provide your organization with certification services.

The Telepathy WTLS gateway is built using the Telepathy WAP security Toolkit, as are several other vendor's security offerings. The toolkit includes C libraries on Windows 32, Solaris 2.5+, HP-UX 10.2+ and Linux platforms, which allows developers to create secure encrypted sessions between networked applications. The toolkit includes an implementation of WTLS 1.1that you can build into your applications, and a high level API to hide a number of encryption and signature algorithms including RSA, DH, RC5, DES, 3DES, IDEA, SHA-1 and MD-5.

Keyon WTLS Gateway

Keyon are another WTLS gateway vendor. Keyon are based in Switzerland and, like Baltimore, have chosen to develop a WTLS gateway that is independent of the WAP gateway. The purpose is to provide a WTLS implementation that can be interposed between the mobile device and any WAP 1.1 gateway that does not have a native WTLS implementation. The WTLS gateway handles all of the security functionality and communicates with the WAP gateway using UDP/IP. It therefore adds a level of indirection and proxies the mobile device. The product is implemented in Java and runs on any Java capable platform. It is also unusual in providing both a class 1and class 2 WTLS implementation. More information is available on http://www.keyon.ch.

F-Secure

One aspect of security that we have not discussed in this chapter is the issue of viruses and other malicious code. As of the time of writing, there are no reported incidents of viruses specifically associated with WAP. There has recently been the first recorded instance of a virus targeting GSM mobile phones, although this had nothing to do with WAP and did not infect the phones themselves – it was propagated by e-mail and used SMS to bombard mobile phone numbers taken from the e-mail client's address book with messages disparaging a telecommunications company. The virus was a nuisance rather than harmful, but it serves as a timely reminder of the possibilities for abuse that arise as a result of advances in communications technology.

Sooner rather than later, WAP will become a target for writers of malicious code, so it is worthwhile taking steps to secure your environment. This includes all of the normal precautions that you would take to secure any device on your network, although the WAP gateway is likely to be an exposed and targeted device, so special care and attention is probably advised. F-Secure Anti-Virus for WAP Gateways is a product that gives you a means of protecting your WAP-enabled clients. Running an anti-virus solution on many mobile devices is not feasible because of the limited processing capabilities of the devices, so most anti-virus products will be deployed in the WAP gateway. The F-Secure anti-virus product is integrated with HP OpenView for alert management, runs on Windows NT, and supports the Nokia WAP gateway.

Summary

Security is a key issue for almost every enterprise that is looking to implement a WAP solution. There is a lot of uncertainty in the market as to what exactly is available, and how secure the products really are. It is sometimes incorrectly observed that WAP 1.1 does not include security and that security will not be available until WAP 1.2, which is completely incorrect: security was included in WAP 1.1 and there are a number of secure solutions available today. This chapter should have cleared up some of the confusion and misinformation about WAP security.

The issue of the WAP gateway may be over-hyped for all but the most strenuous security requirements. However, that the issue exists is undeniable. If it is a problem for your specific application then there are ways of addressing the issue, depending on how much money you are able to spend and how important an issue it is for you. What is clear is that it is possible to achieve security that is just about comparable with anything available on the Internet, and in the near future it will be possible to achieve levels of security that exceed what is available on the Internet. Do realize, however, that anything that you choose to implement as part of securing your WAP applications is only part of the story: a proper, secure environment requires a full security policy carefully constructed and implemented in order to protect the entire network, environment and all of your clients.

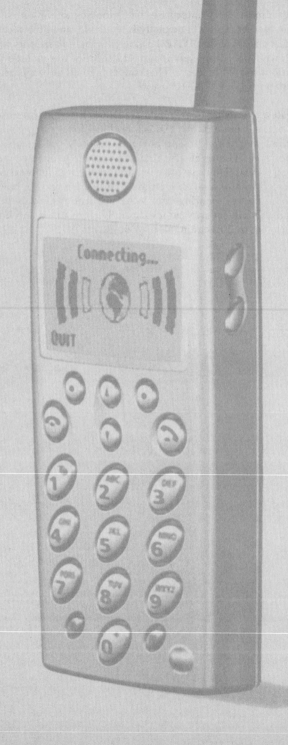

Part Five

Future WAP and Wireless Technologies

The final part of the book looks to the future and focuses on some technologies which are not so easy to implement right now, but which we'll be seeing a lot more of over the next couple of years. So, if you want to get an idea of what's ahead, then read on.

All the WAP examples that we have seen so far in this book require the end-user to make a request to the origin server. However, there are many circumstances where we might want to push information to a WAP device – for example, when a user wants to be notified about the arrival of an important e-mail, or when a goal in a soccer game is scored. Push technologies are part of the 1.2 WAP specifications, but there are no devices on the market right now that implement this (although there are some tools from Phone.com that do implement a notification mechanism). In Chapter 16, we'll examine the WAP Push Framework, and also look at a simple example that implements a type of push mechanism via SMS.

There are many scenarios where the ability to access telephone functionality from WML would be useful. For example, imagine searching for a restaurant and then simply clicking on a hyperlink in order to dial the number to book a table. Or maybe you want to give users the ability to add contact information from a WML card to the phone book on their own mobile. WTA (Wireless Telephony Applications) is part of the WAP 1.1 specifications, and designed to provide functionality just like this. Like Push, however, it is not yet implemented in any of the first generation of WAP-enabled phones. Chapter 17 will introduce WTA, examine the architecture, and also some of the security and privacy implications of such a technology. It also covers WTAI (Wireless Telephony Application Interfaces), which is the set of functions that allows the programmer to implement WTA.

Next, in Chapter 18, we'll finally move away from WAP, and look at a related technology instead: VoiceXML. Mobile phones have limited data input capabilities, and whatever advances in technology occur, this is unlikely to change. The advantage of a mobile phone is just that – it's mobile. No one wants to lug a full 'qwerty' keyboard around with them. With parallel developments in voice recognition and voice synthesis, we are almost at the point where we can implement a genuinely useful voice interface for users to interact with computer applications. Voice is the natural interface for use with a phone. VoiceXML is an XML-based markup language that provides us with a simple way to define human-computer voice interactions.

Finally, in Chapter 19, we'll take a whistle-stop tour of some of the wireless technologies further away on the horizon, examine how these may affect the long-term viability of WAP, and see what the future may hold for a wireless world.

16

Push Technologies

In the preceding chapters, we have discussed various aspects of WAP that enable content to be delivered to a wireless device, but **only** when the user of such a device requests or "pulls" the content from the network. In other words, the content is constantly present in the network, but the user only gets to view it if they voluntarily requests it, at least for the first time in a content pull session. (Once some content is executing in the device, it is possible for script content to be programmed to involuntarily make requests for more content.)

However, when we look at real-life applications, we realize that there is a lot of information that is useful to a user, but which a user does not see because they do not know when it is available or when there is a change in the status of the information. Ideally, information should be "**pushed**" to the user, either at predefined intervals or when certain events occur that would then make the information useful to the user. Some examples of possible push situations are the arrival of new e-mails and stock market information when certain stock price thresholds have been crossed.

This brings us to the subject of push technologies, which define a complete framework for delivering content to a user in an asynchronous manner, without the user being required to request the information. The push architecture is defined for the first time in the WAP 1.2 specifications.

In this chapter, we will explore push technologies in detail. The initial part of the chapter is an introductory discussion on mechanisms similar to push that have been available for the Internet for sometime now (although most of these models are really "**smart-pull**", because the client is the one that either makes and keeps a constant connection with the server or polls the server frequently to receive new information). We then move on to a discussion of why we need such a model for the wireless world. We will look at the push framework, including all the components and protocols that are used. Finally, we look at a sample application which implements push services.

In outline, this chapter will involve looking at:

❑   Internet-based push models, the problems associated with them, and the rationale behind WAP push

❑   The WAP push framework, including the Push Access Protocol (PAP) and Push Over-the-Air (OTA) protocol.

❑   Practical problems that could occur when using push technologies

❑   A case study, where we look at a sample push application using SMS

Internet Push Model

Push models are already defined for the Internet/intranet, albeit using proprietary technologies from various companies such as Microsoft, Netscape, Marimba, and PointCast among others. Even though these technologies make you believe that content is being pushed to you, the truth is, under the hood these are just smart clients that actually make connections to servers to receive frequently changing information. However, push technologies haven't really taken off like the more traditional web pull model has, and so we have been seeing some of the companies closing shop. Some of the reasons behind this could be:

❑   Lack of standardization. Because no standard protocol has been defined for the exchange of push information between push servers and applications receiving such content, it is impossible for clients or servers of different vendors to talk to one another. Providers of push content can never depend on software from one vendor because they are unsure whether it would ever reach a large user base. Similarly, users did not want to use 3 or 4 different push clients to receive content from different providers, and at the same time wouldn't have liked to be stuck with a particular content provider, just because they were using a client from one particular vendor. Standardization is what makes competition thrive and make technologies succeed in the marketplace. This fact is very evident from the runaway success of GSM mobile phone systems all across the world, when there were other systems that were slightly better in terms of efficient use of radio spectrum.

❑   Widespread use of other simpler mechanisms, like e-mail (especially HTML e-mail), to deliver content and notifications to a user on the Internet. You can't push information to a user unless that user is actually using their PC/Workstation, and if the person is in front of it, you might as well push information using standard e-mail. Since they already monitor their inboxes regularly, it doesn't make sense to try to grab their attention using some other mechanism.

❑   Initial push implementations were bandwidth hogs, which scared service providers and corporate users alike into blocking such services. This was because implementations were not sophisticated or efficient, so that a lot more data was being received than needed.

Rationale of a WAP Push Model

Unlike the Internet, the push model for WAP has been well defined in the WAP 1.2 specifications. This should make implementations of push standardized and independent of vendor. Besides, WAP content is targeted towards personal devices that users usually have with them, unlike the Internet, where the users can be away from their computers for substantial periods. Therefore, it makes a lot more sense to have a standardized push model in WAP; it is more likely to succeed than its counterpart on the Internet. In addition, the rivalry between mechanisms like e-mail and push is also not there. In fact, the WAP push model assumes e-mails would be notified using push, so that the user can then make a decision on whether to download it.

As a matter of fact, push services already exist in mobile phone networks, using the well-known Short Message Service (SMS) and the Cell-Broadcast mechanism in GSM networks. Many people already use SMS regularly, for information on key news items, scores from a sports game, or notification that a new message has arrived in their voice mailbox. There is, however, a very important element missing in all these services; the service is not interactive.

Currently if you receive notification that you have a voicemail, you still need to dial the number that gives you access to your voicemail separately. No interactive mechanisms exist that offer you a menu of choices to act upon your voicemail in an interactive manner as soon as the notification has arrived.

Consider another example, where you have registered with your online investment broker to provide you with short messages as soon as a certain stock price crosses a threshold (defined by you). On receiving the information, if you choose to buy or sell the particular stock, you will need to separately communicate with your broker to place the order, as would be the case in SMS. On the other hand, if this whole transaction was defined using WAP push technologies, the notification message could be combined with a menu option to follow a link to a site where you can buy or sell stock.

It is therefore important to make a distinction between the following:

- ❑ SMS and Cell-Broadcast services that have already been widely deployed to push pager-like text messages to users.

- ❑ WAP-based push services that use SMS or Cell-Broadcast as the bearer to transmit packets over the wireless network. In this case, SMS or Cell-Broadcast can become a viable WAP bearer that would not only use existing network infrastructure but also provide the required interactive behavior that characterizes WAP based push.

Push services in wireless networks offer a definite advantage over its Internet counterpart – that is, the ability to produce location-based push content. Because we can discover the users location, it opens up an opportunity to provide local content and information. For example, tourist or hotel information specific to a particular geographical area can be pushed to wireless device users in that area. This is clearly impossible in Internet-based push.

The Push Framework

Within the push framework, the protocols used by the origin server that initiates the push content are separated from the protocols used in the WAP domain. This is achieved by placing an intermediary, known as the **Push Proxy Gateway** (**PPG**), between the push origin server, known as the **Push Initiator** (**PI**), and the **WAP client** on the wireless device. Note that it is possible to draw similarities between the WAP pull model that we have seen in the previous chapters and the push framework. The most obvious similarity is that both models use an intermediary, and mostly for similar reasons.

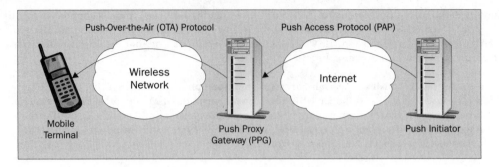

The above framework seems like the most logical one. The **Push Access Protocol (PAP)** is designed to work on top of one of the application level protocols, like HTTP or SMTP on the Internet. In other words, PAP is **tunneled** over a commonly available application layer protocol on the Internet. In this chapter, we will assume that a HTTP POST mechanism is used for tunneling PAP messages. However, this doesn't mean that a PPG implementer cannot devise a way to use SMTP. The specifications only suggest some mechanisms for the tunneling, and an implementer could always use a different mechanism and still be standards compliant

Push Over-the-Air (OTA) protocol, on the other hand, is used on top of the WSP layer of the WAP stack of protocols.

The Push Proxy Gateway (PPG) has to implement the entire WAP protocol stack in addition to the above two push specific protocols, PAP and push OTA. It therefore makes sense to have push functionality as a component or add-on for a WAP Gateway.

Many of the protocols, as well as some of the content, in the push framework are applications of XML. For example, PAP is an XML language. It is therefore reasonably easy for PPG and PI implementers to implement most of their functionality, because XML parser libraries are widely and freely available.

We will examine the protocols used in some detail shortly, but first we take a look at the addresses used to target mobile devices.

Client Addressing

The Push Initiator (PI) needs to know the address of the client device so that the information can be sent to the correct Push Proxy Gateway (PPG), which can then route the push information to the right client. The PI identifies clients using a textual address that can be transformed by the PPG into an address that is valid in the type of wireless network that it is using to deliver the push content.

Two forms of addressing are possible:

❑ User-defined identifiers

❑ Device addresses

We first describe each of these before going on to show how they are used within the generic client address format.

User-Defined Identifiers

User-defined identifiers have no meaning in the wireless network, but the PPG has a mapping from these identifiers into meaningful device addresses. Such identifiers can be useful in a variety of ways:

❑ By not disclosing a bearer-level address, the privacy of a user is ensured. If a user, who had initially subscribed to receive some push content, later requests the PPG administration to remove any further push services, it would be impossible for any PI to then push unsolicited content to that user. Refer to the section *Problems in Push Technologies* in this chapter for more information on privacy issues.

❑ A single user-defined identifier could be aliased to multiple bearer-level device addresses and can therefore serve as a multicast address from a PI's perspective. For example, this concept could be used to construct the equivalent of e-mail mailing lists. Here's a sample user-defined address: `nasdaq-news@ppg.carrier.com`. The PPG may have a mechanism through which users can subscribe to this service. The PI in this case would probably be a content provider who keeps track of NASDAQ and has a tie-up with PPG to simply send a single push message at regular intervals or when there is news to be reported. It would then be the responsibility of the PPG to distribute the message over-the-air to all subscribed users. The PI would not have to send scores of push messages to get the same information across to a bunch of users. The advantages of this mechanism should be obvious.

For example, an e-mail address provided by the service provider/network operator who also has a PPG in their network, can serve as a user-defined identifier. The identifier could actually be any arbitrary text as long as the PPG is aware of the mapping.

Device Addresses

Device addresses are values that have meaning in a wireless network (the network uses them to identify and route voice/data to the device) and they can be used to uniquely identify every device in the wireless network. The most common types of device addresses are:

❑ **IPv4 addresses**: This is the common 32 bit Internet address, normally expressed as a dotted quad of the form *aaa.bbb.ccc.ddd*.

❑ **MSISDN addresses**: This is the "Mobile Station International Subscriber Directory Number" or, in other words, a normal mobile phone number of the form +91-98450-00007, which contains the mobile country code, the mobile network code, and the subscriber number in the network. The format for this address can have minor variations depending on whether the network is of type GSM, CDMA, IS-136, AMPS, PDC, PHS, IDEN or any of the other bearer network types defined in the WDP 1.2 specifications.

❑ **IPv6 addresses**: This evolving addressing format of IP would address the shortage of IPv4 addresses that we are currently facing. IPv6 addresses are 128 bits in length and the addressing space is so large that even at double the current population of the earth, each individual can still have the square of a thousand trillion addresses reserved for themselves. Despite all the interoperability problems with IPv4 that are there, if IPv6 addresses are used sometime in the near future, WAP is ready for them.

Client Address Format

The generic client address format is expressed in Augmented Backus Naur Form (ABNF) notation in the specifications.

ABNF notation is normally used for expressing programming language grammar, to give a precise and concise definition of the syntax.

Refer to the "WAP PPG Service" specification available at `http://www.wapforum.org/` for more details. We will present it here in a somewhat simplified form.

The generic format is as follows:

```
WAPPUSH=<client_user_or_device_address>/TYPE=<address_type>@<ppg_specifier>
```

`<address_type>` should be `USER` for a user-defined identifier, `IPv4` or `IPv6` for the respective device addresses, or `PLMN` for addresses that are phone numbers. (PLMN stands for Public Land Mobile Network.) The `<ppg_specifier>` should be the domain name specifier, with format `ppg.carrier.com`, which identifies the host where the PPG is located.

Here are a few examples of different kinds of addresses. This is taken directly from the "WAP PPG Service" specification.

Addresses using user-defined identifiers, a comma at the beginning of the line indicates that line is a comment:

```
WAPPUSH=john.doe%40wapforum.org/TYPE=USER@ppg.carrier.com
; user-defined identifier for john.doe@wapforum.org
wappush=47397547589/type=user@carrier.com
; user-defined identifier for 47397547589
WAPPUSH=47397547589/TYPE=USER@carrier.com
; equivalent to previous one
WAPPUSH=+155519990730/TYPE=USER@ppg.carrier.com
; user-defined identifier that looks like a phone number, but isn't
```

Addresses using device addresses:

```
WAPPUSH=+155519990730/TYPE=PLMN@ppg.carrier.com
; device address for a phone number of some wireless network
WAPPUSH=FEDC:BA98:7654:3210:FEDC:BA98:7654:3210/TYPE=IPv6@carrier.com
; device address for an IP v6 address
WAPPUSH=195.153.199.30/TYPE=IPv4@ppg.carrier.com
; device address for an IP v4 address
```

The Push Proxy Gateway (PPG)

A PPG is comparable in certain functionalities to a WAP gateway. It forms the point of access to the wireless world for Push Initiators (PIs) on the Internet to push content towards mobile devices. Some of the functionalities of a PPG are:

❑ Push submission processing, including:

    ❑ Access control: Push Initiator (PI) identification and authentication

    ❑ Parsing the XML based PAP control information and detecting errors in **PAP Document Type Definition (DTD)** conformance and well-formedness

- ❑ WAP client address resolution and transformation

- ❑ Content binary encoding and/or compilation if required and if feasible.

- ❑ Over-the-Air protocol implementation for delivery of messages to the client

- ❑ Selection of the bearer to deliver the push content

Bearers Suited for WAP Push Services

Bearers that are well suited for WAP pull services are not necessarily ideal to push content to mobile devices. Among the bearers used for all kinds of WAP service, we can classify them into three classes of bearers:

- ❑ Mobile Circuit Switched Data (CSD) on all kinds of mobile phone networks.

- ❑ Short Message Service (SMS) available on GSM, CDMA, North American IS-136, Japanese PDC etc. The underlying technology and protocols are completely different from each other in these networks but most of them define a mechanism for sending and receiving short text messages.

- ❑ Packet based mobile/wireless networks like AMPS-CDPD, IS-136 packet data or GPRS. Not all of these are very common currently. (Live GPRS networks will be commercially available during the second half of 2000.)

The CSD class of bearers is quite unsuited for push services. Although mobile users might be willing to use CSD to connect to a WAP site to access information (this is the most common mechanism for accessing WAP content at the time of writing), PPG providers would be quite unwilling to bear the airtime costs to push content over expensive CSD services.

Despite having huge round-trip delays, SMS is suited to push content that is small (like notifications of events). Once a user is notified this way, they can perform further actions by visiting a relevant WAP site using the pull model.

The ideal bearer for both pull and push services is, of course, a packet-based wireless network. Such networks make efficient use of Over-the-Air resources, so that the cost of the service is reduced and, in the future, operators could even afford to make services that do not require large bandwidths free. Users and content providers of WAP services need to wait until such networks and devices are commercially available in large volumes to benefit from them. As application designers, we should start designing content and applications for new technology and deploy them with a combination of SMS and CSD, so that as soon as new network technology is in place, they are ready to offer content right away.

The Push Access Protocol (PAP)

PAP is a protocol that is used for delivering content from the Push Initiator (PI) to the Push Proxy Gateway (PPG), which in turn delivers it to the wireless device(s). The syntax and semantics of the protocol are easy to understand and implement. This is because PAP is an XML application and, like all XML applications, a concise Document Type Definition (DTD) is sufficient to define the syntax and semantics precisely. (Refer to Chapter 9 for a brief introduction to XML.)

PAP defines the following operations as part of the protocol:

Operation	Message	Direction	Implementation status as required by the specifications
Push Submission	Push Message	PI ⇨ PPG	Mandatory
	Push Response	PI ⇦ PPG	Mandatory
Result Notification	Result Notification Message	PI ⇦ PPG	Mandatory
	Result Notification Response	PI ⇨ PPG	Mandatory
Push Cancellation	Cancel Message	PI ⇨ PPG	Optional
	Cancel Response	PI ⇦ PPG	Optional
Status Query	Status Query Message	PI ⇨ PPG	Optional
	Status Query Response	PI ⇦ PPG	Optional
Client Capabilities Query (CCQ)	CCQ Message	PI ⇨ PPG	Optional
	CCQ Response	PI ⇦ PPG	Optional
Bad Message Response	Bad Message Response	PI ⇦ PPG	Mandatory

Below, we will explain each of these operations in detail, together with some examples. But first note that a PAP message can consist of the following entities:

❏ **Control Entity**: This is a mandatory entity as defined by the PAP DTD (http://www.wapforum.org/DTD/pap_1.0.dtd). This entity contains all the control information required to deliver the content to the wireless device. For example, it contains the address(es) of the wireless device(s) where the content has to be delivered. Similarly, it also contains other metadata that would provide more information on the particular operation being carried out.

❏ **Content Entity**: This is an optional entity present only in the <push-message> element. The entity format depends entirely on the content-type of the content being pushed. This forms the actual content from the PI to be delivered to the wireless device. This is the reason why only one PAP message, <push-message> actually contains this entity. The format can be simple text, an XML entity or any another MIME type suited for delivery to a wireless device.

❏ **Capabilities Entity**: This provides the assumed or actual wireless device capability. In the case of <push-message>, it will be the assumed capabilities of the device by the PI. In the case of a "Client Capabilities Query (CCQ) Response Message", it is the actual capabilities of the device returned by the PPG to the PI.

If more than one of the above entities must be sent (depending on the type of message), they are sent as MIME multipart/related messages. For detailed information on MIME multipart/related message format, please refer to RFC2387 (http://www.ietf.org/rfc/rfc2387.txt). However, the examples that will be discussed below should make clear the basics of constructing a multipart/related message.

Push Submission

This operation, not only involves pushing the content from the PI to the PPG, but also giving the PPG enough information so that the message can be delivered Over-The-Air to the device(s).

Push Message

The push message is sent as a MIME multipart/related message that always contains a control entity in XML format and a content entity that could be of any format. An optional client capabilities entity could also be sent, indicating the capabilities of the client as assumed by the PI. This is in the Resource Description Framework (RDF) format as defined in the UAPROF specifications available at `http://www.wapforum.org/`. An example capabilities entity is given in the "CCQ Response" Message further down in the chapter.

A simple push message example is given below. Note, however, that each element has more attributes and sub-elements than we show here. A glance through the DTD would give you all the details you need:

```
Content-Type: multipart/related; boundary=my_first_multipart_message;
                    Type="application/xml"

--my_first_multipart_message
Content-Type: application/xml

<?xml version="1.0">
<!DOCTYPE pap PUBLIC "-//WAPFORUM//DTD PAP 1.0//EN"
http://www.wapforum.org/DTD/pap_1.0.dtd>

<pap>
   <push-message push-id="v04210109b50b0aebf02c@pi.wrox.com
    ppg-notify-requested-to="http://pi.wrox.com/cgi-bin/res-notify.cgi">
       <address address-value="WAPPUSH=164.164.56.2/TYPE=IPv4@ppg.wrox.com" />
       <address address-value="WAPPUSH=+919845000007/TYPE=PLMN@ppg.wrox.com" />
   </push-message>
</pap>

--my_first_multipart_message
Content-Type: text/plain

You have received your first WAP push message

--my_first_multipart_message
```

In the above message, we are delivering a plain text string to the device. It could equally well be of any other MIME type like WML, but for our illustration of a push message here, plain text content would suffice. The `ppg-notify-requested-to` is an optional attribute of the `push-message` element, which if present, is a request to the PPG to contact the specified URL after the success or failure of the delivery of content to the device. In other words, "Result Notification" is a PAP procedure that would be applicable *only* if the above-mentioned attribute is present in the push message.

> Note that the unique **push-id** identifies the pushed message so that it is possible for the PPG as well as the PI to track a push transaction. Two push messages that are still being processed or tracked cannot have the same **push-id** . It is analogous to the Message-ID header that we see in SMTP based e-mail headers. It is generated in the PI and it can use any random string as long as it ensures that no two IDs are the same.

Push Response

The push response is used to convey back to the PI the result of initial acceptance (or failure to do so) of the push-message, and possibly some information about the initial processing of it by the PPG. If an error occurs, it is only reported in the push response, and not in the application layer protocols, such as HTTP. If there are errors in the syntax of the push-message, the HTTP response code that must be sent by the PPG is "202 Accepted" (if HTTP is used for tunneling). This means that any control information that is to be conveyed when a PAP message is received is always through another PAP XML message and *not* through the response codes or headers of the protocol used for tunneling these messages. Note that the HTTP codes that are received, or the HTTP headers present in the request or response, have not been in included in the examples given here to ensure that they don't clutter the code.

An example push response is given below:

```
Content-Type: application/xml

<?xml version="1.0">
<!DOCTYPE pap PUBLIC "-//WAPFORUM//DTD PAP 1.0//EN"
http://www.wapforum.org/DTD/pap_1.0.dtd>

<pap>
    <push-response push-id="v04210109b50b0aebf02c@pi.wrox.com">
        <response-result code="1001" desc="Accepted for Processing" />
    </push-response>
</pap>
```

Note that the first four lines are then the same for each message, so we will not include them from here on. In the above <response-result> element, we find two attributes: code, which is a numeric value useful for the application processing the response, and desc, a description useful if presented to a human. The code 1001 indicates that the push-message request has been accepted for processing. These codes are similar to HTTP or FTP protocol response codes that you may be aware of. Unlike HTTP/FTP codes that are usually made up of 3 digits, PAP response codes have 4 digits to ensure that we don't run out of response codes in the future evolution of PAP. These attributes are present in some of the messages that we discuss later. The code attribute can be classified into 5 classes:

❑   1xxx: Success – The action was successfully received, understood, and accepted.

❑   2xxx: Client Error – The request contains bad syntax or the client cannot fulfill it.

❑   3xxx: Server Error – The server failed to fulfill an apparently valid request.

❑   4xxx: Service Failure – The service could not be performed. The operation may be retried.

❑   5xxx: Mobile Device Abort – The mobile device aborted the operation.

For the complete set of response codes and their descriptions, refer to "WAP 1.2 Push Access Protocol Specification" available at http://www.wapforum.org/.

Result Notification

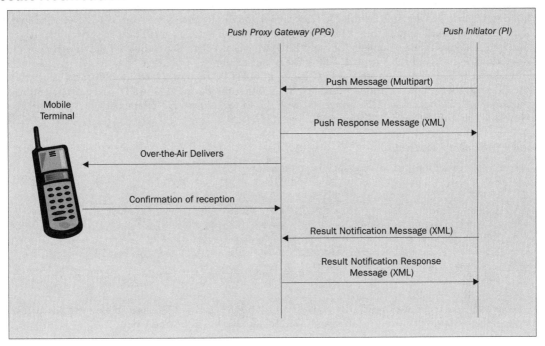

The PPG informs the PI of the outcome of a previous push submission using this operation. This operation informs the PI of one of the following outcomes:

- ❑ Push content was transmitted Over-the-Air to the wireless device.

- ❑ Push content was transmitted Over-the-Air to the wireless device, and a confirmation was received from the device.

- ❑ The push message expired. This is determined by the PPG based on the `deliver-before-timestamp` and `deliver-after-timestamp` attributes of push message (discussed later in the chapter).

- ❑ The push message was cancelled explicitly by the PI using a "cancel message".

- ❑ An error occurred.

> **The rationale of having a result notification is due to the inherent uncertainty in the delivery of the message to the device. For example, the user, may have switched off the device or may be out of range of network coverage. Once this message reaches the PI, there is a guarantee that the message has reached the destination although it is still possible for the user to have discarded it without looking at it.**

If an error is reported in the push response, then the PPG will not send a result notification. A PPG can send a result notification only if the `ppg-notify-requested-to` attribute of the push message element is set to a URL (or another form of return address) where the PI could be contacted.

601

Note that each operation that we describe here could be on a separate application-layer protocol transaction. For instance, the push message/push response might have happened on a particular HTTP connection that was initiated by the PI. This connection might have been terminated and a little while later, the PPG could contact the PI for result notification on a separate HTTP connection that it initiated. Looking at the behavior of PI and PPG, we can say that, depending on the direction of the operation, both PI and PPG act as HTTP servers. For example, in the case of a <push-message>, the PI makes a TCP connection with the PPG to send the HTTP request. Here, the PPG acts as a server and the PI is the client. If we consider a message in the other direction (PPG to PI), like a result notification message, the PPG makes a TCP connection with the PI to send the HTTP message for the PAP message. Now, the roles of PPG and PI are reversed.

Result Notification Message

An example result notification-message is given below:

```
  ...
  <pap>
     <resultnotification-message push-id="v04210109b50b0aebf02c@pi.wrox.com"
     message-state="delivered" code="1000" desc="OK">
        <address address-value="WAPPUSH=164.164.56.2/TYPE=IPv4@ppg.wrox.com" />
     </resultnotification-message>
  </pap>
```

The `message-state` attribute in the above `resultnotification-message` element indicates the state of the message identified by the `push-id`. It can take the following values :

Message-state	Description
rejected	Indicates that the message was not accepted.
pending	Indicates that the message is in process.
delivered	Indicates that the message was successfully delivered to the device.
undeliverable	Indicates that the message could not be delivered because of a problem.
expired	Means that the message exceeded the time limit allowed by PPG policy, or could not be delivered by the time specified in the push submission.
aborted	Indicates that the device/user aborted the message.
timeout	Indicates that the delivery process timed out.
cancelled	Indicates that the message was cancelled through the cancel operation at the PI. This is discussed in the section, *Push Cancellation*, a little later.
unknown	Indicates that the PPG does not know the state of the message.

Result Notification Response

The result notification response is used to convey the result of processing the result notification message at the PI. This message is used to notify the PPG that an error has occurred while processing the result notification message at the PI. PAP messages are always in pairs with the latter being an acknowledgement message.

An example result notification response is given below:

```
...
<pap>
    <resultnotification-response push-id="v04210109b50b0aebf02c@pi.wrox.com"
    code="1000" desc="OK">
        <address address-value="WAPPUSH=164.164.56.2/TYPE=IPv4@ppg.wrox.com" />
    </resultnotification-response>
</pap>
```

Push Cancellation

The PI might choose to cancel a particular push submission. Although it is not mandatory for a PPG to support this operation, there are some reasons why this might be useful:

❏ The PI did not get confirmation, by way of a result notification, that the content had been delivered to the device and a timeout for the delivery of the content had occurred. This timer could be much smaller than the retry timer at the PPG.

❏ Soon after the push submission has occurred, it is possible that the PI detects new information that overrides the content that has already been pushed. The PI can then attempt to cancel a submitted message to reduce unnecessary transmissions. For example, when a notification of the number of new e-mails has been sent to the PPG without the PI receiving result notification and the PI detects more new e-mails. Under such circumstances, the PI can attempt to cancel the previous message and send a new one. If the PI doesn't, there is a risk of delivery of stale content.

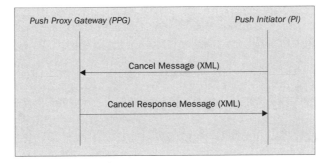

> The delivery of the content to the device doesn't always happen in real-time because the networks could be overloaded, or the user may have switched off the device.

Cancel Message

A cancel message example is given below:

```
...
<pap>
    <cancel-message push-id="v04210109b50b0aebf02c@pi.wrox.com">
        <address address-value="WAPPUSH=164.164.56.2/TYPE=IPv4@ppg.wrox.com" />
    </cancel-message >
</pap>
```

The push-id is the ID for the message. This is what identifies the message to cancel.

Cancel Response

The cancel response is used to convey the result of processing the cancel message at the PPG. The error code number 3003 means that the cancellation could not be actioned.

An example cancel response is given below:

```
...
<pap>
   <cancel-response push-id="v04210109b50b0aebf02c@pi.wrox.com">
      <cancel-result code="3003" desc="Not Possible">
         <address address-value="WAPPUSH=164.164.56.2/TYPE=IPv4@ppg.wrox.com" />
      </cancel-result>
   </cancel-response>
</pap>
```

Status Query

The PI can find out about the status of a previous push submission using this operation. This would typically be used before a result notification message has arrived. The PPG however, is not required to implement this operation.

Status Query Message

A status query message example is given below:

```
...
<pap>
   <statusquery-message push-id="v04210109b50b0aebf02c@pi.wrox.com">
      <address address-value="WAPPUSH=164.164.56.2/TYPE=IPv4@ppg.wrox.com" />
   </statusquery-message >
</pap>
```

Status Query Response

The status query response is used to convey the result of processing the status query message at the PPG.

An example status query response is given below:

```
...
<pap>
   <statusquery-response push-id="v04210109b50b0aebf02c@pi.wrox.com">
      <statusquery-result message-state="pending" code="1000" desc="OK">
         <address address-value="WAPPUSH=164.164.56.2/TYPE=IPv4@ppg.wrox.com" />
      </statusquery-result>
   </statusquery-response>
</pap>
```

The message-state attribute indicates the state of the message with values as discussed in the section, *Result Notification Message*.

Client Capabilities Query (CCQ)

A PI might want to know about the capabilities of the client device that the content is to be pushed to, so that it can customize the content accordingly. The capabilities are reported in the **Resource Description Framework (RDF)** format, which was introduced in Chapter 9.

CCQ Message

A CCQ message example is given below:

```
...
<pap>
    <ccq-message query-id="first_query_id@pi.wrox.com">
        <address address-value="WAPPUSH=164.164.56.2/TYPE=IPv4@ppg.wrox.com" />
    </ccq-message>
</pap>
```

The `query-id` attribute above is useful as the PI can use it to match multiple responses to multiple requests that it might have made. This is a unique string generated by the PI.

CCQ Response

The CCQ response is a multipart message with both a control entity and a capabilities entity. An example this is shown below:

```
Content-Type: multipart/related; boundary=my_second_multipart_message;
Type="application/xml"

--my_second_multipart_message
Content-Type: application/xml

<?xml version="1.0">
<!DOCTYPE pap PUBLIC "-//WAPFORUM//DTD PAP 1.0//EN"
http://www.wapforum.org/DTD/pap_1.0.dtd>

<pap>
    <ccq-response query-id=first_query_id@pi.wrox.com code="1000" desc="OK">
        <address address-value="WAPPUSH=164.164.56.2/TYPE=IPv4@ppg.wrox.com" />
    </ccq-response>
</pap>

--my_second_multipart_message
Content-Type: application/xml

<?xml version="1.0">
<rdf:RDF xmlns:rdf="http://www.w3.org/1999/02/22-rdf-syntax-ns#"
xmlns:prf="http://www.wapforum.org/UAPROF/ccppschema1.0#">
<!-- WAP Browser vendor site: Default description of WAP properties -->
    <rdf:Description>
        <prf:WapVersion>1.2</prf:WapVersion>
        <prf:WmlDeckSize>1400 octets</prf:WmlDeckSize>
        <prf:WapDeviceClass>A </prf:WapDeviceClass>
        <prf:WapPushMsgSize>1400 octets</prf:WapPushMsgSize>
        <prf:WmlVersion>
            <rdf:Bag>
                <rdf:li>1.1</rdf:li>
            </rdf:Bag>
        </prf:WmlVersion>
    </rdf:Description>
</rdf:RDF>

--my_second_multipart_message
```

In the above capabilities entity, the description of the device includes the information that it is WAP 1.2 compliant, the WML deck size it can handle is 1400 octets, the size of the push message it can handle is 1400 octets, the device class is A (currently A, B or C are possible) and a list of WML versions supported (only 1.1 here). The device class indicates the type of WAP features that the device has implemented. A data profile class (Class C) client or server device will provide all mandatory data features of the WAP specifications. A data and telephony profile class (or Class B) client or server device will provide all mandatory data and telephony features of the WAP specifications. A complete data and telephony profile class (or Class A) client or server device will provide all mandatory and all optional data and telephony features of the WAP specifications.

Bad Message Response

This PAP message does not come under any particular category of operation and is only used when the PPG is not able to determine the format of a received message. In other words, the received message was completely unrecognizable for the receiver to be able to parse the PAP entity. This may occur if some other Internet client (mistakenly or otherwise) tries to connect to a PPG and sends data that the PPG cannot understand.

```
...
<pap>
    <badmessage-response bad-message-fragment="<message-fragment>">
</pap>
```

In the above example, `<message-fragment>` is the fragment of the unrecognized message that was received.

Other Important PAP Elements and Attributes

quality-of-service Element

The PAP element `quality-of-service` is optionally available in many of the PAP messages (Push, Result Notification and Status Query Response Messages) that require or indicate differentiation in delivery quality (priority of message delivery, type of network or bearer, etc.). In the case of the Push Message, it indicates the requested quality of service, whereas in the others it indicates the quality of service that was used to deliver the message over-the-air. Within this element, it is possible to specify the following attributes:

- One of the three available priority classes: `high`, `medium` or `low`. The value `high` indicates the fastest delivery is desired. The value `low` indicates the slowest delivery. The actual delivery latencies associated with these qualities are implementation specific.

- One of the four possible delivery methods: `confirmed`, `preferconfirmed`, `unconfirmed` or `notspecified`. When delivery-method is `confirmed`, the PPG must use confirmed delivery of the message to the device over the air. The different types of delivery over the air are discussed later in the section *Push Over–the-Air (OTA) Protocol*. Note that a PI may request confirmation from the device without requesting `ppg-notify-requested-to`; the result is that the message is confirmed over the air but the PPG does not inform the PI. The value `preferconfirmed` allows the PI to inform the PPG of the preferred delivery method. The PPG should try to deliver the message as indicated, but may use another method if it is unable to use the preferred choice. The value `unconfirmed` means that the message *must* be delivered in an unconfirmed manner. The value `notspecified` indicates that the PI does not care whether the PPG uses confirmed delivery or unconfirmed delivery – the choice is up to the PPG.

❑ Type of network to be used for Over-the-Air delivery.

❑ Type of bearer to be used for Over-the-Air delivery.

Attributes that specify date and time

`<push-message>` has two attributes `deliver-before-timestamp` and `deliver-after-timestamp` which the PI can submit the message as before, but control when the content is actually delivered Over-the-Air to the wireless device.

> **If the message could not be delivered before the time given in the `deliver-before-timestamp` attribute, the message is considered to have expired.**

The `received-time` attribute of `<resultnotification-message>` specifies the time at which the message was received at the PPG (from the PI). It may be used by the PI to calculate latency between the push submission time and the time at which the message was received at the PPG. Depending on the PAP tunnel protocol used (say SMTP), there is a possibility of a noticeable delay. The `event-time` attribute of the result notification message specifies the time at which the message reached the device. The timestamp in all time related attributes are represented in Coordinated Universal Time (UTC as it is normally known, despite the expected order of letters), which is a 24-hour timekeeping system of the form:

```
YYYY-MM-DDThh:mm:ssZ
```

where:

❑ YYYY is a 4 digit year ("0000", ..., "9999")

❑ MM is a 2 digit month ("01"=January, "02"=February, ..., "12"=December)

❑ DD is a 2 digit day ("01", "02", ..., "31")

❑ hh is a 2 digit hour, 24-hour timekeeping system ("00", ..., "23")

❑ mm is a 2 digit minute ("00", ..., "59")

❑ ss is a 2 digit second ("00", ..., "59")

❑ Z is UTC. This indicates that the current time string is in the UTC format

An Example: "2000-05-30T23:20:00Z" means 11:20 PM on the 30th of May 2000.

Commonly used WAP Push Content Types

Until now, we have not mentioned the actual content that is pushed. Although it is possible to push any type of content to the wireless device, it might not be feasible to directly push larger sized content, such as entire WML decks. This is because it is possible that a device user is already using the device for other WAP services and the amount of memory and processing power in the device might be even more limited than it is normally. Under such circumstances, it makes a lot of sense to push a notification to the device so that the client can then pull the actual content in a manner that wouldn't disturb any of their ongoing activity.

Therefore, WAP defines two new content types that can be classified as push content: **Service Loading (SL)** and **Service Indication (SI)**. As before, these are XML applications.

Service Loading (SL)

It is possible to cause a user agent on a wireless device to load and execute a service identified by a Uniform Resource Identifier (URI) with the use of Server Loading. The service can be in the form of a WML deck, and executing it would mean rendering on the microbrowser. This mechanism is defined so as to load the service without the user realizing that it is happening. Hence, it is possible to force the user to take notice of a particular event by loading the service before the user has a chance to abort it.

Because it is possible for the content to be loaded without the user realizing it, there is an opportunity for misuse and therefore some security measures must be taken when SL is implemented in the device:

❑ The user agent on the client provides a means to disable acceptance of SL content type

❑ The user agent on the client provides specific security policies that only allow certain URLs or domains to be referenced

❑ A PPG provides a means to control which PIs are allowed to push SLs

The only information sent in this content is the URI of a service. Here is a possible application scenario of SL:

❑ Forcing an end-user with a prepaid subscription for the wireless phone/date service to take action on a low balance, maybe by loading a WML deck from the operator's WAP site where the subscription could be renewed.

Once the device receives the SL content, the content is acted upon as soon as possible and the service identified by the URI is loaded using the usual WSP GET pull mechanism.

Here is an example SL element:

```
<?xml version="1.0"?>
<!DOCTYPE sl PUBLIC "-//WAPFORUM//DTD SL 1.0//EN"
"http://www.wapforum.org/DTD/sl.dtd">
<sl href="http://wap.carrier.com/ppaid.wml" action="execute-high" />
```

The allowed values for the action attribute are execute-high, execute-low or cache:

❑ execute-high: This will interrupt the user if they are using another service.

❑ execute-low: This will never result in the user being interrupted.

❑ cache: The service identified by the URI is loaded but instead of executing it, it is put in the cache of the device, if one is available. If a cache is not supported in the device, the SL is silently discarded.

The SL content-type can also be encoded into a compact binary form to reduce the number of octets sent over-the-air.

Service Indication (SI)

This content type provides a mechanism for asynchronous event notifications, for example, notifying the user of the arrival of e-mail. It is similar to SL in many ways, but there are several differences between the two, which are summarized in the table on the following page.

Service Loading	Service Indication
A URI to the service to be automatically loaded is conveyed in this content.	A short text notification message is conveyed along with the URI of the service to be invoked when the user acts upon the notification.
The user is not presented with any information until after the service has been loaded by the pull mechanism.	The user is presented with the text message available in the push content. It may also contain additional implementation-specific information for the user to see, before the service identified by the URI is loaded.
Primarily used in applications that require the user to take certain action when an event that cannot be ignored has happened (at least from the PI's point of view).	The user is allowed to specify whether the service should be loaded or postponed. This is more useful in applications that require a mechanism to notify the user, but it is assumed that the information is not critical and the user can discard it if they choose.

Here is an example SI element:

```
<?xml version="1.0"?>
<!DOCTYPE sl PUBLIC "-//WAPFORUM//DTD SI 1.0//EN"
"http://www.wapforum.org/DTD/si.dtd">
<si>
    <indication href="http://wap.carrier.com/voicemail.wml"
    created="2000-04-01T16.00.00Z"
    si-expires="2000-04-01T16.01.00Z"
    action="signal-low">
        You have new voicemail
    </indication>
</si>
```

Similar to the SL type, the amount of permitted user intrusion is controlled with the `action` attribute. The possible values for this attribute are `signal-none`, `signal-low`, `signal-medium`, and `signal-high` or `delete`. The `created` attribute gives the date and time when the resource identified by the `href` attribute was created or modified. The date and time is in UTC. The `si-expires` attribute specifies when the current SI expires, so that the device can delete them or mark them expired. If this attribute is not specified, the SI will not be removed automatically from the device.

Also similar to the SL type, the SI type can be encoded into a compact binary representation for Over-the-Air delivery.

Push Over-the-Air (OTA) Protocol

This is the protocol for delivering the push content from the PPG to the device over the wireless network. OTA is a thin protocol layer that is implemented in both the mobile device and the PPG. This layer uses WSP service primitives to push content. It forms the bridge between a push user agent and the WSP layer.

There are different types of OTA push:

❑   Connectionless push

❑   Unconfirmed connection-oriented push

❑   Confirmed connection-oriented push

A connectionless push is the simplest mechanism of the three options given above. Two registered WDP ports, one secure and the other non-secure, are reserved in every client capable of connectionless push. On receiving this message in the device, the OTA layer forwards it to the correct application, based on the application ID provided in the message headers.

The connection-oriented push mechanisms are a little more complex, as they involve the use of an active WSP session. However, it is not possible for the PPG to actually create a WSP session with the client. A simple workaround for this problem has been defined in the specification, so that a session can be created using an indirect mechanism. This is described next.

Client-Side Infrastructure

Apart from the OTA layer that is present in the device, we need two other entities to support push services:

❑ A Session Initiation Application (SIA)

❑ An Application Dispatcher

Session Initiation Application (SIA)

The SIA is introduced into every client that supports connection-oriented push mechanisms. If there are no active WSP sessions with the client, then the PPG sends a **session request** connectionless message to the client. The OTA layer delivers this message to the SIA application, which then goes on to create a new WSP session with the PPG that initiated the session request (or another server specified in the session request message).

Application Despatcher

This is the entity in the device that examines the push message header, `X-Wap-Application-Id`, given to it by the OTA layer and decides which application should receive it. For example, `<sia>` is an application ID for the SIA, described above. The default application ID is the WML user agent for both the connectionless push and the connection-oriented push, unless the default is negotiated in the push session establishment. If the despatcher finds that an application for which a push message has arrived does not exist, it reports an error to the PPG of its inability to accept the content. It is also responsible for confirming push operations to the PPG when the content has been received by the correct application and has been acknowledged.

Problems with Push Technologies

As we all know, wireless devices are a lot more personal than, let's say, a PC. Users have the devices with them all the time and tend to use them heavily. Because of the nature of usage, there are privacy and unsolicited content issues associated with pushing content, whatever the mechanism is.

Rogue PIs can push junk that could disturb users. Any content that the user has not previously registered for can be considered junk. Normal advertising content will become junk if the user does not want it. Advertisers must somehow get permission from users to push such content. Any content cannot be called junk if the user wants it! What is normal content to one is junk to another. Therefore, this distinction is to be made on a per-user basis. Privacy is of the utmost concern when using wireless devices.

Currently the most widely used form of push uses SMS text messages. As an example of the problem of unsolicited content, an incident occurred in Delhi, India where a vendor managed to bribe someone working with the service provider to obtain a thousand phone numbers and push unsolicited advertisement text to all of them using SMS.

With some packet-based wireless networks like GPRS, junk push content could become a major problem, as the device user ends up paying for the airtime (for both incoming and outgoing packets). Unlike fixed networks, radio resources are expensive and scarce. Therefore, billing would be done for both incoming as well as outgoing data. Even legitimate push initiators should only push user notifications that are small in size and allow the user the choice of whether to load a service that might involve a lot more airtime usage. In spite of filter rules and PI authentication mechanisms being available with the PPG provided by the network operator, it may be possible for an anonymous PI to setup a PPG on the Internet to push unsolicited content. This is totally dependent on the type of bearers used for push and security policies implemented by the wireless operator. If a packet network is used and if anyone is allowed to initiate traffic towards the devices, users are in trouble. But if security policies are strict and only trusted parties (who have contractual arrangements with the operator) are allowed to initiate traffic towards the devices, users are safer from spam/junk attacks. On the other hand, with bearers like SMS, it may be virtually impossible to solve spam/junk attacks unless the service is stopped entirely. This is because of the way SMS works.

There are three possible ways to send SMS messages from an application program:

❑   Get access to a network operator's Short Message Service Centre (SMSC) by signing agreements. Use SMS gateway software, such as the one available from `http://www.kannel.org/` or sendSMS available at `http://www.bai.de/sendsms/manual.shtml` to send and receive messages. Not an easy or inexpensive method and because of agreements, it will not be possible to generate spam.

❑   Use exisiting web and e-mail interfaces that a network operator is already providing for sending short messages. A good candidate for spam but the network operator can restrict the total amount of messages going to a single device.

❑   GSM specifications define a DTE : DCE interface (where DTE stands for Data Terminal Equipment, a PC for example, and DCE stands for Data Communication Equipment, for example, a a mobile phone). Using this well-defined interface, it is not only possible to send SMS messages but also to retrieve messages that the mobile receives. All that one needs is a GSM mobile phone, a PC, a PC-phone interface cable or card, SMS gateway software, and a prepaid subscription for anonymity, to spam users. This becomes a very feasible solution for SMS spam.

Using Phone.com Tools

At the time of writing, no vendors have implemented the WAP 1.2 specifications, which define the WAP push model. Therefore, we do not have devices, or the network, to support WAP push. However, we do have the Phone.com tools that implement some kind of alert notification mechanism, which we will discuss here for the sake of completeness. The downside of this implementation is that it is entirely proprietary and does not fit into the WAP scheme of things, which is much more powerful.

A push alert tool, known as `SendNtfn`, is available together with the UP.SDK download provided by phone.com at `http://updev.phone.com`, which uses a proprietary protocol to push alerts.

Here's a sample screenshot of this tool:

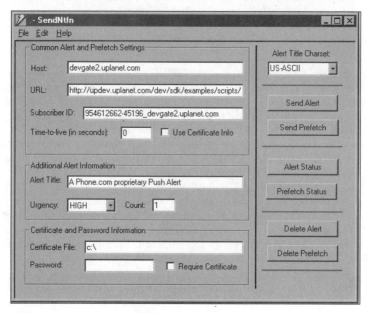

Phone.com provides two logical delivery channels for notifications:

- ❑ **The push channel**: WML services can use the push channel to push notifications asynchronously to any UP.Browser over either packet-switched or circuit-switched networks (possibly using SMS). The UP.Link server attempts to deliver push channel notifications immediately. If the UP.Browser is not available, the UP.Link server periodically attempts to deliver the notification.

- ❑ **The pull channel**: Normally, WML services use the pull channel to send notifications that contain less time-sensitive information. You can include any UP.Link-supported content type in a pull-channel notification. You can't count on the UP.Link server delivering a pull notification immediately. On packet-switched networks, the UP.Link server attempts to deliver pull notifications as quickly as possible (with only UP.Browser availability, the network transport layer, and web server latency impeding delivery time). On circuit-switched networks, the UP.Link server *never* initiates contact to deliver a pull-channel notification. The UP.Browser must open a circuit and initiate contact with the UP.Link server before the it delivers the notification. A prefetch notification is an example for pull-channel notification.

To push alerts, it is necessary to create a subscriber ID in the public Phone.com WAP gateway/push gateway. Unlike some other vendors, who provide an evaluation copy of their gateway software, Phone.com provides a working gateway for developers to test their applications without the need to install their own gateway. To use the public gateway, it is necessary for you to be registered with the Phone.com developer program. Once you have registered and logged on to the developer program, you can to go to the UP Link Provisioning link, log on to it and add subscriber IDs.

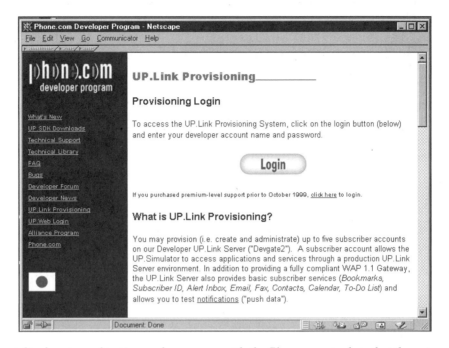

The biggest disadvantage of testing push messages with the Phone.com tools is that the gateway has to initiate a TCP connection to the host on which the UP.Simulator is executing. Now, if you are behind a firewall that does not allow any incoming traffic, it is impossible to test this push mechanism, unless some firewall ports are opened up for incoming traffic (port 4445 for non-secure notifications or 3356 for secure notifications). Depending on the security policy of the company, this may or may not be allowed. An alternative is to use a dial-up or leased line connection from an Internet Service Provider that does not involve a firewall. If you use a dial-up connection, typically the server assigns an IP address dynamically to your computer. If this is the case, you will have to log on to UP.Link Provisioning and use the utility Sync Phone to tell the Phone.com public gateway of your current IP address where the UP.Simulator is being run.

COM (Component Object Model) and C++-based Notification Libraries are provided with the UP.SDK download, using which we could build our own push application. In fact, the SendNtfn tool makes use of the Notification Library, and the source code for the tool is provided too.

Push Alert Example

Here is an example of push alert and prefetch submission with the specific HTTP headers that would be sent when connecting to the Phone.com public gateway "devgate2.uplanet.com".

Note that the following Phone.com push submission protocol has been discovered using spy.pl, *a socket listen program. These are undocumented pieces of information and it is recommended that you don't directly use them. Instead, it is better to use one of the Phone.com notification libraries. These examples are provided only as an illustration of proprietary extensions that Phone.com has provided for pushing content to the Phone.com device.*

```
POST /ntfn/add HTTP/1.0
Content-Length: 197
x-up-upnotifyp-version: upnotifyp/3.0
x-up-subno: 954612662-45196_devgate2.uplanet.com
x-up-ntfn-ttl: 0
x-up-ntfn-channel: push
Content-Location: http://wrox.com/cgi-bin/fetch.cgi?NEXT=MEETING&PREFETCH=YES
Content-Type: application/vnd.uplanet.alert

<?xml version="1.0"?>
<!DOCTYPE ALERT PUBLIC "-//PHONE.COM//DTD ALERT 1.0//EN"
"http://www.phone.com/dtd/alert1.xml">
   <ALERT LABEL = "v4.0 Pushed Alert"
   COUNT = "1"
   HREF = ""
   URGENCY = "MEDIUM" />
```

Prefetch Example

```
POST /ntfn/add HTTP/1.0
x-up-upnotifyp-version: upnotifyp/3.0
x-up-subno: 954612662-45196_devgate2.uplanet.com
x-up-ntfn-ttl: 0
x-up-ntfn-channel: pull
Content-Location: http://wrox.com/cgi-bin/fetch.cgi?NEXT=MEETING&PREFETCH=YES
```

The content types, the XML entities, and the HTTP-headers are all Phone.com specific and do not conform to WAP-based PAP messages. The above mechanism is not even similar to the push model defined in WAP in any sense, as we can see that HTTP headers are used to convey some control information on how to deliver the message to the device. This is completely different from the WAP push philosophy where XML PAP entities are used to convey the control information and HTTP is simply used as a tunnel protocol. This latter arrangement allows push submission to be done using other protocols, like SMTP for example, if the gateway supports this.

An SMS Text Based Push Example

A much more powerful, yet simple, mechanism to push information to a mobile phone is through Short Message Service (SMS). SMS is one of the most widely supported services. For this reason, we will present a case study of an SMS application.

Many mobile network operators provide web or e-mail to Short Message Service Center (SMSC) interfaces to make it easy to send messages. Even though a standardized message submission model is not defined, it is sufficient for us to take one particular case study and customize it later to suit the submission mechanisms provided by your own network operator.

Many of us carry a mobile phone with us all of the time. Let's compare that to our proximity to e-mail. It is quite possible that you are on the move all day, in and out of meetings or traveling around. You might still want to be notified of the arrival of e-mail messages from key people in your organization. Obviously, it would be perfect if notifications about the sender, the subject, the time of arrival and a small fragment of the e-mail body, arrived on your mobile phone. Such an application is very simple to build and is provided here.

The application is built in Perl. It is necessary for us to run the application on a UNIX-like operating system, with the commonly used sendmail based e-mail system (because of the method used to detect new e-mail messages). It is possible to implement such an application on any e-mail system that provides a POP3 or IMAP interface. However, the application would then have to keep polling instead of the mailing system executing an application or script whenever new e-mails arrive. On the other hand, the mechanism that we are going to describe is not based on frequent polling. The e-mail system can be configured to execute a script or a program for every e-mail that arrives and therefore is a much better mechanism than the one based on frequent polling. Another example of a system that triggers a a script when an event occurs (like the arrival of new e-mail) is in Microsoft's Exchange Server. By using something known as Collaboration Data Objects (CDO), it is possible to implement asynchronous email notifications. (Refer to `http://www.cdonline.com` for more information on this mechanism.)

It is also important for us to find out the type of mechanism that the network operator provides for submission of short messages. (It is normally possible to find out from their website.) For example, the operator in my geographical area provides a web-based interface using an HTML form to submit the message. You will therefore need to customize the sample application depending on the mechanism provided by your network operator. The source-code will be marked appropriately if it applies to a specific case.

Three different methods we can use to implement e-mail notifications are:

1. Every incoming email is considered and a notification sent. We can implement this mechanism using the `.forward` mechanism available on UNIX-based systems. In this case, when an e-mail arrives, it is forwarded to all the e-mail addresses stored in the `.forward` file in the home directory. It is also possible for the mail delivery system to pipe the message to another program for further processing.

2. E-mails that match certain criteria are considered and notifications are sent only for these. Filtered notifications are possible using the "procmail" e-mail filter mechanism. Using this, it is possible to specify rules to select particular messages to act on, based on extended regular expression-based pattern matching. Once a message is selected, different actions can be specified for them. The actions are quite similar to the previous case and can either be forwarding the message, storing the message in a specified folder, or piping it to a program. All these rules are to be specified in a file called `.procmailrc` in the home directory.

3. Sending periodic notifications (say, every hour or so) to indicate whether new e-mails have arrived. Due to its periodic nature, this method makes it possible to be implemented with POP3 or IMAP interfaces, where the notification program connects to the mailserver periodically and retrieves the mail headers (and body if required) to send the notifications to the device.

In any of the above mechanisms, it isn't required that the host is a mail server. It depends on the network and mailing system. Again there are about three different types:

1. Sendmail based mailservers on UNIX-based systems and the other nodes largely being Windows-based, where e-mail clients on these nodes use POP3/IMAP interfaces to the mail server to retrieve the mails. For example, most ISPs work in this manner (the nodes may not be permanent because of using dialup connections)

In the above case, the mail server will have a login ID for every e-mail user. The user should then telnet or remote login to the server and store either the .forward *or* .procmailrc *file in the home directory on the server. The Perl program that processes the e-mails and sends the required notifications must also be stored on this server, so that the mailing system can execute the program when required.*

2. Sendmail based mail server(s) on UNIX-based system(s) and the other nodes entirely made of UNIX-based workstations and servers. In this scenario, a combination of NIS+ (Network Information Service), NFS (Network File System) and automounting are used to make it possible to get the same environment, work space and settings regardless of where a user logs on in the network.

❑ NIS is a central database containing data such as UNIX login/password information, home directories of users, hostname- IP address translations, email aliases, and so on. Using NIS, it is possible for users to login on any UNIX workstation in the network using the same user ID and password credentials. The system consults the central NIS database to authenticate a user logging in.

❑ NFS is a mechanism by which files stored on the hard disk of a different host in the network can be accessed as though they were available locally. The process of making such a remote file system available locally is called NFS mounting. NFS is commonly available on all flavors of UNIX and can interoperate with each other which means that a Linux box can mount a SUN filesystem. Even Windows implementations of NFS are available, even though they are unlikely to be commonly used. Using this mechanism, it is possible to have the home directory of a user stored on, say a central server to make system administration tasks easy and still be able to uniformly access it from any host in the network. For example, with a login ID shash, I can simply login to any workstation on the network with the same password and find my home directory mounted on to the same path (say, /home/shash) from wherever it is physically stored

❑ Automounting is a mechanism where a file system stored on the hard disk of another host is NFS mounted on demand when a user or a process makes a reference to a file on such a file system. It is also unmounted after a configurable period of no reference to a file on the system. For example, if you are logged in on a host called *nomad* and try to access the password file on a host called *crusader*, it is possible for example to use the path "/net/crusader/etc/passwd" to access the file. The automounting system will take care of mounting the remote NFS and provide local access to the files.

In this scenario, it is sufficient for a user to login on any system and simply store either the .forward *or* .procmailrc *file in the home directory (doesn't matter where it is physically stored). The Perl program that processes the e-mails and sends the required notifications must be stored in a path accessible to the mailing system.*

3. With mail systems such as MS Exchange, Banyan Mail, Microsoft Mail, the nodes on the network (of any type of system) use POP3/IMAP interfaces to retrieve mail. Such mailing systems also provide mechanisms where programs can be written to act upon e-mails as they arrive in the server.

Using the above system, notification methods (1) and (2) can be implemented using mechanisms like CDO. The .forward *and the* procmail *mechanisms don't apply here. On the other hand notification method (3) could be used here. In such a case, the notification program can run on any type of system as long as it has network access to the mailserver.*

In both notification methods (1) and (2), we will be using the option of piping the email to a program to send email notifications.

.forward Mechanism

In this mechanism, create a file called `.forward` with the following line in it:

```
\<username>, " | <path_to_perl_filter> "
```

In the above line, <username> should be the UNIX login name or the username part of your e-mail ID, and <path_to_perl_filter> should be the absolute path where the Perl filter program that we will describe later, is stored. `.forward` files normally contain a comma-separated list of e-mail addresses. However, in this case, it contains one e-mail address (just a username without the domain part of an e-mail address since it is implicitly known to be the current domain) and the path to a program to be executed.

For example, the following line in my `.forward` file would both store the e-mail in my inbox and also pipe it to the Perl program:

```
\shash, "| /home/shash/bin/mail2mobile.pl "
```

In the above example, . We use the "\" character so that the same forwarding rules are not applied repeatedly, which would cause an infinite loop in forwarding.

procmail Mechanism

Using this mechanism, we can create powerful filters to weed out all the unimportant e-mails and to select only the most important e-mails for sending via the SMS notification. This mechanism is particularly useful if you receive a large volume of e-mail and you wish to be notified about only a few select ones. For instance, a system administrator who gets e-mails about server crashes would want to be notified immediately wherever she is located but not about other general information. Filters can be constructed using the extended regular expressions to look out for specific patterns in the e-mail header.

For example, create a file called `.procmailrc` in your home directory. Suppose I only want to be notified if there is an e-mail from someone in Wrox Press:

```
:0 hci:
#mails from anyone at Wrox
* ^[Ff][Rr][Oo][Mm].*@wrox.com
| /home/shash/bin/mail2mobile.pl
```

We explain this example below. First note, that the above example has a fairly simple rule. Each rule is called a 'recipe' in procmail jargon. This is the format of a procmail recipe:

```
:0 [flags] [ : [locallockfile] ]
        <zero or more conditions (one per line)>
        <exactly one action line>
```

The flags that I have included have the following meanings:

- ❏ h: Feed the header to the pipe (default).
- ❏ c: Generate a carbon copy of this mail. With this flag, not only is the e-mail piped to an external program but it is also delivered to the default inbox.
- ❏ i: Ignore any write errors on this recipe (these are usually due to an early closed pipe).

The condition line in our example above is a simple extended regular expression to select all e-mails with the sender address having a `wrox.com` in it. In the regular expression pattern, we have `[Ff] [Rr] [Oo] [Mm]` matches a case insensitive occurrence of "from". It will therefore match "From", "fRom", and so on, so the header can be read regardless of how it arrives.

Finally, the last line in the example is a pipe "`|`" action line, with the name of the Perl program to be run.

> *To find out more about procmail and how to write powerful filters, you should refer to the procmail(1) and procmailrc(5) manual pages. However, exercise caution as you might lose important e-mails or cause e-mail loops if you are not careful.*

mail2mobile.pl Perl Script

In the above examples, the e-mails are piped to a Perl script called `mail2mobile.pl`, which we will explain here. There are three sections in the script:

- ❏ Extracting the `From:`, `Subject:` and `Date:` headers, and the body of the e-mail (only if required).
- ❏ Constructing the message to be sent depending on the submission format expected by your mobile operator.
- ❏ Submitting the message using one of the submission mechanisms provided by your mobile operator (such as web or e-mail based submission).

The latter two sections are very much mobile network operator specific and have therefore been encapsulated in two Perl subroutines called `construct_message()` and `sendsms_http()`. The script described here is only useful for mobile subscribers of Spice Telecom, which is a mobile network operator/service provider in the state of Karnataka, India. You must modify the `construct_message()` and `sendsms_http()` subroutines to suit the mechanisms provided by your network operator.

> There is no generic mechanism or format for the submission of SMS text messages. Each operator provides a proprietary interface, although the implementation of SMS in GSM networks is very much standardized and is defined in the GSM specifications. If we had used WAP based push instead, the only information that would be different from users under one operator to another would be the location of a PPG, and the rest of the protocol (PAP) would be the same. Except for the push message construction, the rest of the code/mechanisms could be used under a WAP push framework.

The main program flow of the script with plenty of explanatory comments is provided below. Not that to follow this code, you'll need basic understanding of Perl programming and a rudimentary knowledge of perl regular expressions.

```perl
#!/usr/bin/perl
# Change the above to the path where the Perl interpreter is installed

# constants that I have used which you will have to modify

# maximum length of a single SMS message that your operator allows in characters
$max_sms = 160;

$http_proxy = "http://squid.sasi.com:3128/";
$mobile_number1 = "98440";
$mobile_number2 = "13004";
$websms_uri = "http://www.spicetele.com/content/WebSmsThanks.asp";

# Main Program

######################################################################
# Read the message and split it into header and body at the first   #
# blank line. Email messages have headers first, a blank line       #
# (implies two consecutive newlines ) and body.                     #
######################################################################

#This undefines the input record seperator so that the next read will read the
# entire file

undef $/;

# The right hand side of the assignment is a simple pattern match with grouping
# of the header and the body of the email message using ()s.
# The return value of the RHS is a list of values equal to the grouped
# sub-expressions in the regular expression. Since two grouped sub-expressions
# are returned, they can be conveniently assigned to $hdr and $body

($hdr, $body) = (<STDIN> =~ /(.*?\n)(\n.*)/s);

# The above line is equivalent to three statements,
# <STDIN> =~ /(.*?\n)(\n.*)/s;
# $hdr = $1;
# $body = $2;

######################################################################
# The From: mail header is extracted and will be sent as part of    #
# the push message                                                  #
######################################################################

if ( $hdr =~ /^(from:[ \t].*\n)/mi ) {
# eg. "From: Vic <someone@wrox.com>"
  $from = $1;
} elsif ( $hdr =~ /^from[ \t]([^ \t]*?)/i ) {
# eg. "from <someone@wrox.com>"
  $from = "From: $1\n";
} else {
  $from = "From: (anonymous)\n";
# If we can't figure the sender
}
```

619

```
##########################################################################
# The Subject: mail header is extracted and will be sent as part of   #
# the push message                                                    #
##########################################################################

if( $hdr =~ /^(Subject:[ \t].*\n)/mi ) {
# eg. "Subject: Finished the chapter?"
  $subject = $1;
} else {
  $subject = "Subject: (not specified)\n";
}

##########################################################################
# The Date: mail header is extracted and will be sent as part of      #
# the push message                                                    #
##########################################################################

if( $hdr =~ /^(Date:[ \t].*\n)/mi ) {
#eg. "Date: Mon, 10 Apr 2000 18:23:00 +0100"
  $date = $1;
}

############################################################################
# Extract the MIME type and subtype of the email body from the Content-Type: #
# header                                                                   #
############################################################################

if( $hdr =~ /^Content-Type:[ \t](\w*?)\/(\w*)/mi ){ #eg. "Content-Type: text/plain"
  $mime_type = $1;
  $mime_subtype = $2;
}

############################################################################
# We can send part of the email body only if it is                        #
# in text/plain format and if the length of the message is less than the  #
# maximum allowed per message in SMS                                       #
############################################################################

if( ($length_msg = length($msg_to_send)) < $max_sms &&
    $mime_type =~ /text/i &&
    $mime_subtype =~ /plain/i )
  {
    $length_body_to_send = $max_sms - $length_msg;
    $body_to_send = substr $body, 0, $length_body_to_send;
  }

##############################################################################
# Construct the HTTP POST body which should be the same as what would be sent #
# through the WEB/HTML form based SMS text submission, for the               #
# particular network operator                                                #
##############################################################################

$post_msg = &construct_message( $from, $subject, $date, $body_to_send );

##############################################################################
# Send the SMS using HTTP . Another operator might provide an email interface #
# in which case you can define a new perl subroutine sendsms_smtp() and use  #
# it instead. The program exit code will be the same as the code returned by #
# sendsms_http()                                                             #
##############################################################################

exit &sendsms_http( $websms_uri, $post_msg, $http_proxy );
```

construct_message() Function

This function implements the construction of an SMS push message suitable for submission to a web-based interface provided by one single mobile operator. Depending on how SMS is submitted as discussed in the section on the problems with push technologies, this function can be customized. If a WAP based push framework were being used, this function would probably dynamically generate a WML deck for the presentation of the notification along with the PAP Push Message Control Entity.

You will need to install the `URI::Escape` and `Mail::Address` Perl packages if they are not already installed. An error of the form `"Can't locate URI/Escape.pm in @INC"` will be printed if the script is run and the packages are not installed. In such a case, you will either have to ask your system administrator to add the required packages after downloading them from `http://www.perl.com/CPAN/`, or compile the Perl source and add all the packages after downloading them from the above website. Use the command `"perldoc <modulename>"` to get module specific documentation.

```
# function interfaces    |  IN  |  OUT  |  Description
#-----------------------+------+-------+----------------------------------
# $from                  |  •   |       |  Sender of the email
# $subject               |  •   |       |  Subject of the email
# $date                  |  .•  |       |  Date when the email was sent
# $body                  |  •   |       |  Optional Body of the message
# $post_msg              |      |   •   |  Message suitable for pushing to
#                        |      |       |          a particular SMS operator

sub construct_message {
    my $from = shift;
    my $subject = shift;
    my $date = shift;
    my $body = shift;
    my $post_msg;
    my $fromname;
    my $fromuser;
    my $fromdomain;

    # We have to escape the message as the HTTP POST
    # that will be used for pushing the message can only consist
    # of a restricted set of characters

    use URI::Escape;
    my $subj_date_url_encoded = uri_escape($subject.$date);
    my $body_url_encoded = uri_escape($body);

    use Mail::Address;
    my @addrs = Mail::Address->parse($from);
    $fromname = uri_escape($addrs[0]->name());
    $fromuser = $addrs[0]->user();
    $fromdomain = $addrs[0]->host();

    $post_msg = "requesttype=REMINDER_SERVICE&";
    $post_msg .= "servicetype=WEB&";
    $post_msg .= "accesscode=123456&";
    $post_msg .= "fromname=$fromname&";
    $post_msg .= "mobileno1=$mobile_number1&";
    $post_msg .= "mobileno2=$mobile_number2&";
```

```
    $post_msg .= "mailid1=$fromuser&";
    $post_msg .= "mailid2=$fromdomain&";
    $post_msg .= "choicemessage=$subj_date_url_encoded&";
    $post_msg .= "messagetext=$body_url_encoded";

    return $post_msg;
}
```

sendsms_http () Function

This function uses HTTP POST to submit a previously constructed push message using the specified URL. Although this function is being used for submitting an SMS push message, it can very well be used in a WAP push message with HTTP as the tunnel protocol. This is possible because the construction of the push message is done elsewhere.

You will need to install the "Library for WWW access in Perl" module, also known as LWP. You can get the latest version from http://www.linpro.no/lwp/. Before installing this module, you will also need to install the following modules: URI, HTML::Parser, MIME::Base64, Net::FTP, and Digest::MD5. It seems like a lot of work, but it is not much when compared to making socket connections, writing all the HTTP headers, reading the HTTP responses and interpreting all the response codes yourself over the connection.

```
# function interfaces    |  IN  |  OUT  | Description
#------------------------+------+-------+------------------------------------
# $posturl               |  •   |       | URL where push msg is to be submitted
# $postmsg               |  •   |       | push msg content in suitable syntax
# $httpproxy             |  •   |       | HTTP Proxy Server to be used if any
# return code            |      |   •   | 0 for success or 1 for failure

sub sendsms_http {
    my $posturl = shift;
    my $postmsg = shift;
    my $httpproxy = shift;

    # Create a user agent object
    # "Library for WWW access in Perl" module should be
    # available
    use LWP::UserAgent;

    my $ua = new LWP::UserAgent;
    $ua->agent("Wroxware_SMS_Send/0.1 " . $ua->agent);

    if( $ENV{"http_proxy"} ) {
        $ua->env_proxy();
        # Load the proxy location from the "http_proxy" environment
    } elsif ( !($httpproxy) ) {
        $ua->proxy('http', $httpproxy);
    }

    # Create a request
    my $req = new HTTP::Request POST => $posturl;
    $req->content_type('application/x-www-form-urlencoded');
    $req->content($postmsg);

    # Pass request to the user agent and get a response back
    my $res = $ua->request($req);
```

```
# Check the outcome of the response
if ($res->is_success) {
    return 0;
} else {
    return 1;
}
}
```

Summary

In this chapter, we have discussed push technologies using the Internet, WAP and SMS. However, the main focus has been the WAP based push model. WAP push has only been defined in the WAP 1.2 specifications and implementations are not available as yet, so the examples presented in this chapter were based on Phone.com tools and SMS text messaging, but should give an idea of what push involves. This will be useful for building non-WAP based push applications on the Internet until implementations of WAP 1.2 devices and networks are commercially available.

After discussing the push framework, we focused on a detailed description of the Push Access Protocol (PAP), since this knowledge is necessary for content providers wishing to make use of push technologies.

In the next chapter, we talk about Wireless Telephony Application (WTA), which is again is not yet implemented. Combining push and WTA, it is possible to make the mobile phone, a truly interactive device.

WTA – Interacting with the Mobile Phone

Although there are numerous WAP-enabled PDAs on the market at the moment, the majority of WAP-enabled devices are mobile phones. The WAP 1.2 specifications refer to Wireless Telephony Applications (WTA), which will be particularly relevant to such devices. This also applies to any class of WAP enabled device that supports voice telephony and network text (short messages) functionality. For example, WTA might also be relevant and implemented in a futuristic PDA-like device that also supports many voice telephony features, possibly with voice recognition and other advanced technologies. In this chapter, we will be exploring such applications in the wireless world.

These are the aspects of WTA that we'll cover in this chapter:

- ❑ An introduction to WTA

- ❑ The WTA architecture and the identifiable components in the architecture

- ❑ Security aspects of telephony applications

- ❑ The interface libraries available to content providers for authoring different WTA services

- ❑ A discussion on WTA specific components, such as the repository and event handling

- ❑ Some example applications and application scenarios for WTA

Note that a full listing of the functions provided in the WTAI libraries can be found in Appendix D.

What is WTA?

Wireless Telephony Applications (WTA) are those applications that have mechanisms defined to interact with the telephony related functions present in the mobile phone and those provided by the phone network. Here are some of the telephony related functions that are available on a commonly available mobile phone:

- Making a mobile originated call
- Receiving a call (mobile terminated call)
- Sending and receiving Short Text Messages
- Adding, searching and removing phonebook entries
- Examining call logs, calls made, received or missed on the phone in the past
- Sending DTMF tones during an active voice call
- Pressing keys on the keypad during a call

Some of the other telephony functions available the phone network are:

- Call Hold
- Call Transfer
- Call Forwarding
- Conferencing
- Voicemail
- IN (Intelligent Network) Services

Such functions may or may not be available in all types of mobile phone networks (GSM, CDMA, North American IS136, Japanese PDC etc.)

The WAP 1.2 specifications have defined WTA with a more precise manner than the previous versions. Once mobile phone implementations of WAP 1.2 are commercially available in the market, the mobile phone will become a truly interactive device. It will represent the first practical implementation of different technologies bringing together both the interactive information access – possible today only with computers – and the simplicity of a no-hassles electronic device, making such a device easy to use for people at any skill level. Such a device is the ideal thin-client, as opposed to the ones that are now touted under such a classification, while being a lot more complex to operate.

Every mobile phone, regardless of the type of phone network or the vendor of the phone, defines a **Man Machine Interface (MMI)** or, for the politically correct, **Human Computer Interface (HCI)**, for different uses – phone interactions, to make voice calls, receive them, manipulate the phonebook or send and receive short text messages. Even though each HCI finally accomplishes the same task, the look and feel of the interface can differ between phone models and vendors. Not only is the user interface different, but we also don't have a consistent, device independent and operating environment independent mechanism in which to write telephony applications. In other words, we have no idea how the phone software interacts with the phone operating system, for example for voice call control. Yet it would be good if we could write some simple code to get every WAP phone to behave in a consistent and predictable manner for phone and network specific functionality.

We now present a wish list of features that WTA should have. We will see how WAP takes care of these later in the chapter:

❑ Basic features like making and receiving voice calls should be possible in an interactive, yet device and network independent, manner.

❑ If the network operator/service provider so chooses, it should be possible to provide mechanisms to operate on telephony features like call forwarding, call redirection, call conferencing, and possibly a whole lot of others, with the same user interface for all users, regardless of the vendor of the WAP phone being used.

❑ From simple browsing applications, it should be possible to initiate phone calls just by selecting hyperlinks in a WML deck that is being displayed on the phone.

❑ A URI based naming model should be available to access not only basic telephony features, but also Intelligent Network (IN) services, voicemail or any other network specific features.

Intelligent Networks

According to the ITU-T (International Telecommunications Union) definition, an IN (intelligent network) is "*a telecommunications network architecture that provides flexibility for facilitating the introduction of new capabilities and services, including those under customer control*". What this means is that every subscriber can have value-added services enabled, possibly at an additional cost, and then use it as well as customize it to their needs. Such services are more or less common to both fixed as well as wireless phone networks. Some examples of such services are: call deflection, call forwarding on *busy*, call forwarding on *no reply*, unconditional call forwarding, restriction of calling line identification, explicit call transfer, conferencing, time dependent routing of calls to different numbers, and origin dependent routing of calls to different numbers, for example, forwarding the call automatically to voicemail if your boss calls you during the weekend.

This would be a feature of the network and not of a particular model of phone (such as Nokia, which emulates similar call blocking features, reverse charging to receive calls at the subscriber's own expense and so on). Note that many of the above services are those that were available even before the IN concept, and therefore are not a new feature with IN services. But what makes these features useful when implemented in the IN architecture is that, it is easy for operators to implement newer services at a much lower cost while having the flexibility of customizing it on a per-subscriber basis.

Telecommunications standards define protocols like INAP (Intelligent Network Application Protocol) to communicate with network elements known as IN nodes to enable, configure or disable many features and services. Currently, in most fixed and wireless phone networks, such services are available by dialing operator specified numbers. However, with WAP 1.2 phones and using the WTA architecture, it is possible to have interactive, hyperlinked URI based access to such services. The subscriber doesn't ever have to remember sometimes long phone numbers to access different services.

Fundamentals of the WTA Architecture

The WTA architecture primarily defines the components required in a client device to make telephony services available to WAP content. It also defines the role played by certain network elements. These are the components that constitute the WTA framework:

❑ WTA user agent

❑ WTA server

❑   WTA interface (WTAI) libraries – see the section *WTA Interfaces (WTAI)* – these are libraries implemented on WAP 1.2 capable phones to perform telephony functions when referenced from WML and WMLScript code

❑   A persistent storage or "Repository" – see the section *Repository*

We will discuss the user agent and server in more detail, shortly followed by the WTAI libraries, and repositories will be left until a little later in the chapter.

The following figure illustrates the typical components of the WTA architecture:

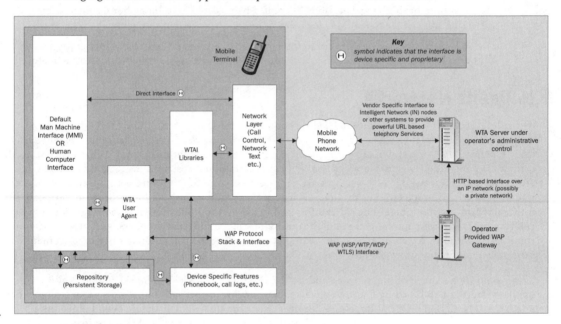

In the above figure, we have ignored a few of the logical components inside a mobile phone (principally the WAE user agent) for the sake of clarity.

WTA User Agent

This user agent is quite similar to a WAE user agent in that it has the ability to execute and present WML and WMLScript content to a user. In fact, it is a WAE user agent in almost every respect including executing content within the boundary of a well-defined context. The primary difference is that a WTA user agent has a very rigid and real-time context management component. For example, it drops stale or outdated network events, does not place intermediate results on a history stack and typically terminates after a network event has been handled if it was not executing before the occurrence of the particular network event. In a WAE user agent, previously loaded decks are stored on the history stack. It is akin to the history of previously visited web pages stored in a web browser, which can be visited using the browser's Back button. Unlike web browsers, the lifetime of some context variables in a WAE User Agent can last longer than a single deck and such variables are typically stored on the history stack, and are known as stored intermediate results. In the case of a WTA user agent, this doesn't happen.

WTA Server

A **WTA server** is nothing more than a web server where WTA content and services are hosted. The primary distinction from any other origin server is that the mobile network operator regards it as a 'Trusted Content Server'. Typically such servers are under the administrative control of the operator so that the nature of the services provided is under the operator's complete control. It is also possible for the operator to delegate the administration and management of WTA server(s) to one or more trusted third party WTA providers. The term 'trusted' in this case means that the third party providers are contractually obliged to ensure that no security lapses occur while providing the WTA services. The reasons a WTA Server must be a trusted server will become clear in the next section on *WTA Security*.

> There is no such thing as a non-operator controlled WTA server, since the operator directly or indirectly controls the WTA services that can be offered. It is therefore not possible for any content provider on the Internet to provide the complete set of WTA services. This requirement comes directly from WAP 1.2 specifications for WTA and any standards compliant implementation will adhere to this.

The WTA server can also have proprietary extensions and interfaces to a 'Mobile Switching Center' and other mobile network elements for enabling more IN services. These services can be referenced through a URL. The server-side executable content can then interface with the mobile network elements to get access to such services. For example, a voicemail system can have a URL such as `http://wta.operator.com/voicemail`. This consistent URL interface, together with the ability to program the mobile phone by loading some content on to its persistent storage, means that it is possible for a mobile operator to provide access to its services automatically; the most the user has to do is switch on the mobile phone! Refer to the separate sections on *Repository* and *Event Handling* for a complete picture.

As a matter of fact, it would not matter which vendor or model of the phone a subscriber is using or which services it supports through the default user interface (or HCI), as long as the phone supports the WAP 1.2 specifications. Of course, this is possible only if a WTA server is provided and the required WDP Port is enabled on the WAP Gateway. This mechanism provides a powerful model to seamlessly integrate services available locally on the mobile phone with the value-added services an operator is providing, while keeping the user interface the same. As long as the phone is WAP 1.2 compliant, it should make no difference who the manufacture of the particular handset is. In this manner, the operator can provide the same user instructions for the WTA services it offers, without having to say, for example, "Nokia phone users please use the following procedure A, Ericsson users follow B, ..."

WTA Security

Telephony services have a stronger security requirement than other types of WAP services. The nature of the operations possible when executing WTA content mean it is not wise for the architecture to allow just anybody to write WTA content and execute it on a user's phone. If an unknown third party content developer on the Internet could have access to the complete set of WTA operations, it would be quite easy to write malicious WML and WMLScript code, for example, to erase an entire phonebook, make random phone calls or send all your personal phonebook data through SMS to a mobile spammer.

The question that we are now faced with is, "How is it possible for the architecture to prevent anyone from writing WTA content and getting it executed on a user's mobile phone?"

Some of the measures and architectural decisions taken to ensure security have been listed here:

❑ The WTA user agent uses a secure WDP port on the WAP gateway for the WSP sessions it needs. The WDP specification specifies that the port number 2805 on the WAP gateway be used for 'WAP WTA secure connection-less session service'. The WTA user agent is also required to discard any content received outside a session established over a non-secure port. The term for a WSP session established over the secure port is now a **WTA session**.

❑ The WAP gateway has to ensure a secure link between itself and the WTA server, either using a private network or by means of strong authentication mechanisms.

❑ The user configures the mobile phone to specify user permissions for the execution of different WTAI library functions. WTA specifications currently do not specify the default user permissions that would apply when you buy the mobile phone. But every phone implementation for the sake of security will probably require user approval, at least the first time a particular WML deck starts using a specific WTAI function, unless the user chooses to change the permissions. There are three user permission types.

In the following table, we have used the term **executable**. In the current context of discussion it refers to any content that calls at least one WTAI function (either in the URL or the Script form). Therefore, we can say that the following qualify to be called executables:

❑ WML or WMLScript content originating from a WTA server that makes calls to WTAI library functions when it executes in the WTA user agent.

❑ WML or WMLScript content stored in the phone's **repository** that makes calls to the WTAI when it executes in the WTA user agent. A repository is a persistent storage module to store WTA content and is discussed in detail in the section, *Repository*.

❑ WML or WMLScript content originating somewhere on the Internet that executes in a WAE user agent and references one or more functions in the Public WTAI Library.

The user permission types are summarized in the table below:

Permission Type	Description
Blanket permission	The user gives blanket permission to the executable for the specified WTAI library function. The executable uses the original permission for all subsequent WTAI functions called whenever it is running.
Context permission	The user gives permission to the executable for the specified WTAI function during a specific run-time context. The executable subsequently has the user's permission for identified WTAI functions while the executable context is still running.
Single action permission	The user gives a single permission to the executable for the specified WTAI function; if the executable subsequently wishes to call the WTAI function again, it must request the user's permission once more, for the WTAI function.

The onus of providing an acceptable level of security lies with the mobile network operator. It is possible to do this only if:

❏ The mobile network operator has administrative control over the WTA server or at least has a trust relationship with the provider of the WTA server.

❏ The mobile network operator controls or at least has a trust relationship with the provider of a WAP gateway that is used by its subscribers

This is only possible as long as the phone or device is configured to use the network operator's gateway. If you configure your mobile phone to use a WAP gateway that is not trusted, then there is a security threat. For example, if you are browsing with the WTA user agent using a non-trusted WAP gateway, the gateway could have been programmed to deliver malicious content that could snoop on your phonebook and send network text messages of the information to somewhere where it could be collected. This opens up a Pandora's box of privacy and security issues.

> **It is recommended that you disable all WTA services if you are temporarily using a WAP gateway other than the one provided by someone you trust (for example, your mobile network operator).**

If you follow the above suggestions, WAP security models will ensure that we would never have to experience a mobile phone virus, probably the wireless world equivalent of the recent 'LOVE BUG' e-mail virus that affected millions of users of Microsoft Outlook software.

Initiation of WTA Services

WTA services can be initiated in a number of ways:

❏ *The user can initiate access by selecting a URL whose content is hosted on the WTA server:* For example, call forwarding identified by a URL. Another example is when a user initiates access to a URL and the content that is normally retrieved has been stored in the repository in a channel. In this case the content is retrieved directly from the repository.

❏ *Via push content over a secure WTA session:* For example, the WTA server may send a new voicemail notification when it is informed of this by the voicemail system.

❏ *A WTA event triggering an event handler:* For example, an incoming call selection WML deck that presents the user a list of choices on how to handle an incoming call (accept, reject, deflect or forward to with voicemail).

WTA Interfaces (WTAI)

All mobile phones that support the WAP 1.2 specifications implement interface libraries on the phone that can be used to build telephony applications. These interface libraries consist of functions for various telephony and network services and they can be invoked either as URLs in a WML card/deck or via WMLScript functions executing in a WTA or WAE user agent context. Content providers can therefore write simple WML and WMLScript code for invoking the telephony functions of the mobile phone.

Such a library provides a device independent and network independent interface that is completely under the control of the content provider, unlike the default HCI provided by each device. (In addition to the standard libraries there are also network specific libraries, like the ones that have been defined for GSM, North American IS136 and Japanese PDC systems that are not network independent).

The libraries are akin to the Java and JavaScript libraries that are available on a plethora of operating environments. Each one provides the same interface to application developers for carrying out a task, although the implementation will be specific to the vendor and model of the phone.

The function libraries are broadly classified into three types:

❑   Public WTAI function libraries

❑   Network common WTAI function libraries

❑   Network specific WTAI function libraries

The WTA specification is a more definitive guide on the specifics of each function in the above libraries, but we'll be looking at some of the most interesting in this chapter, and you can find a full listing of these functions in Appendix D.

First, however, we take a look at how these library functions are called.

Calling WTAI Functions

There are two ways of calling WTAI functions: as a URI within a WML deck or as a WMLScript function.

URI Schemes

The URI scheme used to access WTAI functions begins with a `wtai://`. All URI escaping rules apply to the WTAI URI and therefore many of the disallowed characters will have to be encoded as `%XX` entities, where XX is a hexadecimal number that identifies the particular character. The generic syntax is as follows:

```
wtai://<library>/<function>;<parameter>;<parameter>![<result>];[<result>]
```

Where:

❑   `<library>`: Name of the library. An example is "vc" which is for Voice Call Control.

❑   `<function>`: Identifier of the specific function in the library. An example is "rc" which identifies the Release Call function in the Voice Call Control library.

❑   `<parameter>`: The parameters for the function. One or more can be included separated by semi-colons.

❑   `<result>`: Zero or more return values can be specified delimited by a semi-colon. The WTAI function fills up the variables with any return values.

The square brackets above signify an optional value. The exclamation mark (!) is required only if a return value is specified.

Here's an example in the URI form of the function and you can compare this with the WMLScript version discussed in the next paragraph. Both of them are equivalent calls to the same WTAI function. We use the Release Call from the WTA Voice Call Control library:

```
wtai://vc/rc;0!retval
```

In the above example, 0 is a parameter that is passed to the function and the returned value is stored in the variable `retval`.

WMLScript Syntax

When calling a function using WMLScript, each library is identified by a name that is different from the one used when calling the function using a URI in a WML deck. For example, the Voice Call Control library is identified by the name WTAVoiceCall when using WMLScript, but is identified as vc" when using a URI. Similarly every interface function inside the library is also identified by a name that is different from the corresponding function name used in the URI scheme. For example, the Voice Call Control library function for Release Call, that is rc in the URI format, is release in WMLScript.

Here's an example of a WTAI function call in WMLScript:

```
WTAVoiceCall.release("0");
```

Public WTAI Functions

These are the most basic set of functions; they can be called from content originating from any server and not just a trusted WTA server and on the WAE user agent.

As we know by now, content originating from any web server will be executed by the WAE user agent, while the same content will only be executed by the WTA user agent if it originates from a trusted WTA server in the service provider's mobile network. There is a limited set of telephony functions available to any third-party content provider, and they execute on the WAE user agent. All such functions have been grouped under this Public WTA Library.

There are currently only three functions in the public library:

- ❑ Make a call
- ❑ Send DTMF tones
- ❑ Add a phone book entry.

If you are a third-party content provider who has no arrangements with a mobile service provider for WTA services, then these functions are the only ones you need to know about. A third-party content provider will make arrangements with the operator by way of signing contracts and Memorandums of Understanding (MoUs). The operator-provided WAP Gateway would then authenticate the provider's WTA server so that WTA content originating from this provider is allowed by the gateway.

Make a Call

This function initiates a call, originating from a mobile device, using the specified phone number. Implementations of this function are required to display the phone number before the call is made. Such a call cannot be terminated using another function from the public library. Users will have to rely on standard HCI mechanisms provided by their mobile phones to terminate the call (such as the off button). Here is an example, first in URI form:

```
wtai://wp/mc;+91805553232!retcode
```

Note that we have used an international phone number with country code, area code and the phone number. As a web programmer you might think that the + character needs to be URL escaped, but that is not required here because the above URL does not actually reference a remote location, just a WTAI function which accepts the unescaped + sign. The WTAI specifications allow only the characters + and 0-9 to be used wherever a phone number is expected.

Here is the WMLScript form of the function:

```
var retcode = WTAPublic.makeCall("+91805553232");
```

> In the above example (as well as for the rest of the WTAI library functions) we have
> used the variable **retcode**, which holds the return value of the corresponding
> function call. If the value is negative (< 0), it indicates that an error was
> encountered.

Here's a more complete example that simply asks the user to enter a phone number and places a call to
the number that you enter:

```
<?xml version="1.0"?>
<!DOCTYPE wml PUBLIC "-//WAPFORUM//DTD WML 1.2//EN"
"http://www.wapforum.org/DTD/wml12.dtd">

<wml>
  <card id="makecall" title="Simple Make Call Example">
    <do type="accept">
      <go href="wtai://wp/mc;$number" />
    </do>
    <p>
        Enter a phone number to call:
        <input name="number" format="*N" emptyok="false" />
    </p>
  </card>
</wml>
```

At the time of writing, no phone vendor supports WAP 1.2 completely and therefore nobody supports
all the functions defined in WTAI. However, some phone vendors, like Ericsson and phone.com
support the Public WTAI library, although Nokia is yet to support a WTA feature. Even Ericsson's
R380 Emulator recognizes the 'Make Call' URL in WML code and we are able to see the following
messages on the display of the emulator. It is just an example of how one particular emulator would
behave since it is not possible to emulate WTA functions as completely as WAE browsing:

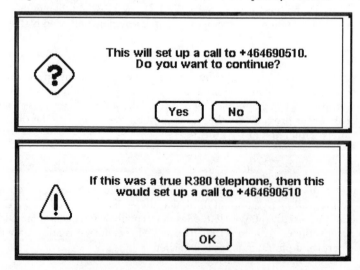

Send DTMF Tones

This function is used to send tones corresponding to certain characters (that can be generated on any phone by pressing the keys on the keypad) through an active voice connection. The allowed characters are the digits 0-9, *, #, ",", A, B, C and D. Typically such tones are sent to automated call servers, such as PABXes, to convey more information after the voice call is setup. For example, if someone is calling my office, they must first dial my office phone number and then, once the switchboard answers the call and the automated greeting is heard, they must dial my extension number. The extension number is sent as DTMF (Dual Tone Multi Frequency) tones that is decoded by the switchboard, to transfer the call correctly. Another example is in automated telephone banking where menu choices are conveyed by way of DTMF tones.

Here is an example for the usage of the sd, send DTMF tone, function, first in URI form:

```
wtai://wp/sd;7000#4366#9087!retcode
```

In the above code, the entire string, 7000#4366#9087, forms the DTMF tone string that would cause the phone to send these tones over an active voice call. The above sequence for example, allows me to log on to my voicemail system. So 7000 is the extension that identifies the voicemail, 4366 is my extension number and 9087 is my password to log on to the system. This sequence of DTMF tones will obviously vary from vendor to vendor of your PABX and voicemail systems.

Here is the WMLScript form:

```
var retcode = WTAPublic.sendDTMF("7000#4366#9087");
```

Add a Phonebook Entry

Every mobile phone provides a phonebook containing many records, each having a name and a phone number. This function is used to add an entry into the default phonebook available in the mobile phone. It is possible in some types of phone systems to have more than one phonebook, one of which will be considered as the default phonebook. For example, GSM phones typically allow a phonebook to be stored in the memory of either the phone or the SIM card. Most phones allow you to cause entries to be added to only one phonebook at any given time. Here is an example, first in URI form:

```
wtai://wp/ap;+91805553232;Shashi!retcode
```

And then in WMLScript form:

```
var retcode = WTAPublic.addPBEntry("+91805553232", "Shashi");
```

Although the provision of this function in the public library may be perceived as a security risk, there is actually no risk of losing any data. The worst that a malicious content provider on the Internet can do is to fill up your phone book with junk entries and this will not have any effect on the existing entries. The user can always erase the junk entries and stay well away from the particular site that caused this.

Network Common WTAI

The functions defined in this class of libraries apply to all types of mobile phone networks that support WAP. All phones implementing WTA are required to implement this class of libraries. However, only content that executes in a WTA user agent, which means content originating from a trusted WTA server, can make calls to the functions defined in this class of libraries. It is therefore not possible for content from any third-party content providers on the Internet, for example, to use these functions.

In addition to functions that are similar to the ones defined in the Public WTAI, this set of libraries provides many more functions that enable the writing of fine-grained telephony applications. Apart from the provision for making function calls to use a telephony feature, it is also possible for a WTA user agent to be notified of certain network events that may or may not occur as a direct result of a prior action. Such events can be captured using the WML <onevent> element, and suitable actions can then be taken. For example, an 'incoming call indication' event may result in a message being displayed on the phone and the WML code might then make a call to the 'accept call' library function to accept the incoming call.

Before we take a closer look at these libraries, let's first examine network events.

Network Events

Unlike the Public WTAI library, where telephony actions are always initiated by the mobile device, the Network Common WTAI has many network originating telephony events for which WTA events are defined. Whenever a network event occurs (for example, an incoming call), it is the responsibility of the WAP/WTA implementation in the mobile phone to deliver the event to the WTA user agent if the agent is being executed and event handling has been defined for that event. If a network event has occurred, the WTA user agent has not been initiated or no event handling is defined, the network event is handled by the default HCI of the phone. Refer to the section *Event Handling* later in this chapter if you are curious about how such events are handled. Right now, we will only list all the predefined WTAI network events and their meanings.

> The WAE user agent is not able to receive and react to telephony and network text events, such as SMS. Only the WTA user agent is allowed to do this.

In the following table, *Event Name* is a short form for the name of the event, *EventID* is the identifier that can be used in WML code to write event handlers, *Parameters* refers to the information that would be available upon handling each of those events, and *Description* offers additional information on when an event occurs:

Event Name	EventID	Parameters	Description
cc/ic	wtaev-cc/ic	<id>, Internal Identity of the call. <callerID>, The phone number of the calling party if available.	**Call Control/Incoming Call Indication** event that can be picked up by the calling the WTAI function 'Accept Call'.
cc/cl	wtaev-cc/cl	<id>. <result>, Indicates why the call was cleared.	**Call Control/Call Cleared** event. The connected call, or the call that has been placed but not yet connected, is disconnected.
cc/co	wtaev-cc/co	<id>. <callerID>.	**Call Control/Call Connected** event. The called party has accepted the incoming call.
cc/oc	wtaev-cc/oc	<id>. <callerID>.	**Call Control/Outgoing Call Indication** event. An outgoing call is being placed by the user.

Event Name	EventID	Parameters	Description
cc/cc	wtaev-cc/cc	`<id>`.	**Call Control/Outgoing Call Alert Indication** event. An outgoing call is now ringing at the destination party's phone.
cc/dtmf	wtaev-cc/dtmf	`<resultstring>`, DTMF character sequence.	**Call Control/DTMF sequence Sent** event.
nt/it	wtaev-nt/it	`<id>`. `<sender>`, The address or phone number of the sending party if available.	**Network Text/Incoming Text Indication** event. A Network Text message (SMS for example) has been received.
nt/st	wtaev-nt/st	`<Text-ID>`, Internal identity of the text sent.	**Network Text/Network Text Sent** event. (For example, an SMS message).

ms/ns	wtaev-ms/ns	`<camping>`, Boolean TRUE if the phone is able to make and receive calls, otherwise FALSE.
		 `<networkName>`, Name of the network to which the phone is connected.
		 `<notCampingCause>`, Reason for not being able to connect to the network:
		   0 (No Network Found)
		   1 (Only Forbidden Networks Found)
			Miscellaneous/Network Status Indication event. This event is typically sent when certain network parameters change. For example, when there is a handover from one base station to another during the course of a call, when there is a change in the location of the phone in the network in idle mode or when there is a change in the network to which the phone is communicating with.

The WML or WMLScript content can reference the above event parameters using a numbering scheme starting from top to bottom in the parameter list. For example, the first parameter is referenced by a variable $1, the second as $2 and so on.

> *WAP 1.2 specifications require that a WTA user agent will have enough space to hold at least 10 event parameters and 250 characters (for all parameters in a single event put together). Currently there are no events with 10 parameters; the greatest number is three.*

Voice Call Control Library

This library contains a total of six functions to handle the commonly available voice call control functionality of all kinds of wireless phone networks. Its name is vc in URI form, or WTAVoiceCall as part of WMLScript. It includes functions for setting up a new call and accepting and releasing a call. It can also be used to send DTMF (dual tone multi frequency) tones and to check the call status.

An example of its application is for routing calls through a switchboard automatically. It should be possible to configure a script to dial a switchboard and then dial through to an extension for you. It is likely that this would be as part of an event handler. Imagine this example: a script could initiate a call to the voicemail when a text message informing the client that a new message has been recorded, is received.

It can also be used to initiate a call from a WML deck, and could be very useful when combined with push technology (as discussed in the previous chapter). The call functions are similar in functionality to the Public WTAI 'make call' function. However, unlike its counterpart in the Public WTAI, the functions provided in this library can terminate or release the call as well.

vc Library Functions Example

Finally, we will end this section with an example. The example presents a list of food choices to a user and sets up a call to the corresponding phone number where the particular type of food can be ordered:

```
<?xml version="1.0"?>
<!DOCTYPE wml PUBLIC "-//WAPFORUM//DTD WML 1.2//EN"
"http://www.wapforum.org/DTD/wml12.xml">

<wml>
  <card id="eFood">
    <p>
      <do type="accept">
        <go href="wtai://vc/sc;$FoodNum;1" />
      </do>
      Choose Food:
      <select name="FoodNum">
        <option value="5556789">Pizza</option>
        <option value="5551234">Chinese</option>
        <option value="5553344">Sandwich</option>
        <option value="5551122">Burger</option>
      </select>
    </p>
  </card>
</wml>
```

In this scenario the WML code may have been browsed on a trusted gateway or may have been pushed to the user.

Network Text Library

This library provides functions to send and receive network text messages (SMS is one name for this type of messages). The URI form of the function calls, that we have been using in the previous two libraries, is unavailable in this library. These functions are only available from WMLScript functions. The library for is called WTANetText.

Functions provided include 'Send Text', which takes a phone number and a string and transmits the message. Errors including failure to send and wrong number can be tested with the return value. Messages can be read and deleted with the use of scripting and we can also get information about the message, including the time it was sent, the senders address as well as its status (unread, read, written and sent).

Phonebook Library

This library provides functions that store, retrieve or search for entries in the default phonebook present in every mobile phone. Again the URI form of the functions is unavailable. The WMLScript library name is WTAPhoneBook and the associated functions are write(), read(), remove(), getFieldValue() and change().

Lets see an example function that uses the `remove` function of the library:

```
function removePBEntryByName( name ) {
  var structfield = WTAPhoneBook.read( "name", name );
  if( $structfield != "" ) {
    var pbentryid = WTAPhoneBook.getFieldValue( $struct, "id" );
    WTAPhoneBook.remove(pbentryid);
  }
}
```

This function is passed a parameter name, which is the name of the phonebook entry. The function begins with a call to `read()`, which returns a string containing all the fields for that entry. Each field can then be extracted by name using the `getFieldValue()` function of the WTAPhoneBook library by passing it the returned string and the name of the field whose value we wish to extract.

The `change()` function allows us to update values for any of the fields in a phonebook entry. The phone number can be updated, for example, by passing the function the name of the phonebook entry, the field name and the new value for the field.

WTAPhonebook example

The following is a WMLScript file called `addpbentry.wmls`. It implements the required functions to add an entry into the phonebook:

```
extern function addPbEntry( nametoadd, phoneno )
{
```

We use this function to determine where to add the entry in the phone book. We check for the last entry in the phonebook using the function `LastIDinPhoneBook()` (which we will see in a moment) and add the entry into the book. The name and phone number of the entry are passed as parameters of the function, as you can see above.

```
var lastid = LastIDinPhoneBook();
var ret;
var ret = WTAPhoneBook.write( lastid + 1, nametoadd, phoneno );
```

If there is an error, `ret` is set with a negative value, and a browser variable, `Msg`, is set with the value `"Error"` and the browser is then forwarded to a card called `displayMsg`. All this card does is display the value in `Msg`:

```
if( ret < 0 )
{
  WMLBrowser.setVar("Msg", "Error");
}
else
{
  var str = "Entry Successfully Written at id: ";
  str += nextid;
  WMLBrowser.setVar("Msg", str );
}
// Go to the card whose id is "displayMsg"
Browser.go("displayMsg");
}
```

We saw `LastIDinPhoneBook()` being called earlier. This function iterates through each entry in the phonebook until it finds an empty one and then returns the ID of the last non-empty phonebook entry:

```
function LastIDinPhoneBook()
{
  var ret;
  var id;
  while( (ret = WTAPhoneBook.read( "id", "" )) != "" )
    {
      id = ret;
    }
  return id;
}
```

The front end of the example is a WML file called `addpbentry.wml`, which takes a name and a phone number and calls the function in `addpbentry.wmls` to add the entry:

```
<?xml version="1.0"?>
<!DOCTYPE wml PUBLIC "-//WAPFORUM//DTD WML 1.2//EN"
"http://www.wapforum.org/DTD/wml12.xml">

<wml>
  <card id="phonebookupdate">
    <do type="accept">
      <go href="addpbentry.wmls#addPbEntry($name, $number)" />
    </do>
    <p>
      Enter the name of the person for whom the Phonebook is to be updated:
      <input name="name" format="*A" emptyok="false" />
      Enter the his/her phone number:
      <input name="number" format="M*N" emptyok="false" />
    </p>
  </card>
  <card id="displayMsg">
    $Msg
  </card>
</wml>
```

In the above script, the format string `"*A"` means that the entry of any upper-case alphabetic or punctuation character is allowed. Similarly the string `"M*N"` means that the first character can be anything in order to accommodate a + sign, and after that only numbers can be entered. Recall that formatting user input was discussed back in Chapter 5.

Call Logs Library

Every mobile phone has a mechanism to store a set of logs (or call registers) for phone calls made, received or missed. The Call Logs library provides functions to read such logs. Again, the URI forms of the functions are unavailable. The name of library is `WTACallLog` and includes the functions `dialled()`, `missed()`, `received()` and `getFieldValue()` of course.

`dialled()` retrieves the last called number whose index is passed in the argument. The index is zero based from newest to oldest as usual. `missed()` is the list of calls missed by the user, which covers those calls where the caller hung up before the call was dealt with. `received()` works in the same way as `dialled()` but for incoming calls and `getFieldValue()` works as usual.

Miscellaneous Library

This library contains functions that cannot be classified under any particular category of functions. Again the URI form of the functions is unavailable in all cases except one. The library is called, understandably enough, WTAMisc and covers mainly configuration of the phone with regards to the WTA and telephony functions. Functions include indication(), endcontext() (ec within WML), and protected().

indication() controls turning on or off the indication of the occurrence of various functionalities of the phone. In English, this means turning on/off being notified when a voicemail, e-mail or text message has arrived, notification of incoming fax or data call or indeed notification of incoming voice calls.

endcontext() terminates the context for the user agent. This would be whenever the function that it serves and possible future operations have been carried out or resolved. For example, a WML deck stored in the repository handling incoming calls simply needs to terminate as soon as the user has selected one of the possible choices that were displayed to him. Unlike a WAE user agent, where there might be an almost infinite set of hyperlinks to traverse, the code would have just one function and so a limited set of hyperlinks. Once the deck completes the required actions and terminates the context, it might be a while before the user uses another WTA service.

protected() allows us to control whether or not a WTA can be interrupted during an operation. Typically, this function is used to indicate whether the context can be interrupted by the arrival of WTA events. For example, sometimes the author of the WTA content might not want the display of the content to be interrupted by, say an incoming call or an incoming short message. The URI form is not available.

Network Specific WTAI

Apart from the above common set of WTAI libraries, there are some mobile phone network type specific libraries. Currently libraries have been defined for GSM, IS136 and PDC (Japan) based systems. Each one of these defines functions that carry out actions specific to the type of network. For example, the GSM library defines additional network events to handle 'Unstructured Supplementary Services Data' (USSD) message strings, call held and call active indications. It also defines functions to do call transfer, call reject, call deflection, join multiparty or provide location information. Refer to the network specific addenda available at http://www.wapforum.org/. A very important GSM specific function is the one that provides location information. The information returned contains the mobile country code, the mobile network code, the location area code and the cell identifier. Applications can make use of this to deliver customized content that depends on the geographic area where the user currently is located.

WTA State Model

The WTA state model is an extension of the standard WAE model and shares all the aspects of session management, user agent context and handling push content. The extension in the model occurs in:

- ❑ Call state management, which defines how an ongoing call should be handled when the user agent context is terminated
- ❑ Content repository
- ❑ A framework for handling WTA network events and managing the parameters associated with the events.

We will now examine these extensions in order.

Call State Management

WTA defines how a call, which is established in the context of a WTA service that is currently executing, must be handled when that context is terminated. If a call has been established by a service in another context or by way of the default HCI, it will not be affected. The content author for the WTA service can set the mode of the call state management to one of the modes given below, by setting a <mode> parameter in the Setup Call and Accept Call functions in the Voice Call library. The mode parameter can take one of these values:

- ❑ **DROP** (mode value 0) – indicates that the call state is tightly coupled with the WTA context in which the call was established. In the event of the WTA context terminating before the call is dropped, the user agent MUST terminate the call.

- ❑ **KEEP** (mode value 1) – indicates no coupling between the call state and the WTA context in which the call was established. In the event of the WTA context terminating before the call is dropped, the user agent MUST NOT terminate the call. It is up to the user to terminate the call using the HCI mechanism for this.

Repository

The **repository** is a persistent storage module within the mobile phone that may be used to eliminate the need for network access when loading and executing frequently used WTA services. This forms an important component of the WTA framework because it removes the latency associated with pulling the content over the network before executing it. Most users are accustomed to slight delays when they are browsing using a WAE user agent, mostly because they are aware that the content might be hosted far away from where they are trying to access it. However, in the case of telephony applications, they will expect responses to be received instantaneously. This is especially true for WTA applications, because a large number of telephony applications are written so that they can replace the phone provided default HCI mechanisms for such services. For example, if a certain application displays a list of choices to the user to handle an incoming call, the user would expect the choices to be offered as soon as the incoming call is detected – not after a delay. However, this delay would be necessary if the content needed to display the choices had to be downloaded from a remote location.

The physical storage from which the memory is derived for such a repository is implementation dependent, but typically it will either be non-volatile RAM present in the mobile phone, or memory on the SIM card. Entire WML decks together with all embedded hyperlinks (images, WMLScript files that have been referenced in the deck, etc.) will be stored in the repository.

> *Provisioning of a repository for WTA Services is analogous to having web pages available for offline browsing, the way it is possible in Internet Explorer 5. Note that a repository is only provided for WTA Services and not shared or provided to other WAE Services, as per WAP 1.2 specifications. However, the repository is not analogous to a browser cache because it is not in the hands of the user or the content provider to control what is stored or deleted in it.*

The WTA specifications are used to classify the content stored in the repository; they have coined some new terms for the stored content, namely **channels** and **resources**.

Resources

Resources are data that have been downloaded to the mobile device using WSP (for example, a WML deck or a WBMP image), and are stored along with their meta-data (for example, content type, HTTP 1.1 entity-tag and location (URL)).

Channels

A channel is a special resource that contains a set of links to other resources and some control information, including one that would uniquely identify it from other channels stored in the repository. It provides the required framework for storing content in the repository. Channels have an identity and 'freshness' associated with them. The freshness of a channel is determined by the HTTP meta-data expiry-date header that is associated with it. If a channel has expired, it is considered 'stale' and can be removed automatically by the user agent whenever it performs some kind of garbage collection.

A logical representation of the repository is illustrated in the diagram below:

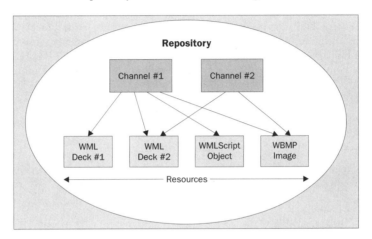

A resource may be referenced by more than one channel, as illustrated in the above diagram. A resource is considered 'stale' if it is NOT referenced by at least one channel which has itself not been marked stale. A channel is accessible to the WTA user agent only after all the resources referenced by it are available in the repository. To reiterate, a channel is like the HTML page that references images, sections of script and the markup contained in it. Resources are the images and scripts and WML decks that are linked together by a channel or channels.

Programming the Repository

A separate **Channel Content Format** has been defined in order to program the repository with the channel and resources – that is, to add a new channel or modify an existing one together with its corresponding resources. A document in the above format is called a **Channel Document** and is defined using a language called **Channel**, an XML language like other content formats used in WAP. To store the content identified by resources in the repository – WML decks, WMLScript decks, WBMP images and so on – it is sufficient to somehow deliver the channel document to the WTA user agent.

The delivery of the channel document could be done in one of the following ways:

❑ Pushing the channel document to the mobile phone using the push framework (see Chapter 17) either directly or using a Service Indication (SI). A possible scenario, where push could be used, is when a mobile user has bought a new subscription for their phone and has just turned the phone on. The network can recognize that such a subscriber is online for the first time and could indicate to the WTA server that it needs to install the new channels for the added services to the mobile phone. The WTA server can use a push framework to deliver one or more channel documents. The WTA server therefore acts as a Push Initiator.

643

❑ The operator can advertise the URL for a WML deck that is hosted on the WTA server, which contains a list of channels that could be downloaded. A user then accesses the advertised URL using the WTA user agent, and selects URLs in the WML deck that will then deliver channel content over the WSP GET or POST response.

> **Once the channel document is made available to the WTA user agent, the responsibility of downloading all the resources referenced by the channel and storing them in the repository lies with the WTA user agent.**

The MIME media type and subtype for the channel document are textual form (text/vnd.wap.channel) and tokenized form (application/vnd.wap.channelc). An example channel document is given below and some of the most important channel XML elements and entities will be discussed immediately after the example. This example references the following resources "incoming.wml", "operatorlogo.wbmp" and "script.wmls". These are relative URLs with respect to the base URL "http://wta.operator.com/".

```
Content-Type: text/vnd.wap.channel

<?xml version="1.0">
<!DOCTYPE channel PUBLIC "-//WAPFORUM//DTD CHANNEL 1.0//EN" channel_1.0.dtd>

<channel
    maxspace="2048"
    base="http://wta.operator.com/"
    EventId="wtaev-cc/ic"
    success="success.wml"
    failure="failure.wml">

    <title>
        IncomingCall
    </title>

    <abstract>
        Incoming Call Selection Service
    </abstract>

    <resource href="incoming.wml" lastmod="957118708" etag="000002"
        md5="4gV5V2/b0qg+BsZRydnWEw==" />
    <resource href="operatorlogo.wbmp" lastmod="957118801" etag="000001"
        md5="Q2hlY2sgSW50ZWdyaXR5IQ==" />
    <resource href="script.wmls" lastmod="957118618" etag="0000010"
        md5="d2kljsdf+8jknsu6qweipw==" />
</channel>
```

maxspace Attribute

The maxspace attribute specifies the maximum memory, in bytes, that is used by the channel. The server will have to guarantee that the sum of all the bytes in all the resources of the channel will not exceed this value. The client may opt not to install the channel should the maxspace be excessive or otherwise unacceptable (for example, too large for its available memory). In the above case it is given that the channel will not be more than 2kb in combined size.

base Attribute

This specifies the base URL for the contents of the channel so that relative URLs can be used to specify the location of the resources. Because this is an XML "#IMPLIED" attribute, if it is absent, the resource URLs must be absolute.

success and failure Attributes

The WTA user agent will make a request for the success URL present in the value of the success attribute upon successful installation of the channel resources. Quite obviously, the user agent will make a request for the failure URL present in the failure attribute in case of failure in the installation. The content thus retrieved is executed and presented to the user; this can be used for error handling.

EventID Attribute

In the above example, you can see that the EventID attribute for the channel element has been specified to be "wtaev-cc/ic", which is the Call Control/Incoming Call event. What this means is that, on the occurrence of such an event, the content present in the channel must be executed by the WTA user agent, subject to certain event binding conditions (which will be discussed in the section *Event Handling* in a moment). Does it mean that all channels present in the repository *must* be associated with an event? The answer is no. For channels that are not associated with any WTA event, this attribute specifies the identity of the channel. For instance, a channel might be present to send network text and, since only the user invoking it can trigger the execution of content in this channel, no event is associated with it.

lastmode, etag and md5 Attributes in the Resource Element

If present, these attributes help in determining the freshness of the resources already present in the repository. lastmode is the last time the resource was changed and etag specifies the relationship between versions of a resource.

For instance, let's say that Channel#1 and Channel#2 both reference Resource#1 and the resources required for Channel#1 have already been installed in the repository. When Channel#2 is somehow delivered to the WTA user agent, the user agent should download all the resources referenced by it, but in this case maybe with the exception of Resource#1. If the WTA user agent determines that any of these attributes differ for Resource#1 between the one present in the repository and the one in the Channel#2 document that was just received, it will request the resource from the server replacing the one in the repository, so that the latest and correct version can be stored in the repository.

- ❏ lastmode gives the last modified time of the resource on the origin server. The format of the lastmode attribute is an unsigned integer number representing the number of seconds from January 1, 1970, 00:00 UTC.

- ❏ etag is called the entity tag. Entity tags are used for comparing two or more versions of the same resource. The user agent can check the differences in the etag attribute to determine how fresh a resource is.

   For more details on the above attributes, you should refer to HTTP/1.1 specifications – RFC2616 available at http://www.ietf.org/rfc/rfc2616.txt.

- ❏ md5 is an MD5 digest of the resource-content for the purpose of providing an **end-to-end message integrity check (MIC)** of the resource-content. (Note: a MIC is good for detecting accidental modification of the entity-body in transit, but is not proof against malicious attacks.)

> *An MD5 digest is a base64 representation of a 128 bit binary code that can be calculated using the MD5 message digest algorithm defined in RFC1321 available at* `http://www.ietf.org/rfc/rfc1321.txt.` *Any modification in the resource-content during transit will result in a mismatch between the computed digest and the digest present in the XML attribute.*

Event Handling

The WTA user agent can be programmed so that it can take the necessary actions upon receiving WTA events. Due to the real-time nature of telephony events, it is necessary for the user agent to be able to respond immediately and execute the code appropriate to the event. This is the primary reason that events can only be associated with:

❑　Content present in the repository, using the `EventID` attribute in the channel document

❑　Content currently being executed by the WTA user agent in a well-defined context, using the `<onevent>` element

Such content is known as an **Event Handler**.

> **It is NOT possible to associate WTA events with content available remotely in a WTA server. Event Handlers must either be in the repository or must be currently executing in the context of the WTA user agent. It is therefore not possible to write code that would say "on occurrence of a particular event, download the content from the WTA server and execute it in the WTA user agent context".**

If an event handler for a particular event is present in the repository, we say that a **Global Binding** exists for that particular event. Similarly, if an event handler for a particular event is present in the content currently being executed by the WTA user agent, we say that a **Temporary Binding** exists for that particular event. Globally bound handlers are called every time the event occurs regardless of the currently executing content, unless a temporary binding to the event has been defined in the current deck. If neither of the above bindings exists for a particular event, we can say that **Fallback Handling** of the event is required. This might also be required when a WTA context is protected, which means that the incoming event is not allowed to interrupt the currently executing WTA context. The fallback handling for any event is carried out by the default device specific HCI.

We will now list the different conditions to be met for each of the above types of event handling. This applies to all the WTA events.

Handling by a Global Binding

❑　Currently no WTA service is running in the WTA user agent AND a matching global binding exists

❑　A WTA service is running in the WTA user agent but no matching temporary binding exists AND the context is not protected AND a matching global binding exists

Handling by a Temporary Binding

❑　A WTA service is running in the WTA user agent AND a temporary binding exists

Fallback handling by the default HCI

❑ Neither a global binding nor a temporary binding exists for a particular event, regardless of whether a WTA service is running in the WTA user agent or not.

❑ A WTA service is running in the WTA user agent AND a temporary binding does not exist AND the context is protected from interruption

❑ It is not possible to load the event handling content because it failed for some reason

Interruption of a WTA Context

If a WTA event is detected while an active WTA context exists, the user agent must determine whether to interrupt the current WTA user agent activity in order to execute the event handler using any of the above mechanisms. However, it is possible to control whether content executing in a WTA context can be interrupted to handle an event using the WTAI Miscellaneous library function WTAMisc.protected(1).

In the situation that an active WTA context is interrupted, the following actions are taken depending on the state of the WTA user agent:

WTA User Agent State	WTA User Agent Action
The WTA user agent is in a stable state and a card is being displayed.	Interrupt the current WTA context. Then process the WTA event.
Execution of WTAI function is in progress.	Wait until execution of WTAI function has been completed. Then interrupt the current WTA context and process the WTA event.
Execution of a WMLScript is in progress.	Interrupt the execution of the WMLScript. Then interrupt the current context and process the WTA event.
A local navigation (to a card in the same deck, to the local cache or to the repository) is in progress.	Wait until navigation has been completed. Then interrupt the current context and process the WTA event.
One or more WSP method requests (GET, PUT etc.) are in progress.	Abort all WSP method requests in progress with the WSP S-Method-Abort service primitive. Then process the WTA event.

Temporary Event Bindings

Consider a situation where a WTA service is executing in the WTA user agent, and it has been set as protected from an event handler or the default HCI interrupting, and yet we want to handle such events gracefully. The only way to do it would be to define a temporary event handler in your content using the <onevent> WML element. The task specified in the <onevent> element is executed. An example for this is discussed in the next section.

WTA Application Scenarios

Here we will take a look at two example scenarios, the first involving a "automatic retry" application of your mobile phone, and the second involving a voicemail application.

"Automatic Retry" Application

Here is an example of a temporary event binding, as discussed in the previous section. If I find the called party's phone number to be busy, it would be a good idea if I could receive some kind of notification as soon as the party is finished with the call, without having to poll frequently by trying to make calls. Such notification systems are available in many telephone exchanges as an additional feature. But most of the time, such a feature might not be available or possible in the phone network that you normally use.

A quick and dirty way to have an **automatic retry mechanism** until the call is setup is given below. Note that this is not exactly the equivalent in operation to the notification mechanism, because this would keep the calling party's phone line busy. Let's say that you see an advertisement on TV for a hot deal offering a limited number of free tickets to a movie premiere to anyone who calls a particular number. There would surely be a limited number of lines for the phone number, so a large number of people calling in would keep the lines busy. In such a case, you would probably wish for an automatic retry option without having to manually disconnect and retry every time. The following WML/WMLScript code implements an automatic retry option.

The first WML deck is called `keepcalling.wml`. It starts as usual with a declaration:

```
<?xml version="1.0"?>
<!DOCTYPE wml PUBLIC "-//WAPFORUM//DTD WML 1.2//EN"
"http://www.wapforum.org/DTD/wml12.dtd"><!-- notice the dtd wml12-->
```

The following event handler looks for an outgoing call being initiated by the user. When this event occurs, the event handler sets a browser variable `callerID` with the value represented by the `<caller ID>` parameter of the event. Finally the browser is redirected to the card, `connecting`:

```
<wml>
   <card id="main">
      <onevent type="cc/oc">
         <go href="#connecting">
            <setvar name="callerID" value="$2" />
         </go>
      </onevent>
```

This is a standard event handler that calls `retry.wmls`'s `keepCalling()` function:

```
      <do type="accept">
         <go href="retry.wmls#keepCalling($number)" />
      </do>
```

The main card prompts the user for a phone number:

```
      <p>
         Enter the Phone Number to call repeatedly until success:
         <input name="number" format="*N" emptyok="false" />
      </p>
   </card>
```

The next set of cards cover the three stages of the retry action. The first informs the user that a connection is being attempted. The middle card looks for a connected event and if so redirects the browser to the connected card. This card is essentially invisible to the user and defines a handler for the connected event. The card informs the user that they are connected:

```
<card id="connecting">
    <p>Calling Number $(callerID). Please Wait...</p>
</card>

<card id="retry_oc">
    <onevent type="cc/co">
        <go href="#connected">
            <setvar name="callerID" value="$2" />
        </go>
    </onevent>
</card>

<card id="connected">
    <p>
        Connected to $(callerID)
    </p>
</card>
</wml>
```

The function used by the above deck is found in the WMLScript called `retry.wmls`:

```
function keepCalling( number ) {

    var id;

    while( (id = WTAVoiceCall.setup(number, 0)) < 0 ) {
        if( id > -5 && id < -7  ) break;
    }
    return id;
}
```

The function checks for three error codes: party busy, network busy or no answer (which take the values -5, -6, -7). The `while` statement loops as long as one of the three values is returned. For all other values the function returns control to the WML deck. Notice we have not set an error deck for this for brevity's sake. The return value for this function will be an error code.

You can see how, with only a few libraries, the WTA functionality can provide us with powerful applications. Let's now look at another example: the voicemail system. Given the information above, any capable programmer should be able to implement this.

Voicemail Application

This example illustrates how a voicemail service could be established within the WTA framework. In this scenario the user is notified that he has received new voicemails and he then chooses to listen to one of them. The scenario becomes a little more complex if more than one voicemail message has to be played in the same phone call.

Here, we'll only be looking at a possible data flow of how such a system could be implemented. The code required to implement this is not given here because the interface between the WTA server and the voicemail system is proprietary and is not defined in WAP specifications. Network operators will be privy to such information; they would use it to build the necessary WTA Services.

The diagram below illustrates how this application might work in one scenario:

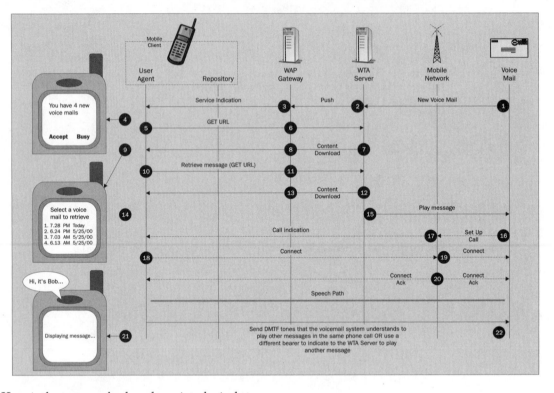

Here is the test case broken down into logical steps.

1. The voicemail system notifies the WTA server that there are new voicemails, and at the same time sends a list of the voicemails.

2. The WTA server creates new service content based on the list received from the voicemail system. The content is stored on the server, and its URL pushed to the client using the Service Indication (SI), discussed in Chapter 16. The Service Indication is sent to the WAP gateway using push. The Service Indication's message could read along the lines of, "You have four new voicemails".

3. The WAP gateway sends the Service Indication to the client, also using push.

4. The user is notified about the Service Indication via a message that is delivered with the Service Indication. The user chooses to accept the Service Indication.

5. A WSP GET request is sent to the WAP gateway (URL provided by the Service Indication).

6. The WAP gateway makes a WSP/HTTP conversion.

7. The WTA server returns the earlier created voicemail service.

8. The WAP gateway makes a HTTP/WSP conversion.

9. The voicemail service is now executing in the client. The user is presented with a list of voicemails originating from the voicemail system (a WML "Select List" created in Step 2). The user selects a certain voicemail to listen to.

10. Another WSP GET request is sent to the WAP gateway. The requested deck identifies the selected voicemail.

11. The WAP gateway makes a WSP/HTTP conversion.

12. The WTA server returns the requested deck. The deck only contains one card with a single WML "<go href=...>" task. The URL is automatically called when the card is executed and it refers to a card in the earlier downloaded voicemail content which binds the incoming call event (cc/ic) so that the subsequent call from the voicemail system will be answered automatically. The WTA server is also informed about which voicemail the user has chosen to retrieve.

13. The WAP gateway makes a HTTP/WSP conversion.

14. The incoming call event (cc/ic) is temporarily bound so that the call from the voicemail system will be answered automatically. In order to avoid the voicemail service answering a call from someone else other than the voicemail system, the calling party's phone number (id) is preferably checked.

15. The WTA server instructs the voicemail system to play the selected voicemail.

16. The voicemail system instructs the mobile network to set up a call to the client.

17. The mobile network sets up a call to the client.

18. The client answers the call automatically.

19. The mobile network informs the voicemail system that the client has accepted the call.

20. Acknowledgements are sent to the client and the voicemail system.

21. A speech path is established between the voicemail system and the client, and the message is played.

22. If the user wishes to play another message without disconnecting the speech path already established with the voicemail system, then things become trickier. If the mobile phone does not allow the WTA user agent to execute WSP methods over a separate WTA session on a separate bearer like SMS or GPRS while a speech path is active, the only possible way is to send DTMF tones that the voicemail system understands over the active speech path. This would be equivalent to making a phone call to the voicemail system using the default HCI provided by the device and hitting keypad numbers to control the voicemail system, the way we normally access voicemail. Such a system would defeat the whole purpose of using WTA to access voicemail. Mobile phones need to address this problem in future.

Other Applications

As we saw earlier, the WTAI Public library functions can be used by any third party content provider for content intended to be executed by the WAE user agent (not originating from the WTA server). Typically WTA has applications in whatever services there are that involve the need for a phone call. For example, you can author a WML deck, displaying a choice of restaurants in your locality that allows 'click to phone' functionality, that would allow the user to make phone calls to the restaurant to make table reservations. Similarly WML decks can be provided that list all essential, emergency and public utility services, with hyperlinks that would make calls to the corresponding phone numbers. Users then would not have to remember the phone numbers for many services. It would also be possible for numbers to change without the users having to know about it.

Summary

In this chapter, we have discussed the WTA architecture and various applications. Since WAP WTA has been defined sufficiently in detail only in the WAP 1.2 specifications, implementations are not readily available for network operators to provide telephony applications. However, some of the phone vendors already provide implementations of the WTAI public library functions. Examples have been provided for third-party content developers to enable them to include 'click to phone' functionality in applications wherever required. Users of WAP phones will now need a little bit of patience until commercial WAP 1.2 phones and network operator support is available, to be able to see everything you have read in this chapter actually functioning in practice.

In the next chapter, we'll see how we can go one step further towards creating a more natural interface for accessing Internet content and services from a phone. Voice recognition technologies have now progressed to such an extent that the ability to create a voice interface for applications is fast becoming a reality. We'll be looking at one such initiative to achieve this next – VoiceXML.

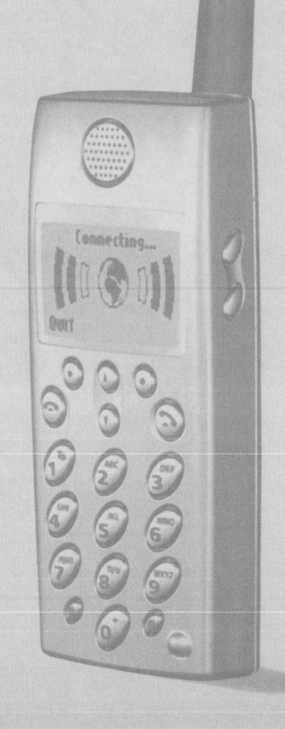

18

VoiceXML-Voice Markup language

The Web has made it possible for people to access information at the click of a mouse. In recent years, the meaning of what a client is has grown from desktop computers to other clients like TV set-top boxes and cell phones. Many of these new client types have limited input capabilities, so usability becomes an even more complex topic. This is where voice control comes in. It can be used over any phone, anywhere. You don't have to put up with entering data using a tiny keypad, but rather you can interact with the service in a very natural manner. After all, we've been using our voice to communicate for many thousands of years, but a keyboard for only a few decades.

Having said this, it must be noted that voice-based navigation can get complex. When implementing information services on a web browser, we can include a glut of information on the page, and overload paths to resources to make sure users reach their required destination whatever their approach to searching for it. In voice applications, it becomes more important to clearly define the information. Voice data is transient; it depends on the users memory and ties in much more closely with preconceptions and experience. Finally, our ability to focus on any one voice-source among many is limited.

The need to avoid ambiguity in the Question / Answer pattern of voice interaction can be the cause of very complex systems, and it becomes more difficult to maintain location information; keeping the user aware of where they are in the application and where they are in relation to other parts of the application, such as the home page, the end and so on. It is characteristic of unpopular applications that the user feels lost and out of control.

The growing awareness of catering for a variety of needs, abilities and devices has highlighted the importance of voice control services, and also the importance of making them usable. Voice entry of textual data is very much easier than using a phone keypad. Current developments in wireless technology and increases in processor speeds have made speech-based applications a reality. With powerful servers for both speech processing and wireless-based thin clients, like mobile phones and PDAs, it is now possible to interact with the user using audio input and output.

In this chapter, we will examine XML's role as a markup language for voice-based interactions. Although XML has many roles to play in IT, its classic role is as a language for inter-application communication. Being an open standard, many applications now support the XML specification. The chapter will focus on VoiceXML, a standard for voice-based communication. VoiceXML is an XML language, which plays the role of the language of communication in voice applications, similar to the role played by HTML in web applications.

Also, like other XML technologies, VoiceXML seamlessly integrates with existing web-based technologies and can be used with any existing server-side technology such as ASP, and Java servlets. The content in this chapter is intended to give the reader an overview of voice technology-based applications and how they are implemented in web-based architecture. In particular, the possible implementations of VoiceXML technology are discussed. The final part of the chapter focuses on next generation user interfaces in wireless applications.

How to get started

VoiceXML is a relatively new specification. It has its roots in a language designed by Motorola by the name of VoxML, another specification for presenting services and data in a voice medium. We will not discuss VoxML here, but you should know that the Motorola WAP SDK does support VoxML and similar results to those available here can be achieved with it.

In order to test the example applications here, there is a VoiceXML package available from IBM Alphworks' Voice Server SDK. All the code in this chapter has been tested using the Voice Server together with an Apache-Tomcat setup.

Voice Browser by IBM Alphaworks

IBM Alphaworks implements a sample voice browser for browsing VoiceXML documents, the only VoiceXML browser available at present. It can be downloaded free-of-charge from the IBM Alphaworks site at `http://www.alphaworks.ibm.com.`(you should be warned it is 65Mb). The Voice browser is implemented on the Java platform. It requires JDK/JRE 1.2, and JMF 2.0 for implementing the `<audio>` and `<record>` elements. Currently, only a Windows version is available.

The VoiceXML browser is shipped as an easy to install set up program which copies the different files required and the examples. This Voice browser supports two modes – live mode and text mode. Live mode allows the user to browse in an interactive audio environment, which requires IBM ViaVoice to be installed on the system. (This can be purchased from `http://www.ibm.com/.`) Text mode allows users to test VoiceXML documents in a text-based environment where input is given in the form of a text file. Output is also in the form of text. The installation copies two batch files, `text.bat` and `live.bat`, that are useful tools for browsing in text mode and live mode respectively. The browser program is contained in a JAR file.

Introduction to VoiceXML

VoiceXML is a member of the XML family, a W3C specification for organizing data in a document using a set of elements. (See Chapter 9 for a brief overview of XML.) Rules governing the document can be specified as either a Document Type Definition (DTD) or a schema. VoiceXML is one such schema specification. It consists of a set of rules that detail how to describe a voice transaction using a markup language. For example, it defines elements that direct the browser both to collect input from the user and present content to the user.

Here is a typical transaction between a user (USER) and a voice-based application (SERVICE) which may look something like the following:

```
SERVICE     'Welcome to Mobilestore. Your clothes store location information
             center'
SERVICE     'Please choose one of the following. Discount store, Fashion, Label
             goods'
USER        'Discount'
SERVICE     'Please select phone number or address'
USER        'Address please'
SERVICE     '120 The High Street, Anywhere Town, Somewhere.'
            'Do you wish to continue?
USER        'No'
SERVICE     'Thankyou for using Mobilestore'
```

In this transaction, the user is greeted and prompted for the type of clothes store they wish to visit. The service then returns the name and address or phone number of the nearest store. This simple transaction can be represented in VoiceXML as:

```xml
<?xml version="1.0"?>
<vxml version="1.0">
  <form>
    <block>
      Welcome to Mobilestore. Your clothes store location information center.
    </block>

    <field name="store">
      <prompt>
        Please choose one of the following. Discount store, Fashion, Label goods
      </prompt>
      <grammar src="map.gram" type="application/x-jsgf/" />
    </field>

    <field name="info">
      <prompt>
        Please select phone number or address
      </prompt>
        <grammar src="map.gram" type="application/x-jsgf/" />
    </field>

    <submit next="http://www.process.geoplanet/findplace.asp" />
  </form>
</vxml>
```

Here, you can see that VoiceXML is used to provide the user with a speech-based interface, while the actual task is performed by an ASP document, `findplace.asp`. We can use this VoiceXML snippet as a data island within an ASP document, providing the client supports VoiceXML.

We will be explaining exactly how the elements in this code work in later sections. For the moment, however, note that VoiceXML defines *what* to do with the content, rather than *how* to convey the content, like the original approach to HTML. It is up to the client to render the document.

As given in the VoiceXML forum specification (see `http://www.voicexml.org`), the advantages of using VoiceXML as the language of audio are that VoiceXML:

❑ Minimizes client/server interactions by specifying multiple interactions per document.

❑ Shields application developers from low-level and platform specific details.

❑ Separates the user interaction code (which is given in VoiceXML) from service logic.

❑ Promotes service portability across implementation platforms. VoiceXML is a common language for content providers, tool providers and platform providers.

❑ Is easy to use for simple interactions, and yet provides language features to support complex dialogs.

Architectural Overview

Before we go on to discuss VoiceXML in detail, we will look at the architecture needed to implement VoiceXML applications. The architectural design of VoiceXML is very flexible and integrates well with existing web technology. The model makes use of existing web server technology to deliver data over a network, and uses a VoiceXML client (browser/gateway) to interpret and execute the document.

The actual translation process between voice and VoiceXML can be done either at the VoiceXML gateway or at the browser. This will depend mainly on how 'thin' the client is. In either case the request is translated into VoiceXML and transmitted via HTTP to the content server whether IIS, Apache, Netscape or some other. This is illustrated in the diagram below:

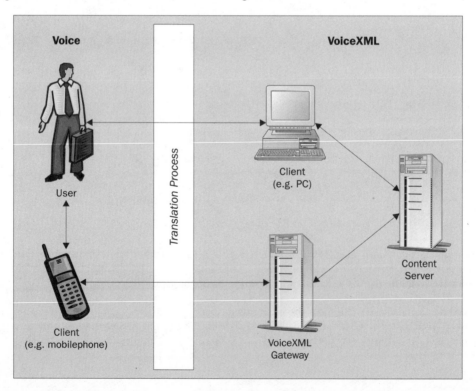

In this architecture, VoiceXML is used as the language of communication between the origin server and the VoiceXML browsing gateway or VoiceXML browser. The browser or gateway works in a VoiceXML context, which is responsible for event handling and maintaining state. For example, if the user connects to the VoiceXML gateway using a telephone call, the gateway context may need to listen for an incoming call and request an initial VoiceXML document. Using a VoiceXML gateway, voice browsing can be made available to a wide variety of existing clients, including ordinary telephones.

One example of a VoiceXML application, that may be accessed through a telephony device, is a voice-based browser for a music store. In this application, the user can download or hear streamed samples of songs through a telephone and can then order them. The process begins when a user dials a number from their mobile phone to connect to the VoiceXML gateway, which maintains a context for listening to platform specific events, like accepting the incoming calls. The VoiceXML context in the gateway, which accepts the call, starts by loading an initial VoiceXML document and transfers control to the VoiceXML browser. The initial VoiceXML document runs on the browser and either transfers control to the next document or finishes the conversation. The VoiceXML context will always be listening for events such as `exit` which would cause the application to terminate.

Now that we have an idea of what VoiceXML is and how it works, it's time we took a look at this technology in a little more detail.

VoxML

VoxML is a markup language for speech that was proposed by Motorola and is used in their telephony applications and IVR (Interactive Voice Response) systems. Motorola and other companies later formed the VoiceXML forum to make an industry standard markup language for voice.

Motorola's VoxML implementation contains three components – a content server, a voice browser and a telephone. The Voice Interpreter and context form the browser implementation. The user connects to a VoxML gateway by dialing its number. On establishing the connection, the interpreter loads the startup VoxML page from the content server, which is then executed. Motorola provides a browser gateway that allows you to access VoxML applications. More information on this can be found at `http://www.voxml.com/voxml.html`, where you can download their application development kit.

Elements of the VoiceXML Implementation

We have already seen that the VoiceXML architecture contains a VoiceXML browser, which interacts with other components and operating systems to make voice browsing a reality. Typically, the implementation of a VoiceXML browser will be as shown below:

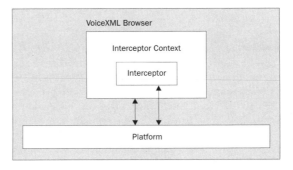

The interpreter context will be responsible for platform specific methods, for example receiving a request and sending a response, while the interpreter itself will maintain the state for applications.

To render the VoiceXML document, a browser also requires a TTS (Text To Speech) conversion engine, a speech recognition engine and sometimes, a natural language processing engine. Typically these are supported as external components.

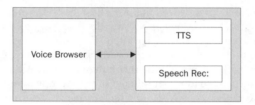

A TTS conversion engine synthesizes text to speech, possibly with the help of a markup language such as JSML, Java Speech Markup Language. The browser may communicate with these components using a standard API, such as Speech API in Windows Platform (http://www.research.microsoft.com) or Java API for Speech (http://jsp.java.sun.com/products/java-media/speech/). Commercial TTS and Speech recognition engines such as LernOut & Hauspie for Speech API or ViaVoice for IBM are suitable for this purpose.

A speech recognition engine converts speech to the information required by the application, for example, integers or text, based on the specified grammar. The grammar contains the rules for validating the speech. Like TTS, a speech recognition engine can be implemented as software, hardware or a combination of both. A speech recognition engine can only convert speech into raw information – the user is expected to give input exactly .A natural language processor can then be used to process the raw information generated by a speech engine based on natural language processing algorithms, extracting the exact information required.

Powerful hardware-based speech processors, which can convert text to speech and vice versa, are also available. One example is Lucent Technologies Speech Server, which also implements VoiceXML. Lucent Technologies server supports a programmable API in Java and C++, which runs on Solaris.

Voice Browsing from Mobile Devices

We've seen that VoiceXML is intended for browsing in an audio environment. It requires either:

❑   A voice browser implemented as VoiceXML plug-in for a microbrowser

❑   A telephony based connection to a VoiceXML gateway (as in the implementation of VoxML by Motorola)

For mobile phones, VoiceXML applications can be accessed like any other telephony based application, if we access VoiceXML documents through a VoiceXML gateway. The major advantage of this option is that the client needs no additional hardware or software to access the functionality. But browsing content using audio only leads to an unnatural conversation with the user. This type of system mainly finds its applications in telephone-based interactive voice response systems (IVRs) used in fields such as railway timetable information, weather forecasts and so on. Also, as the penetration of telephones in daily life is much higher than any other system of communication, this is particularly useful to access the content. To illustrate this, VoiceGenie recently launched a service to deliver existing content to telephony-based systems using VoiceXML.

VoiceXML applications can also be accessed through VoiceXML plug-ins for microbrowsers. A Voice browser like IBM Alphaworks can be used in mobile devices, like PDAs.

At present there are no browsers or mechanisms that support switching of voice-based markup and text markup, such as WML. In future, there may be VoiceXML plug-ins for commercial content browsers, so that VoiceXML can be used along with WML. The application may use a mixture of audio content and text markup content depending on the nature of the application.

Overview of VoiceXML

We will now look at VoiceXML in some detail, to get an understanding of both the structure and content of VoiceXML applications. The nature of VoiceXML applications is such that information must be extracted and presented in a **linear** way. While an intelligent design can allow experienced users to cut down on the time it takes to get to the information, there is a limitation in the divergence from this linear model. Each stage of the application requires a number of decisions to be made by the user.

As a result VoiceXML applications are designed to follow a certain pattern of question and answer. And, as an enabling technology, actual processing is limited to that needed to extract and verify the information. Once the information has been entered, the VoiceXML application typically submits the relevant data to a server-side application that handles service logic and database operations, and subsequently returns a result.

Grammar

In a moment, we'll take a look at how the extraction of information is managed, but first we'll examine the data verification process. A **grammar** defines the allowable inputs submitted by the user. Typically, it is very difficult to implement a listener that can recognize any word without giving it context. To allow the speech recognition software to achieve reasonable accuracy and response time, we can define a set of possible inputs, which simplifies the recognition process enormously. There are also several grammars pre-defined that we can use such as a digit grammar and a character grammar. So, for the question, "Which department would you like to be connected to?" we could define a grammar that allows the response "Marketing", "Personnel", and "Shop Floor", but not "Correspondence".

The syntax method for specifying grammar in VoiceXML is JSGF or **Java Speech Grammar Format**. JSGF is a specification from Sun MicroSystems, and more details on this can be found at `http://java.sun.com/products/java-media/speech/forDevelopers/JSML/`.

Let's briefly look at a simple example:

```
<grammar>
   Catatonia                    {Catatonia}
   | Manic Street Preachers    {manics}
   | Manics                     {manics}
   | Stereophonics              {stereophonics}
   | Tom Jones                  {tomjones}
<grammar>
```

Each possible selection is listed, separated by the OR (|) character. In addition, we can specify what value is submitted to the application for each matching value. The example above illustrates an occasion where two possible answers give the same result. Alternative result values are included in curly braces ({}). We can also use square brackets to signify optional additional values, for example, Tom [Jones] would match either Tom or Tom Jones.

The understanding of grammar is essential to voice applications. We can specify various scopes for the grammar that can allow a user to take shortcuts through the application. By allowing some options that can be accepted throughout the application, in the current forms or only for the current field value we require, we can mix various values to allow the user to change their mind or start again and generally feel in control. In particular, all platform implementations support user choices such as 'Help' and 'Exit' that will elicit further information about what is required from the user or exit the application respectively.

Structure of VoiceXML Applications

A VoiceXML application is a collection of VoiceXML **documents**, which are themselves composed of **dialogs**. A voice application is basically a negotiation between the user and the application. The user wants some information or a service, and the service needs to extract as much information as is necessary. This is done by breaking up each dialog into forms that contain a list of all the data and decisions we require from the user.

Each dialog normally breaks down to one of two types: **forms** and **menus**. Forms allow the user to enter information and to navigate the application. Menus are a type of form which list the available options to the user before allowing them to make a choice. Most often these are used only for navigation. In order to get the information from the user, the form contains prompts and other information that will describe what is needed.

Each application has a root document. The root document contains variables and code that is shared by the other documents. A user often starts the application by opening the root document, and this document will remain loaded in the browser/gateway as long as the user interacts with the application. If another document is loaded which specifies a different root document, then that root document will be loaded in place of the previous one, together with the requested document.

This process is continued across the documents within an application, until the last dialog of the application is reached. Any stored data is global to the application. This structure is illustrated in the following diagram:

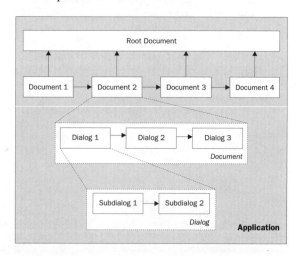

Subdialogs are self-contained forms that elicit specific information from the user. You can think of them as functions that perform an often-used operation. For example, one frequently used subdialog requests credit card information from the user. Since this is a standard operation and is self contained, it can be isolated in its own dialog that can then be used by any application. This is not limited to applications residing on the server, as we will see; it is possible to call documents and dialogs in any location that can be pointed to with the use of a URL.

The way is which a browser works through a form can be described by an algorithm. Whenever the form is loaded, it is initialized. The variables are initialized and set to their default value or to undefined. The browser now enters the main iteration. The form selects the next field to be filled, prompts the user and waits for input, and then processes that input. When it has done that, it loops through the form again selecting the next field, and so on.

Each field and prompt also includes an attribute that specifies whether or not it should be visited by the browser. Usually this value is set as `false` (field has not been visited) at the initialization stage and is then set to `true` (just before the field is visited). In addition, the condition for visiting the field can be specified at run time by including sections of script that evaluate to a Boolean. With fields, if the variable has a value other than undefined it is deemed filled and not visited again unless its value is cleared. When an appropriate form item is visited it is done in the following way. Any prompts are visited. It is possible to specify a value that stipulates at what iteration (or re-iteration) a prompt should be queued for output. Thus, we can specify several different prompts that will execute depending on how many times the browser has requested them to be filled. Non-interactive items are set to visited and queued to output.

When the user has successfully entered a value, this value is processed. We can specify an event handler that deals with a successfully entered value that is called <filled>, which we will look at later. If the entry belongs to a grammar other than the current one, the current form terminates, and another form is initialized with the input given. If the input is an event, such as `exit` or `help` the appropriate event handler is executed. Otherwise the filled event handler is executed. If none of the above conditions apply, the next iteration of the loop begins and the next item for processing is selected.

The browser continues to step through the application in this way until an exit is specified, whether at the end of the application or by user request.

Different Types of Forms

The main problem in voice applications is that they are time consuming. As users become familiar with the application they wish to speed up the process of stepping through the applications. As we saw in Chapter 7, catering for the various levels of familiarity of users with the application is important to keep those customers. The way that this is provided for is through the use of directed and mixed initiative forms.

Directed Forms

Typically, a VoiceXML form is interpreted and executed in a sequential order. Elements within each form are also executed in a given order. Sequential types of forms are typically used when the number of fields in the form is small. In this type of form, the computer directs the entire conversation. The user must follow a set number of steps as directed by the application to get the information they require. This contrasts with a visual form that allows user initiative – the user can choose to follow the dialog or can skip steps and the system can then clarify points that aren't focused enough. For example, imagine an application for accessing information about time zones around the world. This is a global application, that allows several locations names. Suppose the user asks for the time zone in Washington – Washington could be the well known location in the USA, or one of several villages in the United Kingdom. The user can either go through the form step-wise (first naming the country, then political area, and finally town or city name), or can directly say the name of a location. If the name is ambiguous, then the application narrows down the search by taking further information if necessary.

Mixed Initiative Forms

A mixed initiative form is analogous to an event driven environment, where both the user and the computer can affect the conversation. The form contains fields that can be filled by a user in any order. Mixed initiative forms start with an initial item, specified by an <initial> element. The content in the <initial> element gives information that sets the background and explains to the user what information is available.

The rest of the form can then be filled in any order according to the user's input. In addition, more than one field can be filled in a single utterance of the user. So, in a music store application the user can go through the application in a linear way if they so wish, but can also match any of the fields, thus cutting down on the time taken to navigate through it. This also allows for a more natural interaction. Take a look at the following interaction:

```
SERVICE    'Welcome to Mobile Store.'
           'Please choose a department, Classical, Pop, Rock?'
USER       'Rock'
SERVICE    'Choose Artist.'
USER       'Foo Fighters'
SERVICE    'Please select album title.'
USER       'The color and the shape'
SERVICE    'Do you wish to buy this title or listen to it?'
```

The above interaction is equivalent to this one, spoken by an experienced user:

```
SERVICE    'Welcome to Mobile… '
USER       <User interrupts>'I want to listen to The Color and the Shape by Foo
           Fighters'
```

In either case the appropriate fields would be filled and the result submitted to the appropriate CGI or other server-side application. In addition some information can carry implicit qualifiers, that is, it is possible to infer that *The Color and the Shape* refers to the *Foo Fighters* album of the same name.

We can see how this can make for a powerful and easy to use application. Mixed initiative forms implement conversations of the latter type in VoiceXML. They contain an <initial> element, the contents of which are executed first. After that, the user can fill any field of the form, depending on how the conversation progresses. Whenever a user gives an entry, it will be verified against all active grammar fields and will be filled into the appropriate field. The <initial> element acts as a buffer so that the user can enter all the values simultaneously. They will be filled in the appropriate fields and processed depending on the application logic. If the user does not fill the values simultaneously, the initial statement expires and hands the control to individual prompts for information.

A Form Dialog

Probably the most important part of a VoiceXML document, is the form. A form holds together different input fields, variable declarations, events to handle the input data and events to handle errors and logic. A form contains different fields, which accept input from user as speech.

We can set the scope of the grammar using the scope attribute of the <form> element within which the grammar is set. If the scope has value document, then the grammar is active throughout the particular document. If it has value dialog, then the scope of the grammar is limited to the form. Therefore, a grammar within a form in the root document that has scope = "document" is available throughout the application.

An item within a form implementing a particular action is called a field and is defined by the `<field>` element. The form itself acts as a container for these elements.

Fields

A `<field>` element declares an input field variable in a form that takes its value from user input. VoiceXML variables follow ECMAScript syntax. Later in this chapter, you will see that ECMAScript can be also used for scripting in VoiceXML using the `<script>` tag. The values of different field variables collected by a dialog during execution are submitted to the next dialog in the chain. The `<field>` element has several attributes including `name` and `expr` that define the attribute's name and an initial value. This can be a default value and will not be visited unless the service logic requires an alternative value from the user, in which case the value would be cleared, signaling to the browser that it should visit the field. The possible inputs can be specified as a built in data type such as `integer`, `boolean`, `date`, `digits`, `time` or `currency` or using a grammar, whether external or in-line.

Inside the `<field>` element, a `<prompt>` element is used.

If the `type` attribute of the `<field>` element is used, then the data that is input to the field will be validated using this type. Below we see an example of the use of the `type` attribute. It specifies the type of data that the interpreter should expect:

```
<field name="somenumber" type="integer" >
   <prompt>
       Please say a number between 1 and 10
   </prompt>
</field>
```

An invalid input such as, "I don't want to" would trigger the `nomatch` event that would call a handler either provided by the developer or the default system one, for example, "I'm sorry that is not an option". It would be up to the application to validate the rule, 0<value<11. In this case a grammar would probably be more appropriate.

The `<prompt>` element is designed to prompt the user for some input. At the VoiceXML browser, the content within the `<prompt>` element is queued for playing to the user. The `<prompt>` element also causes the VoiceXML interpreter to collect the user input, interpret it and execute the relevant action. Attributes of `<prompt>` include `cond`, an expression that determines whether the prompt should be spoken and `bargein`, that specifies whether the user can interrupt the prompt, for example if they have heard it before, or are not interested.

In addition to specifying what prompt is spoken to the user, we can also specify a `timeout` value – the maximum time that the application should wait for user input. This attribute can be used in combination with the `count` attribute to provide tapered prompts. The `count` attribute can be used to provide multiple prompts that either progressively get more verbose or less depending on function. Let's look at this in more detail. Imagine that we define a prompt that should be self-explanatory. If the user fails to enter a value successfully, we can provide progressively more verbose prompts as shown:

```
<prompt count="1">Which department do you require:</prompt>
<prompt count="2">Please choose a department, Classical, Pop, Rock</prompt>
<prompt count="3">Music is listed under categories in this store. In order to
                see our titles you will need to choose a department. Please
                say Classical, Pop or Rock</prompt>
```

In this example, if the user did not respond to the prompt or attempted to make an invalid choice –
such as "Hip Hop" – then they would hear progressively more information.

In this case, a `<grammar>` element is used to specify the rules needed to validate the input. The
VoiceXML specification recommends Java Speech Grammar Format (JSGF) as the standard to be used for
specifying the grammar. Usually, the grammar is contained in a file with a `.gram` extension of standard
MIME type `application/x-jsgf`. We can specify the URL of the grammar using the `src` attribute,
and the MIME type using the attribute `type`.

In the document below, the grammar is specified by an external file, namely, `continent.gram`:

```
<field name="continent" >
   <prompt>
       Say the continent you want to go to
   </prompt>
   <Grammar src = "../grammars/continent.gram" type="application/x-jsgf" />
</field>
```

First, the browser prompts the user to enter a continent. It then collects the input and validates it
according to a grammar specified in `continent.gram`, an external grammar file in JSGF:

```
<grammar type="application/x-jsgf">
    Asia {asia} | Africa {africa} | America {america} | Australia {australia}|
    Antartica {antartica} | Europe {europe}
</grammar>
```

Recording Input

As seen above, the `<field>` element is used for collecting user input. The `<record>` element, on the
other hand, is used to record the user input as voice. We can think of the `<field>` element as
analogous to a human speaking with another human or Interactive Voice Response system, while the
`<record>` element is more analogous to a voice mailbox, which asks the caller to leave a message, like
leaving a greeting.

The recorded voice is stored in a variable within the `<record>` element, from where it can either be
used on the client-side or can be uploaded to the server. The attributes of the `<record>` element
define the maximum recording time, whether a beep prompts the user to begin recording, the audio
file type used (this would normally be platform specific), and the interval of silence that signifies the
user has finished.

The `<record>` element may contain the `<prompt>` element to prompt the user. It usually also contains
a `<noinput>` element. The following example shows a simple use of the `<record>` element:

```
<record name="yourname" beep="true" finalsilence="2000ms"
        maxtime="10s" type="audio/wav" >
   <prompt>
       Hi, Say your name so that we can call you by your name
   </prompt>
   <noinput>
       Please say your name
   </noinput>
</record>
```

This code typically may be executed as:

```
SERVICE    'Hi, Say your name so that we can call you by your name'
USER       < The user, Paul, remains silent for some time >
SERVICE    'Please say your name'
USER       'Paul Newman'
```

Here we have used the `noinput` tag to specify an additional prompt. The recording, maximum length 10 seconds, will be preceded by a beep and the browser will assume the user is finished if they are quiet for 2 seconds.

Blocks and Objects

We've now seen two elements in a form used for user input, namely `<field>` and `<record>`. There are also items in VoiceXML forms that are used for content presentation and manipulation. For example, the `<block>` element contains mark-up content and this can be conditionally executed by the browser. A block element holds non-interactive content.

The `<block>` element is executed based on the value of the field variable associated with the block. If the `name` attribute is specified, the associated field variable takes that name; else it will be associated with a default internal Boolean variable of the form. In this case, once the block is executed, the internal variable maps to `true`, which indicates that the block has been visited. As long as this variable is `true`, that particular block is never executed again. This is particularly useful when we use the `<block>` element to specify the title of the form, which we only want to be executed once. If we want more control over the execution of a block, we can specify the `name` attribute and modify that field variable to control the execution. For example:

```
<form>
   <block>
      Welcome to MobileStore
   </block>
<!-- some code here -->
<!-- some further content here -->
</form>
```

In the above code snippet, no name is specified for the field variable of the block, which means the `<block>` element can only be visited once.

Objects are used to declare and execute sections of code. The `<object>` element in VoiceXML is very similar to its counterpart in HTML. An object used for user authentication is given below:

```
<object name="usergate"
          classid="method://userverification/verifyAndEnter"
          data="http://mobilestore.com/geoplanet/objects/authencication.jar">

   <param name="username" expr="getusername.vxml" />
   <param name="pwd" expr="password.vxml" />
</object>
```

This object, `usergate`, is located inside a Java archive. It collects two field variables by using two VoiceXML documents, and authenticates a user.

A Menu Dialog

The menu dialog in VoiceXML is intended to allow the user to make a selection from a set of choices. For example, in our VoiceXML music shopping portal, the application asks the user whether they want to buy titles on classical music, pop or rock using a menu. This menu leads the user to another dialog, which will depend on their selection. A simple menu type dialog to this effect is given below:

```
<menu>
   <prompt>
      Welcome to Music Portal. Select the category you want to go to:
      <enumerate />
   </prompt>

   <choice next= "http://www.mobilestore.com/vxml/classical.vxml">
      Classical
   </choice>
   <choice next= "http://www.mobilestore.com/vxml/pop.vxml">
      Pop
   </choice>
   <choice next= "http://www.mobilestore.com/vxml/rock.vxml">
      Rock
   </choice>

   <noinput>
      Please make a choice
      <enumerate />
   </noinput>
</menu>
```

lists all available options to the user. This code essentially defines a prompt and enumerates through the choices. In the example above each choice directs the user to a different section of the application through a hyperlink. The final section defines the prompt to be spoken if the timeout value is exceeded. If the user does not speak within a specified time, the application reiterates the choices.

A typical outcome of the menu document given above is as follows:

```
SERVICE     'Welcome to Music Portal. Select the category you want to go to:
            Classical, Pop, Rock.'
USER        <idle for some time>
SERVICE     'Please make a choice: Classical, Pop, Rock.'
USER        'Classical'
SERVICE     <Takes the user to http://www.mobilestore.com/vxml/classical.vxml>
```

The entire menu-type dialog is enclosed within a <menu> element. Inside the <menu> element, there are other elements intended to prompt the user for input and to collect this input.

As an alternative to text to speech (TTS) traslation we can provide audio content using the <audio> element. For example, in the above <prompt> element, the presentation before the user is specified using PCDATA, interpreted by the VoiceXML browser. However, in the code snippet given below, the presentation content is specified in the form of an <audio> element:

```
<menu>
    <prompt>
        Welcome to Music Portal, Select the category you want to go to
        <audio src="http://www.mobilestore.com/sounds/soundblast.wav" />
        <enumerate/>
    </prompt>
    <choice next= "http://www.mobilestore.com/vxml/classical.vxml">
        Classical
    </choice>
```

On interpreting the above VoiceXML document, the browser plays the `soundblast.wav` audio file at the same time as the speech, "Welcome to Music Portal, select the category you want to go to". The attribute `src` of the `<audio>` element is similar to `src` in the `<img>` element of WML.

Although a `.wav` file is used here, the VoiceXML specification does not insist on any specific file format. However, it is recommended in the specification that the implementation should support PCM and WAV, the most popular file formats. (For more information on these file formats, go to `http://www.sonicspot.com`.)

Sub Dialogs within a Form

We have seen subdialogs earlier and we will revisit them here. A subdialog in a form is a dialog within the scope of another dialog. In addition to the reasons we saw earlier, subdialogs are helpful for giving structure to a dialog; for example, complex logic and input fields in a dialog can be split off into subdialogs. In the case of a VoiceXML application for user registration, many fields and complex entries are needed, which will be easier to manage if a subdialog mechanism is used. Subdialogs are linked to a main dialog using the `<subdialog>` element:

```
<!-- Maindlg.vxml -->
<?xml version="1.0"?>
<vxml version="1.0">
<form id="sampleform">
    <var name="cost" type="currency"/>
    <subdialog name="subdlg" src="subdlg.vxml#costdetails">
        <filled>
            <assign name="bookcost" expr="subdlg.cost" />
        </filled>
    </subdialog>
</form>
</vxml>
```

```
<?xml version="1.0"?>
<vxml version="1.0">
<form id="costdetails">
    <field name="cost" type="currency">
        <prompt>
            This is from Subdialog, what is the cost of this book
        </prompt>
    </field>
</form>
</vxml>
```

The dialog itself does not know it is a subdialog. It is only the way that it is called from within another form that means it is a subdialog in this context. If the dialog performs a function that can either serve in a self-standing application or can be used as an add on, this can be done by either loading the dialog directly into the browser or calling it from another dialog as shown above.

Transitions between Dialogs

We've already seen that a VoiceXML application consists of a set of dialogs, and that the dialogs can submit data to other dialogs or a document. In practice, the information is passed between documents in the content server. The two elements used for transferring execution between forms or documents are `<goto>` and `<submit>`.

The `<goto>` element is generally used to transfer execution either from one form to another form, from one item to another item within the same form, or to another document. The different attributes used by the `<goto>` element contain the necessary information for transition from one point to another, and are listed below:

- ❑ next specifies the URI of the form to pass control to.

- ❑ expr is an expression which results in a URI to pass control to, in ECMAScript. Either expr or next can be specified, but not both. expr is provided in order to allow the decision of where to transfer to to be made at run time, according to, for example, a variable whose value is set by user input or similar.

- ❑ nextitem is used when the transition is between items in the same form

- ❑ expritem is used if the URI is determined at run-time by a section of ECMAScript

For example, in the sample application given below, the first dialog says 'Hello' and the second dialog says 'world'. The execution is transferred from the first to the second dialogs by the `<goto>` element with the next attribute:

```
<!-- First form which says Hello -->
<form id= "hello">
   <block>
       Hello
       <goto next="#world" />
   </block>
</form>

<!-- Second form which says world -->
<form id="world">
   <block>
       world
   </block>
</form>
```

It should be noted that the `<goto>` element can only be placed inside the `<block>`, `<filled>` and `<nomatch>` elements. As we saw, an expression that gives a URI as a result can also be used to direct the execution to another form. For example, the first form above could be modified to:

```
<block>
    Hello
    <goto expr="'#' + 'world'" />
</block>
```

The transition can also be made between documents. If we split the code of the previous example into two files, hello.vxml and world.vxml, the <goto> statement will look like this:

```
<!-- hello.vxml -->
<?xml version="1">
<vxml version="1">
<!-- First form which says Hello -->
<form id= "hello" >
    <block>
        Hello
        <goto next="world.vxml" />
    </block>
</form>
</vxml>
```

```
<!-- world.vxml -->
<?xml version="1">
<vxml version="1">
<!-- Second form which says world -->
<form id="world">
    <block>
        world
    </block>
</form>
</vxml>
```

The <goto> element can also be used in a similar way using the nextitem or expritem attribute to transit between different items within the same form.

As we have seen, we can use the <goto> element when we want to jump from part of a VoiceXML document to another part of the document or even to another document. Any form level variables are lost during this operation, so in order to pass parameters between dialogs global variables (declared in the root document) are needed. In these situations, we use the <submit> element which allows us to submit a set of parameters using HTTP GET or POST methods.

Like the <goto> element, the <submit> element takes the next and expr attributes. Other commonly used attributes of the <submit> element are:

❑ namelist – a collection of variables to pass. This contains individual variable references to be submitted.

❑ method – contains the request method, either GET, the default or POST.

❑ enctype – gives the encoding type of the submitted document. The default is application/x-www-forum-urlencoded, although there may be other proprietary encoded types.

The example given below shows how to pass variables using a <submit> element:

```
<?xml version="1.0"?>
<vxml version="1.0">
<form id="continents">
    <block>
        Welcome to MobileStore
    </block>
```

671

```
<field name="MyStore">
   <prompt>
      Say the name of the department you want to go to
   </prompt>
   <grammar src="stores.gram" type="application/x-jsgf" />
</field>
<block>
 <submit namelist="MyStore" next="http://localhost:8080/servlet/Stores" />
</block>
</form>
</vxml>
```

The code above asks the user to speak out the name of a store, which it submits to a servlet using `<submit>` element, which may explain the different features of that store. The grammar file used, `stores.gram`, is given below:

```
#JSGF V1.0;
grammar stores;
public <MyStore> = Classical | Pop| Rock;
```

The grammar used for validating speech input is specified in `stores.gram`, which has MIME type `application/x-jsgf`.

Variables and Actions in VoiceXML Dialogs

Variables can be declared in VoiceXML using the `<var>` element. This element is named using the name attribute and can be set with a default or initial value using the `expr` attribute. This can then be cleared if the default value is not sufficient, in which case it will be visited by the browser at its next iteration.

Variables are also declared by form items, like `<field>` and `<record>`. VoiceXML variables are similar to ECMAScript variables, although those beginning with an underscore character (_) are reserved for internal use. As with grammars, variables can have session level, application level, document level, dialog level and element scope. Session level variables cannot be declared by VoiceXML documents, but the standard session level variables are declared and modified by the VoiceXML interpreter context. This includes `session.telephone.ani`, which if available automatically identifies the telephone number of a caller. Application level variables are variables declared in root document, document: dialog level variables are variables declared inside a document and dialog respectively, while an element level variable is declared within elements like `<block>`.

The `<assign>` and `<clear>` elements are designed to assign a value to a particular variable and reset the value of a variable to undefined respectively. `<assign>` differs from `<clear>` somewhat, in that while `<clear>` can be used to reset the values of one or more items, `<assign>` can be applied to only one variable at a time. The snippet of code below shows these statements in action. It declares the variable country, assigns a value to the existing variable continent and then resets the values of both these variables:

```
<var name="country" expr="India" />
<assign name="continent" expr=" 'a' + 'sia'" />
<clear namelist=" continent country " />
```

Resetting using the `<clear>` element means assigning the value `undefined` to all variables specified within the element.

The execution flow of a VoiceXML document is controlled by **conditional elements**. These types of elements are either event-related – designed to execute some action of a particular field in response to an event, like the `<filled>` element – or logical statement elements like the `<if>` element.

Conditional logic in VoiceXML is handled by the `<if>` element, and the optional `<else>` and `<elseif>` elements. We can also make use of the usual ECMAScript operators, for example > and <, but these must be escaped:

```
<if cond="latitude==55">
   <if cond="longitude==8">
      <assign name="place" expr="Trivandrum" />
   </if>
   <assign name="place" expr="some other place"/>
</if>
```

Here, if latitude is equal to 55 and longitude is 8, the value of the variable `place` is assigned the value `Trivandrum`; else it is assigned `some other place`.

The `<filled>` action handler element in VoiceXML contains code that is to be interpreted when the user has entered value(s) in a particular field or fields. The `<filled>` element can be contained either in a form or in a field.

When used within a `<field>`, the `<filled>` element acts when that particular field is filled:

```
<field name="continent">
<!-- some code here -->
   <filled>
      <if cond="continent==Antartica" >
         <prompt>
            Antartica is a very cold place, where penguins live!
         </prompt>
      </if>
   </filled>
</field>
```

In the above snippet of code, a user fills the field `continent`. It triggers the `<filled>` element, which checks if `continent` is `Antarctica` and if so, plays the prompt.

Inside a `<form>`, the `<filled>` element is triggered if combinations of fields are filled by user input, these fields being specified by the attribute `namelist`. The common attributes of the `<filled>` element are:

❏ `namelist` – contains the fields that trigger the `<filled>` element within a `<form>`. These are space delimited.

❏ `mode` – this can take the values `any` or `all`. If it takes `all`, the event is triggered only when all fields in the specified `namelist` are filled. If it takes `any`, the event is triggered when any of the fields specified are filled. The default is `all`. We can specify this attribute only if `<filled>` is a child of `<form>`.

673

This element is illustrated by the following example:

```
<form>
    <field name="latitude">
<!-- some code here -->
    </field>
    <field name="longitude">
<!-- some code here -->
    </field>
    <filled namelist="longitude latitude">
        <!-- Executed when longitude and latitude are filled -->
    </filled>
</form>
```

Event Handling in VoiceXML

The presentation of content is generally event driven. As in HTML and WML, the browser listens to the user and acts based on their input. But in this technology, which presents information in time rather than space, events become more important. Most normal, expected events are catered for. However, as VoiceXML is not intended for processing, unexpected runtime error support is limited.

The event handling is mainly used for unexpected events, such as the caller hanging up, missing resources or broken links, and so on. In the event model of VoiceXML, the interpreter context, in conjunction with the platform, listens for events to be generated. When a particular event is triggered, it passes the event to the current document/dialog, which may handle this event unless a document-specific one has been provided. Critical events like `telephone.hangup` are implemented so that the VoiceXML interpreter context itself terminates the execution. The diagram below illustrates the event model of VoiceXML:

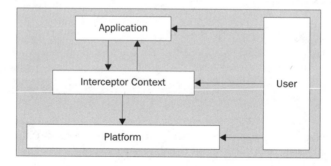

As shown above, the user is in the outermost part of the event model for a VoiceXML application. The platform and application generate events, which are handled by the interpreter context or application. The event flow in the diagram is shown by arrows.

Like in many languages, the VoiceXML event model contains two elements, `<throw>` and `<catch>`. The `<throw>` element throws a particular event to an application, while the `<catch>` element listens for a particular event.

The `<throw>` element has only one attribute called `event`, which contains the event to be thrown. The event can be either a standard event or a custom event. The events provided by the implementation include:

- ❏ cancel (loading of document)

- ❏ error (missing resource, divide by zero, etc)

- ❏ exit

- ❏ help (this is usually active for the whole document)

- ❏ noinput

- ❏ nomatch

- ❏ telephone.disconnect

For example:

```
<!-- A Predefined event 'nomatch' is thrown -->
<throw event="nomatch" />
```

The code to be interpreted on the occurrence of a particular event is generally contained within <catch>. The attributes of <catch> specify the event to handle, and an optional condition that defines at runtime, if this is the most qualified handler for this error. This also includes the count attribute that allows us to specify different handlers for different occurrences of an event, for example, each handler can be different for the first, second, third events, and so on. One thing to note is that intermediate values can be missed, perhaps to allow an alternative handler for recurring errors. We can see this below:

```
<!-- associated form or field -->
<catch event="nomatch noinput" count="1">please input the value</catch>
<catch event="nomatch noinput" count="6">There has been an error<exit/></catch>
```

In this case, the first five failures to gather successful input will re-prompt the user. On the sixth, the application will exit with an error message. While the above error code is not very elegant it should illustrate what is possible.

The event caught may be either standard or application defined. In the code snippet below, the standard event nomatch is caught by the <catch> element and prompts some advice to the user. The <nomatch> event is raised when the input entered by the user is not according to grammar specified:

```
<form id="continents">
   <block>
      Welcome to GeoPlanet
   </block>
   <field name="MyContinent">
      <prompt>
         Say the name of the continent you want to go to
      </prompt>
      <grammar src="conts.gram" type="application/x-jsgf" />
      <catch event="nomatch" >
         <prompt>
            To use this application, you need to learn the names of continents!
         </prompt>
      </catch>
<!-- some code here -->
</form>
```

There are also some standard `<catch>` events in VoiceXML. One example is `<nomatch>`, which is equivalent to `<catch event= "nomatch">`. We can rewrite the above code using `<nomatch>` as:

```
    </prompt>
    <grammar src="conts.gram" type="application/x-jsgf" />
    <nomatch>
        <prompt>
            To use this application, you need to learn the names of continents!
        </prompt>
    </nomatch>
```

In a similar way, the `<noinput>` element is equivalent to `<catch event= "noinput">`. `<help>` and `<error>` are defined similarly (the latter catches all types of errors).

Other Elements of VoiceXML

In addition to the more common elements described above, there are other elements used for providing additional facilities. The different elements covered here are:

❑ Java Speech Markup Language (JSML) elements, which act as markup for speech in VoiceXML and are designed exclusively for telephony applications

❑ The `<script>` element

❑ Telephony elements

JSML Elements

It is nearly impossible for devices to synthesize human speech from text in an effective manner since humans blend a lot of expressions into speech. One may stress important sentences or whisper secrets. No text to speech conversion can be expected to be smart enough to learn all the words and language grammar needed to enable an intelligent algorithm to add 'emotions' to speech without additional help on how to render the content. This means that there is a need for a markup language like HTML for speech. Just as HTML or WML elements, like the `<b>` element to direct the browser to display the characters in bold font, speech markup language provides elements to emphasize content, based on the system the speech engine uses.

JSML or Java Speech Markup Language is one such markup language for speech, proposed by Sun Microsystems for their Java platform. The JSML standard involves different elements to express speech with the right intonation, emphasis, pitch, speed and so on. VoiceXML adopted a limited set of the JSML elements for expressing speech markup. A table of those JSML elements that are used in VoiceXML is given here:

JSML element	Description	Important attributes
`<break>`	Used to insert a pause in speech.	`msecs`: Time of the pause in milliseconds; `size`: Duration of pause in a relative sense; values can be `none`, `small`, `medium` or `large`.
`<div>`	Indicates that the text is a separate paragraph or sentence.	`type`: value can be `sentence` or `paragraph`. This will usually cause an audible break.

JSML element	Description	Important attributes
`<emp>`	Specifies that the enclosed text should be emphasized.	`level`: Contains rate of emphasis, which can be `strong`, `moderate` (default), `none` or `reduced`.
`<sayas>`	Specifies the grammar that the content belongs to.	`class`, `sub` and `phon`, which are explained below.

The `<sayas>` element mainly contains information about 'what is spoken'. This information is contained in the `class` attribute, which can have values such as `date`, `digits`, `currency`, `number`, `time` etc. The `sub` attribute contains the substitute text to be spoken instead of the contained text. This would allow us to make the browser spell out a word rather than attempting to enunciate it, and to do conversion of type. The `phon` attribute contains the IPA or Unicode International Phonetic Alphabet characters to be spoken instead of the contained text. If the browser implementation does not support a type, it should say the words instead.

Scripting in VoiceXML

Like many other markup languages, VoiceXML enables the use of client-side scripting. Client-side logic, which is written as ECMAScript in the form of Character data (CDATA), is enclosed within a `<script>` element.

The following piece of code illustrates the use of script inside VoiceXML:

```
<?xml version = "1.0"?>
<vxml version = "1.0" >
<script>
    <![CDATA [function IncreNumber(num)
      {
        return (num+1);
      }]]>
</script>
<form>
    <field name="aninteger" type="integer" >
        <prompt>
            Say a number, I will  increment it!
        </prompt>
        <filled>
            <prompt>
                Next number is <value expr="IncreNumber(num)" />
            </prompt>
        </filled>
    </field>
</form>
</vxml>
```

Client-side scripting is particularly useful for some validation of user input and providing dynamic content.

Telephony Elements

The development of VoiceXML is at present mainly targeted at **telephony applications**. In a telephony application, the end-client will be the user who establishes a connection by dialing a number to a VoiceXML browser, which acts as a gateway between the content server and the end-user. These types of applications normally give the user the option to enter input either by speech, or by touch-tone key grammar – DTMF (Dual Tone MultiFrequency Tones) – the encoding method used to send keypad digits in a digital line. For example, users will sometimes prefer to enter the selection of a particular menu by pressing a key on a keypad, rather than giving input through speech.

677

The element <dtmf> is used to specify a DTMF grammar, as follows:

```
<dtmf src="Source URI" type="mime-type" />
```

In the grammar, we would specify the allowable key presses and define the corresponding string value that describes the significance of the input.

Like the <grammar> element, the <dtmf> element has the attributes src and type. However, VoiceXML does not specify or require support for any specific grammar format, like JSGF in <grammar>. The implementation platform or interpreter can specify its own standard MIME type.

In a menu dialog, we can include a dtmf attribute in a <choice> element, to give the user the option to enter a choice using DTMF, that is, by pressing the appropriate number on their phone.

A Sample VoiceXML Application

The following GeoPlanet VoiceXML application is a sample VoiceXML application intended to show how VoiceXML works and also to illustrate the difficulties of voice browsing. The application has been tested on the voice browser of IBM Alphaworks discussed above together with Tomcat as a servlet content server. The working is shown here in text mode.

This application brings together the different VoiceXML elements we have explained in different parts of this chapter. Its function is to provide information about different geographical locations around the world. Note that only the VoiceXML interface of the application is explained and illustrated, while the servlets used are not; they are available for download with the rest of the code from this book.

This application does two things:

❑   Finds a place if a latitude and longitude are entered

❑   Finds the latitude and longitude of a particular place

We'll first look at the root document, which acts as a startup form:

```
<!-- root document geo.vxml -->
<?xml version="1.0"?>
<vxml version="1.0">
<form>
   <block>
      Welcome to Geoplanet
      <goto next="geomain.vxml" />
   </block>
</form>
</vxml>
```

After giving a greeting, the root document directs the user to geomain.vxml, where the user makes the choice of whether to find a place by latitude and longitude or to get the latitude and longitude of a particular place:

```
<!-- geomain.vxml -->
<?xml version="1.0"?>
<vxml version="1.0" application="geo1.vxml">
   <menu>
      <prompt>
         Please select the category you want to use
         <enumerate/>
      </prompt>
      <choice next="findaplace.vxml">
         Find a Place
      </choice>
      <choice next="getlat.vxml">
         Get a Latitude and Longitude
      </choice>
      <noinput>
         Please make a choice
         <enumerate/>
      </noinput>
   </menu>
</vxml>
```

If the user decides to find a place by giving a latitude and longitude, they are sent to
findaplace.vxml:

```
<?xml version="1.0"?>
<vxml version="1.0" application="geo1.vxml">
<form>
   <field name="latitude" type="number">
      <prompt>
         Please give the latitude
      </prompt>
   </field>
   <field name="longitude" type="number">
      <prompt>
         Please give the longitude
      </prompt>
   </field>
   <filled namelist="latitude longitude">
   </filled>
   <block>
      <submit next="http://localhost:8080/servlet/get_place"/>
   </block>
</form>
</vxml>
```

As seen, findaplace.vxml asks the user for the latitude and longitude and submits the data to a
servlet, if both values are filled. The query string will look like:

```
http://localhost:8080/servlet/get_place?latitude=XX&longitude=XX
```

The servlet returns the name of a place. Normally this would be queued in TTS, if working in live
mode, and executed.

If the user had decided to find the latitude and longitude of a given place, they are sent to `getlat.vxml`:

```
<!-- getlat.vxml -->
<?xml version="1.0"?>
<vxml version="1.0"   application="geo1.vxml">
<form>
   <field name="place">
      <prompt>
         Please say the name of a place
      </prompt>
      <grammar src="places.gram" type="application/x-jsgf"/>
   </field>
   <block>
      <submit next="http://localhost:8080/servlet/get_lat_long" />
   </block>
</form>
</vxml>
```

The functionality of this document is similar to `findaplace.vxml`, but it has a grammar for speech input rather than having a `type` specified in the `<field>` element. The grammar file contains the names of different places that the application knows. If the field is filled, the data is submitted to another servlet, which returns the latitude and longitude.

VoiceXML and WAP

The description of VoiceXML given so far has sketched what is possible, although we are aware we have only skimmed the subject. It should however give you an idea of the possibilities and, having seen the limitations of current devices it should be clear what VoiceXML has to offer in terms of improved usability to our WAP applications. We can see how combining VoiceXML and WAP/WML for data input/output can be a powerful way of developing applications.

Possible examples are a credit card telephone booking and information site for a cinema. This allows the user to find cinema information, in this case having the ability to present the film information as text is better than saying it, but much of the interaction is better done spoken especially such input as film names. We can think of many other applications for a VoiceXML-enabled WAP site and we can look forward to the further development of this area.

Next Generation Interfaces and Multi Modal Technology

We now turn to the future to see what it may hold for voice-based applications.

Voice Browsing: Design and Limitations

So far, we have seen how voice browsing can be made a reality using VoiceXML and a voice browser. However, voice browsing in its fullest sense may not be acceptable to users for a number of reasons:

❑ Users cannot retain different menu items for long

❑ Users will always prefer familiar types of conversations rather than automated formal ones

For example, to get a particular railway time, users may prefer the conversation:

```
TRAVELLER    'What time does the train to Bangalore start from Trivandrum?'
ASSISTANT    'Half past three.'
```

Rather than the typical automated conversation like:

```
SERVICE      'Welcome to the railway timetable.
             Please say from where you want to travel?'
USER         'From Trivandrum.'
SERVICE      'Where do you want to go to?'
USER         'Bangalore.'
SERVICE      'The next train is at 3:30 PM.'
```

Taking these facts into account, a VoiceXML application should be designed so that it will lead the user to the correct solution by a conversation which mimics natural conversation as much as is possible. Researches in user interface technologies show that voice browsing should be based on a natural language dialog, and not be a simple translation of the functionality of a graphical-based user interface to voice-based interface to be successful.

Consider the case of an e-mail client application. Typical graphical elements of the application are an Inbox, Outbox, Sent items, and Trash Folder. We will take the example of Microsoft Outlook, which is shipped with MS Office:

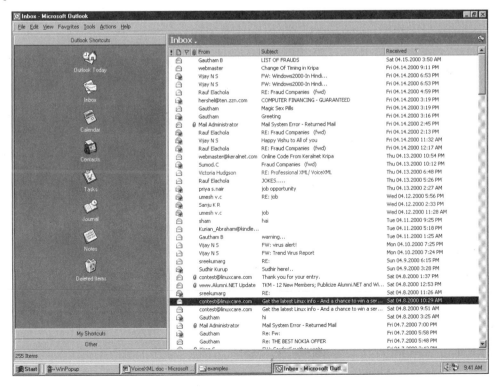

681

In the left pane, we can see different short cuts for navigating to folders, whose details are shown in the right pane. Different actions can be performed either by selecting menus or by shortcut keys. A straight translation of this user interface to a voice environment might be something like:

```
SERVICE:     'Welcome to Outlook, Please say the folder you want to go to.
             Inbox, Sent Items, Deleted Items,...'
USER:        'Inbox.'
SERVICE:     'Which action do you want to perform? Send and Receive,
             Send, Receive, Delete a mail, ...'
USER:        'Receive.'
SERVICE:     'You have 2 mails, from Victoriah, Thomas Roehrich.
             You can say Open to Open mail. Delete to... '
USER:        'Open mail from Victoriah.'
SERVICE:     'Hi, Send the chapter a.s.a.p. regards, Victoria, Wrox.'
USER:        'Open mail from Thomas Roehrich.'
SERVICE:     'Send the Patch as soon as possible.'
USER:        'Close Program'
```

Normally, nobody will be happy to use this application more than one or two times. This is because the mode of conversation between user and program is not natural. Based on my personal use of Outlook, I may want to know if there are mails from a particular person, to know if there are any important mails, to send some mail to somebody in particular, and so on. A VoiceXML application will be more natural if the design is based on natural dialogs, with mixed initiative forms. For example:

```
SERVICE      'Welcome to OutLook, Say help for ...'
USER         <barges in> 'Do I have any mails from Victoria?'
SERVICE      'Yes, Shall I read it?'
USER         'Yeah.'
SERVICE      'Hi, Send the chapter a.s.a.p. regards, Victoria, Wrox.
             Send a reply?'
USER         'Yeah, I'll send it tomorrow evening. Send a mail to Gulzar.'
SERVICE      'Please say…'
USER         <barges in> 'How's your trip?...'
```

This type of dialog sounds like a natural language conversation to the user.

Designing a voice-only user interface is a more difficult task than a straight WML interface because the contents at any moment should be kept to a minimum and navigation should be as natural as possible. This is where it would be nice to mix the two and allow both VoiceXML and WML on the same application. This would normally rely on support for both and may be difficult to implement so that either stands in its own right. This depends to a great extent on the use of the language and the psychology of different people.

Voice Applications and Mobile Devices

As we have seen throughout this book, microbrowsers in clients (mainly mobile phones) are characterized by limitations. These limitations led to a new protocol called WAP and a new markup language called WML, based on XML. Even though the technical limitations are solved to an extent as we saw earlier, the user interfaces available still leave a lot to be desired.

The user usually struggles to enter any text using the keypad of a mobile phone or a PDA. In telephony applications, DTMF and shortcut keys configured by device manufacturers can be used to solve these limitations to a certain extent.

MultiModal Interfaces

MultiModal interfaces allow the user to make use of different mediums of interaction and give the designer the ability to present content by integrating different interfaces like speech and graphics. MultiModal technology is well suited to the field of wireless communication as it is inherently characterized by the limitations that wireless devices have.

In MultiModal interfaces, the user is allowed to use their most natural way of input, which may be either speech-based or graphical-based. MultiModal technology can be applied to application level control as well as individual form level control. For example, in the case of a CAD application, the procedure usually adopted by the user to draw a solid block of iron is:

- ❑ Select primitives from the toolbox
- ❑ Construct the block on the drawing area with the help of a pointing device such as a mouse
- ❑ Assign the material as Iron

On redesigning this interaction based on a MultiModal interaction, the user could:

- ❑ Move a pointing device to the drawing area
- ❑ Select the primitive from the tool palette by saying the type of the primitive
- ❑ Draw using a mouse and then say 'Iron' to assign the material as iron

Once the user gets familiarized with the interface, this will save many hours of designer time in real life. In a similar way, an application can use MultiModal technology to give the user output on a simulation process. If the user analyzes the stress of different parts in a CAD application, our application may typically speak the details as the user moves over them with the pointing device.

Shown below is a prototype MultiModal application, called ProfilTec:

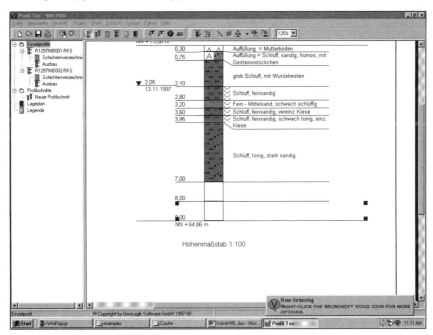

In this application, Microsoft Speech API is used to fill the geographical information of a particular layer selected. Here the user can select the particular geographical layer with a pointing device like a mouse and fill in the information by speaking out.

Similarly, in WAP based wireless applications, users can navigate to a particular field using the conventional keypad and fill the field by speaking out.

Recently, Microsoft Research demonstrated a research prototype of their PDA called MiPad, which works entirely on MultiModal technology. They call these types of interfaces 'Tap and Talk'. To enter text in MiPad, users can select an edit box with a pointing device and speak to fill the edit box with content. The PDA was demonstrated in a Wireless LAN. Since bandwidths and research at speech technology show a steep curve of growth, these types of PDAs may be available in the near future.

At present in desktop computers with the Java Platform, we can make use of the Java Speech API to make applets MultiModal. Also, with Wireless modems, VoiceXML and the PDAs presently in the market like the Palm Pilots, MultiModal technology can be made a reality to some extent.

Summary

In this chapter, we have seen an overview of how a voice-based interface can be specified using VoiceXML. VoiceXML applications consist of many documents, each of which contains dialogs. These dialogs take the form of menus or forms. Forms can be constructed in different schemes – direct or mixed initiative.

The implementation of VoiceXML can be either telephony-based or browser-based. In the case of telephony-based implementations, the user connects to a VoiceXML gateway through the telephone, which itself connects to a content server. However, for browser-based implementations the user interacts directly with a browser that connects to the content server. The browser or gateway interacts with a TTS (Text To Speech) engine and speech recognition engine, which may be implemented in hardware or software to render VoiceXML dialogs to the user.

As both voice browsing and visual browsing in mobile devices are characterized by limitations, MultiModal interactions are the best choice for delivering content to the user and for collecting information from the user. With advances in speech technology research and wireless communication, these kinds of interfaces should become a reality in the near future.

19

What the Future Holds

Predicting the future direction of any technology and its impact on the way we live and work is always fraught with risk. All too frequently, last year's certainties are at best slightly off target and at worst downright ludicrous with hindsight.

All the usual clichés regarding technological change apply to WAP and a range of other leading edge wireless technologies; rapid change and development, huge speculative investments by an enormous range of companies from tiny start-ups to some of the largest companies in the world such as Nokia, Microsoft and Vodafone Airtouch, enormous uncertainties, huge potential market opportunities to fight for – you've heard them all a dozen times before. In many ways they mirror the emergence and growth of the Internet, with its associated changes and opportunities.

However, we are currently at a stage where we can (with some certainty!) identify a number of key elements that will have an impact on the development of the wireless data market in the months and years ahead. The precise balance of these forces, in terms of their relative impact and importance, is in a state of flux. However, they each form a part of the overall wireless data jigsaw, which in turn will influence the future role of WAP within the overall picture.

We have already seen the near future and what we should expect in the next year or so in terms of the development of WAP, WML and it's associated technologies, we now look further to the long term and what we should expect.

In this chapter, we'll take a brief overview of some of these different forces, in the hope that if you are reading this in 2001 or a little later you will at least recognize and identify with some of these ideas and feel that they were indeed reasonable and rational at the time.

High Bandwidth – Key Enabler or Disappointment?

At the time of writing, we are witnessing an incredible economic and commercial phenomenon in Europe: the spectacle of a number of huge existing mobile telephony carriers together with a sprinkling of hopeful new entrants, bidding literally billions of pounds, euros and (through the participation of US partners) dollars to obtain UMTS wireless spectrum licenses (UMTS is the so called 3rd Generation or 3G technology that will eventually supercede the existing GSM mobile telephony standard). Theoretically, these exciting new 3G networks will one day deliver data at up to 2Mb per second to wireless devices, but despite the establishment of a European wide standard for 3G, there are still many technical hurdles to be overcome. In practice there will only be around 384 Kbps for the first few years of deployment and many are highly skeptical of even that data rate being achieved under normal operating conditions.

The multi-billion dollar question is, of course, will these companies achieve anything like a viable return on the huge investment in licenses and the construction of the networks? This is a key point with regards to WAP. If commercial reality results in the financial markets losing faith in the promise of 3G, this will lead to lower investment and uptake of WAP-based services. This will invert the current trend of high investment, which in turn helps foster interest in and uptake and development of numerous new WAP based services and supporting technologies, such as GPRS and 3G.

We will consider the evidence for consumer and business demand for wireless data services in the next section. First, let us look at the anticipated developments in carrier technology, leading on from the existing GSM based standards through to full 3G networks.

GSM is a circuit-switched technology. The implications of this are that a caller needs to establish a connection and maintain it in order to effect data transfer in either direction. On the other hand, packet-switched technologies – such as GPRS and 3G – allow users of mobile devices to establish a connection with their carrier, which is then maintained indefinitely. Data can be sent or received with billing based on data transferred as opposed to connection time as with current GSM systems. There is no need to re-establish a connection, or go through the tedious dial in and hand-shaking procedures that are involved using the current generation of circuit-switched networks. A GPRS connection will respond to a data transfer request in less than 0.25 seconds. Typically, it can take at least 30 seconds to dial in and start data transmission with GSM.

This feature of all packet-switched systems is extremely important. It provides the user with permanent connectivity, removing one of the major frustrations of GSM, namely dropped connections and the inconvenience and delay of having to dial up repeatedly to perform a WAP-based transaction or interaction over GSM, or indeed any other circuit-switched network.

In addition to permanent connectivity, even the very first packet-switched services such as GPRS will deliver higher data transfer rates than the 9.6 Kbps currently possible over GSM. This will naturally further boost the convenience and capability of these systems. Initially GPRS services will probably deliver between 20 and 30 Kbps. This may improve somewhat, depending on the investments the carriers make in this technology prior to the migration to 3G. EDGE is a further enhancement of GSM based technology and may eventually offer data transmission rates that match those of 3G networks. EDGE stands for Enhanced Data Rates for Global Evolution. As with all the carrier systems beyond GSM it is packet switched. It is anticipated that EDGE will be available in the market for deployment by existing GSM operators.

It is noteworthy that existing WAP handsets (i.e. GSM based devices) will not work with GPRS or any of the other new carrier technologies. Whilst we are likely to see a number of dual carrier compatible devices in the future, that support GSM and GPRS or GPRS and EDGE, or even all three standards within one phone, the existing GSM WAP phones cannot be upgraded to cope with the new carrier technologies. From the point of view of the uptake and success of WAP, the benefits associated with the migration from GSM to any of the packet switched systems give users another reason to upgrade their handsets. The larger the number of up to date handsets out in the user community, the better the chances of WAP succeeding. Improvements in the hardware, browsers, keypads etc. will mean that newer phones are more effective, powerful and useful tools than the current first generation GSM offerings on the market.

The diagram below illustrates the data transmission rates as given by the 'official' estimates quoted in the popular press:

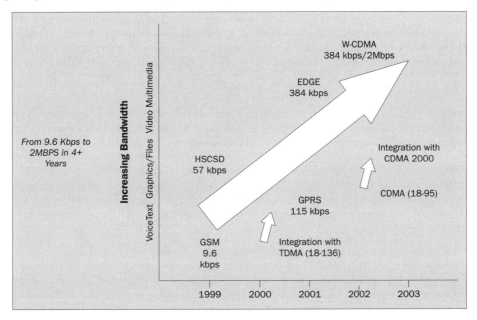

Given the cost of establishing 3G services, there has been some speculation that EDGE-based 2.5G services, which are essentially an enhanced version of GSM technology, might offer strong competition to the 3G providers. Amongst the facts mitigating against this happening are that all of the companies best placed to deploy EDGE in the UK (and most probably throughout the rest of Europe as well) have won 3G licenses and therefore have a strong incentive to provide full 3G services as quickly as possible to start recouping their investment. In addition, in the event that mobile data services prove to be as popular as the carriers hope, EDGE will struggle to serve large numbers of concurrent users with high data demands.

With regard to the situation in the US, GSM based services are far less firmly established. There are only about 5 million GSM users in the US (this compares to well over 200 million outside the US), with a high proportion of non-GSM analogue devices still in use. Due to the numerous competing standards currently in place across the US and the more patchy coverage offered by many carriers in that market, it is almost a certainty that the roll-out of 3G services across the US will lag behind Europe and most of Asia. Most analysts estimate a delay of 18 months to 2 years, although such estimates should be treated with caution as it is difficult to compare such vastly different geographical regions. Once the major US cities have their coverage in place, most users will probably be satisfied with the level of service. Given the vast areas of the US with very low population densities, it is doubtful that it would make much sense to provide full 3G (or indeed any other network) coverage across all of these. Within Europe the population density is far higher, therefore the European market can be thought of as one extended urban and suburban area from the point of view of wireless service providers.

So, what does all of this mean for WAP? Regardless of the precise degree of improvement and the associated timescales, there can be no doubt that we will see increases in bandwidth over the coming years, along with all the other benefits associated with the migration from circuit-switched to packet-switched transmission. According to most projections, by 2002, 80% of European subscribers will have access to a GPRS or even higher-speed network, enabling WAP services to use a greater bandwidth. Most of Asia will gain at least comparable levels of access to more advanced networks, with the US lagging somewhat.

One line of logic would therefore suggest that one of the current benefits of WAP, namely the efficient mechanism it applies to compressing data for transmission, will become less important in a higher bandwidth world. This argument assumes the overall quantities of data remain constant. However, as has happened consistently in the wired world, as more and more bandwidth and computing power become available, new applications and enhancements come along that gobble up all the increased resources. This is highly likely to occur in this situation, making effective compression an ongoing necessity. This is one area in which WAP has a definite advantage over current HTML-based wireless protocols.

There is also likely to be a lag between the first packet-switched data services operating at relatively modest (even if better than GSM) data transmission rates and full-blooded 3G services. During this 'lull before the data transmission storm', WAP will have ample time to become established as a foundation block for all subsequent developments. The greater the number of users connecting via GPRS within a given carrier cell, the lower the average data rate each will enjoy. In practice, the headline burst transmission speed of up to 115Kbps (theoretically even 171Kbps) will be reduced to about 32Kbps or even lower. Everything will hinge on the number of concurrent users within a given cell and their specific data transmission demands. In other words, bandwidth will still be a scarce resource for several more years at least.

WAP will be successful and become firmly established if the market for wireless data services grows dramatically during the 2.5G phase, a period which may last for about 2 years or so. If the market for whatever reason fails to materialize, then clearly the matter of WAP versus any competing technologies becomes a largely irrelevant contest to determine the tallest of the seven dwarves. However, there is considerable reason to be optimistic. We will consider the growing body of evidence for the growth of the wireless market in the next section.

Evidence for the Existence of a Wireless Market

Up until a couple of years ago, mobile telephony was just that – mobile voice telephony. With the advent of SMS messaging and a range of more sophisticated voice services such as voicemail, we have begun to use mobiles for much more than just synchronous voice calls. The uptake of SMS messaging has been phenomenal. Deutsche Telekom sometimes handles up to 5000 messages per second and this figure continues to grow rapidly. In terms of the evolution of mobile phones from telephony device to Wireless Information Devices (or WIDs), SMS is extremely significant. It demonstrates that users believe the benefits of such a service outweigh the inconvenience of miserly keypads and tiny screens. It is a reasonable assumption that as WAP and the supporting devices and carrier technologies improve dramatically in the near future, users will migrate to WAP with it's added benefits.

Currently, the most convincing example of the mass market potential for wireless data services comes from Japan. In February 1999, NTT DoCoMo (Japan's largest mobile telecom operator) launched its I-Mode service. Using a proprietary HTML based browser and a GPRS packet-switched carrier system, I-Mode phones have a relatively large screen and a keypad that is fairly typical in terms of size compared to the current generation of European mobile phones. I-Mode phones can only be used with the NTT DoCoMo service, although a number of different manufacturers produce them.

At the time of writing, I-Mode has nearly 10 million subscribers, having far exceeded NTT DoCoMo's most optimistic forecasts for adoption and resulting in a temporary halt to the recruitment of new users as systems are upgraded to meet demand. The number of people in Japan accessing the Internet via their mobile phones now exceeds the number of fixed wire access users. This is the first market in which this has happened, but others will follow in the coming years. The all-important ARPU (Average Revenue Per User) has also exceeded all expectations. In addition to a high monthly user tariff, a broad range of premium services incur a range of charges that go directly to the carrier. These are in addition to the actual costs of goods and services purchased in a transaction.

The range of services offered by I-Mode is already quite broad. Many of the traditional Internet based facilities are available – shopping for books, CDs and cinema tickets, as well as financial services and information and entertainment content. At the time of writing, I-Mode offers content from 420 different content partners and provides about 550 different sites. These are only accessible via a link from the DoCoMo mobile portal. In addition to these partner sites, there are around 8000 so called 'voluntary' sites. These have also been designed for I-Mode access (although they are not developed in direct partnership and association with NTT – hence the designation 'voluntary'), and are accessible either by inputting a URL into the phone, or via of the 20 search engines. These search engines operate in an analogous manner to normal wired Internet search engines, accepting category or keyword searches.

Unsurprisingly, e-mail has proved to be one of the core killer applications on I-Mode. Many younger users in particular are prepared to wrestle with the small keys to write long messages and it is clear that many subscribers regard this service and voice telephony alone as ample justification for having an I-Mode phone. One of the most popular additional services is in fact a daily cartoon, which can be downloaded for the equivalent of a few pence per month, a clear indication that there will indeed be many opportunities to innovate and create new services for the m-commerce age.

Whilst I-Mode uses an HDML (Hand Held Device Mark-up Language) browser, from the users' perspective the types of services and its form of operation are not significantly different from what is feasible with WAP. The lesson from Japan is that there is a huge potential market for wireless data services and – on the premise that the WAP standard prevails – there will be huge demand for all the skills and technologies associated with WAP. Take a look at `http://www.nttdocomo.com` if you are interested in finding out more about I-Mode.

Many interesting examples of wireless innovation within Europe can be found in the Scandinavian countries, where market adoption rates of both wired and wireless technologies are amongst the highest in the world. Based in Helsinki, a small start-up firm called WapIT (`http://www.wapit.com`) provides a wide range of services to users of their wireless portal. Address books, calendars, custom icons, as well as a range of more esoteric services such as horoscopes, jokes, a vegetarian recipe of the day and highlights of Finnish players in the U.S. National Hockey League, are all available. WapIT has more than 100 content partners who develop many of the services offered. Content is provided by most partners on a revenue-sharing basis, although some provide it for free. WapIT also provides a range of standard practical applications such as package tracking, flight information and emergency phone numbers.

Another Finnish company, Iobox (`http://www.iobox.com`) lets users enter personal data like calendar entries, address book and Web bookmarks which are then stored on Iobox's servers. Having entered this data via a conventional Web site, it can then be accessed via a WAP phone. SMS based reminders can be set up and are then sent by Iobox to warn you of meetings, anniversaries etc. Room33 (`http://www.room33.com`) is a Swedish company that offers a suite of personal information services including e-mail, weather, financial news and travel information. Whilst currently focusing on WAP based services, Room33 emphasize their commitment to whatever markup languages may win in the future. Thus, through the use of templates they are able to deliver WML, XHTML or Palm Web Clipping content to the appropriate devices.

There will doubtless be a ferocious battle over who 'owns' the end customer for wireless data services. The current dominant players are, of course, the wireless carriers, however they will come under increasing pressure from a broad array of content providers, new and existing Web portal businesses and ISPs. These forces should promote the establishment of standards such as WAP, since any player attempting to protect their customer relationships through the use of proprietary technology is unlikely to succeed in the longer term. Carriers offering a 'Walled Garden' approach, whereby the consumer is only allowed access to a limited number of pre-configured sites and services controlled by the carrier (either directly or through partnerships with banks, shops, travel agents etc.) may believe that they will be able to reap more revenue than those offering unlimited access to all sites and services. However, as was the case with players like AOL and CompuServe in the world of the wired Web, customers will ultimately demand free unfettered access across the Web. You and I will want to choose the services we want from all those available, not a narrow sub-set as defined by the network provider. The walled garden may be comfortable, but the huge freedom of choice available beyond is even more attractive in the medium to longer term.

The Future for Client Devices and Operating Systems

When considering devices and client operating systems, a good starting point is to review and understand the most basic general aspects of mobile data devices. To begin with, while handheld computers have massive theoretical processing capability, they will always rely on batteries of some sort or other. Running powerful applications requires significant energy. Although advances in chip technology could radically reduce power usage (for example, Transmeta's Crusoe chip should use only 1 – 2 Watts compared to an Intel mobile chip's 10 – 15 Watts, and ARM processors use even less) and battery technology is improving steadily, power is always likely to be a limiting factor for mobile devices. Server-based applications are one way to improve on the load on devices.

Security issues are also paramount. A secure network-based architecture is clearly preferable to carrying around sensitive data on a small device that is so easily lost or stolen.

We already have a vast array of different form factors of devices, ranging from tiny mobile phones to laptop-sized devices, which in future should have WAP capability. Psion's NetBook is likely to have a WAP browser available for it in the very near future. The range of devices is likely to increase even further, as suppliers seek to exploit new market niches and differentiate their offerings. It is safe to conclude that we will not see PC form factor type standardization in this market. Web browsers such as Netscape's Communicator and Microsoft's Internet Explorer are not truly scalable to handheld wireless devices. What is needed is an intelligent self-optimizing protocol, with complementary microbrowsers and user interfaces. WAP has a clear role to play in this world of 1001 different form factors managing data across an evolving set of carrier technologies. Ease of use, reliability and general fitness for purpose are essential to the broad uptake of mass-market devices and services. Were Nokia, Ericsson or Motorola to sell several million WAP phones with the same unreliability and ease of use issues to general users as some personal computer systems have suffered from, they would probably be bankrupted by demands for customer service.

So how do the current contenders on the operating system side compare against these criteria? The Palm OS has been a spectacular consumer success on pen-driven PDAs. The form factor, ease of use, simplicity, battery life, connectivity and general overall convenience have made Palm products the choice for many users around the world. A large user base has driven the trend of third party applications development, in turn driving further demand. Technically, the Palm OS has a number of shortcomings, which present the company with severe constraints as we enter the wireless data world.

The rudimentary 16-bit architecture does not lend itself to the plethora of device form factors that it will need to support and the integration of key wireless technologies into the OS will be a challenge. A radical evolution of the Palm OS to a new 32-bit architecture is needed. This will be an even more dramatic evolution than was the move from EPOC16 to EPOC32 for Psion a few years ago.

The EPOC32 operating system, originally developed by Psion, is now controlled by the Symbian consortium. Designed and built from the ground up for mobile computing, it is without doubt the best of the three major platform contenders for wireless client devices in terms of its capabilities and architecture. There are Development SDKs available for the EPOC32 OS at http://www.symbiandevnet.com. Symbian intend to license the EPOC operating system as widely as possible, the UIKON interface support enables individual licensees to customize the user interface as a means of differentiating their products whilst maintaining full compatibility with applications written for EPOC. EPOC is extremely compact and efficient, while being extremely robust and resilient with the full multi-tasking and multi-threading capabilities associated with traditional PC type operating systems that require far greater memory and processing resources.

Assuming everything goes to plan, from early in 2001 onwards we should see a wide array of devices running EPOC. These will range from 'Smart Phones', to more sophisticated 'Communicators' with larger screens and enhanced capabilities. Given the Symbian partners' dominance of the mobile phone handset market (between them Nokia, Motorola, Ericsson and Matsushita produce more than 60% of the world's mobile phones), it is a near certainty that once the Symbian products become available, should these manufacturers choose to do so they could deliver huge numbers of these devices via their existing distribution channels. This would include the conventional carrier subsidized offers for both monthly billed and pre-paid mobile use. For the likes of Palm and Microsoft's Windows CE/Pocket PC licensees like Compaq and HP, this represents a formidable challenge.

Given Symbian's wholehearted endorsement of and commitment to WAP, the likely success of Symbian based devices in 2001 and beyond can only be good news for all advocates of WAP. Palm's proprietary Web Clipping technology is unlikely to move beyond Palm OS based devices, however WAP browsers are already available for the Palm platform and may eventually supersede Web Clipping.

Following a number of false starts, Microsoft has changed the name of Windows CE to Pocket PC in the latest version of its mobile operating system. Early versions of Windows CE were slow, power hungry, unstable and had a user interface that put off all but the most dedicated users. Much of the early hardware designed by Microsoft's licensees left a lot to be desired, especially when compared to slicker more elegant products from Palm and Psion. Whilst Microsoft is clearly learning and applying lessons already learned by its competitors, it is by no means certain that it will be able to catch up, either with Palm's market share of the current generation of palmtop PDA devices, or Symbian's overall technical superiority and commercial positioning in the area of handheld operating systems for the emerging types of wireless device. Having said that, the very latest Pocket PC powered PDAs from Compaq, HP and Casio have been received very well by reviewers and clearly offer a number of compelling features such as advanced synchronization capabilities with desktop systems, built in MP3 players and high quality color screens.

In a recent development, which may prove significant, Sony has chosen to license EPOC from Symbian. Given that Sony already has a strong relationship with Microsoft (all of Sony's highly successful Vaio laptop PCs use the Windows platform) and the fact that Microsoft undoubtedly lobbied hard to win over Sony to Pocket PC, the influential consumer electronics firm nevertheless chose EPOC. It can be assumed that Sony represents a highly qualified 'neutral' party in this battle. They were free to select whichever platform they believed would bring the greatest commercial success to them as an organization.

There is also a contrary argument that says that the client device OS is largely an irrelevance. Given that what we are dealing with is likely to be an ultra-thin client, provided that they support some sort of standard browser (such as a WAP browser), the underlying system is of no great importance. Applications will consist of a series of plug-in applets that are downloaded from the network as and when needed, removing all the problems of having to maintain a sophisticated client environment. Should this model emerge, it will also support the establishment and maintenance of a standard such as WAP.

Synchronization standards such as the SyncML initiative announced a few months ago could theoretically lead to rapid and simple interchange of data between competing device technologies. SyncML is currently being developed by a consortium that includes Psion, Palm, IBM and Motorola. Its aim is to develop a common protocol for synchronization between all SyncML compatible devices and applications. This should ultimately permit seamless exchange and interoperability over all wired and wireless networks, assuming that the initiative is successful. As with all such standards based efforts, the key driver that will determine success is whether or not a critical mass of compliant systems, devices and applications becomes established within a reasonable time frame. Once such a market share is achieved, manufacturers and software developers have more to lose by remaining outside the standard than they stand to gain by joining it.

Bluetooth, Voice Recognition and Positioning Technology

Originally conceived by Ericsson in 1994 as MC Link, Bluetooth can be considered as a wireless metaphor for universal serial bus (USB). It offers inexpensive, easy to build and use, low power consumption, wireless communication over short distances by means of small radio chips that can be built into just about any electronic device. Bluetooth uses unlicensed spectrum to broadcast within a 10 meter radius at around 720 Kbps. It is not dependent on line-of-sight connection and can operate through walls and most solid objects.

Without taking your Bluetooth-enabled PDA out of your pocket, you will be able to synchronize it with your PC or establish a wireless link via your mobile phone to your PDA. There are still a few glitches and issues to be resolved with the technology, but we can expect to see Bluetooth-enabled devices in volume in 2001. As with all such technologies, reaching a critical mass of relevant devices in the field is key: after all, as Alexander Graham Bell may once have said, 'It's not much fun being the owner of the world's first and only telephone.' Bluetooth, like a number of other key technologies such as voice recognition, improved displays and keyboards, will make the user experience more convenient and rewarding for wireless devices. This in turn will generate increased uptake, stimulating demand for WAP based services. You can find more information about Bluetooth at http://www.bluetooth.com/.

Whilst Bluetooth will help overcome the fiddliness of wires and sockets for connectivity, apart from providing a means of linking a mobile device to a normal keyboard or monitor, it will do nothing to improve the ease of interaction with the mobile device itself. By abandoning keyboards altogether, Palm Pilots sacrificed data input convenience for other benefits which users found to be an acceptable trade-off. But, imagine if a Palm could achieve perfect voice recognition, capturing your words both for input and as a means of navigating through existing information. The usability and attractiveness of the device would take a leap forward if this could be implemented well. With the exception of Orange's *Wildfire* product, which accepts and responds to a range of voice commands, very few voice recognition solutions have been deployed in the mobile communications industry with any success. The urgent need for such technology and the rapid progress being made with the use of voice to control PCs is likely to drive the delivery of such solutions in the next few years. There is huge interest within the industry in such technologies and the PC experience suggests that successful deployments will combine voice input and control with visual displays and various forms of mechanical input – would you want to keep saying 'Scroll' to your PDA?

The Belgian company Lernout and Hauspie, which recently acquired another leading voice recognition company called Dragon Systems, is currently one of the leaders in the field. The deployment of their technology within the PDA/wireless device market is a high strategic priority for them.

GPS and associated positioning technologies are becoming well established. We will soon see these integrated into mobile phones and wireless data devices. We've already seen how powerful the marriage between Push and location-awareness could be.

In the US, the Federal Communications Commission has stipulated that wireless carriers must be capable of identifying the physical location of mobile phones and other wireless devices to within a few meters by 2002. This is to enable the emergency services to pinpoint callers. The E-911 emergency law has allowed the development of some exciting new location specific promotions and one-to-one location related marketing exercises. For example, the Zagat restaurant guide, which is widely known and used in the US, has been made available to wireless data subscribers. Zagat is extending its services outside the US, including a version for Tokyo, which will be launched in collaboration with I-Mode. In a number of US cities, restaurant and bar owners already offer location specific information and special offers based on a customer's actual location in the city. This concept could clearly be extended across a whole range of retail and travel services.

It should be noted that there are of course a number of legal issues regarding the use of a wireless users' position information. This data is currently controlled by the carriers and will have enormous potential value in the medium to longer term, assuming a suitable legal framework can be established around its use and dissemination to third parties.

The Post PC World Will be Wireless

Where, ultimately, are these developments taking us and what will the technological landscape look like in 5 or 10 years time? All around us we can see strands of technology and patterns of human behavior that may lead us decisively into a post PC world.

In this environment, the primary personal computational and information device will not be a desk bound or laptop PC, reliant on wired networks to be a communication tool. It is more likely to be a highly portable device similar in outward design to today's PDAs. However, these devices – let's call them Wireless Information Devices or WIDs for convenience – will be far smarter than anything currently available. Using fully built out 3G networks they will deliver seamless real time video conferencing, enabling you to see one or more people you are talking to. You will also be able to record, send and play video mails. Voice recognition will provide near perfect speech to text and text to speech services, enabling you to perform keyboard intensive tasks quickly and easily. Unified messaging, combining voice, e-mail, video mail, fax and any other messaging service imaginable will become a reality.

Should you still wish to use a conventional keyboard, or a full size monitor or overhead display screen or even a printer, your WID will connect wirelessly to such peripherals, which will become commodity office items, as ubiquitous and interchangeable as office chairs and flip charts. All the really personal and powerful information will be stored remotely on a secure server. You will be able to access it as necessary using your WID as the primary access control mechanism, even if you use other tools to display and interact with the data. You will determine just how much of your own information you hold locally on the device at any time and your company's IT policy will determine the rules on corporate data that you can access and use on your device.

There will be many slips and stumbles along the way and doubtless even 10 years may prove too short a time horizon for many of these things to be realized. Let us not forget just how long it has taken the original Apple Newton to evolve into the successful Palm. What we are talking about here are several further leaps forward. However, we can see the foundation technologies, ideas and services all around us. The first generation WAP phones operating over GSM networks may be slow, awkward and at many times very frustrating to use. Nevertheless, even these early pioneering commercially available devices are capable of delivering compelling and valuable services and information and the ultimate potential is clear to see for all but the most blinkered observer.

Let the innovating begin.

WML Elements

This section lists all of the WML elements in alphabetical order, along with all their attributes (where relevant), a description of the function of each, and details of support for each element on four types of browser - Microsoft's Mobile Explorer, Phone.com (UP.Browser), Nokia and Ericsson. The support of each element/attribute for each browser type will be represented by a 4-letter code in brackets after it's description:

The **first** letter denotes support by Microsoft Mobile Explorer, and will be 'M' if it is properly supported, and 'm' if it is not.

The **second** letter denotes support by Up.Simulator, and will be 'U' if it is properly supported, and 'u' if not.

The **third** letter denotes support by Nokia (6110, 6150 and 7110), and will be 'N' if properly supported, 'n' if not.

The **fourth** letter denotes support by Ericsson (our testing performed on the R380 simulator), and will be 'E' if properly supported, 'e' if not.

So, for example, an attribute supported by Up.Simulator and Ericsson, but not by Nokia or Microsoft would have (mUnE) after its description.

The last section of this appendix deals with some specialized elements that are specific to the Up.Browser, and so consequently won't be recognized by other microbrowsers. It is strongly recommended that you bear this in mind when considering the interoperability issues of your WML decks!

Universal Attributes

One more thing before we plunge into the list - there are three attributes that can be applied to nearly every single element in this list, we will detail them here:

xml:lang Specifies the natural language for the element and its contents. (MUNE)
Id Specifies the name of the element. (MUNE)
Class Specifies the class name for the element. (muNe)

So, unless specified otherwise in the individual element descriptions, these attributes can be applied to any element.

<a>

Specifies a link to another card. (MUNE)

Attributes

href Specifies the destination URI – the name of the card to display.(MUNE)
title Specifies a brief text string identifying the link.(mUNE)

<access>

Allows the writer of the card to limit access to the document to only certain other cards, by location - domain and path. It is contained within <head> tags.(MUNE)

Attributes

domain sets a domain that can access the card.(MUNE)
path sets a path that can access the card.(MUNE)

<anchor>

Specifies an anchor.(MUNE)

Attributes

title Specifies a brief text string identifying the link.(MUNE)

<b>

Specifies bold text.(MUNE)

Note

The Ericsson seems to display **all** text formatting (all of the tags listed in this appendix) as bold, except big. Text formatting doesn't appear to work inside a link.

<big>

Specifies large font text.(MUNE)

Tells the browser to add a line break to the text at the point the element is written.(MUNE)

<card>

Specifies a single interaction between the user and the device.(mUNE)

Attributes

title	Specifies a label for the card.(MuNE)
newcontext	Default is false, but if set to true, the current browser context is re-initialized upon entry to this card and clears the navigational history state, and resets the implementation-specific state to a default value (which may vary with browser). newcontext is only performed as part of the go task.(MUNE)
ordered	This attribute gives an indication to the user agent about how the card content is organized. This indication can be used to organize the content presentation or to otherwise influence the layout of the card. If ordered="true", the card is naturally organized as a linear sequence of field elements, for example, a set of questions or fields, which are naturally handled by the user, in the order in which they are specified in the group. If ordered="false", the card is a collection of field elements without a natural order.(mUNE)

<do>

Specifies a general mechanism for the user to act upon the current card. The action to do, when activating a do element can be specified by the elements **go, prev, noop** or **refresh.** See relevant sections.(MUNE)

Attributes

type	Specifies a hint to the microbrowser about the author's intended use of the element. The table below shows the predefined do-types.(MUNE)

Do-type	Description
accept	Positive Acknowledgement.
prev	Backward history navigation.
help	Request for help.
reset	Clearing or resetting state.
options	Request for options or additional operations.
delete	Delete item or choice.
unknown	Generic type.
"" (empty string)	Equivalent to unknown.
x-*, X-*	Experimental type.
vnd.*, VND.*	Vendor or user agent specific type of the kind vnd.*co-type*, where *co* is a company name and *type* is the do-type.

label	Specifies a text string suitable for dynamically labeling a user interface component.(MUNE)
optional	If this attribute value is true, the microbrowser can ignore the element, otherwise it is set to "false" (the default), and it is not allowed to.(MUNE)
name	Specifies a name for the element. If a card level and a deck level do element have the same name, the card level element will override the deck level element.(MUNE)

<em>

Specifies emphasized text, in a very similar fashion to the effect of the <b> tag.(MuNE)

<fieldset>

When <fieldset> brackets are put around sections of paragraph content, it is supposed to tell the browser to separate them out into "subpanes", to give the card a better look, and lay the information out in a more logical way. At the moment, browsers do not support it very well. They either completely ignore the element, or don't display the text inside the tags. (mune)

<go>

Specifies a task that navigates to a URI. xml:lang is not an associated attribute. (MUNE)

Attributes

href	Specifies the destination URI – the name of the card to display. (MUNE)
sendreferer	Defaults to false. If set to true, the user agent needs to specify the URI of the deck containing this task in the server-bound request. (mUNE)
method	Specifies the HTTP request method, either **get** or **post**. (MUNE)
accept-charset	Must be followed by a list of character encodings for data that the origin server must accept when processing input. (mUNE)

<head>

This element specifies an optional header for the wml document. It is used to contain **<Access>** and **<meta>** information that relates to the whole document. (MUNE)

<i>

Specifies italicized text. (MuNE)

<img/>

Specifies a picture to be inserted. (MUNE)

Attributes

Some of you may find that the behavior of some of these attributes (paying particular attention to height and width) may differ on the emulators as compared to the real phones. For example, it was found that the height and width attributes crashed on the nokia 7110 toolkit, but worked on the actual phone.

src	Specifies the URI for the image to display. If the localsrc attribute (see below) specifies a valid icon, this attribute is ignored. (MUNE)
alt	Specifies the alternative text to display if the device does not support images or neither the localsrc attribute or src attribute name a valid image. (MUNE)
localsrc	Specifies a predefined icon. If this attribute specifies a valid icon, the src attribute and alt attributes are ignored. (MUne)
align	Specifies how the image is aligned relative to the current line of text. It can be given one of three values, "top" "middle" or "bottom". (mUnE)
vspace	Specifies the white space to allocate above and below the image. (muNE)
hspace	Specifies the white space to allocate to the left and right of the image. The Up.Browser will only allow the amount specified in pixels. (mUNE)

height	Specifies the suggested height for the image. (MuNE)
width	Specifies the suggested width for the image. (MuNE)

`<input/>`

Specifies a point that the user is prompted to enter text. (MUNE)

Attributes

name	The user will be prompted a name, which is then stored as a variable specified in the attribute. e.g. name="var1" will cause entered text to be stored as variable var1. (MUNE)
value	Allows you to set a default value for the entry, which the user can then simply ok if they do not wish to change it. (MUNE)
type	Sets the type of text entry. The default is **text**, which will allow normal text entry. The other option is **password**. When this is chosen, text entered will be replaced by asterisks out - a simple security option. (MUNE)
title	Suggests a title for the text entry screen, displayed when entering text.(mUNE)
maxlength	Sets a maximum length for entered strings. (MUNE)
format	Sets a format that the entered text is forced to stick to, e.g. format=" AA\-NNNN" states that the entered text has got to be "two uppercase letters, followed by a dash, followed by four numbers". See chapter XXX for more details on the code system. (MUNE)
emptyok	Simply states that it is ok for the user to not enter anything. (MUNE)
tabindex	Allows you to set the mode of movement between input boxes, so that the user could 'tab' between them, using specialized control keys. (MUNE)
size	Specifies the width, in characters, of the input area. (MUNE)

`<meta/>`

General, normally browser specific meta data of any sort, data that describes the content of the document, and is both user and machine readable. It is contained within **<head>** tags. If the browser doesn't understand this data, it simply ignores it.(mune)

Attributes

content	Sets the content type value. (mune)
name	gives the meta data a name. The user agent will ignore named meta data, and Network servers will not emit WML content named with this attribute. (mune)
http-equiv	Can be used in place of name, indicates that the data should be interpreted as an HTTP header. Meta data named with this attribute is converted to a WSP or HTTP response header if the content is tokenized before arrival at the user agent. (mune)
forua	Controls whether the meta data was intended to reach the user agent. If true, it must do. If false, then it must be removed at an intermediate stage. (mune)
scheme	Specifies a form or structure that may be used to interpret the data value. (mune)

`<noop>`

Specifies that nothing should be done. (MUNE)

`<onevent>`

Declares that, when the event detailed by the attribute occurs, the action(s) contained within the tags will be taken. (MUNE)

Attributes

type Sets which type of event the code is waiting for to occur. The types are:-
"onenterbackward" - This waits for the user to go to the card backwards (e.g. navigating
backwards through the history stack), then executes the action. (MUNE)
"onenterforward" - This waits for the user to navigate to the card forwards (in anyway
except through the history stack), then executes the action. (MUNE)
"ontimer" - This will wait for a declared timer (declared using **<timer>** - see relevant
section) to finish counting before executing the action. (MUNE)

<option>

A set of <option> tags is needed to specify each individual item in a list (see <select>). (MUNE)

Attributes

value Gives the option a shorthand value, e.g. an initial for a name. This value can be given to a
variable, or be used to set it's option as the default choice, using the <select> attributes
name and value respectively. (MuNE)

index Gives the option an index number for it to be referred to. The number can be used to
specify it's option as the default choice in the list using the **<select>** attribute ivalue, or
it's value can be given to a variable specified by **<select>** attribute iname. (MuNE)

title a name can be given to each option in the list for the browser to display. However, it
doesn't seem to work on most browsers and is rather pointless anyway. (mUNE)

onpick Related to some of the **<onevent>** attributes, this attribute allows you specify the id of a
card to navigate to when you pick an option in a list. (MUNE)

<optgroup>

Sets of **<optgroup>** brackets can be put around **<options>** in a **<select>** list. The effect of this is
breaking the list up into options in submenus. (mUNE)

Attributes

title Gives a title to each submenu, which is also the option that will represent that submenu in
the main menu. (mUNE)

<p>

Specifies a paragraph of text with alignment and line wrapping properties. The up.browser never resets
the alignment.(MUNE)

Attributes

align The three available values, "left", "center", and "right" specify line alignment. If you do
not specify the align attribute, the line is reset to "left" alignment. (MUNE)

mode Has two possible values, "wrap" and "nowrap", used to Specify the line-wrapping mode. If
you do not specify the mode value, the device uses the last specified mode value. (MUNe)

<postfield>

Allows variables to be posted to other pages and scripts. (MUNE)

Attributes

name Gives the value a name. (MUNE)

value Specifies which variable is to be posted by this particular element. (MUNE)

<prev/>

Specifies navigation to the previous URI in the history. xml:lang is not an associated attribute.(MUNE)

<refresh/>

Specifies a refresh task, stating a need for an update of the user agent context as specified by the contained **<setvar>** elements (see relevant section). User-visible side effects of the update can occur during the processing of the **<refresh>**. (MUNE)

<select>

Allows the definition of a list, embedded in a card, to allow the user to choose inputs from a list rather than having to type something in. (MUNE)

Attributes

name	Sets a variable name that will be assigned a value equal to the specified value attribute of the **<option>** that gets selected (see **<option>**). (MUNE)
iname	Sets an index variable name that will be assigned the index value of the **<option>** that gets selected.(MUNE)
value	Allows a default selection to be specified by using the option's value. (MUNE)
ivalue	Allows a default selection to be specified by using the option's index number. (MUNE)
title	Allows you to give the list a title for the browser to display. (mUNE)
multiple	Has two values, true and false. The default is false, but if you specify true, the user will be able to select multiple entries from the list. (MUNE)
tabindex	Allows you to set the mode of movement between selection boxes, so that the user can 'tab' between them, using specialized control keys. (MUNE)

<setvar>

Sets a variable. Can only be included inside **<refresh>** and **<go>** tags. (MUNE)

Attributes

name	The value used will be the name given to the variable set. (MUNE)
value	The value used will be the value given to the variable set. (MUNE)

<small>

Specifies text using a small font.(MuNE)

<strong>

Specifies strongly emphasized text.(MuNE)

<table>

Specifies a table.(MUNE)

Attributes

title	Specifies a brief text string that may be used in the presentation of the table.(muNE)
align	Specifies the layout of text and images within the columns of the table. The available settings are "left", "center" and "right". ("L", "C" and "R" will also work.) The default is "left", or "L". In the Nokia Toolkit, excluding the 7110, this attribute seems to be obeyed, except that it takes L, C and R as values only.(MUNE)
columns	Specifies the exact number of columns in the table.(MUNE)

\<td\>

Used to define individual cell contents in each row of a defined table.(MUNE)

\<timer/\>

sets a timer that starts counting. Not much use on its own, but combine it with **\<onevent type="ontimer"\>**, to immediately see a useful application. (MUNE)

Attributes

value   Sets the length of time to count, in tenths of seconds. (MUNE)

\<tr\>

Defines each row in an already defined table. (MUNE)

\<u\>

Specifies underlined text. (MUNE)

\<wml\>

Specifies a WML deck. (MUNE)

Up.Browser specific elements

If you want to use these elements, you must change the DOCTYPE header to the following line:

```
<!DOCTYPE wml PUBLIC "-//PHONE.COM//DTD WML 1.1//EN"
"http://www.phone.com/dtd/wml11.dtd" >
```

\<catch\>

Specifies an exception handler.

Attributes

name   Specifies which exception is to be handled in this particular instance. If no name is specified, then any exception will be handled by this **\<catch\>**.

onthrow Tells the engine what to do if and when the exception occurs.

\<exit\>

Declares an exit task - the current context is then stopped.

\<link/\>

Carries out a very similar task to that of **\<a\>**; it declares a link to appear on the display

Attributes

href	Specifies the URI for the link to navigate to.
sendreferer	Defaults to false. If set to true, the user agent needs to specify the URI of the deck containing this task in the server-bound request.
rel	Specifies what relationships exist between the deck containing the link, and the card to be navigated to.

<receive/>

Receives data sent from another context.

Attributes

name	Specifies the name of the variable to be received.

<reset/>

Clears all of the variables declared in the current context.

<send/>

Specifies a single variable to be sent to the relevant parameter block position.

Attributes

value	Specifies which value to send.

<spawn>

Declares a spawn task - creates a child context, and spawns a URL.

Attributes

href	Specifies the URI to be navigated to.
sendreferer	Defaults to false. If set to true, the user agent needs to specify to URI of the deck containing this task in the server-bound request.
accept-charset	Must be followed by a list of character codes for data that the origin server must accept when processing input.
method	Specifies the HTTP request method, either **get** or **post**.
onexit	Specifies the URI to navigate to, upon completion of the child context, through the performing of an exit action.
onthrow	Specifies to URI the navigate to , upon termination of the child context, through the performing of a **<throw>** action.

<throw>

Declares a throw task - that an exception should be raised at the current context.

Attributes

name	Specifies the name of the correct exception to be raised.

B

WMLScript Reference

This appendix outlines the syntax of the WMLScript language:

- ❑ WMLScript Operators:

  - **a.** Arithmetic
  - **b.** Logical
  - **c.** Bitwise Shift
  - **d.** Bitwise Logical
  - **e.** Assignment
  - **f.** Comparison
  - **g.** Miscellaneous

- ❑ WMLScript Operator Precedence
- ❑ WMLScript Statements/Functions

  - **a.** Declarations
  - **b.** Loops
  - **c.** Execution Control statements

- ❑ Pragmas
- ❑ Comments
- ❑ Escape Codes

WMLScript Operators

A. Arithmetic Operators

Name	Example	Result
Addition	v1 + v2	Sum of v1 and v2.
		Concatenation of v1 and v2, if they are strings.
Subtraction	v1 - v2	Difference of v1 and v2
Multiplication	v1 * v2	Product of v1 and v2
Division	v1 / v2	Quotient of v2 into v1
Integer Division	v1 div v2	Integer quotient of v2 into v1 (ignoring the remainder)
Modulus	v1 % v2	Integer remainder of dividing v1 by v2
Prefix Increment	++v1 * v2	(v1 + 1) * v2
Postfix Increment	v1++ * v2	(v1 * v2). v1 is then incremented by 1
Prefix Decrement	--v1 * v2	(v1 - 1) * v2
Postfix Decrement	v1-- * v2	(v1 * v2). v1 is then decremented by 1

B. Logical Operators

These operators should return one of the Boolean literals, true or false. However, this may not happen if either v1 or v2 is neither a Boolean value nor a value that easily converts to a Boolean value, such as 0, 1, null, the empty string, or undefined.

Name	Example	Result
Logical AND	v1 && v2	Returns true if both v1 and v2 are true, false otherwise. Will not evaluate v2 if v1 is false.
Logical OR	v1 || v2	Returns false if both v1 and v2 are false, true otherwise. Will not evaluate v2 if v1 is true.
Logical NOT	!v1	Returns false if v1 is true, true otherwise.

C. Bitwise Shift Operators

These operators work by converting the value in v1 to a 32 bit binary number and then moving the bits in the number to the left or the right by the number of places specified by v2.

Name	Example	Result
Left Shift	v1 << v2	Shifts v1 to the left by v2 places, filling the new gaps in with zeros
Right Shift	v1 >> v2	Shifts v1 to the right by v2 places, ignoring the bits shifted off the number
Zero-Fill Right Shift	v1 >>> v2	Shifts v1 to the right by v2 places, ignoring the bits shifted off the number and adding v2 zeros to the left of the number

D. Bitwise Logical Operators

These operators work by converting the values in both v1 and v2 to 32 bit binary numbers and then comparing the individual bits of these two binary numbers. The result is returned as a normal decimal number.

Name	Example	Result
Bitwise AND	v1 & v2	ANDs each pair of corresponding bits
Bitwise OR	v1 | v2	ORs each pair of corresponding bits
Bitwise XOR	v1 ^ v2	XORs (that is, exclusive ORs) each pair of corresponding bits
Bitwise NOT	~v1	Inverts all the bits in the number

E. Assignment operators

Name	Example	Meaning
Assignment	v1 = v2	Setting v1 to the value of v2
Shorthand Addition *or*	v1 += v2	v1 = v1 + v2
Shorthand Concatenation		
Shorthand Subtraction	v1 -= v2	v1 = v1 - v2
Shorthand Multiplication	v1 *= v2	v1 = v1 * v2
Shorthand Division	v1 /= v2	v1 = v1 / v2
Shorthand Integer Division	v1 div= v2	v1 = v1 div v2
Shorthand Modulus	v1 %= v2	v1 = v1 % v2
Shorthand Left Shift	v1 <<= v2	v1 = v1 << v2
Shorthand Right Shift	v1 >>= v2	v1 = v1 >> v2
Shorthand Zero-Fill Right Shift	v1 >>>= v2	v1 = v1 >>> v2, adding 2 padding zeros after assignment.
Shorthand AND	v1 &= v2	v1 = v1 & v2
Shorthand XOR	v1 ^= v2	v1 = v1 ^ v2
Shorthand OR	v1 |= v2	v1 = v1 | v2

711

F. Comparison operators

These operators return the Boolean literal values, `true` and `false`. If v1=1 and v2=2, the following statements are all true.

Name	Example	Meaning
Equal	`v1 == 1`	True if two operands are strictly equal.
Not Equal	`v1 != v2`	True if two operands are not strictly equal.
Greater Than	`v2 > v1`	True if LHS operand is greater than RHS operand.
Greater Than Or Equal	`v2 >= v2`	True if LHS operand is greater than or equal to RHS operand.
Less Than	`v1 < v2`	True if LHS operand is less than RHS operand.
Less Than Or Equal	`v1 <= v1`	True if LHS operand is less than or equal to RHS operand

G. Miscellaneous operators

There are several other miscellaneous operators in WMLScript.

Name	Example	Description
Conditional Operator	`evalquery ? v1 : v2`	If `evalquery` is true, the operator returns v1, else it returns v2.
Comma Operator	`eval1, eval2`	Evaluates both `eval1` and `eval2` while treating the two as one expression. Can also be used to declare or set multiple variables at the same time.
`typeof`	`typeof v1` `typeof (v1)`	Returns a number representing the type of v1, which is not evaluated. The numbers 0, 1, 2, 3, 4 represent the types integer, floating point, string, Boolean and invalid.
`isvalid`	`isvalid x`	Returns a Boolean: `true` if x is not of type invalid, and `false` if x is of type invalid.

Operator Precedence

Does `1 + 2 * 3 = 1 + (2 * 3)` = 7 or does it equal `(1 + 2) * 3` = 9?

The table shows precedence with highest at the top, and like operators grouped together. The third column explains whether to read 1+2+3+4 as ((1+2)+3)+4 or 1+(2+(3+(4))).

Operator type	Operators	Evaluation order for like elements
Postfix	`[] () expr++ expr--`	left to right
Unary	`++expr --expr +expr -expr ~ !`	right to left
Type	`typeof isvalid`	right to left
Multiplicative	`* / div %`	left to right
Additive	`+ -`	left to right
Shift	`<< >> >>>`	left to right
Relational	`< > <= >=`	left to right
Equality	`== !=`	left to right
Bitwise AND	`&`	left to right
Bitwise Exclusive OR	`^`	left to right
Bitwise Inclusive OR	`|`	left to right
Logical AND	`&&`	left to right
Logical OR	`||`	left to right
Conditional	`? :`	right to left
Assignment	`= += -= *= /= div= %= &= ^= |= <<= >>= >>>=`	right to left
Comma	`,`	left to right

WMLScript Statements/Functions

The following tables describe WMLScript statements

A. Declarations

Statement	Example	Description

`var`	`var Number;`
	`var Number = 6;`
	`var N1, N2, N3 = 6;`
		Used to declare a variable. Initializing it to a value is optional at the time of declaration.

Table continued on following page

Statement	Example	Description

function	`extern function doItNow()`
	
	`{`
	
	   `statements`
	
	`};`
		Used to declare a function with the specified parameters.
		
		To return a value the function must use the `return` statement.

	`extern function doThis(p1, p2, p3)`
	
	`{`
	
	   `statements`
	
	`};`
		`extern` is used so that the function is available outside of where it is defined.

use	`use url script2 "http://www.somewhere.com/WMLScripts/script2.wmls";`	`use` is used to enable the script to use pragmas (see table below).

B. Loops

Statement	Example	Description

for	`for (var i=0; i<15; i++)`
	
	`{`
	
	   `x += i;`
	
	   `doSomething(x);`
	
	`}`
		Creates a loop controlled according to the three optional expressions enclosed in the parentheses after the `for` and separated by semicolons. The first of these three expressions is the initial-expression, the second is the test condition, and the third is the increment-expression.

if...else	`if (x <= y)`
	
	`{`
	
	   `thing += x;`
	
	   `x++;`
	
	`}`
	
	`else`
	
	   `thing += y;`
		Executes a block of statements if the condition evaluates to true. If the condition evaluates to false, another block of statements can be executed using `else` (this is optional).

while	`while(y < 3)`
	
	`{`
	
	   `doSomething();`
	
	`}`
		Executes a block of statements if a test condition evaluates to `true`. The loop then repeats, testing the condition with each repeat, ceasing if the condition evaluates to `false`.

C. Execution Control Statements

Statement	Example	Description

break	```var x = 0;```
	```while (x < 20)```
	```{```
	``` if (10 == x)```
	``` break;```
	``` x++;```
	```}```
	```return x*b;```
		Used within a while or for loop to terminate the loop and transfer program control to the statement following the loop.

continue	```var count = 0;```
	```while (count < 16)```
	```{```
	``` if (0 == (++count % 2))```
	``` continue;```
	``` return count*c;```
	```}```
		Used to stop execution of the block of statements in the current iteration of a while or for loop; execution of the loop continues with the next iteration.

return	```extern function```
	```returnSthg(x, y)```
	```{```
	``` return x/y;```
	```}```
		Used to specify the value to be returned by a function, or simply to exit from the current function.

Pragmas

Pragma	Example	Description
url	use url *ID* "*URL*"	Used to specify the URL of the WMLScript file containing the functions we want to use, in *URL*, and can then access these functions using the name specified in *ID*.
access	use access domain "*domain*" path "*path*";	Used to specify the *domain* and *path* from which access is allowed to functions in the current WMLScript.
meta	use meta *type property content scheme*	Used to supply additional information. type represents the type of pragma, property the name of the header you wish to set, content the value you want to set the header, and scheme the formatting of the header.

Comments

Comments are notes which the script engine ignores, and which can be used to explain the code.

```
//this is the syntax for a one line comment...
```

```
/* and this is the syntax for a multiple line comment. The comment can be of any
length, as long as it is contained within the "star slash" brackets */
```

Escape Codes

The following table lists all the literal string escape codes.

Escape Code	Represents
\ '	Single quote
\ "	Double quote
\ \	Backslash
\ /	Frontslash
\b	Backspace
\f	Form feed
\n	Newline
\r	Carriage return
\t	Horizontal tab
\x*hh*	Character *hh* from the Latin-1 character set (ISO 8859-1), specified in hexadecimal format as two digits
ooo	Character *ooo* from the Latin-1 character set (ISO 8859-1), specified in octal format as three digits
\u*hhhh*	Character *hhhh* from the Unicode character set, specified in hexadecimal format as four digits

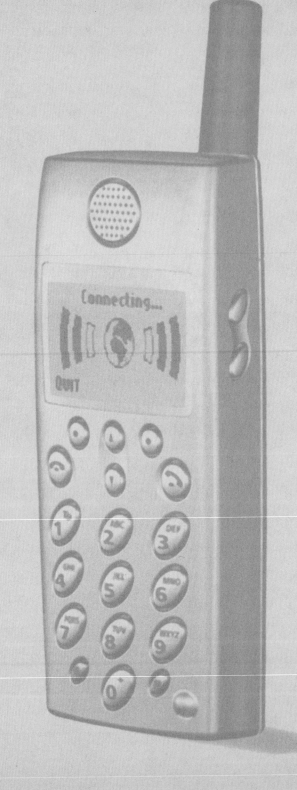

C

Standard WMLScript Library Functions

Dialogs

This library contains functions used to produce simple user interface cards.

alert

Usage: alert(message)
Parameters: message – of type string, the warning to be displayed to the user
Comments: This function displays the message passed to it as a warning and when the user confirms
             they have read the message returns them to the previous card
Example: `Dialogs.alert("There has been an error");`

confirm

Usage: confirm(message, ok, cancel)

Parameters: message – of type string, the question to ask the user
ok – of type string, the positive option to offer the user
cancel – of type string, the negative option to offer the user

Returns: a Boolean, `true` if the user chooses ok, `false` if they choose cancel

Comments: This function is used to prompt the user when a question, and in particular a confirmation, is required.

Example: bleResult = Dialogs.confirm("Are you sure you wish to do this", "Yes", "Not really");

prompt

Usage: prompt(message, default)

Parameters: message – of type string, the text to display prompting the user for input
default – of type string, the default text to fill the input box with

Returns: a string, the text the user has entered

Comments: This function just presents the user with an input box to fill.

Example: strResult = Dialogs.prompt("Enter your name", "Bob");

Float

This library contains functions for the manipulation and conversion of floating point numbers.

ceil

Usage: ceil(value)

Parameters: value – a floating point number

Returns: An integer, which is nearest in size to the value, but not smaller than it.

Comments: Be careful when using negative numbers, ceil(-2.7) = -2 and NOT -3

Example: x = Float.ceil(4.1);
// x is assigned the value 5

floor

Usage:	floor(value)
Parameters:	value – a floating point number
Returns:	An integer, which is nearest in size to the value, but not greater than it
Comments:	Be careful when using negative numbers, floor(-4.1) = -5 and NOT -4
Example:	x = Float.floor(1.9); // x is assigned the value 1

int

Usage:	int(value)
Parameters:	value – a floating point number
Returns:	The integer part of the floating point value
Comments:	This simply returns the integer part of the value; it doesn't round the number
Example:	x = Float.int(2.9); // x is assigned the value 2

maxfloat

Usage:	maxFloat()
Parameters:	None
Returns:	The maximum size floating point number that can be represented
Comments:	This will typically be 3.4028235E38
Example:	x = Float.maxFloat(); // x is assigned the value 3.4028235E38

minfloat

Usage:	minFloat()
Parameters:	None
Returns:	The smallest non-zero floating point number that can be represented
Comments:	This will typically be 1.17549435E-38
Example:	x = Float.minFloat(); // x is assigned the value 1.17549435E-38

pow

Usage:	pow(number1, number2)
Parameters:	number1 – a floating point number number2 – a floating point number
Returns:	The result of raising number1 to the power of number2
Comments:	This function performs the calculation $(number1)^{number2}$
Example:	x = Float.pow(2.5, 3); // x is assigned value 15.625

round

Usage:	round(value)
Parameters:	value – a floating point number
Returns:	An integer as a result of rounding the value
Comments:	The normal mathematical rules for rounding apply.
Example:	x = Float.round(3.7); // x is assigned value 4

sqrt

Usage: sqrt(value)
Parameters: value – a floating point number
Returns: The result of taking the square root of the number
Comments: If an attempt is made to take the square root of a negative number, it returns invalid
Example:
```
x = Float.sqrt(31.36);
// x is assigned value 5.6
```

Lang

This library contains core WMLScript functions.

abort

Usage: abort(message)
Parameters: message – an error message of type string
Returns: None
Comments: This function stops the current execution of WMLScript and hands control back to the browser
Example:
```
Lang.abort("Calculation failed");
```

abs

Usage: abs(number)
Parameters: number – number of any number type
Returns: The absolute value of the number
Comments: The return type is of the same type as the parameter passed to the function
Example:
```
x = Lang.abs(-3)
// x is assigned value 3
```

characterSet

Usage: characterSet()
Parameters: None
Returns: An integer that gives the MIBEnum value from IANA
Comments: See `ftp://ftp.isi.edu/in-notes/iana/assignments/character-sets` for list of character sets
Example:
```
x = lang.characterSet();
// x is assigned the integer that represents the present character
set
```

exit

Usage: exit(value)
Parameters: value - a number of any type
Returns: None
Comments: This function stops the the execution of the script and returns control to the WMLScript interpreter.

Example:
```
Lang.exit(3);
x = 6;
// The script is exited with return value of 3
// The assignment never takes place
```

float

Usage: float()
Parameters: None
Returns: A Boolean indicating whether the interpreter supports floating point numbers
Comments: The result of this function will obviously vary from one browser to another
Example:
```
x = Lang.float();
// If the interpreter supports floating point numbers then
// x is true, otherwise it is false
```

isFloat

Usage: isFloat(value)
Parameters: value – a value of any type
Returns: A Boolean indicating whether the value can be successfully converted to a floating point number
Comments: If the interpreter doesn't support floating point numbers then the return value is invalid
Example:
```
x = Lang.isFloat("3.53322");
// x is assigned the value true
```

isInt

Usage: isInt(value)
Parameters: value – a value of any type
Returns: A Boolean indicating whether the value can be successfully converted to an integer
Comments:
Example:
```
x = Lang.isInt("1243");
// x is assigned the value true
```

max

Usage: max(number1, number2)
Parameters: number1 and number2 are numbers of any numerical type
Returns: The larger of the two numbers.
Comments: If the numbers are the same in size then the first is returned
Example:
```
x = Lang.max(8, 12.4);
// x is assigned 12.4
```

maxInt

Usage: maxInt()
Parameters: None
Returns: The largest integer supported by the browser
Comments:
Example:
```
x = Lang.maxInt();
// x is an integer and has the largest value that an
// integer can be
```

min

Usage: min(number1, number2)
Parameters: number1 and number2 are numbers of any numerical type
Returns: The smaller of the two numbers
Comments: If the numbers are the same size then the first is returned
Example: x = Lang.min(4.5, 9)
                // x is assigned 4.5

minInt

Usage: minInt()
Parameters: None
Returns: The smallest integer supported by the browser
Comments:
Example: x = Lang.minInt();
                // x is an integer and has the smallest value that an
                // integer can be

parseInt

Usage: parseInt(value)
Parameters: value, which is the string to be converted
Returns: The result of converting the value to an integer
Comments: If this cannot be done, the function returns invalid
Example: x = Lang.parseInt("5");
                // x is an integer with value 5

random

Usage: random(value)
Parameters: value – the highest number that will be acceptable
Returns: An integer randomly chosen from the range 0-value
Comments: The value parameter must be a positive number
Example: x = Lang.random(5);
                // x is an integer anywhere in the range 0-5

seed

Usage: seed(value)
Parameters: value – a value to seed the random number generator
Returns: An empty string if the function succeeds
Comments: This function should be used before the random function for best results
Example: Lang.seed(7);
                // The random number generator is seeded with the number 7!

String

The string library contains functions for the manipulation and conversion of strings.

charAt

Usage:	charAt(string, number)
Parameters:	string – a string
	number – an integer offset for the string
Returns:	The character from the string at the position given by the number
Comments:	The numbering of positions starts at 0
Example:	`x = String.charAt("Hello world", 6);`
	`// x is assigned "w"`

compare

Usage:	compare(string1, string2)
Parameters:	string1 and string2 – both of string type
Returns:	-1 if string1 < string2
	1 if string1 > string2
	0 if string1 = string2
Comments:	The result of this calculation is of course dependent upon the character set that is used
Example:	`x = String.compare("a string", "a string");`
	`// x is assigned the value 0`

elements

Usage:	elements(string, separator)
Parameters:	string and separator are both strings
Returns:	The number of elements in the given string where an element is defined as a substring separated by the given delimiter
Comments:	The separator should not be an empty string or the return value will be of type invalid
Example:	`x = String.elements("This has, three, elements", ",");`
	`// x is assigned the number 3`

elementAt

Usage:	elementAt(string, index, separator)
Parameters:	string and separator – strings
	index – an integer index
Returns:	The element in the string at the given index where an element is a section divided by the separator
Comments:	The indexing of the elements starts from 0
Example:	`x = String.elementAt("This has, three, elements", 1, ",");`
	`// x is assigned " three"`

find

Usage:	find(string, sub)
Parameters:	string – a string
	sub – a substring to find in the string
Returns:	An integer index of where the substring appears in the string
Comments:	The indexing starts from 0
Example:	`x = String.find("this is a string", is");`
	`// x is assigned the number 5`

format

Usage: format(format, value)

Parameters: format – a formatting string

value – value to be converted to a string using the formatting string parameter

Returns: The result of formatting the value using the format parameter

Comments: A formatting string is a string that can contain a format specifier. This format specifier begins with a % and can then be followed by a width or precision before its type is given. The three formatting types are d – integer, f – floating point and s – string. So, to give a format parameter that means "seven characters wide with an integer" use: %7d. To give a format parameter that means "seven characters wide, with a precision of four" and using an integer, use: %7.4d

Example:
```
x = String.format("Number-%7.4d", 12);
// x is assigned "Number-    0012"
```

insertAt

Usage: insertAt(string, element, index, separator)

Parameters: string – the string into which the new element is to be inserted

element – the new string element that is to be inserted

index – the index in the string where the element is to be inserted

separator – the string that is used to separate the different elements

Returns: A string that comprises of the given string with the element inserted at the index, where elements are sections separated by the given separator

Comments: The indexing starts at 0

Example:
```
x = String.insertAt("one, two, three", " one and a half", 1, ",");
// x is assigned "one, one and a half, two, three"
```

length

Usage: length(string)

Parameters: string – the string to calculate the length of

Returns: The length of the string passed as a parameter

Comments:

Example:
```
x = String.length("Hello");
// x is assigned 5
```

isEmpty

Usage: isEmpty(string)

Parameters: string – the string, that we want to test for being empty

Returns: A Boolean indicating whether the string has length 0 or not

Comments:

Example:
```
x = String.isEmpty("");
// x is assigned true
```

removeAt

Usage: removeAt(string, index, separator)

Parameters: string – the string to remove an element from

index – the position of the element to be removed

separator – the string that is used to separate the elements

Returns: A string with the element at the given index removed
Comments: Indexing starts from 0, an element is defined as a section of the string separated by the given separator
Example:
```
x = string.removeAt("zero, one, two", 1, ",");
// x is assigned "zero, two"
```

replace

Usage: replace(string, old, new)
Parameters: string – a string, which will have some of its substrings replaced
old – a string which is to be replaced
new – a string to replace the old string with
Returns: The result of substituting the substring new into the string for every substring old
Comments:
Example:
```
x = String.replace("Hello, world!", "world", "goodbye");
// x is assigned the value "Hello, goodbye!"
```

replaceAt

Usage: replaceAt(string, element, index, separator)
Parameters: string – a string of elements
element – an element to be inserted into the string at the given index
index – the position within the string of the element to be replaced
separator – the string which divides the elements
Returns: The result of replacing the element at the index in the string with the string given by the element parameter, where elements in the string are divided by the given separator
Comments: The index starts from 0
Example:
```
x = String.replaceAt("zero, one, two", " 1", 1, ",");
// x is assigned "zero, 1, two"
```

squeeze

Usage: squeeze(string)
Parameters: string – the string to be squeezed
Returns: A string where all whitespaces have been reduced to a single space character
Comments:
Example:
```
String.squeeze("Hello,       goodbye   !");
// x is assigned the value "Hello, goodbye !"
```

subString

Usage: substring(string, index, length)
Parameters: string – the string to take the substring from
index – the position in the string to take the substring from
length – the number of characters to take from the string for the substring
Returns: A substring, formed by taking a string of the given length from the given string at the position given by the index
Comments:
Example:
```
x = String.subString("Hello world!", 6, 5);
// x is assigned "world"
```

trim

Usage:	trim(string)
Parameters:	string – the string to be trimmed
Returns:	The string with all leading and trailing whitespace removed
Comments:	
| **Example:** | ```
x = String.trim("   Hello, world!    ");
// x is assigned "Hello, world!"
``` |

toString

Usage:	toString(value))
Parameters:	value – the value to be converted to a string
Returns:	The result of converting the value to its string representation
Comments:	
| **Example:** | ```
x = String.toString(27);
// x is assigned the string "27"
``` |

URL

This library contains functions for the manipulation and validation of URLs.

escapeString

Usage:	escapeString(string)
Parameters:	string – the string to be escaped
Returns:	A string as the result of using normal URL escaping rules on the given string
Comments:	URL escaping is the process of taking characters that are illegal or have special meaning in a URL and replacing them with %xx, where xx is a code representing the character
| **Example:** | ```
x = URL.escapeString("The # character has to be escaped");
// x is assigned "The %23 character has to be escaped"
``` |

getBase

Usage:	getBase()
Parameters:	None
Returns:	The current URL but without the details of the present WMLScript function
Comments:	If you call some script using http://www.companyname.com/testscript.wmls#function the base is http://www.companyname.com/testscript.wmls
| **Example:** | ```
x = URL.getBase();
// x is assigned the current URL but without the details of the
// present WMLScript function
``` |

getFragment

Usage:	getFragment(string)
Parameters:	string – an URL
Returns:	The fragment part of the URL given as the string parameter
Comments:	The fragment part of a URL is the part following the # that is used to determine the specific WMLScript function or WML card

Example: `x = URL.getFragment("http://www.companyname.com/test.wml#main");`
                 `// x is assigned the value "main"`

getHost

Usage:	getHost(string)
Parameters:	string – an URL
Returns:	The host part of the URL given as the string parameter
Comments:	In a URL of the form `http://www.companyname.com/testscript.wmls#function` the host part is `www.companyname.com`.
Example:	`x = URL.getHost("http://www.companyname.com/test.wml#main");` `// x is assigned the value "www.companyname.com"`

getParameters

Usage:	getParameters(string)
Parameters:	string – an URL
Returns:	A string of parameters from the URL given as the string parameter
Comments:	Parameters are given at the end of a URL and are separated by semi-colons (;)
Example:	`x = URL.getParameters("http://www.companyname.com/test.wml;10;12");` `// x is assigned "10;12"`

getPath

Usage:	getPath(string)
Parameters:	string – an URL
Returns:	A string of the path from the URL.
Comments:	The path is the location of the card on the current host
Example:	`x = URL.getPath("http://www.companyname.com/wap/test.wml#main");` `// x is assigned "/wap/test.wml"`

getPort

Usage:	getPort(string)
Parameters:	string – an URL
Returns:	The port as a string from the URL
Comments:	The port number is given at the end of the domain and is separated from it by using a colon (:).
Example:	`x = URL.getPort("http://www.companyname.com:8080/test.wml#main");` `// x is assigned the value "8080"`

getQuery

Usage:	getQuery(string)
Parameters:	string – an URL
Returns:	The query part of the URL as a string
Comments:	The query part of a URL is placed at the end of a URL and its beginning is marked by a question mark (?), each parameter assigned is separated with an ampersand (&).
Example:	`x=URL.getQuery("http://www.companyname.com/test.wmls#main?x=10&y=43");` `// x is assigned "x=10&y=43"`

getReferer

Usage: getReferer()
Parameters: None
Returns: The relative URL of the resource that called the current WMLScript
Comments: If there was no referrer, then the function returns an empty string ("")
Example:
```
x = URL.getReferer()
// x is assigned a relative URL to the resource that called the
// present WMLScript unit
```

getScheme

Usage: getScheme(string)
Parameters: string – an URL
Returns: The scheme as a string of the URL given as the string parameter
Comments: The scheme is the protocol given at the front of a URL.
Example:
```
x = URL.getScheme("http://www.companyname.com/test.wmls#main");
// x is assigned the string "http"
```

isValid

Usage: isValid(string)
Parameters: string -- an URL
Returns: A Boolean indicating whether the URL given as the string parameter is in a valid form for a URL
Comments:
Example:
```
x = URL.isValid("http://www.companyname.com/test.wmls#main");
// x is assigned the Boolean value true
```

loadString

Usage: loadString(url, type)
Parameters: url – a string representation of an URL
type – a string giving the MIME type of the URL which is to be loaded
Returns: If the document at the location given by the URL parameter is of the same type as the type parameter, then this document is returned as a string – otherwise the function returns an integer to signal an error
Comments: The type of the URL to be loaded as a string must be a text type, i.e. the MIME type must start "text/"
Example:
```
x = URL.loadString("http://www.companyname.com/test.wml","text/vnd.wap.wml");
// x is a string which is the full contents of the WML text file located
// at http://www.companyname.com/test.wml
```

resolve

Usage: resolve(base, relative)
Parameters: base – a string representing a base URL
relative – a string representing a relative path to a resource
Returns: The result of embedding the relative URL into the base URL
Comments:

Example:
```
x = URL.resolve("http://www.company.com", "test.wml");
// x is assigned the string "http://www.company.com/test.wml"
```

unescapeString

Usage: unescapeString(string)
Parameters: string – the string that is to be unescaped
Returns: A string as a result of applying unescaping rules to the string given as a parameter
Comments: The process of unescaping involves finding escape codes, which are of the form %xx (where xx is the number representing a character), and converting them back to their actual characters
Example:
```
x = URL.unescapeString("The %23 character has been unescaped");
// x is assigned "The # character has been unescaped"
```

WMLBrowser

The WMLBrowser library contains functions for controlling the WMLBrowser. These functions have an effect when the script has finished executing and returns control back to the WMLBrowser.

getCurrentCard

Usage: getCurrentCard()
Parameters: None
Returns: A string giving a relative URL to the card that is presently being displayed by the browser
Comments:
Example:
```
x = WMLBrowser.getCurrentCard()
// x is assigned a string that gives a relative URL to the card
// currently being displayed
```

getVar

Usage: getVar(variable)
Parameters: variable – a string containing the name of a WML variable
Returns: The value of the WML variable whose name is given as a parameter
Comments: If the variable doesn't exist then an empty string ("") is returned
Example:
```
x = WMLBrowser.getVar("wmlVar1");
// x is assigned the value of the WML variable with name wmlVar1
```

go

Usage: go(string)
Parameters: string – an URL
Returns: An empty string ("")
Comments: When the execution of the current script finishes and control is returned to the browser, the card at the location given in the string parameter will be loaded by the browser
Example:
```
WMLBrowser.go("http://www.company.com/test.wml#main");
// When the present script has finished executing, the card at the
// location http://www.company.com/test.wml#main will be loaded
```

newContext

Usage:	newContext()
Parameters:	None
Returns:	An empty string ("")
Comments:	This function clears the history stack and all WML variables; it has the same effect as using the newcontext="true" attribute in a WML <card> element

Example:	WMLBrowser.newContext();
	// When control is returned to the WML browser all WML variables
	// have been destroyed and the history lost

prev

Usage:	prev()
Parameters:	None
Returns:	An empty string ("")
Comments:	When returning control to the browser, the prev task will be called. This will cause the browser to return to the previous card

Example:	WMLBrowser.prev();
	// when control returns to the browser, the previous card will be
	// displayed

refresh

Usage:	refresh()
Parameters:	None
Returns:	An empty string ("")
Comments:	When returning control to the browser, the refresh task will be called. This will cause the browser to refresh the display of the card – this is particularly useful if the card displays some WML variables that have been altered in the script
Example:	WMLBrowser.refresh(); // when returning to the browser, the display will be refreshed

setVar

Usage:	setVar(variable, value)
Parameters:	variable – the name of a WML variable value – the new value to assign to the WML variable
Returns:	A Boolean, true if it succeeds, false otherwise
Comments:	This function sets the value of the WML variable, named in the variable parameter, to the value given as the value parameter – if the value is not a string then it is converted to a string first
Example:	WMLBrowser.setVar("WMLvar1", 12); // The WML variable WMLvar1 is assigned the string "12"

D

WTAI Libraries

In this appendix we will give the details of the network common WTAI libraries that were introduced in Chapter 17. For each library we will give the library name in both URI and WMLScript form (where appropriate), and describe the functions the library contains. For each function we give the general syntax along with some examples, and any associated events. Associated events are those that occur after a call to a function has been made, occurring as a direct or indirect result of the function call.

Voice Call Control Library

This library consists of six functions, and is used in the obvious way – to control voice phone calls. Its `<library>` value is vc in the URL form and `WTAVoiceCall` in the WMLScript form.

Setup Call

The URI syntax for this function (which has an obvious meaning) is as follows:

```
wtai://vc/sc;<number>;<mode>!<retcode>
```

and in WMLScript form, this is:

```
var <retcode> = WTAVoiceCall.setup(<number>, <mode>);
```

`<number>` is the phone number of the party to whom the call is being made.

<mode> indicates the state model: 0 indicates the call should be dropped when the current WTA user agent context is cleared, 1 indicates the call should be kept when the current WTA user agent context is cleared.

<retcode> is the call id of the call setup. An error code will be returned in case of error. The id of the call that was returned is necessary to reference the particular call that was setup. For example, the id would be necessary to release the call programmatically using the "Release Call" function. The id is particularly useful to track calls when there is more than one call in progress at the same time. (You might have put one call on hold while answering the other).

Here is an example, first in URI form:

```
wtai://vc/sc;+91805553232;0!retcode
```

then in WMLScript form:

```
var retcode = WTAVoiceCall.setup("+91805553232", 0);
```

The function has the following associated events:

```
cc/cl, Call Cleared
cc/co, Call Connected
```

Accept Call

This function accepts an incoming voice call and accomplishes the equivalent of lifting the handset off the hook. It is normally called when content executing in the WTA user agent has an event handler for the "cc/ic" – Incoming Call Indication event. It has the URI syntax:

```
wtai://vc/ac;<id>;<mode>!<retcode>
```

and the WMLScript form:

```
var <retcode> = WTAVoiceCall.accept(<id>, <mode>);
```

<id> is the internal identity of the call being accepted.

<mode> has the same possible values as in the previous section.

<retcode>, again, has the same meaning as in the previous section.

Here is an example, first in URI form:

```
wtai://vc/ac;0;0!retcode
```

then in WMLScript form:

```
var retcode = WTAVoiceCall.accept(0, 0);
```

It has the associated events:

```
cc/cl, Call Cleared
cc/co, Call Connected
```

As you can see, the associated events above do NOT include "cc/ic" even though this function is typically called when a "cc/ic" event occurs. This is because "associated events" are those that occur after a call to this function has been made and clearly "cc/ic" is not such an event.

Release Call

This function releases the specified call and accomplishes the equivalent of replacing the handset. The URI syntax for releasing a call is:

```
wtai://vc/rc;<id>!<retcode>
```

or in WMLScript form:

```
var <retcode> = WTAVoiceCall.release(<id>);
```

`<id>` is the call id.

`<retcode>` is the return code.

Here is an example, first in URI form:

```
wtai://vc/rc;0!retcode
```

then in WMLScript form:

```
var retcode = WTAVoiceCall.release(0);
```

This function would release (i.e. hang up) the call whose id is zero.

It has the associated events:

```
cc/cl, Call Cleared
```

Send DTMF Tones

This function is used to send the DTMF tone sequence for the specified characters over the specified voice call. Here is the syntax, first in URI form:

```
wtai://vc/sd;<id>;<dtmf>!<retcode>
```

and then in WMLScript form:

```
var <retcode> = WTAVoiceCall.sendDTMF( <id>, <dtmf> );
```

`<id>` is the call id, this is the internal identity of the call.

`<dtmf>` is the dtmf character sequence, one or more of '0' – '9', 'A' – 'D', '#', '*', ','.

`<retcode>` is as above.

Here is an example, first in URI form:

```
wtai://vc/sd;0;5276108#4366!retcode
```

then in WMLScript form:

```
var retcode = WTAVoiceCall.sendDTMF( 0, "5276108#4366" );
```

The function has associated event:

```
cc/dtmf, DTMF sent
```

Call Status

With this function, you can retrieve parameters associated with a specific phone call. Note that, with a single function call, it is possible to retrieve only one parameter.

```
wtai://vc/cs;<id>;<fieldval>!<retcode>
```

in WMLScript form:

```
var <retcode> = WTAVoiceCall.callStatus( <id>, <fieldval> );
```

`<id>` is the id of the call.

`<fieldval>` is the name of the parameters to be retrieved and takes one of the following values:

- ❏ `number` : The number of the other party.

- ❏ `name` : The name of the other party if it is available. If not, the 'number' field is returned instead.

- ❏ `duration` : The duration of the phone call up to the current state. The duration info could be in a device specific or user preference defined format.

- ❏ `durationHMS` : The duration of the call is returned in the form HHHMMSS which is based on the ISO8601 format. Check out `http://www.iso.ch/markete/8601.pdf` for the standard. 3 digits for hours, two for minutes and two again for seconds. Any one phone call is limited to no more than 999 hours, 59 minutes and 59 seconds!

- ❏ `state` : The current state of the call: `active`, `hold`, `waiting`, `connecting`, `disconnecting`, `released`.

- ❏ `mode` : The mode as defined during call setup. Possible values are `keep` or `drop`.

`<retcode>` is as above.

Here is an example, first in URI form:

```
wtai://vc/cs;0;state!retcode
```

then in WMLScript form:

```
var retcode = WTAVoiceCall.callStatus( 0, "state" );
```

This asks for the state of the call, whose ID, is zero.

List Call

Returns the identities of the calls currently handled within the device. This only lists those that are available to the WTA user agent. The URI syntax is:

```
wtai://vc/lc;<call_index_number>!<retval>
```

and the WMLScript syntax is:

```
var <retval> = WTAVoiceCall.listCall(<call_index_number>);
```

`<call_index_number>` is the index number of the call from zero to n in order of age (0 newest).

`<retval>` can be used as a call id for other functions of the library.

Here is an example in URI syntax:

```
wtai://vc/lc;0!callid0
```

then in WMLScript form:

```
var callid0 = WTAVoiceCall.listCall(0);
```

Network Text Library

This library contains functions that control text messages. The URI format is unavailable, so we show only the WMLScript syntax. The `<library>` name for this is WTANetText

Send Text

This function sends a text message to a destination address if such a service is available and supported in the network. The syntax is:

```
var <retcode> = WTANetText.send(<number>, <message>);
```

<number> is the telephone number of the called party or service to whom the text is being sent.

<message> represents the text string that is to be sent.

<retcode> is an integer value reporting on the success of the operation. A negative value indicates failure.

Here is an example:

```
var retcode = WTANetText.send("+919845007190", "Hello World");
```

This sends the message "Hello World" to the mobile phone whose number is 91 9845 007190.

The function has the associated event:

```
nt/st, Network Text Sent
```

Read Text

This function returns the network text data (the message that was previously received and stored in the device) in the form of a string. This string is made up of a multi-field structure. The individual fields including the network text string can be retrieved using the getFieldValue() function.

The syntax for this function is:

```
var <struct> = WTANetText.read(<id>);
```

<id> is the index number of the message (0 is newest).

<struct> is the resulting string composed of several fields.

Here is an example:

```
var structfield = WTANetText.read(1);
```

This returns the message data for the second oldest message.

Remove Text

This removes a message previously stored in the phone. The generic WMLScript form is as follows:

```
var <retcode> = WTANetText.remove( <id> );
```

<id> is the same as in the previous section.

<retcode> is an integer value, if below zero it indicates failure.

Here is an example:

```
var retcode = WTANetText.remove(1);
```

Get Field Value

With this function, you can retrieve fields associated with a specific network text message that was read into a variable. The generic WMLScript form is as follows:

```
var <fieldval> = WTANetText.getFieldValue( <struct>, <field> );
```

`<struct>` is the name of the variable into which the read() function returned the message.

`<field>` is the name of the fields to be retrieved in the form of predefined strings:

❏ `text` : Body of the Network Text Message.

❏ `tstamp` : A string containing the time stamp when the message was sent. It is based on ISO8601 format and is of the form YYYYMMDDHHMMSS, i.e. `<year><month><date><hour><minutes><seconds>`.

❏ `tstamp_off` : An integer containing the above time stamp's offset from Co-ordinated Universal Time(GMT) in multiples of 15 minutes.

❏ `tstamp_rec` : The local time stamp value when the text message was received.

❏ `address` : The string containing the message originating address. This could be a phone number if it originated from the mobile or another number that identifies a particular service.

❏ `status` : Status of the message. Possible values are unread, read, written, sent.

`<fieldval>` is the value of the field returned. If the field is not supported, a value that is less than zero is returned. If a field is supported, but is not present or if it cannot be retrieved, an empty "" string is returned.

Here is an example:

```
var fieldval = WTANetText.getFieldValue( $structfield, "address" );
```

Phonebook Library

The control of the phonebook present in the mobile phone is managed by functions in this library. Again the URL forms of the functions are unavailable. The `<library>` is WTAPhoneBook in the WMLScript format.

Write Phonebook Entry

This function is used to add a new entry to the phonebook. Any previous entry with the same identity is overwritten. The generic WMLScript form is as follows:

```
var <result> = WTAPhoneBook.write( <id>, <number>, <name> );
```

`<id>` is the identity of the phonebook entry. This is just a number that could identify the position of the entry in the phonebook.

`<number>` is the phone Number to be stored.

<name> is the name to be associated with the phone number.

<result> gives an error code that is below zero in case of failure.

Here is an example:

```
var retcode = WTAPhoneBook.write( 0, "+441902989898", "Victoria");
```

Read Phonebook Entry

With this function, you can retrieve specific entries by specifying any one of the <id>, <name> or <number> fields of a phonebook entry. The generic WMLScript form is as follows:

```
var <result> = WTAPhoneBook.read( <field>, <fieldval> );
```

<field> is the name of the fields to be retrieved in the form of predefined strings:

- ❑ id : Search for the entry is based on the <id> field with the value specified in the next parameter.
- ❑ number : Search for the entry is based on the <number> field with the value specified in the next parameter.
- ❑ name : Search for the entry is based on the <name> field with the value specified in the next parameter.

<fieldval> is the value of the field which the phonebook search is to be carried out using.

<result> is a string that is composed of many fields of the phonebook entry. Each field can be retrieved using the getFieldValue() function in the Phonebook library. The result can be an empty string if no matching entry was found.

Here is an example:

```
var structfield = WTAPhoneBook.read ( "name", "Victoria" );
```

Remove Phonebook Entry

This function removes an entry in the phonebook. The <id> of the entry must be known. If only the <name> or the <number> field of an entry that is to be removed is known, the previous function *Read Phonebook Entry* can be used to search for the required entry and find its <id>. The generic WMLScript form is as follows:

```
var <result> = WTAPhoneBook.write( <id> );
```

<id> is the identity of the phonebook entry.

<result> is an error code that is below zero in case of failure.

Here is an example:

```
var retcode = WTAPhoneBook.remove( 0 );
```

Get Field Value

With this function, you can retrieve fields associated with a specific phonebook entry that was read into a variable. The generic WMLScript form is as follows:

```
var <fieldval> = WTAPhoneBook.getFieldValue( <struct>, <field> );
```

`<struct>` is the name of the variable into which the read() function returned the message.

`<field>` is the same as in *Read Phonebook Entry*.

`<fieldval>` is the value of the field returned. If the field is not supported, a value that is less than zero is returned. If a field is supported, but is not present in the variable `<struct>`, an empty "" string is returned.

Here is an example:

```
var fieldval = WTAPhoneBook.getFieldValue( $structfield, "id" );
```

Change Phonebook Entry

You can change the contents of an existing phonebook entry with this function. The generic WMLScript form is as follows:

```
var <result> = WTAPhoneBook.change( <id>, <field>, <fieldval> );
```

`<id>` is the identity of the phonebook entry.

`<field>` is the same as fields defined in *Read Phonebook Entry*.

`<fieldval>` is the value of the field which the phonebook search is to be carried out using.

`<result>` is the `<id>` for the particular entry returned in case of success or an error code in case of failure.

Here is an example:

```
var id = WTAPhoneBook.change( 0, "number", "+441902777565" );
```

Call Logs Library

This library is used to control the logs that are made of calls that are made or received. Again the URL forms of the functions are unavailable. The `<library>` name is `WTACallLog` in the WMLScript form

Last Dialed Numbers

Returns an entry from the list of "last dialed numbers" call log or register. The generic WMLScript form is as follows:

```
var <struct> = WTACallLog.dialled( <id> );
```

<id> is the identity of the call log entry. A value of "0" returns the entry corresponding to the last dialed number, a value of "1" returns the entry corresponding to the second last dialed number, and so on. If id is empty (""), the entry corresponding to the last dialed number is returned.

<struct> is a string that is composed of many fields of the last dialed call log entry. Each field can be retrieved using the getFieldValue() function in the Call Logs library. The possible fields in the string are:

❏ number : String containing the phone number without any blanks in.

❏ timestamp : Indicates when the entry was written to the log which is practically equivalent to the time when the call was made.

Here is an example:

```
var structfields = WTACallLog.dialled( 0 );
```

Missed Calls

Returns an entry from the list of phone calls that were missed (calls for which the calling party disconnects before the call could be accepted by the phone user) The generic WMLScript form is as follows:

```
var <struct> = WTACallLog.missed( <id> );
```

<id> is the identity of the call log entry. A value of "0" returns the entry corresponding to the last missed call, a value of "1" returns the entry corresponding to the second last missed call, and so on. If id is empty (""), the entry corresponding to the last missed call is returned.

<struct> is a string that is composed of many fields of the missed call log entry. Each field can be retrieved using the getFieldValue() function in the Call Logs library. The fields provided by the Last Dialed Numbers function are all available here. In addition to these, one more field is provided:

❏ class : String that contains a reason, if the number field does not contain a phone number.

Here is an example:

```
var structfields = WTACallLog.missed( 0 );
```

Received Calls

Returns an entry from the list of phone calls that were received/accepted/answered. The generic WMLScript form is as follows:

```
var <struct> = WTACallLog.received( <id> );
```

`<id>` is the identity of the call log entry. A value of "0" returns the entry corresponding to the last received call, a value of "1" returns the entry corresponding to the second last received call, and so on. If id is empty (""), the entry corresponding to the last received call is returned.

`<struct>` is a string that is composed of many fields of the received call log entry. Each field can be retrieved using the `getFieldValue()` function in the Call Log library. The fields provided by the *Missed Numbers* function are all available here.

Here is an example:

```
var structfields = WTACallLog.received( 0 );
```

Get Field Value

With this function, you can retrieve fields associated with a specific call log entry that was read into a variable. The generic WMLScript form is as follows:

```
var <fieldval> = WTACallLog.getFieldValue( <struct>, <field> );
```

`<struct>` is the name of the variable into which one of the previous call log functions returned the message.

`<field>` is the same as fields defined in the previous call log functions.

`<fieldval>` is the value of the field returned. If the field is not supported, a value that is less than zero is returned. If a field is supported, but is not present in `$structfield`, an empty "" string is returned.

Here is an example:

```
var fieldval = WTACallLog.getFieldValue( $structfield, "timestamp" );
```

Miscellaneous Library

This library brings together all other functions that are not classified under the other headings. Most of these only have WMLScript syntax. The `<library>` name is ms in the URI form and `WTAMisc` in the WMLScript form.

Indication

This function allows turning on or off of some kind of logical indication to indicate the occurrence of one of the predefined conditions or events. The generic WMLScript form is as follows:

```
var <result> = WTAMisc.indication( <type>, <operation>, <count> );
```

`<type>` is a number identifying a predefined condition:

- ❑   0 : incoming speech call
- ❑   1 : incoming data call
- ❑ · 2 : incoming fax call
- ❑   3 : call waiting
- ❑   4 : received text
- ❑   5 : voice mail notification
- ❑   6 : fax notification
- ❑   7 : email notification
- ❑   8-15 : extra notifications

`<operation>` is to set or reset the indicator:

- ❑   1 : Set the indicator
- ❑   2 : Reset the indicator

`<count>` is the number of new text messages, voicemails, emails, for example.

Here is an example:

```
var result = WTAMisc.indication( 7, 1, 1 );
```

The above code causes the phone to display some kind of visual or audible indication to the user that one new email has arrived.

Terminate WTA User Agent

This function terminates the context for the user agent. It is generally used when all the required WTA actions that the current WML deck has to carry out are complete. The generic URI form is as follows:

```
wtai://ms/ec[!<result>]
```

and the generic WMLScript form is:

```
var <result> = endcontext;
```

<result> is zero if successful or a value less than zero in case of failure.

Protect WTA User Agent Context

This function allows you to control whether or not a WTA user agent context can be interrupted from whatever it is currently doing. The generic WMLScript form is as follows:

```
var <result> = WTAMisc.protected( <mode> );
```

<mode> takes the values:

- ❏   0 : Do not protect the context.
- ❏   1 : Protect the context.

<result> is the value of the <mode> after the operation is carried out.

Here is an example:

```
var callid0 = WTAMisc.protected(1);
```

The WBMP Image Format

In the future, the WBMP specification may be extended to support different image types, which may include color, animation and image compression. However, at present the WBMP format only supports black and white images with no compression. These are called **type 0** WBMPs.

A WBMP consists of two sections, the header and the image data. In this description of the format given below, the word **octet** is used to mean an 8-bit value.

Header

This consists of four parts, in the following order: type, fixed header, width and height. The type is one octet and should be zero (see above). The fixed header is also one octet and should be zero. The width and height parts of the header give the width and height of the image in pixels. These are **multi-byte integers**.

A multi-byte integer is either a single octet or sequence of octets. The most significant bit (the first bit) in each octet is set to 1 if more octets are to follow and 0 if it is the last octet. The other seven bits contain the actual value.

Image Data

Each row of the picture consists of a sequence of octets. Each bit in each octet represents one pixel in the image. If the width of an image is not a multiple of eight, then the remaining bits in the last octet must all be set to 0 (zero). The default color-coding in the WBMP format is white, which is represented by a 1, and black, which is represented by a 0.

Apache and Tomcat Installation

In order to install Apache and Tomcat, note that you must have JAVA 2 1.3 installed.

Apache

1. Download the latest version of the Apache self-installing win32 binary from:

`http://www.apache.org/dist/binaries/win32`

2. Install Apache by double clicking on the icon and accepting all defaults. This will install to `c:\Program Files\Apache Group\Apache`

3. If you have another server installed on your system, open the `httpd.conf` in `c:\Program Files\Apache Group\Apache\conf` using Notepad.

4. Find the line that reads:

`Port 80`

and change it to:

`Port 8000`

5. Find the line that reads:

```
#servername new.host.name
```

    a. If you are on a LAN, change it to:
```
servername <DNSname> - where DNSname is the name of your computer.
```

    b. If you have an IP address, change it to:
```
servername <ip address>
```

If your IP address is assigned dynamically, you must specify your computers DNS name.

    c. If you have a URL, change it to:
```
servername www.<yourservername>.com
```

6. Open a MS-DOS command prompt window, change directory to `c:\Program Files\Apache group\Apache` and enter

```
apache
```

7. To test that Apache has installed correctly, open your favorite browser and enter the following URL:

```
http://<yourservername>:8000/
```

You should now have displayed the "Powered by Apache" homepage and are now the webmaster of your own Apache server.

8. To switch Apache off you will need to open another MS-DOS window, change directory to `c:\Program Files\Apache Group\Apache` and enter

```
apache.exe -k shutdown
```

Tomcat

1. Download the self-installing `Jakarta-tomcat.zip` file from:

```
http://jakarta.apache.org/builds/tomcat/release/v3.1/bin/
```

2. Double click on the `Jakarta-tomcat.zip` icon and change the installation directory to `c:\Program files\Apache Group`

3. If you are using Windows 95 & 98:

    a. Change the `autoexec.bat` file to include the following lines
```
set TOMCAT_HOME=c:\Program Files\Apache Group\Jakarta-tomcat
set JAVA_HOME="<your Java JDK home directory>"
```

b. Also in `autoexec.bat`, add the locations for JDK and Java to your `path` command, for example:

```
path=%path%;"c:\javasoft\jre\1.3\bin";"c:\jdk1.3"
```

c. It may also be necessary to increase the memory space needed to store environment variables. To do this, add the following line to your `config.sys` file:

```
shell=\command.com /E:2048 /P
```

The emboldened number above can be increased in 1024 increments if needed.

4. If you are using Windows 2000:

Add:

```
TOMCAT_HOME= c:\Program Files\Apache Group\Jakarta-tomcat
```

to the system variables. You can find these in START/SETTINGS/CONTROL PANEL. Choose SYSTEM, click on the ADVANCED tab followed by ENVIRONMENT VARIABLES and finally choose NEW in the lower section, titled System Variables.

Variable Name is `TOMCAT_HOME`

Variable Value is `c:\Program Files\Apache Group\Jakarta-tomcat`

The default is `c:\Program Files\Apache Group\Jakarta-tomcat`

5. Open a MS-DOS command prompt window and change directory to `c:\Program Files\Apache Group\Jakarta-tomcat\bin`. Enter:

```
tomcat run
```

This will set up a new `.conf file called tomcat-apache.conf in c:\Program Files\Apache Group \Jakarta-tomcat\conf`.

6. Edit `c:\Program Files\Apache Group\Jakarta-tomcat\Conf\tomcat-apache.conf` and place quotes around the paths referred to in the `/examples and /test` aliases.

7. Change the file attribute of `tomcat-apache.conf` to read-only by entering:

```
attrib tomcat-apache.conf +r
```

We have to do this because each time Tomcat is run a new `tomcat-apache.conf` file is created. This means that the changes in point 6 will have to done each time Tomcat is used, which is not the most ideal of situations.

8. Edit the file `httpd.conf` in `c:\Program Files\Apache Group\Apache\conf` and add the following line to the bottom of the file:

```
include "c:\Program Files\Apache Group\Jakarta-tomcat\Conf\tomcat-apache.conf"
```

Please note the use of quotes.

9. Download the file `ApacheModuleJServ.dll` from:

`http://jakarta.apache.org/builds/tomcat/release/v3.1/bin/win32/i386/`

and copy it to `c:\Program Files\Apache Group \Apache\Modules`.

10. To test Tomcat, ensure that Apache is running (see above), open your favorite browser, and enter the following URL:

`http://<yourservername>(:optionalportnumber)/examples/`

where `(:optionalportnumber)` is the port number specified in point 4 of the Apache installation.

You should now have displayed the "Index of /examples" directory and are now the webmaster of your own Apache-Tomcat server.

11. Stop Tomcat by opening a new MSDOS command prompt window, changing directory to `c:\Program Files\Apache Group\Jakarta-tomcat\Bin` and entering:

`tomcat stop`

Shortcuts

To simplify things you may prefer to set up shortcuts to switch Apache and Tomcat on and off.

Apache Shortcuts

1. Right click on the desktop and choose NEW/SHORTCUT.

2. Enter:

`"c:\Program Files\Apache Group\Apache\apache.exe" -d "c:\Program Files\Apache Group\Apache" -s`

as the command line, and choose a name for the shortcut, e.g. Start Apache.

3. Right click on the desktop and choose NEW/SHORTCUT.

4. Enter:

`"c:\Program Files\Apache Group\Apache\apache.exe" -d "c:\Program Files\Apache Group\Apache" -k shutdown`

as the command line, and choose a name for the shortcut, e.g. Stop Apache.

Tomcat Shortcuts

1. Right click on the desktop and choose NEW/SHORTCUT.

2. Enter:

   ```
   "c:\Program Files\Apache Group\Jakarta-tomcat\bin\tomcat" run
   ```

   as the command line, and choose a name for the shortcut, e.g. Start Tomcat.

3. Right click on the desktop and choose NEW/SHORTCUT.

4. Enter:

   ```
   "c:\Program Files\Apache Group\Jakarta-tomcat\bin\tomcat" stop
   ```

   as the command line, and choose a name for the shortcut, e.g. Stop Tomcat.

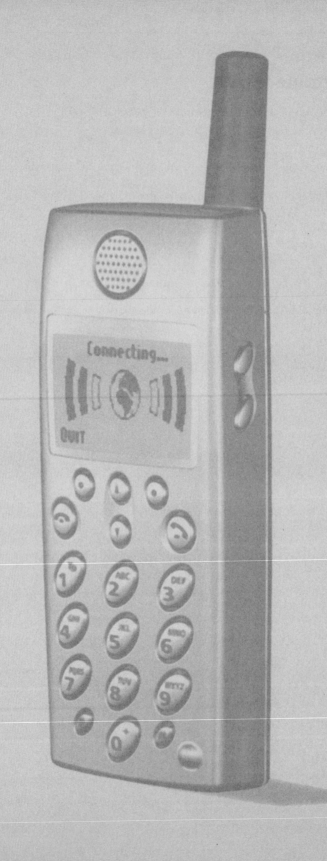

G

Glossary

3G: or **3rd generation mobile technology** is the generic term used to describe the next generation of mobile telephony systems. 3G systems will expand mobile telephony capabilities to include voice, text and data transmission over wireless networks.

ACL: Asynchronous Connectionless Link, type of data packet (data only).

ACL: Access Control List.

AT-commands: Set of protocols that allow mobile phones and modems to be controlled.

Baseband: Part of the Bluetooth Protocol stack, enabling the physical radio frequency link between Bluetooth units on a piconet.

Bluetooth: Low power radio technology developed to replace cables and infrared links for distances of up to 10 metres.

Bluetooth SIG: Bluetooth Special Interest Group. Founded in May 1998 by Ericsson, IBM, Intel, Nokia and Toshiba, the Bluetooth SIG is a forum for the development, promotion and enhancement of Bluetooth technology. The Bluetooth SIG, now led by the Promoter Group (composed of the founding members plus Lucent, Motorola, Microsoft and 3Com) now has some 2000 adopter members.

CAMEL: Customized Application for Mobile networks Enhanced Logic is a feature of GSM that allows users to roam between networks. CAMEL is a standard that is now starting to be deployed.

CC/PP: Composite Capability/Preferences Profiles is a set of **CPI**s.

CCQ: Client Capabilities Query.

CDMA: Code Division Multiple Access is a technology that enables multiple users to access a single radio frequency channel through the allocation of a unique code sequence.

CDP: Cellular Digital Packet data.

Cell Broadcast: Technology designed for the simultaneous delivery of short messages to multiple mobile users within a specified region. This is a one-to-many version of SMS.

Communicator: PDA type equipment integrated with or attached to a mobile phone, for example Nokia Communicator 9110, Ericsson MC218.

COO: Cell Of Origin is a mobile location system.

CPI: Capabilities and Preferences Information is the generic term used to describe the information relating to a particular device, the network it operates on and the user's preferences as to content reception. This information is stored on a **CC/PP** server.

CSD: Circuit Switched cellular Data.

CTIA: Cellular Telecommunications Industry Association.

DECT: Digital European Cordless Telecommunications.

Dual-Band: Characterizes a handset that is able to operate on two different frequencies.

E-OTD: Enhanced Observed Time Difference is a mobile location system that uses differences between time of arrival, at the handset and at a nearby locator, of a signal transmitted by the mobile network to pin-point the devices position.

ECMA: European Computer Manufacturer Association.

EDGE: Enhanced Data for GSM Evolution is an ETSI standard. It is a higher bandwidth version of GSM, allowing for transmission speeds of up to 384 Kb per second, that makes use of existing GSM infrastructure.

EPOC: Operating system specifically designed for mobile devices by Symbian, a consortium formed of Psion, Ericsson, Matsushita, Nokia and Motorola. It is best known for its implementation on Psion PDAs and Ericsson R380 mobile phones.

ETSI: European Telecommunication Standards Institute.

FTP: File Transfer Protocol.

GPRS: General Packet Radio Service is an ETSI standard and is the first implementation of a packet switched wireless protocol within a GSM infrastructure. Its main difference compared to GSM, which uses a predominantly circuit switched protocol, is that GPRS only uses the network when data is to be sent. GPRS enables users to send data at speeds of up to 115 Kb per second. GPRS is often referred to as "always on" technology. Because it is particularly well suited to a "bursty" type of data transmission, it effectively brings IP capabilities (e-mail, Internet access) to a GSM network.

GPS: Global Positioning System is a satellite based radio positioning system that uses the US's NAVSTAR system to accurately provide positioning, velocity and time information to GPS enabled device users.

GSM: Global System for Mobile communication is the prevailing mobile standard for Europe and the Asia Pacific region. GSM operates in the 900 MHz and 1800 MHz (1900 MHz in the US) frequency bands.

H.323: is an ITU standard that defines a protocol for the transmission of multimedia (audio, video and data) packets over packet switching networks (for example, GPRS). These networks may include the Internet, enterprise LANs, or WANs.

HDML: Handheld Device Markup Language is a subset of HTML and is a text-based way of defining data, sent for display on handheld devices through the use of a microbrowser. HDML's use is likely to disappear in favor of WML or Web Clipping.

HSCSD: High Speed Circuit Switched Data is a circuit switched (as opposed to packet switched) protocol that extends the capabilities of GSM to increase its transmission speeds by up to 4 times its GSM equivalent (57.6 Kb per second). It achieves this by using 4 GSM time slots rather than one.

HTML: Hyper Text Markup language is a text-based way of describing data for transmission over the Internet.

HTML-NG: HTML Next Generation.

HTTP: Hyper Text Transfer Protocol is a protocol that defines the way in which a web server and a web client contact (handshake) each other.

ICQ: Online instant messaging program developed by Mirabilis Ltd.

IDEN®: is Motorola's proprietary technology for Integrated Digital Enhanced Networks. It allows business users to take full advantage of wireless technology by combining the capabilities of a digital mobile phone, a two-way radio, an alphanumeric pager and a data/fax modem in a single mobile device.

IETF: Internet Engineering Task Force is an international organization that defines and develops Internet standards specifications.

IMAP: Internet Message Access Protocol, a protocol for retrieving e-mail messages.

IMT-2000: International Mobile Telecommunications 2000 is an ITU concept that defines the group of technological solutions that will enable 3rd Generation mobile systems.

IP: Internet Protocol, defined by the IETF for the transmission of information over the Internet. It works by dividing transmitted data into packets, and attaching to each packet a header containing the addressing information.

IrDA: Infrared Data Association.

IRIDIUM®: is a communication system that uses a 66 strong satellite network orbiting the earth. The system was first developed by Motorola and established itself as a separate company in 1991. It provides a mobile wireless communication network across the world and is connected to terrestrial telephone systems. It allows a mobile user to place and receive calls from anywhere in the world.

IrMC: Infrared Mobile Communications.

ITU: International Telecommunications Union is an international organization for the development and specification of global telecom networks and services standards.

LAN: Local Area Network.

L2CAP: Logical Link and Control Adaptation Protocol (a Bluetooth Specific Protocol).

LMP: Link Manager Protocol is the layer of the Bluetooth protocol stack responsible for the set up of the link between Bluetooth devices. This includes security aspects (authentication, encryption), the control and negotiation of packet sizes, power mode control and connection states of a Bluetooth unit in a piconet.

MExE: Mobile Execution Environment is a protocol for the integration of Java onto mobile phones. MExE will extend the capabilities of WAP (Wireless Application Protocol) and offer greater security features.

Microbrowser: Software that allows the user to access the Internet from a mobile device.

MIM: Mobile Instant Messaging is a technology similar to ICQ and will allow mobile users to check for instant availability and communicate instantly with other users on a non-voice basis.

MSISDN: Mobile Station International Subscriber Directory Number, commonly known as a phone number.

OBEX: Object Exchange Protocol, is a session protocol developed by the IrDA that allows the exchange of data in a simple and spontaneous manner. Previously known as IrOBEX, it provides the same basic functionality as HTTP.

OTA: Over-The-Air.

PAP: Push Access Protocol (see also under WAP).

PCMCIA: Personal Computer Memory Card International Association.

PDA: Personal Digital Assistant is the generic term used to describe a family of mobile devices offering users PIM functionality in the form of an electronic phone book, calendar and notepad.

PI: Push Initiator (see also under WAP).

PIM: Personal Information Manager.

PKI: Public Key Infrastructure.

POP: Post Office Protocol, a protocol used to retrieve e-mail from a web server.

PPG: Push Proxy Gateway.

PPP: Point to Point Protocol, defined by the IETF. This protocol defines the means to transfer IP packets to and from a LAN.

Profile: is basically a schema that encapsulates the display characteristics of a device or network.

Push Message: is a message from a PI, which is pushed to one or more (Multicast Message) clients.

RFC: Request For Comments.

RFCOMM: Serial cable emulation protocol, protocol that emulates serial cable control and data signals and that provides transport capabilities in a wireless environment for protocols that use serial line as their usual transport mechanisms.

SAT: SIM Application Toolkit is a technology that extends the capabilities of the SIM card by being programmable. It allows for personalization of the functionality of a mobile phone.

SCO: Synchronous Connection Oriented, type of data packet (may include audio).

SDK: Software Development Kit.

SDP: Service Discovery Protocol, allowing for the query of devices and services on a wireless network.

Session: In the context of a wireless transmission, a session is the series of exchanges of information or data that exists between two programs (typically one on the server and one on the client).

SET: Secure Electronic Transaction is a standard for credit card payments across networks.

SI: Service Indication (see also under WAPSI).

SIM Card: Subscriber Identity Module found in a mobile phone that stores authentication information and the GSM encryption algorithms that mobile phones need for connecting and securing a call over a GSM network.

SL: Service Loading.

Smartcards: can be viewed as SIM cards with an integrated microprocessor. These are able to provide the user with extended capabilities in the form of "card-based" applications.

Smartphone: Mobile phone with extended capabilities (such as display, or keyboard) and functionalities (for example, e-mail, fax).

SMPP: Short Message Peer to Peer.

SMS: Short Messaging Service is a technology for the transmission of text messages to and from mobile phones. It allows for up to 160 alphanumeric characters. This technology is best used for pushing information from one-to-one or one-to-few.

SMSC: Short Message Service Center.

SSL: Secure Socket Layer.

Symbian: Joint venture between Psion, Motorola, Nokia, Ericsson and Matsushita, formed to develop and promote the use of the EPOC operating system for wireless devices.

Synchronization: the act of updating data between different devices.

TCP: Transport Control Protocol, defined by the IETF. This is a protocol used for communication across the Internet.

TCS BIN or TCS Binary: Telephony Control Specification Binary is a bit oriented protocol that defines call control signaling for the establishment of speech and data calls between Bluetooth devices.

TDMA: Time Division Multiple Access is a wireless access standard based on the allocation of unique time slots over a single radio frequency to access a network, thus limiting the possibility of interference. In use in particular in the United States, TDMA technology is considered as a 2nd generation wireless system.

TIPHON: Telecommunications and Internet Protocol Harmonization Over Networks is an ETSI project that will define a protocol for communication between packet switched and circuit switched networks.

TOA: Time Of Arrival is another mobile location technology.

Tri-Band: Characterizes a handset that is able to operate on three different frequencies.

UDP: User Datagram Protocol, defined by the IETF. This is a protocol used for communication across the Internet.

UMS: Unified Messaging Systems is a technology that should allow users to access messages sent in different formats through one single interface.

UMTS: Universal Mobile Phone System is the European implementation of the ETSI's 3G system. The advertised data rates for UMTS are: 144 Kb per second for vehicular transmissions, 384 Kb per second for pedestrian and 2 Mb per second for in-building communication.

UP: Unwired Planet® is a set of technologies that enhances the number of services available for handheld devices, for example the UP-Browser.

URL: Uniform Resource Locator.

USSD: Unstructured Supplementary Services Data allows for the transmission of information via a GSM network. Contrasting with SMS, it offers real time connection during a session. A USSD message can be up to 182 alphanumeric characters in length. This is a WAP bearer service.

vCAL: Electronic or virtual Calendar, developed by the versit consortium and now controlled by the Internet Mail Consortium. This open specification defines the format of electronic personal calendar entry and scheduling information.

vCard: Electronic or virtual Card, developed by the versit consortium and now controlled by the Internet Mail Consortium. This open specification defines the format of an Electronic Business Card.

VoiceXML: VoiceXML, a markup language for speech, is a standard being pushed by the VoiceXML Forum driven by Motorola, AT&T and Lucent and is aimed at allowing voice recognition for accessing the internet via a phone, whether wired or not.

VoIP: Voice over IP is a protocol that allows the transmission of voice over Internet networks by using IP encoding.

VoxML: A markup language for speech proposed by Motorola for their telephony applications.

W3C: World Wide Web Consortium is an international standards organization whose aim is to define and develop technical specifications for the development of the Web.

W-CDMA: Wideband CDMA.

WAE: Wireless Application Environment is part of the WAP stack of protocols. It consists of a framework containing all the elements allowing for the development of wireless applications. This includes WML, WMLScript, the WAE User Agent and supported media types.

WAP: Wireless Application Protocol, open, global standard for wireless solutions. This technology permits the design of interactive, real time wireless services for wireless devices.

WAP Forum: Standards committee first founded by Unwired Planet (now Phone.com) whose role is the development of specifications for the WAP standard.

WAP Push Access Protocol: or PAP, is a protocol used for the transmission of information that should be pushed to a client. This protocol controls the transmission of push information between the Push Initiator (Server) and the Push Proxy/Gateway. The transmission between the Push Proxy/Gateway and the network client is controlled by the **WAP Push OTA Protocol**.

WAPSI: Wireless Application Protocol Service Indication is a content type that allows content providers to send notifications to users in an asynchronous manner. In its most basic form a SI will be a short message with an attached URL.

WBMP: Wireless Bitmap, is a graphic format optimized for the transmission of bitmaps over wireless networks.

WBXML: WAP Binary XML content is a binary representation of XML. The binary nature of the representation means a reduction in the resources required to transmit XML documents to wireless devices.

WCMP: Wireless Control Message Protocol is part of the WAP stack and provides an error reporting mechanism for the WDP (Wireless Datagram Protocol). These errors can be captured and managed.

WDP: Wireless Datagram Protocol.

Web Clipping: Palm proprietary format for the delivery of web based information to Palm devices via synchronization or wireless communication (Palm VII).

WIM: Wireless Identity Module is part of WTLS that stores the information necessary for the protocol to execute its security and authentication functions. SIM cards and Smartcards are implementations of WIM.

WML: Wireless Markup Language is a subset of XML and has been developed especially for WAP. It provides 4 major functionalities: allows for text display on a device, card and deck organization, navigation and linking, and state management.

WMLScript: is a scripting language specifically designed to be used for programming mobile devices. It is based on the ECMAScript specification but has been optimized for low bandwidth communication and thin clients.

WMLScript Libraries: are sets of libraries that allow programmers to access and take full advantage of WMLScript's core functionality.

WSP: Wireless Session Protocol is the layer of the WAP Protocol stack that controls the transmission between a remote client and a server (or proxy). At its core, WSP is the wireless version of HTTP and therefore manages all aspects of a session (from the time that the connection to the network is established to the time the user ends that connection). WSP should provide both push and pull data transfer capabilities.

WTA: Wireless Telephony Application is an extension of the WAE (Wireless Application Environment) by providing a set of interfaces to the telephony functionality of a mobile device.

WTAI: Wireless Telephony Application Interface is a set of Interfaces that extend the WAE (Wireless Application Environment) to include telephony applications.

WTLS: Wireless Transport Layer Security is that part of the WAP Stack that defines and controls the security features of a wireless transaction.

WTP: Wireless Transaction Protocol is that part of the WAP protocol stack that controls and manages sessions. It effectively controls the interaction between a user agent and a content server.

XML: eXtensible Markup Language.

XSLT: eXtensible Stylesheet Language Transformation.

Resources

This book has covered a lot of territory, including many different programming languages. In order to make the book as manageable as possible, explanations of some of these languages, and of some other concepts, have had to be kept short. In this appendix, we aim to amalgamate resources from the text for your convenience, together with other resources that should help you, should you wish to find out more about any of the mentioned technologies.

General WAP Resources

There are many current resources for WAP that can be found on the Internet using the standard search engines, and many more may be expected as WAP moves out of its infancy. Below we list some of these resources, just to give you a head start:

❑ The WAP forum at `http://www.wapforum.com`. At this site, the current WAP specifications can be found, together with suggested future specifications.

❑ The WAP group at `http://www.thewapgroup.com`. Here you can gain access to a network of professionals, all working towards the widespread dispersal of knowledge and the development of WAP technologies.

❑ Anywhereyougo at `http://www.anywhereyougo.com/`, formerly known as WAPtastic, provides links to news items, articles, discussion groups and much more.

❑ Gelon at `http://www.gelon.net/` includes links to WAP services, discussion forums and a WAP browser emulator (see below).

- ❑ YourWAP at `http://www.yourwap.com` allows you to manage data such as email accounts and address books from your mobile device. It also includes a web based WAP browser.

- ❑ MobileThink at `http://www.mobilethink.com` is trying to help companies take advantage of the new mobile world, for example by producing usability studies.

- ❑ The site at `http://www.wirelessdevnet.com/` is useful for industry news and other information resources

- ❑ Lists of further WAP related links can be found at `http://www.waplinks.com`

- ❑ The independent WAP and WML FAQ at `http://wap.colorline.no/wap-faq/` may prove useful for any queries you may have.

- ❑ At `http://www.wapwednesday.com` you will find a forum for people interested in WAP.

- ❑ Links to other resources, news and reviews of current WAP devices can be found at `http://www.wap-uk.com`

- ❑ An Asia Pacific WAP developer forum can be found at `http://www.wap.com.sg/`

- ❑ For a library containing many free WBMP files, try `http://www.hicon.nl`.

WAP Browsers and Emulators

In Chapter 2 we discussed the WAP browsers and browser emulators currently on the market. As we saw in some detail, downloadable toolkits including browser emulators are available from the following sites:

- ❑ Nokia: `http://forum.nokia.com/`

- ❑ Phone.com: `http://updev.phone.com/`. (For a list of phones using the Phone.com browser, see `http://updev.phone.com/dev/ts/`.)

- ❑ Ericsson: `http://www.ericsson.com/developerszone/`

- ❑ Motorola: `http://www.motorola.com/MIMS/MSPG/spin/mix/mix.html`

A browser is also available for Palm PDA type devices:

- ❑ Palm: `http://palmsoftware.tucows.com/tucows_int_web.html`

Finally, there are a number of other WAP emulators, including those based on the following web sites:

- ❑ Winwap: `http://www.slobtrot.com/winwap/`

- ❑ Gelon: `http://www.gelon.net/`

WAP Gateways

The following list contains vendors of some of the current WAP Gateway products. More information on some of these may be found in Chapter 3.

- Audicode WAP Server: http://www.audicode.com/eng/index.html

- CMG, WAP Service Broker: http://www.cmg.com/

- Dr. Materna Gmbh: http://www.materna.com/

- Ericsson: http://www.ericsson.se/WAP/

- Integra Micro Systems: http://www.integramicro.com/ or: http://www.VSellinIndia.com/jataayu/index.html

- Kannel, Open-Source WAP Gateway: http://www.kannel.org/

- KNO Software, Free Personal WAP Gateway: http://www.kno.fi/

- Mobileways: http://www.mobileways.de/

- Nokia: http://www.forum.nokia.com/wap/tools.html

- Phone.com, UP.Link Server Suite: http://www.phone.com/products/uplink.html

- Silicon Automation Systems WAP Gateway: http://www.sasi.com/telecom/

- Kipling Information Technology, Trinity WAP Gateway: http://www.kipling.se/wap.html

- Virtuacom or Edge consultants: http://www.virtuacom.com/

- Gnuws project for an open source UNIX gateway: http://www.wapgw.org/

Usability

The issues surrounding usability were discussed in detail in Chapter 7. Many of the major browser-owning companies have published usability guidelines for their products. These include:

- Phone.com: http://updev.phone.com/dev/ts/

- Nokia: http://www.forum.nokia.com/

In addition, Telenor, the largest Norwegian telecom company, has released some user interface design guidelines, available from http://wap.telenor.no/go/docs/fase0/no/ressurser/WAP_guidelines.pdf.

ASP

In Chapter 8, ASP and ADO were used to create a dynamically generated WAP application. For more information on these technologies, see the following books from Wrox Press:

- *Professional ASP 3.0*, by Richard Anderson et al, ISBN 1861002610

- *Professional ADO 2.5 Programming*, by Ian Blackburn et al, ISBN 1861002750

Also see ASPToday at http://www.asptoday.com, which amongst other things provides daily articles, and techniques, tips and tricks on ASP programming and related technologies.

XML

XML was introduced briefly in Chapter 9. Note that you can obtain the specifications and other XML documentation from the W3C web site at http://www.w3.org/. Within this site is a section devoted to the Mobile Access Group (at http://www.w3.org/Mobile), and an 'Activity' statement that describes in detail their initiative of working towards comprehensive web access from mobile devices.

For more information, also see http://www.xml.com, which aims to provide a mix of information and services for the XML community.

There are a wide range of Wrox Press books covering the various XML technologies used in Chapter 9 and elsewhere in the book. These include:

❑ *Professional XML*, by Richard Anderson et al, ISBN 1861003110

❑ *XSLT Programmer's Reference*, by Michael Kay, ISBN 1861003129

❑ *Beginning XHTML*, by Frank Boumphrey et al, ISBN 1861003439

XML Parsers and XSLT Processors

An XML parser is needed in order to interpret an XML document. Such parsers include:

❑ Apache: http://xml.apache.org/

❑ Sun: http://www.sun.com/

❑ James Clark's xp: http://www.jclark.com/xml/

For information on the conformance testing of XML parsers, see the conformance study at http://www.xml.com/pub/1999/09/conformance/summary.html, with follow-up discussions in the next two issues.

In chapter 10 we also needed an XSLT processor, an example of which is:

❑ James Clark's xt: http://www.jclark.com/xml/

Java

The Java programming language has been used in a number of chapters in this book to produce example applications. For example, in Chapters 13 and 14 Java servlets were used, while in Chapter 10 JSP were used.

Servlet-enabled Web Servers

There are a number of web servers that can be used in association with servlets, including:

❑ Apache + JServ J: http://www.apache.org/

❑ Apache + Tomcat: http://www.apache.org/

❑ Apache + JRun: http://www.jrun.com/

- ❏ Acme Web Server: http://www.acme.com/java/software/
- ❏ Avenida AWS: http://www.avenida.co.uk/
- ❏ Sun JWS: http://www.sun.com/
- ❏ Oracle Application Server: http://www.oracle.com/
- ❏ Gefion Web Server Lite: http://www.gefionsoftware.com/LiteWebServer/

Apache, Tomcat, JServ and Acme are all free. Apache is fully functional and in use across the majority of commercial web servers, but can sometimes overwhelm with options that can be confusing for a first-time user. The installation of Apache and Tomcat are explained in Appendix F.

Avenida is not free but has a friendlier user interface, and reasonable documentation. Note that the user interface only works with JDK 1.1.x, but the daemon will run under JDK 1.2.x without problem.

The above list is just a small selection of what is currently available. See the following for other choices:

- ❏ http://www.servlets.com/resources/urls/engines.html
- ❏ http://www.gamelan.com/
- ❏ http://www.davecentral.com/

Note that whichever web server you choose, you must define the WML MIME types for successful WML serving (as described in Chapter 2). For detailed information on MIME multipart/related message format, please refer to RFC2387 to be found at http://www.ietf.org/rfc/rfc2387.txt.

Java Servlets

There are numerous books on Java servlets on the market. These include:

- ❏ *Professional Java Server Programming*, by Danny Ayers et al, from Wrox Press, ISBN 1861002777
- ❏ *Java Servlet Programming*, by William Crawford et al, from O'Reilly, ISBN 156592391X

The Wrox tome excels with superior real-world examples of servlets integrating with databases, XML, JNDI, LDAP, Jini, Javaspace, etc. It also has a chapter for each of Jserv, ServletRunner and JRun that will ease the pain of configuring your web server.

JSP

JSP were introduced and used to dynamically generate a WAP application in Chapter 10. The syntax for JSP is quite straightforward and compact: it all fits on a double-page syntax card available from Sun at http://java.sun.com/products/jsp/syntax.pdf.

Note that JRun (2.3 and later) from www.allaire.com/Products/JRun/ is an example of a self-standing JSP engine.

For more information on JSP, see the following titles from Wrox Press:

❑ *Professional Java XML Programming with Servlets and JSP*, by Tom Myers and Alexander Nakhimovsky, ISBN 1861002858.

❑ *Professional JSP*, by Karl Avedal et al, ISBN 1861003625

ColdFusion

Although ColdFusion-based WML development is still in its infancy, there are a few web sites devoted to ColdFusion/WML programming. Ones to check out include:

❑ The Cold Fusion WAP Developer Area, located within the wapuseek site. The actual URL for the area is `http://www.wapuseek.co.uk/wap_cf.cfm`, although you must register (for free) to access that page. It offers several interesting ideas and observations.

❑ Systemanage.com has an area devoted to ColdFusion/WML coding, at `http://www.systemanage.com/wml/`

Hopefully there will be more over time.

Allaire has started to offer a number of resources for WML development. One of them is a "reference desk" page on WAP, at `http://www.allaire.com/developer/TechnologyReference/wap.cfm`. There are some interesting pointers to other resources, and if Allaire keeps it updated it would be a good resource to bookmark.

There's also a very interesting Q&A article at Allaire's web site, in the form of an interview with noted ColdFusion expert and Allaire evangelist Ben Forta (see `http://www.allaire.com/developer/referenceDesk/index.cfm`) . It includes several interesting discussions of Allaire's position regarding WML as well as upcoming changes that may come in ColdFusion to add further support (including integration in Allaire Spectra, their content management system).

It's also important in the early phases to find others who are using CF and WML.

The Allaire forums, at `http://forums.Allaire.com`, are an excellent resource. There is a forum devoted to ColdFusion programming, and it generates hundreds of questions and answers per day. There is no area (yet) devoted to WML programming issues, and there are currently only a relatively small number of WAP based discussions, but that's sure to change as WML programming catches fire in the ColdFusion community.

There is another relatively new list devoted specifically to WML programming with ColdFusion. To join the list, send an email to `cf-wap_subscribe@bromby.com` with the following information:

subscribe cf-wap *firstname lastname*

using your first and last names, of course. This is not to be put in the SUBJECT, but the BODY (nothing is needed in the subject). Once you receive a confirmation e-mail, you can then send notes to the list by sending mail to `cf-wap@bromby.com`. If these instructions fail, see the site `http://www.houseoffusion.com`, which also offers instructions for joining this and other CF mailing lists.

As for identifying WML sites that are using ColdFusion, it's often difficult to tell when a site uses ColdFusion. (You'd have to notice the `.cfm` extension being used, which is hard in ever-popular framed sites as well as in WML browsers that don't show the URLs for links being taken.) However, there are a couple of ColdFusion sites that are providing WML pages, including `http://wap-gate.ch` and `http://info-wap.ch`.

Look for some of the large, commercial ColdFusion sites to begin adding WML capabilities as well. (You might be surprised at the roster of large, popular ColdFusion sites!)

Conversion

The subject of conversion of content from web to WAP format was treated in Chapter 12. Here we bring together the relevant Internet resources.

The following companies market conversion tools:

- ❑ Phone.com: `http://www.phone.com/`
- ❑ Oracle: `http://www.oracle.com/` and `http://www.mobileoracle.com/`
- ❑ Argo: `http://www.argogroup.com/`
- ❑ Spyglass: `http://www.spyglass.com/`
- ❑ Orchid: `http://www.webshaper.net`

There is also a Perl HTML to WML conversion tool that can be found at `http://wap.z-y-g-o.com/tools/` amongst various other WAP Perl tools.

Each of the following list of sites has a conversion demonstration for you to try:

- ❑ Digital Paths: `http://www.digitalpaths.com/`
- ❑ Orchid: `http://www.orchidsys.com/wap11.wml`
- ❑ Google: `http://www.google.com/`
- ❑ SpyGlass: `http://www.spyglassmobile.com/`

The number of sites delivering content (or partial content) that has been converted from HTML is growing all the time, but currently includes:

- ❑ Oracle: `http://www.mobileoracle.com/`
- ❑ BT Cellnet: `http://www.genie.co.uk`

Finally, the following site contains tools for converting GIF, JPEG and BMP files to WBMP format:

- ❑ Teraflops,: `http://www.teraflops.com/wbmp/`

LDAP

LDAP was the subject of Chapter 14. For further information on LDAP, see

- ❏ *Implementing LDAP*, by Mark Wilcox, from Wrox Press, ISBN 1861002211.
- ❏ *Programming Directory-Enabled Applications With LDAP*, by Tim Howes and Mark Smith, from Macmillan, ISBN 1578700000.

We also saw JNDI and ADSI in use in this chapter. For more information on these technologies, see the following from Wrox Press:

- ❏ *Professional JSP* and *Professional Java Server Programming* each have a chapter on JNDI. (See above for their details.)
- ❏ *Professional ADSI Programming*, by Simon Robinson, ISBN 1861002262.

Security

The Security chapter of this book (Chapter 15) discussed encryption in enough detail for the understanding of the chapter. For more information on this subject, see:

- ❏ *Applied Cryptography*, by Bruce Schneier, from John Wiley & Sons, ISBN: 0471128457
- ❏ *Implementing Elliptic Curve Cryptography*, by Michael Rossing, from Manning Publications, ISBN: 1884777694.

See also The Code Book, by Simon Singh, from Doubleday, ISBN: 0385495315, which is an excellent popularization of cryptography through the ages.

For further information on the security of mobile device applications, see:

- ❏ Baltimore Technologies: `http://www.baltimore.com/`
- ❏ Certicom Encryption: `http://www.certicom.com/`
- ❏ Diversinet Corporation: `http://www.dvnet.com/`

Voice Mark Up Languages

Chapter 18 was predominantly concerned with VoiceXML, for which the WAP forum specification can be found at `http://www.voicexml.org`.

Information on VoXML, the Motorola proprietary voice mark up language, can be found at `http://www.voxml.com`.

IBM Alpha works implements a sample voice browser for browsing VoiceXML documents. It can be downloaded freely from the IBM Alpha works site `http://www.alphaworks.ibm.com`.

Support, Errata and p2p.wrox.com

One of the most irritating things about any programming book is when you find that the bit of code you've just spent an hour typing simply doesn't work. You check it a hundred times to see if you've set it up correctly and then you notice the spelling mistake in the variable name on the book page. Of course, you can blame the authors for not taking enough care and testing the code, the editors for not doing their job properly, or the proofreaders for not being eagle-eyed enough, but this doesn't get around the fact that mistakes do happen.

We try hard to ensure no mistakes sneak out into the real world, but we can't promise that this book is 100% error free. What we can do is offer the next best thing by providing you with immediate support and feedback from experts who have worked on the book and try to ensure that future editions eliminate these gremlins. We also now commit to supporting you not just while you read the book, but once you start developing applications as well through our online forums where you can put your questions to the authors, reviewers, and fellow industry professionals.

In this appendix we'll look at how to:

- ❏ Enroll in the peer to peer forums at `http://p2p.wrox.com`
- ❏ Post and check for errata on our main site, `http://www.wrox.com`
- ❏ E-mail our technical support a query or feedback on our books in general

Between all three of these support procedures, you should get an answer to your problem in a speedy manner.

The Online Forums at p2p.wrox.com

Join one or more of the three mobile mailing lists for author and peer support. Our system provides **programmer to programmer™ support** on mailing lists, forums and newsgroups all in addition to our one-to-one e-mail system, which we'll look at in a minute. Be confident that your query is not just being examined by a support professional, but by the many Wrox authors and other industry experts present on our mailing lists.

How To Enroll For Support

Just follow this four-step system:

1. Go to http://p2p.wrox.com in your favorite browser.
Here you'll find any current announcements concerning P2P – new lists created, any removed and so on.

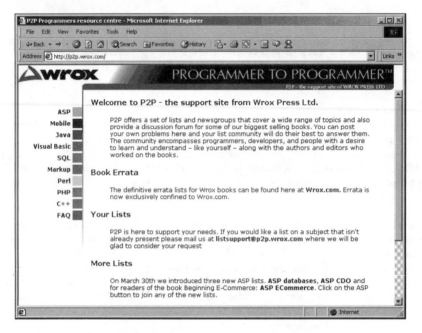

2. Click on the Mobile button in the left hand column.

3. Choose to access one of the three lists (wrox_symbian, wrox_wap or wrox_wml).

4. If you are not a member of the list, you can choose to either view the list without joining it or create an account in the list, by hitting the respective buttons.

5. If you wish to join, you'll be presented with a form in which you'll need to fill in your e-mail address, name and a password (of at least 4 digits). Choose how you would like to receive the messages from the list and then hit Save.

6. Congratulations. You're now a member of one of the Wrox p2p mailing lists.

Why this system offers the best support

You can choose to join the mailing lists or you can receive them as a weekly digest. If you don't have the time or facility to receive the mailing list, then you can search our online archives. You'll find the ability to search on specific subject areas or keywords. As these lists are moderated, you can be confident of finding good, accurate information quickly. Mails can be edited or moved by the moderator into the correct place, making this a most efficient resource. Junk and spam mail are deleted, and your own e-mail address is protected by the unique Lyris system from web-bots that can automatically hoover up newsgroup mailing list addresses.

Online Errata at www.wrox.com

The following section will take you step by step through the process of posting errata to our web site and getting help with known errata. The sections that follow, therefore, are:

- ❏ Wrox Developer's Membership
- ❏ Finding a list of existing errata on the web site
- ❏ Adding your own errata to the existing list
- ❏ What happens to your errata once you've posted it (why doesn't it appear immediately)?

So that you only need view information relevant to yourself, we ask that you register as a Wrox Developer Member. This is a quick and easy process, that will save you time in the long-run. If you are already a member, just update membership to include this book.

Wrox Developer's Membership

To get your FREE Wrox Developer's Membership click on Membership in the top navigation bar of our home site – http://www.wrox.com. This is shown in the following screenshot:

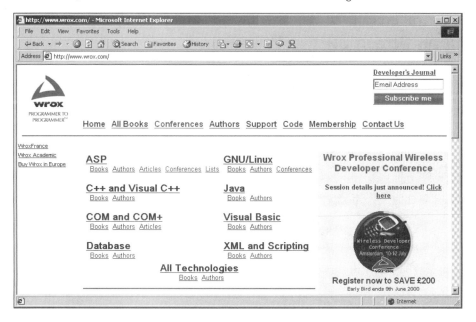

Then, on the next screen (not shown), click on New User. This will display a form. Fill in the details on the form and submit the details using the Register button at the bottom. Before you can say 'The best read books come in Wrox Red' you will get the following screen:

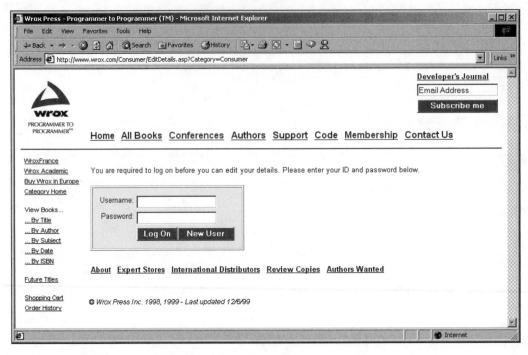

Type in your password once again and click Log On. The following page allows you to change your details if you need to, but now you're logged on, you have access to all the source code downloads and errata for the entire Wrox range of books.

Finding an Errata on the Web Site

Before you send in a query, you might be able to save time by finding the answer to your problem on our web site – http://www.wrox.com.

Each book we publish has its own page and its own errata sheet. You can get to any book's page by clicking on Support from the top navigation bar.

Halfway down the main support page is a drop down box called Title Support. Simply scroll down the list until you see Professional WAP. Select it and then hit Errata.

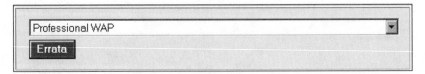

This will take you to the errata page for the book. Select the criteria by which you want to view the errata, and click the Apply criteria button. This will provide you with links to specific errata. For an initial search, you are advised to view the errata by page numbers. If you have looked for an error previously, then you may wish to limit your search using dates. We update these pages daily to ensure that you have the latest information on bugs and errors.

Add an Errata : E-mail Support

If you wish to point out an errata to put up on the website or directly query a problem in the book page with an expert who knows the book in detail then e-mail support@wrox.com, with the title of the book and the last four numbers of the ISBN in the subject field of the e-mail. A typical e-mail should include the following things:

> The **name, last four digits of the ISBN** and **page number** of the problem in the Subject field.
>
> Your **name, contact info** and the **problem** in the body of the message.

We won't send you junk mail. We need the details to save your time and ours. When you send an e-mail it will go through the following chain of support:

Customer Support

Your message is delivered to one of our customer support staff who are the first people to read it. They have files on most frequently asked questions and will answer anything general immediately. They answer general questions about the book and the web site.

Editorial

Deeper queries are forwarded to the technical editor responsible for that book. They have experience with the programming language or particular product and are able to answer detailed technical questions on the subject. Once an issue has been resolved, the editor can post the errata to the web site.

The Authors

Finally, in the unlikely event that the editor can't answer your problem, s/he will forward the request to the author. We try to protect the author from any distractions from writing. However, we are quite happy to forward specific requests to them. All Wrox authors help with the support on their books. They'll mail the customer and the editor with their response, and again all readers should benefit.

What We Can't Answer

Obviously with an ever-growing range of books and an ever-changing technology base, there is an increasing volume of data requiring support. While we endeavor to answer all questions about the book, we can't answer bugs in your own programs that you've adapted from our code. So, while you might have loved the chapters on file handling, don't expect too much sympathy if you cripple your company with a routine which deletes the contents of your hard drive. But do tell us if you're especially pleased with the routine you developed with our help.

How to Tell Us Exactly What You Think

We understand that errors can destroy the enjoyment of a book and can cause many wasted and frustrated hours, so we seek to minimize the distress that they can cause.

You might just wish to tell us how much you liked or loathed the book in question. Or you might have ideas about how this whole process could be improved. In either case, you should e-mail feedback@wrox.com. You'll always find a sympathetic ear, no matter what the problem is. Above all you should remember that we do care about what you have to say and we will do our utmost to act upon it.

Index

Symbol

<!ATLIST> element, SGML
DTD, 269

A

<a> element, 124
description, support and attributes, 700
Abstract Syntax Notation One
see ASN.1 specification
ACAP
competing standard to LDAP, 557
Access control, 80
restricting specific content, 80
Access Control Lists
see ACLs.
<access> element
description, support and attributes, 700
access pragma, 193
Active Directory
definition, 549
Active Directory Servce Interface
see ADSI
Active Server Pages
see ASP
ADO, 233
description, 233
ADO command syntax, 555
ADsPath, 555
example, 555
properties, 555
scope, 555
search filter, 555
ADO object model, 236
Command object
uses, 236
connecting to database, 236
objects created implicitly, 236
objects, create explicitly, 236
connecting to database example, 236
Connection object, create, 237
ConnectionString specifying, 237
DSN, using, 237
OLE DB, using, 237
Connection object
explicitly close, 238
uses, 236
Connection pooling, 239
querying the database, 237
Recordset object stores result of query, 237
Recordset object
explicitly close, 238
uses, 236

ADSI
access functionality from WMLScript, 549
ADO command syntax, 555
ADsPath, 550
string passed to getObject(), 550
analagous to JNDI, 549
can use from any COM-aware language, 549
cannot search from scripting languages, 555
COM objects
does not have fixed set of, 550
definition and description, 549
providers, 549
providers
diagram, 550
IIS provider, 549
LDAP provider, 549
Novell Netware directory providers, 549
WinNT provider, 549
searching Active Directory, 555
searching performed with ADO, 555
update properties of dictionary objects, 551
ADSI methods, 550
GetObject() method, 551
SetInfo() method, 551
aliases
definition, 525
alt attribute
displays text, 132
<anchor> element, 123
description, support and attributes, 700
Apache
configuring MIME types, 48
installation, 751
shortcuts, 754
Apache Cocoon
adding new media device, 457
caching system, 436
features, 436
HTMLExtractor, 459
installation, 451
testing, 451
Java and servlet-based, 436
Phone.com simulator
adding, 457
WML output from XML input
testing, 451
Apache Cocoon components
Formatters, 449, 450
Processors, 449, 450
Producers, 449
creating and testing, 459
getDocument() method, 458
getStream() method, 458
Apache Xalan, 451
Apache Xerces, 445, 451

N

wrox
PROGRAMMER TO PROGRAMMER™

Wrox writes books for you. Any suggestions, or ideas about how you want information given in your ideal book will be studied by our team. Your comments are always valued at Wrox.

Free phone in USA 800-USE-WROX
Fax (312) 893 8001

UK Tel. (0121) 687 4100   Fax (0121) 687 4101

Professional WAP - Registration Card

Name _____

Address _____

_____

_____

_____

City _____ State/Region _____

Country _____ Postcode/Zip _____

E-mail _____

Occupation _____

How did you hear about this book? _____

☐ Book review (name) _____

☐ Advertisement (name) _____

☐ Recommendation _____

☐ Catalog _____

☐ Other _____

Where did you buy this book? _____

☐ Bookstore (name) _____ City _____

☐ Computer Store (name) _____

☐ Mail Order _____

☐ Other _____

What influenced you in the purchase of this book?

☐ Cover Design

☐ Contents

☐ Other (please specify) _____

How did you rate the overall contents of this book?

☐ Excellent   ☐ Good

☐ Average   ☐ Poor

What did you find most useful about this book? _____

_____

What did you find least useful about this book? _____

_____

Please add any additional comments. _____

_____

What other subjects will you buy a computer book on soon? _____

_____

What is the best computer book you have used this year?

_____

Note: This information will only be used to keep you updated about new Wrox Press titles and will not be used for any other purpose or passed to any other third party.

wrox

PROGRAMMER TO PROGRAMMER™

NB. If you post the bounce back card below in the UK, please send it to:

Wrox Press Ltd., Arden House, 1102 Warwick Road,
Acocks Green, Birmingham B27 6BH. UK.

——— *Computer Book Publishers* ———

NO POSTAGE
NECESSARY
IF MAILED
IN THE
UNITED STATES

BUSINESS REPLY MAIL
FIRST CLASS MAIL   PERMIT#64   CHICAGO, IL

POSTAGE WILL BE PAID BY ADDRESSEE

WROX PRESS INC.,
29 S. LA SALLE ST.,
SUITE 520
CHICAGO IL 60603-USA